SIXTH EDITION

PUBLIC ADMINISTRATION AND PUBLIC AFFAIRS

Nicholas Henry

Georgia Southern University

 Prentice Hall, Englewood Cliffs, New Jersey 07632

Library of Congress Cataloging-in-Publication Data

Henry, Nicholas, [date]

    Public administration and public affairs / Nicholas Henry. - - 6th
ed.

      p. cm

  Includes bibliographical references and index.

  ISBN 0-13-081779-1

  1. Public administration. I. Title.

JFH1351.H45 1995

350—dc20   93-46949

Editorial director: *Charlyce Jones Owen*
Assistant editor: *Jennie Katsaros*
Project manager: *Joanne Riker*
Cover design: *Marjory Dressler*
Production coordinator: *Mary Ann Gloriande/Robert Anderson*

Printed in the United States of America

10 9 8 7 6 5 4 3 2 1

ISBN 0-13-081779-1

Prentice-Hall International (UK) Limited, *London*
Prentice-Hall of Australia Pty. Limited, *Sydney*
Prentice-Hall Canada Inc., *Toronto*
Prentice-Hall Hispanoamericana, S.A., *Mexico*
Prentice-Hall of India Private Limited, *New Delhi*
Prentice-Hall of Japan, Inc., *Tokyo*
Simon & Schuster Asia Pte. Ltd., *Singapore*
Editora Prentice-Hall do Brasil, Ltda., *Rio de Janeiro*

To Muriel

CONTENTS

PREFACE

This edition of *Public Administration and Public Affairs* is notable in part because it marks the book's twentieth anniversary (in 1995, to be precise) as what my publisher tells me is a leading text in the field. I am pleased, because *Public Administration and Public Affairs* is my first book and still stands as my favorite among those that I have written. Some of it has appeared as articles in various journals and compendia, parts of it have been published in Spanish, and it has been published in its entirety in Japanese (Bunshindo Publishers, Tokyo). I would like to think that it has made a mark on my field of study, as only books which are written with a definite perspective can make a mark. *Public Administration and Public Affairs* has always had a particular point of view on matters managerial, and the sixth edition is no exception.

Among the new or significantly expanded discussions contained in the sixth edition are

- the differences between administrators in the public sector and administrators in the private sector;
- the mental process of making decisions;
- patterns of power in the organizational hierarchy;
- organizational socialization;
- the kinds of people in organizations who are the most effective in getting organizations to change in significant ways;
- how public organizations deal with a declining environment;

- the power bases of leadership;
- the impact of national cultures on organizational behavior;
- geographic information systems;
- the federal experience with Inspectors General;
- Total Quality Management in the public sector;
- the implications of the Government Performance and Results Act of 1993, performance evaluation and productivity measurement;
- the effects of deficit spending in the United States;
- recent developments in budgetary thinking at all levels of government in the United States, including Target Base Budgeting and cutback management;
- changing federal policies toward whistle-blowers;
- the recent court decisions regarding affirmative action and the Civil Rights Act of 1991;
- sexual harassment in the public sector;
- the changing demographics of the American workforce;
- the new and smaller world of public employee unions;
- strategic planning and decision making in the public sector;
- the "revolving door" in federal procurement practices, and the growing roles of lobbyists for both domestic and foreign interests in the federal government;

- privatization in state and local governments, including perceptions of the business community in contracting with governments;
- the expanding significance of volunteers in delivering government services;
- the management of government corporations;
- the implications of "reinventing government" and "entrepreneurial government";
- the impact of federal mandates and money on policy formulation in states and communities;
- a history of the public productivity movement in the United States;
- new and far-reaching proposals for sorting out intergovernmental relations;
- the problematic place of counties in the American governmental context;
- the hasty withdrawal of federal dollars from state and local budgets;
- new findings on the practice of ethical public administration in state and local governments.

Also given new treatment in the sixth edition are the extensive appendices that have made *Public Administration and Public Affairs* a useful reference work to both students and practitioners since its initial publication in 1975. Appendix A is a compendium of annotated information sources in public administration and related fields. Not only are bibliographies, dictionaries, directories, encyclopedias, and guides in public administration explained but also are comparable works in political science, management, American government, law, statistics, and the social sciences. Library of Congress call numbers for each work are listed, a feature which should ease library searches.

Similarly, Appendix B, which is an expanded list of selected journals relevant to public admin-istration, also features Library of Congress call numbers as well as brief explanations of the journals listed. Appendix C lists selected academic, professional, and public interest organizations, with descriptions and addresses, and Appendix D provides the correct form of address for public officials.

Appendix E is also updated and explains what kinds of jobs are available in the public sector, and the salaries that one might expect for all levels of government for various administrative positions. It offers a sample résumé that reflects the latest thinking in résumé writing, and which is designed to assist one in putting his or her best foot forward in applying for jobs in the public sector.

An attempt has been made in the sixth edition to eliminate the more miasmic detail that accretes in a volume after two decades of writing and rewriting it, and a special effort has been made to provide one-sentence definitions of terms used in the text. When these definitions are provided, the term being defined is italicized.

Public Administration and Public Affairs reflects the continuing evolution and growing self-confidence of the field. The developments in the fields that the sixth edition reports are developments that reflect a field maturing, growing more intellectually powerful, and making greater contributions to the society that supports it. Writing the sixth edition of *Public Administration and Public Affairs*, has been, as with the case in previous editions, a happy exercise.

N. H.
Statesboro, Georgia

ACKNOWLEDGMENTS

In the first edition of this book, I stated that I owed an intellectual debt to at least three of my teachers: Lynton Keith Caldwell, Jack T. Johnson, and York Y. Wilbern. I further noted that they taught me most of what I know about public administration, politics, and how to survive in a bureaucracy. I still owe my teachers that intellectual debt, and one that I continue to acknowledge. Although it has been quite a while since I sat in their classrooms, their impact has waxed, not waned, over the years. This is especially true for Jack T. Johnson, who continues to advise me on matters managerial, even if by long distance.

I have since added a fourth person to this small circle: Frank J. Sackton. Professor Sackton (also Lieutenant General Sackton, retired) introduced me to the classroom of the practical world during the dozen years that I spent at Arizona State University. It was a rare education indeed, and one that I shall always treasure.

I am indebted to my editor at Prentice Hall, Jennie Katsaros, who has been unflagging in her support; and to the reviewers for their comments: Paula D. McClain, University of Virginia; Lawton Bennett, University of Texas at Tyler; David S. Calihan, Longwood College; April Hejka-Ekins, California State University at Stanislaus.

Ginger Malphrus, the chief word processor in the Office of the President at Georgia Southern University, did a superb job in producing the significantly revised manuscript for the sixth edition, and I am genuinely grateful. Marilyn Leon, Jo Ann Marsh, Ruth Ann Rogers, and Angie Waters of my immediate staff warrant high accolades for keeping my administrative days on track and the President's Office in order. I am indebted to my colleagues, students, and those anonymous reviewers who have had such a constructive impact on the continuing evolution of *Public Administration and Public Affairs.*

As always, my wife Muriel, and my children, Adrienne and Miles, provided the deepest level of support. The book is for them.

NH
Statesboro, Georgia

PART ONE

PARADIGMS OF PUBLIC ADMINISTRATION

Bureaucracy and democracy are antithetical. The former is hierarchical, elitist, specializing, and informed; the latter is communal, pluralist, generalizing, and ill-informed if not ignorant. With the usual quantum of exceptions, these are the realities of the civic culture in advanced industrial democracies such as the United States.

Reconciling these realities is not a task for the timorous. Yet, such a reconciliation is essential if societies are to continue to be advanced, industrial, and democratic. The nexus of where democratic mass and technological elite meet—where this reconciliation occurs (or fails to occur) in the most central and deepest terms—is in the public bureaucracy.

The place of the public bureaucracy in a democracy, and the role that public administrators play in a democracy, is what Part One is about. These descriptions are brushed in broad strokes, although we do become more detailed when we review the intellectual evolution of public administration as an area of study. This review is important because how public administrators see themselves and their proper field of action in a democracy is a perspective that is formed more in the halls of academe than in the corridors of power. Hence, we devote some pages to the history of ideas in public administration.

So, welcome to *Public Administration and Public Affairs*, welcome to Part One, and welcome to one of the most exciting and rewarding career possibilities that is available today.

CHAPTER 1

BIG DEMOCRACY, BIG BUREAUCRACY

Consider the dilemmas of two presidents in dealing with the government bureaucracy.

More than three decades ago, President John F. Kennedy was pestered by his brother, Attorney General Robert Kennedy, over the fact that there was a large sign directing drivers to the Central Intelligence Agency's Langley, Virginia, headquarters. The Attorney General saw this sign every day that he commuted to work, and grew increasingly irked; he believed that its presence was in violation of federal policy by advertising the address of the supersecret spy agency. After listening to the intensifying complaints of his brother, President Kennedy ordered an aide to have the sign removed, who in turn, directed the Interior Department to remove it. Nothing happened. A few days later, the president repeated his order. Again, nothing happened. Aggravated by both the bureaucracy and his brother's persistence, the president personally called the official in charge of signs: "This is Jack Kennedy. It's eleven o'clock in the morning. I want that sign down by the time the attorney general goes home tonight, and I'm holding you personally responsible." The sign was removed and the president had learned a lesson: "I now understand that for a president to get something done in this country, he's got to say it three times."[1]

Such an understanding of supposed bureaucratic inertia is held, in fact, by most presidents. But quite the opposite can occur. Consider the experience of President Jimmy Carter. President Carter's daughter, Amy, was having difficulty one Friday afternoon on a homework problem about the industrial revolution. Amy asked her mother for help, who asked an aide if she knew the answer. The aide called the Labor Department for assistance. Labor was pleased to oblige. On Sunday, a truck pulled up to the White House with Amy's answer: a massive computer printout, costing several hundred thousands of dollars and requiring a special team of analysts to work overtime. The department thought it was responding to an order from the president. Amy received a "C" for her homework assignment.[2]

GOVERNMENT AND THE HOSTILE AMERICAN

These episodes, trivial in and of themselves, symbolize the problem of public bureaucracy. It is not that government is too lethargic or too efficient, too futile or too effective: The public bureaucracy is, in the view of some, simply unresponsive to the directives of the citizenry and its elected executives.

This viewpoint is reflected in various polls. The people's trust in government has declined precipitously from around 80 percent in the late 1950s to levels ranging from as low as 17 percent to as high as 23 percent in the 1980s, depending upon the type of government (*i.e.*, the executive branch of the federal government, state government, or local government).[3] By the early 1990s, roughly half of Americans believed that waste in government would grow, and that government was not working as well as it used to.[4]

An important point, however, is worth noting in these depressing statistics: Much of the decline in public confidence in government, as well as many other institutions of society, seems to be less a loss of faith in the institutions themselves, and more a distrust of the leadership of those institutions. For example, the Gallup Poll, which has measured public confidence in institutions since 1973, found that the confidence in institutions in the mid-eighties was 50 percent to 70 percent higher than was public confidence in the leadership of those institutions, and, while faith in leadership has fallen dramatically, the levels of confidence in the institutions which those leaders head have remained relatively unchanged since 1973.[5] Over half of Americans believe that the country's elected leaders are not paying attention to the long-range needs of the country, and almost half think that elected leaders do not care about "people like you," and are too influenced by special interest groups.[6] As two observers put it, "In the past, American ideals of appropriate leader behavior have been fairly high and constant despite frequent disillusionments. This may be changing. . . . [perhaps] the American mentality is reaching a point in a couple of decades that it took the French mentality several centuries to cultivate."[7]

The American disaffection with the leaders of government that is held by those who are governed, however, appears to be more complex and to run deeper than merely a cynicism *à la francais*. Americans reject involvement in public life if they perceive it as "politics," but they are extraordinarily engaged in the civic culture if they see themselves as solving common problems.[8]

When do Americans define (and detest) public life as "politics"? When they associate it with

politicians and lobbyists, issue avoidance, and special concessions to special interests. When do Americans define (and drive) public life as problem solving? When they connect it with community associations, neighbors, and problems that they feel they understand and which have been seriously addressed by civic leaders. Americans are angered when important public issues are exploited by politicians with sound bites, and trivialized by a shallow media. "When people sense that they do have a voice, they begin to sense that there is some possibility to make a difference."[9]

Interestingly, public administrators themselves reflect these currents, and seem to share a faith in the institution of government, but question its leadership. Gregory B. Lewis pulled the responses of government employees from a larger sample of respondents to surveys and compared the responses of the government employees to these surveys with those of the general population. He found that public employees have no more confidence in the people running governmental institutions than the average citizen, and are no less likely to have confidence in the people running other social institutions. The same pattern essentially held true for top public bureaucrats culled from the surveys, although this group held the leaders of the military, organized labor, and the medical community in significantly less esteem than did either all government employees or the general public.[10]

Figure 1-1 indicates this sinking level of trust that Americans have in government by comparing the threat perceived by Americans concerning the rise of Big Government relative to Big Labor and Big Business. Clearly, Big Government is far more worrisome to the average American than either of the other two institutions.

Fiscal reality has reflected these trends in popular opinion, and this is particularly true at the grassroots levels of government. Although California's notorious Proposition 13 of 1978, voted in by a two-to-one popular margin and which slashed property taxes in the state, became the symbol of the revolt against government and taxes in the popular mind, it is clear that the real revolt had begun years earlier. Between 1942 and 1976, the public sector at the state and local levels was a high-growth industry. For thirty-four years, state and local spending burgeoned at

FIGURE 1-1   The Public's Perception of the "Biggest Threat to the Country in the Future," Selected Years, 1959-1985

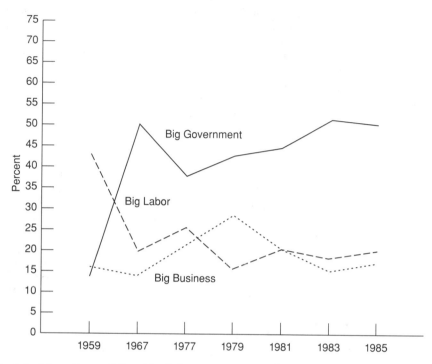

Source: Data derived from George Gallup, *The Gallup Poll: Public Opinion, 1983* (Wilmington, Del.: Scholarly Resources, 1984), pp. 127-128, and 1987, p. 25.

a rate almost three times faster than that of the economy. But after 1976, combined state and local spending in real terms began a decline that has yet to be reversed. (The decline began in 1974 for local governments, and in 1976 for state governments.)

The revolt continues. Twenty-two states have imposed taxation and expenditure limitations upon themselves since 1977. Forty-three states have imposed eighty-four taxation and expenditure limitations on their local governments, most of which limit local jurisdictions' capacity to collect property taxes—the traditional fiscal mainstay of counties and municipalities.[11]

BIG GOVERNMENT: "THE INCREDIBLE BULK"

Americans, in short, have made it clear that they are fed up with something called "Big Government," or at least the leadership of "Big Government." But is the cause of their frustration actual or illusory? Is American Government really all that huge? Yes, it is, although how huge depends to a degree on one's perspective. Despite grassroots efforts to rein in government, it nonetheless stands as the "incredible bulk." At all levels, government spending (but not, by any means, government revenues, at least not at the federal level) now exceeds $1.9 trillion, and government expenditures account for almost 35 percent of the Gross Domestic Product.[12] The real tax burden on the middle class has increased by more than 90 percent since 1953.[13] The number of full- and part-time public employees at all levels of government stands at close to 18 million, or one-fourth of the nation's civilian labor force. This figure does not include an estimated 3 million employees who work in the private sector, but who are paid entirely through federal contracts, and another 2 million military personnel.[14]

These are impressive figures. Even so, however, it is worth keeping in mind that American governments appear to loom less large in the lives of their citizens than do their counterparts elsewhere. In 1989, the tax revenues collected by all American governments amounted to slightly over 30 percent of the Gross Domestic Product. But the tax revenues collected at all levels by the governments of the seventeen Western European democracies, Australia, Canada, Japan, New Zealand, and Turkey amounted to almost 39 percent of their respective GDPs, on the average[15]—a considerably higher take than in the United States.

Relatively speaking, perhaps, American governments do not amount to "Big Government." But they do seem big in the eyes of most Americans. The surveys taken during the 1980s indicate that two-thirds of the general public believed that their own taxes were too high, and when asked whether they would favor more spending by government on eleven items dealing with foreign and domestic concerns, only five items were identified as policy areas worthy of greater public funding. (These areas were, in order of support, crime, education, health, drugs, and the environment; 65 percent to 61 percent of the general public thought that the government was spending too little on these areas.) The responses of public administrators to these questions were almost identical to those of the general public.[16] Americans, in short, including public administrators themselves, clearly have reservations about how big American governments have grown.

In addition, Americans have a reputed disdain for "the bureaucrat." Politicians run against bureaucrats and bureaucracy in an unending campaign for votes. One analysis of introductory college textbooks on American government found that over three-fourths of them portray public administrators as "government employees who stay on forever," and two-thirds depicted government bureaucracy as "all powerful and out of control."[17] Do Americans really feel this way?

BUREAUCRATS AND THE APPROVING AMERICAN

Evidently not. When we scratch the surface, and examine the one-on-one relationships that citizens have with their bureaucrats, we find quite different results. For example, a national Harris poll asked Americans if they had ever gone to a federal, state, or local agency to get "the government" to do something that was not related to routine matters, such as applying for drivers' licenses or paying taxes. Among those who indicated that they had sought some kind of personal objective within the public bureaucracy about two-thirds stated that they had found their public bureaucrats to be helpful, and most were satisfied with the services that they received (46 percent, in fact, were highly satisfied with their treatment by federal civil servants).[18] Table 1-1 indicates the results of the survey by levels of government and citizen satisfaction.

Another national poll conducted at approximately the same time was designed to probe more deeply about the level of satisfaction obtained by the average citizen when dealing with the government bureaucracy. These respondents were asked if they had ever gone to a government agency for help in several areas ranging from looking for a job to obtaining retirement benefits. Sixty-nine percent of these respondents pronounced themselves to be very satisfied or fairly well satisfied with the way the government

TABLE 1-1 Public Opinions on Helpfulness of and Satisfaction with Public Bureaucrats

Did you find the people you went to at (the federal/your state/your local) government helpful or not helpful?

	Federal	*State*	*Local*
Helpful	73%	66%	64%
Not helpful	24	29	34
Not sure	3	5	2

Did you come away from that experience with (the federal/your state/your local) government highly satisfied, only somewhat satisfied, or not satisfied at all?

	Federal	*State*	*Local*
Highly Satisfied	46%	39%	39%
Only somewhat satisfied	29	26	26
Not satisfied at all	24	34	35
Not sure	1	1	0

Source: Confidence and Concern: Citizens View American Government, A Survey of Public Attitudes by the Subcommittee on Intergovernmental Relations on the Committee on Government Operations, U.S. Senate (Washington, D.C.: U.S. Government Printing Office, 1973), p. 315.

TABLE 1-2 Public Satisfaction with Public Bureaucrats and Related Opinions

How satisfied were you with the way the office handled your problem? Would you say you were very satisfied, fairly well satisfied, somewhat dissatisfied, or very dissatisfied?

Very satisfied	43%
Fairly well satisfied	26
Somewhat dissatisfied	12
Very dissatisfied	14
Don't know, no answer	5

How much effort did the people at the office make to help you? Would you say it was more than they had to, about right, less than they should have, or no effort at all?

More than they had to	16%
About right	57
Less than they should have	12
No effort	9
Don't know, no answer	6

How efficient did you think the office was in handling your problem? Was it very efficient, fairly efficient, rather inefficient, or very inefficient?

Very efficient	43%
Fairly efficient	31
Rather inefficient	9
Very inefficient	11
Don't know, no answer	6

Do you feel you were treated fairly or unfairly by the office?

Fairly	76%
Unfairly	12
Mixed	5
Don't know, no answer	7

Source: Daniel Katz, Barbara A. Gutek, Robert L. Kahn, and Eugenia Barton, *Bureaucratic Encounters* (Ann Arbor: Institute for Social Research, University of Michigan, 1975), p. 64. Copyright ©1975 Institute for Social Research. Reprinted with permission.

office handled their problems. Sixteen percent said that the people in the office did more than they had to do to help them, and another 57 percent said that the level of effort to resolve their problem was about right. Nearly three-quarters of the respondents said that the government office was very efficient or fairly efficient in handling their problems, and more than three-fourths said that they were treated fairly; only 12 percent in fact said that they were treated unfairly.[19] Table 1-2 indicates the results of this survey.

There are additional surveys, both national and local, that have found results comparable to these.[20] One "meta-analysis" of 261 citizen surveys taken during the 1980s, and covering more than 200,000 respondents, found "generally favorable assessments" by citizens of their local governments' services.[21]

What we seem to have are two different streams of thought running parallel with each other. On the one hand, there is a clear and genuine disaffection with "Big Government." On the other hand, however, there is a remarkably positive attitude found among Americans who have dealt with their public bureaucrats on a person-to-person basis, and a general satisfaction regarding their efficiency in delivering public services. As one reviewer of the data concluded, "When queried in certain ways, the American public does not appear as disdainful of bureaucrats as the projected media image would indicate."[22]

There is a third facet of the role of government and the government bureaucrat in American democracy: the attitude of elected officials toward the public bureaucracy.

The opinions held by elected officials about public administrators are mixed. As Table 1-3 (which summarizes a national survey) indicates, politicians view bureaucrats as unimaginative, prim, dull, and (unsurprisingly) "bureaucratic." Citizens are much less critical on these dimensions. But elected office holders are far more positive about bureaucrats when it comes to such basic matters as their honesty and incorruptibility; in these areas, citizens are more skeptical than are elected officials, although even on these dimensions Americans can hardly be categorized as critical.

Consider, then, the dilemma of both the public administrator and the citizen. Public administrators in American democracy must deal with a citizenry that seems pleased with their professional abilities, yet is distrustful of the institutions where public administrators work, and the officials who head those institutions. The citizenry's elected representatives, unlike the people who elected them, seem to hold public administrators in low-keyed contempt—a difficult situation for public administrators who are ultimately responsible to these elected officials. And, despite their best efforts, American citizens have not really shrunk government. With the exception of a modest downturn in public employment

levels in the early 1980s, government continues
to grow. Why?

WHY BUREAUCRACY?

Although many explanations about why government grows have been put forth (including the
guile of bureaucrats themselves), we shall review
only the principal ones: political pluralism, the
displacement/concentration hypothesis, and technological complexity.

Political Pluralism

Our first explanation is one that is favored by
political scientists.[23] Although it is not usually
employed to explain the growth of government,
but rather to demonstrate how the political
process is supposed to work, the pluralist model
nonetheless has some utility as an explanation of

**TABLE 1-3   How the Public and Elected Officials
View Public Bureaucrats**

Description	Public (percentage agreeing)	Elected Officials (percentage agreeing)
Do things by the book	23%	60%
Play it safe	21	48
Bureaucratic	14	58
Make red tape	12	25
Dull	6	14
Corrupt	4	0
Honest	16	34

*Source: Confidence and Concern: Citizens View American
Government*, A Survey of Public Attitudes by the
Subcommittee on Intergovernmental Relations on the
Committee on Government Operations, U.S. Senate
(Washington, D.C.: U.S. Government Printing Office, 1973),
p. 310.

why government has burgeoned in society. The
basic model is: Society is comprised of a number
of competing groups that have a broad range of

A PARABLE OF MICE AND MEN

The following incident really happened in 1977 and 1978. It is offered without comment.

It is not only Congress but also the White House
mice that have been teaching Jimmy Carter the limits
of Presidential power.

When the members of the Carter entourage arrived
from their country homes in Plains, Georgia, they
were surprised to discover that their new city mansion
at 1600 Pennsylvania Avenue was plagued with mice.

Indeed, the story goes that one night when
President Carter was deep in conference with Frank B.
Moore, his Congressional liaison chief, in his little
hideaway office, two mice scampered across the carpet. The alarm went out to the General Services
Administration (G.S.A.), which does the housekeeping
for Federal buildings, and the President turned to more
weighty affairs.

But the mouse problem proved intractable. Just
before the Latin American heads of government
arrived in Washington for the signing of the Panama
Canal treaties, one small gray creature climbed up the
inside of a White House hall and died. The Oval
Office was bathed with the odor of dead mouse.

Desperately, the President called the G.S.A. again.
But the agency insisted that it had killed all the mice
inside the White House and that therefore this mouse
must have come from outside the building.

According to the agency, this meant that the offensive mouse was an "outside" mouse, a wayward ward
of the Interior Department, which tends the grounds
around the White House.

But the Interior Department demurred. It must be
an "inside" mouse, said Interior officials. Moreover,
regardless of its origins, it was obviously now the
G.S.A.'s worry because the carcass was imbedded
inside a White House wall.

"I can't even get a damned mouse out of my
office," the President moaned to Jody Powell, his
press secretary.

In frustration, he summoned two officials from
each agency and lined them up before him in the
stench of the Oval Office to break the bureaucratic
deadlock. As a compromise solution, one aide
quipped, "it took an interagency task force to get that
mouse out of here."

Now, vigilant against future crises, the White
House has gone on the offensive. As Mr. Powell
remarked, "You can't open a desk drawer around here
without getting your hand caught in a rat trap."

*Copyright © 1977 by New York Times Company.
Reprinted by permission.*

interests which may or may not be compatible with one another. Thus, blacks, for instance, may wish to wrest certain concessions from policymakers to accomplish their own particular ends (for example, busing children to achieve integrated school districts), but that such a gain for one group is achieved ultimately at the cost of other groups (or so it is perceived by other groups)— for instance, the inconvenience to whites that busing may incur. Hence, in the classic pluralist model one group's gain becomes another group's loss. Pluralists believe that such a process results in a social "good" on the grounds that the majority of people benefit from this contention of interest groups—provided, of course, that the basic human rights of a group or individual are not destroyed by the process, and government is the institution charged with society's responsibilities to protect these rights.

But how does the pluralist interpretation of the political process relate to a theory concerning the growth of government? The intellectual jump is not a difficult one to make, but it is worth some explanation. If government has an increasingly expanding economy from which to draw resources (*i.e.*, taxes), or if government simply taxes more, it becomes increasingly easier for policymakers to placate any given group, but not necessarily at the expense of other groups. With larger tax bases, more and more demands can be met by government, but without employing the traditional but difficult device of reallocating resources to do so.[24]

When government's resources are scarce, however, and policymakers must take away resources from one program to provide funding to another program, it follows that what one group gains in the form of a new or expanded policy, another group consequently loses. But with a growing economy, or just an expanded tax base, reallocative decision making is not required, or, at least, less required. Old programs can be maintained and new programs started by reason of an increasingly expanding resource base in the forms of growing industrialization, productivity, employment, and concomitant tax increases. Therefore, government can meet, for example, the traditional demand for adequate national defense by letting lucrative contracts to businesses in the defense industries, and simultaneously assure the adequate safety of workers in those industries by setting up such devices as an Occupational Safety and Health Administration, thus meeting the demands of other groups whose values are not necessarily profit-motivated.

A secondary consequence of such a situation is that demands for government services by various groups have resulted both in more government services that are wanted by some groups, but which are not wanted by others. The tensions resulting from this situation may have contributed to the popular distrust and dislike of government. Nevertheless, it is this basic dynamic of competing interest groups demanding more and more resources from government—but only in the context of more resources—that serves as the basic pluralist theory explaining the growth of government.

The Displacement/Concentration Hypothesis

The traditional pluralist model of political scientists as an explanation of the growth of government is not particularly satisfying. This is not to say that the model is "wrong," but it is to say that it is awfully simple. A more sophisticated interpretation of the growth of government is provided by economists.[25] As Alan T. Peacock and Jack Wiseman observe in this context, economists, for the most part at least, do not base their theories on "any all-embracing theory of the state," as the political scientists implicitly do. Indeed, the assumptions of the economists in explaining the growth of government are that: "Governments like to spend more money, citizens do not like to pay more taxes, governments need to pay some attention to the wishes of their citizens."[26]

Peacock and Wiseman, for example, argue cogently that the growth of government may be attributed to two distinct features in the twentieth century. One is that certain major disturbances, such as wars, shift public revenues and expenditures to new and heretofore unimagined public revenues and expenditures to new and heretofore unimagined levels. When the disturbance has run its course, new ideas emerge of what a tolerable tax level is, and higher plateaus of government activity in the economy are achieved and maintained; invariably, these plateaus represent a higher portion of the Gross Domestic Product than was the case prior to the social disturbance. It is this phenomenon that Peacock and Wiseman call "the displacement effect." Economists do not assert that all social disturbances inevitably are accompanied by lasting increases in governmental expenditures, nor that the more permanent influences on the behavior of government, such as population shifts and growth, are irrelevant, but it is inescapable that the growth of government has been a reality in the twentieth century and can be traced, using economic statistics, to major periods of social disturbance. As Peacock and Wiseman observe, the upward displacement of government revenues and expenditures came during and after two major wars in Great Britain.

The displacement effect often is followed by an "inspection process" in society. The disturbance calls to the attention of citizens and governments new knowledge about their own society. Thus, for example, public education was seen as a desirable and social goal when the Napoleonic wars first exposed the educational deficiencies in the European lower classes. More recently, the development of British social services in World War II, which were the result of war-time bombing that had made the replacement of voluntary hospital services necessary, eventually grew into the National Health Service.[27]

Concomitant with the displacement effect and the ensuing inspection process, at least in some societies, is the "concentration process." The concentration process does not refer so much to increases in the total volume of government expenditures, but rather to the "concentration" of those expenditures at *higher* levels of government. Obviously, the concentration process can occur only in societies that have a federal form of government, such as the United States; thus, the national government acquires responsibility for public services, such as welfare, that traditionally have been the preserve of state or local governments. As we shall see in our chapter on intergovernmental administration, such a concentration process has been occurring in the United States with particular rapidity during the last twenty years.

The concentration process is quite distinct from the displacement effect in the view of most economists. Economic reality, rather than social disturbance, works toward the increasing centralization of economic power by the national government relative to the state and local units. Thus, "local autonomy usually has many defenders, and its preservation is frequently a matter of political importance. At the same time, economic development produces changes in the technically efficient level of government, and also produces demands for equality of treatment (*e.g.*, in services such as education) over wider geographical areas. . . . Clearly, this evolution is distinct from the displacement effect, since the forces just described operate in normal as well as disturbed times."[28]

Even so, social disturbances which displace the level of government expenditures upward also are going to have some bearing on the concentration process. Traditional political considerations often are swept aside during periods of major disturbance in a society, and some of these traditional political considerations may concern certain functions of government that "always" have been the exclusive preserve of sub-national jurisdictions. As Peacock and Wiseman observe, "Periods of displacement are also going to be periods of interest" from the viewpoint of the concentration process.[29]

Technobureaucracy: Bureaucracy as Interpreter of Technology

There is a third theory (there are many more, of course, but we are considering only the major explanations in this chapter), and one that owes much of its intellectual development to the futurists as opposed to the political scientists and economists.[30] Like the pluralist and displacement/concentration models, this explanation does not contradict any of the others; instead it merely amplifies the preceding two, and it will serve as this book's primary explanation of the burgeoning bureaucracy. It holds that bureaucracy is the inescapable political expression of technology. Technology, in this sense, refers to the growing complexity of society that has been brought about not merely by scientific discoveries of profound social significance, but also by the proliferating economic and social interrelationships that are associated with industrialization. Not only are purely technical complexities evident, but new and varied social relationships also become apparent. "Technology," in this context, has certain conceptual relationships to what economists call "technical efficiency," and to what political scientists call "values," which are represented to policymakers by interest groups competing for resources in a pluralist political system; thus, in the political scientist's sense, both "technology" and "efficiency" are but two of many "values" to be "represented" by groups in the political process.

But the futurists' argument that technology lies behind the growth of government goes further and perhaps has more power as an explanation, than either the theories of the political scientists or the economists, and one of the best empirical examples of the futurists' interpretation is provided by America. The United States is a technological society; indeed, the United States may be the archetype of technological societies. Computers, automation, and advanced modes of transportation and communication often are developed in America first. The rest of the world adopts its technologies as experiments when they are already commonplace there. But technology brings with it new and interesting political problems. ("May you live in interesting times" is considered a curse in China.) Consider a simple one—highways.

Highway technology is one that most people can understand. The Romans, indeed, understood highways as a technology supremely well 2,500 years ago. Yet American society has grown so complex that highways have taken on new meanings as a technology. For example, in the late 1960s the U.S. Department of Housing and Urban Development (HUD) found that large and disproportionate numbers of urban rioters, notably in Watts and Newark, had lived in the riot areas for a year or less. Moreover, these people had recently moved to the riot-torn areas because they had been displaced from their original homes by such projects as urban renewal and highway construction. As a result, neighborhood "fabrics" were torn and former residents scattered—people became new residents in other areas; they had nothing to lose and no neighborhood to protect. Hence, building large highways through large urban areas, according to HUD officials, may have influenced the intensity of the urban riots of the late 1960s.

In sum, although most of us consider the highway to be relatively simple technology, it has resulted in complicated social and political problems that ultimately must be settled by the public at large. But how is the public to understand the more complex aspects of technological problems? Highways provide only one example; there are many others. Consider the problem of the computer and its role in the protection of privacy and in the gathering of social data on which to form public policy—where is the line to be drawn between the right to privacy, the need for information, and the right to know? Or consider the environment and its relationship with the energy dilemma—where does full employment end and the potential degradation of the earth begin? Still another problem is the population explosion—where does the right to life end and the rights of the individual woman begin? Of course, these are not merely technological questions; they are also deeply moral and ethical ones. Technology, in the forms of industrialization, "the pill," and electronic data processing techniques, to mention only a few, has injected new layers of complexity that are only beginning to be understood by experts in their respective fields. Yet the political questions and the public problems that these technologies and others raise require that policies concerning them be formulated in the broadest public sense conceivable. Nevertheless, the question stands: How is the public in a democracy to understand such issues as they pertain to these extraordinarily complex and technical questions?

The answer that has emerged in fact, if not necessarily in theory, is the public bureaucracy. Bureaucrats are hired to be specialists. They are, in a sense, experts in their particular fields. Because technology requires expertise, bureaucrats have been saddled with the responsibility of interpreting complex technological and political problems so that as many citizens as possible might understand the issues involved. Whether or not the bureaucrats do a particularly good job of this chore is another question altogether. But their abilities as specialists are one reason why they are there.

We have been suggesting in the preceding paragraphs that bureaucracy grows in large part because technology requires expertise, and bureaucrats are the political actors who have been saddled with the responsibility of interpreting and translating complex technological and social problems into policy. By adopting this explanation of the *raison d'être* of the bureaucratic phenomenon as our primary thesis, we have posited a fundamental tension between bureaucracy and democracy. On the one hand are the bureaucrats-as-experts, the specialists with knowledge about particular professions and techniques. On the other hand are "the people," those who represent what are considered human values. To carry this dichotomy even further, we have the "computers"—the "technocrats"—squaring off against "humanity." This dichotomization, which obviously is grossly overdrawn, is nonetheless representative of the root tension between "the bureaucrats" and "the people." We consider this tension in upcoming chapters on organization theory, but for now it is enough to note that there is an inherent gap in any society between expertise, including the expertise of public administration, and populist democratic values.

BUREAUCRATIC POWER

Regardless of why the bureaucracy exists, and irrespective of why the number of bureaucrats has grown, the fact remains that the bureaucracy has power. The Founding Fathers of the United States never really addressed this "fourth branch" of government, nor did most of the Founding Fathers of other nations. For example, Karl Marx, the intellectual father of numerous, formerly socialist nations and the few remaining ones, never comprehended the power of bureaucracy.

Staying Power

One major form of power that the bureaucracy has is simply its staying power. Perhaps the most infamous example of the staying power of public bureaucracies is the International Screwthread Commission, which one observer called the "commission that will not die."[31] Formed in 1918 by Congress with the stipulation that its life span would not exceed sixty days, it survived until 1933, when President Franklin Roosevelt ordered it abolished. But the Commission simply reformed itself as the Interdepartmental Screwthread Commission,

which eventually was reestablished as the present Commission. Although most observers agree that the Commission's work was accomplished many years ago, it is still going strong.

Herbert Kaufman completed the first empirical research on the staying power of public bureaucracies and concluded, reluctantly, that it was awesome. Kaufman wanted to find out whether or not government organizations, in effect, "lived forever." To ascertain this, Kaufman determined how many U.S. government agencies had "died" (that is, were actually terminated, not just changed in name) between 1923 and 1973. He found 175 identifiably separate agencies within the government in 1923, and by 1973, not only were 109 of these same agencies still in operation, but also the government agency "population" had exploded to 394 separate agencies. Only 15 percent of the original 175 had disappeared. When Kaufman compared the "death rate" of government agencies with the rate of business failures over the fifty-year period, he found that in any given year the rate of business failure exceeded the rate of agency death.[32]

Subsequent research has questioned Kaufman's conclusions about the relative immortality of government agencies, arguing that Kaufman's analysis was based on a sample of organizations which was incomplete; that his methodology was flawed in that it ignored, among other items, the large number of federal agencies that were created during the New Deal and World War II, and which were terminated following the resolution of those crises; and that his definition of what would constitute a "dead" agency was far too stringent. If one were to adopt a more flexible concept of agency succession, then a far greater "death rate" of federal agencies would be evident.

B. Guy Peters and Bryan W. Hogwood took precisely this approach, and found that from the 1930s through the 1970s, 2,245 initiations, terminations, and various kinds of successions involving 889 federal organizations occurred over the course of this fifty-year period. As the authors concluded, "there has been a great deal of change in government of the fifty year period we investigated. This change has included the birth of new organizations, the death of many more than might have been expected, and the metamorphoses of even more." Among other findings, "having a basis in an act of Congress does not protect an organization from termination or succession."[33]

In a sense, it is difficult to argue with either approach, in that Kaufman's approach is in many ways more straightforward, while Peters and Hogwood's tack is more flexible, and in many ways more complete. Nevertheless, it is a reasonable conclusion that most Americans believe, regardless of what evidence may be provided to them, that government organizations are indeed "immortal." Whether or not agencies outlive their usefulness is a question that the researchers of agency life cycles have not addressed.

Political Power

Perhaps even more important than staying power is policymaking power. It is increasingly obvious in the twentieth century that bureaucracy is the major policymaking arm of government. Consider some examples. Two little black girls are sterilized by family planning officials in Alabama. The U.S. Food and Drug Administration reverses past policy and bans cyclamates because of a single but determined biologist in its employ. A vice president of the United States resigns as the unanticipated but ultimate consequence of an investigation by a lone Justice department lawyer in Maryland. The Pentagon Papers are released by a conscience-stricken analyst in the Air Force's RAND Corporation. Watergate erupts as the result of premeditated law-breaking by members of the Cabinet, the White House staff, and a former president of the United States.

The preceding instances are examples of public policy being made by public administrators. Some of these policies are good, others bad. Some are confined in their social impact, others are reweaving the fabric of the American polity. All of these public policies, however, were made primarily by bureaucrats, with little or no influence from legislators or judges, and all affect the lives of people.

One should place, however, the power of bureaucrats to make public policy in perspective. In a careful, empirical, and original analysis of the federal policymaking process, John W. Kingdon found that while "no one set of actors

dominates the process" of agenda setting and policymaking, "elected politicians and their appointees come closer than any other."[34] Kingdon, in fact, concluded from his study that the president and members of Congress were quite important in the initiation of new ideas and the formation of the policy agenda for the nation. Almost equally important were top presidential appointees (who actually were ranked higher than the president), White House staffers, and congressional staffs. Of course, these latter groups are not elected officials, and may be considered public administrators (although they are not in the "career civil service"). Career civil servants, on the other hand, were considerably less important in originating new ideas for public policy and setting the national agenda, but they were extremely significant in structuring the alternative solutions that could be applied to recognized public problems. Kingdon found that "the customary distinction between line and staff bureaucrats is . . . important, because line people are particularly preoccupied with administering existing programs while staff people might have more time to concentrate on policy changes. Thus one does find staff people . . . who concentrate on legislative proposals, studies of future problems, and thinking about the directions public policy might take. . . . The career civil servants [on the other hand] may have more impact on the specification of alternatives. . . . With respect to agenda setting, then, a top-down model of the executive branch seems to be surprisingly accurate."[35]

BUREAUCRATIC SOVEREIGNTY

Besides being powerful, policy-making figures within the constitutional and legitimate confines of the system, public administrators have encroached beyond their recognized bounds, and appear to have wrested control over critical policy areas from elected officials, both legislators and chief executives.

Bureaucrats and Legislators

Let us consider first the political relationships between bureaucrats and legislators. At the local level, there is a small raft of research indicating that appointed city managers view themselves as legitimate, appropriately powerful policymakers in their cities, whereas elected city council members (who hire and fire city managers) tend to see their managers more as administrators of council policy as well as appreciated policy experts whose involvement in the policy process is useful, and whose advice is generally worth heeding.[36] These studies have found, quite consistently, that (to quote one review of this literature) "virtually all managers always or nearly always participate in the formulation of policy and set the council agenda. Most initiate policy and play a leading role in policymaking."[37] A significant minority (a sixth to a fifth) of local government managers report that they also engage in local politics,[38] and one national survey found that 12 percent of urban managers regularly helped incumbent council members win re-election![39] Far more local managers believe that their policymaking power and local political influence will increase, rather than decrease, over time.[40]

This kind of clout comes with costs, but the costs themselves constitute additional evidence of the bureaucrats' clout. One analysis of why city managers were fired or pressured out of office by their councils found that the managers' personal "style" and open policy disagreements between managers and council members were the leading causes.[41]

Studies of other legislative bodies also tend to validate the hypothesis that public administrators are policymakers. For example, in a classic study of policymaking in school boards, which are usually composed of members elected by the community, it was found that the professional school superintendent was the major formulator of board policy: "School governance has never completely fallen under the sway of the superintendent's office, but there is no question that the first half of the twentieth century saw enormous gains of power for the office."[42] In fact, the researchers concluded that, in comparison to city managers in council-manager governments, superintendents exercised relatively more power over their boards than did managers over their councils.[43] A later study of school boards and superintendents found that boards adopted the policies recommended by their superintendents an astonishing 99 percent of the time; "the super-

intendent—far more than the board—is identified publicly as the 'governor' of education. Although superintendents are rarely selected by public election, they are, because of the expectations placed upon them, the symbol of school government."[44]

One might expect that chief executive officers who are appointed by elected officials would, at least to some degree, "naturally" assume the reigns of power in their jurisdictions. But it also seems to be the case that bureaucrats who are appointed merely as staff assistants are becoming increasingly influential in legislative bodies. Legislative staffs at both the state and national levels have burgeoned precipitously.

In 1960, no state legislature staffed its standing committees in both chambers, and only nine legislatures accorded their own legislative leaderships even partial staff assistance. Now, however, more than two-thirds of the legislatures staff their standing committees in both chambers, and all states have a standing legislative bureaucracy. Almost two-fifths of the legislatures fund personal staffs year round and the remainder do so when the legislature is in session.[45] Currently, the nation's 7,482 state legislators pay more than 16,000 full-time legislative employees year-round, a number that balloons to 25,000 employees when the legislatures are in session.[46]

A parallel growth is evident at the national level. In 1947, there were fewer than 2,500 personal and committee congressional staffers. Today, there are approximately 21,000 personal and committee staffers, or about thirty-seven staff members for each Senator and Representative, and the annual cost of Congress, in large part as a consequence of staff salaries, is nearly $2.5 billion per year.[47]

About a quarter of these 21,000 staffers and other employees serve congressional committees; the remainder work for individual members of Congress. In addition to these personal and committee staffs, there is a growing legislative bureaucracy to which members of Congress have exclusive access. This bureaucracy includes the Congressional Budget Office, the General Accounting Office, the Office of Technology Assessment, and the Library of Congress. These are only the principal nonpartisan staffs of the legislative bureaucracy in Washington, and they number approximately 20,000 people. When combined with Congress' 21,000 personal and committee staffers, the congressional bureaucracy totals over 40,000 employees.

We noted earlier that Kingdon's study of the policymaking process in Washington concluded that congressional staffers had significant levels of influence in the policymaking process.[48] Other studies confirm this. For example, one especially thorough examination of congressional staffing observed that "staffers exert a strong influence on material with which they deal because of their position astride the office communications process, their control of factual data, and the expertise and professional judgment which they bring to their jobs . . . today's staff are more expert and are becoming increasingly specialized. . . . On occasion, they argue vigorously for or against a certain policy position."[49]

The role of staffs at the state level, particularly in such heavily staffed legislatures as those in California, New York, and Illinois, indicate a similar experience. As a former staffer in the highly professionalized legislature in California put it, "The most remarkable discovery that I made during my tenure as a staff member was the amount of power I had over the bills on which I worked. The members relied almost entirely on staff to accurately summarize the legislation and also to develop compromises among the many interests which were brought into conflict by these bills."[50]

Bureaucrats and the Elected Executive

Just as the public bureaucrats have gained and are gaining autonomy as policy makers at the expense of legislators, public administrators also have encroached on the political independence of elected chief executives. Elected chief executives, notably presidents, are deeply aware of this encroachment. Consider some of the following comments made by presidents of the United States about "their" bureaucracy.

- Franklin Delano Roosevelt, who lamented his condition "under the shadow of the bureaucrat," bemoaned the impossibilities inherent in changing the U.S. Navy: "To change anything in the Na-a-v-y is like punching a feather bed. You punch it with your right, and you punch it with your left, until you are finally

exhausted, and then you find the damn bed just as it was before you started punching."[51]
- Harry Truman: "I thought I was the president, but when it comes to these bureaucrats, I can't do a damn thing."[52]
- Dwight D. Eisenhower expressed himself as "amazed" over the naiveté of his successor in dealing with the bureaucracy, who "seemed unaware of the limitations on presidential power to enforce decisions."[53]
- John F. Kennedy, Ike's successor, soon lost his innocence, and told a caller, "I agree with you, but I don't know if the government will."[54]
- Richard Nixon: "We have no discipline in this bureaucracy! We never fire anybody! We never reprimand anybody! We never demote anybody!"[55]
- Jimmy Carter, who, in the final year of his presidency, remarked, "Before I became president, I realized and was warned that dealing with the federal bureaucracy would be one of worst problems I would have to face. It has been worse than I had anticipated."[56]

The frustrations that elected chief executives endure in dealing with their own bureaucracies are legion, and it is little wonder that a primary objective of elected chief executives, particularly presidents, has been to gain control over their bureaucracies. Most presidents fail in this attempt.

In an enlightening study of "the administrative presidency," Richard P. Nathan analyzes how recent presidents have attempted to gain control over their bureaucracies, and how they have, by and large, failed. Lyndon Johnson, for example, thought that he had found the sole solution to the problem of controlling the bureaucracy, which Nathan calls the "single-solution syndrome," and relied on a single professional group—economists—to implement a management control system for all of the federal government. The crux of his management control system was a budgeting technique (which we discuss in Chapter 8) called Programming-Planning-Budgeting (PPB). One day (August 25th, 1965, to be precise), and with no forewarning, Johnson dictated that the entire government was now on a PPB footing, and, while the idea may have been a grand one, its efficacy in terms of gaining presidential control over the federal bureaucracy was dubious at best. With the exception of the Department of Defense, the federal government (and many state and local governments, which were too quick to adopt it) abandoned PPB about as soon as Johnson departed the White House.

Johnson's successor, Richard Nixon, took an entirely different approach to gaining control over the bureaucracy, but also failed. At first, Nixon adopted a legislative strategy, in which he tried to push laws through Congress that would give him more control over the federal administrative apparatus, and, when that approach proved futile, he switched to an administrative strategy, in which he attempted to replace his initial appointments with Nixon loyalists. That tactic also was doomed to failure, and, as Nathan notes, "Although Nixon was on the right track, true to form he proceeded in a heavy-handed way that might well have failed even without Watergate."[57]

Jimmy Carter, who introduced a highly centralized and personal style of management to the White House, attempted to, in effect, implement his policies almost single-handedly, and became heavily involved in the details of agency operations. As one speechwriter in the Carter White House noted, Carter was a "perfectionist and accustomed to thinking that to do the job right you must do it yourself."[58] Obviously, that approach, too, failed.

These examples of presidential failure in controlling the federal bureaucracy seemed to constitute the rule of the administrative presidency, but, like any rule, there are exceptions, and among the most notable exception to this rule was the administration of Ronald Reagan, whose strategy was largely emulated by his successor, George Bush. Like Nixon, Reagan used both a legislative and an administrative approach to gaining managerial control of the bureaucracy, but, unlike Nixon, "the Reaganauts" employed a dual approach to gaining control of the federal bureaucracy (with the notable exception of the Department of Defense) by combining both the legislative and administrative strategies, rather than using first one tack, and then the other, as Nixon had tried. Moreover, Reagan initiated his attempts to control the federal administrative apparatus immediately upon entering the White

House, whereas Nixon made his attempt well into his presidency. As Nathan observes, Reagan "avoided the pitfalls of Nixon's heavy-handedness, Johnson's grand design, and Carter's atomic-submarine approach to management."[59]

Because Reagan was more successful than many other elected chief executives in gaining control over the public bureaucracy, we shall devote some discussion to his tactics and why they worked. Nevertheless, it is important to keep in mind how difficult Reagan's successes were to achieve, and how limited they were.

Reagan's approach to controlling the bureaucracy was comprised of five ingredients. The first was to choose cabinet officers who were loyal to both Reagan personally and to the ideology that he brought to the White House. Although appointing politically loyal men and women to cabinet positions would seem to be an obvious move, a far more typical presidential approach to cabinet appointments is to reach out to former (the president hopes) rivals, and appoint people of disparate political views and differing constituencies in an effort to heal the wounds of the campaign. When appointments such as these are made, the result frequently is an intense and immediate level of bureaucratic infighting among the cabinet secretaries and their subordinates.

A second ingredient of Reagan's administrative presidency focused on the appointment of subcabinet officials. Jimmy Carter had left such appointments to his cabinet secretaries, and this soon proved to be a serious error. Consider the following quotation from one assistant secretary who served under Carter: "There is a belief that some assistant secretaries are in business for themselves. Officially, when they testify on the Hill, they say the right thing in respect to the President's budget and legislative program, but privately, they tell committee staff members, 'I don't really think that.'"[60]

Reagan did not permit this kind of administrative undermining of his agenda. Instead, his strategy was "one of having his most doctrinaire supporters in these [subcabinet] positions instead of in the more visible and exposed cabinet positions where they are more likely to be lightening rods for public criticism."[61]

A third component of Reagan's administrative presidency was how he motivated public officials. Moreso than most presidents, Reagan understood the more subtle levers of managerial power in Washington. Invitations to state dinners, favorable or unfavorable rumors emanating from the White House about an appointee's actions, an upbeat mention at a press conference, phone calls, notes, and favorable budget decisions, among other motivators play an enormous role in Washington, and in government generally, relative to the private sector. Reagan also placed greater stock in making sure that his political appointees stayed home, rather than traveling abroad, so that they would have a better understanding of their own agencies, and often communicated with them directly, avoiding middlemen as much as possible.

Another tactic that Reagan used in gaining control of the federal bureaucracy involved the budget, and we discuss this approach more thoroughly in Chapter 8. Suffice it to note here, however, that Reagan was extraordinarily successful in implementing a budgetary process that, more than any of its predecessors, enabled the president to gain control over the bureaucracy.

Finally, Reagan understood that to truly control the bureaucracy, one had to decentralize. Nixon and Carter, perhaps moreso than any other presidents, did not comprehend this admittedly paradoxical rule of bureaucratic control. Nixon provides an especially telling case in point. Rather than delegating authority to loyal subcabinet officials, Nixon, at the beginning his second term, attempted to concentrate authority in a small group of senior advisors. This group rapidly became entangled in a miasma of details, and, as a consequence, the powers of subcabinet career officials were enhanced, rather than reduced. This strengthening of subcabinet careerists was precisely what Nixon wanted to avoid, but Nixon was late in learning that "the penetration of political officials into administrative processes is not a job that can be done, or even supervised, from the White House."[62]

We review these components of how an elected chief executive officer can gain control over his or her bureaucracy because they appear to work, at least when compared to other approaches, and because they have been used so infrequently in the past. Reagan, as we have noted, was the exception who proved the rule in bringing the public bureaucracy to heel, but even in his administration there were spectacular failures of administrative control. Consider, for example, grotesque cost overruns in the Department of Defense; corruption and blatant political favoritism in the Department of Housing and Urban Development that eventually cost the taxpayers millions of dollars; the spectacular failure of the savings and loan associations, which was a direct result of irresponsibly lax federal regulation and criminals in the private sector; and "Iran-Contra," in which laws governing foreign policy were apparently broken by White House aides.

Control of the public bureaucracy by elected chief executives, it appears, is a highly relative notion.

Whether it is hemming in elected legislators or elected executives, it is clear that the public bureaucracy has waxed into a policymaking power of no mean proportion. Is this development "good" or "bad" for the public? We will not attempt to answer that question here, but the point stands that bureaucratic power is real, growing, and in the views of many, worrisome.

KNOWLEDGE MANAGEMENT: THE BASE OF BUREAUCRATIC POWER

How has the bureaucracy grown so in political importance? The fundamental response must be that, in a highly complex and technologically oriented society such as the United States, those who control and manipulate information gain power. The old saw that "knowledge is power" never has been more true than it is today. As Max Weber, the famous theorist on bureaucracy observed nearly a century ago:

> The pure interest of the bureaucracy in power, however, is efficacious far beyond those areas where purely functional interests make for secrecy. . . . in facing a parliament, a bureaucracy, out of a sure power instinct, fights every attempt of the parliament to gain knowledge by means of its own experts or from interest groups. . . . bureaucracy naturally welcomes a poorly informed and hence a powerless parliament—at least insofar as ignorance somehow agrees with the bureaucracy's interests . . .[63]

More modern administrative theorists, though usually less savage in their assessments, have not seen fit to counter Weber's basic statement and, indeed, have reinforced it. As one contributor to a symposium on this very topic, published in *Public Administration Review* (the field's major journal) summarized, "Administration is knowledge. Knowledge is power. Administration is power," continuing that "this simplistic syllogism" is a major reality of our post-industrial age.[64]

In a more empirical mode, investigators have noted the relationship between organizational complexity in political settings and the subsequent control that appointed administrators appear to gain. In the study of school boards cited earlier, it was found that the professional school superintendent had far more power relative to members of the school board in the big cities, substantially less power in the suburbs, and even less power in the small towns.[65] Similarly, a national survey of city managers found that the larger the city, the likelier the manager would be intensely involved in municipal policymaking.[66] Both analyses indicate that, as the political system became more complex, administrators gained more power.

Political complexity renders politically sensitive information more valuable. In the national survey of city managers just noted, the single most consistent finding in the study was that, in cities of all types, more than 60 percent of the managers voiced strong opposition to a full-time, professionally paid city council: "This item evoked the strongest expression of opinion in the entire series of questions."[67] Moreover, a majority of managers opposed the provision of a full-time separate staff for the mayor and 77 percent of the respondents reported that they always or nearly always resisted council involvement in "management issues."

These strongly held opinions on the part of city managers indicate that the appointed urban chief executive is well aware that one of his or her major bases of political power is the control of information. (Richard Nixon's chief adviser for domestic affairs, John Ehrlichman, also showed an understanding of this point when he said, "operations is policy"[68]) A full-time professional staff for the mayor and a full-time, hard-working city council that is interested in "man-

agement issues" are anathema to the typical city manager. The urban manager is an example of the politics of expertise, a peculiar kind of political control that provides the manager with an ability to have his or her policies adopted by elected officials, primarily because he or she controls a major source of information, the city bureaucracy itself.

EXPLORING BUREAUCRACY, UNDERSTANDING GOVERNMENT

For the better part of the twentieth century, the public bureaucracy has been not only at the center of public policy formation and the major political determinant of where this country is going, but also it has expressed more articulately than any other American institution the mounting tensions between the values of the technological and information elite and the democratic and populist mass. The government bureaucracy also is the biggest conglomerate of organizations and employs more highly educated professional people than any other institution in the United States. It appears, therefore, that the public bureaucracy is worthy of some study, whether as an intellectual enterprise (so that we may learn more about how an advanced industrial democracy works), as an altruistic endeavor (so that we may learn how to promote the public interest more effectively), or as a personal investment (so that we will be more qualified for a job in government). The study and practice of public bureaucracy is called public administration, and public administration is what this book is about. We examine the peculiar nature and evolution of public administration as a field of academic enterprise in the following chapter.

NOTES

1. John F. Kennedy, as quoted in Peter Goldman, *et al*, "The Presidency: Can Anyone do the Job?" *Newsweek* (January 26, 1981), p. 41.

2. United Press International, "Amy's Homework Aid Likely Costs Thousands," *The Arizona Republic* (February 9, 1981).

3. Terrence R. Mitchell and William G. Scott, "Leadership Failures, The Distrusting Public, and Prospects of the Administrative State," *Public Administration Review*, 47 (November/December,

1987), p. 445; Lewis Harris and Associates, *Public Opinion Survey: Confidence in Leaders of Social Institutions* (New York: 1980 and 1984); and "Public More Trusting?" *I.S.R. Newsletter* (Autumn 1983), p. 4.

4. "America's Biggest Worries," *Washington Post* (November 4, 1991). This was a Washington Post/ABC News Poll.

5. *Gallup Report* (Princeton, N.J.: February 7, 1985).

6. "America's Biggest Worries."

7. Mitchell and Scott, "Leadership Failures, the Distrusting Public, and Prospects of the Administrative State."

8. The Harwood Group, *Citizens and Politics: A View from Main Street America* (Washington, D.C.: The Kettering Foundation, 1991).

9. David Mathews, "Putting the Public Back into Politics," *National Civic Review*, 80 (Fall 1991), p. 349.

10. Gregory B. Lewis, "In Search of Machiavellian Milquetoasts: Comparing Attitudes of Bureaucrats and Ordinary People," *Public Administration Review*, 50 (March/April 1990), p. 224.

11. As derived from: Advisory Commission on Intergovernmental Relations, *Significant Features of Fiscal Federalism*, 1992 edition, Volume I, M-180 (Washington, D.C.: U.S. Government Printing Office, 1992), pp. 14-18.

12. Advisory Commission on Intergovernmental Relations, *Significant Features of Fiscal Federalism*, 1991 edition, Volume 2, M-176-II (Washington, D.C.: U.S. Government Printing Office, 1991) pp. 7, 38.

13. Advisory Commission on Intergovernmental Relations, *Significant Features of Fiscal Federalism, 1980—81* (Washington, D.C.: U.S. Government Printing Office, 1982), p. 48. Between 1953 and 1980, the total tax burden on the American family with an average income ($21,500 in 1980) increased by 92 percent. Most of this hike was the result of tax increases by the federal government.

14. Advisory Commission on Intergovernmental Relations, *Significant Features of Fiscal Federalism*, 1991 edition, Volume 2, p. 218; and Barbara Blumenthal, "Uncle Sam's Invisible Army of Employees," *National Journal* (May 5, 1979) p. 732. Data are for 1989 except for the estimate of 3 million "indirect employees" who were paid through federal contracts during the years 1979-1980. In 1989, full- and part-time civilian public employees numbered 17,879,000. More than 3 million worked for the federal government, more than 4.3 million worked for state governments, and 10.4 million worked for local governments.

15. As derived from: U.S. Bureau of the Census, *Statistical Abstract of the United States, 1992* (Washington, D.C.: U. S. Government Printing Office, 1992), p. 836, Table 1381.

16. Lewis, "In Search of Machiavellian Milquetoasts," p. 222.

17. Beverly A. Cigler and Heidi L. Neiswender, "Bureaucracy in the Introductory American Government Textbook," *Public Administration Review*, 51 (September/October 1991). p. 444.

18. Harris survey as cited in Charles T. Goodsell, *The Case for Bureaucracy: A Public Administration Polemic*, 2nd ed. (Chatham, N.J.: Chatham House, 1985), p. 22.

19. University of Michigan Survey Research Center, as cited in *ibid.*, p. 24.

20. Several of these additional studies are cited in *ibid.*, pp. 25-26. See also: Steven A. Peterson, "Sources of Citizens' Bureaucratic Contracts: A Multivariate Analysis," *Administration and Society*, 20 (August 1988), pp. 152-165.

21. Thomas I. Miller and Michelle A. Miller, "Standards of Excellence: U. S. Residents' Evaluations of Local Government Services," *Public Administration Review*, 51 (November/December 1991), p. 503.

22. Goodsell, *The Case for Bureaucracy*, p. 106.

23. The single best description of the pluralist model remains that put forth in *The Federalist*, particularly "No. 10" by James Madison, but L. Harmon Zeigler and G. Wayne Peak's *Interest Groups in American Society*, 2nd ed. (Englewood Cliffs, N.J.: Prentice Hall, 1972), is a very good elaboration on the pluralist viewpoint in a more modern context.

24. As noted in the text, we are now moving slightly away from the traditional pluralist model. By introducing the notion of resources to pluralism, we implicitly are expanding the concept to include game theory. Many contributors to the theory of games, however, identify with political science. Game theory is explained more amply in Chapter 6 on "The Systems Approach," but suffice it to note here that game theorists would call the situation described in the text a "non-zero-sum game," or a "win/win scenario."

25. The bulk of this discussion is drawn from Alan T. Peacock and Jack Wiseman, assisted by Jindrich Veverka, *The Growth of Public Expenditure in the United Kingdom*. A study by the National Bureau of Economic Research (Princeton, N.J.: Princeton University Press, 1961), pp. xxi—xxxi.

The displacement/concentration hypothesis as developed by Peacock and Wiseman is a refinement of the theories originated by Adolph Wagner in the late nineteenth century. Wagner set forth the "law of increasing state activity" which, to phrase it very crudely, contended that with social progress (a less than objective term in and of itself) came increased activity by government, thus intensifying the government's impact on the national economy as a whole. To quote Wagner, "Historical comparisons of different countries, at different times and places, show that in the case of culturally progressive peoples . . . we can point to a regular expansion of the activity of the state and of public agencies in general. . . . The central and local governments constantly undertake new functions while they perform both old and new functions more completely and efficiently. In this way, increasingly more of the economic needs of the people . . . are satisfied more fully and in a better manner by the state and these other public agents. The clear proof of this development is seen in the increase of the financial needs of the central and local governments." (See Adolph Wagner, *Grundlegung der Politichen Oekonomie*, 3rd ed., Leipzig: C. F. Winter'sche Verlags Handlung, 1893, p. 893, as quoted in: Frederick C. Mosher and Orville F. Poland, *The Costs of American Governments—Facts, Trends, Myths* (New York: Dodd, Mead, 1964), p. 20.

26. Peacock and Wiseman, *The Growth of Public Expenditure in the United Kingdom*, p. xxiii.

27. R. M. Titmuss, "Problems of Social Policy," *History of the Second World War*, Civil Series, London, 1950, Chapter xv, as cited in Peacock and Wiseman, *The Growth of Public Expenditure in the United Kingdom*, p. xxviii.

28. *Ibid.*, p. xxv.

29. *Ibid.*, p. xxv.

30. Actually, there is no single literature of which I am aware that explains the growth of bureaucracy in precisely the same terms that I am using in the text. Nevertheless, a number of authors identified with "futures research" seem to imply it, or state the explanation in different ways. A popular example, if admittedly dated, would be Theodore Roszak's *The Making of a Counter Culture* (Garden City, N.Y.: Doubleday, 1969).

31. Jim Clark, "The International Screwthread Commission," *The Washington Monthly*, as reprinted in *Doing Public Administration: Exercises, Essays, and Cases*, Nicholas Henry, ed. (Boston: Allyn & Bacon, 1978) pp. 41-42.

32. Herbert Kaufman, *Are Government Organizations Immortal?* (Washington, D.C.: Brookings Institution, 1976).

33. B. Guy Peters and Bryan W. Hogwood, "The Death of Immortality: Births, Deaths, and Metamorphoses in the U.S. Federal Bureaucracy, 1933-1982," *American Review of Public Administration*, 18 (June 1988), p. 131.

34. John W. Kingdon, *Agendas, Alternatives, and Public Policies* (Boston: Little Brown, 1984), p. 47.

35. *Ibid.*, pp. 33-34.

36. See, for example: Ronald A. Loveridge, *The City Manager and Legislative Policy* (Indianapolis, Ind.: Bobbs-Merrill, 1971); Robert J. Huntley and Robert J. McDonald, "Urban Managers: Urban Managers: Managerial Style and Social Roles," *Municipal Year Book, 1975*, (Washington, D.C.: International City Management Association, 1975), pp. 149-159; Betty A. Zisk, *Local Interest Politics: A One-Way Street* (Indianapolis, Ind.: Bobbs-Merrill, 1973), p. 58; R. E. Green, "Local Government Managers: Styles and Challenges, *Baseline Data Report*, 19 (March 1987), pp. 1-11; and James H. Svara, *Official Relationships in the City* (New York: Oxford University Press, 1990).

37. James H. Svara, "Council and Administrator Perspectives on the City Manager's Role: Conflict, Divergence, or Congruence?" *Administration and Society*, 23 (August 1991), p. 231.

38. D. N. Ammons and Charles Newell, "City Managers Don't Make Policy: A Lie; Let's Face It," *National Civic Review*, 57 (April 1988), pp. 124-132.

39. Huntley and McDonald, "Urban Managers," p. 152.

40. Richard J. Stillman II, "Local Public Managers in Transition: A Report on the Current State of the Profession," *Municipal Year Book, 1982* (Washington, D.C.: International City Management Association, 1982), p. 171.

41. Gordon P. Whitaker and Ruth Hoogland De Hoog, "City Managers Under Fire: How Conflict Leads to Turnover," *Public Administration Review* 51, (March/April 1991), pp. 159-160.

42. Harmon Zeigler and M. Kent Jennings, with the assistance of G. Wayne Peak, *Governing American Schools: Political Interaction in Local School Districts* (North Scituate, Mass.: Duxbury, 1974), p. 27.

43. *Ibid.*, p. 251.

44. Harvey J. Tucker and L. Harmon Zeigler, *Professionals Versus the Public: Attitudes, Communication, and Response in School Districts* (New York: Longman, 1980), p. 143. The percentage figure is found on page 144.

45. As derived from Table 30, Council of State Governments, *The Book of the States, 1980-81* (Lexington, KY: Council of State Governments, 1980), p. 128; and Council of State Governments, 1961 survey, as cited in Herbert L. Wiltsee, "Legislative Service Agencies," *The Book of the States, 1961-62* (Lexington, KY: Council of State Governments, 1962), p. 67.

46. William Pound, "The State Legislatures," *The Book of the States, 1982-83* (Lexington, KY: Council of State Governments, 1982), p. 181. Figures are for 1980.

47. Mike Causey, "Hill Staff, Then and Now," *Washington Post* (September 30, 1991).

48. Kingdon, *Agendas, Alternatives, and Public Policies*, p. 34.

49. Harrison W. Fox, Jr. and Susan Webb Hammond, *Congressional Staffs: The Invisible Force in American Law Making* (New York: The Free Press, 1977), p. 144.

50. Michael J. BeVier, *Politics Backstage: Inside the California Legislature* (Philadelphia: Temple University Press, 1979), p. 229.

51. Franklin D. Roosevelt, quoted in Marriner Eccles, *Beckoning Frontiers*, Sidney Hyman, ed. (New York: Alfred A. Knopf, 1951), p. 336.

52. Clinton Rossiter, *The American Presidency* (New York: New American Library, 1956), p. 42.

53. Dwight D. Eisenhower, *The White House Years: Volume II. Waging Peace, 1956-1961* (Garden City, N.Y.: Doubleday, 1965), p. 713.

54. John F. Kennedy, as quoted in Richard P. Nathan, *The Administrative Presidency* (New York: Macmillan, 1983), p. 1.

55. Richard Nixon, as quoted in Richard P. Nathan, *The Plot That Failed: Nixon and the Administrative Presidency* (New York: John Wiley and Sons, 1975), p. 69.

56. Jimmy Carter, as quoted by Haynes Johnson, "Tests," *The Washington Post* (April 30, 1978).

57. Nathan, *The Administrative Presidency*, p. 87.

58. James Fallows, "The Passionless President," *The Atlantic Monthly* (May 1979), p. 38.

59. Nathan, *The Administrative Presidency*, p. 88.

60. Dom Bonafede, "Carter Sounds Retreat from 'Cabinet' Government," *National Journal* (November 18, 1978), p. 1852.

61. Nathan, *The Administrative Presidency*, p. 90.

62. *Ibid.*, p. 93.

63. Max Weber, *From Max Weber: Essays in Sociology*, H. H. Gerth and C. Wright Mills, eds. (New York: Oxford University Press, 1946), p. 233.

64. James D. Carroll, "Service, Knowledge, and Choice: The Future as Post-Industrial Administration," *Public Administration Review*, 35 (November-December 1975), p. 578. It is recommended that the reader see the "Symposium on Knowledge Management," James D. Carroll and Nicholas Henry, Symposium Editors, in the same issue.

65. Zeigler and Jennings, *Governing American Schools*, pp. 177-178.

66. Huntley and McDonald, "Urban Managers," p. 153.

67. *Ibid.*, p. 150.

68. John Ehrlichman, quoted in Nathan, *The Plot that Failed*, p. 62.

CHAPTER 2

PUBLIC ADMINISTRATION'S CENTURY IN A QUANDARY

Public administration is a broad-ranging and amorphous combination of theory and practice; its purpose is to promote a superior understanding of government and its relationship with the society it governs, as well as to encourage public policies more responsive to social needs and to institute managerial practices attuned to effectiveness, efficiency, and the deeper human requisites of the citizenry. Admittedly, the preceding sentence is itself rather broad-ranging and amorphous, but for our purposes it will suffice. There are, however, additional characteristics of public administration that fill out the model we shall be using in the following chapters.

As Stephen K. Bailey noted, public administration is (or should be) concerned with the development of four kinds of theories:[1]

1. *descriptive theory*: descriptions of hierarchical structures and relationships with their sundry task environments;
2. *normative theory*: the "value goals" of the field—that is, what public administrators (the practitioners) ought to do given their realm of decision alternatives, and what public administrationists (the scholars) ought to study and recommend to the practitioners in terms of policy;
3. *assumptive theory*: a rigorous understanding of the reality of the administrative person, a theory that assumes neither angelic nor satanic models of the public bureaucrat;
4. *instrumental theory*: the increasingly refined managerial techniques for the efficient and effective attainment of public objectives.

Taken together, Bailey's quartet of theories forms three defining pillars of public administration: organizational behavior and the behavior of people in public organizations; the technology of management and the institutions of policy implementation; and the public interest as it relates to individual ethical choice and public affairs.

In this chapter we review the successive definitional crises of public administration—that is, how the field has "seen itself" in the past. These paradigms of public administration are worth knowing, first, because one must know where the field has been to understand its present status and second, because this book represents a departure from past paradigms. We contend that public administration is unique, that it differs significantly from both political science (public administration's "mother discipline") and management (public administration's traditional alter ego) in terms of developing certain facets of organization theory and techniques of management. Public administration differs from political science in its emphasis on bureaucratic structure and behavior and in its methodologies. Public administration differs from management in that the evaluative techniques used by nonprofit public organizations are not the same as those used by profit-making private organizations, and in that profit-seeking organizations are considerably less constrained in considering the public interest in their decision-making structures and in the behavior of their administrators.

Public administration has developed as an academic field through a succession of five overlapping paradigms. As Robert T. Golembiewski has noted in a perceptive essay,[2] each phase may be characterized according to whether it has *locus* or *focus*. *Locus* is the institutional "where" of the field. A recurring locus of public administration is the government bureaucracy, but this has not always been the case and often this traditional locus has been blurred; moreover, this traditional locus is changing. *Focus* is the specialized "what" of the field. One focus of public administration has been the study of certain "principles of administration," but again, the foci of the discipline have altered with the changing paradigms of public administration. As Golembiewski observes, the paradigms of public administration may be understood in terms of locus or focus; when one has been relatively sharply defined in academic circles, the other has been conceptually ignored and vice versa. We shall use the notion of locus and focus in reviewing the intellectual development of public administration.

THE BEGINNING

Woodrow Wilson largely set the tone for the early study of public administration in an essay entitled "The Study of Administration," published in the *Political Science Quarterly* in 1887. In it, Wilson observed that it "is getting harder to *run* a constitution than to frame one," and called for the bringing of more intellectual resources to bear in the management of the state.[3]

Wilson's seminal article has been variously interpreted by later scholars. Some have insisted that Wilson originated the "politics/administration dichotomy"—the naive distinction between "political" activity and "administrative" activity in public organizations that would plague the field for years to come. Other scholars have countered that Wilson was well aware that public administration was innately political in nature, and he made this point clear in his article. In reality Wilson himself seems ambivalent about what public administration really was. Wilson failed,

> to amplify what the study of administration actually entails, what the proper relationship should be between the administrative and political realms, and whether or not administrative study could ever become an abstract science akin to the natural sciences.[4]

Nevertheless, Wilson unquestionably posited one unambiguous thesis in his article that has had a lasting impact on the field: Public administration was worth studying. Political scientists would later create the first identifiable paradigm of public administration around Wilson's contention.

PARADIGM 1:
THE POLITICS/ADMINISTRATION DICHOTOMY, 1900-1926

Our benchmark dates for the Paradigm 1 period correspond to the publication of books written by Frank J. Goodnow and Leonard D. White; these dates, like the years chosen as marking the later periods of the field, are only rough indicators. In *Politics and Administration* (1900), Goodnow contended that there were "two distinct functions of government," which he identified with the title of his book. "Politics," said Goodnow, "has to do with policies or expressions of the state will," while administration "has to do with the execution of these policies."[5] Separation of powers provided the basis of the distinction. The legislative branch, aided by the interpretive abilities of the judicial branch, expressed the will of the state and formed policy; the executive branch administered those policies impartially and apolitically.

The emphasis of Paradigm 1 was on locus—where public administration should be. Clearly, in the view of Goodnow and his fellow scholars, public administration should center in the government's bureaucracy. While the legislature and judiciary admittedly had their quanta of "administration," their primary responsibility and function remained the expression of the state will. The initial conceptual legitimation of this locus-centered definition of the field, and one that would wax increasingly problematic for academics and practitioners alike, became known as the politics/administration dichotomy.

The phrase that came to symbolize this distinction between politics and administration was, "there is no Republican way to build a road." The reasoning was that there could only be one "right" way to spread tarmac—the administrative engineer's way. What was ignored in this statement, however, was that there was indeed a Republican way to decide whether the road needed building, a Republican way to choose the location for the road, a Republican way to purchase the land, a Republican way to displace the people living in the road's way, and most certainly a Republican way to let contracts for the road. There was also, and is, a Democratic way, a Socialist way, a Liberal way, even an Anarchist way to make these "administrative" decisions as well. In retrospect the politics/administration dichotomy posited by Goodnow and his academic progeny was, at best, naive. But many years would pass before this would be fully realized within public administration's ranks.

Public administration received its first serious attention from scholars during this period largely as a result of the "public service movement" that was taking place in American universities in the early part of this century. Political science, as a report issued in 1914 by the Committee on Instruction in Government of the American Political Science Association stated, was concerned with training for citizenship, professional preparations such as law and journalism, training "experts and to prepare specialists for governmental positions," and educating for research work.[6] Public administration, therefore, was something more than a significant subfield of political science; indeed, it was a principal reason of being for the discipline.

As an indication of public administration's importance to political science, a Committee on Practical Training for Public Service was established in 1912 by the American Political Science Association and, in 1914, its report recommended with unusual foresight that special "professional schools" were needed to train public administrators, and that new technical degrees might also be necessary for this purpose.[7] This committee formed the nucleus of the Society for the Promotion of Training for the Public Service, founded in 1914—a forerunner of the American Society for Public Administration, which was established in 1939.

The relations between the "public administrationists" (*i.e.*, the academics) and the public administrators (*i.e.*, the practitioners) were at this time quite close—indeed, little distinction was made between the two. The New York Bureau of Municipal Research, founded in 1906 by public-spirited philanthropists, was created to improve the management of local government, and in 1911 it established (and ran) the nation's first school of public administration, the Training School for Public Service, with Charles A. Beard as its first director, later succeeded by Luther Gulick. In 1924, the School, which had produced the nation's first trained corps of public administrators, was transferred lock, stock, and student body to Syracuse University, where it became the nation's first public administration program to be associated with a university—the Maxwell School of Citizenship and Public Affairs.[8]

In 1915, the Bureau of Municipal Research created the Government Research Association as a means of bringing together its Training School's graduates for annual conferences, a practice that it continued until 1932, when the Depression struck. The Association was, along with the Society for the Promotion of Training for the Public Service, an early forebear of the American Society for Public Administration.[9]

Public administration began picking up academic legitimacy in the 1920s; notable in this regard was the publication of Leonard D. White's *Introduction to the Study of Public Administration* in 1926, the first textbook entirely devoted to the field. As Waldo has pointed out, White's text was quintessentially American Progressive in character and, in its quintessence, reflected the general thrust of the field: Politics should not intrude on administration; management lends itself to scientific study; public administration is capable of becoming a "value-free" science in its own right; the mission of administration is economy and efficiency, period.[10]

The net result of Paradigm 1 was to strengthen the notion of a distinct politics/administration dichotomy by relating it to a corresponding value/fact dichotomy. Thus, everything that public administrationists scrutinized in the executive branch was imbued with the colorings and legitimacy of being somehow "factual" and "scientific," while the study of public policymaking and related matters was left to the political scientists. The carving up of analytical territory between public administrationists and political scientists during this locus-oriented stage can be seen today in universities: It is the public administrationists who teach organization theory, budgeting, and personnel; political scientists teach such subjects as American government, judicial behavior, the presidency, state and local politics, and legislative process, as well as such "non-American" fields as comparative politics and international relations.

A secondary implication of this locus-centered phase was the isolation of public administration from such other fields as business administration, which had unfortunate consequences when these fields began their own fruitful explorations into the nature of organizations. Finally, largely because of the emphasis on "science" and "facts" in public administration and the substantial contributions by public administrationists to the emerging field of organization theory, a foundation was laid for the later "discovery" of certain scientific "principles" of administration.

PARADIGM 2:
THE PRINCIPLES
OF ADMINISTRATION, 1927-1937

In 1927, W. F. Willoughby's book *Principles of Public Administration* was published as the second full-fledged text in the field. Although Willoughby's *Principles* was as fully American

Progressive in tone as White's *Introduction*, its title alone indicated the new thrust of public administration: Certain scientific principles of administration existed; they could be discovered; and administrators would be expert in their work if they learned how to apply these principles.

It was during the phase represented by Paradigm 2 that public administration reached its reputational zenith. Public administrationists were courted by industry and government alike during the 1930s and early 1940s for their managerial knowledge. Thus the focus of the field—its essential expertise in the form of administrative principles—waxed, while no one thought too seriously about its locus. Indeed, the locus of public administration was everywhere, since principles were principles and administration was administration, at least according to the perceptions of Paradigm 2. By the very fact that the principles of administration were indeed *principles*—that is, by definition, they "worked" in any administrative setting, regardless of culture, function, environment, mission, or institutional framework and without exception—it therefore followed that they could be applied successfully anywhere. Furthermore, because public administrationists had contributed as much if not more to the formulation of "administrative principles" as had researchers in any other field of inquiry, it also followed that public administrationists should lead the academic pack in applying them to "real-world" organizations, public or otherwise.

Among the more significant works relevant to this phase were Mary Parker Follet's *Creative Experience* (1924), Henri Fayol's *Industrial and General Management* (1930), and James D. Mooney and Alan C. Reiley's *Principles of Organization* (1939), all of which delineated varying numbers of overarching administrative principles. Organization theorists often dub this school of thought "administrative management," since it focused on the upper hierarchial echelons of organizations. A related literature that preceded the work in administrative management somewhat in time, but which was under continuing development in business schools, focused on the assembly line. Researchers in this stream, often called "scientific management," developed principles of efficient physical movement for optimal assembly-line efficiency. The most notable contributions to this literature were Frederick W.

Taylor's *Principles of Scientific Management* (1911) and various works by Frank and Lillian Gilbreth. While obviously related in concept, scientific management had less effect on public administration during its principles' phase because it focused on lower-level personnel in the organization.

The lack of locus, if not, perhaps, the sharpening new focus of public administration during this period, made itself evident within the university community. In 1935, the Public Administration Clearing House held a conference at Princeton University, and the conference's report was radically different from the report issued in 1914 by the Committee on Practical Training for Public Service of the American Political Science Association. Suddenly political scientists had great difficulties with the idea of founding separate schools of public administration and believed instead that existing courses in political science departments and in other relevant disciplines, such as law, economics, and management, provided, if they were correctly combined, an education that was entirely adequate for budding government bureaucrats. The conference, therefore, found itself "unable to find any single formula which warrants the establishment of an isolated college or university program which alone will emphasize preparation exclusively for the public service." Only a "university-wide approach" would be satisfactory, since the problem of public administration education exceeded the "confines of any single department or special institute or school."[11]

As a more modern scholar has since observed, "A logical consequence of this reasoning" as expressed by the Princeton Conference of 1935, "could have been the elimination of public administration as a discrete field of study within the universities."[12] Such were the dangers of not having a firm and stationary intellectual locus on which to build a curriculum.

Despite these difficulties, however, scholars who identified with the study of public administration nonetheless found it useful to establish, four years after the publication of the Princeton report, the American Society for Public Administration (ASPA), which continues to function as the nation's primary association of scholars and practitioners of public administration, and as the sponsoring organization of the field's premier journal, *Public Administration Review*. But the creation of ASPA was less a response to the difficulties that public administration was having within universities generally, and more a reaction to what public administrationists were experiencing within political science departments specifically. As Dwight Waldo has put it, "The sense that political science as an academic discipline did not adequately represent and nurture the needs of those interested in improving performance in public administration was a strong motivating force in creating the new organization. In retrospect, it is clear that ASPA represented above all an attempt to loosen public administration from the restraints of political science. . . ."[13]

But the founding of ASPA was more than that: It was also an attempt to loosen public administration from the restraints of the citizenry. ASPA was created by practitioners and scholars of public administration for practitioners and scholars of public administration; its founding also was a secession from the Government Research Association, which was comprised not only of practitioners and scholars, but also of taxpayers, citizen-based government reform groups, elected politicians, and philanthropists as well. Darrell L. Pugh, ASPA's historian and archivist, puts it cogently: "ASPA's formation . . . symbolized an end to the historic union by facilitating its fragmentation in favor of a new coalition based on professionalism."[14] Professionalism is, by definition, a phenomenon predicated on planned career ladders, closely held in-group values, an eschewing of popular "politics," and intimate ties with the universities; ASPA was all of these.

As with any proposed secession, its execution was not easy. Public administrationist Donald C. Stone recalls the emotions involved at ASPA's founding: "Questions of loyalty, sedition, intrigue, separatism, and schism kindled emotions."[15] Golembiewski has summed it up: The birth of ASPA was "an expression of the felt needs of the burgeoning graduates and faculty of suddenly virile programs of public administration. So much was at stake, practically as well as intellectually."[16]

The secession succeeded, and it symbolized public administration's conscious need to become a profession and a discipline. But professions have their own orthodoxies, and the "high noon of orthodoxy," as it often has been called, of public administration was marked by the publication in 1937 of Luther H. Gulick and Lyndall Urwick's *Papers on the Science of Administration*. This landmark study also marked the high noon of prestige for public administration. Gulick and Urwick were confidantes of President Franklin D. Roosevelt and advised him on a variety of matters managerial; their *Papers* were a report to the President's Committee on Administrative Science.

Principles were important to Gulick and Urwick, but where those principles were applied was not; focus was favored over locus, and no bones were made about it. As they said in the *Papers*,

> It is the general thesis of this paper that there are principles which can be arrived at inductively from the study of human organizations which should govern arrangements for human association of any kind. These principles can be studied as a technical question, irrespective of the purpose of the enterprise, the personnel comprising it, or any constitutional, political or social theory underlying its creation.[17]

Gulick and Urwick promoted seven principles of administration and, in so doing, gave students of public administration that snappy anagram, POSDCORB. POSDCORB was the final expression of administrative principles. It stood for:

P lanning
O rganizing
S taffing
D irecting
C
O ordinating
R eporting
B udgeting

That was public administration in 1937. To be fair, Gulick and Urwick (although perhaps more so in Gulick's case) clearly understood that their "principles" were not immutable facts of nature, but were simply helpful touchpoints in conveying an understanding of how organizations worked. Nevertheless, over time, they became rigid "scientific principles" in the minds of the

many readers of their work — a process encouraged, no doubt, by the predilections of later scholars to erect straw men that they then could happily demolish.[18]

THE CHALLENGE, 1938-1947

In the year following the publication of Luther and Gulick's defining opus, mainstream public administration received its first real hint of conceptual challenge. In 1938 Chester I. Barnard's *The Functions of the Executive* appeared. Its impact on public administration was not overwhelming at the time, but it later had considerable influence on Herbert A. Simon when he was writing his devastating critique of the field, *Administrative Behavior*. The impact of Barnard's book may have been delayed because, as a former president of New Jersey Bell Telephone, he was not a certified member of the public administration community.

Dissent from mainstream public administration accelerated in the 1940s in two mutually reinforcing directions. One objection was that politics and administration could never be separated in any remotely sensible fashion. The other was that the principles of administration were something less than the final expression of managerial rationality.

Demurring to the Dichotomy

Although inklings of dissent began in the 1930s, a book of readings in the field, *Elements of Public Administration*, edited in 1946 by Fritz Morstein Marx, was one of the first major volumes to question the assumption that politics and administration could be dichotomized. All fourteen articles in the book were written by practitioners and indicated a new awareness that what often appeared to be value-free "administration" actually was value-laden "politics." Was a technical decision on a budgetary emphasis or a personnel change really impersonal and apolitical, or was it actually highly personal, highly political, and highly preferential? Was it ever possible to discern the difference? Was it even worth attempting to discern the difference between politics and administration if, in reality, there was none? Was the underpinning politics/administration dichotomy of the field, at best, naive? Many academics and practitioners alike were beginning to think so.

In his superb analysis of "The Trauma of Politics" and public administration, Allen Schick observes that the intellectuals' abandonment of the politics/administration dichotomy in the 1940s has been overstated in more recent years, and that those advocating its abandonment never intended to argue that something called "administration" and something called "politics" were totally inseparable. The challengers of the forties only wished to emphasize that public administrators, as well as legislators, made political decisions and public policies:

> Public administration always has served power and the powerful. . . . the service of power was *pro bono publico*, to help power holders govern more effectively. The presumption was that everyone benefits from good government . . . the constant concern with power was masked by the celebrated dichotomy between politics and administration. But the dichotomy, rather than keeping them apart, really offered a framework for bringing politics and administration together . . . the dichotomy provided for the ascendancy of the administration over the political: efficiency over representation, rationality over self-interest. . . . In the end, the dichotomy was rejected not because it separated politics and administration but because it joined them in a way that offended the pluralist norms of postwar political science.[19]

Puncturing the Principles

Arising simultaneously with the challenge to the traditional politics/administration dichotomy of the field was an even more basic contention: There could be no such thing as a "principle" of administration. In 1946 Simon gave a foreshadowing of his *Administrative Behavior* in an article titled "The Proverbs of Administration" published in *Public Administration Review*. The following year, in the same journal, Robert A. Dahl published a searching piece, "The Science of Public Administration: Three Problems." In it he argued that the development of universal principles of administration was hindered by the obstructions of values contending for preeminence in organizations, differences in individual personalities, and social frameworks that varied from culture to culture. Waldo's major work also reflected this theme. His *The Administrative State: A Study of the Political Theory of American Public Administration* (1948) attacked the notion of unchanging principles of administration, the inconsistencies of the methodology used in determining them, and the narrowness of the "values" of economy and efficiency that dominated the field's thinking.

The most formidable dissection of the principles notion, however, appeared in 1947: Simon's *Administrative Behavior: A Study of Decision-Making Processes in Administration Organization.*

Simon showed that for every "principle" of administration there was a counterprinciple, thus rendering the whole idea of principles moot. For example, the traditional administrative literature argued that bureaucracies must have a narrow "span of control" if orders were to be communicated and carried out effectively. Span of control meant that a manager could properly "control" only a limited number of subordinates; after a certain number was exceeded (authorities differed on just what the number was), communication of commands became increasingly garbled and control became increasingly ineffective and "loose." An organization that followed the principle of narrow span of control would have a "tall" organization chart (see Figure 2-1).

Span of control made sense up to a point. Yet, as Simon observed, the literature on administration argued with equal vigor for another principle: If organizations were to maximize effective communication and to reduce distortion (thereby enhancing responsiveness and control), then there should be as few hierarchical layers as possible—that is, a "flat" hierarchical structure. The logic behind this principle was that the fewer people who had to pass a message up or down the hierarchy, the more likely it would be that the message would arrive at its appointed destination relatively intact and undistorted. This, too, made sense up to a point. The "flat" hierarchy required to bring the bureaucracy in accord with this principle of administration would have an organization chart like that in Figure 2-2.

Obviously to Simon and now to us, the two

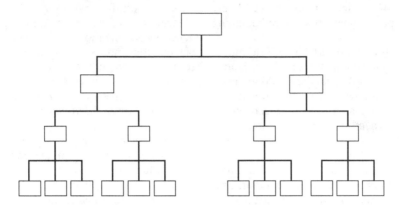

FIGURE 2-1   The "Principle" of Narrow Span of Control

"principles" were mutually contradictory and therefore by definition could not be principles. This dilemma encompassed the whole of the traditional public administration literature, but it was never more than suspected of being so stark a case until Simon published his book.

But Simon went beyond merely pointing out inconsistencies in the traditional literature of public administration. More importantly, he reconceived the entire field.

Simon understood that administrative decision makers wanted to make rational choices (*i.e.*, the single "best" choice), but that there were a lot of variables standing in the way of locating the single most rational decision. In his book, Simon made the field aware that there were limits on information and computational abilities within any human institution. Where the purveyors of administrative principles had erred, in Simon's view, was in their assumptions that all alternatives were known, that the consequences of choosing any one of those alterna-

tives were equally known, and that decision makers doggedly searched until they found the single best alternative from the standpoint of their own preferences. In questioning these assumptions, Simon argued that choices had to be discovered by searching for them; that typically only a relatively few alternatives could be considered; that information also had to be sought through a search process; and that decision makers did not select the single best alternative, but instead "satisficed," or chose the alternative that both satisfied and sufficed from their point of view.

Simon's perspective was less economic than behavioral. In contrast to the literature that argued for principles of administration, Simon suggested a more human process of decision making. Hence, Simon argued that the constraints on organizational choices should include not only those external factors found in the task environment of organizations, but should include as well those constraints that existed as part of

FIGURE 2-2   The "Principle" of Maximized Communications

the human condition, such as limits on memory, rationality, and information. These notions ultimately waxed into Simon's theory of "bounded rationality," or the idea that people are rational decision makers—within limits. The ultimate effect of Simon's *Administrative Behavior* (other than earning him the Nobel Prize in 1978) and related critiques appearing in the late 1940s was to bury the belief that principles of administration, public or otherwise, could be discovered in the same sense that laws of science and nature could be.[20]

By mid-century the two defining pillars of public administration—the politics/administration dichotomy and the principles of administration—had been abandoned by creative intellects in the field. This abandonment left public administration bereft of a distinct epistemological and intellectual identity.

REACTION TO
THE CHALLENGE, 1947-1950

In the same year that Simon decimated the traditional foundations of public administration in *Administrative Behavior*, he offered an alternative to the old paradigms. For Simon, a new paradigm for public administration meant that there ought to be two kinds of public administrationists working in harmony and reciprocal intellectual stimulation: those scholars concerned with developing "a pure science of administration" based on "a thorough grounding in social psychology," and a larger group concerned with "prescribing for public policy." This latter enterprise was far-ranging indeed. In Simon's view, prescribing for public policy "cannot stop when it has swallowed up the whole of political science; it must attempt to absorb economics and sociology as well." Nevertheless, both a "pure science of administration" and "prescribing for public policy" would be mutually reenforcing components: "There does not appear to be any reason why these two developments in the field of public administration should not go on side by side, for they in no way conflict or contradict."[21]

Despite a proposal that was both rigorous and normative in its emphasis, Simon's call for a "pure science" put off many scholars in public administration. For one thing, there already existed a growing irritation in the field with POSDCORB and other "principles of administration" on the basis of their implicit claims of representing a "pure science"; the challengers of the late 1940s had shown that the "principles of administration" were hardly the final expression of science, and consequently public administrationists were increasingly skeptical that the administrative phenomenon could be understood in wholly scientific terms. Second, Simon's urging that social psychology provided the basis for understanding administrative behavior struck many public administrationists as foreign and discomfiting; most of them had no training in social psychology. Third, since science was perceived as being "value-free," it followed that a "science of administration" logically would ban public administrationists from what many of them perceived as their richest sources of inquiry: normative political theory, the concept of the public interest, and the entire spectrum of human values. While this interpretation may well have rested on a widespread misinterpretation of Simon's thinking (understandable, perhaps, given the wake of *Administrative Behavior*), as Golembiewski contends,[22] the reaction nonetheless was real.

The threat posed by Simon and his fellow challengers of the traditional paradigms was clear not only to most political scientists but to many public administrationists as well. For their part the public administrationists had both a carrot and a stick as inducements not only to remain within political science but to strengthen the intellectual linkages between the fields. The carrot was the maintenance of the logical conceptual connection between public administration and political science—that is, the public policymaking process. Public administration considered the "internal" stages of that process: the formulation of public policies within public bureaucracies and their delivery to the polity. Political science was perceived as considering the "external" stages of the process: the pressures in the polity generating political and social change. There was a certain logic in retaining this linkage in terms of epistemological benefits to both fields. The stick, as we have noted, was the worrisome prospect of retooling only to become a technically oriented "pure science" that might lose touch with political and social realities in an effort to cultivate an engineering mentality for public administration.

As we also have noted, political scientists, for their part, had begun to resist the growing independence of public administrationists and to question the field's action orientation as early as the mid-1930s. Political scientists, rather than advocating a public service and executive preparatory program as they had in 1914, began calling for, in the lucid and graceful phrases of Lynton K. Caldwell, "intellectualized understanding" of the executive branch, rather than "knowledgeable action" on the part of public administrators.[23]

In 1952 Roscoe Martin wrote an article appearing in the *American Political Science Review* calling for the continued "dominion of political science over public administration."[24]

By the post-World War II era political scientists were well under the gun, and could ill afford the breakaway of their most prestigious subfield. The discipline was in the throes of being shaken conceptually by the "behavioral revolution" that had occurred in other social sciences. The American Political Science Association was in financially tight straits. Political scientists were aware that not only had public administrationists threatened secession in the past, but now other subfields, such as international relations, were restive. And in terms of both science and social science, it was increasingly evident that political science was held in low esteem by scholars in other fields. The formation of the National Science Foundation in 1950 brought the message to all who cared to listen that the chief federal science agency considered political science to be the distinctly junior member of the social sciences, and in 1953 David Easton confronted this lack of status directly in his influential book *The Political System*.[25]

The capitulation of the public administrationists to pressures brought on them by political scientists and their own self-doubt about where the field was and should be going was expressed beyond cavil in the major public administration journal in 1950. John Merriman Gaus, a prestigious public administration scholar, penned his oft quoted dictum in the tenth anniversary issue of *Public Administration Review*: "A theory of

public administration means in our time a theory of politics also."[26] The die was cast.

PARADIGM 3:
PUBLIC ADMINISTRATION
AS POLITICAL SCIENCE, 1950-1970

As a result of these essentially political concerns and the icy intellectual critiques of the field, public administrationists leaped back with some alacrity into the mother discipline of political science. The result was a renewed definition of locus—the governmental bureaucracy—but a corresponding loss of focus. Should the mechanics of budgets and public personnel policies be studied exclusively? Or should public administrationists consider the grand philosophic schemata of the "administrative Platonists" (as one political scientist called them),[27] such as Paul Appelby? Or should they, as urged by Simon, explore quite new fields of inquiry such as sociology, business administration, and social psychology as they related to the analysis of organizations and decision making?

In brief, this third phase of definition was largely an exercise in reestablishing the conceptual linkages between public administration and political science. But the consequence of this exercise was to "define away" the field, at least in terms of its analytical focus, its essential "expertise." Thus, writings on public administration in the 1950s spoke of the field as an "emphasis," an "area of interest," or even as a "synonym" of political science.[28] Even long-standing friends of public administration expressed their concern during this period. Frederick Mosher, for example, concluded, "Public administration stands in danger of . . . senescence",[29] while Martin Landau stated his deeply held worry that public administration, "that lusty young giant of a decade ago, may now 'evaporate' as a field."[30]

These concerns, which focused largely on the research agenda of the field, were reflected in the curriculum of public administration as well. A survey conducted in 1961 of graduate education in public administration found such enormous diversity of forms and emphases in university programs[31] that one observer could accurately state, "The study of public administration in the

United States is characterized by the absence of any fully comprehensive intellectual framework."[32] Public administration, as an identifiable field of study, began a long, downhill spiral.

Things got relatively nasty by the end of the decade and, for that matter, well into the 1960s. In 1962 public administration was not included as a subfield of political science in the report of the Committee on Political Science as a Discipline of the American Political Science Association. In 1964, a major survey of political scientists indicated a decline in faculty interest in public administration generally.[33] In 1967, public administration disappeared as an organizing category in the program of the annual meeting of the American Political Science Association. Waldo wrote in 1968 that "many political scientists not identified with Public Administration are indifferent or even hostile; they would sooner be free of it," and added that the public administrationist has an "uncomfortable" and "second-class citizenship."[34] Between 1960 and 1970, only 4 percent of all the articles published in the five major political science journals dealt with public administration.[35] In the 1960s, "P.A. types," as they often were called in political science faculties, pretty much shuffled through political science departments.

At least two developments occurred during this period that reflect in quite different ways the gradually tightening tensions between public administrationists and political scientists: the growing use of the case study as an epistemological device, and the rise and fall of comparative and development administration as subfields of public administration.

Case Studies

The development of the case method began in the 1930s, largely under the aegis of the Committee on Public Administration of the Social Science Research Council.[36] Typically, cases were reports written by practicing public administrators on managerial problems and how they solved them. This framework gave way in the mid-1940s to a new version conceived in the Graduate School of Public Administration at Harvard University (as it was then called) which followed the lines of the public administration case as we know it today. A joint, four-university

program with foundation support resulted, called the Committee on Public Administration Cases. The Committee, in turn, engendered adequate interest in the case method to encourage the establishment in 1951 of the Inter-University Case Program.

The Inter-University Case Program published a spate of excellent public administration case studies, but began to falter in the 1970s; fortunately, the cause of the case study was taken up in 1977 by the newly formed Education for Public Service Clearing House Project, supported by grants from the Ford and Sloan Foundations. The Project lasted only a year, but succeeded in publishing a useful bibliography of public administration cases. In 1978, a successor organization, the Public Policy and Management Program for Case/Curriculum Development, was created via grants provided by the Sloan and Exxon Education Foundations, and was housed in the Intercollegiate Case Clearing House, a group that had been founded in 1957 with the purpose of developing case studies for business schools. The Intercollegiate Case Clearing House expired in 1980, but the Public Policy and Management Program for Case/Curriculum Development survived (and thrived) until 1985; it ultimately published three additional bibliographies of case studies, and developed a number of new cases. Currently, case development in public administration is conducted by the Association for Public Policy and Management, which took over the activities (but not the grants, which terminated in 1985) of the Public Policy and Management Program for Case/Curriculum Development.[37]

The significance of the case study to the development of the field of public administration is a somewhat peculiar one, quite aside from the innate value of the case method as a simulation-based teaching device and as an extraordinarily effective vehicle for illuminating questions of moral choice and decision-making behavior in the administrative milieu. Waldo believes that the emergence of the case method in the late 1940s and its growth throughout the 1950s reflect the response of public administrationists to the "behavioral revolution" in the social sciences generally. On the one hand, the traditional public administrationists, particularly those who entered the field in the 1930s, welcomed the case method as a means of being empirical and "behavioral," and thus provided an additional way of reestablishing the linkages between their field and political science. The case study also offered a comfortable alternative to Simon's call for a rigorous, "pure science of administration" that could—probably would—necessitate a methodological retooling on their part. On the other hand, those public administrationists who entered the field later, and who had been academically reared in political science departments when behaviorism was very much in vogue, were not especially at home with the case study as public administration's answer to the challenge of the behaviorists, but temporarily agreed to the case method as an uneasy compromise. There was also a third grouping of public administrationists in the fifties and sixties who embraced the case study: the retired government bureaucrats, who occasionally were hired by political science departments when public administration was held in low academic esteem but in relatively high student demand. This group appreciated an intellectual approach to the field that identified closely with administrative experience.

The scholarly uneasiness surrounding the use of the case method (which has never had the impact on public administration education that it has had in the business schools, although there are hopeful signs that use of the case method in public administration may be making a comeback) reflects the condition of public administration at the time: a band of dispirited scholars, isolated from their colleagues, but trying to cope in the only way they knew how. But this generalization did not apply to another group of "P. A. types": those who tilled the modish (and financially fertile) fields of comparative and development administration.

Comparative and Development Administration

Cross-cultural public administration, as the comparative approach also is called, is a fairly new development in the field. Prior to the abandonment of the principles of administration, it was assumed that cultural factors did not make any difference in administrative settings because

principles, after all, were principles. As White said in 1936, a principle of administration "is as useful a guide to action in the public administration of Russia as of Great Britain, of Irak as of the United States."[38] But, as Dahl and Waldo, among others, would later point out, cultural factors could make public administration on one part of the globe quite a different animal from public administration on another part.[39] By the late 1940s, in fact, courses in comparative public administration were appearing in university catalogs, and by the early 1950s the American Political Science Association, the American Society for Public Administration, and the Public Administration Clearing House were forming special committees or sponsoring conferences on comparative public administration. The real impetus came in 1962 when the Comparative Administration Group (CAG, founded in 1960) of the American Society for Public Administration received financing from the Ford Foundation that eventually totaled about $500,000.

The Ford Foundation's support of comparative administration (which has since stopped) appears to have stemmed from an altruistic interest in bettering the lot of poor people in the Third World through the improvement of governmental efficiency in the developing nations, and from a political interest in arresting the "advance of communism," especially in Asia, by entrenching bureaucratic establishments composed of local elites—remember, the Ford Foundation's initial decision to support the field in a big way came at the height of the Cold War.

The Foundation's emphasis on the Third World was especially enriching to a semiautonomous subfield of comparative public administration called development administration, which concentrates on the developing nations. Ironically, as we shall shortly see, the practical (if somewhat naive) motivations of the Ford Foundation underlying its funding of comparative and development administration were seldom shared by the recipients of the Foundation's grants.

Comparative public administration, as Ferrel Heady has explained, addresses five "motivating concerns" as an intellectual enterprise: the search for theory; the urge for practical application; the incidental contribution of the broader field of comparative politics; the interest of researchers trained in the tradition of administrative law; and the comparative analysis of on-going problems of public administration.[40] Much of the work in comparative public administration revolves around the ideas of Fred W. Riggs, who "captured" (to quote one assessment)[41] the field's early interest in public administration in the developing nations, and who was simply a very prolific writer and substantial contributor to the theoretical development of the subfield in its early stages. From 1960 to 1970, when the subfield dominated comparative public administration, Riggs chaired ASPA's Comparative Administration Group.[42]

It was and is Riggs' intention and the intention of the comparative public administrationists generally to use their field as a vehicle for stiffening and strengthening theory in public administration. To borrow Riggs' terminology, comparative public administration is to do this by being empirical, nomothetic, and ecological; that is, put crudely, factual and scientific, abstracted and generalizable, systematic and nonparochial. In this emphasis, there always was a quantum of distaste in the ranks of CAG for studies that are rooted solely in the American experience.

Public administration has two differences with its comparative subfield. One is that the larger field is forthrightly and frankly culture-bound. The defense of American public administration's "parochialism" is much the same as that for "parochialism" of the behavioral sciences generally, and it is comprised of four main points:

1. All empirical theory rests on the values of science that guide the conduct of the scientific method;
2. The choice of subjects to study usually reflects the researcher's socialization in and the needs of his or her own society;
3. Since humankind is the object of study in the behavioral sciences, then humanity's values, viewpoints, and culture must be included as part of the theory to be developed, notably as intervening variables in correlational analyses;
4. The uses to which public administration theory and data are put in practice inevitably must be culture-bound.

A second difference that public administration generally has with comparative public administration specifically is the question of action versus theory. From its origins, American public administration has attempted to be "practitioner-oriented" and to be involved with the "real world," while comparative public administration, from its origins, has attempted to be "theory-building" and to seek knowledge for the sake of knowledge. Increasingly, this purely scholarly (as opposed to professional) thrust of comparative public administration has boded ill for the subfield. A spokesperson for the chief financier of CAG, the Ford Foundation, asked what "all this theorizing and all this study will amount to" in terms of improving the practice of public administration, and no one in comparative public administration ever really answered him.[43] In fact, the dominant theme among the members of CAG (although perhaps less emphatically among those involved in development administration) seemed to be to stick to their intellectual guns, and keep building theory as they perceived it. A survey of the CAG membership conducted in 1967 revealed that there was not a

> strongly stated appeal for linking the theoreticians with the practitioners . . . nor for an investment of resources in stimulating empirical research, nor for pursuing the work of the CAG into such practical realms as training and consulting. . . . [P]roposals to channel CAG efforts into the sphere of action received very short shrift among respondents.[44]

Not surprisingly, perhaps, the Ford Foundation terminated its support of CAG in 1971.

Comparative public administration has been productive and active as a subfield; reports of its death are premature, although comparative public administration does appear to have reached a critical point of development. Although CAG had achieved a membership of more than 500 by 1968, in 1973 it was disbanded and merged with the International Committee of the American Society for Public Administration. Relatedly, the field's major journal, *The Journal of Comparative Administration*, was terminated in 1974 after five years of publication. Analyses of core course requirements in Master of Public Administration degree programs across the country found that by the mid-1970s courses in comparative and development administration were virtually never required in the core MPA curriculum, and were almost never taken by students.[45]

Perhaps Golembiewski best sums up the dilemma (or what he calls the "fixation") of comparative and development administration by noting, "public administration should take full notice of the fact that comparative administration's failure rests substantially on a self-imposed failure experience. It set an unattainable goal, that is, in its early and persisting choice to seek a comprehensive theory or model in terms of which to define itself."[46]

While this goal may be unattainable, there are signs that comparative public administration is continuing to make progress. Robert C. Fried sketches the challenges in developing a comprehensive theory of comparative public administration (and, implicitly, lets us know that the mainstream scholars of comparative public administration are still trying to construct such a theory). In his discussion of "Why Universal Theory Remains Elusive," he notes, among other problems, that national administrative systems are far more difficult to study than are other social institutions because of the difficulty in assessing their performance, their boundaries are difficult to pinpoint, cultural differences among nations, and a host of other phenomena.[47] On the other hand, one study of twenty journals conducted over a five-year period, found that the articles on comparative public administration were far more practitioner-oriented, more empirically rooted, more likely to make policy recommendations, and more concerned with developing methodologies, than were articles on this topic in the past. Nevertheless, "the field as a whole. . . . lacks features that give it clear identity . . . and thus the overall status of comparative public administration remains ambiguous."[48]

Political Science:
The Impact of a Parent

Political science—the biological parent, the "mother discipline" of public administration—clearly has had a profound affect on the character of the field. Public administration was born in the house of political science, and its early rearing occurred in its backyard. The fundamental precepts of American political science—the self-evident worth of democracy, a pluralistic polity, political participation, equality under law, and due process are examples of these precepts — continue to hold sway among even the most independently minded public administrationists. While it can be convincingly argued that the American civic culture inculcates these values among all its intellectuals, and that American public administrationists would cherish democratic values regardless of their experiences in political science, it nonetheless seems valid that the environment of political science sharpened and deepened the commitment of public administrationists to the country's core constitutional concepts. If, to indulge in speculation, public administration had been born and bred in the nation's business schools, would we have the same kind of academic field that we have today? Perhaps not. In any case, one can argue that, despite the disdain with which political science often treated public administration, political science was a salutary former of the field in laying its philosophic and normative foundations.

Beyond providing a base of democratic values, however, political science was, and is, of scant utility to the education of public administrators. David L.Weiner argues that, because the personal skills of political actors are typically excluded (or considered only as external variables) in the dominant pluralist theories propounded by political scientists, political science has little relevance to either theory in public administration or to the training of practitioners. Even the bounty of descriptive studies of executive behavior by political scientists is of limited use, since so few attempts are made to explicitly link commonalities and make comparisons among individuals. "What can political science contribute to the improvement of practitioner skill . . . ? An overview of the major intellectual approaches within political science suggests the answer is 'not much.'"[49]

PARADIGM 4:
PUBLIC ADMINISTRATION
AS MANAGEMENT, 1956-1970

Partly because of their second-class citizenship status in a number of political science departments, some public administrationists began searching for an alternative. Although Paradigm 4 occurred roughly concurrently with Paradigm 3 in time, it never received the broadly based favor that political science garnered from public administrationists as a paradigm. Nonetheless, the management option (which sometimes is called "administrative science" or "generic management") was a viable alternative for a significant number of scholars in public administration and, for some, it still is. But in both the political science and management paradigms, the essential thrust was one of public administration losing its identity and its uniqueness within the confines of some "larger" concept. Management is a field that covers organization theory and behavior, planning, decision making, various techniques of "management science" such as path analysis and queuing theory, human resources management, leadership, motivation, communication, management information systems, budgeting, auditing, productivity, and occasionally, marketing.

As a paradigm, management provides a focus but not a locus. It offers techniques, often highly sophisticated techniques, that require expertise and specialization, but in what institutional setting that expertise should be applied is undefined. As in Paradigm 2, administration is administration wherever it is found; focus is favored over locus.

A number of developments, many stemming from the country's business schools, fostered the alternative paradigm of management. In 1956 the important journal *Administrative Science Quarterly* was founded by a public administrationist on the premise that public, business, and institutional administration were false distinctions, that administration was administration. Public administrationist Keith M. Henderson, among others, argued in the mid-1960s that organization theory was, or should be, the overarching focus of public administration.[50] And it cannot be denied that such works as James G. March and Herbert Simon's *Organizations* (1958), Richard Cyert and March's *A Behavioral Theory of the Firm* (1963), March's *Handbook of Organizations* (1965), and James D. Thompson's *Organizations in Action* (1967) gave solid theoretical reasons for choosing management, with an emphasis on organization theory, as the paradigm of public administration.

In the early 1960s "organization develop-

ment" began its rapid rise as a specialty of management. As a focus, organization development represented a particularly tempting alternative to political science for many public administrationists. Organization development as a field is grounded in social psychology and values the "democratization" of bureaucracies, whether public or private, and the "self-actualization" of individual members of organizations. Because of these values, organization development was seen by many younger public administrationists as offering a very compatible area of research within the framework of management: Democratic values could be considered, normative concerns could be broached, and intellectual rigor and scientific methodologies could be employed.

From the late fifties through the mid-sixties, a spate of scholars writing in a variety of management journals accelerated the drumbeat of generic management as the logical successor to more "parochial" paradigms, such as public administration and business administration.[51] Weighing heavily in the value structure of these scholars was the interdisciplinary nature of management studies, and the necessity that university policymakers recognize this aspect and reorganize accordingly.

These intellectual currents had a genuine impact on the curricula of universities. A 1961 survey of graduate study in public administration in the United States found that, while the great majority of public administration programs were still located in political science departments, there was nonetheless "a ground-swell development that tends to pervade all others," and this was the idea of "administration" (*i.e.*, the field of management) as a unifying epistemology in the study of institutions and organizations, both public and private.[52] Similarly, by 1962, as many as a fifth of the business administration programs in the United States, Canada, and Mexico joined the study of business administration with economics, public administration, and other social sciences.[53]

The first institutional expression of the generic management "ground swell" came in the 1950s with the founding of the School of Business and Public Administration at Cornell University, and over the years three models of the generic management school developed.[54] The "purest" of these are those schools of administrative science that were created consciously (indeed, on occasion, ideologically) as generic, and offer master's degrees only in "administra-tion" or "management." Closely related to the school of administrative science is the school of management. "Public management" is offered as a minor option within its degree programs, and the implicit philosophy of these schools is what is good for business is good for government. The third variant of the generic management model is the combined school of business and public administration. Typically, these schools offer a common core curriculum for all students, but house separate departments of public administra-tion that offer their own degree programs.

During the sixties and early seventies in par-ticular, the generic management concept was especially modish. Suddenly it seemed that a number of public administrationists were discov-ering the line in Woodrow Wilson's seminal essay of 1887 that, "the field of administration is a field of business. It is removed from the hurry and strife of politics. . . ."[55]

Perhaps it was this statement by Wilson that initially encouraged an attitude among some management scientists that strikingly paralleled the long-standing attitude held by political scien-tists about public administration: that is, public administration amounted to a subfield of their larger field. In the case of Paradigm 4, however, the "larger" field was management rather than political science. To some degree, such an atti-tude depends upon the perspective of the viewer. In a useful analysis, James L. Perry and Kenneth L. Kramer have clarified what this sense of per-spective means in terms of public administration and management.[56] If, for example, an analyst believes that the primary purpose of an organiza-tion is to achieve social goals (*e.g.*, education), as opposed to instrumental goals (*e.g.*, profits); that similarities and differences among organiza-tions can best be understood by comparing orga-nizations as a whole (*e.g.*, the Department of the Interior and Ford Motor Company), rather than parts of organizations (*e.g.*, the accounting departments); that selected similarities and dif-ferences among organizations carry more weight and are more important than others (*e.g.*, the influence of politics on public agencies in con-trast to private firms), as opposed to according equal importance to all similarities and differ-ences; and that an analytical approach focusing

on the discovery of patterns of organizational behavior (*e.g.*, technology and organizational change), rather than case studies (*e.g.*, "International Widget Markets in East Anglia: Lessons for Us All"), then that analyst likely will conclude that public administration is quite a bit different from private management. Analysts who hold opposite beliefs and approaches proba-bly will contend that the supposed differences between the two are artificial: Management is management is management. Table 2-1 summa-rizes these perspectives.

Just as individual scholars can have differing viewpoints on the question of where public administration fits, so can the larger literature that they both write and use in their own research.

In the case of the management literature, and despite occasional protestations by management scholars to the contrary, the administrative phe-nomenon is typically cast in terms of the busi-ness world. A glance at virtually any introducto-ry text in management brings this point home; government, when it is mentioned at all, often is treated as a "constraint" in the "organizational environment" of the corporation.

As we review in Part Two, the data indicate that the "real-world" skills needed by public administrators and business managers differ markedly, and those successful businesspersons who have become public managers are among the first to deny that there are significant similar-ities between the public and private sectors; pub-lic administrators who enter the corporate world experience comparable difficulties of transi-tion.[57] In addition, as we also see in Part Two, the growing research literature that empirically compares public and private organizations casts grave doubt that the public and private adminis-trative sectors can be fruitfully approached as a single entity except in the broadest strokes con-ceivable. The emerging consensus of public administrationists increasingly appears to be that public and private management are, to cite Wallace Sayre's old saw, fundamentally alike in all unimportant respects.

It follows that if public and private manage-ment are alike in all unimportant respects, then those disciplines which attempt to understand these separate managerial sectors must rely to a significant degree on different sets of knowledge.

TABLE 2-1   Perspectives of Analysts Who Assess Similarities and Differences between Public and Private Management

Issues raised in drawing comparisons	*Perspectives of analysts who conclude that public and private management are more similar than different*	*Perspectives of analysts who conclude that public and private management are more different than similar*
What is an organization's proper role toward its external environment?	To achieve instrumental goals	To achieve social goals
Can similarities and differences in the management of organizations be understood by looking at the parts or at the whole of management?	The similarities and differences can be understood by looking at the parts.	The similarities and differences can only be understood by looking at the whole.
Are all similarities and differences of equal importance?	The similarities and differences are weighted equally.	Some similarities and differences are more important than other similarities and differences.
Should proof of the existence of similarities and differences between organizations be based on case experiences or on dominant patterns within the entire population of organizations?	Case experiences	Dominant patterns

Source: James L. Perry and Kenneth L. Kraemer, "Part Three: Is Public Management Similar to or Different From Private Management?" in *Public Management: Public and Private Perspective,* James L. Perry and Kenneth L Kraemer, eds. (Palo Alto, Calif.: Mayfield, 1983), p. 56.

And research indicates this to be the case. A careful study of eight major, representative generic schools of management found that there were a total of thirty different courses comprising the "common" core of courses for a masters degree.[58] Although there was some limited agreement among the generic schools with regard to eight courses that emphasized operations research, statistics, economics, accounting, finance, and organization theory, there nonetheless remained a "substantial amount of disagreement about the commonality of administrative tools and techniques."[59]

The upshot of Paradigm 4 insofar as many public administrationists were and are concerned is that the field of public administration would exchange, at best, being an "emphasis" in politi-cal science departments, for being, at best, a subfield in generic schools of management.

Management: The Impact of a Foster Parent

If political science was profoundly influential on the evolution and underlying values of public administration, management was less so. But, in many ways, the impact of management on public administration was also more positive. In part, this was because management entered into the upbringing of public administration when the field was beginning its adolescence, and, unlike political science, it was not a blood relative; consequently, public administration was granted more independence and breathing room to grow and develop on its own. This is not to say that the household environment created by the field of management for public administration was one of warmth and succor. It was not. But instead of treating public administration like an abusive parent, as political science occasionally did, management let public administration stay in its house like an absent-minded aunt who was never quite sure who was living in which room, and who often forgot to serve meals.

Management had at least three distinct and beneficial influences on public administration: It forced public administrationists to examine more closely what the "public" in "public administration" meant; it convinced many public administrationists that a whole new set of management methodologies was needed; and it provided public administration with a model of how to assess what, as a field, it was teaching and why.

Understanding the "Public" in Public Administration. One of the principal effects of the management paradigm on public administration concerned the distinction between "public" versus "private" administration. Defining the "public" in public administration has long been a knotty problem for academics. In part, this is because Western culture has never completely sorted out what Stanley I. Benn and Gerald F. Gaus call the "complex-structured concept" of "publicness" and "privateness" in society,[60] and this larger dilemma has had its effects on understanding what constitutes *public* administration.

Fortunately, Benn and Gaus provide one of the better analyses of the components of this complex-structured concept. They contend that publicness and privateness in society are comprised of three dimensions: agency, interest, and access.

Agency, in this sense, refers to the "basic distinction . . . between an agent acting privately, *i.e.*, on his own account, or publicly, *i.e.*, as an officer of the city. . . . The public/private distinction is thus important in answering the questions: What is your standing as an agent? What significance do your actions and decisions have for the status of other people?"[61]
Interest "is concerned with the status of the people who will be better or worse off for whatever is in question."[62] Hence, it is the

interest of the private firm to benefit only the people in it and who own it through salaries and profits. "By contrast, the supposed end of a public enterprise is to serve the public interest (providing a . . . service to any or every member of the community . . .)."[63]
Access refers to the degree of openness that distinguishes publicness from privateness. Access encompasses access to activities (*e.g.*, town meetings are public because they are open to all, but corporate board meetings are private because only board members have access to them); space (the town hall versus the corporate board room); information (everyone may read the minutes of the town meeting, but only board members may peruse those of the board meeting); and resources ("Access to lawnmowers is generally private; access to a . . . drinking fountain can be public in the sense that anyone may use it").[64]

These three dimensions of publicness and privateness are helpful in our understanding of how public administration's experience in its management paradigm defined its public role, for agency, interest, and access all have bearing. We consider them in turn.

The institutional definition. Traditionally, when public administrationists thought about what the "public" in public administration meant at all, they thought about it in *institutional* terms, that is, the management of tax-supported agencies that appeared on government organization charts—the government bureaucracy. The bureaucracy—the agencies—constituted the "locus" of public administration that held sway over the field's focus during the periods of Paradigms 1 (the politics/administration dichotomy) and 3 (public administration as political science). It amounts to an institutional definition of the "public" in public administration, and it is a virtual "match" with Benn and Gaus's thinking about the "agency" dimension of publicness and privateness. (Indeed, even the term "agency" seems to be uniquely suitable to public administration.)

The institutional definition of "public" still dominates thinking in the field. One review of some of the more important literature on public organizations concluded that the vast majority of writers (70 percent of the books reviewed) took an "agency" perspective, as opposed to an "interest" or "access" view in analyzing public organizations.[65]

Nevertheless, there are real problems with an agency, or institutional, definition, and public administration's experience with Paradigm 4 helped tease these out. The most notable problem, and one with which the better theorists in all fields are familiar, is that of the real world; the real world makes an institutionally centered definition of public administration problematic at best and untenable at worst. The research and development contract; the military-industrial complex; the roles of regulatory agencies and their relations with industry; the emergence of "third sector," or nonprofit and voluntary organizations; and the developing awareness of what one author has called "the margins of the state"[66] in reference to such phenomena as the expansive growth of government corporations and the privatization of public policy, all have conspired to make *public* administration an elusive entity, at least when attempts are made to define it in empirical terms that are based on an institutional construct.

The management paradigm was particularly useful in exposing these real-world deficiencies that are inherent to an institutional definition of public administration. Of course, the motivation of the management scientists to do so (occasionally with great glee) may have stemmed as much from a desire to claim public administration as an inseparable part of the management field as from a dedication to shed intellectual light on the problem. But understanding the shortcomings of defining public administration's locus as simply government agencies was nonetheless needed, and the management professors provided this critique. So public administrationists began searching for an alternative framework for understanding the "public" in public administration.

The normative definition. During the 1970s, the alternative that emerged was a normative one, and it reflected Benn and Gaus's concept of "interest" as a dimension of the public/private concept. Inspired in part by the "new public administration" movement (which we explain in greater detail shortly) and its ethical overtones, the normative definition of public administration focused not on government agencies as such, but on those phenomena that affected the public interest. This more dynamic philosophic approach could include not only government agencies and the actions of those agencies, but a plethora of other institutions, technologies, and interrelationships as well. Thus, rather than concentrating on the Department of Defense, for example, as its proper public locus, and leaving, say, Lockheed Corporation to students of business management, public administrationists began to understand that the Department's contractual and political relationships with Lockheed should now be their central object of study, since these relationships clearly involved the public interest. This new, noninstitutional and normative definition of the "public" in public administration was brought about in large part by the difficulties encountered by public administrationists who were working within the confines of generic schools of management in explaining their field to their academic colleagues—who, on occasion, were somewhat less than sympathetic to the role of government in society and even to the notion of the public interest.[67]

The organizational definition. The normative definition of public administration clearly had advantages over the institutional one, but there were problems with it, too. It was, after all, not terribly precise; one person's idea of the public interest might not be shared by another. For example, the president of Lockheed, the Secretary of Defense, and a pacifist might have very different views of what constituted the public interest, or even if the relationships between Lockheed and the Department of Defense were a proper subject of study for those who wished to discern what the public interest was.

Hence, a third option for defining the "public" in public administration presented itself: the organization. Specifically, were public organizations, such as government agencies, public authorities, voluntary associations, and nonprofit corporations, different from private organizations, such as IBM, and if so, how?

Public administrationists had muddled around for years with the notion that public and private organizations were distinctly different, but many of them drew this conclusion more from ideological beliefs than from empirical research.

Beginning in the late 1970s, however, a spate of new research appeared that focused on the public organization. As we explain in Part Two, this research is relatively unambiguous in concluding that there is at least one, absolutely critical difference between the public organization and its private counterpart, and from which many other important differences derive: the impact of the organization's task environment on its inner workings and general behavior. The "task environment" of an organization is that "outside" milieu of other organizations and forces with which the organization must deal to survive. For General Motors, for example, the task environment is the marketplace; for the Interstate Commerce Commission it is a welter of political, economic, social, and market forces. What the new (and, for that matter, the old) literature on public organizations is contending is that the task environment is much more influential and critical to the behavior of public organizations than to private ones.

This idea that the impact of the task environment is central to an understanding of the unique properties of public organizations corresponds nicely with Benn and Gaus's idea of "access" as a dimension of the public/private concept. In contrast to private firms, public agencies are exceptionally accessible. Private citizens, legislators, special interests, other organizations, and many other groups can and do involve themselves in the workings of public organizations far more readily than in private ones. They can determine or significantly influence the level of a public organization's resources (*e.g.*, its annual budget), how those resources will be used (its enabling legislation), and can second-guess (or even reverse) the decisions made by its administrators much more minutely and authoritatively because they have vastly greater access to the information relied upon by the public organization's administrators to make decisions than they have for private organizations.

These realities of organizational access render the public organization (and its administration) a very different creature from the private one, and constitute our third definition of the "public" in public administration.

Our definitions of *public* administration—institutional, normative, and organizational—are in no way mutually exclusive; rather, like Benn and Gaus's dimensions of "publicness" and "pri-

vateness" (agency, interest, and access), they are mutually reinforcing. Together, they form the "public" in public administration, the locus of both the field and the profession.

The New Methodologies.   A second impact that Paradigm 4 had on public administration was methodological. Public administrationists associated with political science departments had long known (or at least it was dawning on them with accelerating speed) that the methodologies of political science were inappropriate to the concerns of public administration. Often these scholars looked to the management schools for illumination and guidance. In many cases, because the public administrationists of Paradigm 3 did not fully understand the methodologies employed by the management scientists, they put great (and frequently inappropriate) stock in their potential utility. In other instances, public administrationists of the Paradigm 3 mode rejected the methodologies of management out of hand because they found them threatening, or were ignorant of them.

The combined consequence of these reactions to the management methodologies was the ultimate recognition by the more committed public administrationists (whether they were found in political science departments or in management schools) that wholly new methodologies were needed for the field. Indeed, the development of these methodologies was central to the emergence of "self-aware" public administration.

In some cases, adapting on a selective basis existing methodologies of both political science and administrative science was appropriate, such as survey research (from political science) and operations research (from management). But, by and large, new methods were needed, and "evaluation research" or "program evaluation" have become the terms that we presently associate with many of the developing bundles of methodologies that public administration calls its own.[68] The emphasis of these methodologies is on whether public programs are effective, efficient and, increasingly, whether they are needed. They borrow techniques from a variety of disciplines, and have a clearly "applied research" cast.

Closely related to evaluation research are the continually evolving methods of budgeting, ranging from line-item to Zero-Base. Increasingly, these "budgetary" concepts are becoming management control strategies that use the methodologies of program evaluation in determining budget allocations.[69]

Finally, there are a number of existing quantitative techniques that fall under the general (and unsatisfactory) rubrics of "public decision making" or "public management" that are being increasingly transformed and adapted to a governmental context. These include probability theory, statistical comparisons, linear correlations and linear programming (particularly sensitivity analysis and the simplex method), government accounting, critical path method, benefit-cost analysis, decision trees, queuing theory, public choice theory, simulations, and management information systems, among others. There have been a number of recent works that do a fine job in applying these and other methods to problems of the public sector.[70]

Learning How to Take Oneself Seriously. A final area in which the management paradigm influenced the evolution of public administration as a field of study was the relatively serious way in which the business schools took their enterprise. Compared to political science departments, at least, the process of educating students in generic schools of management and in business schools was and is far more focused, self-analytical, systematic and, well, *serious*. This is not to say that individual political scientists or public administrationists take their classroom responsibilities lightly; by and large, they do not. But as a field, political science has never put itself through the long-term self-examination and critical assessment that business education has.

During the decade of the 1950s, business educators inflicted upon themselves a well-financed and searching examination of their curricula and instructional programs. The resulting reports—two thick volumes often containing sharp criticism of current practices—had profound effects on business education.[71] By contrast, the only comparable effort conducted by political science during this period resulted in a book that has been dismissed by political scientists themselves as one whose "very triteness and superficiality... made it important."[72] A later attempt to redress this problem focused more specifically on public administration education, but still as it was conducted within the environment of political science, and the results were much the same.[73] Public administrationists criticized the report as

dealing with "venerable and eminently fatiguing issues,"[74] and its only lasting impact seems to have been that it led to the field's concern with a "new public administration."[75] The major opus born by the "new public administration" (Frank Marini's *Toward a New Public Administration* of 1971), however, ultimately had little impact on the public administration curriculum, beyond, perhaps, sensitizing the field to the importance of educating for ethics.

These reports on education for the public service appeared in 1951 and 1967, when public administration was dominated by political science, and their superficiality in dealing with the problems they sought to address was rendered all the more stark when compared to the reports of 1958 that had been prepared by business educators. This lesson has not been lost on the current generation of public administrationists. A proliferating number of analyses of all aspects of public administration education by individual scholars have appeared since the mid-1970s (only a few of which have been cited in this chapter), indicating a renewed concern with the problem. More significantly, however, the National Association of Schools of Public Affairs and Administration has grown into a body of more than 220 member institutions, and is maturing into an organization that has the greatest likelihood of producing a self-evaluation of public administration education that parallels in scope and quality the analyses of business education conducted in the 1950s.[76] Perhaps the model of a searching and systemic self-assessment that has been provided by the business education community may become the single most constructive effect that Paradigm 4 ultimately has on the field of public administration.

THE FORCES OF SEPARATISM 1965-1970

Even at its nadir during the period of Paradigms 3 and 4, public administration was sowing the seeds of its own renaissance. This process—quite an unconscious one at the time—took at least three distinct but complementary forms. Two were largely academic. One was the development of interdisciplinary programs in "science and society," "science, technology, and public policy," or similar titles in major universities, and the other was the appearance of the "new public administration." The third phenomenon was a growing pride among public administrators, particularly at the federal level; in retrospect, this resurgence of self-esteem seems wholly natural, coming, as it did, during the peak of Lyndon Johnson's "Great Society," a period of dramatic government expansion and expansiveness.

"Science, Technology, and Public Policy"

The evolution of "science and society" curricula in universities occurred largely during the late 1960s and was the intellectual forerunner of a later and deeper scholarly interest in the relationships between knowledge and power, bureaucracy and democracy, technology and management, and related "technobureaucratic" dimensions.[77] These programs, although broadly interdisciplinary, often were dominated by public administrationists located in political science departments. By the late 1960s, there were about fifty such programs and they were situated for the most part in the top academic institutions of the country. It was largely this new focus on science, technology, and public policy that gave those public administrationists connected with political science departments any claim to intellectual distinction during the 1960s, and helped offset the loss of a disciplinary identity that then beset public administration. This renewed identity came in part because the focus of science, technology, and public policy did not (and does not) rely conceptually on the pluralist thesis favored by political science. Instead, the focus is elitist rather than pluralist, synthesizing rather than specializing, and hierarchical rather than communal.

"The New Public Administration"

The second development was that of the "new public administration." In 1968, Dwight Waldo, as Albert Schweitzer Professor in Humanities of Syracuse University, sponsored a conference of young public administrationists on the new public administration, the proceedings of which subsequently were published as a book in 1971, titled *Toward a New Public Administration: The Minnowbrook Perspective*. The volume remains the key work of this focus.

The focus was disinclined to examine such traditional phenomena as efficiency, effectiveness, budgeting, and administrative techniques. Conversely, the new public administration was very much aware of normative theory, philosophy, and activism. The questions it raised dealt with values, ethics, the development of the individual member in the organization, the relation of the client with the bureaucracy, and the broad problems of urbanism, technology, and violence. If there was an overriding tone to the new public administration, it was a moral tone. Nevertheless, with hindsight the "new P.A." can be viewed as a call for independence from both political science (it was not, after all, ever called the "new politics of bureaucracy") and management (since management always had been emphatically technical rather than normative in approach).

The science-and-society and the new-public-administration movements were short-lived. Science, technology, and public policy programs eventually devolved into specialized courses on such topics as information systems, growth management, and environmental administration, while the new public administration never lived up to its ambitions of revolutionizing the discipline. Nevertheless, both movements had a lasting impact on public administration in that they nudged public administrationists into reconsidering their traditional intellectual ties with both political science and management, and contemplating the prospects of academic autonomy.

Pride to the Practitioners!

While these intellectual currents were coursing through the halls of academe, an entirely separate phenomenon was roiling in the corridors of power. For want of a better term, we will call it "practitioner pride," and it, too, fostered the rise of an independent field of public administration.

Practitioner pride means that public administrators simply began to assert themselves and their profession as being worthwhile to society. This assertiveness was in no way defensive, arrogant, or angry; it was paramountly an expression of self-confidence.

The symbol of this rising pride in the professionalism of public administration was the

PUBLIC ADMINISTRATION AS NEITHER MANAGEMENT NOR POLITICAL SCIENCE

The following selection discusses why public administration differs significantly from management. In it, Luther Gulick, public administrationist and confidante of President Franklin D. Roosevelt, suggests that the "politico-administrative system" is unique and warrants a unique educational treatment.

My point is best illustrated by a lesson I learned from President Franklin D. Roosevelt. In January 1937, Brownlow, Merriam and I finished our report to the President on the administrative management of the government. He sent it to the Congress in January. Some months later the hearings began and dragged on into that long, hot summer. Unfortunately, Brownlow and Merriam had to go abroad for conferences in Paris and left me with Joe Harris in Washington, to wrestle with Jimmy Byrnes and Congress over the "reorganization bill." As the only member of the committee "in residence," I had a number of sessions with President Roosevelt to test our further ideas on which we were then at work, in our search for greater efficiency and economy in national administration.

One of our technical teams had reached the tentative conclusion that the whole accounting system under social security was meaningless and highly wasteful. As you will remember, both the old age pension and the unemployment laws provided for contributions by the employer and the employee and the setting up of individual accounts under the name of each man and women covered. Millions of personal accounts were involved, with many more millions of accounts to come, and in those days, with electronic accounting still in its infancy, such accounting was very complex.

When it come to making payments to those who retired or were unemployed, however, payments were to be made on the basis of legally defined amounts, which had little or no relation to the cash balances in the individual accounts. Thus the individual cash accounts were quite superfluous for the administration of the system. Moreover the grand total of assets in the

several funds were not invested as such. They were not even segregated in the Treasury.

The technical experts thus reached the conclusion that individual accounts were totally unnecessary, and were a great administrative waste. I presented the idea to Frank Bane, Arthur Altmeyer, Harry Hopkins, Henry Morgenthau, Beardsley Ruml, Alvin Hanson and others, and then to the President. He asked a number of questions, and said to come back. Something apparently troubled him about the suggestion.

Some days later he had me up to his room where he generally had breakfast in bed. He asked me to restate the proposition, and then said: "I don't see any hole in the argument, but the conclusion is dead wrong. The purpose of the accounts for Tom, Dick, and Harry is not to figure what we collect or pay. It is to make it impossible when I am gone for the . . . Republicans to abolish the system. They would never dare wipe out the personal savings accounts of millions. You can't do that in America!"

Immediately I knew he was right. His reasoning rested not solely on the dramatic political insight stated so simply, but also on the psychological impact of personal accounts on the recipients and on those who paid into the social security account.

The error we technical management and accounting experts almost fell into was the inadequate definition of the system which we were analyzing. We did a good job on the law, on the bookkeeping, on administrative mechanics, and the fiscal and cost analysis. But we missed two dimensions of the problem, the political and the psychological, and we overlooked the problem of strategy which was always so important in the mind of the President.

Luther Gulick
Public Administration Review

founding in 1967 of the National Academy of Public Administration. Originally comprised of past presidents of the American Society for Public Administration, its primary founder was James E. Webb, the dynamic Administrator of the National Aeronautics and Space

Administration when the nation's space program was in its heyday.

Webb and his colleagues wanted to create an association of the nation's most distinguished public administrators and academics who could serve as a resource in the solution of public problems—much as the National Academy of Sciences serves as the nation's single most authoritative advisor to government on scientific matters. Like the National Academy of Sciences, in fact, the National Academy of Public Administration is chartered by Congress, and it is the only other Academy in the country that holds a congressional charter.

Although the National Academy of Public Administration has yet to rival the status of the National Academy of Sciences (which was founded in 1863), it has waxed into the single most prestigious group of public administrators at all levels of government, scholars of public administration, and people who have distinguished themselves in some form of public service. Membership is determined by vote of slightly more than 300 Fellows of the Academy, and it is functioning much in the manner that its founders anticipated.

In sum, both the academic and practitioner communities of public administration were, in the last years of the sixties, moving toward an enhanced self-awareness. By 1970, the separatist movement was underway.

PARADIGM 5: PUBLIC ADMINISTRATION AS PUBLIC ADMINISTRATION: 1970-?

In 1970, the National Association of Schools of Public Affairs and Administration (NASPAA) was founded. The formation of NASPAA represented not only an act of secession by public administrationists, but a rise of self-confidence as well.

NASPAA's origins lay in the Council on Graduate Education for Public Administration, which had been founded in 1958 by a small number of graduate programs in the field. The decision in 1970 to dramatically expand the scope of this somewhat cozy group (and later, in 1983, to decide to become a formal professional accrediting agency for Master of Public Administration programs) indicated a determination by public administration educators to take public responsibility for upgrading the educational backgrounds and technical competence of the nation's government managers. By 1970, as represented by the founding of the National

Association of Schools of Public Affairs and Administration, public administration could properly call itself, and increasingly be recognized as, a separate, "self-aware" field of study.

The profile of public administration as a "self-aware" field reflects in many ways what Simon predicted it should become in 1947. Although there is not yet a focus for the field in the form of a "pure science of administration," progress, particularly in the area of organization theory and information science, has been made in this direction. Additionally, considerable progress has been made in refining the applied techniques and methodologies of public administration. There has been, perhaps, less movement toward delineating a locus for the field, or what Simon called "prescribing for public policy." Nevertheless, public administration does appear to be emphasizing such areas as state and local government, executive management, administrative law, and all those questions that seek to explain what "the public interest" is in a technobureaucratic, "Big Democracy."

The emerging curriculum of graduate public administration education reflects these emphases. A more-or-less agreed upon core curriculum seems to have developed for public administration education at the graduate level, and it centers on the environment of public administration (*i.e.*, general introductory courses that focus on the role of the bureaucracy in a democracy), quantitative methods, public budgeting and financial management, organization theory, and human resources administration in the public sector. The average number of required hours in these core areas has grown, with the primary expansion being in quantitative methods, public budgeting, and financial management. [78]

The increase in required courses in the core curriculum reflects to some degree the growing clout of the National Association of Schools of Public Affairs and Administration, which strongly favors a common core curriculum at the graduate level. Over a hundred universities and colleges have been accredited by NASPAA, and accreditation by NASPAA increasingly is held in high esteem by academics, students, and employers alike. Surveys indicate that administrators of Master of Public Administration degree programs find that accreditation by NASPAA brings with it a higher prestige for the MPA program, a

TABLE 2-2   ORGANIZATIONAL PATTERNS OF PUBLIC ADMINISTRATION PROGRAMS, SELECTED YEARS, 1973-1991

ORGANIZATIONAL PATTERN	*1973*	*1977*	*1981*	*1985*	*1991*
	N=101	N=156	N=192	N=193	N=222
1. Separate Professional Schools	25%	21%	17%	14%	13%
2. Separate Departments in Large Units	23	31	33	34	38
3. P.A. Programs Combined With Another Professional School or Department (*e.g.* Business Administration)*	17	8	10	15	9
4. P.A. Programs Within Political Science	36	40	39	31	36
5. Unclassified Organization**	0	0	1	6	6
TOTAL	100	100	100	100	100

*In 1991, 4 percent of public administration programs were combined with another professional school, and 5 percent with another professional department.

**Includes interdisciplinary programs and institutes reporting to the central university administration and other organizational structures.

Source: Derived from National Association of Schools of Public Affairs and Administration, *1992 Directory*, p. x. Percentages have been rounded.

more effective program, and an enhanced ability to recruit higher quality faculty and students.[79]

National surveys indicate that public administration's secession from the fields of political science and management is real. Table 2-2 displays the results of these surveys for selected years. Nineteen eighty-five was the first year that public administration programs within political science departments did not constitute a plurality among the possible organizational patterns available for public administration programs in the universities. Instead, for the first time, separate departments of public administration comprised a plurality. The number of separate departments of public administration has more than tripled since 1973, and between them, separate schools and departments of public administration amount to over half of all university public administration programs that are members of NASPAA.

Similarly, the number of public administration programs that are housed within professional schools or departments— typically, schools or departments of business administration or management—has declined precipitously over the years, from 17 percent in 1973 to 9 percent currently. This decline reflects yet another aspect of the secession, but in this case, a secession from business schools rather than political science departments.

This move toward an autonomous academic field appears to have been good for public administration. Research indicates that the most effective MPA programs are those which are administered by free-standing schools and departments of public administration.[80]

There are some 25,000 students enrolled in masters degree programs in public administration and public affairs, up from fewer than 11,000 in 1973, and over 9,000 undergraduate majors.[81] Of these students, 49 percent are women, 13 percent are black, and 7 percent are of Hispanic origin. Most MPA students are part-time and are holding jobs while they attend classes.

Meeting the educational needs of these students, whether graduate or undergraduate, and, in the process, supplying the public with capable managers, is no easy task. As the president of Harvard University, which houses the John F. Kennedy School of Government, put it:

> The universities have a major opportunity and responsibility to set about the task of training a corps of able people to occupy influential positions in public life. What is needed is nothing less than the education of a new profession. . . . I can scarcely overemphasize the importance of this effort. . . . Since universities are primarily responsible for advanced training in our society, they share a unique opportunity and obligation to prepare a profession of public servants equipped to discharge these heavy responsibilities to the nation.[82]

NOTES

1. Stephen K. Bailey, "Objectives of the Theory of Public Administration," in *Theory and Practice of Public Administration: Scope, Objectives, and Methods*, James C. Charlesworth, ed. Monograph 8 (Philadelphia: American Academy of Political and Social Science, 1968), pp. 128-29.

2. Robert T. Golembiewski, *Public Administration as a Developing Discipline, Part I: Perspectives on Past and Present* (New York: Marcel Dekker, 1977).

3. Woodrow Wilson, "The Study of Administration," *Political Science Quarterly*, 2 (June 1887), pp. 197-222; reprinted 50 (December 1941), pp. 481-506.

4. Richard J. Stillman, II. "Woodrow Wilson and the Study of Administration: A New Look at an Old Essay," *American Political Science Review*, 67 (June 1973), p. 587. More accurately, in formulating his politics/administration dichotomy, Wilson apparently misinterpreted some of the German literature that he read on public administration. In any event, the politics/administration dichotomy clearly had an impact on the early evolution of public administration. See, for example: Paul Van Riper, "The American Administrative State: Wilson and the Founders—An Unorthodox View," *Public Administration Review*, 43 (November/December 1983), pp. 477- 490, and Daniel W. Martin, "The Fading Legacy of Woodrow Wilson," *Public Administration Review*, 48 (March/April 1988), pp. 631-636.

5. Frank J. Goodnow, *Politics and Administration* (New York: Macmillan, 1900), pp. 10-11.

6. *Proceedings of the American Political Science Association, 1913-1914*, p. 264, as cited in Lynton K. Caldwell, "Public Administration and the Universities: A Half-Century of Development," *Public Administration Review*, 25 (March 1965), p. 54.

7. Committee on Practical Training for Public Service, American Political Science Association, *Proposed Plan for Training Schools for Public Service* (Madison, Wis.: American Political Science Association, 1914), p. 3.

8. The financier of the Bureau's Training School for Public Service was Ms. E. H. Harriman, who raised some \$250,000 and turned it over to the Bureau of Municipal Research for a school. Ms. Harriman had preferred that her school be in a university in the first place, but could find no takers; the presidents of Harvard, Yale, and Columbia were approached by her, but she found them to be "polite but amused" by her proposal. See Luther Gulick, "George Maxwell Had a Dream," *American Public Administration: Past, Present, Future*, Frederick C. Mosher, ed. (Syracuse, N.Y.: Maxwell School of Citizenship and Public Affairs and the National Association of Schools of Public Affairs and Administration, 1975), p. 257.

9. Darrell L. Pugh, "ASPA's History: Prologue!" *Public Administration Review*, 45 (July/August, 1985), p. 475.

10. Dwight Waldo, "Public Administration," in *Political Science: Advance of the Discipline*, Marian D. Irish, ed. (Englewood Cliffs, N.J.: Prentice Hall, 1968), pp. 153-189.

11. Morris B. Lambie, ed. *Training for the Public Service: The Report and Recommendations of a Conference Sponsored by the Public Administration Clearing House* (Chicago: Public Administration Clearing House, 1935).

12. Caldwell, "Public Administration and the Universities," p. 57.

13. Dwight Waldo, "Introduction: Trends and Issues in Education for Public Administration," in *Education for Public Service: 1979*, Guthrie S. Birkhead and James D. Carroll, eds. (Syracuse, N.Y.: Maxwell School of Citizenship and Public Affairs, Syracuse University, 1979), p. 15.

14. Pugh, "ASPA's History," p. 476.

15. Donald C. Stone, "Birth of ASPA—Elective Effort in Institution Building," *Public Administration Review*, 35 (January 1975), p. 87.

16. Golembiewski, *Public Administration as a Developing Discipline*, p. 23.

17. Lyndall Urwick, "Organization as a Technical

Problem," in *Papers on the Science of Administration*, Luther Gulick and L. Urwick, eds. (New York: Institute of Public Administration, 1937), p. 49.

18. For a good analysis of this point see: Thomas H. Hammond, "In Defence of Luther Gulick's 'Notes on the Theory of Organization,'" *Public Administration*, 68 (Summer 1990), pp. 143-173.

19. Allen Schick, "The Trauma of Politics: Public Administration in the Sixties," in Mosher, *American Public Administration*, p. 152.

20. Ironically, the notion of "principles" of public administration has been quashed so thoroughly, that there is some scholarly activity underway to bring principles back. As one writer in the field has contended, "The utility of tested administrative principles . . . is as great as it was in 1939." However, this author, as well as others, argues that we should define the concept of administrative principle in considerably less rigid terms than did the fields intellectual forebears, and has suggested that, "A principle is a generalized normative statement based on experience and does not purport to be the universality of a theory or law." See, Ronald C. Moe, "Traditional Organizational Principles and the Managerial Presidency: From Phoenix to Ashes," *Public Administration Review*, 50 (March/April 1990), p. 136.

A principle as a "generalized normative statement" seems to be what Luther Gulick had in mind when he wrote "Notes on the Theory of Organization," in his and Urwick's *Papers on the Science of Administration of 1937* (pp.1-45). And while I agree that there are some general precepts that public administrators would be well advised to follow (*e.g.*, authority should match accountability), and that it is the responsibility of the academics to, in conjunction with the practitioners, develop these precepts, I do not believe that changing the definition of the word, "principle," is the way to do it. Its somewhat casual use by Gulick and Urwick in 1937 not only set them up for scholarly attack later, but the attacks themselves probably deflected needed research on how public organizations work, and this was a disservice. Nevertheless, the first condition in any field of academic and professional endeavor should be retaining clarity and precision of language; hence, redefining or fogging up what "principle" means is not a particularly fruitful way of advancing the discipline.

21. Herbert A. Simon, "A Comment on 'The Science of Public Administration,'" *Public Administration Review*, 7 (Summer 1947) p. 202.

22. Golembiewski, *Public Administration as a Developing Discipline*, pp. 20-22.

23. Caldwell, "Public Administration and the Universities," p. 57.

24. Roscoe Martin, "Political Science and Public Administration—A Note on the State of the Union," *American Political Science Review*, 46 (September 1952), p. 665.

25. David Easton, *The Political System* (New York: Knopf, 1953). Easton pulled no punches in his appraisal of the status of political science. As he noted (pp. 38-40), "With the exception of public administration, formal education in political science has not achieved the recognition in government circles accorded, say, economics or psychology." Or, "However much students of political life may seek to escape the taint, if they were to eavesdrop on the whisperings of their fellow social scientists, they would find that they are almost generally stigmatized as the least advanced."

26. John Merriman Gaus, "Trends in the Theory of Public Administration," *Public Administration Review*, 10 (Summer 1950), p. 168.

27. Glendon A. Schubert, Jr., "'The Public Interest' in Administrative Decision Making," *American Political Science Review*, 51 (June 1957), pp. 346-368.

28. Martin Landau reviews this aspect of the field's development cogently in his "The Concept of Decision-Making in the 'Field' of Public Administration," *Concepts and Issues in Administrative Behavior*, Sidney Mailick and Edward H. Van Ness, eds. (Englewood Cliffs, N.J.: Prentice Hall, 1962), pp. 1-29. Landau writes (p. 9), "Public administration is neither a subfield of political science, nor does it comprehend it; it simply becomes a synonym."

29. Frederick C. Mosher, "Research in Public Administration," *Public Administration Review*, 16 (Summer 1956), p. 171.

30. Landau, "The Concept of Decision Making in the 'Field' of Public Administration," p. 2.

31. Ward Stewart, *Graduate Study in Public Administration* (Washington, D.C.: U.S. Office of Education, 1961).

32. William J. Siffin, "The New Public Administration: Its Study in the United States," *Public Administration*, 34 (Winter 1956), p. 357.

33. Albert Somit and Joseph Tanenhaus, *American Political Science: A Profile of a Discipline* (New York: Atherton, 1964), especially pp. 49-62 and 86-98.

34. Dwight Waldo, "Scope of the Theory of Public Administration," in Charlesworth, *Theory and Practice of Public Administration*, p. 8.

35. Contrast this figure with the percentage of articles in other categories published during the 1960-1970 period: "political parties," 13 percent; "public opinion," 12 percent; "legislatures," 12 percent; and "elections/voting," 11 percent. Even those categories dealing peripherally with "bureaucratic politics" and public administration evidently received short shrift among the editors of the major political science journals. "Region/federal government" received 4 percent, "chief executives" won 3 percent, and "urban/metropolitan government" received 2 percent. The percentages are in Jack L. Walker, "Brother, Can You Paradigm?" *PS*, 5 (Fall 1972), pp. 419-422. The journals surveyed were *American Political Science Review*, *Journal of Politics*, *Western Political Quarterly*, *Midwest Political Science Journal*, and *Polity*.

36. This discussion relies largely on Waldo, "Public Administration," pp. 176-179.

37. Christopher E. Nugent, "Introduction," *Cases in Public Policy and Management: Spring, 1979* (Boston: Intercollegiate Case Clearing House, 1979),

p. v; and Colin S. Diver, "PPMP's Swan Song," *Public Policy and Management Newsletter*, 7 (May 1985), p. 1.

38. Leonard D. White, "The Meaning of Principles of Public Administration," in *The Frontier of Public Administration*, John M. Gaus, Leonard D. White, and Marshall E. Dimock, eds. (Chicago: University of Chicago Press, 1936), p. 22

39. See, for example, Robert A. Dahl, "The Science of Public Administration: Three Problems," *Public Administration Review*, 7 (Winter 1947), pp. 1-11, and Dwight Waldo, *The Administrative State* (New York: Ronald, 1948).

40. Ferrel Heady, "Comparative Public Administration: Concerns and Priorities," in *Papers in Comparative Public Administration*, Ferrel Heady and Sybil Stokes, eds. (Ann Arbor, Mich.: Institute of Public Administration, 1962), p. 3. But see Heady's excellent work, *Public Administration: A Comparative Perspective*, 3rd ed. (New York: Marcel Dekker, 1984), especially Chapter 1.

41. Keith M. Henderson, "A New Comparative Public Administration?" in *Toward a New Public Administration: The Minnowbrook Perspective*, Frank Marini, ed. (Scranton, Penn.: Chandler, 1971), p. 236.

42. Heady, *Public Administration*, pp. 15-16. Riggs' classic work in development administration remains his *Administration in Developing Countries: The Theory of Prismatic Society* (Boston: Houghton Mifflin, 1964), but see also Riggs' *Prismatic Society Revisited* (Morristown, N.J.: General Learning Press, 1973).

43. George Grant, as quoted in Henderson, "A New Comparative Public Administration?" p. 239.

44. *CAG Newsletter* (June 1967), pp. 12-13.

45. Nicholas Henry, "The Relevance Question," in Birkhead and Carroll, *Education for Public Service: 1979*, p. 42.

46. Golembiewski, *Public Administration as a Developing Discipline*, p. 147.

47. Robert C. Fried, "Comparative Public Administration: The Search for Theories," in Naomi B. Lynn and Aaron Wildavsky, eds., *Public Administration: The State of the Discipline* (Chatham, N. J.: Chatham House, 1990), pp. 322-325.

48. Montgomery Van Wart and N. Joseph Cayer, "Comparative Public Administration: Defunct, Dispersed, or Redefined?" *Public Administration Review*, 50 (March/April 1990), p. 238. The authors surveyed twenty "likely journals" published between 1982 and 1986, and analyzed 256 articles on comparative public administration.

49. David L. Weiner, "Political Science, Practitioner Skill, and Public Management," *Public Administration Review*, 52 (May/June 1992), p. 241.

50. Keith M. Henderson, *Emerging Synthesis in American Public Administration* (New York: Asia Publishing House, 1966).

51. See, for example: Edward H. Litchfield, "Notes on a General Theory of Administration," *Administrative Science Quarterly*, 1 (June 1956), pp. 3-29; John D. Millett, "A Critical Appraisal of the Study of Public Administration," *Administrative Science Quarterly*, 1 (September 1956), pp. 177-188; William A. Robson, "The Present State of Teaching and Research in Public Administration," *Public Administration*, 39 (Autumn 1961), pp. 217-222; Andre Molitor, "Public Administration Towards the Future," *International Review of Administrative Sciences*, 27, No. 4 (1961), pp. 375-384; Ivan Hinderaker, "The Study of Administration: Interdisciplinary Dimensions," *Summary of Proceedings of the Western Political Science Association*, Supplement to *Western Political Quarterly*, 16 (September 1963), pp. 5-12; Paul J. Gordon, "Transcend the Current Debate in Administration Theory," *Journal of the Academy of Management*, 6 (December 1963), pp. 290-312; and Lynton K. Caldwell, "The Study of Administration in the Organization of the University," *Chinese Journal of Administration* (July 1965), pp. 8-16.

52. Stewart, *Graduate Education in Public Administration*, p. 39.

53. Delta Sigma Pi, *Eighteenth Biennial Survey of Universities Offering an Organized Curriculum in Commerce and Business Administration* (Oxford, Ohio: Educational Foundation of Delta Sigma Pi, 1962).

54. Much of the following discussion is drawn from Kenneth L. Kraemer and James L. Perry, "Camelot Revisited: Public Administration Education in a Generic School," *Education for Public Service: 1980*, Guthrie S. Birkhead and James D. Carroll, eds. (Syracuse, N.Y.: Maxwell School of Citizenship and Public Affairs, Syracuse University, 1980), pp. 87-102.

55. Wilson, "The Study of Administration," p. 209.

56. James L. Perry and Kenneth L. Kramer, "Part Three: Is Public Management Similar or Different From Private Management?" in *Public Management: Public and Private Perspectives*, James L. Perry and Kenneth L. Kramer, eds. (Palo Alto, Calif.: Mayfield, 1983), p. 56.

57. See, for example, Michael Blumenthal, "Candid Reflections of a Businessman in Washington," *Fortune* (January 29, 1979); Donald Rumsfeld, "A Politician Turned Executive," *Fortune* (September 10, 1979); A. J. Cervantes, "Memoirs of a Businessman-Mayor," *Business Week* (December 8, 1973); and James M. Kouzes, "Why Businessmen Fail in Government," *New York Times* (March 8, 1987).

58. Kraemer and Perry, "Camelot Revisited," p. 92. The investigators found twenty-two universities by their own count that used a generic model in teaching management.

59. *Ibid.*

60. Stanley I. Benn and Gerald F. Gaus, "The Public and the Private: Concepts and Action," in *Public and Private in Social Life*, S. I. Benn and G. F. Gaus, eds. (New York: St. Martin's, 1983), p. 5.

61. *Ibid.*, p. 9.

62. *Ibid.*, p. 10.

63. *Ibid.*

64. *Ibid.*, p. 9.

65. James L. Perry, Hal G. Rainey, and Barry Bozeman,

"The Public Private Distinction in Organization Theory: A Critique and Research Strategy," paper presented at the 1985 Annual Meeting of the American Political Science Association, New Orleans, August 29-September 1, 1985, Table 1.

66. Ira Sharkansky, *Wither the State? Politics and Public Enterprise in Three Countries* (Chatham, N.J.: Chatham House, 1979), p. 11.

67. An admittedly unfair (and possibly fictitious) example of this problem is provided by a university, at which I was once a faculty member. It allegedly housed "the largest business school in the Free World." (It had then some 12,000 students.) The story goes that a lone student stood up in the back of a lecture hall containing several hundred business administration students and asked the instructor, "Sir, what is the social responsibility of business?" The professor replied unhesitatingly, "Son, business has no social responsibility." On hearing the answer, the class burst into applause.

68. Perhaps the seminal statement of evaluation research as it has been adopted by the field of public administration is Carol H. Weiss, *Evaluation Research: Methods of Assessing Programs* (Englewood Cliffs, N.J.: Prentice Hall, 1972).

69. A detailed and excellent study of this process at the federal level is contained in: Hugh Heclo, "Executive Budget Making," paper presented to the Urban Institute Conference on Federal Budget Policy in the 1980s, Washington D.C.: September 29-30, 1983. But see also: Joseph White, "Much Ado About Everything: Making Sense of Federal Budgeting," *Public Administration Review*, 45 (September/October 1985), pp. 623-630.

70. Five good examples of this emerging literature are: Susan Welch and John C. Comer, *Quantitative Methods for Public Administration: Techniques and Applications* 2nd ed.(Homewood, Ill.: Dorsey, 1988); E. S. Quade, *Analysis for Public Decisions*, 2nd ed. (New York: North Holland, 1982); Christopher K. McKenna, *Quantitative Methods for Public Decision Making* (New York: McGraw-Hill, 1980); Richard D. Bingham and Marcus E. Etheridge, eds. *Reaching Decisions in Public Policy and Administration: Methods and Applications* (New York: Longman, 1982); and John Kenneth Gohagan, *Quantitative Analysis for Public Policy* (New York: McGraw-Hill, 1980). For an applied version of some of these techniques, see: Nicholas Henry, ed., *Doing Public Administration: Exercises in Public Management*, 3rd ed., Dubuque, Iowa: William C. Brown, 1991).

71. Robert Aaron Gordon and James E. Howell, *Higher Education for Business* (New York: Columbia University Press, 1959); and Frank Pierson, *The Education of American Businessmen* (New York: Carnegie Corporation, 1959).

72. Albert Somit and Joseph Tannenhaus, *The Development of Political Science* (Boston: Allyn & Bacon, 1967), p. 188. Somit and Tannenhaus are referring to: Committee for the Advancement of Teaching, American Political Science Association, *Goals for Political Science* (New York: Sloane, 1951).

73. John C. Honey, "A Report: Higher Education for Public Service," *Public Administration Review*, 27 (November 1967), pp. 301-319.

74. Peter Savage, "What Am I Bid for Public Administration?" *Public Administration Review*, 28 (July 1968), p. 391. See also James S. Bowman and Jeremy F. Plant, "Institutional Problems of Public Administration Programs: A House Without a Home," *Public Administration Education in Transition*, Thomas Vocino and Richard Heimovics, eds. (New York: Marcel Dekker, 1982), p. 40.

75. Schick, "The Trauma of Politics, p. 162.

76. As this is written, in fact, NASPAA continues to struggle with an in-depth examination of the public administration curriculum. The funding for this project is provided by the Mellon Foundation and is being conducted largely at Princeton University's Woodrow Wilson School of Public and International Affairs. However, it is unclear at this point if the final product will be comparable in depth and thoroughness to the studies of business education conducted in the fifties. It is, perhaps, comforting to know that professors of public administration take the challenge of developing a more useful curriculum seriously. For a stinging critique of public administration education, see: Curtis Ventriss, "Contemporary Issues in American Public Administration Education: The Search for Educational Focus," *Public Administration Review*, 51 (January/February 1991), pp. 4-14.

77. Representative works of the Science, Technology, and Public Policy movement that had lasting impacts include: Michael D. Reagan, *Science and the Federal Patron* (New York: Oxford University Press, 1969) and Lynton Keith Caldwell, *Environment: A Challenge to Modern Society* (Garden City, N.Y.: Natural History Press, 1970).

78. Khi V. Thai, "Does NASPAA Peer Review Improve the Quality of PA/A Education?" *Public Administration Quarterly*, 8 (Winter 1985), pp. 446, 450.

79. Mark R. Daniels, "Public Administration as an Emergent Profession: A Survey of Attitudes About the Review and Accreditation of Programs," paper presented at the National Conference of the American Society for Public Administration, New York, April 1983, and J. Norman Baldwin, "Comparison of Perceived Effectiveness of MPA Programs Administered Under Different Institutional Arrangements," *Public Administration Review*, 48 (September/October 1988), pp. 876-884.

80. Baldwin, "Comparison of Perceived Effectiveness of MPA Programs Administered Under Different Institutional Arrangements," p. 876. Baldwin surveyed 207 MPA program directors, and received responses from 158, over a 76 percent response rate.

81. National Association of Schools of Public Affairs and Administration, *1992 Directory of Programs* (Washington, D.C.: National Association of Schools and Public Affairs and Administration, 1992), p. xi. All the following data are taken from this source, pp. ix-xii.

82. Derek Bok, "The President's Report, 1973-74," *Harvard Today*, 18 (Winter 1975), pp. 4-5, 10.

PUBLIC ORGANIZATIONS: THEORIES, CONCEPTS, AND PEOPLE

Part Two packs in an unusually large number of notions and asks you to (with some help from the text) sort them out and try to match them with your own experiences in and with bureaucracies and bureaucrats. Part Two may be that portion of this book which will have the most lasting value for you as you enter the world of organizations. It covers the intellectual evolution of organization theory and organizational behavior, the major theoretical and behavioral concepts in the field, discusses why bureaucrats behave in the ways they do, and attempts to help you gain a bit of insight about what to expect should you find yourself working in the public sector. Throughout Part Two, an effort is made to show how public organizations differ from private organizations, although, of course, there are similarities as well.

Fundamentally, organizations are people. Keep this in mind not only when you read Part Two, but also when you deal with organizations.

CHAPTER 3

THE THREADS OF ORGANIZATION THEORY

In this and the following chapters, we shall examine various perspectives on organizations, pertinent concepts about how organizations work, and the kinds of people one finds in organizations.

MODELS, DEFINITIONS, AND ORGANIZATIONS

The notion of "models," a useful epistemological device in the social sciences, has considerable utility in discussing what an organization is. A *model* is a tentative definition that fits the data available about a particular object. Unlike a definition, a model does not represent an attempt to express the basic, irreducible nature of the object, and is a freer approach that can be adapted to situations as needed. Thus, physicists treat electrons in one theoretical situation as infinitesimal particles and in another as invisible waves. The theoretical model of electrons permits both treatments, chiefly because no one knows exactly what an electron is (that is, no one knows its definition).

So it is with organizations. Organizations are different creatures to different people, and this

phenomenon is unavoidable. Thus, organizations are "defined" according to the contexts and perspectives peculiar to the person doing the defining. For example, Victor A. Thompson states that an organization is "a highly rationalized and impersonal integration of a large number of specialists cooperating to achieve some announced specific objective"; Chester I. Barnard defines an organization as "a system of consciously coordinated personal activities or forces of two or more persons"; E. Wight Bakke says an organization is "a continuing system of differentiated and coordinated human activities utilizing, transforming, and welding together a specific set of human material, capital, ideational and natural resources into a unique, problem-solving whole whose function is to satisfy particular human needs in interaction with other systems of human activities and resources in its particular environment."[1]

These models of organizations are all quite different and lead to quite different conclusions on the part of their exponents. Bakke, a social psychologist, has constructed a model of organizations that allows him to dwell on the human effects organizations engender, which he does at length and with little regard for how organizations get their tasks accomplished. Conversely,

Barnard's model permitted him to write about what interested him in organizations as a retired president of New Jersey Bell Telephone Company; that is, how cooperation and coordination were achieved in organizations. Thompson's model, with its emphasis on rationality, impersonality, and specialization, ultimately leads to his taking the radical stance that organizations should have no administrators whatever, only coldly efficient "specialists." Yet, none of these models is "wrong"; they only facilitate what they are to be used to illustrate.

Even though organizations represent different things to different people, it is not enough to "define" organizations, as James G. March and Herbert A. Simon once did, with the phrase, "organizations are more earthworm than ape."[2] As an indication of their simplicity, March and Simon are correct, to be sure, but it is possible to ascertain additional characteristics of organizations that will be useful in our model for the remainder of this book. Organizations

1. are purposeful, complex human collectivities;
2. are characterized by secondary (or impersonal) relationships;
3. have specialized and limited goals;
4. are characterized by sustained cooperative activity;
5. are integrated within a larger social system;
6. provide services and products to their environment;
7. are dependent upon exchanges with their environment.

These features make up our working model of organizations, both public and private.

Organization theorists, using essentially this list of characteristics but stressing different features of it, have produced a vast body of literature on the nature of organizations. The literature can be trisected into these major streams: the closed model, the open model, and what James D. Thompson called "the newer tradition," which attempts to synthesize both models.[3] These three streams, each with its own "schools" and substreams, constitute the threads of organization theory. The remainder of this chapter considers each literary stream, the thinking of its principal contributors, and the relationships and distinctions among the streams. In reading this chapter, you may wish to refer to Table 3-1 occasionally, as it summarizes these literatures by theoretical school.

THE CLOSED MODEL OF ORGANIZATIONS

Traditionally the closed model of organizations has perhaps had the largest influence on the thought of public administrationists. The model

TABLE 3-1   The Models of Organization Theory

The Closed Model	The Literature of Model Synthesis: Uncertainty Reduction	The Open Model
1. Bureaucratic theory (Weber)	(Barnard, Simon, March and Simon, Cyert and March, Thompson)	1. Human relations (Roethlisberger and Dickson, Maslow, Mayo, Herzberg)
2. Scientific management (Taylor, the Gilbreths)		2. Organization development (Lewin, McGregor, Bennis, Bechard, French and Bell, Lippitt, Shepard, Blake Benne, Bradford, Argyris, Golembiewski)
3. Administrative, or generic management (Mooney and Reiley, Gulick and Urwick, Fayol, Follett)		3. The organization as a unit in its environment (Barnard, Selznick, Clark, Downs, Warwick, Meyer)

goes by many names. Bureaucratic, hierarchical, formal, rational, and mechanistic are some of them, and there are at least three permutations, or schools, that have thrived within its framework: bureaucratic theory, scientific management, and administrative management (sometimes called generic management).

Characteristics

Tom Burns and G. M. Stalker have provided a useful listing of the principal features of the closed model of organizations that will suffice for our purpose:[4]

1. Routine tasks occur in stable conditions.
2. Task specialization (i.e., a division of labor) is central.
3. Means (or the proper way to do a job) are emphasized.
4. Conflict within the organization is adjudicated from the top.
5. "Responsibility" (or what one is supposed to do, one's formal job description) is emphasized.
6. One's primary sense of responsibility and loyalty is to the bureaucratic subunit to which one is assigned (e.g., the accounting department).
7. The organization is perceived as a hierarchic structure (i.e., the structure "looks" like a pyramid):

8. Knowledge is inclusive only at the top of the hierarchy (i.e., only the chief executive knows everything).
9. Interaction between people in the organization tends to be vertical (i.e., one takes orders from above and transmits orders below), but not horizontal.
10. The style of interaction is directed toward obedience, command, and clear superordinate/ subordinate relationships.
11. Loyalty and obedience to one's superior and the organization generally are emphasized, sometimes at the expense of - performance.

12. Prestige is "internalized," that is, personal status in the organization is determined largely by one's office and rank.

So runs our closed model of organizations. One should recall that, like any model, it is what Max Weber called an "ideal type."[5] An *ideal type* is what an organization (or any other phenomenon) tries to be. Once we know what something wants to become (such as a little girl who wants to become a firefighter), we can predict with some accuracy how it will behave (the same little girl probably will want a toy fire engine for her birthday). In this logic, closed-model organizations behave in such a way as to fulfill the twelve characteristics posited by Burns and Stalker, although this is not to say that any actual organization meets all twelve features in practice. For example, of organizations that are widely known, the Pentagon and the American military organization likely come closest to accomplishing the requisites of the closed model, but the Pentagon's exceptions to the model are obvious: Nonroutine tasks, unstable conditions, and externalized prestige are frequent facts of organizational life in the military. Nevertheless, the military behaves in such a way as to minimize these exceptions to the closed model, along which it is basically patterned.

Bureaucratic Theory

The first school of the closed model that warrants consideration is that of bureaucratic theory. Its chief theorist and best known representative is Max Weber, a remarkable German sociologist who also gave us the sociology of religion, a theory of leadership and, with them those phrases familiar to scholars and practitioners in public administration: "the Protestant work ethic" and "charisma." In what is perhaps a too succinct summary of Weber's model of bureaucracy, the features of bureaucracy amounted to:

1. hierarchy,
2. promotion based on professional merit and skill,
3. the development of a career service in the bureaucracy,
4. reliance on and usc of rules and regulations, and

5. impersonality of relationships among career-professionals in the bureaucracy and with their clientele.

Organization theorists working in the open model stream of organization theory have been most critical of Weberian bureaucratic theory, largely because it has been the most influential of all the schools in the closed model and most clearly represents the values of the closed model. Open-model theorists dislike the rigidity, the inflexibility, the emphasis on means rather than ends, and the manipulative and antihumanist overtones of Weberian bureaucratic theory. But, in Weber's defense, these criticisms often have been overdrawn and certainly have not been leveled with Weber's own social context in mind. Although the origins of bureaucracy can be traced at least as far back as Cardinal Richelieu's machinations to unify the French kingdom and Frederick the Great's project to turn poverty-ridden, land-locked Prussia into an efficient, military nation, Weber was writing at a time when "Blood-and-Iron" Bismarck was in the final stages of engineering his consolidation of the German states and when positions of public trust still were assigned on the basis of class rather than ability. To Weber, an impersonal, rule-abiding, efficient, merit-based career service provided the surest way of fulfilling the public interest in the face of a politically fragmented but culturally unified Germany and an arrogant, powerful, yet somewhat silly *Junker* class. Justice based on rational law would replace what Weber called "*Kadijustice*," or justice based on the whim of a charismatic leader; the rationalism of the bureaucracy would offset the romanticism of the polity, and this was to the good of society. In short, Weber, in a large sense, was not antihumanist in his thinking, but the effects of the bureaucracy that he so loudly touted often were, both to the citizens who were governed by the bureaucracy, and to the bureaucrats themselves.

Scientific Management

Another major literary stream encompassed by the closed model is represented by the theories of scientific management. Scientific management refers to what is more popularly known as time-motion studies; it flourished at the beginning of the twentieth century, and remains very much in use today in industry.

Scientific management had (and has) its intellectual home in America's business schools. Its motivating concern was to improve organizational efficiency and economy for the sake of increased production. Perhaps the most firmly entrenched characteristic of scientific management was its view of humanity. Human beings were perceived as being adjuncts of the machine, and the primary objective of scientific management was to make them as efficient as the machines they operated. This view of humanity applied solely to workers on the assembly line and in the lower organizational echelons; it did not apply to upper-echelon managers—it was to them that the scientific management literature was addressed.

The key representatives of the scientific management school are Frederick Taylor (who gave scientific management its name with his 1911 volume, *Principles of Scientific Management*) and Frank and Lillian Gilbreth.[6] The person-as-machine conception, replete with all its discomfiting moral overtones, are on clear display in the writings of Taylor and the Gilbreths. A notorious example of the conception occurs in Taylor's (likely fictional[7]) story of Schmidt, the pig-iron hauler, whom Taylor unabashedly declared to be "stupid . . . phlegmatic . . . [and] more nearly resembles in his mental make-up the ox than any other type."[8] After Taylor analyzed Schmidt's physical movements, he ordered him to change how he moved his body and, as a result of these "scientific" alterations in Schmidt's physical behaviors, Schmidt's production went up from twelve and a half tons of pig-iron hauled per day to forty-seven tons. Taylor is obviously proud of his feat in rendering Schmidt a more efficient, machine-like man, and because of such feats he was eminently successful as a time-motion expert in his day. Similarly, Frank and Lillian Gilbreth developed the concept of the "therblig," each one of which represented a category of eighteen basic human motions—all physical activity fell into a therblig class of one type or another. (The scientific management experts rarely were constrained by false modesty; try reading "therblig" backwards.)

The person-as-machine model of scientific management doubtless has a distasteful aura.

People are not machines. They do not have an array of buttons on their backs that merely need pressing for them to be machines. This distaste with the person-as-machine conception, however, has often been extended by some critics to include a distaste for the notion of efficiency. Outside the realms of theory, few are against efficiency in government, least of all the governed. So one must be wary of dismissing the value of efficiency along with "Taylorism" (as scientific management also is called), as occasionally has been done by humanist critics of the school.

One also should be cautious of relegating Taylorism to the intellectual slag heap on the assumption that its scholar/practitioners were consciously tools of the robber barons and premeditated exploiters of the working class. To a degree they were, but Taylor and the Gilbreths would likely be shocked by the suggestion. Taylor's Schmidt, it should be recalled, was employed according to the standard industrial system of the age: the piece-work method. For every ton Schmidt hauled, he was paid accordingly. Thus, to increase his daily production meant that Schmidt, as well as his bosses, was better off. Moreover, Taylor himself had served as an apprentice workman in a steel company and knew what that side of life was like. For their part the Gilbreths applied their therbligs to surgery techniques in hospitals, and the sharply-ordered "Scalpel! Sponge!" we watch being slapped into a surgeon's palm by a hyperefficient nurse on television is a direct result of Gilbreth's operating-room studies. Prior to the Gilbreths' analysis, surgeons rustled around for their own instruments with one hand, evidently holding open the incision with the other. Efficiency can serve humanism as well as any other value, and this aspect sometimes is overlooked by open-model critics.

As a final note, it is worth observing that Taylorism has been used—and is being used—by the federal government, occasionally in such a way as to render the person-as-machine model painfully apparent. One example is the use of "psychotechnology" by the National Aeronautics and Space Administration (NASA) in its training of astronauts. The objective of NASA's use of psychotechnology is to "integrate" the astronaut with the technological environment of his space capsule, both mentally and physically, in order to reduce his or her response time. Psychotechnology is essentially scientific management updated, but with the added fillip of psychoemotional as well as physical conditioning being practiced.

Administrative Management

The final literature based on the closed model is administrative management, which also is called generic management. Luther Gulick and Lyndall Urwick's *Papers on the Science of Administration* is an outstanding example of administrative management in public administration, although James D. Mooney and Alan C. Reiley's *Principles of Organization* is more frequently cited as exemplary.[9]

Administrative management presumed that administration is administration, wherever it was found (hence, its other title, "generic"), and therefore devoted its energies to the discovery of "principles" of management that could be applied anywhere. Once an administrative principle was found, it logically should work in any kind of administrative institution: government bureaucracies, business management, hospitals, schools, universities, prisons, libraries, public health or international institutions—wherever. Thus, Gulick and Urwick gave us POSDCORB, and Mooney and Reiley contributed four principles of organization: the coordinative principle, the scalar principle (or hierarchial structure), the functional principle (or division of labor), and the staff/line principle. There were other exponents, of course, such as Mary Parker Follet and Henri Fayol.[10] Their impact on public administration has been detailed in Chapter 2.

Administrative management is closer in concept and perceptions to Weberian bureaucratic theory than to Taylorian scientific management. The major reason for this is that bureaucracies are less concerned with time-motion economies than are assembly lines, and both bureaucratic theorists and administrative management analysts primarily were concerned with the optimal organization of administrators rather than production workers. But, like both bureaucratic theory and scientific management, administrative management holds economic efficiency (or "rationalism") as its ultimate criterion.

The difference between traditional bureaucratic theory and administrative management largely is one of theory as opposed to implementation. Weber and his academic peers were interested in learning how bureaucracies functioned, why they functioned as they did, and what their implications for the large society were. Mooney and Reiley, Gulick and Urwick, Follett, Fayol, and their colleagues thought they knew how bureaucracies functioned and why, and they were interested in applying the principles of administration they had derived from their knowledge to actual administrative organizations to enable administrators to operate more efficiently and effectively.

There also was a second, more subtle difference between bureaucratic theory and administrative management, one that provides a linkage between the closed and open models of organizations. Weber, like Taylor, did not think much about underlings and toilers in organizations beyond their capacities for obedience (in Weber's case) and production (in Taylor's case), and both capacities were regarded as being almost limitless, provided managers took their respective writings to heart. But with the emergence of the theorists on administrative management, a hint surfaced that underlings and toilers in organizations conceivably might have minds of their own. Indeed, it was not much of a hint, barely an inkling. But it was there, and it is noticeable in Mooney and Reiley's contention that the "indoctrination" of subordinates is vital to well-managed organizations. In fact, Mooney and Reiley attributed the durability of the Roman Catholic Church to its ability to indoctrinate—a talent which has maintained a viable, continuing organization for nearly two thousand years, and in their view is a highly praiseworthy method of organizational control and survival.

Such a grudging concession to the thinking powers of subordinates did not amount to much in terms of high esteem for the subordinates' mental prowess generally. But it represented a recognition that subordinates were people (like managers) and could think (almost like managers). It was left for certain writers using the open model to assert that underlings and toilers could indeed think, feel, and behave on their own, and often differently from the ways they were supposed to. Some of these writers would argue that subordinates could outthink, outsmart, and outfox their superordinates—and did—with both ease and frequency.

THE OPEN MODEL OF ORGANIZATIONS

The open model of organizations traditionally has had a greater influence on business administration than on public administration, although this situation has been changing in recent years. Like the closed model, the open model goes by many names. Collegial, competitive, freemarket, informal, natural, and organic are some of them, and, like the closed model, three literary streams run through the model's overarching framework. These streams, or schools, are, first, the human relations school; second, the newer field of organization development; and third, the literature that views the organization as a unit functioning in its environment. It is this final stream that has a unique utility to public administration.

The historical origins of the open model precede the intellectual roots of the closed model, originally developed by Max Weber, by more than a century and a half. In a perceptive essay, sociologist Alvin W. Gouldner[11] attributes the open model's original conceptualization to Count Louis de Rouvroy Saint-Simon, the brilliant French social thinker, and to his protege Auguste Comte, the "father of sociology." Saint-Simon and Comte wrote during a span of time that began in the corrupt *ancien régime* of Louis XIV, continued through the bloody French Revolution and the rule of the military despot and national hero, Napoleon Bonaparte, and ended under the reign of Louis Napoleon. Partly as a reaction to the administrative stultification of the last days of the French kings and the explosiveness of the Revolution, Saint-Simon, and later Comte, speculated on what the administration of the future would be like. They thought that it would be predicated on skill rather than heredity, "cosmopolitanism" (by which Saint-Simon meant the development of new professions based on technology) would be the order of the day, and organizations themselves would be a liberating force for humanity. Throughout, Saint-Simon and Comte stressed the value of spontaneously created organizations that developed "naturally" as they were needed. On reflection, Saint-Simon and Comte's views on organizations and society sound like a seventeenth-century version of Alvin Toffler's concept of "Ad Hocracy" in his book *Future Shock*.[12]

Characteristics

Once again we rely on Burns and Stalker's research for a listing of the principal features of the open model.[13]

1. Nonroutine tasks occur in unstable conditions.
2. Specialized knowledge contributes to common tasks (thus differing from the closed model's specialized *task* notion in that the specialized *knowledge* possessed by any one member of the organization may be applied profitably to a variety of tasks undertaken by various other members of the organization).
3. Ends (or getting the job done), rather than means, are emphasized.
4. Conflict within the organization is adjusted by interaction with peers, rather than adjudicated from the top.
5. "Shedding of responsibility" is emphasized (*i.e.*, formal job descriptions are discarded in favor of all organization members contributing to all organizational problems).
6. One's sense of responsibility and loyalty is to the organization as a whole.
7. The organization is perceived as a fluidic network structure (*i.e.*, the organization "looks" like an amoeba):

8. Knowledge can be located anywhere in the organization (*i.e.*, everybody knows something relevant about the organization, but no one, including the chief executive, knows everything).
9. Interaction between people in the organization tends to be horizontal (*i.e.*, everyone interacts with everyone else), as well as vertical.
10. The style of interaction is directed toward accomplishment, "advice" (rather than commands), and is characterized by a "myth of peerage," which envelops even the most obvious superordinate/subordinate relationships (*e.g.*, a first-name "familiarity" exists even between president and office boy, on the logic that the maintenance of an image of intimacy is somehow "friendlier").
11. Task achievement and excellence of performance in accomplishing a task are emphasized, sometimes at the expense of obedience to one's superiors.
12. Prestige is "externalized" (*i.e.*, personal status in the organization is determined largely by one's professional ability and reputation, rather than by office and rank).

So runs our open model of organizations, which, like the closed model, is an ideal type. It seldom if ever exists in actuality, although a major university might come close (which is why the open model occasionally is called the "collegial" model). A Big Ten or Ivy League university could meet many of the requisites of the open model, notably specialized knowledge located throughout the organization, largely horizontal interaction, and externalized prestige. But exceptions to the model also are apparent; tasks (*e.g.*, teaching, research, studying) are relatively routine and, at least among the faculty, one is likely to find a higher degree of loyalty to the subunit (*i.e.*, the academic department) than to the organization as a whole.

Human Relations

Human relations, the first of three schools of the open model, focuses on organizational variables never considered in the closed model: cliques, informal norms, emotions, and personal motivations, among others. Paradoxically, this focus resulted from what originally was intended to be a research undertaking in scientific management, a literature at the opposite end of the continuum in terms of the values held by its theorists.

In 1924 Elton Mayo and Fritz J. Roethlisberger began a series of studies (later known as the Hawthorne studies, for the location of the plant) of working conditions and worker behavior at a Western Electric factory. Their experiment was predicated on the then-plausible Taylorian hypothesis that workers would respond like machines to changes in working conditions. To test their hypothesis they intended to alter the intensity of light available to a group of randomly selected workers. The idea—that when the light became brighter, production would increase, and when the light became dimmer, production would decrease—is all very common-sensical, of course. The workers were told they would be observed as an experimental group. The lights were turned up and production went up. The lights were turned down and production went up. Mayo and Roethlisberger were disconcerted. They dimmed the lights to near darkness, and production kept climbing.

Among the explanations of this phenomenon that later came forth were

1. Human workers probably are not entirely like machines.
2. The Western Electric workers were responding to some motivating variable other than the lighting, or despite the lack of it.
3. They likely kept producing more in spite o poor working conditions because they knew they were being watched.

Mayo and his colleagues were so impressed by these initial findings that they ultimately conducted a total of six interrelated experiments over an eight-year period. In part because of the massive size of the undertaking, the Hawthorne studies number among the most influential empirical researches ever conducted by social scientists. Most notably they produced the famous term, "Hawthorne effect," or the tendency of people to change their behavior when they know that they are being observed. But even more important, the studies were interpreted by succeeding generations of management scientists as validating the idea that unquantifiable relationships (or "human relations") between workers and managers, and among workers themselves, were primary determinants of workers' efficiency; conversely, material incentives and working conditions, while relevant, were less significant as motivators of productivity.

A reinterpretation of the Hawthorne data, using statistical techniques that were unavailable to Mayo and Roethlisberger, has turned the "human relations" interpretation upside down. In an important analysis of the original data, Richard Herbert Franke and James D. Kaul concluded that human relations were *not* the reasons behind worker efficiency, but rather such traditional motivators as "managerial discipline," fear (in the form of the Depression), reduction of fatigue (the experimental groups were given rest periods), and money (the groups also were given group pay incentives) were the real reasons underlying increased productivity.[14]

Although the notion that workers produce more because of relations among themselves and management has been recently and seriously questioned, the Hawthorne studies nonetheless marked the continuation of the Saint-Simonian tradition after a century-long gap, and the beginning of human relations as we know it.

Much of human relations has concerned itself with the informal work group at the assembly-line level. What makes them work or not work? How do they behave and why? Yet increasingly, human relations has had the managerial echelons as its investigative object, and this has contributed to the study of public administration.

Notable in terms of the impact of the human relationists on public administration is their research on motivation and job satisfaction. Much of this research centers around the "hierarchy of human needs" developed by A. H. Maslow. Maslow perceived human desires to be based first on (1) physiological needs, which provided the foundation for the human's next greatest need, (2) security, then (3) love or belongingness, (4) self-esteem, and finally (5) self-actualization. For the record, Maslow later added a sixth and highest need, "metamotivation,"[15] but Maslow's self-actualization need has spawned the most analysis in public administration. *Self-actualization* refers to the individual growing, maturing, and achieving a deep inner sense of self-worth as he or she relates to his or her job and organization. In terms of the person and the organization, Maslow wrote that these "highly evolved" self-actualized individuals assimilated "their work into the identity, into the self, *i.e.*, work actually becomes part of the self, part of the individual's definition of himself."[16]

Frederick Herzberg stimulated much of the empirical research that related to Maslow's hierarchy of needs.[17] Herzberg developed the concept that there were two basic classes of phenomena which made people feel bad or good about their jobs. One class related to the *context* of the job, and included such factors as relations with co-workers and supervisors, working conditions, organizational policies and procedures, and salary; Herzberg called these "extrinsic" dimensions *hygienic factors*, and they correspond more or less with the base of Maslow's pyramid of human needs, where physiological and security needs are found.

Herzberg's second category related to the *content* of the job, and included such factors as professional and personal challenge and growth in the position, appreciation of a job well done by supervisors and peers, a sense of being responsible for important matters, and achieving goals; Herzberg called these "intrinsic" aspects *motivator factors*, and they relate by and large to the upper reaches of Maslow's pyramid: belongingness, self-esteem, and self-actualization.

Although, as we describe in Chapter 5, Maslow's hierarchy of needs does not appear to translate well into cultures other than that of the United States, limited testing in other cultures of Herzberg's motivation theory indicates that his theory does appear to work in different cultural contexts. In a comparative study of American and Korean public employees, it was found that "Herzberg's two-factor theory of job motivation applies with equal force in both national settings."[18]

Herzberg's framework (itself a derivative of Maslow's need hierarchy) and various modifications of it have produced a voluminous body of literature that attempts to test such hypotheses as "participative decision-making, interesting jobs, and related organization variables correlate positively with job satisfaction," and "job satisfaction correlates positively with job performance." But, at least one review of this literature concludes that there is not a clear-cut body of empirical results that relates organizational effectiveness to "the humanistic model of organizational motivation."[19]

Organization Development

An important subfield of the open model is called organization development (OD). The overlappings of OD with the human relations literature are manifold, but it nonetheless can be considered a separate school because it attempts to go beyond the locus of small group theory and is almost missionary in its zeal to "democratize" bureaucracies.

Organization development is a planned, organization-wide attempt directed from the top that is designed to increase organizational effectiveness and viability through calculated interventions in the active workings of the organization using knowledge from the behavioral sciences. This intervention often is accomplished through third-party consultants. The stress in this definition of OD is on planned change, systemic analysis, top management, and the objectives of organizational effectiveness and "health." These emphases distinguish OD from other kinds of efforts to change organizations, such as sensitivity training or "management development," which are not action-oriented, and operations research, which is not human value-oriented.[20]

Organization development can be viewed as having evolved along two distinct if intertwining branches, both of which owe much of their initial impetus to the social psychologist, Kurt Lewin: The "laboratory-training stem" and the "survey research feedback stem."[21]

The laboratory approach focuses on small group methods; its origins may be traced to conferences held in 1946 and 1947, headed by Lewin and others, which led to the founding of the National Training Laboratories for Group Development—a significant force in the development of T-group (therapy group) and sensitivity training techniques. By the early 1960s it was becoming apparent that the laboratory approach could be used for entire organizations, not just small groups. Douglas McGregor, working for Union Carbide, and J. S. Mouton and Robert Blake, working for Esso Standard Oil, used the first versions of a "managerial grid" concept.[22]

These efforts represented the initial attempt to involve top management in the human development of the organization, take measurements of individual behaviors, trace feedback effects, and use "third party" outside consultants to foster organizational innovation. These exercises in *intergroup* development represented a real departure from the standard T-group approach.

The survey research feedback stem can be traced to Lewin's Research Center for Group Dynamics at the Massachusetts Institute of Technology, which he founded in 1945. On Lewin's death in 1947 the Center's senior staff moved to the Survey Research Center at the University of Michigan and formed the Institute for Social Research. The people involved in the Institute began the initial studies of measuring employee and management attitudes concerning their organization. Feedback from these surveys was maximized through the use of interlocking group conferences. Thus, as these techniques developed, the individual participant in the organization was given a sense of the whole and the particular roles that he or she played, as well as others, as they pertained to the organization.

Since its beginnings in the late 1940s, OD has been used in a number of ways. While many of its applications have been in business organizations, its influence in public bureaucracies and the broad-ranging field of community development has been accelerating since the early 1960s. Chris Argyris applied OD techniques in 1967 to the United States Department of State in an effort to resolve intergroup conflicts between Foreign Service officers and administrative officers. OD has been used for such diverse purposes as maximizing communications between a Community Action Agency and an Indian tribe, and facilitating the organization of a new junior high school. The goals of these and many other OD projects have been and are broadly humanistic and reflect the underlying values of the field. The mission of organization development is to:

1. improve the individual member's ability to get along with other members (which the field calls "interpersonal competence"),
2. legitimate human emotions in the organization,
3. increase mutual understanding among members,
4. reduce tensions,
5. enhance "team management" and intergroup cooperation,
6. develop more effective techniques for conflict resolution through nonauthoritarian and interactive methods, and
7. evolve less structured and more "organic" organizations.

OD advocates strongly believe that achieving these goals of the field will render organizations more effective in the rapidly changing environment of technological societies. "The basic value underlying all organization-development theory and practice is that of *choice*. Through focused attention and through the collection and feedback of relevant data to relevant people, more choices become available and hence better decisions are made."[23] The techniques used by OD to maximize organizational choice include the use of confrontation groups, T-groups, sensitivity training, attitude questionnaires, third-party change agents in the form of outside consultants, data feedback, and the "education" of organizational members in the values of openness and participatory decision making.

Although it is commonly believed that OD is used primarily by the private sector, it may be that as many as half of all the applications of organization development are in government agencies. In a study of 47 percent of all known public-sector applications, it was found that these exercises, for the most part, were far-reaching and successful: "public-sector OD interventions tend to hunt the bigger game: racial tension; conflict . . . ; basic reorganization."[24] Moreover, 84 percent of the respondents in this survey reported that organization development had had "highly positive and intended effects" on their agencies, or that there had been a "definite balance of positive and intended effects"; only 9 percent reported negative effects. These rates were quite comparable to the private sector's experience with OD.[25]

Human Relations and Organization Development: A Humanistic Caveat— and a Managerial One

Both the human relations and organization development schools of the open model draw on, and have been heavily influenced by, a branch of psychology called humanistic psychology, or third-force psychology. Humanistic psychology, like OD, emerged in the 1940s in the United States, and in many ways its aims and values are identical to those of organization development: the flowering of the human being into his or her full potential, or a kind of self-actualization. Maslow, in fact, is considered to be at least as much a central contributor to humanistic psychology as he is to human relations and OD. Other major figures in third-force psychology are Carl Rogers (who is closely identified with the growth movement and encounter groups), Arthur Janov (the originator of primal scream therapy), Ida P. Rolf (of "rolfing" fame), Alexander Lowen (promoter of bioenergetics), Fritz Perls (of Gestalt therapy), R. D. Laing, and Werner Erhard.[26] There are, of course, others.

A Humanistic Caveat. Most of the third-force psychologists are therapists—what would be known in public administration circles as practitioners. They believe that psychology can be a much more positive force in society than its traditional use of merely helping the neurotic. And, perhaps because they are practitioners rather than theorists, they are more interested in developing and applying techniques of intervention (such as rolfing, primal scream therapy, and encounter groups that are designed to "open up" people and free them of the psychological repressions of civilization) than they are in developing and testing theory.

This bias toward action, as opposed to analysis, which is implicit in humanistic psychology, clearly is reflected in the practice of organization development. As one theorist of organization development noted, "The point is not to analyze [organizations] *but to change them!*"[27] More fully expressed, the goal of the humanistic psychologists is to create a spiritually aware, happy, loving person who is unencumbered by society's hang-ups. How such a "primal man"—a twentieth-century version of Jean Jacque Rousseau's natural man—might relate to the institutions of society does not concern the humanistic psychologists; society is not their field, people are, and simply because civilization is neurotic, it does not follow that people must be, too. Nevertheless, the intervention techniques created and

used by the humanistic psychologists seem to be powerful; people often do appear to be altered after having experienced them. But what those changes really mean to both the individuals undergoing them and to others who later must relate to these new, rolfed, bioenergized, primal people is unclear.

The third-force psychologists have deliberately set themselves apart from the field's more established traditions, notably the behaviorists and the Freudians. These traditions are insufficiently upbeat, visionary, and change-oriented for their tastes. But whether the humanistic psychologists have been able to offer a serious alternative to mainstream psychology is an open question, and at least one observer has noted that most of the literature of third-force psychology is "more or less pop psychology marked by carelessness and a lack of concern for the scientific method."[28] (It should be noted, however, that, in the views of many humanistic psychologists, their lack of scientific rigor is not a criticism, since they typically see themselves as practicing something beyond science, or at least irrelevant to it.)

There is, certainly, a bright side to humanistic psychology: In its rejection of the behaviorists (at least as represented by B. F. Skinner), it overtly rejects on ethical grounds the idea that controlling the behavior of others through the manipulation of their immediate environment is acceptable. As Rogers puts it,

> Who will be controlled? Who will exercise control? What type of control will be exercised? Most important of all, toward what end . . . will control be exercised? It is on questions of this sort that there exist . . . deep differences [between the humanistic psychologists and the behavioral psychologists].[29]

The third-force psychologists, in sum, may argue that there is human salvation beyond science, but they would never suggest that there is human happiness (as Skinner contends) "beyond freedom and dignity,"[30] and this is likely to their credit.

There is, however, a dark side of the (third) force. In their dismissal of the Freudians, the third-force psychologists risk dismissing the ego as well.

Sigmund Freud posited four dimensions of personality structure: the id, the libido, the ego, and the superego.[31] The *id* is the oldest and most basic element of personality; it is inherited, unconscious, utterly amoral, has no direct relationship to the external world, and exists solely to satisfy its own needs. The *libido* is the id's energy, its tension-release mechanism; the id functions through the libido. The *ego* is the conscious and preconscious part of personality, and is formed by a person's experiences; unlike the id, which is guided by the pleasure principle, the ego is directed by the reality principle, relates to the external world, and acts as a check on the id and libido. It is the ego that does such "unnatural" things to us as sublimate, repress, and make us fall in love. Finally, the *superego* is our conscience. It is a specialized part of the ego, is entirely conscious, and is that portion of the ego that is on the front line of its ongoing battle with the id and libido. (Obviously, we have grossly simplified Freud's theory of personality, but then this is not a book about psychology.)

Where the humanistic psychologists differ from the Freudians is on the question of whether the id and libido are less or more important than the ego and superego; the humanistic psychologists take a considerably greater interest in the former, and hold the id and libido in significantly higher esteem than the Freudians. Ego and superego, in their view, are associated with the repressiveness of society, while the id and libido relate to the holistic, primal person that they are trying to release from the forces of repression and guilt through their therapy techniques.

This emphasis seems to relate to a perspective held by the third-force psychologists that humanity is fundamentally better (in moral terms) than the Freudians believe; the id is not all that bad. As a distinguished humanistic psychologist said, "So when a Freudian . . . tells me . . . that he perceives man as 'innately evil' or more precisely, 'innately destructive,' I can only shake my head in wonderment. . . . How could it be that [we], working with such a similar purpose in such intimate relationships with individuals in distress, experience people so differently?"[32] As one writer astutely observes, the humanistic psychologist's greater faith in the goodness of humanity leads to a greater emphasis on the idea that the ego and superego are indistinguishably integrat-

ed with—are part and parcel of—the id and libido. "For Freud, the id was basic; for [the humanistic psychologists] it existed simultaneously and equally with the superego."[33] This conception by the humanistic psychologists of the *inseparability* of the amoral id and the conscience-stricken superego, in contrast to the Freudian view of the virile id and lusty libido being held in tenuous and not-always-successful check by a repressed ego and guilty superego, made for much nicer people.

Nicer? Nicer in terms of being at peace with themselves, nicer in terms of being freed from the repressions of a neurotic society, nicer in terms of feeling good and doing it. The third-force psychologists believe that nicer people—peaceful, unrepressed, happy people—are more moral people, and this is a logical conclusion if one believes, as the third-force psychologists do, that people are inherently good; people are not "innately evil" or "innately destructive." But "moral" to the humanistic psychologists is not an interactive concept, as it is to the Freudians and the behaviorists. To be loving and at peace with oneself is moral, and that seems to be about it. Morality is not defined in external and social terms (society, after all, is perceived as repressive, neurotic, and part of the problem), but in internal and individual terms; to be happy is to be moral.

By contrast, the Freudians and the behaviorists do define morality in external and social terms. One can be unhappy—indeed, curmudgeonly—and still be moral. Morality is defined by the Freudians and behaviorists in terms of the individual and the external world, of a reality "out there," of behavior.

The humanistic psychologists are less concerned than the Freudians and behaviorists with developing people who fit in well with society, and are more interested in helping people fit in well with themselves. Releasing the personality from the forces of repression is releasing people's inherent goodness. And, because the ego and superego are the personality's vessels of society's repression, it follows that the id and libido should be granted greater freedom from them. The intervention techniques practiced by the third-force psychologists are designed to do just that. Ultimately, the ego and superego lose.

Recall, however, that the ego is that part of

the personality which is directed by the reality principle. When it goes (or so the Freudians believe), so does a person's ability to make his or her own choices on the basis of experiences with the external world. The result is a vacuum into which many substitutes may enter. But when the reality check provided by the ego is diminished, the resulting vacuum is not "filled" by the pleasure-loving id (which is off having a good time on its own); it is filled instead by some other reality check, a substitute ego provided by the external world that defines reality in terms of *its* own experience. These substitutes for the ego can be authority figures who may be "good" (at least as defined by society), such as the Pope, or "evil," such as David Koresh, leader of the sixty-seven Branch Davidians, who in 1993 self-immolated in their compound in Waco, Texas, on Koresh's orders; or Jim Jones of Jonestown, Guyana, who in 1977 persuaded 912 of his followers to commit mass suicide because they accepted his version of reality.

It is of note in this regard that 22 percent of the followers of Bhagwan Shree Rajneesh (all of whom had turned over all their worldly goods to the Bhagwan and worked full-time for him), who resided in the commune of Rajneeshpuram in central Oregon during the early 1980s, had university degrees in psychiatry or psychology, and half of these held advanced degrees. Yet, according to one observer who studied the commune over a period of years, "with all the years of academic training represented, there was not, as far as I could determine, a single straight Freudian or straight behaviorist" among the Bhagwan's followers; all ascribed to third-force psychology.[34]

So what? Consider this statement, made by a Rajneeshee named Ava, after the Bhagwan had fled the country and Rajneeshpuram's leaders had been imprisoned for fraud, poisoning their fellow Rajneeshees (including Ava) and a number of outsiders, bugging the quarters of most of the Bhagwan's followers (and the Bhagwan himself), and attempted murder:

> "I conveniently forgot things because they seemed impossible to remember. . . . I forgot the tape . . . of a conversation with Bhagwan which showed he was involved, well, in

things he said he wasn't. . . . For three days, I was just so *angry* at Bhagwan. But I'm over that now."

Ava called in a third time to say that she hoped that she had not sounded too negative before. She had been in a bad space, but now she had accepted everything and Bhagwan was still her Master.[35]

One might infer that such is the fate of those who release their egos to others, and release of the ego is implicit in humanistic psychology, and, to a lesser extent, in human relations and organization development. One does not necessarily have to substitute another person—a "Master"—for one's ego. One can substitute one's organization and one's work for it instead. This is, recall, what Maslow meant by self-actualization: "work actually becomes part of the self."[36]

A Managerial Caveat. To move from bureaucracy to commune, as we have done in this discussion, may seem to wander too far afield. This is, after all, a book about making public organizations and public administrators more effective, not about opening up the id and libido of public employees.

True, but here our apparent digression leads us to another aspect of human relations and organization development that is worth positing as a managerial caveat, as opposed to a humanistic one, about OD in particular. The third-force psychologists seem to have convinced some of those third-party change agents (*i.e.*, OD consultants), who are hired by managers to make their organizations more effective, that helping organizations become more productive should not necessarily be at the top of their agendas; instead, making the organization's employees more self-actualized, fulfilled, and liberated human beings should lead the OD consultants' agendas. Attaining this objective, of course, is not why OD consultants are hired by managers; they are hired by managers to make their organizations more effective and productive in their organizational environments, and if happier, more self-actualized employees are the means to this end, then all is well and good. But, from the manager's viewpoint, the means are not the end; the end is the end, and management's end is a more productive and effective organization, but not necessarily happier employees.

We are not suggesting that OD consultants and the values they represent are not useful to organizations and, indeed, to the public interest; they are. But the possible disconnect between the agendas and objectives of the practitioners of organization development and the practitioners of administration, both public and private, is worthy of note as a managerial caveat.

In a revealing article about this potential difference in agenda between third-party change agents in the OD tradition and administrators, Thomas H. Fitzgerald questions the propriety and morality of third-party change agents taking the side of the executives who hire them, and facilitating their interests. He writes that some OD consultants

> often share the mindset of management. . . .
>
> More than a decade ago, feminist writers pointed out male body language and condescending gestures, their special idiom for keeping women defined in pejorative ways— but people in the rank and file see these behaviors all the time in managers and executives.
>
> Some consultants display similar managerial bearing. They are breezy, self-assured, and excessively articulate, and they take charge of the discussion. Employees soon figure out whose side they are on. . . . That style . . . permits consultants to gloss over the grubby realities of worklife. . . . [37]

This viewpoint of an OD consultant—that his OD compatriots have sold out their humanistic values to the economic values of management— should alert the managers who hire OD consultants that they may be getting more than they bargained for. Expecting their OD experts to facilitate an "opening up" of their organizations which will lead to greater organizational effectiveness, managers may get instead an organization peopled by sullen workers whose resentment of "breezy, self-assured, and excessively articulate" managers has merely been exacerbated by "third-party change agents."

Ironically, it may be that even when organiza-

tion development succeeds in achieving its own expressed goals—that of opening up people—its success may not lead to an improved organization. Opening up individual psyches requires an organization culture that is tolerant of all human foibles, and some foibles may be more useful to the organization than others. As yet another practitioner of organization development observes:

> The culture [that] organization development professionals intend to create allows all to be themselves. . . . But the techniques we use burr off people's rough edges, and frequently those rough edges are essential ingredients. . . . We teach the perfectionist patience with others, and he stops demanding the best. We teach the creative genius the slowness with which a group learns, and she stops sharing her unorthodox leaps. We teach the ogre of operations that fear is an unseemly emotion and do not understand why the factory meanders out of control. We intend to moderate, but instead we debilitate. [38]

If these quotations are representative of the difficulties inherent in organization development—the potential undermining of managerial authority and the possible quashing of individual talent—then those who hire OD consultants to benefit their organizations should at least be aware of them.

The Public Organization as a Unit in its Environment

A third school of the open model is less bulky as a literature but nonetheless is separate and identifiable. Notable among its early contributors are Chester I. Barnard, Philip Selznick, and Burton Clark,[39] although this literary stream is currently undergoing a significant revitalization. It is characterized by use of the organization as a whole as its analytical unit (in contrast to the other schools' preference for the small group), its theme of the organizational pressures and constraints emanating from the environment, and organizational strategies designed to cope with environmentally spawned problems.

Because this literary stream emphasizes so heavily the organization's relations with its task environment, a word of explanation about what the term *environment* means in the context of organization theory may be helpful. Herbert Kaufman explains the concept well:

> Speaking metaphorically, you might liken the [organization's task] environment to a reticular pattern of incessant waves constituting a perpetually varying net or screen sweeping continuously through the total aggregation of interlocked organizations that form in the human population. The openings in the ever-changing screen constantly assume different shapes and sizes. At the same time, the organizations themselves are always changing as they try to avoid being swept away. If the two sets of changes are such that an organization can "fit" through the "holes" when the screen passes, the organization survives; if not, it is carried off.[40]

Kaufman's vivid description of the impact of the task environment on the organization—a description that implies the task environment is far more important to the success or failure of an organization than are such "internal" variables an organizational leadership or managerial competence—"goes double" for public organizations. Unlike private organizations, whose environment amounts to little more than the marketplace itself, public organizations must endure in an environment comprised of far more complex, aggressive, and intrusive forces, among them politics, culture, law, economics, and organizational interdependencies not present in the corporate world. Perhaps because of this reality, organization theorists who are interested in such issues as strategic management and planning find themselves studying business firms (to manage, plan, and strategize require, after all, some independence from outside forces), while scholars more interested in the organization's relations with its task environment incline more toward the study of government agencies (where the impact of the environment on the inner workings of the organization is considerably more apparent than in private companies).

It is with this appreciation of the relationship between an organization and its task environment in mind that Selznick, for example, developed his "co-optation" concept in his book on the establishment of the Tennessee Valley Authority (TVA).[41] Co-optation referred to the strategy employed by the TVA Board of Directors in gaining the acceptance, and ultimately the strong support, of initially hostile local interests by granting their representatives membership on the board. TVA, as a result, influenced and cajoled the local interests far more profoundly than the local interests influenced the TVA; in short, TVA co-opted the local interests but was required to modify slightly its own purposes in so doing.

There may have been a "sleeper effect" in the TVA's board's co-optation of local interests. In a more recent analysis of TVA at the grassroots, Richard A. Couto found that those local interests that had been co-opted by the top administrators of the Tennessee Valley Authority had, nearly forty years later, become considerably more powerful, and, in fact, were able to develop a sufficient level of power that they could "foster new operative goals for TVA and to prevent TVA initiated modifications of those goals."[42] Couto concludes that, while Selznick was essentially correct in his description of co-optation, co-optation is a more dynamic process than Selznick initially posited, and he found that co-optation was, in reality, a "process of participation and representation rather than a stable, enduring outcome of bureaucratic process."[43] Most significantly, co-optation legitimated an agency's leadership in the eyes of both the agency and the co-opted groups (as Selznick found), but, in contrast to Selznick's findings, the supposedly co-opted groups, under certain conditions, could acquire real power over the agency, and co-optation often functioned as a very effective form of participation and representation for some groups that traditionally had been relatively powerless.

Given its relatively small numbers, the theoretical school dealing with organizations as units in their environment has had a disproportionate impact on public administration. This is understandable, however, for the stream is primarily concerned about the "public" (*i.e.*, the "environment"), and its political relationship with the organization. In this emphasis, the organization/environment literature is uniquely concerned with the problems of public administration.

Perhaps it is predictable, then, that more

recent organization theorists in this stream have begun to address directly the unique aspects of public organizations, and the emphasis of their thinking is on how the task environment of public organizations differs from that of private organizations, and how these differences affect public organizations.[44] Although one may categorize these distinctions along many dimensions, the following are reasonably straightforward: the high importance of the demands being made on the public organization by its task environment relative to internal management needs; the unique impact of the task environment on the public organization's structure and bureaucracy; its decision making; the motivation of public managers; their satisfaction with their work; the public organization's internal management; and even the performance of its administrators.

Internal Needs versus External Demands.

If the literature on the differences between public and private organizations agrees on anything, it is that upper-echelon public administrators must spend considerably more time and attention on their agency's external environment, and less on matters of internal management, than their counterparts in business.[45]

This reality brings with it several corollaries. On the one hand, public bureaucrats, for example, must deal with far more constraints and controls (most typically in the form of legal requirements) over their organizations than must private managers.[46] However, these constraints can be "informal" and political, as well as legal, and at least equally controlling.[47] Two national surveys of local public works directors in the United States, for example, found that working in a "political environment" constituted a primary set of "impediments to effective management."[48]

On the other hand, the political environment (which is a specialized type of the task environment in which all organizations find themselves) in which public organizations must work provides opportunities and challenges as well as limitations. Support for the public agency is "out there," often waiting to be mobilized, in the forms of clients (or prospective clients), interest groups, other organizations sympathetic to the agency's goals, legislators, and other constituents.[49] It is this condition that forces public executives, as noted earlier, to expend consider-

ably more effort on their organization's external relations, and accords them a more political and expository role than their colleagues in the private sector.[50]

Structure and Bureaucracy.

Perhaps the most notable impact of the relative importance of environmental demands on public organizations is how they alter organizational structure. Anthony Downs was among the first to assess the impact of the public organization's task environment on its internal structure. In *Inside Bureaucracy*, Downs argued that organizations deprived of free market conditions in their environments (*i.e.*, government agencies) were more pressured to create additional layers of hierarchy than were organizations that functioned in the marketplace. Because it was so much more difficult for public organizations to measure output than it was for private organizations (which had an "automatic" measure of output called the profit margin), internal rules were needed to control spending, assure fair treatment of clients, and coordinate large-scale activities. The presence of these rules, in turn, demanded extensive monitoring to ensure compliance, and such monitoring meant more reports, and more effort spent on internal communications. Thus, Downs's "Law of Hierarchy" is a function of an organization's task environment, and whether or not that environment provides market mechanisms.[51]

Donald P. Warwick later expanded on Downs's main points by explicating those elements in the environment that shape the internal structure of public organizations: Legislatures may do so by statute, accounting and budgeting bureaus may mandate highly bureaucratized record-keeping procedures, interest groups may pressure for internal changes, and so forth.[52]

A somewhat different conception of the role that environmental factors play in the dynamics of public organizations is provided by Marshall W. Meyer. Meyer agrees that the task environment has an unusually salient impact on public organizations, and also concurs that public organizations react to these impacts by "bureaucratizing"—that is, by adding on increasingly complex mechanisms. But, in contrast to the implications of Downs and Warwick, Meyer contends that such bureaucratization is not a sign of resistance to new demands from the environment, but is instead one of eagerness to accommodate those demands; additional layers of bureaucracy in a public organization may be used not only to control but also to serve and connote a desire to deliver more programs to more people in more ways: "Contrary to stereotypes, bureaus tend to be very open and vulnerable to their immediate environments . . . increasing the bureaucratization of public agencies through additional rules and layers of hierarchy results in part from their openness to their environments."[53]

Although Meyer is more upbeat than are Downs and Warwick in his assessment of how the task environment affects the structure of a public organization, these and other analysts agree that, because of the public organization's greater vulnerability and openness to its task environment relative to its counterpart in the private sector, the public organization is significantly different in additional ways from the private organization. Certainly these differences include decision making, motivation, satisfaction, management, and performance evaluation.

Decision Making. The unique qualities of the public organization's exchanges with its task environment result in some unique qualities of decision making and management within public organizations. Decision making is less autonomous than in the private sector,[54] and procedures are more constricting.[55] Practitioners who have served in both the public and private sectors at high levels note that legislators (who are the equivalent of a board of directors in the business world) are less likely to agree with public administrators on organizational goals, are less expert and less informed on substantive issues, and are less likely to be consistent in dealing with government executives and external constituents than are board members.[56] Such phenomena have a distinct impact on the decision-making process of public organizations and require that decision makers be more aware of their symbolic leadership role and "image management," deal with vastly more decision criteria and decision-making participants, and have a broader scope and greater complexity of decision; as a consequence, decision making in the public sector is slower than in the private sector.[57]

In one of the largest empirical and systematic studies of public and private decision making, it was found that decision makers in public organizations did not necessarily make decisions slowly as a conscious act, but there seemed to be a clear tendency toward a "vortex-sporadic" style of decision, by which was meant that decision makers in public organizations tended to intermittently swirl through a series of intense meetings and conversations with each other when making decisions. The study, which involved intensive longitudinal research of strategic decision processes in thirty British public and private service and manufacturing organizations, also found that decision makers in public organizations were much more likely than those in private organizations to engage in formal and informal interaction with other members of the organization when making decisions.[58]

An even larger survey of 210 "upper managers" in thirty-nine public and private organizations in Syracuse, New York, substantiated the findings of other studies that decision making is more participative and sporadic in the public sector than in the private sector: "Publicness is associated with greater decision participation but not smoothness."[59]

Another analysis based on the Syracuse data was more explicit: "The image of public organizations that emerges is one of little organizational coherence in the identification of strategic decisions. In addition, the ability of top-level managers to control the decisions and actions of their organizations is called into question." The researchers concluded that whether the sector is public or private "creates substantive differences" in decision making.[60]

In further support of the notion that the impact of the task environment affects decision making in public organizations more than in private ones, it was found, in a study of more than fifty federal agencies which were headed by boards, that the Federal Government in the Sunshine Act of 1976, in the opinions of the members of those boards, had adversely affected the level of collegiality in agency decision making; many agency officials felt "that the strictures of the law weakened them in executing their responsibilities and weakened agency performance, especially in policy development."[61] In the views of the officials heading those agencies, the more collegiality was reduced, the more of the quality of agency decision making suffered.

It would appear from this literature that not only do public organizations have a unique style of decision making—intense, sporadic, highly interactive, collegial, and slow—but also that the impact of the outside environment, which is considerably stronger than it is in the private sector, can disrupt even these unique features of decision making in the public sector, and, in the view of the decision makers themselves, reduce the quality of decision making in public organizations.

Motivation. What turns public administrators on? Is what turns them on different from what turns on managers in the private sector?

The answer to the latter question is, yes. Public administrators have a very different set of motivations than do their private counterparts (although there are exceptions), and these differences result in very different ways in which executives in the public and private sectors lead their administrative staffs.

Among the earlier students of these differences was James F. Guyot, who compared federal managers with those in business, and concluded that middle managers in the federal service had higher needs for achievement than did their private sector colleagues (a finding that runs directly counter to the popular stereotype of indolent government bureaucrats), about the same needs for power as business managers, and lower affiliation needs (*i.e.,* their concern with acceptance or rejection by their colleagues).[62] Later research largely supports Guyot's findings; one study of graduating college students found that those students entering the nonprofit sector had a greater need to dominate, were more flexible, had a higher capacity for status, and lower needs for wealth than students entering the for-profit sector.[63]

Most of the research agrees that "public managers, as compared to comparable groups in business, give lower ratings to the importance of high financial rewards as career goals and higher ratings to the importance of worthwhile social or public service."[64] This is the most consistent conclusion of this literature.

Most of the studies also concur that "public employees have greater security-seeking tendencies than private employees"[65]—a finding that supports the conventional wisdom of security-obsessed bureaucrats. In an important exception to this generalization, however, Dennis Wittmer notes that, whereas this rule may apply to *government* employees, it does not seem to pertain to the employees of *other public sector organizations*, notably those in non-governmental, not-for-profit organizations. When these workers are taken into account, the "stereotype that public employees are preoccupied with job security is not supported. . . . On the contrary, the data indicates that private managers, to a statistically significant degree, rate job security as more important."[66] Despite these differences in motivation among administrators in the two sectors, however, both groups work hard, and effort levels are roughly equal to each other in this respect.[67] "The findings . . . do not indicate a terrible malaise in the public sector if the private sector is used as a baseline."[68]

It appears from this literature that the public sector may be attracting people who are more difficult to manage than is business. Public administrators seem to have a higher need to achieve program objectives, are more likely to be loners, have more dominant personalities, are wilier (or what the literature euphemistically calls "flexible"), and are more demanding of status than are their counterparts in commerce. Moreover, although public administrators have power drives comparable to those of business managers, they may be less vulnerable to being bought off with monetary bonuses, since the available research suggests that public bureaucrats are less interested in growing wealthy and more committed to achieving results than are business executives. While these motivations may indeed be in the public interest, they do bring with them unique problems of public management.

Satisfaction. Just as differing motivations account for a person's decision to enter the public sector or the private one, so it is that, once employed in one sector or the other, people derive satisfaction from their work for quite different reasons.

The different bases underlying work satisfaction in the two sectors appear to be starkly separate from each other. One study found that, although employees in both sectors emphasized intrinsic factors in deriving satisfaction from their work (or Herzberg's motivator factors, such as opportunities for growth and attaining goals), public employees "tended to value the extrinsic or hygienic factors [such as relations with co-workers, working conditions, and organizational policies] significantly higher than those in the private sector."[69] More focused research supports the idea that public administrators gain considerably higher levels of satisfaction from a "sense of being able to make a difference in what gets done in their organizations" than do private managers.[70]

Beyond differing bases for job satisfaction, however, it seems equally clear from a growing body of research that employees in the public sector are less than happy campers compared to their counterparts in the private sector. Increasingly, research indicates that public administrators are less satisfied, and less loyal to their organizations, than are private managers.[71] Surveys taken of public administrators and private managers, particularly during the 1960s, indicate that public administrators are much less likely to feel that pay in their organizations depends upon performance, and that their own pay represents a reward for good performance. Public managers generally express feelings that they have less security, less autonomy, and are less "self-actualized" than are their counterparts in the private sector.[72] As a rule, it does seem that the typical public manager in the United States is more frustrated and dissatisfied in his or her work than is the typical private manager.

This generalization is brought home, at least to some degree, when we compare similar dimensions between public and private managers in other countries. Two independently conducted studies of public and private executives in Israel are quite striking in this regard. One, which compared 125 top managers in public enterprises to 125 top managers in private enterprises in Israel, concluded that there were no differences in terms of perceived relations between rewards and performance, personal freedom, delegation, and participation.[73] The other study, which focused on chief executives in ninety-one private firms and forty public enterprises in Israel, did find the public administrators to be somewhat lower in

terms of their satisfaction with financial rewards and challenge (although the researcher concluded that these differences were not important statistically), but found no differences in terms of how public chief executives perceived the impact of external influences on their decision processes in comparison with private managers—a striking difference with studies that have compared public and private administrators in the United States on the decision-making dimension.[74]

Nevertheless, most of the research indicates that many—perhaps most—public administrators in the United States experience less satisfaction with work than do most private managers in the United States. But there are some significant exceptions to this possible rule. ("Possible" because the exceptions that have been found in the research are so large that the rule may not be valid.) For example, it has been found that, while federal administrators typically register very low levels of satisfaction with their work on the various surveys that have been taken of them, this generality seems to break down by type of federal worker. In an extensive study undertaken in the early 1960s, it was found that, while college graduates and certain kinds of professionals, such as scientists and engineers, were less satisfied with their work than were their counterparts in the private sector, federal executives were quite comparable to business executives in terms of job satisfaction.[75] It also seems that blue-collar workers in the public sector are more satisfied with most of their work than are blue-collar workers in the private sector. On the other hand, white-collar public sector workers are much less satisfied with co-workers, supervision, and a general interest in their work, than are their counterparts in business.[76]

There also may be differences in satisfaction with work by level of government. For example, state workers may be more satisfied with their work than are both their corporate and federal counterparts. In a study that compared 150 mid-level public, predominately state, administrators with 125 counterparts in the private sector, it was found that, while the public administrators reported lower levels of satisfaction with co-workers, promotions, and rewards, there was no difference between the two groups in terms of role conflict, ambiguity, clarity of goals, motivation, and job involvement.[77]

But perhaps the most intriguing finding is that local administrators seem to defy most completely and consistently the despondency and dissatisfaction found among federal managers when compared with executives in the corporate sector. In a study of three different surveys taken of private sector managers, federal career executives, and city managers in California, the differences among the three sets of respondents were striking. A remarkable 72 percent of the U.S. Government executives stated that they did not feel that they would ever fulfill their life's ambition, compared to only 17 percent of the city managers and 18 percent of the private sector executives who did not feel that they would ever fulfill their life's ambition. City managers and private sector executives were quite consistent in the level of optimism that they felt about economic, social, and political trends, and organizational and personal prospects; both city managers and private sector administrators were consistently more optimistic on all these variables than were federal executives. Fully two-thirds of the city managers would advise bright young people to seek careers in local government, while less than a fourth of federal executives would advise bright young people to seek careers in the federal government.[78]

While there is reason for concern about the relative dissatisfaction of public administrators with their jobs in comparison with their counterparts in the private sector, this concern seems to concentrate at the federal level, rather than at the state and local ones. Moreover, there are indications that the level of satisfaction of federal employees with their work may have deteriorated over time.[79]

Why many public administrators are relatively dissatisfied with their careers remains an enigma. Their dissatisfaction may be a consequence of uniquely high psychological needs among public administrators for achievement and status, as the research consistently verifies relative to private managers, or their dissatisfaction may be attributable to objective reality: The low levels of their satisfaction, which seems to concentrate in the areas of promotions and rewards for work well done, "could simply reflect more stringent norms or expectations among government managers" of their colleagues than are held by corporate executives.[80]

Management. These differences that we have reviewed between the public and private administrators in decision making, motivation, and satisfaction correlate with differences in management. Most obviously, public managers are faced with "accomplishing" enormously complex but horrendously ill-defined objectives. Goals are vague, and public organizations are appropriately sprawling as structures meant to achieve the vagaries of large but poorly conceived organizational missions; performance criteria, consequently, are as loosely construed as are the organization's goals themselves. Again, these unique problems of management in public organizations are attributable to forces in their highly politicized task environments, such as legislatures, pressure groups, and elected chief executives, that constantly try to use public organizations for political as well as programmatic, economic, and social purposes.[81]

Although one draws short (far short) of describing the managerial milieu of public organizations as chaotic, it does appear to be less bureaucratically rational (in Weber's sense of the word) than private organizations. As a result, caution prevails, and innovation is less likely.[82] Studies of executive behavior in the public and private sectors have found that public executives spend considerably more time in contact with the directors of outside groups than do executives in the private sector. Moreover, the style of interaction that the public manager has with directors and external interest groups is far more formal, as well as more frequent, than the mode of interaction experienced by private sector managers.[83]

But if there is a greater formality in public administrators' exchanges with their clienteles, there also is a greater sensitivity displayed by public managers relative to private managers. One review of the findings on this topic concluded that,

> The "insensitive" stereotype [of public administrators] typically evokes images of public employees who are uncaring, inflexible. . . . and generally inept in dealing with the public.

Although the numerous findings related to this image are generally mixed, the modal finding indicates that public employees are more sensitive than private employees. [Overall, this research shows that] public employees value qualities associated with sensitivity, empathy, broad mindedness, good interpersonal relations, forgiveness, politeness, helpfulness—more than or equal to private employees.[84]

Formality, frequency, and sensitivity of public management's dealings with its clienteles aside, it may be that more open management—open in the sense that more people are dunning and hassling the managers—may lead to less effective management. In a survey of 20,000 students, teachers, and principals in 500 public and private high schools, it was found that principals and teachers in the public schools perceived outside authorities to wield a much stronger influence on their management than did principals and teachers in private schools. This stronger influence in the public schools than in the private ones by outside authorities was accompanied by weaker parental involvement in the public schools, weaker faculty influence on the curriculum, more managerial and less professional orientations among the principals, less emphasis on academic excellence, more formal constraints on personnel policy, and less clarity of goals and disciplinary policies.[85]

As the foregoing discussion implies, subordinates are treated differently in public organizations, too. Delegating authority to subordinates and controlling the behavior of subordinates are more difficult in the public sector than in business,[86] in part because public executives are allowed to select significantly fewer of their own subordinates than are corporate executives, and in part because subordinates often can develop allies to assist them in undermining their superiors in the highly politicized task environment outside their agency.

It also appears that priority setting, planning, and information management—all fundamental tasks of management—differ markedly in the public sector. Planning and setting priorities are considerably more difficult because of less focused organizational goals and more rapid turnover among top executives.[87] The difficulties of setting priorities and planning accordingly

seem to exist in an informational milieu that is unique to public organizations. An empirical study of high-level data managers in 622 public organizations and 383 private ones concluded that data managers in the public sector had to deal with "greater levels of interdependence across organizational boundaries. . . . higher levels of red tape. . . . [and] more procedural steps for a specific management action" than did those in the private sector.[88] Although planning for and purchasing management information systems in public organizations appeared to be more difficult and complex than in private organizations, the directors of public management information systems typically occupied a lower rung on the organizational hierarchy than did directors of private management information systems.[89]

Evaluating Executive Performance. These differing realities affect administrators in the two sectors in different ways. Not only do managers in the two sectors behave differently, *but even what constitutes effective management can be polar opposites in each sector*! One study of executive work behavior compared forty managers in city governments with forty managers in industry, and concluded that the public managers believed—and, in fact, accurately so—that they had little control over how they used their time, and thus accorded scant effort to "time management," relative to the corporate managers. Urban managers were considerably more victimized by forces in their organizations' task environments than were their counterparts in the private sector; they spent less time alone in their offices, less time on planning, were more "rushed" to get things done, and spent nearly twice as much time on the telephone than did private managers.[90]

Other studies confirm this kind of office life style. Research on U.S. Navy civilian executive and executives from a number of private service and manufacturing firms found that, while there were similarities in the work of the two kinds of managers, the public managers devoted far more time to crisis management than did the private managers.[91]

More significantly, *effective* managers display quite different work behaviors depending on whether they work in the public or private sectors. In the study of urban and industrial managers, it was found that *more effective public administrators* were more flexible, planned less, and had less control over their time than did industrial managers. In fact, the *less effective public administrators* spent more time on planning their time than did the more effective public managers, while quite the reverse held true in the private sector: Less effective industrial managers spent less time planning their time than did more effective industrial managers![92]

Other research substantiates the idea that, because public administrators must deal with a more intrusive task environment than private managers, both the nature of their work and the evaluation of their performance differ. A study of managers in four federal agencies and twelve large (*Fortune* 500) private corporations concluded that private managers performed better than public administrators when it came to expressing and achieving organizational goals. This superiority, however, was attributable to an absence of clear measures of performance (*e.g.*, profits) for public administrators. Because private managers were able to define organizational objectives more definitively than were public managers, and because intraorganizational procedures in the twelve companies were less subject to influence by outside interests than in the four agencies, more strategic planning was made possible and used more frequently by private managers. This greater freedom among private managers to engage in strategic decision making enabled them to score higher than their public counterparts on such measures of leadership as "conceptualization" and "use of oral presentations." It is, after all, comparatively easy to articulate and drive home points when one is in a position to decide autonomously about an organization's future, with relatively little fear of being challenged by elements outside one's own organization.[93]

Perhaps because of these factors, public administrators express considerably greater frustration and dissatisfaction over how their performance and that of their co-workers is evaluated by their superiors than do private managers.[94] Similarly, public-sector supervisors consistently state their concerns over constraints on their ability to reward and discipline subordinates.[95] Nor do public managers hold their co-workers in as high esteem as do their counterparts in the private sector;[96] in fact, although the findings are mixed, they often do not think that their colleagues are very able,[97] a view whose jaundice may be more a product of a disruptive task environment than of the innate abilities of public administrators.

Public administration, it appears, is different.

THE CLOSED AND OPEN MODELS: THE ESSENTIAL DIFFERENCES

We have reviewed two eminently disparate models of organizations and their respective literary emphases. In essence, their fundamental differences may be reduced to four: (1) perceptions of the organizational environment, (2) perceptions of the nature of human beings, (3) perceptions of the use of manipulation in organizations, and (4) perceptions of the role and significance of organizations in society. For purposes of review, we shall consider each of these differences.

Perceptions of the Organizational Environment

The closed model is predicated on the belief that organizations exist in a stable, routine environment, and the open model is predicated on the belief that organizations must function in an unstable environment, replete with surprises. Both models, however, assume that organizations will act in order to survive and, ultimately, to thrive.

The beauty in these two differing perceptions of organizations is that both models work in the respective environments posited for them. That is, an open-model organization likely would "die" in a stable environment, and a closed-model organization probably would wither in an unstable environment. To recall Kaufman on the task environment, one way or the other, an organization must adapt so that it can "fit" through the "holes" of the environmental screening equipment that sweeps incessantly through it if it is to survive.

To elaborate, when an organization that is superbureaucratic, rigid, and routinized around long-standing patterns of well-ordered and predictable stimuli that have emanated from a habitually stable environment suddenly is confronted with a "new," unstable environment, the organi-

BUREAUCRACY VERSUS HUMANISM: TWO VIEWS ON THE HUMAN BEING IN THE CLOSED AND OPEN MODELS OF ORGANIZATIONS

The following passages illustrate by contrast the differences between the closed and open models of organization theory. While closed-model theorist Max Weber and open-model theorist Frederick Herzberg address the plight of the bureaucrat in bureaucracies from vastly different perspectives, their basic agreement on the point that the individual remains in a genuine bind in bureaucratic settings is illuminating.

Once it is fully established, bureaucracy is among those social structures which are the hardest to destroy. Bureaucracy is the means of carrying "community action" over into rationally ordered "societal action." Therefore, as an instrument of "societalizing" relations of power, bureaucracy has been and is a power instrument of the first order—for the one who controls the bureaucratic apparatus.

Under otherwise equal conditions, a "societal action," which is methodically ordered and fed, is superior to every resistance of "mass" or even of "communal action." And where the bureaucratization of administration has been completely carried through, a form of power relation is established that is practically unshatterable.

The individual bureaucrat cannot squirm out of the apparatus in which he is harnessed. In contrast to the honorific or avocational "notable," the professional bureaucrat is chained to his activity by his entire material and ideal existence. In the great majority of cases, he is only a single cog in an ever moving mechanism which prescribes to him an essentially fixed route of march. The official is entrusted with specialized tasks and normally the mechanism cannot be put into motion or arrested by him, but only from the very top. The individual bureaucrat is thus forged to the community of all the functionaries who are integrated into the mechanism. They have a common interest in seeing that the mechanism continues its functions and that the societally exercised authority carries on.

The ruled, for their part, cannot dispense with or replace the bureaucratic apparatus of authority once it exists. For this bureaucracy rests upon expert training, a functional specialization of work, and an attitude set for habitual and virtuoso-like mastery of single yet methodically integrated functions. If the official stops working, or if his work is forcefully interrupted, chaos results, and it is difficult to improvise replacements from among the governed who are fit to master such chaos. This holds for public administration as well as for private economic management. More and more the material fate of the masses depends upon the steady and correct functioning of the increasingly bureaucratic organizations of private capitalism. The idea of eliminating these organizations becomes more and more utopian.

Every audience contains the "direct action" manager who shouts, "Kick him!" And this type of manager is right. The surest and least circumlocuted way of getting someone to do something is to kick him in the pants—give him what might be called the KITA.

There are various forms of KITA, and here are some of them:

Negative physical KITA. This is a literal application of the term and was frequently used in the past. It has, however, three major drawbacks:

(1) it is inelegant; (2) it contradicts the precious image of benevolence that most organizations cherish; and (3) since it is a physical attack, it directly stimulates the autonomic nervous system, and this often results in negative feedback—the employee may just kick you in return. These factors give rise to certain taboos against negative physical KITA.

The psychologist has come to the rescue of those who are no longer permitted to use negative physical KITA. He has uncovered infinite sources of psychological vulnerabilities and the appropriate methods to play tunes on them. "He took my rug away"; "I wonder what he meant by that"; "The boss is always going around me"—these symptomatic expressions of ego sores that have been rubbed raw are the result of application of:

Negative Psychological KITA. This has several advantages over negative physical KITA. First, the cruelty is not visible; the bleeding is internal and comes much later. Second, since it affects the higher cortical centers of the brain with its inhibitory powers, it reduces the possibility of physical backlash. Third, since the number of psychological pains that a person can feel is almost infinite, the direction and site possibilities of the KITA are increased many times. Fourth, the person administering the kick can manage to be above it all and let the system accomplish the dirty work. Fifth, those who practice it receive some ego satisfaction (one-upmanship), whereas they would find drawing blood abhorrent. Finally, if the employee does complain, he can always be accused of being paranoid, since there is no tangible evidence of an actual attack.

Now, what does negative KITA accomplish? If I kick you in the rear (physically or psychologically), who is motivated? I am motivated; you move! Negative KITA does not lead to motivation, but to movement. So:

Positive KITA. Let us consider motivation. If I say to you, "Do this for me or the company, and in return I will give you a reward, an incentive, more status, a promotion, all the quid pro quos that exist in the industrial organization," am I motivating you? The overwhelming opinion I receive from management people is, "Yes, this is motivation."

I have a year-old Schnauzer. When it was a small puppy and I wanted it to move, I kicked it in the rear and it moved. Now that I have finished its obedience training, I hold up a dog biscuit when I want the Schnauzer to move. In this instance, who is motivated—I or the dog? The dog wants the biscuit, but it is I who want it to move. Again, I am the one who is motivated, and the dog is the one who moves. In this instance all I did was apply KITA frontally: I exerted a pull instead of a push. When industry wishes to use such positive KITAs, it has available an incredible number and variety of dog biscuits (jelly beans for humans) to wave in front of the employee to get him to jump.

Why is it that managerial audiences are quick to see that negative KITA is not motivation, while they are almost unanimous in their judgment that positive KITA is motivation? It is because negative KITA is rape, and positive KITA is seduction. But it is infinitely worse to be seduced than it to be raped; the latter is an unfortunate occurrence, while the former signifies that you were a party to your own downfall. This is why positive KITA is so popular; it is in the American way. The organization does not have to kick you; you kick yourself.

---

zation either must "loosen up" and adapt or die. Eventually, the long-standing and rigid routines of the closed organization, which once may have worked very well because they were closely keyed to predictable task environment, would bear no relationship to the organization's radically changed environment, and the organization would fail. For example, it is unlikely that a house of *haute couture*, which must be extremely sensitive to changes and trends in its task environment, would last long with a "tall" organizational structure staffed by Prussian officers who ran the fashion house along the lines of Kaiser Wilhelm's army.

Conversely, when an organization is superfluidic and tackles each challenge emanating from its environment as something unique, new, and fresh (which indeed may be the case), with no attempt to discover commonalities among tasks and to categorize and routinize them along "rational" lines, is confronted over time with a highly stable and structured environment, the organization either must adapt or die from its own inefficiency and absence of structure and routine relative to its environment. For example, it is dubious that Bethlehem Steel Corporation, which functions in a very routinized market environment, would survive long if it were staffed by volunteers who operated "crash pads" for runaway youths.

To summarize, in terms of matching environmental stability or lack of it, both the closed and open models make sense. From this perspective, it also makes sense that the closed model of organizations traditionally has had a greater impact on the study of public administration than the open model. When the nation was younger and simpler, the government smaller, and public bureaucracy less ambitious and complex, a closed model suited the American milieu. Lately, however, as the nation and government have grown, faced domestic upheavals, weathered technological change, and confronted future shock, the public bureaucracy has taken on new tasks, assumed new duties, and grasped new powers. The environment has changed and is changing rapidly, and the public bureaucracy must adapt to these changes or, if not die, become part of the problem. Thus, the literature of the open model seems destined to have growing influence on the thinking of public administration.

Perceptions of the Nature of the Human Beings

The second basic difference between the closed and open models parallels the first, in that their respective models of human beings match the models of organization. Douglas McGregor called these two models "Theory X" and "Theory Y."[98] Theory X applies to the closed model, particularly to bureaucratic theory. Its underlying belief structure assumes that work is not liked by most people, most people prefer close and unrelenting supervision, most people cannot contribute creatively to the solution of organizational problems, motivation to work is an individual matter, and most people are motivated by the direct application of threat or punishment. It is apparent that organizations exemplifying the closed model not only would fit, but possibly might also be appealing to Theory X people.

Theory Y, which goes by other titles as well, such as System 4, Self-Actualization, Intrinsic Motivation, and Eupsychian Management, has quite another underlying belief structure. Theory Y assumes that, given the right conditions, most people can enjoy work as much as play, most people can exercise self-control and prefer doing jobs in their own way, most people can solve organizational problems creatively, motivation to work is a group matter, and most people often are motivated by social and ego rewards. It is apparent that organizations predicated on the open model likely would attract Theory Y people.

There is another aspect to the nature of the human being posited by the open and closed models, and that is the problem of rationalism. In the closed model, *rational* means that everyone in the organization has the same goals and agrees on how to achieve those goals in an optimal fashion. Consider a hypothetical example. In International Widget, a closed-model organization, we may assume that (1) everyone wants to achieve the officially stated goals of the organization, which are to make widgets and profits, and (2) everyone agrees on how widgets should be made and profits reaped with maximum efficiency and economy.

In the open model, however, *rational* has quite a different meaning—it means that everyone in the organization has his or her own personal goals and has his or her own personal way to achieve those goals. Both goals and the ways to achieve them are unique to each individual in the organization.

If we turned our example of International Widget into an open-model organization, then the production of widgets and the reaping of profits would be incidental considerations at best to most members of the organization. Their real goals (*i.e.*, their "rationality") would revolve around such values as getting ahead, acquiring status (through salary, position, and reputation), and receiving various other psychological and social satisfactions. Some of these goals are in conflict (for instance, several executives vying for the same promotion) and others are not, although they still may be quite disparate (for instance, one member of the organization may have deeply set needs for organizational prestige, while another may want nothing more than the opportunity to do his or her own thing, such as auditing). The point is, however, that the official goals of the organization rarely are the real goals of the organization's people.

Moreover, people with similar goals in the organization will likely differ on how those goals should be fulfilled. Two executives competing for a promotion may have quite different means for attaining the same end; one may prefer to cultivate those in influential positions and another may prefer to be judged on his or her merits, such as one's sales record. It should be recalled, however, that in the open model even "merit" will mean different things to different people and, in certain organizational situations, "brown-nosing" may be regarded as a highly meritorious and rational activity. In sum, rationality in organization theory depends on what organization, group, or person you are talking about.

Perceptions of the Concept of Manipulation

Manipulation in an organizational context simply means getting people to do what you want them to do. Getting one's way, of course, may be accomplished through a wide variety of methods, ranging from brute force to no force at all, and the particular techniques of manipulation correspond with organizational perceptions on the nature of the human condition.

The open model, most notably its organization development school, occasionally appears to argue against the practice of manipulation of people by other people. Manipulation is seen as dehumanizing, "dematurizing" (to use Argyris's term),[99] and generally nasty. Indeed, manipulation inhibits the self-actualization of organizational members and reduces their sense of self-worth. By contrast, the closed model, particularly its bureaucratic theory school, has no qualms about employing manipulative methods. It advocates "using" people for the sake of the organization's ends. Moreover, the callous use of authoritative coercion in manipulating people is seen as entirely legitimate.

The preceding paragraph may overstate the case, but it nonetheless is representative of the differing values of the two models concerning manipulation. In actuality, their difference over manipulation is one of style. In the ideal-type closed model, force is always a possibility; we can conceive of an administrator smashing the nearest chair over a subordinate's cranium in an effort to induce the hapless underling to do things his or her way. In fact, similar incidents have happened; public administrators in the government of the Third Reich (as close to a prototype of a closed-model organization as one is likely to find) were known to level Lugers at the necks of subordinates when they displayed reluctance to follow orders and be "a good German." Conversely, the use of coercion in open-model organizations is considered reprehensible and is actively discouraged. Manipulation in the open model takes on a far more subtle hue; suggestions replace orders, persuasion supplants coercion, education is favored over obedience, socialization is used instead of force, and cooperation displaces authority. The fundamental idea is to so manipulate organizational members that they "want" to work for the organization.

An example of what this line of thought means in practice is Robert T. Golembiewski's discussion of the "inappropriate 'good morning'" in *Behavior and Organizations*. If administrators are to induce a feeling of supportive relationships among subordinates, goes the reasoning, then they must be aware of the more subtle requisites of the social context. It follows that one should not say "good morning" inappropriately when speaking to subordinates. An explosively cheery "good morning" is likely to put off, say, a secretary as being phony and overdrawn, while a snarled "good morning" or a grunt is likely to make him or her wary and sulky. "Good mornings" must be tailored appropriately in tone to the persons receiving them if individual self-actualization via supportive relationships is to be attained, and thereby benefit organizational productivity.[100]

Not all the theorists of the open model are as straightforward in their acceptance of manipulation as Golembiewski. In part, this is because manipulation itself goes against the grain of the open model. As Allen Schick observes, Argyris, one of the intellectual leaders of organization development, "for two decades . . . has resisted his own findings that organization demands and individual needs are incongruent, and he still labors to develop models of compatibility."[101] Schick suggests in this light that, "The reconciliation of man and his organization has proved to be an essential but perhaps hopeless task. Either the individual is autonomous or the organization is dominant, for the very notion of individualism wars against even benevolent organization."[102]

In sum, manipulation is necessary in the open model as well as in the closed model of organizations. Only the techniques of manipulation differ. The closed-model theorists, in the tradition of Weber, believed in orders and obedience, rules and regulations, punctuality and punctiliousness. The human dysfunctions of these manipulative techniques are obvious; rigidity, impersonality, alienation, narrowness, and stultification number among the human and organizational liabilities of authoritarian manipulation. But there are also human advantages to the crudities of the closed-model's manipulative techniques: People in closed-model organizations "know where they stand." The authoritarianism of the closed model is for people who like things straightforward and clearcut.

Just as the disadvantages of the closed-model's manipulative techniques are apparent, so the advantages of the open-model's methods of manipulation are clear; humanism, openness, communication, teamwork, and innovation are enhanced by the use of OD concepts. But there are also liabilities to the social-psychological brand of manipulation employed by the open model. The more refined manipulative methods stemming from small-group theory, supportive relationships, myths of peerage, and appropriate "good mornings" tend to camouflage the unavoidable exercise of power in organizations. As a result, people in open-model organizations may never be sure "where they stand." More significantly, if they think that they do know where they stand, their knowledge may be the end-product of a manipulation of their psyches so subtle as to render them analogous to the "conditioned" human shell of the protagonist in George Orwell's *Nineteen Eighty-four*, who uncontrollably shrieked "Long Live Big Brother!" even as he despised him. Eric Fromm expresses this idea more succinctly with his concept of "willing submissiveness"; that is, although organizational subordinates may appear to have "team spirit" (and actually may have been so successfully manipulated as to believe they have it), the psychological techniques used to create their willing submissiveness induces in reality a subliminal and deep internal resentment toward their superiors bordering on hatred.[103]

Perceptions of the Social Role of Organizations

The fourth principal difference between the closed and open models is particularly germane to the study of public administration, and centers on how their respective theorists have viewed the organization and its relationships with the larger society. In considering

this dimension, we are examining from a different perspective the moral question of organizational manipulation.

Weber provides an especially solid example of a closed model theorist who makes his values explicit in this regard. Weber believed a highly rational bureaucracy to be essential in achieving the goals of the tumultuous, charisma-dominated society that whirled beyond its confines. Without bureaucracy, society would achieve nothing; it would not "progress," it would not replace *Kadijustice* with the rule of rational law. To exaggerate but to nonetheless state the point, bureaucracy, replete with its own internal injustices, dehumanizing rules, and monocratic arbitrariness, was vital in its very rigidity and rationalism to the unorganized societal lunacy that it offset. If Weber's conception of the bureaucracy's station in society could be illustrated, it would look something like Figure 3-1.

Weber was not unsympathetic to the plight of the individual bureaucrat. In fact, he deplored what the mechanization and routinization of bureaucratic settings could do to the human spirit. But, when all was said and done, Weber could accept the dehumanization of society's social servants, who were somehow apart from the other citizens, on the grounds that the bureaucracy was essential to social progress and the elimination of injustice. There was, in sum, a higher morality that provided the *raison d'être* of bureaucracy and, if a few unfortunates were hurt inside the bureaucracy, so be it.

In contrast to Weber, the open-model theorists have a completely different conception of the organization's role in society. To them, virtually everyone in society is encased in some sort of organization. Thus, for the public bureaucracy to manipulate and dehumanize its own bureaucrats in order to further society's goals and establish

**FIGURE 3-1   The Closed Model's View:
Organizations *and* Society**

**FIGURE 3-2   The Open Model's View:
Organizations *as* Society**

rational social justice is self-defeating because the bureaucrat and the citizen are one and the same. The open model's view of the role of the organization in society is a complex of interlocking and interacting organizations; society itself is a series of organizations, and there is no unorganized, irrational society "out there," functioning beyond the organizations' boundaries. The open-model's concept of society and the bureaucracy looks like Figure 3-2.

The contrast between the closed and open modelists is that the closed modelists distinguished between citizens and bureaucrats, whereas the open modelists feel that essentially all citizens are "bureaucrats"—that is, all citizens belong to or are affected by organizations in some ways. The lack of distinction between citizens and bureaucrats, and between society and its organizations, has led the open-model theorists to see moral choice and the concept of the public interest as essentially intraorganizational phenomena. Thus, to treat a member of an organization, particularly a subordinate, badly is immoral because there is no higher morality to excuse such treatment, as there is in Weber's construct. In the open model, what is good for the individual is also good for the society.

THE LITERATURE OF MODEL SYNTHESIS

Students of organizations may be initially confused by the fundamentally different paradigms of organization theory represented by the closed and open models. One model assumes monolithic, organizational rationality, the other model assumes "nonrationality," by which is meant a pluralist state of many unique, individual rationalities. One model assumes a stable environment, the other assumes an unstable environment. One assumes a Theory X view of human beings, the other assumes a Theory Y view. One assumes that society is unstructured, but predictable, the other assumes that society is highly structured, but unpredictable. These are basic differences. Can they be reconciled and, if so, how?

The answer to the first part of the question is a qualified "yes," and the attempt to do so is represented by the "newer tradition" of organization theory as exemplified by Herbert A. Simon's *Administrative Behavior*, James G. March and Simon's *Organizations*, Richard Cyert and March's *A Behavioral Theory of the Firm*, and James D. Thompson's *Organizations in Action*, although there is, of course, a much larger literature extant. Barnard's *The Functions of the Executive* also can properly be considered a key work in this stream, as well as a major contribution to the open-model.

In terms of reconciling the two models, it first must be appreciated that our culture really does not facilitate our thinking of opposites as harmonious. It requires some hard concentration to think about something half closed, half open; half certain, half uncertain; half regulated, half spontaneous; and half rational, half nonrational. Yet, this is precisely what Simon, March, Cyert, Thompson, and others try to do, and they largely succeed.

The essence of the literature of model synthesis is that it starts with the open model (that is, it assumes that organizations are spontaneous collectivities of people with their own goals and drives; who are operating in an uncertain environment), but explains organizational behavior as being motivated by a need to routinize and rationalize the organization's internal workings and its relationships with its environment whenever and wherever possible. This is essentially a Darwinian notion (adapt or die). Another way of saying the same thing is that organizations try to become rational. Consider the same concept from another perspective: Organizations try to make all variables (*e.g.*, member behavior, technological and environmental developments) predictable. Visualized differently, we can perceive that organizations try to achieve closure. Yet another (and perhaps the best) way of expressing the same idea is to say that organizations try to reduce uncertainty.

Thus, the two models are synthesized, and the synthesis is predicated on three very reasonable assumptions:

1. Organizations and their environments can and do change.
2. Organizations and the people in them act to survive.
3. Organizations and the people in them can and do learn from experience, including failures and successes.

The key to understanding the literature of model synthesis is that all organizations must deal with uncertainty. Kaufman provides some useful insights in this regard. He suggests that organizations will try to grow as large as they can (since growth is seen as the basic stratagem for assuring organizational survival), and that the necessity of reducing uncertainty stands as the central problem in trying to grow; hence, "organizations are averse to uncertainty."[104]

Uncertainty may spring from two sources: those sources that are internal to the organization and those that are external to it. If the sources of organizational uncertainty are internal, then the organization will strive to reduce uncertainty by centralizing. Centralizing techniques include "control . . . of all communication to the members of the vexing suborganizations . . . so that nonconforming thought (and therefore deviant behavior) is prevented; intensifying surveillance to discourage nonconformity by increasing the probability of exposure and punishment; detaching key operations [such as taking away the control of funds and rewards from suborganizations] . . . thus reducing their self-containment and increasing their vulnerability to central direction; . . . indoctrinating all members . . . to respond only to commands from the central leadership and from no other source. . . . [and finally, expelling] the offending suborganization, [an act amounting to] a contraction of boundaries constituting a withdrawal from internal sources of uncertainty."[105]

If, however, the sources of organizational uncertainty are external, then the organization will seek to expand its boundaries—to grow. Often, decentralization is required if an organization is to expand. The organization will attempt to incorporate external sources of uncertainty into the organization. Selznick's co-optation, described earlier, is one form that this incorporation of external uncertainties might take; the effort by an organization to control some facet of the natural environment (for example, to engage in flood control or weather prediction) is another form; to merge or ally with competitive organizations is yet another.

If the expansion of an organization's boundaries is blocked, then the organization will seek to reduce its exchanges with its environment—"withdrawal from the source of uncertainty, as it were."[106] A firm uncertain about its future supplies or service needs might decide to stockpile or produce its own manufacturing components, or develop its own service staffs. Entire nations, particularly in Asia, have been known to reduce *their* external uncertainties by radically reducing exchanges with other nations and launching self-sufficiency policies; the invariable consequence, however, is an elevation of costs and a lowering of living standards.

The preceding points are important, and we shall be referring to them implicitly in the next chapter, which is about some concepts of organization theory.

NOTES

1. See the following: Victor A. Thompson, *Modern Organization* (New York: Knopf, 1961), p. 5; Chester I. Barnard, *The Functions of the Executive* (Cambridge, Mass.: Harvard University Press, 1938), p. 11; and E. Wight Bakke, *Bond of Organization* (New York: Harper & Row, 1950), pp. 8-9.
2. James G. March and Herbert A. Simon, *Organizations* (New York: John Wiley, 1958), p. 4.
3. James D. Thompson, *Organizations in Action* (New York: McGraw-Hill, 1967).
4. Tom Burns and G. M. Stalker, *The Management of Innovation* (London: Tavistock, 1961).
5. Max Weber, *From Max Weber*, in H. H. Gerth and C. Wright Mills, eds. (New York: Oxford University Press, 1946).
6. See especially Frederick W. Taylor, *Principles of Scientific Management* (New York: Harper & Row, 1911); and Frank G. Gilbreth, *Primer of Scientific Management* (New York: Van Nostrand, 1912).
7. Charles D. Wrege and Amedeo G. Perroni, "Taylor's

Pig-Tale: A Historical Analysis of Frederick W. Taylor's Pig-Iron Experiment," *Academy of Management Journal*, 17 (March 1974), pp. 6-27.

8. Taylor, *Principles of Scientific Management*, p. 59.

9. See especially Luther Gulick and L. Urwick, eds., *Papers on the Science of Administration* (New York: Institute of Public Administration, 1937); and James D. Mooney and Alan C. Reiley, *The Principles of Organization* (New York: Harper & Row, 1939).

10. See, for example, M. P. Follett, *Creative Experience* (New York: P. Smith Company, 1924); and Henri Fayol, *General and Industrial Management* (London: Pitmann, 1930).

11. Alvin W. Gouldner, "Organizational Analysis," in *Sociology Today*, Robert K. Merton, Leonard Broom, and Leonard S. Cottrell, Jr., eds. (New York: Basic Books, 1959), pp. 400-428.

12. Alvin Toffler, *Future Shock* (New York: Random House, 1970).

13. Burns and Stalker, *The Management of Innovation*.

14. The original Hawthorne studies are in: Fritz J. Roethlisberger and William J. Dickson, *Management and the Worker* (Cambridge, Mass.: Harvard University Press, 1939). The reinterpretation of Hawthorne is in: Richard Herbert Franke and James D. Kaul, "The Hawthorne Experiments: First Statistical Interpretation," *American Sociological Review*, 43 (October 1978), pp. 623-643.

15. See Abraham Maslow, "A Theory of Metamotivation: The Biological Rooting of Value-Life," *Humanitas*, 4 (1969), pp. 301-343.

16. Abraham Maslow, *Eupsychian Management: A Journal* (Homewood, Ill.: Dorsey, 1965), p. 1.

17. See, for example, Frederick Herzberg, *Work and the Nature of Man* (Cleveland, Ohio: World Publishing, 1966).

18. Chunoh Park, Nicholas P. Lobrich and Dennise L. Soden, "Testing Herzberg's Motivation Theory in a Comparative Study of U.S. and Korean Public Employees," *Review of Public Personnel Administration*, 8 (Summer 1988), p. 40.

19. Frank K. Gibson and Clyde E. Teasley, "The Humanistic Model of Organizational Motivation: A Review of Research Support," *Public Administration Review*, 33 (January-February 1973), pp. 89-96.

20. Richard Beckhard, *Organizational Development: Strategies and Models* (Reading, Mass.: Addison-Wesley, 1969), pp. 20-24.

21. Wendell L. French and Cecil H. Bell, Jr., *Organization Development: Behavioral Science Interventions for Organization Improvement* (Englewood Cliffs, N.J.: Prentice Hall, 1973).

22. Douglas McGregor, *The Professional Manager* (New York: McGraw-Hill, 1967); and Robert R. Blake and J. S. Mouton, *The Managerial Grid* (Houston, Tex.: Gulf Publishing, 1964).

23. Warren G. Bennis, *Organizational Development: Its Nature, Origins, and Prospects* (Reading, Mass.: Addison-Wesley, 1969), p. 17.

24. Robert T. Golembiewski, Carl W. Proehl, Jr., and David Sink, "Success of OD Applications in the Public Sector: Toting Up the Score for a Decade,

More or Less," *Public Administration Review*, 41 (November/December 1981), p. 681. The authors counted 574 OD applications in the public sector conducted between 1945 and 1980.

25. Peggy Morrison, "Evaluation in OD: A Review and an Assessment," *Group and Organization Studies*, 3 (March 1978), pp. 42-70; and Jerry Porras, "The Comparative Impact of Different OD Techniques and Intervention Intensities," *Journal of Applied Behavioral Science*, 15 (April 1979), pp. 156-178.

26. Representative works (besides Maslow's, cited earlier) include: Carl R. Rogers and Barry Stevens, *Person to Person: The Problem of Being Human* (Lafayette, Calif.: Real People Press, 1968); Carl R. Rogers, *On Encounter Groups* (New York: Harper & Row, 1970); Arthur Janov and E. Michael Holde, *Primal Man: The New Consciousness* (New York: Crowell, 1975); Ida P. Rolf, *Rolfing: The Integration of Human Structures* (Santa Monica, Calif.: Dennis-Landman, 1977); Alexander Lowen, *Bioenergetics* (New York: Penguin, 1975); R. D. Laing, *The Facts of Life: An Essay on Feelings, Facts, and Fantasy* (New York: Pantheon, 1976); and Walter Truett Anderson, *The Upstart Spring: Esalen and the American Awakening* (Reading, Mass.: Addison-Wesley, 1983).

27. Robert Kahn, quoted in Thomas H. Fitzgerald, "The O.D. Practitioner in the Business World: Theory vs. Reality," *Organizational Dynamics*, 16 (Summer 1987), p. 28. Emphasis is original.

28. Frances FitzGerald, *Cities on a Hill: A Journey through Contemporary American Cultures* (New York: Simon & Schuster, 1986), p. 284.

29. Carl R. Rogers and B. F. Skinner, "Some Issues Concerning the Control of Human Behavior," *Science*, 124 (1956), pp. 1057-1065, as reprinted in: Richard I. Evans, *Carl Rogers: The Man and His Ideas* (New York: E. P. Dutton, 1975), p. lxii.

30. B. F. Skinner, *Beyond Freedom and Dignity* (New York: Bantam, 1972).

31. Sigmund Freud, *The Ego and the Id* (London: Hogarth 1947), and *Civilization and Its Discontents* (London: Liverwright, 1930).

32. Carl Rogers, describing a conversation with the noted Freudian, Karl Menninger, and quoted in Howard Kirschenbaum, *On Becoming Carl Rogers* (New York: Delacorte, 1979), p. 250.

33. *Ibid.*, p. 251.

34. FitzGerald, *Cities on a Hill*, p. 275.

35. *Ibid.*, pp. 380—381.

36. Maslow, *Eupsychian Management*, p. 1.

37. Fitzgerald, "The O.D. Practitioner in the Business World," pp. 25, 27

38. John Cowan, *Small Decencies: Reflections and Meditations on Being Human at Work* (New York: Harper & Row, 1992), pp. 92-93.

39. See, for example, Chester L. Barnard, *The Functions of the Executive*; Philip Selznick, *TVA and the Grass Roots* (Berkeley: University of California Press, 1949); and Burton R. Clark, *Adult Education in Transition* (Berkeley: University of California Press, 1956).

40. Herbert Kaufman, *Time, Chance, and Organizations:*

Natural Selection in a Perilous Environment (Chatham, N.J.: Chatham House, 1985), p. 67.

41. Selznick, *TVA and the Grass Roots.*

42. Richard A. Couto, "Co-optation in TVA: Selznick Updated," paper delivered at the 1981 Annual Meeting of the American Political Science Association, New York, September 3-6, 1981, abstract page.

43. Richard A. Couto, "TVA's Old and New Grass Roots: A Reexamination of Cooptation," *Administration and Society*, 19 (February 1988), p. 453.

44. Among the best reviews of this literature, and its manifold methodological problems, are: Hal G. Rainey, "Public Organization Theory: Current Contributions and Research Directions," paper presented at the 1984 Annual Meeting of the American Political Science Association, Washington, D.C.: August 30-September 2, 1984; Hal G. Rainey, "Public Management: Recent Research on the Political Context and Managerial Roles, Structures, and Behaviors," *Journal of Management*, 15 (April 1989), pp. 229-250; James L. Perry and Hal G. Rainey, "The Public-Private Distinction in Organization Theory: A Critique and Research Strategy," *Academy of Management Review*, 13 (April 1988), pp. 182-201; and Hal G. Rainey, "Public Management: Recent Developments and Current Prospects," in Naomi B. Lynn and Aaron Wildavsky, eds., *Public Administration: The State of the Discipline* (Chatham, N.J.: Chatham House Publishers, 1990), pp. 157-184.

45. Both the experiential and academic literatures agree on this point. For examples of the former, see: W. Michael Blumenthal, "Candid Reflections of a Business Man in Washington," *Fortune* (January 29, 1979), pp. 2, 6-49; and Donald Rumsfeld, "A Politician-Turned-Executive Surveys Both Worlds," *Fortune* (September 10, 1979), pp. 88-94. For examples of the latter, see: Bruce Buchanan II, "Red-Tape and the Service Ethic: Some Unexpected Differences Between Public and Private Managers," *Administration and Society*, 6 (February 1975), pp. 423-488; Louis C. Gawthrop, *Bureaucratic Behavior in the Executive Branch* (New York: Free Press, 1969); Bruce Buchanan II, "Government Managers, Business Executives, and Organizational Commitment," *Public Administration Review*, 35 (July/August 1975), pp. 339-347; and Robert T. Golembiewski, *Humanizing Public Organizations* (Mt. Airy, Md.: Lomond, 1985).

46. Lewis C. Mainzer, *Political Bureaucracy* (Glenview, Ill.: Scott, Foresman, 1973), p. 14; and John D. Millett, *Organization for the Public Service* (Princeton, N.J.: Van Nostrand, 1966), p. 10. The point is sufficiently basic that the list of sources supporting it could be expanded almost *ad infinitum.*

47. Paul Appleby, *Big Democracy* (New York: Knopf, 1945); Gawthrop, *Bureaucratic Behavior*; Robert T. Golembiewski, "Organization Development in Public Agencies: Perspectives on Theory and Practice," *Public Administration Review*, 29 (July/August 1969), pp. 367-368.

48. Claire L. Felbinger, "Impediments to Effective Management in Local Bureaucracies: The Perceptions of Public Works Directors," *Public Productivity and Management Review*, XIV (Fall 1990), pp. 12, 15. The American Public Works Association conducted these surveys in 1981 and 1987.

49 J. A. Stockfisch, *The Political Economy of Bureaucracy* (New York: General Learning Press, 1972); Gary L. Wamsley and Mayer N. Zald, *The Political Economy of Public Organizations* (Lexington, Mass.: D. C. Heath, 1973); and Herman L. Weiss, "Why Business and Government Exchange Executives," *Harvard Business Review* (July/August 1974), pp. 129-140.

50. Stockfisch, *The Political Economy of Bureaucracy*; and Henry Mintzberg, *The Nature of Managerial Work* (New York: Harper & Row, 1973), p. 108.

51. Anthony Downs, *Inside Bureaucracy* (Boston: Little, Brown, 1967), pp. 52-59, 145-146.

52. Donald P. Warwick, *A Theory of Public Bureaucracy* (Cambridge, Mass.: Harvard University Press, 1975), pp. 73-80, 188-191.

53. Marshall W. Meyer, *Change in Public Bureaucracies* (London: Cambridge University Press, 1979), p. 5.

54. Buchanan, "Government Managers, Business Executives, and Organizational Commitment"; Louis C. Gawthrop, *Administrative Politics and Social Change* (New York: St. Martin's, 1971); and Mainzer, *Political Bureaucracy.*

55. Mainzer, *Political Bureaucracy*; Millett, *Organization for the Public Service*; and Edward A. Holdaway, *et al.*, "Dimensions of Organizations in Complex Societies: The Educational Sector," *Administrative Science Quarterly*, 20 (March 1975), pp. 37-58.

56. Blumenthal, "Candid Reflections of a Businessman Washington"; Rumsfeld, "A Politician-Turned-Executive Surveys Both Worlds"; and Weiss, "Why Business and Government Exchange Executives."

57 *Ibid.*; Robert A. Dahl and Charles E. Lindblom, *Politics, Economics and Welfare* (New York: Harper & Row, 1953); and Golembiewski, *Humanizing Public Organizations.*

58. D.J. Hickson, R.J. Butler, D. Cray, G.R. Mallory, and D.C. Wilson, *Top Decisions: Strategic Decision Making in Organizations* (San Francisco: Jossey-Bass, 1986).

59. David Coursey and Barry Bozeman, "Decision Making in Public and Private Organizations: A Test of Alternative Concepts of 'Publicness,'" *Public Administration Review*, 50 (September/October 1990), p. 525.

60. Gordon Kingsley and Pamela Norton Reed, "Decision Process Models and Organizational Context: Level and Sector Make a Difference," *Public Productivity and Management Review*, XIV (Summer 1991), p. 409.

61. David M. Welborn, William Lyons, and Larry W. Thomas, "The Federal Government in the Sunshine Act and Agency Decision Making," *Administration and Society*, 20 (February 1989), p. 483.

62. James F. Guyot, "Government Bureaucrats *Are* Different," *Public Administration Review*, 22

(December 1962), pp. 195-202.

63. James R. Rawls and Oscar T. Nelson, Jr., "Characteristics Associated with Preferences for Certain Managerial Positions," *Psychological Reports*, 36 (June 1975), pp. 911-918; James R. Rawls, Robert A. Ulrich, and Oscar T. Nelson, "A Comparison of Managers Entering or Reentering the Profit and Nonprofit Sectors," *Academy of Management Journal*, 18 (September 1975), pp. 616-622; and Warren H. Schmidt and Barry Z. Posner, "Values and Expectations of City Managers in California," *Public Administration Review*, 47 (September/October 1987), pp. 404-409.

64. Hal G. Rainey, "Reward Preferences Among Public and Private Managers: In Search of the Service Ethic," *American Review of Public Administration*, 16 (Winter 1982), p. 290. See also Dennis Wittmer's excellent analysis of this research: "Serving the People or Serving for Pay: Reward Preferences Among Government, Hybrid Sector, and Business Managers," *Public Productivity and Management Review*, XIV (Summer 1991), pp. 369-383.

65. J. Norman Baldwin, "Public Versus Private Employees: Debunking Stereotypes," *Review of Public Personnel Administration*, 11 (Fall 1990-Spring 1991), p. 7.

66. Wittmer, "Serving the People or Serving for Pay," p. 379.

67. Hal G. Rainey, "Public Agencies and Private Firms: Incentive Structures, Goals, and Individual Roles," *Administration and Society*, 15 (August 1983), pp. 207-242; and U.S. Office of Personnel Management *Federal Employee Attitudes* (Washington, D.C.: U.S. Government Printing Office, 1979).

68. Hal G. Rainey, Carol Traut, and Barry Blunt, "Reward Expectancies and Other Work-Related Attitudes in Public and Private Organizations: A Review and Extension," paper presented at the 1985 Annual Meeting of the American Political Science Association, New Orleans, August 29-September 1, 1985, p. 9.

69. Ebrahim A. Maidani, "Comparative Study of Herzberg's Two-Factor Theory of Job Satisfaction Among Public and Private Sector," *Public Personnel Management*, 20 (Winter 1991), p. 441.

70. Santa Falcone, "Self-Assessments and Job Satisfaction in Public and Private Organizations," *Public Productivity and Management Review*, XIV (Summer 1991), p. 394.

71. Buchanan, "Government Managers, Business Executives, and Organizational Commitment"; and Buchanan, "Red Tape and the Public Service Ethic."

Although the literature that compares public and private managers by and large concludes that public administrators are less committed to their organizations than are private managers, this may not be an entirely negative factor insofar as the public interest is concerned. While it is generally assumed that the high level of personal commitment to one's organization is desirable, researchers in this area have argued that "high levels of commitment to the organization may have severe negative consequences where individuals

within the organization and for organizations themselves." See: Donna M. Randall, "Commitment and the Organization: The Organization Man Revisited," *Academy of Management Review*, 12 (September 1987), p. 460.

72. Frank T. Paine, Stephen J. Carroll, and Burt A. Leete, "Need Satisfactions of Managerial Personnel in a Government Agency," *Journal of Applied Psychology*, 50 (June 1966) pp. 247-249; J.B. Rhinehart, *et al.*, "Comparative Study of Need Satisfaction in Governmental and Business Hierarchies," *Journal of Applied Psychology*, 53 (June 1969), pp. 230-235; Lyman W. Porter and Edward E. Lawler, *Managerial Attitudes and Performance*, (Homewood, Ill.: Irwin, 1968; Buchanan, "Government Managers, Business Executives, and Organizational Commitment"; Buchanan, "Red Tape and the Service Ethic"; Hal G. Rainey, Carroll Traut, and Barrie Blunt, "Reward Expectancies and Other Work-Related Attitudes in Public and Private Organizations: A Review and Extension," *Review of Public Personnel Administration*, 6 (Summer 1986), pp. 50-72.

73. E. Solomon and M. Greenberg, "Organizational Climate in the Public and Private Sectors," paper presented at the annual meeting of the Academy of Management, New York, 1982.

74. Ran Lachman, "Public and Private Sector Differences: CEOs' Perceptions of their Role Environments," *Academy of Management Journal*, 28 (June 1985), pp. 671-679.

75. F.P. Kilpatrick, M.C. Cummings, Jr., and M.K. Jennings, *The Image of the Federal Service*, (Washington, D.C.: Brookings Institution, 1964).

76. Michael P. Smith and Smith L. Nock, "Social Class and the Quality of Life in Public and Private Organizations," *Journal of Social Issues*, 36 (June 1980), pp. 59-75.

77. Rainey, "Perceptions of Incentives in Business and Government," and Rainey, "Public Agencies and Private Firms."

78. Schmidt and Posner, "Values and Expectations of City Managers in California," p. 408. Schmidt and Posner compared surveys of 1,498 managers from the private sector taken in 1981, 803 career executives in the federal government taken in 1982, and 213 California city managers taken in 1983.

79. Rhinehart, *et al.*, "Comparative Study of Satisfaction in Government and Business Hierarchies"; Paine, Carroll, and Leete, "Need Satisfactions of Managerial Personnel in a Government Agency"; and Buchanan, "Government Managers, Business Executives, and Organizational Commitment."

80. James L. Perry and Lyman W. Porter, "Factors Affecting the Context for Motivation in Public Organizations," *Academy of Management Review*, 7 (January 1982) p. 96.

81. See, for example: Laurence E. Lynn, *Managing the Public's Business* (New York: Basic Books, 1981); Herbert Kaufman, *The Administrative Behavior of Federal Bureau Chiefs* (Washington, D.C.: Brookings Institution, 1981); Richard Elling, "The Relationships Among Bureau Chiefs, Legislative Committees, and

Interest Groups: A Multi-State Study," paper presented at the Annual Conference of the American Political Science Association, Chicago, September 1-4, 1983; and Randall B. Ripley and Grace A. Franklin, *Policy-Making in the Federal Executive Branch* (New York: Free Press, 1975).

There are numerous examples of books and articles devoted to the unique problems of public management, but not very many with a perspective that is distinctively drawn from organization theory; most are written in the tradition of the literature of public policymaking.

82. Charles L. Schultze, "The Role of Incentives, Penalties, and Rewards in Attaining Effective Policy," in Robert H. Haveman and Julius Margolis, eds., *Public Expenditures and Policy Analysis* (Chicago: Markham, 1970), pp. 145-172; Golembiewski, "Organization Development in Public Agencies"; and Golembiewski, *Humanizing Public Organizations*.

83. Henry Mintzberg, *The Structuring of Organizations* (Englewood Cliffs, N.J.: Prentice Hall, 1979), and L.E. Kurke, and H.E. Aldrich, "Mintzberg Was Right? A Republication and Extension of *The Nature of Managerial Work*," *Management Science*, 29 (Winter 1983), pp. 975-984.

84. Baldwin, "Public Versus Private Employees," p. 9.

85. John E. Chubb and Terry M. Moe, *Politics, Markets, and America's Schools*, (Washington, D.C.: Brookings Institution, 1990). See also, Chubb and Moe, "Politics, Markets, and the Organization of Schools," paper presented at the meeting of the American Political Science Association, New Orleans, September 1985.

86. Blumenthal, "Candid Reflections of a Businessman in Washington"; Rumsfeld, "A Politician-Turned-Executive Surveys Both Worlds"; Golembiewski, "Organization Development in Public Agencies"; Marshall W. Meyer, *Bureaucratic Structure and Authority: Coordination and Control in 254 Government Agencies* (New York: Harper & Row, 1972); and John W. Macy, *Public Service: The Human Side of Government* (New York: Harper & Row, 1971).

87. Buchanan, "Government Managers, Business Executives, and Organizational Commitment"; and Gawthrop, *Bureaucratic Behavior in the Executive Branch*.

88. Stuart Bretschneider, "Management Information Systems in Public and Private Organizations: An Empirical Test," *Public Administration Review*, 50 (September/October 1990), p. 537.

89. *Ibid*. At least one observer has noted that, in his experience, once the information is available, candid discussion of more sensitive points is less likely in government than in business. See: Blumenthal, "Candid Reflections of a Businessman in Washington."

90. Lyman W. Porter and John Van Maanen, "Task Accomplishment and the Management of Time," in *Managing for Accomplishment*, Bernard Bass, ed. (Lexington, Mass.: Lexington Books, 1970), pp. 180-192.

91. Alan W. Lau, Cynthia M. Pavett, and Arthur R. Newman, "The Nature of Managerial Work: A Comparison of Public and Private Sector Jobs," *Academy of Management Proceedings*, (August 1980), pp. 339-343.

92. Porter and Van Maanen, "Task Accomplishment and the Management of Time."

93. Richard E. Boyatzis, *The Competent Manager* (New York: John Wiley, 1982).

94. The research is quite consistent on this point. See, for example, Paine, Carroll, and Leete, "Need Satisfaction of Managerial Level Personnel in a Government Agency"; Porter and Lawler, *Managerial Attitudes and Behavior*; J. B. Rinehart, *et al.*, "Comparative Need Satisfaction in Government and Business Hierarchies"; Ran Lachman, "Perceptions of Role-Environment Among Public and Private Sector Executives," *Academy of Management Proceedings*, (August 1983), pp. 347-351; and Rainey, "Public Agencies and Private Firms."

95. Macy, *Public Service*; and Alan K. Campbell, "Civil Service Reform: A New Commitment," *Public Administration Review*, 38 (March/April 1978), pp. 101-102.

96. Buchanan "Government Managers, Business Executives, and Organizational Commitment"; Buchanan, "Red Tape and the Service Ethic"; and Smith and Nock, "Social Class and the Quality of Life in Public and Private Organizations."

97. For a review of the findings on this point, see: Baldwin, "Public Versus Private Employees," pp. 9-13.

98. Douglas McGregor, *The Theory of Human Enterprise* (New York: McGraw-Hill, 1960).

99. Chris Argyris, *Organization and Innovation* (Homewood, Ill.: Richard D. Irwin, 1965).

100. Robert T. Golembiewski, *Behavior and Organizations* (Chicago: Rand-McNally, 1962).

101. Allen Schick, "The Trauma of Politics: Public Administration in the Sixties," in *American Public Administration: Past, Present, Future*, Frederick C. Mosher, ed. (Tuscaloosa, Ala.: University of Alabama Press, 1975), p. 171.

102. *Ibid.*, p. 170.

103. Eric Fromm, *The Art of Loving* (New York: Harper & Row, 1956).

104. Kaufman, *Time, Chance, and Organizations*, p. 117.

105. *Ibid.*, p. 44.

106. *Ibid.*, p. 43.

CHAPTER 4

CONCEPTS OF ORGANIZATION THEORY

This chapter will review briefly some of the speculations and findings generated by organization theorists about organizations. Our review is hardly definitive; it concentrates on the literature of model synthesis explained in Chapter 3, and it emphasizes those concepts that seem especially germane to organizations in the public sector. The concepts covered are: change and innovation (particularly the roles of technology, task environment, and organizational members); information and intelligence; control, authority, and power; decision making; administration; and organizational assessment. These are not neat categories; their many conceptual overlappings are the result of the pervasive emphasis of decision-making theory in the study of organizations.

With the preceding sketch of the chapter's structure in mind, it is important to add three caveats about organization theory generally. First, organization theory is a broad but shallow field. It melds many concepts from many fields, but occasionally the propositions generated by organization theorists do not appear penetratingly insightful. Second, organization theory does not attempt (at least, it rarely attempts) to tell you how to run your organization "better." That abili-

ty normally is the product of native intelligence, experience, and motivation. Organization theory does attempt to discover what makes organizations tick, how organizations behave, and what accounts for differences among organizations. This knowledge, it is hoped, may ultimately prove useful to students who eventually find themselves working in a public bureaucracy. Third, as we mentioned in Chapter 2, there are no "principles of organizations" that are worth anything. For every principle, there is a counterprinciple, or the principle itself may be tautological. There are however, some enlightening perceptions in the literature about how organizations behave, and it is to a few of these that we now turn.

CHANGE AND INNOVATION

Obviously, being able to change, innovate, alter, adapt, or however one labels it is vital to any form of life, and organizations are no exception. Change in organizations is heavily influenced by at least three factors: (1) the technology of the organization (that is, what the organization does and how it does it—its official or formal goals, and its official or formal structure); (2) the task environment in which the organization must function; and (3) how the people in the organization react and interact to technology, environment, and each other.

Organizational Technologies and Organizational Change

Theorists have attempted to categorize technologies and to relate these categories to other variables in the organization. As technology changes, so will the rest of the organization—that is, the organization's structure and the goals of the organization will alter.

For example, James D. Thompson[1] has classified organizational technologies into three types: *long-linked technology*, such as the assembly line; *mediating technology*, found in such institutions as the telephone company, which must deal with people and other variables both extensively and in standardized ways; and *intensive technology*, used by such organizations as hospitals and scientific laboratories, in which the object of the technology often is a human being and feedback from the technology itself is important to the organization. These three technologies correlate with at least three other organizational variables that are significant to change and adaptation: the *cost* of the operation in terms of decision, effort, and communication; the type of *interdependence* found among people and among parts of the organization; and the style of *coordination* necessary to the organization. To elaborate, a mediating technology would have low operating costs, "pooled" or "generalized" interdependence (*i.e.*, each unit of the telephone company, such as line personnel, contribute to the organi-

zation, but the company could continue functioning despite the elimination of one of its units), and standardization of parts and units as the chief means of coordination. A long-linked technology would have intermediate costs, interdependence would be "sequential" (*i.e.*, no worker on the assembly line can work until the worker preceding him or her has completed his or her task), and planning is the form of coordination favored. An intensive technology would have high costs, "reciprocal" interdependence (every part and person of the organization is dependent upon every other part and person), and would be coordinated through mutual adjustment of the parts. Thompson's view of technology and change in organizations is arranged in summary form in Table 4-1.

Charles Perrow[2] is even more adamant about the significance of technology for organizational change, and he empirically illustrates how technology affects the power structure of organizations. (Thompson only implies this, but, after all, interdependence and coordination are variants of power in any social setting.) Perrow's study of hospitals is intriguing in this regard. He notes that when hospitals used relatively simple technologies, boards of trustees tended to form the central power structure, but when medical technologies became more complex, physicians dominated hospital power relationships. Moreover, as medical technologies became more sophisticated, official hospital goals changed from a "humanistic" and charitable mission to a technically proficient and professionally remunerative mission. Finally, when hospital technologies began to require the use of consultants, specialists, outside experts, and coordination, administrators became the power elite. A change of goals also accompanied this change in technology, and the official

TABLE 4-1   Technology and Organizational Variables

Type of Technology	Type of Interdependence	Type of Coordination	Operating Costs
Mediating (telephone company)	Pooled	Standardization	Low
Long-linked (assembly line)	Sequential	Planning	Intermediate
Intensive (scientific laboratory)	Reciprocal	Mutual Adjustment	High

hospital mission was suddenly perceived as including the social as well as the physical aspects of medicine.

There is little doubt that the technology of an organization can have a profound influence on organizational change. Despite methodological problems involving how "technology" and "organizational structure" are defined by different researchers, differing levels of analysis, and differing measures, the research is unusually consistent in concluding that when an organization's technology alters, so does the structure of the organization itself.[3]

No doubt, this relationship between technology and change pertains to public organizations as well as to private ones (although the literature on technology and organizational structure does not distinguish between public and private organizations). But technology, an "internal" factor affecting change, does not seem to be the primary force in changing public organizations. (We shall return to this point later.) That title, as we observed in Chapters 2 and 3, appears to be held by an "external" phenomenon: the organizational environment.

Organizational Environments and Organizational Change

Environmental changes can have such profound effects that organizations will radically transform themselves to survive in an altered environment. Sheldon L. Messinger has noted how the Townsend Movement, for example, which originally was a politically activist plan to alleviate unemployment in the mid-1930s, gradually converted itself into a recreational club after the Social Security Act was enacted, which effectively knocked the ideological underpinnings from the Plan. Townsendites continued to pay lip service to their plan despite the presence of Social Security.[4]

In an effort to find out how organizational capacity for change related to the nature of the organization's task environment, Tom Burns and G. M. Stalker[5] conducted extensive empirical research at two fundamentally different organizations operating in highly dissimilar environments. Their study of a Scottish yarn factory and a Scottish electrical engineering firm indicates radically different organizational structures as a function of environmental impacts. The engineering company had virtually continuous meetings, no written job descriptions, and no rule book, largely as the result of an unstable, rapidly changing task environment. The firm was quite successful in coping with fast-paced environmental changes because it was geared for them.

The yarn textile company was a well-established firm with a long tradition of industrial success. It had a massive rule book called the "Factory Bible" (which was followed scrupulously), highly formal and infrequent meetings, and painfully clear superordinate/subordinate relationships. But, because of recent changes in the historically hidebound task environment of the textile trade (*e.g.*, polyesters, blends, knits, and new marketing techniques), the firm was in trouble. Lack of structural response to a changing environment was hurting the organization financially.

Relatedly, William R. Dill has observed how the task environment can affect the autonomy and the capacity to effect changes in top management.[6] Dill's study of two Norwegian companies, "Alpha" (a clothing manufacturer) and "Beta" (an electronics firm) concluded that the Alpha management, operating in a stable environment subject to few unexpected contingencies, had far less autonomy than the Beta management. Managers in a stable environment had relatively less freedom to make innovative decisions either in terms of the company's owners or relative to their fellow managers.

Environmentally Induced Innovation: Some Dilemmas and Opportunities for Public Organizations. When environments change, managers (if the organization is to survive) must be granted some freedom of action to adapt to altered circumstances. Unfortunately, organizations in the public sector have inherently less ability to act as freely as do those in the private sector.

Richard L. Meier conducted an intriguing study of a university library that was in the process of administratively breaking down because of too many demands and not enough resources. He examined how institutions without the benefits of functioning in a free-market environment where information inputs could be adjusted through market mechanisms responded to environmental overload.[7] He delineated fourteen strategies used by such organizations to cope with rising levels of environmental stress, including queuing (*e.g.*, keeping library patrons in waiting rooms "outside" the organization); the creation of branch facilities; creation of a mobile reserve (*e.g.*, teams of personnel transferable to units as needed); the evolvement of specific performance standards followed immediately by a reduction of those standards; a "brainstorming" search for a "magic formula"; promotion of self-service (*e.g.*, letting patrons into the stacks, which is a radical strategy because it represents a deliberate reduction of organizational sovereignty); the limitation of work to capacity as determined by rigid, ritualistic rules and characterized by the denial of error and the refusal of challenge; and, ultimately, the dissolution of the organization.

The library, in a very real sense, had no choice but to play out this scenario. It did not have the control over demands from its environment that, say, International Widget would have had. International Widget could simply boost the price of widgets, and thereby reduce demand, or overload. But the library—and, presumably, any public organization—did not have this option. It had to adjust internally.

Although Meier's library was unable to cope with overload, it appears that public organizations do find ways of dealing with a "declining environment" that private organizations seem unable to undertake. In a fifteen-year study of the ten "provinces" of the largest religious order in the United States (the Jesuits), it was found that this "third-sector" organization dealt with an increasingly difficult environment by increasing cooperation among its provinces (or subunits) and placing a priority on the internal exchange of information. "There is little reason to believe that this would have happened without the trigger of decline."[8]

This kind of interorganizational coordination does not appear to occur in private-sector organizations; at least one study has concluded, for example, that cooperative, interorganizational "strategic capacity" in a hostile environment is essentially unobtainable to private firms.[9]

But this possible advantage is not without its costs. The intensifying cooperation and expanding linkages among organizational units render the administrator's role more complex and his or her power weaker: "The administrator's role changes from autocrat to facilitator."[10] So, just as Meier's library experienced a loss of organizational sovereignty when environmental overload swamped it, so the individual public administrator loses managerial autonomy when interorganizational cooperation and information sharing are used as a strategy to cope with an environment which is growing more difficult for the organization to thrive in.

How the Environment Makes Organizations Change: Three Models.   The disproportionate impact of the task environment on public organizations has been noted, but the ways in which the environment causes organizational change is a subject of some debate, and different writers on this topic use different models, or metaphors, in explaining how the environment effects organizational change.[11]

The biological metaphor: The organization as organism.   One model of organizational response to environmental change is biological (or, in the case of Herbert Kaufman, even pre-biological)[12]. The "population ecology" or "organizational ecology" writers are included in this model, and their ranks include Martin Landau, Howard E. Aldrich, and John Child, among others.[13]

The biological model is reasonably straightforward. The organization's task environment easily and intimately penetrates the organization, and changes in the organization occur with changes in its environment; stability in this extraordinarily open system of constant exchange between the organization and its environment occurs because all natural systems ultimately are self-regulating; and successful organizations achieve success by a process of natural selection that rewards the organization's ability to adapt to its environment.

There are problems with the biological model. For one, it assumes, as does the theory of natural selection, that perfect competition exists among organizations in the social world just as perfect competition is present among plants and animals in the natural world; this assumption is untenable. For another, adaptation in the natural world occurs for whole species, not individual organisms, but in the social world survival and extinction are perceived in terms of individual organizations. Organization theorists have developed a lot of taxonomies and classifications of organizations[14] that are based on all sorts of distinctions: domains, structure, function, incentives offered to employees, regulated/unregulated, large/small, old/young, complex/simple, autocratic/democratic, and, of course, our old friend, public/private. But, as Kaufman points out, these different classification schemes serve the personal purposes of different theorists, and, consequently, "What we are still groping toward . . . is a taxonomy [of organizations] that takes account of the developmental implications of evolution and calls attention to connections among the categories as well as to the distinctions between."[15] Finally, the ability to adapt in nature is determined by genetic sport, not exactly the thinking person's reaction to problems, while in society adaptability is a product of both luck (perhaps the social equivalent of genetic sport) and rational action—a quality not found in nature.

The rational metaphor: The organization as omniscient. It is this quality—that is, the thinking capacities unique to human beings—that is central to a second model of organizational response to the task environment: the *rational* model. It is difficult to list specific contributors to this model because its contributors' beliefs about the rational qualities of the organization as constituting the primary explanation of how organizations respond to their environments are implicit rather than stated upfront; indeed, the critics of this model are far more readily ascertained than are its contributors.[16] But much of the business management literature, the research on leadership, and the writings on strategic planning implicitly accept the idea that the rational model best characterizes the organization's relations with its environment.[17]

The essence of the rational model is that people who direct organizations (and, hence, organizations) are, for all practical purposes, omniscient; they know everything that they need to know. They can discern and often accurately interpret events and trends in the environment, rank prospective organizational responses in

order of their effectiveness in dealing with these events and trends, change the organization accordingly, and monitor and adjust to the results; the model has self-evident parallels with the belief sets expressed in the closed model of organizations (described in Chapter 3) and the rationalist model of public policy (described in Chapter 10).

Donald Chisholm perceptively points out that both the biological and rational models of the organization and its environment share a common blind spot: They "treat organizations as elementary, internally non-conflictual, elements within another conflict system."[18] This is a serious flaw because organizations are not happy families; they are, rather, pastiches of many aggressive individuals and coalitions (and passive ones, too), each with their own agendas regarding organizational, coalitional, and individual objectives.

The political metaphor: The organization as actor. Thus, a third model of the organization's relations with its task environment presents itself: the *political* model. Contributors include James G. March, Jeffrey Pfeffer, and James D. Thompson, among others.[19]

The political model is of unusual pertinence to public administration and, in a way, represents a compromise of sorts between the biological and rational models: Neither the environment nor the "rational organization" is recognized as consistently dominant in determining organizational change; instead, organizational change is a product of unremitting political interaction among individuals and groups within the organization who are cutting their own deals with each other *and* with other individuals and groups operating in the organization's external environment. The political model places considerable emphasis on *differentiation*, by which is meant the many divisions of labor, specializations, processes, and goals extant in large bureaucracies, and in the fact that most organizations are comprised of members who can leave if they wish. It follows that many internal differences and few organizational sanctions soon lead to a situation in which organizational change is both "biological," in that the environment is impacting directly and discretely on elements within the organization (and not merely on the organization "as a whole"), and "rational" in that these internal elements, each in their own ways, are rationally dealing with that impact to further their individual goals and preferences about how their organization should change.

Organizational Members and Organizational Change

The causal relationships between technology, environment, and organizational change are obscure, but we do know that alterations in technology and environment are major factors in organizational innovation, and that these factors are "felt" by the organization through the people who make up the organization. For example, James G. March and Herbert A. Simon have noted that when an organization becomes stabilized in terms of technological and environmental change, the phenomenon of "goal displacement" often occurs.[20] That is, means become ends, or suboptimal goals become optimal goals for various parts of the organization. In the hypothetical organization of International Widget, for example, it may happen that the advertising department perceives the optimal end of the company to be creative marketing, rather than selling widgets. But to the president of International Widget, presumably, creative marketing—or, even more to the point, effective advertising—is simply a means of selling widgets. And to the corporation's stockholders, selling widgets is merely a means of making money. In each instance, goals have been displaced.

Change occurs in other ways, too. In an organization characterized by instability, change comes through (to borrow Richard Cyert's and March's term) organizational "drift."[21] Drift refers to the directions in which the organization flows as the result of various member coalitions being formed and reformed within its boundaries.

Of course, despite changes in technology and environment that affect human participants, organizational change can still be hindered by those members who are both powerful and conservative. Anthony Downs has noted the propensity of new organizations to be composed of "climbers," who are ambitious for the advancement that accompanies organizational innovation, and for old organizations to be dominated

by "conservers," who feel more secure in stable, if possibly dying, organizations.[22] At the lower echelons, Michel Crozier has observed the inclination of French workers to resist changes that could be of obvious benefit to the organization's welfare, and ultimately their own, out of a deep psychological sense of *bon plaisir*, or the peculiarly French pride of having a recognizable, bureaucratic, and rational "place" in the organization's structure.[23]

Downs and Crozier oddly parallel each other's thoughts about how organizations change. Downs sees the process as related to an "age lump" phenomenon: Organizations grow old and stultified just as their members do, and when the conservers retire they often do so as a "lump," making way for a resurgence of change-oriented climbers. Thus, organization change alternates between lethargic "drift" and "reorganizational catch-up." Empirical support of Downs' theory of the life cycle of organizations can be found in the experiences of public agencies.[24]

Crozier sees essentially the same effect but with a slightly different dynamic. Because of the growing bureaucratic rigidity brought about by generally shared attitudes of *bon plaisir*, French organizations either must face collapse or revolutionary change from the top. The need to rationalize and bureaucratize is carried to the limit in French organizations, and with little regard for technological and environmental changes. Hence, change, when it comes, is revolutionary yet authoritarian, because it is long overdue and because the *bon plaisir* mentality of organizational members is one cultivated to resist cooperative innovation.

Downs's notion of an age lump in the life cycle of organizations and Crozier's concept that delayed change eventually means revolutionary change have some interesting applications in public administration. Public administration is facing an age lump of its own. The "Depression virtuosos"—those talented administrators who entered government service in the 1930s because they could not find better-paying jobs in business—have retired. Whether the upshot of this will amount to some sort of "revolutionary" change from the top in the public bureaucracy is a moot question, but it is notable that a new breed of climbers (women, ethnic groups, and highly educated youth) is knocking at the conservers' door with rising insistence.

Although the age of individuals in the organization can have an impact on the nature of organizational change, other characteristics are at least as important. One intensive study of "champions of change" in twenty-five large Canadian corporations found that these central agents of introducing successful innovations in information technology to their companies were self-confident, persistent, energetic, and risk-prone; they expressed a "captivating vision," pursued "unconventional action plans," developed the potential of others, and gave credit and recognition to others; they typically had been employees of their organizations for a long period, possessed the authority to make decisions, were very knowledgeable of their industries, and had a wide variety of experience in them. All were middle managers.

Champions of change used three, quite different, "processes" to persuade their organizations to implement the changes they desired. The *rational process* was the presentation of a traditional "solid business case" to win support, and was "by far the most common approach to innovation."[25] The *participative process* capitalized on the culture of some of the organizations studied—cultures which placed a premium on consensus, communication, cooperation, and consideration—and used a combination of logic and emotion to convince colleagues at all levels of the benefits of the changes well before any official decision was made to implement it. Finally, the *renegade process* involved an "end run" around top management, often in violation of corporate rules, putting the innovation in place without authorization to do so; once the advantages of the innovation are apparent, official approval becomes moot, and the earlier transgressions committed by the champion of change are quietly forgotten. "The renegade process is typically used in an organization whose culture produces tremendous resistance to change."[26]

As we noted, "champions of change" in the preceding research were uniformly middle managers, but top managers and chief executive officers must manage environmentally spawned change, too, and sometimes how they manage it can determine the life or death of their organizations. What these executives focus on in determining how they should change their organizations to survive in a changed environment is critical.

In an intriguing comparison of the correspondence of the "senior managers" of fifty-seven large companies in manufacturing, retailing, and transportation which had filed for bankruptcy with the communications of fifty-seven matched counterparts who had survived during the same five-year period in the same environment of declining opportunities, researchers found that the managers whose companies had failed focused on different parts of their organizations and their organizations' environments than did managers whose firms had survived. Those who presided over organizations that "died" concentrated their attention on "input factors," such as creditors and suppliers, and "internal environments," where the firms' owners, employees, and top managers were found, but denied or ignored "output factors" and the "external environment," such as customers and general economic conditions. By contrast, the heads of surviving companies placed equal attention on both the internal and external environments, and more attention to output factors (such as satisfying customers) than to input factors (such as fending off creditors). These successful senior managers were much more externally directed and concerned with their organizations reaching out to a difficult task environment than were their failed colleagues.[27]

Shaping Public Organizations: Technology, Environment, or People?

What is the most critical force in "causing" organizational change, particularly in public organizations: its technology, its environment, or its members? No one knows. However, some speculations have emerged in the research on organizations that are at least worth some discussion.

The (Probably) Limited Role of Technology. First, because the technologies of a public organization—that is, what an organization does—seldom change, it follows that relatively little organizational change will occur because of technological change. The technologies of public organizations tend not to change because legislatures and other elements of the task environment generally inhibit it; the Social Security Administration, for example, is not likely to diversify and start manufacturing widgets, in addition to mailing Social Security checks. But this does not hold for private organizations; U.S. Steel, for example, can diversify, and it has done so to the point that manufacturing steel is now one of its lesser technologies, and it consequently has changed its name to USX.

This is not to say that public organizations are immune to the changes that accompany technological developments; the computer, for example, is a new technology that has altered virtually every other technology used by organizations, including public organizations, and, as we describe in Chapter 6, significant organizational change has accompanied this new technology. Nevertheless, technology seems to be less a factor in changing public organizations than private ones.

Environmental Determinism versus Human Choice. This leaves the task environment and the members of organizations—its people—as the more important variables in motivating change in public organizations. Which is the more important? Kaufman argues in eloquent terms that the more significant factor is the environmental one, and not merely for just public organizations:

> I anticipate . . . that comparisons between organizations that survive and those that expire will in the vast majority of instances disclose no significant differences in their respective levels of ability, intelligence, or leadership. . . . [T]he Tolstoyan view of leaders as chips tossed about by the tides of history rather than masters of events cannot be rejected a priori. . . . [E]ven if leaders *do* appear to be as important as conventional opinions hold them to be, the quality of leadership will nevertheless prove to be randomly rather than systematically distributed among organizations, and chance will therefore remain the main factor in organizational survival.[28]

What, in sum, Kaufman and many of the leading organization theorists seem to be saying is

that people do not count for much in shaping organizations.[29]

But not all organization theorists agree with this assessment; in fact, one exhaustive review of the literature identified the questions of whether the organization's environment or the people in it had the greater influence on an organization's destiny as two of the four "central perspectives" constituting the "debates in organization theory,"[30] and other analysts have described the issue as "one of the most pervasive and central arguments" in the field.[31]

As the theory of organizations grows more sophisticated, some tentative answers to this dilemma begin to emerge, and the answers center around not merely the "perspectives" (*i.e.,* the biases) of individual theorists, but the types of organizations that are being theorized about.[32] And here is where the public/private distinction in organization theory seems to have a special usefulness.

Table 4-2 on page 94–95 is an attempt to categorize some of the more important ideas held by organization theorists regarding the impact of the task environment (or what is sometimes referred to by authors as "determinism"), and the impact of the organization's leaders, managers and members (also known as "choice") on an organization's destiny. At one extreme, some theorists argue that the environment is all important, all pervasive, and that any decisions made by individuals or groups within an organization about the organization's future really make no difference. At the other extreme, some organization theorists, particularly those associated with the generic management field, argue that the human being is supreme and dominant over the forces of the environment; human choice, in this school, sets organizational destiny, not some social form of natural selection.

Quadrant 1 in Table 4-2 sketches the first extreme that we have described. Quadrant 1 lists some of the characteristics found in an organization that essentially is at the mercy of its task environment. Although an example of this kind of organization may be impossible to find in the real world, certainly some of the literature in political science suggests that, on occasion, federal regulatory agencies have been "captured" by the special interests that they are charged with regulating.[33]

The view held by those theorists who adhere to

the paradigm expressed in Quadrant 1 is that environmental forces render organizationally autonomous and self-aware decision making by members of the organization moot, or at the very most, trivial. The organization's relationship with its environment is, to use the metaphor employed earlier, "biological." Change in the organization is achieved by random reactions to random, uncontrollable alterations in the task environment, and the organization's independent standing in society is low due to these environmental constraints. The political behavior of the organization can be characterized as low profile; conflict, both internally and externally, is not high.

The center of organizational control in Quadrant 1 is external to the organization since the environment has such a heavy impact on the organization's behavior. All managers in all organizations tend to have what some authors have called a "generic strategy," by which is meant the recurrent theme of their management posture. In the case of a Quadrant 1 organization, that strategy is a defensive one. Means are emphasized over ends because ends are determined by the task environment, and the role of the manager and the workings of the organization are passive or inactive. Organizational planning is very short-term and oriented toward the immediate solution of problems emerging from the task environment. Much of the literature of organizational ecology, economic history, and political systems has contributed to this view of the organization's relations with its task environment.

In Quadrant 2, we have a situation in which the impact of the task environment upon organizational behavior is strong, but the impact of the organization's members also is strong. Unlike an organization in Quadrant 1, in Quadrant 2 we have a contest among equals; these organizations function in conditions of perfect competition. An example of an organization in this situation might be any major corporation, such as General Motors or IBM, and the people in the organization are seen as being capable of rationally attaining the goals of the larger system. However, the situation described in Quadrant 2 does not envision some sort of Weberian monocrat directing and controlling the organization; rather, parts of the organization and individuals within the organization recognize challenges to the organization surfacing in the environment and have the ability to

respond to them. While some direction from the top is necessary to do this, various groups and individuals comprising the organization are rational actors in their own right, and can respond to the environment rationally in their own way. Hence, these organizational actors do not necessarily follow the wishes of the organization's leaders, but instead are capable of achieving the goals of the larger system (for example, surviving in the free market place) via their own judgments and actions. Hence, the organization's relationship with its environment is "rational" in the sense that we have used this term earlier, but with a distinctly economic emphasis.

Change in the Quadrant 2 organization is achieved by a rational reordering of subsystems within the organization to adapt to changes in the environment, technology, or whatever. Because of the tension between the deterministic forces in the environment and the capabilities for human choice within the organization, the organization is left with a medium level of autonomy. Political behavior is highly conflictual, but this behavior is largely externally directed; the organization is fighting to survive in a highly competitive environment.

The center of organizational control in Quadrant 2 is shared between the organization and its environment. Decisions tend to focus on means, but with a secondary emphasis on achieving efficiency-related ends. The manager's role is largely one of reacting to challenges coming from the environment. Planning, as in Quadrant 1, is short-term and solution-driven, but there is also some "slack search." *Slack search* is a term originated by James G. March and refers to planning activities that are not necessarily driven by the need for finding immediate solutions, and often is not especially well connected with specific organizational needs. March describes it as a process of "dabbling" or nondirected activity.[34] And, in fact, many Quadrant 2 organizations do engage in this kind of slack search.[35] The literary schools that contribute to the Quadrant 2 concept in organization theory include systems theory, structural/functionalism, and contingency theory.

In Quadrant 3, organizations function in a situation in which there is little human choice and little environmental impact. Quadrant 3 is an unstable condition, both internally and externally, and one finds that Quadrant 3 organizations either die

TABLE 4-2 Relations Between Environmental Determinants of Organizational Behavior and Independent Organizational Choice

	Impact of Organization's Leaders, Managers, and Members ("Choice")	
	Weak	*Strong*

Impact of Organization's Task Environment ("Determinism")
 	
Strong
	Example: A government regulatory agency "captured" by the special interest that it is charged to regulate.
	Worldview: Environmental forces render organizationally autonomous and self-aware decision making moot.
	Relation with environment: "Biological."
	    Organizational change: Achieved by random reactions to random, uncontrollable alterations in the task environment.
	Organizational autonomy: Low due to environmental constraints.
	Political behavior: Low, both externally and internally.
	Center of organizational control: External.
	Generic strategy: Defensive.
	Decision emphases: Means over ends.
	Managerial role: Inactive.
	Planning: Solution driven, short term.
	Contributing literatures: Organizational ecology, economic history, political systems.
	
	(*Weak "choice," strong "determinism"*) Q1
		Example: A major automobile manufacturer.
		Worldview: Organizational individuals, departments, and hierarchical levels are capable of rationally attaining the goals of the larger system.
		Relation with environment: "Rational"/economic.
		    Organizational change: Achieved by reordering of subsystems in the organization to adapt to changes in the environment, technology, and so forth.
		Organizational autonomy: Medium.
		Political behavior: Highly conflictual, externally directed, low profile.
		Center of organizational control: Shared.
		Generic strategy: Analytical/cautious.
		Decision emphases: Primarily means, with a secondary emphasis on efficiency-related ends.
		Managerial role: Reactive.
		Planning: Solution driven, short term, with some "slack search."
		Contributing literatures: Systems theory, structural/functionalism, contingency theory.
		
		Q2 (*Strong "choice," strong "determinism"*)

The table is organized as a 2×2 matrix. The top row contains two quadrants (Q3 on the left, Q4 on the right). The axis labels appear at the bottom and along the left side.

	(Weak "choice," weak "determinism") Q3	Q4 (Strong "choice," weak "determinism")
Weak	*Example:* A new nonprofit, voluntary service organization. *Worldview:* Organizations are collectivites of semiautonomous parts that constantly engage in bargaining with each other and outsiders to achieve ends. *Relation with environment:* "Political." *Organizational change:* Achieved by bargaining, negotiating, and mutual political adjustment. *Organizational autonomy:* Low due to constraints within the organization. *Political behavior:* Low. *Center of organizational control:* Latent. *Generic strategy:* Reactive. *Decision emphases:* Means and ends roughly equal. *Managerial role:* Interactive. *Planning:* Sporadic. *Contributing literatures:* Public choice, political pluralism, organization development.	*Example:* A large government corporation. *Worldview:* Organizations are hierarchically structured, rationally behaving, autonomous entities designed to implement the will of the people who head it. *Relation with environment:* "Rational"/legal. *Organizational change:* Achieved by rationally deduced decisions made by top management and implemented by the organization's divisions of labor. *Organizational autonomy:* High. *Political behavior:* Highly conflictual, externally directed, low profile. *Center of organizational control:* Internal. *Generic strategy:* Creative/risk-taking. *Decision emphases:* Primarily ends, with a secondary emphasis on effectiveness-related means. *Managerial role:* Proactive. *Planning:* "Slack search" *Contributing literatures:* Decision theory, strategic planning, business management.
	Weak	*Strong*

Impact of Organization's Leaders, Managers, and Members ("Choice")

Impact of Organization's Task Environment ("Determinism") — *Weak*

Sources: Barton Wechsler and Hal Rainey, "Strategic Management in Political Environments," paper presented at the 1986 Annual Meeting of the American Political Science Association, Washington, D.C.: August 1986; Lawrence G. Hrebeniak and William F. Joyce, "Organizational Adaptation: Strategic Choice and Environmental Determinism," *Administrative Science Quarterly*, 30 (September 1985); and W. Graham Astley and Andrew H. Van de Ven, "Central Perspectives and Debates in Organizational Theory," *Administrative Science Quarterly*, 28 (June 1983).

quickly or reform themselves in such a way as to move to another quadrant. An example of an organization functioning in a Quadrant 3 situation would be a nonprofit voluntary service organization, or any organization that is characterized by a decision process that has been described as "muddling through."[36] Lawrence G. Hrebeniak and William F. Joyce describe the situation expressed in Quadrant 3 as one in which organizations

> have an array of internal strengths and competencies that are appropriate to external opportunities and conditions. . . . It is reasonable to argue that an appropriate mix or insufficient number of internal capabilities will prevent organizations from acting, despite the benignity, munificence, or lack of threat of the environment. In this view, the task of the organization is to develop the capabilities or distinctive competencies needed to take advantage of environmental conditions and thereby alter and escape from the conditions of [Quadrant 3].[37]

The view in Quadrant 3 is that organizations are federations of semiautonomous parts that constantly engage in bargaining with each other and outsiders to achieve their ends. The organization's relationship with its environment is "political" and organizational change is achieved by bargaining, negotiating, and mutual political adjustment. Organizational autonomy is low and the level of political behavior is low. But these low levels of organizational independence and political activism are due less to forces in the environment influencing the organization than to constraints within the organization itself.

The center of organizational control in Quadrant 3 is latent because no real control of any kind has emerged. The organization's generic strategy is reactive; it tends to emphasize means and ends roughly equally. Its managers assume interactive roles with both the environment and with the internal parts of the organization; planning is rare, sporadic, and disjointed. Literatures that have had an impact on the thinking underlying a Quadrant 3 situation include public choice, political pluralism, and organization development.

Finally, Quadrant 4 posits a condition of strong organizational choice and weak environmental determinism. It is the extreme opposite of organizations in Quadrant 1. An example would be a large government corporation. We describe the power of the government corporation in Chapter 11. Suffice it to note for now that government corporations, which are corporations chartered by governments and often granted what amount to both economic and political monopolies, have emerged during the past thirty years as important and independent economic and political policymakers. An example of this power is epitomized by the late Robert Moses, who headed a variety of government corporations in New York. As a biographer of Moses stated, "For thirty-four years, Moses played an important part in establishing [the city of New York's] priorities, and for seven years he established *all* the city's priorities."[38]

It is with this kind of dominance by organizational leaders over their task environments in mind that some writers have characterized organizations as being hierarchically structured, rationally behaving, autonomous entities that have the ability to implement the will of the people who head them. Thus, an organization with the characteristics of Quadrant 4 is eminently "rational," but instead of an economic orientation in this rationality (as is characteristic of organizations found in Quadrant 2), it has a much more legalistic one. Organizational change is achieved by rationally deduced decisions made by top management and implemented along rational lines by the appropriate divisions of labor within the organization. Organizational autonomy is high and the organization's political behavior is highly conflictual, and externally directed against rivals in the environment, but this aggressive political behavior typically is characterized by a low profile.

The center of organizational control in Quadrant 4 is almost entirely internal, and the generic strategy employed by the organization is highly creative and risk taking. The organization emphasizes ends over means, although there is a secondary emphasis on those means that concern how to attain the organizations's ends most effectively. The role of the manager is highly proactive and "slack search" characterizes the planning function. Among the contributing literatures to a Quadrant 4 conception of organizations are decision theory, strategic planning, and business management.

These relationships between the organization's task environment and its capacity for organizational choice, as illustrated in Table 4-2, have a readily apparent bearing on public organizations. In fact, one could argue that the typology posited by Table 4-2 makes a credible case for arguing that public organizations are more diverse and are found in more types of environmental contexts than are private organizations. After all, as Table 4-2 shows, we find that public organizations (a term including "third sector" organizations) appear in three of the four quadrants (Quadrants 1, 3, and 4). While it is entirely possible that examples of private organizations could be used in these same quadrants, there is only one, Quadrant 2, that has obvious bearing on the private organization. One might infer from this that public organizations present a far richer source of study and inquiry than do private ones.

INFORMATION AND INTELLIGENCE IN ORGANIZATIONS

How information, intelligence, and knowledge are used, distorted, and transmitted has considerable significance for what we have just considered in the preceding section: change in organizations. Cybernetist and operations researcher Stafford Beer, in fact, defines information as "what changes us."[39] Additionally, the uses of intelligence have particular significance for the understanding of public bureaucracies, for it is on knowledge and feedback that public policy decisions are made and adjusted.

Hierarchy and Information

Perhaps the most focused research in the field of organizational intelligence has been done by Harold L. Wilensky.[40] Wilensky considered both private and public organizations, but it is clear that public bureaucracies stand to gain or lose the most from how information is used or abused. Wilensky's basic contention is that organizational change and control are achieved through the control of information. He observes that organizational change is hindered by such phenomena as "the significance of slogans," "the power of preconceptions," and, perhaps paramountly, secrecy.

In Wilensky's view, organizational conflict, informational control, and personal power are inextricably intertwined. Consider Wilensky's example of Nazi Foreign Minister Ribbentrop

and his use of the notorious World War II spy, "Cicero," who was the valet of the British ambassador at Ankara. Cicero sent astonishingly accurate and detailed intelligence concerning the Allied invasion plans to Ribbentrop. Although the Foreign Minister had his doubts as to the authenticity of Cicero's reports, his overriding reason for sitting on most of Cicero's information appears to have been interagency rivalry. Ribbentrop was involved in a bitter power struggle with the Reich Security Office, and he loathed von Papen, the German ambassador to Turkey. Because Cicero reported directly to one L. C. Moyzisch, an attache on von Papen's staff employed by the Reich Security Office, Ribbentrop found it most expedient to dismiss Cicero's intelligence. Wilensky concludes from this and other instances that the use of secrecy exaggerates organizational pathologies that already may be present, such as conflict, authoritarianism, lack of feedback, and excessive personal power.

Wilensky also argues that information may be distorted and prevented from reaching the people who need it and can act on it by excessive centralization or decentralization of the organization. As an example of what happens to knowledge in a decentralized (or open-model) organization, Wilensky cites the surprise of American troops at Pearl Harbor during the Japanese attack. The Japanese secret code had been broken, and there is substantial evidence showing that various elements in the military and foreign services knew approximately when and where the Japanese would attack. But the information failed to reach the forces at Pearl Harbor in time.

Partly as a response to the intelligence fiasco of Pearl Harbor, the aptly dubbed Central Intelligence Agency (CIA) was established. The idea was that important messages no longer would be lost in the interorganizational shuffle, as in the Pearl Harbor incident, but would be sent directly to the people who were in a position to respond to new knowledge, including the president.

Nevertheless, information can be blocked in centralized (or closed-model) organizations, too. Wilensky cites the Cuban Bay of Pigs disaster as an example. In this instance, the CIA evidently approached the freshly elected President John F. Kennedy with what it represented as a long-standing, well-formulated, and superbly conceived (not to mention, sure-fire) plan for the

INFORMATION, INTELLIGENCE, ORGANIZATIONS, AND FOUR DEAD HORSES

Information and intelligence in organizations often exist only in the eye of the beholder. In the eyes of a number of beholders in Arizona, neither information nor intelligence characterized a senseless incident involving the Internal Revenue Service (IRS), the Arizona Livestock and Sanitary Board, and a herd of horses.

Carl J. Jatho was a free-wheeling entrepreneur from Kingman, Arizona, a small town in the northern part of the state, who headed a tax-preparation business called The Bookkeeper. For various reasons, Jatho and his bookkeeping ran into legal troubles. For example, he admitted in court to signing up customers for fictitious mining partnerships as part of his tax shelter scheme. Ultimately, Jatho pleaded guilty to five counts of tax fraud that cheated the federal government out of an estimated $45 million in taxes owed by some 3,800 taxpayers. So many of these bilked taxpayers appeared in federal court *en masse* during Jatho's trial that the press took to calling them "The Jatho People." Ultimately Jatho was sentenced to three years in prison, fined $150,000, and ordered to pay $1.2 million for preparing fraudulent tax returns. Jatho was imprisoned in September, 1986.

Among Jatho's remaining assets were thirty-five to forty horses that he kept fenced on his ranch in Kingman. Apparently no one thought too seriously about the fate of Jatho's horses until early January, 1987, when officials from the Arizona Livestock and Sanitary Board, the Internal Revenue Service, and some local agencies met to discuss what to do with them. What precisely occurred at this meeting is unclear. The IRS had the legal authorization to seize the horses as part of its civil case, but decided not to do so because its officials believed that only seventeen of the horses belonged to Jatho, and no one was sure which of the beasts were his. The Mohave County Animal Control Board and the Mohave County Sheriff's Office thought that the animals fell under the jurisdiction of the State Livestock Board, but the Livestock Board decided not to act on the grounds that it believed the IRS had jurisdiction. It did appear from subsequent press reports, however, that neither the IRS nor the Livestock Board had plans to take care of the horses, and that each agency knew that the other was not going to assume responsibility for them either.

Five days after the meeting, the press reported that four of Jatho's horses had died from starvation. When questioned by the press about how and why this had occurred, IRS agent William Bronson stated that the horses were in such poor condition that they could not be sold, adding, "We are a tax collecting agency, not a humane society." At this point, the State Livestock Board acted and seized the horses, noting in the process that hay and other feed had been in the storage shed behind the Jatho house during the entire five months that had passed since Jatho entered prison. In an apparent effort to show that it was on top of the problem, the Livestock Board filed charges of willful neglect and cruelty to animals against Jatho, who had, of course, been in prison since September. Meanwhile, the Phoenix office of the Internal Revenue Service was besieged with phone calls from irate citizens.

At this point, the IRS and the Livestock Board began trading charges. A member of the Livestock Board stated that, "It was the IRS that put the guy in jail. The IRS should have made some provision for those horses." The IRS contended, in turn, that it was the victim of a "cheap shot" by the media and other government agencies; the IRS suggested that the Livestock Board was well aware that it was not planning to take jurisdiction of the horses and thus the Livestock Board should have done so.

The senior Senator from Arizona, Dennis DeConcini, soon got into the act by writing the Commissioner of the IRS that the incident in Kingman was the "result of either a severely flawed policy by the agency or negligent actions taken by IRS personnel," and launched his own inquiry. As an aide to Senator DeConcini noted, "The word 'insane' is used rather frequently in news stories because news stories cover unusual and unexpected things, but I don't ever recall seeing a news story where the word 'insane' was more applicable. . . . You don't just leave forty horses there to die. It's crazy. There's nothing rational about it." The state's largest newspaper, in an editorial, characterized the explanations from both the IRS and the Livestock Board as "lame and ludicrous."

Mohave County Supervisor Becky Foster, after noting that a number of citizens had offered to donate food or money for the benefit of the horses, stated, "This restores your faith in humanity." Then she broke into tears as she watched workers dump the dead horses into a truck.

Sources: Steve Daniels, "Outraged Arizonans Rally to Rescue Starving Horses," The Arizona Republic, *January 14, 1987; Andy Hall and Steve Daniels, "Agencies Trade Blame for Abandoned Horses,"* The Arizona Republic, *January 15, 1987; and "The Cold Hands of the IRS,"* The Arizona Republic, *January 16, 1987.*

overthrow of Premier Fidel Castro's revolutionary government in Cuba. Kennedy, who later implied he had been somewhat awed by the intelligence-gathering capabilities and expertise of the CIA and, in any event, had no comparable organization in terms of prestige to which he could turn for additional intelligence, decided to let the agency carry on, essentially in its own way. Among the other aspects of remarkably poor planning by the CIA, as it turned out, was the agency's ignorance of extensive swamps in the Bay of Pigs area, which entrapped the invasion force on the coastline and made the Cuban expatriates easy pickings for Castro's troops.

Gordon Tullock[41] has argued that organizational decentralization is more conducive than centralization to the preservation of information and the minimization of its distortion in organizations. Tullock constructs an arithmetic "model of hierarchical distortion," in which he reasons that the more an organization grows, the more effort and expense will be required for "internal" administration, to the detriment of the "external" achievements of organizational goals relative to the society. This pathology is unavoidable because the larger the bureaucracy, the more time must be devoted by its members to assuring that information reaches the right administrators relatively intact; in other words, the bigger the bureaucracy, the more people who may stop, distort, take away from, or add to the same information bit, and hence greater effort must be generated to preserve "noise"-free intraorganizational communications at the expense of accomplishing the organization's social mission. As a result of this reasoning, Tullock advocates that bureaucracies be vastly reduced in size so that the society may benefit more directly. Tullock believes that in small organizations the goal and rationality of the organization (*e.g.*, legal assistance for the poor) are more likely to complement the goals and rationalities of the individuals in the organization (*e.g.*, getting ahead) because it is far easier to see causal relationships between individual acts and mission accomplishment in small organizations than in large organizations, and the evaluation of organizational performance is thus much easier. Tullock's recommendation is a radical one relative to the rest of organization theory, which tends to regard organizational growth as a sign of health.

March and Simon also have noticed that information tends to be distorted by multiple levels of hierarchy.[42] They note the pathology of "uncertainty absorption" in bureaucratic organizations, whereby data that initially are regarded as tentative, uncertain, and "soft" by the persons who collect them become increasingly final, certain, and "hard" as they are sent up through the decision-making hierarchy. Thus, we may assume that in the decision by Ford Motor Company to build the Edsel, the corporation's low-level market researchers concluded that there "might" be a market for a middle-range car in the United States, but by the time their findings reached Henry Ford it was being voiced in top management circles that there "was" such a market; uncertainty in the initial information had been absorbed by the various hierarchical levels that handled it on its way to upper management.

These and other studies of informational dynamics in organizations are especially relevant to public administration for a number of reasons. Public organizations tend to be bureaucratic organizations, they do not operate in free-market environments, and they "produce" policies rather than products. Information is of unusual importance to all these characteristics and functions. Herbert Simon has observed that "how to process information" will be the core challenge to executives in our postindustrial age,[43] and studies of top-level officials in local governments have found that these public administrators "spend a significant portion of their work time engaged in myriad information-seeking."[44] And recent developments in public administration indicate that information will be of even more importance to the public bureaucracy and the public. One such development is the growing professionalism and expertise of the public administrator.

Professionalism and Public Knowledge

The professionalization of public administration represents a second development that seems destined to affect the free flow of knowledge in the task milieu of the public bureaucrat. By *professionalization* is meant the evolvement of a core of commonly shared and recognized knowledge and expertise held by members of a group. The rise of the M.P.A. and D.P.A. degrees, the establishment of professional schools of public administration and public affairs, and the appearance of new professional journals and associations all indicate that public administration is professionalizing as never before.

Paradoxically, professionalization of the public service has both benefits and liabilities for the public. As York Willbern noted in a seminal article on the subject,[45] professionalism in public bureaucracies brings

1. increased technical competence;
2. increased respect for technical expertise;
3. the enforcement of minimal ethical and technical standards;
4. insulation from pressure to discriminate against clients;
5. the avoidance of direct democratic control that might be of doubtful utility in some fields;
6. greater interchangeability of personnel among governmental units;
7. the incentive for officials to acquire more skills;
8. the creation of in-group loyalty;
9. the provision of additional satisfactions to employees.

Conversely, however, professionalism also brings with it

1. potential conflicts of interest between the professional group (*e.g.*, school teachers) and larger publics (*e.g.*, taxpayers);
2. the presence of undue influence wielded by special publics through professional ties (such as the medical profession's occasionally debatable impact on public health programs in some states through the American Medical Association);
3. the insulation of public servants from public control;
4. the lack of internal democracy often found in professional associations;
5. the limitation of public services by the professionals' insistence on the maintenance of unrealistic professional standards;
6. the diminishing of transferability of personnel among agencies because of overly specialized training;
7. the lack of interagency coordination because of professional specialization or jealousy;

8. the discouraging of citizen participation by the presence of a professional mystique.

Most if not all of the dysfunctions of professionalism listed by Willbern revolve around the control of knowledge and expertise—or what often passes for expertise. If knowledge is power, then how is professional knowledge (with its antidemocratic implications) to be used to further the goals of society? Obviously, it must be used carefully, for the very idea of being professional carries with it a dangerous footnote for democratic values: "We know more than you, therefore do as we say."

An example of how professional status, mystique, and expertise exercise a control over information that prevents and undermines the manifestation of democratic values is provided by Alan Altshuler in his study of a decision to locate a freeway in the Minneapolis-St. Paul area.[46] The local highway department made a conscious, internal decision to be inflexible on the proposed freeway's route and location and based this decision on the unsophisticated but "professional" criterion of a crude cost/benefit analysis. This analysis formed the core rationale of the department's justification of its decision. More profoundly, however, the department's sole, and quite effective, justification of its decision was that it was made on the basis of professional and technical values, and who could argue with "the facts?" This argument won the day, despite very legitimate pressures brought by blacks, white residents in some of the few remaining middle-class neighborhoods in downtown St. Paul (who had the quiet support of the governor), retailers in the central business district, and the existence of an alternative route developed by the city planner that would have satisfied these many protests. Expertise and the control of information took political precedence because they were presumed to be apolitical.

James D. Carroll has extended the concept of professionalism and has called it "noetic authority," or the power that derives from knowledge. He argues that the politics and administration of the future will be based on who controls information and knowledge rather than who controls wealth and power. Carroll cites the rise of a plethora of political and administrative issues involving the press, telecommunications, urban planning, the environment, education, transportation, and consumerism, among others, as disputes in which the old "politics of greed" is being displaced by the new "politics of knowledge."[47]

Information and Decision Making

As Carroll implies, information and knowledge are more important than ever before in organizational decision making. In light of this argument, however, how is it that, "organizations seem to invest in information and information systems, but their investments often do not seem to make sense. They gather information and do not use it. They ask for reports and do not read them. They act first and receive requested information later, and do not seemed to be concerned about the order."[48]

These are important concerns. Few administrators have not both written and read the useless memorandum—useless, that is, in terms of its alleged relevance to making the decision at hand. The literature is rife with examples of information being generated so that managers might make better decisions and yet having no apparent relationship to those decisions.[49] Why is this so?

Martha S. Feldman and James G. March have phrased the problem of information and decision making in organizations (or what they call "a portrait of important features of information use") in a reasonably rigorous fashion:

1. Much of the information that is gathered and communicated by individuals and organizations has little decision relevance.
2. Much of the information that is used to justify a decision is collected and interpreted *after* the decision has been made, or substantially made.
3. Much of the information gathered in response to requests for information is not considered in the making of decisions for which it was requested.
4. Regardless of the quantity and quality of the information available at the time a decision is first considered, more information is requested.
5. Complaints that an organization does not have enough information to make a decision are voiced at the same time that available information is ignored.
6. The relevance of the information already being provided to decision makers is considerably less conspicuous than the unrelenting insistence by decision makers for more information.[50]

Organization theorists and decision scientists have provided two explanations for these pathologies. One is that "information overload" can occur, and organizations and the people in them simply are unable to process the information they have because of organizational and human limitations.[51] A second explanation often offered is that the information itself is poor or the wrong kind of information, and while there may be a great deal of information (*i.e.*, data), it is not information that we can use (*i.e.*, knowledge).[52]

Feldman and March offer a considerably more creative and original explanation, and one that is a genuine contribution to both organization theory and decision science. They contend that the apparent lack of a "match" between information and decision making in organizations does not, "in general, reflect stupidity on the part of organizations. Rather [this absence of a match between information and decisions] are symptoms of sophistication in understanding the role of information in organizational choice."[53]

Feldman and March go on to argue that the sophistication displayed by organizations that gather more information than they use or seem to need is not necessarily conscious. But the standard operating procedures of an organization that result in the production of such massive amounts of data may, in and of themselves, betoken a high quality of organizational decision making.

Feldman and March make three important points about the role of information in organizations. The first is that organizations tend to gather information in a "surveillance mode" rather than in a "decision mode." Information, in other words, is gathered for the sake of monitoring the environment and the internal workings of the organization on a routine basis. The kind of information gathered in this mode, which is the typical way in which information is gathered in organizations, is not related to specific decisions that are coming up on the organizational agenda.

Second, the standard operating procedures of organizations provide incentives for underestimating the costs of gathering the information relative to the returns that the information provides the organization. Typically, the information-gathering functions of an organization are separate from its information-using functions. Those who use the information are not those who gather it, and information users (*i.e.*, decision makers) seldom provide any particular set of guidelines to the information gatherers (*i.e.*, staffers and researchers). There is also a bias among information users that holds it is better to have more information than is necessary than less, and this also results in more information being gathered. This bias toward caution in gathering information is buttressed by two experiments which found that information that can be used for defensive purposes is more valued by decision makers than information which can be used offensively: "People appear more willing to buy information that may decrease an expected loss than information that may increase an expected gain."[54]

Finally, much of the information used in organizations is subject to "strategic misrepresentation." Information frequently is produced for the purpose of persuading someone to do something; when information is found that would undermine the process of persuasion, it is edited and discarded. At its worst, this process can result in a competition among liars, but organizations and the decision makers in them typically find ways of accounting for this pathology. "Decision makers learn not to trust overly clever people, and smart people learn not to be overly clever."[55]

These organizational realities result in information taking on its own value as a symbol and a signal in the political and decision-making life of an organization. The role of information as symbol and signal has been underestimated by decision theorists. Yet, these symbolic and signaling functions of information have great substantive importance. On the one hand, organizations underestimate the true cost of gathering information, yet on the other hand, place a high value in using information to buttress preferred decisions:

> Individuals and organizations will consistently over invest in information . . . because the acts of seeking and using information in decisions have important symbolic value to them and to the society. . . . Decisions are orchestrated in such a way as to ensure that those making them and those observing them come to

believe that they are reasonable—or even intelligent. The use of information, asking for information, and justifying decisions in terms of information have all come to be significant ways in which we signal that the process is legitimate, that we are good decision makers, and that our organizations are well managed . . . . Since legitimacy is a necessary property of effective decisions, conspicuous consumption of information is a sensible strategy for decision makers. The strategy need not be chosen deliberately. It will characterize processes that work.[56]

By this logic, then, decisions that are information intensive have a greater legitimacy in organizations, and as a result it is ultimately easier to gain organizational acceptance of decisions and their smoother implementation. Because decision makers implicitly recognize this utility of information, it follows that better decision makers would invest more in gathering information than would poor decision makers, even if the information had nothing in particular to do with making the decision itself. Thus, "organizations that exhibit an elaborate information system and conspicuous consumption of information will . . . be more effective decision makers than those who do not."[57]

Organizations that are information-sensitive also will make their decisions more rapidly. A careful study of eight microcomputer manufacturing firms found that fast decision makers used more information in making their decisions than did slower decision makers. Fast decision makers also developed more alternatives in deciding how to deal with problems.[58]

Interestingly, fast decision makers also seemed to rely on counseling with respected colleagues more when making decisions than did slower decision makers. Recall, in this regard, our discussion in Chapter 3 about the differences in decision making in the public and private sectors: Public decision makers indulged in a much more collegial style of decision making than did private decision makers. In the study of decision making in the microcomputer firms, it was found that a pattern of information reliant, advice seeking, rapid decision making led to "superior performance" by executives[59] Yet, in the public sector, decision making seems to have only one of these three components consistently present in the decision process: advice seeking. Both information and rapidity often appear to be absent.

CONTROL, AUTHORITY, AND POWER IN ORGANIZATIONS

Organizational intelligence, noetic authority, information, and decision making as concepts overlap considerably with organizational control and authority. He or she who controls information possesses genuine power in the bureaucracy.

The analyst most noted for his argument that authority is the central variable in organizational behavior is Amitai Etzioni. [60] Etzioni contends that power is all, and that virtually all characteristics of the organization are determined by the kind of authority used in the organization. For example, a prison uses "coercive" power, its method of control is physical (*e.g.*, solitary confinement); the organization acquires participants through the socialization of inmates; both officials (*e.g.*, the warden) and information leaders (popularly respected or feared prisoners with no official position) are present; and "instrumental activities" (mechanical kinds of activities) predominate as the organization's chief technology. At the other extreme of Etzioni's power continuum, a political party uses "identitive," or "normative" power; its method of control is symbolic (*e.g.*, appeals to patriotism); the organization acquires participants both through the socialization of its members and the selection of applicants; only "formal leaders" (or leaders who have both real and official power) are present, and "expressive activities" (or interpersonal activities) predominate as the organization's chief activity. Finally, in the middle ranges of Etzioni's continuum, a business corporation uses "utilitarian" power; its method of control is material (*e.g.*, a salary); participants are acquired chiefly through a selection process; leadership comprises all types (officials, information leaders, and formal leaders), and activities may be both instrumental and expressive. Etzioni's concept is diagrammed in Table 4-3.

Public organizations commonly are a hybrid combining Etzioni's normative and utilitarian forms of organizational power. There is a certain "calling" involved in working for the public service and nonprofit agencies (thus yielding them some identitive power), but there is also a recognized necessity among those wishing to join public organizations that it also would be nice to earn a regular paycheck (thus giving public organizations some utilitarian power). It follows that public organizations would attract (and want) employees with an unusual set of attitudes about how they would like to spend their working lives; Simon has called these attitudes "decision premises."[61]

The Decision Premise: The Objective of Organizational Authority

A *decision premise* refers to the values and perceptions held by each member of the organization, on which he or she bases every decision he

TABLE 4-3   A Continuum of Organizational Power

Type of Power	Method of Control	Acquisition of Participants	Type of Leadership	Type of Activities
Coercive (a prison)	Physical	Socialization	Officials and informal leaders	Instrumental
Utilitarian (a business corporation)	Material	Selection	Officials, informal leaders and formal leaders	Instrumental and Expressive
Indentitive or normative (a political party)	Symbolic	Selection and socialization	Formal leaders	Expressive

or she makes regarding the organization. These individual values and perceptions are unique to the individual, but many can be altered and influenced through the use of organizational means and sanctions available to those in positions of control, the division of labor in the organization and how it affects the individual, standard operating procedures used in the organizations, the socialization and training of new members of the organization, and the kinds of people who are selected to join the organization. Together, these techniques can mold each individual's decision premise in a way that reduces organizational uncertainty by making the individual's decisions predictable. When uncertainty is low (*e.g.*, "I trust Mary to do the right thing . . ."), authority and control often are relinquished or "decentralized" (". . . so I've made her responsible for the job").

Many organizations attempt to control, or at least filter, the decision premises of applicants even before they enter the organization. Some businesses prefer applicants who are business majors and fraternity or sorority members over applicants who majored in sociology and were independents. The rationale is that "B-school" joiners are more likely to cultivate a corporate team spirit than are socially aware loners. After entry, subordinates' decision premises are formed more fully by superordinates through "management training" classes and the more subtle socialization techniques extant in most large organizations.

Empirical research indicates that these organizational efforts at selection and socialization are effective. A tracking of the careers of 171 entry-level auditors in the eight largest accounting firms in the United States found those recruits whose values (and, presumably, their decision premises, which are a type of personal value) most closely matched the values of the firm adjusted more quickly to working life in the firm; recruits who were most vigorously socialized by the firm following their entry fit the firm's values more closely than those who were not; and those recruits whose values best matched those of the firm felt the most satisfied and stayed longer with the firm.[62]

Once recruited, new members of the organization find that there is an astonishing range of resources and techniques that organizations, particularly business organizations, have available to form the decision premise of their members more to their liking. In addressing the topic of "organizational seduction," Roy J. Lewicki suggests that "matching" the values of the organization and those of recruits to the organization is only the first step. Others include providing employees with an opportunity to work for a high-status organization (or at least with opportunities for attaining status within the organization), providing challenges, and providing a pleasant, even luxurious, work environment.[63]

In contrast to business administration, however, public administration has been far less able to control the decision premises of decision-making participants in public bureaucracies. True, there is a selection and socialization process in public bureaucracies but, more than other bureaucracies, public bureaucracies make decisions in situations characterized by unusual degrees of participation from the task environment. Public administrators, especially in recent years that have been characterized by a social milieu advocating "power to the people," increasingly find themselves asking "client-members" of their organizations to participate in the decision-making process. A *client-member* is a person who is both a "customer" and a member of an organization, such as a student in a university or an inmate in a prison. And, it is worth adding that other techniques available to the business organization for forming members' decision premises, such as providing a luxurious work environment, are less available to public organizations. In any event, public administrators often find that they lack the authority and control possessed by administrators in other institutional settings. This situation may well be to the benefit of the polity, but it often does not seem so to the frustrated public administrator confronting what occasionally appears to be organizational and environmental chaos.

Slack, Side Payments, and Bargaining: The Milieu of Power in Organizations

Organization theorists agree that the exercise of control, authority, and power in organizations is a complex, political phenomenon. Cyert and March, Downs, and Thompson more or less share the same concept of how control and authority are achieved in organizations. In their view, "slack," bargaining, "side payments," and coalition formation represent the dynamics of organizational control. Slack refers to those "nonrational" interstices present in even the most rigid bureaucracies that represent opportunities for what is known in the military as "scrounging" (*e.g.*, an unused typewriter in the accounting department mysteriously and "unofficially" finds its way to the advertising department where it receives considerable use). Side payments in organizations would not be possible without organizational slack. Side payments can be made in the form of status (*e.g.*, a new "unofficial" carpet for an individual's office or a promotion in name only, with no increase in salary or authority) or as material rewards (*e.g.*, a salary increment). Side payments are usually made on the basis of discreet bargaining between the representatives of coalitions (*e.g.*, "young Turks," "old guard," whatever) in the organization, and genuine authority in the organization is determined by who represents what coalitions.

Styles of authority and control must change as the organization changes. Thus, the military sociologist Morris Janowitz[64] suggests that the old, closed-model style of authority traditionally favored in the military, that of "domination," is no longer suitable for an organization characterized by such technological and environmental changes as new weapons systems, the adoption of deterrence as a strategy, the routinization of innovation, and the blurring of historic soldier/civilian distinctions. Janowitz urges that a "fraternal type authority" based on the open-model's techniques of manipulation replace the domineering techniques normally used in the military. And, over time, the American military has moved in the direction that Janowitz urged in the 1950s.

The "Two-Wayness" of Power in Organizations

The notion of styles of authority leads us to the problem of the legitimacy—indeed, even the morality—of authority. Chester Barnard was perhaps the first theorist to appreciate that there was more to authority than a boss giving orders to an underling; Barnard pointed out that a subordinate had to *accept* a superior's directive before that superior could ever have something called authority, or power. Even more profoundly,

Barnard contended that, before an order would be accepted by a subordinate, the superior first had to penetrate the subordinate's "zone of indifference." Most of the time, Barnard said, underlings really could care less about what a boss directed. Thus, authority was conceived as a two-way process between subordinate and superior, and this "two-wayness" added to the legitimacy of authority.[65]

Simon, whose early work was intensely influenced by Barnard, extended Barnard's concept of authority by devising a "zone of acceptance" and positing four basic motivations of subordinates to accept the will of a superior: rewards and sanctions, legitimacy, social approval, and the subordinate's confidence in the superior's ability.[66] Of these motivations, those of rewards and sanctions are the most interesting, if for no other reason than that Simon thought the subordinate had more rewards and sanctions at his or her disposal than the superior! The superior had only three: the power to hire and fire; the power to promote and demote, and certain incentive rewards. But the subordinate had at least twice that number: the power to quit, to strike, to slow down, to perform minimally, to perform "literally" (or to do only the jobs specified), and not to perform.

Power in Organizations: The Place of Personal Skill

Simon's idea that the subordinate can have more power in an organization than his or her superior was revolutionary, and it had a lasting impact on the field of organization theory, particularly as it is applied to public organizations. For example, one study of the gubernatorial administrations in California of Ronald Reagan and Jerry Brown concluded that their organizational power was a direct result of their "obedience to roles" expected of them by the organization (in this case, state government) that they led. As the authors put it,

> This obligation to act within the bounds of a role does not decrease as one assumes high positions of authority; a role may grant more discretion in how it is enacted, but there are normative constraints to even the highest level position. The cabinet officers . . . no less than a clerk, were constrained to perform their roles

in such a way as to demonstrate obeisance to norms. . . . One need only recall President Nixon's supposed abuse of office to recognize that no actor within a social system can ignore the rules of a system. To unseasoned actors, behaving capriciously . . . might seem the quintessential evidence of power. But such a strategy cannot endure in an organized setting.[67]

Power Down: Controlling Subordinates. Nevertheless, superiors do retain some authority over subordinates. One review of the literature on organizational control identified six "major control mechanisms":[68]

Supervision, or the direct observation by a supervisor, who provides corrective feedback to the subordinate;

Input control, or the constraining of resources to subunits, a method favored especially by nonprofit organizations because they are limited (according to some analysts[69]) in their use of output controls relative to for-profit organizations;

Behavior control, or the structuring of individual and group activities via procedures, performance standards, and technology;

Output control, a type of control used extensively but not exclusively by for-profit organizations, refers to the monitoring and evaluation of organizational outputs, such as market share, profits, or student test scores;

Selection-socialization, or a kind of control that exists when certain types of norms and values are internalized into the organization— "localized cooptation," discussed earlier, falls into this category;

Environmental control is the constraint on the organization imposed by its task environment, although there are few studies illustrating how administrators capitalize on this constraint in terms of attaining their own organizational ends.

A study of how these six kinds of administrative control mechanisms were used by administrators to control 120 school principals in sixty elementary school districts found that district administrators used all six methods of control in a surprisingly broad and balanced way—at least

when compared to studies of organizational control in private, for-profit enterprises. However, supervision was the least effective form of influence among the six; input control (largely in the form of budget allocations) was used extensively, as was behavior control (although the principals themselves did not perceive behavior control to be a major method used to control them); output control was essentially restricted to student achievement, although the principals thought many more output controls were being used; selection-socialization controls appeared to be heavily present, as were environmental controls in the form of principals relying on the district office to provide them with feedback from their schools' communities.[70]

District administrators "zoned" their control of their principals, in that they tightly held the reigns over administrative matters, but only loosely over instructional ones. Similarly, ends were objects of tight central control, but the means for achieving those ends were not, and were left largely to the principals. The study concluded that "a more complex system of control" based on multiple sources of information "may be used for managers in not-for-profit organizations who have to supervise a workforce employing an unclear technology" (in this case, teaching), leading to greater managerial stress because these public managers are effectively "monitored by everyone around them."[71]

Power Up: Controlling Superordinates. As we have noted, personal power flows in many organizational directions, including up as well as down, and subordinates can gain some control over their superordinates that exceed Barnard's and Simon's "zones" of indifference and acceptance. A major study of sixty-seven American semiconductor companies over a period of twenty-two years found that, while the chief executive officers (CEOs) of these organizations were more likely to be fired by their boards of directors during times of poor organizational performance (an understandable consequence under the circumstances), the more powerful CEOs could survive tough times more frequently than weaker CEOs. A more powerful chief executive officer was found in organizations where the CEO had a larger share of stock in that company (or, to employ the term used in this research, his or her "ownership position" was greater); ownership of the corporation by other shareholders was more widely dispersed; and there was both a greater proportion of "inside board members" (such as company employees) on the board, and a higher percentage of inside board members who had been appointed to the board by the CEO.

In cases where the chief executive officer was powerful and the company was performing below average, there was a marked propensity by the board to retain the CEO, and an equally significant tendency by the CEO to dismiss the managers who reported to him or her, thus "providing evidence of scapegoating. . . . Apparently, powerful chief executive officers buffer themselves from performance responsibility but 'compensate' by replacing top managers of the organization."[72]

Power Up, Down, and Sideways: Power Relationships among and around Directors of Boards.
Just as there are patterns of power relationships between chief executive officers and boards of directors, so there are power patterns among directors themselves. In a study of the boards of directors of 1,200 Canadian nonprofit organizations,[73] five types of power relationships were identified: a CEO dominated board (or the type just discussed, and which provides the chief executive officer with a high level of protection from dismissal, but top managers with a low one), a chair-dominated board, a fragmented power board, a power sharing board, and a powerless board.

With a few exceptions (such as the size and age of the nonprofit organization that the board directs), the personal characteristics of the board members are the prevailing factors in determining the power pattern of the board. In CEO dominated boards, for example, the chief executive officer has considerable seniority, and there are few members who are women, more members who are over sixty years of age, more members who were invited to join because of their personal prestige, and more highly educated or professionally trained members. These characteristics associate with a low level of involvement by board members, creating a power vacuum that is soon filled by a seasoned CEO. Similarly, boards which are dominated by their chairs have significantly more members who were chosen because of their prestige, and who are highly educated or professionally trained.

Fragmented power boards are characterized by members who have relatively low levels of education and prior commitment to the goals of the organization, and associate with boards which supervise larger organizations; it may be that the larger the organization, the more likely it is that the board's agenda will fragment, thus leading to fragmented power within the board itself.

Power sharing boards have significantly higher proportions of women and members who are under sixty years of age, and have a disproportionate number of members who possess low educational levels and professional training, but very high levels of commitment to the goals of the organization prior to their joining the board; like fragmented power boards, power sharing boards usually head large organizations. It perhaps follows that women and relatively young, less educated or professionally trained, and highly committed people would be more willing to share power, thus muting the tendency of boards which direct large organizations to fragment power among members.

Powerless boards typically have more members sixty years old or older, are more highly educated or professionally trained, had low levels of commitment to the organization prior to joining the board, and direct organizations which are relatively new.

This research on the boards of nonprofit organizations has, of course, direct relevance to the public sector, and suggests that third sector agencies can create more dynamic board leadership for themselves by selecting members who are female, young, less educated and professionally trained, and low on prestige but high on commitment.

Power in Organizations: The Role of Hierarchical Structure

As the foregoing research implies, the acquisition of power in organizations is a product of many factors besides that of personal skill. Most theorists agree that power is a matter of organizational structure as well as personal skill,[74] and the proposition appeals to common sense. Thus far, we by and large have been discussing qualities of skill, not hierarchy, in learning about organizational power, but this latter area warrants review, too.

Organizational Structure and Individual Power.   Researchers increasingly suggest, in fact, that, at least for mid-level and low-level personnel, organizational structure may be more important than the skills of individuals in acquiring organizational power.[75] A complex study of a newspaper publishing company found that the "criticality" of a "task position" (that is, the removal of the position would result in a breakdown of workflow), the number of opportunities inherent to the occupant of a position to engage in transactions with people in many other positions, and access to the communication network of the coalition that dominated the organization had a strong, positive relationship with an individual's perceived power in the organization. Access to a variety of communication networks in the organization, particularly control of one's departmental communications, associated strongly with an individual's promotion to supervisory positions.[76] "While personal attributes and strategies may have an important effect on power acquisition," the study contended, "structure imposes the ultimate constraint on the individual."[77]

Organizational Structure and Group Power. Just as structural variables can affect the power of individual people in an organization, so they can influence the power of whole departments. Research indicates that the power of a subunit is a combination of three factors: the subunit's ability to cope with uncertainty; its "nonsubstitutability" (*i.e.*, no other department can do what it does); and its centrality to the larger organization.[78] Of these factors, that of centrality appears to be of greatest relevance to the public organization. But "centrality" can assume many meanings in this context, including a subunit's immediacy, or its ability to severely and quickly impact on the whole organization; its pervasiveness, or how much it interacts with other departments; and its match, or how closely its purpose corresponds to that of the larger organization.

One study of six universities found that the centrality factor, particularly as defined by the pervasiveness dimension, had the single greatest explanatory value in accounting for a subunit's power within the organization.[79] A later study of six other universities demonstrated that centrality, as defined by the department's match to the larger purpose of the organization, was critical in

the subunit's power and its success in acquiring budgetary resources.[80] In fact, even if "peripheral" (*i.e.*, non-central) departments developed their own outside constituencies and resources, their power within the university did not rise significantly (if at all) unless they focused "on broader institutional needs" and brought in "external resources that contribute to the whole."[81]

Studies of different kinds of organizations demonstrate different relationships. Research on five breweries, in stark contrast to the findings on universities, found that a subunit's ability to cope with uncertainty and its central immediacy to the entire organization yielded it a powerful position in the organization.[82] However, a study of four oil and gas companies found only a weak correlation between a subunit's capacity for dealing with uncertainty and its power, but relatively strong relations between high levels of power and the subunit's nonsubstitutability and centrality.[83] The authors of one review of the literature have suggested that "the findings can be used to argue that the relationships between power and its determinants vary with the industry studied,"[84] and, certainly, whether the "industry" is public or private would seem to have a bearing on these relationships.

DECISION MAKING IN ORGANIZATIONS

We noted that Simon's notion of decision premises is central to an understanding of power in organizations; it also provides a convenient introduction to the more general consideration of organizational decision making. Simon argues stringently for the concept that virtually all decisions in organizations are only "satisficing" decisions; that is, decisions do not maximize, they only satisfy and suffice, or (combined) "satisfice."[85]

Simon closely linked his notion of satisficing to his concept of "bounded rationally" (mentioned in Chapter 2), or the idea that the reasoning powers of the human mind are bound to a small and simple plot compared to the vastness and complexity of the territory spanned by the problems that human minds are expected (expected, at least, by traditional theorists in economics and management) to comprehend and solve.

Researchers have since amplified for us the

limitations of our species when it comes to making decisions. The psychologist, George Miller, for example, determined that the mind can distinguish a maximum of seven categories of phenomena at a time, but beyond that number loses track.[86] People tend to use heuristic thinking (*i.e.*, "rules of thumb") in making decisions, which is invariably flawed, and base their decisions on their perception of the status quo, rather than on an objective comparison of known variables; people also are biased in favor of protecting against losses relative to planning for gains in making decisions, so stability is favored over change.[87] (Recall, in this regard, that decision makers prefer information that protects them against anticipated losses over information that they can use to make gains.) Emotion plays a fulsome part in decision making, and a decision seems to be an emotional, or affective, response to one's environment, which is overlain by a later, more rational response.[88] Solutions that provide quick results are preferred to those which result in delayed returns.[89] Stress accompanies decision making, and, as a consequence, avoidance and denial are frequently the handmaidens of the decision process;[90] making decisions within the context of a group seems to narrow the options considered by decision makers even further.[91] Environment generally plays a large role in how a person makes decisions, as Table 4-2 demonstrates.

One's organization, of course, constitutes a major portion of the individual decision-maker's environment, and organization theorists use the findings on satisficing and bounded rationally in studying how organizations make decisions. James D. Thompson and Arthur Tuden,[92] for example, developed a "typology of decision issues," in which they matched decision-making strategies with whether organizational members agreed or disagreed about what causes what, and whether members agreed or disagreed about what the organization should do. For example, in a bureaucracy of specialists, in theory everyone would agree about causation ("If you fill out the form, then you will get your Social Security check"), and they would agree about decision outcomes ("Social Security is worthwhile to society"). In such a bureaucracy, decisions would be made "computationally"; that is, with little or no internal debate about values and with decisions made on the basis of shared technical perceptions.

Other kinds of organizations necessitate other kinds of decision-making strategies; the matrix in Table 4-4 on page 110 summarizes them.

In some ways Thompson and Tuden's typology of decision-making strategy seems a bit farfetched. Some might argue, for instance, that finding very many "inspirational-decision making" organizations in the real world would not be likely. Yet when we approach the area of public organizations, we find few agreements among organizational members, and perhaps public decisions are more inspired than we know.

The Garbage Can Model of Decision Making

Michael Cohen, James G. March and Johan Olsen have given us a creative approach to this dilemma of making sense of how decision makers make decisions when they have pervasive differences of opinion by analyzing what they called "organized anarchies."[93] They used universities as their example of organized anarchies, but with little alteration of their model, we find that governments provide fine examples, too.

Organized anarchies have three characteristics. First, members of the organization do not define their preferences about policies and goals very precisely, and on those rare occasions when preferences are defined in exact terms, they often are in conflict with each other. The organization is a "loose collection of ideas" instead of a coherent structure; "it discovers preferences through action more than it acts on the basis of preferences."[94]

A second characteristic of an organized anarchy is that the technology is as unclear as the preferences. Members do not understand what the organization does. For example, how familiar is the typical faculty member with the operations of the registrar's office? And vice versa?

Finally, participation in the decision-making process of the organization is extremely fluid, even erratic. Participants drift in and out of the decision-making process. Sometimes a member will attend a critical meeting, and sometimes not.

Cohen, March, and Olsen suggest that organized anarchies use a decision-making process that is comprised of four separate streams: problems, solutions, participants, and choice opportu-

TABLE 4-4   A Typology of Decision-Making Strategies

Beliefs about Causation	Preferences about Outcomes	
	Agreement	*Disagreement*
Agreement	Computational decision making (an organization of specialists)	Compromising decision making (Congress agrees that it facilitates social change, but disagrees about how society should be changed)
Disagreement	Judgmental decision making (a college agrees that students should learn, but disagrees on how to cause learning)	Inspirational decision making (an "atomic" organization, such as France in 1958— DeGaulle's Fifth Republic— represented inspirational and authoritarian decision making)

nities. These streams rarely connect with each other. An organized anarchy "is a collection of choices looking for problems, issues and feelings looking for decision situations in which they might be aired, solutions looking for issues to which they might be the answer, and decision makers looking for work."[95]

When these four streams do connect with each other, however, the result is often a major decision. This connecting up of problems, solutions, participants, and choice opportunities is what Cohen, March, and Olsen describe as the "garbage can model." Thus, decisions are the function of a mix of problems, solutions, participants, and participants' resources (*i.e.*, the "garbage can"), and how that mix is processed. The "choice opportunity" is the mix that occurs within the garbage can. Thus, the structure of organized anarchies is a flow of separate streams or processes throughout the organization, and with decision outcomes being heavily dependent upon the coupling of the streams at a given point in time.

The garbage can model of organizational decision making seems to have unusual utility to public organizations; John W. Kingdon, for example, has noted its usefulness in describing the policy-making process (or decision making writ large) of the federal government.[96] An analysis of the Cuban missile crisis of 1962 stated that "Although the Cuban missile crisis shared some characteristics of . . . [the] garbage can model, that model is not wholly appropriate for understanding the group decision-making process during the missile crisis." The author's point is that, while the "missile crisis was in danger of becoming an organizational garbage can," it did not become one because top decision makers "controlled the issues that they allowed to be attached to the crisis," such as heading off the attachment of such side issues to the crisis as the removal of Fidel Castro as prime minister of Cuba.[97] To some readers, this argument that the decisions averting a nuclear World War III in 1962 were not wholly like garbage may be of cold comfort.

ADMINISTRATION IN PUBLIC ORGANIZATIONS

The ambivalency of decision making that is expressed by the garbage can model seems to extend to administration. This ambivalency of administration is common to private as well as public organizations, however, because the art of administration rests on the concept of "coalition management." Every organization is a complex of coalitions and, while technologies, environments, and perceptions will always be unique, politically motivated coalitions will always be common. Thus, one way of expressing what an administrator does is to say that he or she manages coalitions that are contending, cooperating, and coalescing inside his or her organization.

Thompson explains coalition management particularly well:

> In the highly complex organization, power is dispersed. . . . [and] for the organization to be decisive and dynamic, the dispersed power must be . . . exercised through an inner circle. Have we defined such an organization as inevitably lacking a central power symbol, a recognized leader? Certainly we are implying that unilateral power cannot fall to one man in such organizations. Yet we know that an individual can "cast the long shadow" over an organization. . . . In the organization with dispersed power, the central power figure is the individual who can manage the coalition. . . . [but he or she] can do so [only] with the consent and approval of the dominant coalition.[98]

Within the broad context of coalition management, a variety of administrative, or implementation, tactics are possible. Paul C. Nutt, in one of the few empirical investigations of organizational implementation tactics that attempt to assess their frequency of use and rates of success, identified four: persuasion, edict, intervention, and participation.[99] Nutt's study is a particularly useful one because it focuses on the active side of administration—implementing change in organizations, rather than maintaining the *status quo*—and on how the tactics of implementation affect "stakeholders," or those people in the organization whose interests will be helped or harmed by a proposed change.

Persuasion is by far the most commonly used tactic of implementation; of the ninety-one case studies analyzed by Nutt, 42 percent displayed this tactic. *Persuasion*, more than any other type of approach, involves the use of outside consultants, internal staff, or any persons identified as "experts" who attempt to sell a change or policy that they have devised to members of the organization. Persuasion seems to be particularly favored as an administrative tactic among public organizations. One examination of school administrators found that these administrators not only spent a great deal of their time talking with subordinates and peers, "and that this talk accomplishes administration, but that talk is used to do the work of tightening and loosening administrative control."[100]

The next most favored implementation tactic is that of the edict (it was used in 23 percent of the cases). Like the tactic of persuasion, implementing by *edict* is straightforward: The sponsor of the change—which can be an individual member, a part of the organization, the organization as a whole, or all of the foregoing—has a clearcut stake in implementing the change, and simply directs that it be done; the change itself has considerable significance to its sponsor. Using edicts to effect change requires that the sponsor have power in the organization and be prepared to risk it; if the change fails, the sponsor issuing the edict loses.

Intervention (used in 19 percent of the cases) involves top managers (or any key executive with adequate authority) justifying a need for change, establishing new standards by which to judge performance in implementing the change, devising new ways to implement the change, and demonstrating the feasibility of the change and the improvements that result from it. In this tactic, administrators are not merely issuing edicts to change something, or wearing down the opponents of the change through unremitting talk; instead, they are personally pushing the change through, and altering the organization in virtually any way they can to accommodate the change they want. Intervention is the most aggressive of all the tactics of administration.

Finally, implementation of change can be achieved by participation. *Participation* was the least used tactic in the study (it was recorded in only 17 percent of the cases), and refers to stakeholders in the change cooperatively implementing it. Participation can range from only token participation to comprehensive, with all members of the organization (or at least all stakeholders in the change) both framing possible solutions to a perceived problem and then specifying as a group the solution they will implement. In not one case, however, did managers permit full, comprehensive participation by stakeholders.

Which tactic works? Without question, intervention (the approach used almost the least frequently) is the most successful tactic of implementation: 100 percent of the managers who used it were successful in implementing the change they wanted, and, as a tactic, its resource demands were modest. It appears that there is something to be said for "hands-on" administration; the intervention tactic was deemed to be "highly desirable and worthy of active promotion among managers."[101]

By contrast, the other tactics were less effective. The next highest success rate went to the tactics of persuasion and participation, both of which recorded 75 percent success rates, but managers typically underestimated the budget and staff resources needed to make them more effective. Implementation by edict (the second most favored approach after persuasion) clearly was the least successful tactic; in only 42 percent of the cases was it used successfully.

Effective administration, it appears, is not accomplished by decree; it is done by the down and dirty.

Effective administration, however, requires more than administrators who are willing and able to take a hands-on approach; effective administration also requires that administrators be granted the autonomy and freedom to administer in ways that they think will be the most effective, and here, as we discussed in this and the preceding chapter, public administrators have unique problems. The single most characteristic reality of the public sector is the overwhelming impact of the task environment (*i.e.*, "determinism") on the inner workings of the public organization.

Sadly, the heavy impact of the environment on the public organization, and the corresponding loss of autonomy suffered by its public administrators, seem to correlate with a lower quality of administration and decision making. A growing number of empirical investigations all point to this conclusion. Greater organizational autonomy and independence, at least up to a point, associate with a higher quality of administration. To cite some of the more recent studies in this regard:

- A study of nine citizen advisory boards in Michigan concluded that a high level of autonomy of those boards had a direct and beneficial impact on the effectiveness of those boards. "The boards . . . were advisory boards, which do not have the legal power over program, budget, and staff. Rather, these boards

made recommendations to the city commission which were acted on or not acted on at the prerogative of the commission. However, some of the citizen advisory boards were more effective than others in gaining their objectives and this was found to be related to the degree of independence which they attained."[102]

- A study of the impact of the Government in the Sunshine Act of 1976, which affected the meeting procedures of more than fifty federal agencies headed by boards of directors or similar collegial bodies, found indications that the law's opening up of the meetings of those boards diminished the quality of the decision-making process. Most agency officials felt "that the strictures of the law weakened them in executing their responsibilities and weakened agency performance, especially in policy development."[103]

- A ten-year study of the experiences of 20,000 students, teachers, and principals in some 500 public and private schools in the United States concluded that "the best determinate of the school's effectiveness was the degree of autonomy it enjoyed from bureaucracies and other outside interference. None of the other factors that usually preoccupied reformers, including class size, faculty salaries and spending per pupil, mattered as much."[104]

- An analysis of the safety records of twenty-four nuclear power plants in the United States undertaken after the Three Mile Island nuclear crisis of 1979, found that the administrative autonomy of a nuclear plant correlated with a high safety record. "Autonomy is the outcome of a good safety record and contributes to a good safety record. . . . If poor performers are given more autonomy, this analysis suggests, their safety record is likely to improve. . . ."[105]

- A four-year study of American governments, published as a book titled *Reinventing Government* (and which made the best seller list), concluded that much of the perceived unresponsiveness, inefficiency, and ineffectiveness of government is attributable to its lack of autonomy: Public administrators are "trapped in archaic systems that frustrate their creativity and sap their energy," and the authors urge that these systems "be changed, to liberate the enormous energies of public servants—and to heighten their ability to serve the public."[106]

What the research by and large indicates, in short, is that, within the American context of extreme openness, some enhancement of public agencies' administrative independence and organizational autonomy likely will result in more effective and responsive government, with little or no new resources being required.[107]

ASSESSING THE PERFORMANCE OF PUBLIC ORGANIZATIONS

Meier's research on the tribulations of a university library undergoing pressures from its environment was cited earlier as an example of the difficulty that a public organization has in dealing with a task environment that lacks the benefit of a market mechanism. On another plane, Meier's dilemma is one of how to assess the performance and efficiency of all public organizations. As we explain in greater detail in Chapter 7, government agencies, unlike business corporations, normally cannot measure their performance by the fatness of their profits.

Thompson has framed the organizational assessment problem in a more rigorous manner. He observes that organizations may be evaluated according to one of three "tests"; the appropriateness of any one of these tests depends on the nature of the organization. Thompson posits efficiency, instrumental, and social tests as ways of assessing organizational performance,[108] and, in several ways, these tests represent a conceptual extension of Thompson and Tuden's earlier work on decision issues (see Table 4-3).

The *efficiency test* relates to Thompson and Tuden's notion of "computational decision-making," and is applicable to organizations that have "crystallized standards of desirability," and whose members believe they fully comprehend the relationships between causes and effects. For example, executives in our hypothetical corporation of International Widget have a solid notion of what they want to do and how to do it: maximize profits (*i.e.*, their standards of desirability are quite firm and clear, or "crystallized") and manufacture widgets as cheaply as possible (*i.e.*, there is a clear causal connection between high profits and cheap production). Thus, assessing the performance of International Widget as an organization is both objective and easy; efficiency, or economic, tests are applicable.

The *instrumental test* is less objective, less easy to apply, and less optimal in evaluating organizational performance than the efficiency test. But it is the only kind of test that is appropriate for certain kinds of organizations, notably organizations that use "judgmental decision making." Instrumental tests are applicable to organizations that, like International Widget, have crystallized standards of desirability (*e.g.*, high profits) but, unlike International Widget, the organizational members are uncertain about what causes what. As a result of this situation, the efficiency test no longer is a suitable evaluative tool, because when no one is sure about causality there is no way of assessing the effects of what the organization is doing.

An example of such an organization might be a public agency. The Department of Defense, for instance, has a crystallized standard of desirability (adequate deterrent), but its officers are unsure about whether their programs actually are establishing that deterrent. None of them knows if their defense policies are sufficient to deter a nuclear attack (until and unless, of course, one comes). Thus, unlike the officials of International Widget, the Pentagon brass always will be uneasy about whether its programs are maximizing its mission achievement. Hence, we see Defense asking for more money as a means of maximizing its standard of desirability (*i.e.*, its unproven deterrent capacity), but International Widget attempting to reduce its operational costs as a means of maximizing its standard of desirability (*i.e.*, profits).

The *social test* also is applicable to public bureaucracies, particularly those agencies that have ambiguous, rather than crystallized, standards of desirability. Whether or not members believe they understand cause-and-effect relationships does not matter, so the decision-making strategies of such an organization could range from one of compromise to inspiration. Such an agency might be a social service or a university; often, no one in these organizations can quantify, even remotely, the impact of their activities. What, for instance, is meant by "breaking the cycle of poverty"? What is "learning"?

Instrumental, but more especially social, tests

of organizational performance are the kinds of evaluational tools that public bureaucracies find themselves using. Neither test is especially effective, but at least the reasons for their ineffectuality are fairly clear; public organizations, like the polity they administer, lack specificity in expressing their goals and in comprehending the most efficient way to achieve those goals.

Because of this dilemma, organizations that are unclear about causality or standards of desirability have developed a number of variants of instrumental and social tests in an attempt to assess themselves and to prove their worth to their audience outside. Public organizations have been especially adept at this because their very survival depends on the monies and legitimacy that they draw from the polity. Put crassly, this means acquiring prestige. For an organization faced with the necessity of using instrumental or social tests as a method of assessment, prestige and status often become the operational yardsticks of performance.

One way of measuring prestige is by calculating the historical improvement of the agency. This may be done in a number of ways: an increase in organizational visibility, budget increments, ratings by outside observers, proliferation of programs, size of the clientele served, and so forth. Universities, for example, rely to a large degree on accrediting associations, faculty publications, and research grants (all of which are ratings by outside observers) as social tests of performance, while public agencies often rely on the relative size of their annually appropriated budget as an indication of prestige. It is not surprising that organizational growth is associated with high organizational prestige, which in turn relates to an inferred favorable assessment of organizational performance. This is an especially telling point for public bureaucracies. It indicates that we can expect public officials to try to acquire fatter budgets for their agencies in an effort to "prove" their agencies' high level of performance, and then rationalize that their fat budgets represent a measurement of high performance that already was there. Either way, it is the prestige factor that determines how public bureaucracies normally are assessed.

Unfortunately, the prestige factor can be carried to ludicrous lengths as a yardstick of organizational performance. Joseph W. Eaton found that the in-house research units in two "treatment-oriented" organizations were used primarily as a method of acquiring prestige rather than as a method of discovering more objective measurements of true organizational performance.[109] Any "substantive" research projects regarding organizational performance that could be potentially embarrassing were discouraged, while "symbolic" research—noncontroversial research that did not question the organizations' traditional goals nor threaten established power patterns and was essentially useless—was encouraged in the organizations. In this light, it is worth recalling that government generally has less prestige than business organizations among the American populace. This situation can affect relative organizational performance in the two spheres. A study of a public government hospital and a private volunteer hospital concluded that the private institution was better able to fulfill its official mission than the government hospital because of greater prestige in the community. The private hospital received more financial contributions, patients, and popular support.[110]

More recent and systematic studies substantiate how critical social tests can be to the very survival of public-sector organizations, particularly younger ones. (The literature of organization theory generally supports the proposition that newness is a liability among all organizations, and that new organizations are likelier to "die" than are established ones.[111]) An investigation of 389 newly founded, voluntary, nonprofit social service organizations in metropolitan Toronto[112] concluded that the acquisition of "external legitimacy" by these new social service organizations (typically in the forms of obtaining a *Community Directory* listing, a Charitable Registration Number, and a large and distinguished board) far outweighed the use of internal management changes within these organizations in predicting their long-term survival. Changes in the "internal coordination" of these organizations (a term encompassing changes in the organizations' service areas, chief executives, goals, client groups, and structure) bore no relationship (with one exception, that of changing the chief executive) to the survival rates of these nonprofit organizations. Social tests, then (and more precisely, the acquisition of social status), while often times less than measurable, appear to be vitally important to the success of public-sector organizations.

In this chapter, we have reviewed some of the more important ideas found floating in the vast ocean of organization theory. Like ideas in any field, they bob and bump into each other, depending on the prevailing currents. We have tried to point out those ideas that have a special utility to the public sector. In the next chapter, we move to a more lively part of organization theory: people.

NOTES

1. James D. Thompson, *Organizations in Action: Social Science Bases of Administrative Theory* (New York: McGraw-Hill, 1967), pp. 14-82.
2. Charles Perrow, "The Analysis of Goals in Complex Organizations," *American Sociological Review*, 26 (December 1961), pp. 854-866; and "Hospitals: Technology, Structure and Goals," *Handbook of Organizations*, James G. March, ed. (New York: Rand-McNally, 1965).
3. Louis W. Fry, "Technology-Structure Research: Three Critical Issues," *Academy of Management Journal*, 25 (September 1982), pp. 532-552. Fry analyzed 140 articles and books on the subject published between 1965 and 1980 and found that nearly 49 percent of the works showed a statistically significant relationship between technological change and structural change, and that this significance was "roughly equal across different conceptions of technology and structure, different levels of analysis, and different types of measures" (p. 341).
4. Sheldon L. Messinger, "Organizational Transformation: A Case Study of a Declining Social Movement," *American Sociological Review*, 20 (February 1955), pp. 3-10.
5. Tom Burns and G. M. Stalker, *The Management of Innovation* (London: Tavistock, 1961).
6. William R. Dill, "Environment as an Influence on Managerial Autonomy," *Administrative Science Quarterly*, 2 (March 1958), pp. 409-443.
7. Richard L. Meier, "Communications Overload," *Administrative Science Quarterly*, 7 (March 1963), pp. 529-544.
8. Dean C. Ludwig, "Adapting to a Declining Environment: Lessons from a Religious Order," *Organization Science*, 4 (February 1993), p. 54
9. Kathryn R. Harrigan, "Strategic Formulation in Declining Industries," *Academy of Management Review*, 4 (June 1980), pp. 599-604.
10. Ludwig, "Adapting to a Declining Environment," p. 54.
11. Many of the ideas in this discussion are drawn from: Donald Chisholm, "Organizational Response to Environmental Change," paper presented at the 1985 Annual Meeting of the American Political Science Association, New Orleans, August 29-September 1, 1985.
12. Herbert Kaufman, *Time, Chance, and Organizations: Natural Selection in a Perilous Environment* (Chatham, N.J.: Chatham House, 1985). Kaufman likens the organization's relationship with its environment to "a process of 'chemical evolution'" that predates biological evolution (p. 91).
13. See, for example, Martin Landau, "On the Concept of Self-Correcting Organizations," *Public Administration Review*, 33 (November/December 1973), pp. 533-542; Howard E. Aldrich, *Organizations and Environments* (Englewood Cliffs, N.J.: Prentice Hall, 1979); and John Child, "Organization Structure, Environment, and Performance: The Role of Strategic Choice," *Sociology*, 6 (January 1972), pp. 1-22.
14. Kaufman provides a nice overview of these. See Kaufman, *Time, Chance, and Organizations*, p. 153.
15. *Ibid.*, p. 150. Two solid reviews that deal with the problem of organizational taxonomies are: Douglas R. Wholey and Jack W. Brittain, "Organizational Ecology: Findings and Implications," *Academy of Management Review*, 11 (July 1986), pp. 513-533, and Phillip Rich, "The Organizational Taxonomy: Definition and Design," *Academy of Management Review*, 17 (October 1992), pp. 758-781.
16. Examples include: Herbert A. Simon, *Administrative Behavior* (New York: Free Press, 1947); and James G. March and Herbert A. Simon, *Organizations* (New York: John Wiley, 1958). Virtually all the contributors to the open model of organizations and the literature of model synthesis, described in Chapter 3, could be listed in this respect.
17. Perhaps the most straightforward, well-known example of this view is: Thomas J. Peters and Robert H. Waterman, Jr., *In Search of Excellence: Lessons from America's Best-Run Companies* (New York: Warner, 1982).
18. Chisholm, "Organizational Response to Environmental Change," p. 14.
19. See, for example, James G. March, "The Business Firm as Political Coalition," *Journal of Politics*, 24 (November 1962), pp. 662-678; Jeffrey Pfeffer, *Power in Organizations* (Marshfield, Mass.: Pitman, 1981); and James D. Thompson and William J. McEwen, "Organizational Goals and Environment: Goal-Setting as an Interaction Process," *American Sociological Review*, 23 (February 1958), pp. 23-31.
20. March and Simon, *Organizations*, p. 38.
21. Richard M. Cyert and James G. March, *A Behavioral Theory of the Firm* (Englewood Cliffs, N.J.: Prentice Hall, 1963).
22. Anthony Downs, *Inside Bureaucracy* (Boston: Little, Brown), 1967), pp. 92-101.
23. Michel Crozier, *The Bureaucratic Phenomenon* (Chicago: University of Chicago Press, 1964), pp. 220-224.
24. Howard E. McCurdy, "Organizational Decline: NASA and the Life Cycle of Bureaus," *Public Administration Review*, 51 (July/August 1991), pp. 308-315.

25. Jane M. Howell and Christopher A. Higgins, "Champions of Change: Identifying, Understanding, and Supporting Champions of Technological Innovations," *Organizational Dynamics* (Summer 1990), p. 48.

26. *Ibid.*, p. 50.

27. Richard A. D'Aveni and Ian C. MacMillan, "Crisis and the Content of Managerial Communications: A Study of the Focus of Attention of the Top Managers in Surviving and Failing Firms," *Administrative Science Quarterly*, 35 (October 1990), pp. 634-657.

28. Kaufman, *Time, Chance, and Organizations*, pp. 69, 150.

29. For other examples, see Aldrich, *Organizations and Environments*; and Child, "Organization Structure, Environment, and Performance."

30. W. Graham Astley and Andrew H. Van de Ven, "Central Perspectives and Debates in Organization Theory," *Administrative Science Quarterly*, 28 (June 1983), p. 245.

31. Lawrence G. Hrebeniak and William F. Joyce, "Organizational Adaptation: Strategic Choice and Environmental Determinism," *Administrative Science Quarterly*, 30 (September 1985), p. 336.

32. Two important contributions to answering the question are: Barton Wechsler and Hal Rainey, "Strategic Management in Political Environments," paper presented at the 1986 Annual Meeting of the American Political Science Association, Washington, D.C., August 29-31, 1986; and Hrebeniak and Joyce, "Organizational Adaptation." Table 4-2 has been developed using several of the ideas contained in these pieces, as well as the thinking in Astley and Van de Ven, "Central Perspectives and Debates in Organization Theory."

33. See, for example, Roger Miles Blough, *The Washington Embrace of Business* (New York: Columbia University Press, 1975); Mark J. Green, ed., *The Monopoly Makers: Ralph Nader's Study Group Report on Regulation and Competition* (New York: Grossman, 1973); Louis M. Kohlmeier, Jr., *The Regulators: Watchdog Agencies in the Public Interest* (New York: Harper and Row, 1969); Arthur S. Miller, *The Modern Corporate State: Private Governments and the American Constitution* (Westport, Conn.: Greenwood Press, 1976); and Robert Sobel, *The Age of Giant Corporations: A Microeconomic History of American Business, 1914-1970* (Westport, Conn.: Greenwood Press, 1972).

34. James G. March, "Decisions in Organizations and Theories of Choice," in Andrew H. Van de Ven and William F. Joyce, eds. *Perspectives on Organization Design and Behavior* (New York: Wiley Interscience, 1981), pp. 205-244.

35. See, for example, Peters and Waterman, *In Search of Excellence*, pp. 200-234, in which they describe successes enjoyed by major companies that practice what amounts to slack search.

36. Charles E. Lindblom, "The Science of Muddling Through," *Public Administration Review*, 19 (Spring 1959), pp. 79-88.

37. Hrebeniak and Joyce, "Organizational Adaptation," p. 342.

38. Robert A. Caro, *The Power Broker: Robert Moses and the Fall of New York* (New York: Knopf, 1974), p. 38. Emphasis is original.

39. Stafford Beer, "Managing Modern Complexity," *The Management of Information and Knowledge.* Panel on Science and Technology (11th meeting). Proceedings before the Committee on Science and Astronautics, U.S. House of Representatives, 91st Congress, Second Session, January 27, 1970, No. 15 (Washington, D.C.: U.S. Government Printing Office, 1970).

40. Harold L. Wilensky, *Organizational Intelligence* (New York: Basic Books, 1967). The saga of Cicero is on pp. 68-69.

41. Gordon Tullock, *The Politics of Bureaucracy* (Washington, D.C.: Public Affairs Press, 1965).

42. March and Simon, *Organizations*, p. 165.

43. Herbert A. Simon, *Administrative Behavior: A Study of Decision-Making Processes in Administrative Organizations*, 3rd ed. (New York: Free Press, 1976), p. 292.

44. Marc A. Levin, "The Information-Seeking Behavior of Local Government Officials," *American Review of Public Administration*, 21 (December 1991), p. 283. Levin surveyed 200 city and county managers in the San Francisco Bay Area. See also: D. N. Ammons and C. Newell, *City Executives: Leadership Roles, Work Characteristics, and Time Management* (Albany: State University of New York Press, 1989).

45. York Willbern, "Professionalization in the Public Service: Too Little or Too Much?" *Public Administration Review*, 14 (Winter 1954), pp. 13-21.

46. Alan Altshuler, *The City Planning Process: A Political Analysis* (Ithaca, N.Y.: Cornell University Press, 1965).

47. James D. Carroll, "Noetic Authority," *Public Administration Review*, 29 (September/October 1969), pp. 492-500.

48. Martha S. Feldman and James G. March, "Information in Organizations as Signal and Symbol," paper presented at the Western Political Science Association in San Francisco, California, March 27-29, 1980. See also: Feldman and March, "Information in Organizations as Signal and Symbol," *Administrative Science Quarterly*, 26 (June 1981), pp. 171-186. The following quotations in the text are drawn from the paper first cited.

49. See, for example, Thomas D. Clark, Jr., and William A. Shrode, "Public Sector Decision Structures: An Empirically Based Description," *Public Administration Review*, 39 (1979), pp. 343-354; Lindblom, "The Science of Muddling Through," pp. 79-88; Morton H. Halperin, *Bureaucratic Politics in Foreign Policy* (Washington, D.C.: Brookings Institution, 1974); and Michael D. Cohen and James G. March, *Leadership and Ambiguity: The American College President* (New York: McGraw-Hill, 1974).

50. Feldman and March, "Information in Organizations as Signal and Symbol," pp. 12-13.

51. See, for example, Steve Chan, "The Intelligence of

Stupidity: Understanding Failures and Strategic Warning," *American Political Science Review*, 73 (1979), pp. 171-180.

52. See, for example, Irving L. Janis and Leon Mann, *Decision Making: A Psychological Analysis of Conflict, Choice, and Commitment* (New York: Free Press, 1977).

53. Feldman and March, "Information in Organizations as Signal and Symbol," pp. 15-16.

54. James Brown and Zi-Lei Qiu, "Satisficing When Buying: Information," *Organizational Behavior and Human Decision Processes*, 51 (June 1992), p. 471.

55. Feldman and March, "Information in Organizations as Signal and Symbol," p. 20.

56. *Ibid.*, pp. 23-24.

57 *Ibid.*, p. 25.

58. Kathleen M. Eisenhardt, "Making Fast Strategic Decisions in High-Velocity Environments," *Academy of Management Journal*, 32 (September 1989), pp. 543-576.

59. *Ibid.*, p. 543

60. Amitai Etzioni, *Modern Organizations* (Englewood Cliffs, N.J.: Prentice-Hall, 1964).

61. Simon, *Administrative Behavior*, 3rd ed., pp. 48-52. For an interesting discussion of the decision premise in the context of ethical choice in the public sector, see: Debra W. Stewart, "The Decision Premise: A Basic Tool for Analyzing the Ethical Content of Organizational Behavior," *Public Administration Quarterly*, 8 (Fall 1988), pp. 315-328.

62. Jennifer A. Chatman, "Matching People and Organizations: Selection and Socialization in Public Accounting Firms," *Administrative Science Quarterly*, 36 (September 1991), pp. 459-484.

63. Roy J. Lewicki, "Organizational Seduction: Building Commitment to Organizations," *Organizational Dynamics* (Autumn 1981), p. 7.

64. Morris Janowitz, "Changing Patterns of Organizational Authority: The Military Establishment," *Administrative Science Quarterly*, 3 (March 1959), pp. 473-493.

65. Chester I. Barnard, *The Functions of the Executive* (Cambridge, Mass.: Harvard University Press, 1938).

66. Herbert A. Simon, *Administrative Behavior*, 3rd ed., pp. 123-153. But see also the essay by Simon and Robert Bierstedt in *Studies in Managerial Process and Organizational Behavior*, John H. Turner, Alan C. Filley, and Robert J. House, eds. (Glenview, Ill.: Scott, Foresman, 1972), pp. 59-72, and J. Bernard Keys and Thomas L. Case, "How To Become an Influential Manager," *The Executive*, 4 (November 1990), pp. 38-51. Keys and Case summarize much of the research on this topic, and add their own, noting (on p. 38) that because "of the increasing diversity of goals and values of employees and their increasing interdependence, the effectiveness of formal authority is diminishing."

67. Nicole Wollsey Biggart and Gary G. Hamilton, "The Power of Obedience," *Administrative Science Quarterly*, 29 (December 1984), p. 548. In a critique of the authors' research, one reviewer made a comment that amounted to a backhanded acceptance of the view that public organizations are different from private ones: "In making their case . . . [Biggart and Hamilton evoke] a somewhat oversocialized conception of power that may be typical of state government but is restrictive in its broader relevance." See: Walter W. Powell's review of *Governor Reagan, Governor Brown: A Sociology of Executive Power* by Gary G. Hamilton and Nicole Woolsey Biggart (New York: Columbia University Press, 1984), in *Administrative Science Quarterly*, 31 (March 1985), p. 134.

68. Kent D. Peterson, "Mechanisms of Administrative Control over Managers in Educational Organizations," *Administrative Science Quarterly*, 29 (December 1984), pp. 576-581.

69. See, for example, William H. Newman and Harvey W. Wallendar, "Managing Not-for-Profit Enterprises," *Academy of Management Review*, 3 (January 1978), pp. 24-31; and Mayer Zald, *The Political Economy of the YMCA* (Chicago: University of Chicago Press, 1970). This idea of the difficulties of achieving "output control" in nonprofit organizations is essentially another way of saying that public organizations do not have a profit margin with which to gauge performance.

70. Peterson, "Mechanisms of Administrative Control," pp. 584-593.

71. *Ibid.*, p. 595.

72. Warren Boeker, "Power and Managerial Dismissal: Scapegoating at the Top," *Administrative Science Quarterly*, 37 (September 1992), p. 418.

73. Vic Murray, Pat Bradshaw, and Jacob Wolpin, "Power in and Around Nonprofit Boards: A Neglected Dimension of Governance," *Nonprofit Management and Leadership*, 3 (Winter 1992), pp. 165-182.

74. See, for example, Pfeffer, *Power in Organizations*, pp. 130-135.

75. See, for example, Rosabeth M. Kanter, "Power Failures in Management Circuits," *Harvard Business Review* (July-August 1979), pp. 65-75; and Charles Perrow, "Departmental Power and Perspectives in Industrial Firms," in *Power in Organizations*, Mayer N. Zald, ed. (Nashville, Tenn.: Vanderbilt University Press, 1970), pp. 59-89.

76. Daniel J. Brass, "Being in the Right Place: A Structural Analysis of Individual Influence in an Organization," *Administrative Science Quarterly*, 29 (December 1984), pp. 532-533.

77. *Ibid.*, p. 518.

78. David J. Hickson, *et al.*, "The Strategic Contingencies' Theory of Intraorganizational Power," *Administrative Science Quarterly*, 16 (March 1971), pp. 216-229.

79. Carol S. Saunders and Richard Scamell, "Intraorganizational Distributions of Power: Replication Research," *Academy of Management Journal*, 25 (March 1982), p. 194.

80. Judith Dozier Hackman, "Power and Centrality in the Allocation of Resources in Colleges and Universities," *Administrative Science Quarterly*, 30 (March 1985), pp. 61-77.

81. *Ibid.*, p. 75.

82. C. R. Hinings, D. J. Hickson, J. M. Pennings, and R. E. Schneck, "Structural Conditions of Intraorganizational Power," *Administrative Science Quarterly*, 19 (January 1974), pp. 22-24; and Saunders and Scamell, "Intraorganizational Distributions of Power," p. 194.

83. Saunders and Scamell, "Intraorganizational Distributions of Power," p. 198. Centrality is measured by immediacy and pervasiveness, but not its match, which was a concept not used in the study.

84. *Ibid.*, p. 199.

85. *Ibid.*, pp. 240-244.

86. George Miller, "The Magic Number Seven, Plus or Minus Two," *Psychological Review*, 63 (March 1956), pp. 81-97. For an excellent review of this literature, see: George Keller and Ann McCreery, "Making Difficult Educational Decisions: Findings from Research and Experience," paper presented at the 25th Annual Conference of the Society for College and University Planning, Atlanta, Georgia, July 31, 1990.

87. Daniel Kahneman and Amos Tversky, "Choices, Values, Frames," *American Psychologist*, 39 (June 1984), pp. 341-350.

88. Suzanne Langer, *Mind: An Essay on Feeling* (Baltimore, Md.: Johns Hopkins University Press, 1988).

89. Robert Frank, "Shrewdly Irrational," *Sociological Forum*, 2 (September 1987), pp. 21.41.

90. Janis and Mann, *Decision-Making.*

91. Irving Janis, *Victims of Groupthink* (Boston: Houghton-Mifflin, 1972).

92. James D. Thompson and Arthur Tuden, "Strategies, Structures and Processes of Organizational Decision," *Comparative Studies in Administration*, James D. Thompson, *et al.*, eds. (Pittsburgh, Penn.: The University of Pittsburgh Press, 1959), pp. 195-216.

93. Michael Cohen, James G. March, and Johan Olsen, "A Garbage Can Model of Organizational Choice," *Administrative Science Quarterly*, 17 (March 1972), pp. 1-25.

94. *Ibid.*, p. 1.

95. *Ibid.*, p. 2.

96. John W. Kingdon, *Agendas, Alternatives, and Public Policies* (Boston: Little, Brown, 1984), p. 90.

97. Paul A. Anderson, "Decision Making by Objection and the Cuban Missile Crisis," *Administrative Science Quarterly*, 28 (June 1983), p. 216.

98. Thompson, *Organizations in Action*, p. 142.

99. Paul C. Nutt, "Tactics of Implementation," *Academy of Management Journal*, 29 (July 1986), pp. 230-261.

100. Peter C. Gronn, "Talk as Work: The Accomplishment of School Administration," *Administrative Science Quarterly*, 28 (March 1983), p. 1.

101. *Ibid.*, p. 258.

102. David G. Houghton, "Citizen Advisory Boards: Autonomy and Effectiveness," *American Review of Public Administration*, 18 (September 1988), p. 293.

103. David M. Welborn, William Lyons, and Larry W. Thomas, "The Federal Government in the Sunshine Act and Agency Decision Making," *Administration and Society*, 20 (February 1989), p. 483.

104. Don Wycliff, "Market System Urged as Way to Loosen Grip of School Bureaucracy," *New York Times* (June 6 1990). Wycliff is reporting on the study: John E. Chubb and Terry M. Moe, *Politics, Markets, and America's Schools* (Washington, D.C.: Brookings Institution, 1990).

105. Alfred A. Marcus, "Implementing Externally Induced Innovations: A Comparison of Rule-Bound and Autonomous Approaches," *Academy of Management Journal*, 31 (June 1988), p. 249.

106. David Osborne and Ted Gaebler, *Reinventing Government: How the Entrepreneurial Spirit Is Transforming the Public Sector* (Reading, Mass: Addison-Wesley, 1992), p. xviii.

107. In a remarkable feature article in *Fortune*, one of the nation's foremost business magazines, precisely this point was argued, and strongly so. This could be an augury of reform, and movement toward a more autonomous public service. See: David Kirkpatrick, "It's Simply Not Working," *Fortune* (November 19, 1990), pp. 20-21. To be fair, however, not all the research agrees that more autonomy will result in more effective public agencies. See: Diane Vaughan, "Autonomy, Interdependence, and Social Control: NASA and the Space Shuttle *Challenger*," *Administrative Science Quarterly*, 35 (June 1990), pp. 225-257.

108. Thompson, *Organizations in Action*, pp. 83-98.

109. Joseph W. Eaton, "Symbolic and Substantive Evaluation Research," *Administrative Science Quarterly*, 6 (March, 1962), pp. 421-442.

110. Ray H. Elling and Sandor Halebsky, "Organizational Differentiation and Support: A Conceptual Framework," *Administrative Science Quarterly*, 6 (September 1961), pp. 185-209.

111. See, for example, Arthur L. Stinchcombe, "Organizations and Social Structure," in James G. March, ed. *Handbook of Organizations* (Chicago: Rand-McNally, 1965), pp. 153-193; Glenn R. Carroll and Jacques Delacroix, "Organizational Mortality in the Newspaper Industries of Argentina and Ireland: An Ecological Approach," *Administrative Science Quarterly*, 27 (June 1982), pp. 169-196; and John Freeman, Glenn R. Carroll, and Michael T. Hannan, "The Liability of Newness: Age Dependence in Organizational Death Rates," *American Sociological Review*, 48 (October 1983), pp. 692-710.

112. Jitendra V. Singh, David J. Tucker, and Robert J. House, "Organizational Legitimacy and the Liability of Newness," *Administrative Science Quarterly*, 31 (June 1986), pp. 171-193.

CHAPTER 5

PEOPLE IN PUBLIC ORGANIZATIONS

We have seen that organizations are changed according to the ways in which technologies, task environments, and people interact with one another in the organization. We know that people change organizations and this, in its way, is a comforting thought. Less comforting, however, is the thought that organizations change people—that organizations somehow, over time, alter personalities. Was *The Organization Man* described by William H. Whyte[1] the same rigid automaton before he joined "the team," or was he originally a normal human being who was drastically altered by the organization once he was under its influence?

WHAT CAN ORGANIZATIONS DO TO YOU?

It appears that some organizations—what Erving Goffman calls "total institutions," such as prisons, orphanages, barracks, ships, asylums, sanitariums, monasteries, and certain types of schools—can change the people in them.[2] This is logical; the technology (*i.e.*, what the organization does) of total institutions is people, and the

mission of total institutions is to change the "client-members" inside them. The technology of prisons, for instance, is rehabilitation; the technology of schools is education.

Goffman has delineated the characteristics of total institutions as follows:

- All aspects of life are separated from the larger society and are conducted in the same place and under the same authority.
- The activities of client-members generally occur in "large batches" (*i.e.*, they do most things together, and client-members are treated equally).
- Each day's activities are tightly scheduled and regulated.
- Each activity is perceived as being part of an overall plan designed to achieve official goals.
- There is a staff/inmate (*e.g.*, guard/prisoner) split.

In his study of prisons, Goffman observed that life in the "inmate world" was characterized by (1) a "mortification process" that often was perpetrated unconsciously by the staff as the result of managing many people in a small space with limited resources, (2) a "privilege system" that amounted to nothing more than a lack of sanctions, and (3) various forms of adaptation by inmates to the mortification process. These adaptations could include situational withdrawal; rebellion; "colonization," in which inmates grew to prefer prison to the society outside; and "conversion" by those inmates who came to be known as "square johns" because of their total acceptance of the official prison system. In the "staff world," Goffman noted that prison officials, who were pulled between the desires to maintain both humane standards and organizational efficiency, often developed a "theory" of human behavior that rationalized the inmates' hostility toward them.

Another kind of total institution may be closer to home to most readers: colleges and universities. Not all colleges, of course, have totalistic features, but many do. S. M. Dornbusch has written of the ethos prevalent in the United States Coast Guard Academy, which was designed to develop a "bureaucratic spirit" and a sense of solidarity in its students.[3] In this light, voluntary student resignations were speeded and hushed by academy officials, and questionable practices, such as hazing, were justified with such slogans as "separating the men from the boys."

Charles E. Bidwell and Rebecca S. Vreeland[4] have developed a "typology of socializing organizations" for colleges that classifies a college's probability for successfully indoctrinating students for life according to the kinds of goals professed by college officials and the scope of student involvement in the institution. For instance, a "doctrinal-administered communal" college (*i.e.*, a residential college with the goal of inculcating certain ethical and philosophic beliefs in its students) would have a very strong and homo-geneous moral impact on its client-members. An example might be Bennington College, which was set up in 1932 with the idea of liberalizing the daughters of wealthy and often conservative families. Studies by Theodore M. Newcomb[5] at Bennington indicated that, indeed, the college's students adopted more politically liberal attitudes during their college careers and retained these attitudes well into later life. Conversely, a "procedural-administered associational" college (*e.g.*, a commuter college with "technical" goals, such as teaching its students a particular trade) would have no significant moral impact on its client-members. An example might be any public junior college.

Bidwell and Vreeland's conception of how organizations change their client-members is shown in Table 5-1.

If it is true that total institutions alter their client-members (and this contention is by no means conclusively validated by evidence), it does not necessarily follow that bureaucracies somehow change their members. Many (but not all) total institutions acquire their client-members by force, or at least by the application of social pressure (*e.g.*, "Don't you *want* to go to Dad's *alma mater*?"). Bureaucracies rarely add to their memberships in these ways; people join bureaucracies relatively voluntarily. And when they do join, they are not client-members, such as a prisoner or a student. They are full-fledged members of the organization, such as a guard or a faculty member.

Some theorists, however, do argue that bureaucracies, particularly public bureaucracies, change the bureaucrats inside them. Perhaps the classic statement of this argument is Robert K. Merton's essay on the "bureaucratic personality." By the very drive of the bureaucracy to rational-

TABLE 5-1   A Typology of Socializing Organizations

	Scope of Involvement	
Goals	*Communal*	*Associational*
Moral	Doctrinal-administered community: strong, homogeneous moral impact on client-members.	Doctrinal-administered association: moderate, homogeneous moral impact on client-members.
Technical	Procedural-administered community: strong, heterogeneous moral impact on client-members.	Procedural-administered association: no significant moral impact on client-members.

ize (and thus rigidify) its administrative techniques, the bureaucrats in it must be trained and socialized so that they begin to think along the lines and patterns mandated by those techniques. Thus, in Merton's words, the bureaucrat grows to personify "Veblen's concept of 'trained incapacity,' Dewey's notion of 'occupational psychosis' or Warnotte's view of 'professional deformation.'"[6] Yet, after such training, a way of seeing also becomes a way of not seeing. It is an inescapable outcome that bureaucrats become methodical and prudent persons because they must if they are to survive in a bureaucracy that places "tremendous symbolic significance" on rules and their adherence. In fact, the pressures to rationalize the bureaucracy work to produce "overconformity," because that assures a margin of safety in terms of reducing uncertainty in the organization. Additionally, the stress in bureaucracies to depersonalize relationships, combined with the "professional deformation" brought about by socialization, results in the unsympathetic, disinterested, and often uncomprehending bureaucrat perceived by the client who is concerned with his or her special problem and its several unique features. Because of such dynamics between social and organizational forces, the notorious, petty, dense, and arrogant bureaucratic personality has emerged.

Other analysts are less positive that organizations change their members. Ivar Berg, in a methodologically careful empirical study, attempted to ascertain if organizations changed people by examining the attitudes and behavior of "old" and "new" organizational members; in Berg's words, "I tried to measure employees' propensities to accept and act upon their impulses."[7] After much analysis, Berg was forced to concede that he could not draw any final conclusions, although there was a "close fit" between senior members and their organizations. Problems involving personality change, self-selection, and organizational selection were too difficult to separate as intervening variables, and the thesis that the organization *caused* changes in its people was methodologically impossible to "prove." Although research is continuing, whether or not bureaucracies change people must still remain a moot point.

We do know, however, that there are many different kinds of people in organizations, regardless of the forces that may have shaped their personalities. It is to some of these models that we now turn, in an effort to learn what our implicit assumptions about the nature of the administrative human being really are.

ADMINISTRATIVE HUMANITY: CLASSICISM VERSUS SOCIAL-PSYCHOLOGY

Throughout the preceding chapters, we implicitly have been contrasting the early, "classical" views of what people are like and how they behave in organizations with the more useful and more current perspectives on the nature of people in organizations that are derived from social-psychology. In this section, we do so more explicitly.

Administrative Humanity: The Classical View

Under the "classical view," we consider those early theorists who tended to ignore social and psychological variables in the constitutions of members of organizations, and who instead stressed their "rational" and physical dimensions.

The classical model of the bureaucrat was not drawn entirely from Theory X, but it was largely predicated on that concept. Max Weber, for example, perceived the key to getting things done in a bureaucracy to be primarily a matter of "rationalizing" the behavior of bureaucrats—getting each member to do his or her job in such a way that he or she optimally expedited the official goals of the bureaucracy. Frederick Taylor had essentially the same idea, but his theory rationalized the physical behaviors of workers.

Although the classical theorists had more highly refined models of administrative humanity than the preceding description may indicate, they nevertheless were drawn from the basic conception that it expresses.

Administrative Humanity: The Social-Psychological View

In contrast to the classical theorists, theorists relying principally on the open model of organizations and the Theory Y conception of personality focused less on rational, economic concerns and more on psychological and social ones. Representatives of a "pure" social-psychological view of the organization member would include Chester I. Barnard, Herbert A. Simon, James G. March, Richard M. Cyert, and James D. Thompson.[8] In this literary stream, the administrative human being is seen as a biological, physical, emotional, behavioral, and social creature who possesses limited cognitive abilities, but nonetheless has an occasional capacity to perceive and act in his or her self-interest, solve problems, and bargain.

Simon provided a useful description of the social-psychological view in his *Models of Man*.[9] On the one hand, Simon posited *psychological man*, or *Freudian man*, who represented the model used by psychologists to predict the behavior of individual persons. Psychological man was beset by insecurities, quirks, motivations, and emotional needs; "rational" behavior was a totally individual phenomenon; every person had to do his or her own thing. On the other hand, Simon posited *rational man*, or *economic man*, who represented the model used by economists to predict the behavior of the economy as a whole. Economic man was totally rational in the sense that he not only understood thoroughly his own self-interest (*i.e.*, the acquisition of money), but was fully cognizant of all the options available to him and would act on the choice that brought him the most money. Thus, in contrast to psychological man, who had his own unique and highly personal goals that were rational only to him, economic man had precisely the same goal as every other person in the economy, and would behave just like every other person to achieve it.

Administrative man, in Simon's view, provided a conceptual bridge between psychological man and economic man. While administrative man had his own private goals and rationality, he also understood the official goals and formal rationality of his organization. Moreover, he knew that his welfare and that of the organization were somehow related, although this was not to say that he believed what was good for the organization was necessarily good for him. Finally, administrative man could seldom if ever see all his possible options in making a decision, nor could he predict their consequences.

All these models of the human being work—that is, they yield accurate predictions—in their respective disciplines. The social-psychological model of the individual posited by the Barnard-Simon-March-Cyert-Thompson stream of literature works for organization theory.

Understanding the distinctions between the classical and social-psychological interpretations of the human condition in organizations is needed, but it does not take us very far in terms of comprehending the kinds of people with whom we must deal in public bureaucracies. There are at least three distinct literatures written in the social-psychological tradition that are of unique utility in this regard: models of adult development (which focus largely on psychological variables), models of cultural behavior, and models of political behavior (which, at the opposite end of the social-psychological continuum, focus largely on social variables). We consider these approaches in turn.

MODELS OF ADULT DEVELOPMENT

People change. How people change, and what effects those changes might have on the organizations in which they work, have been the subjects of psychological and social-psychological research since the 1930s.[10]

Turning Points

The adult development psychologists, taken together, have identified a series of psychological tasks that everyone must confront as a means of interpreting how people approach each stage of their lives, and with what attitudes. Erik Erikson, for example, posits a progressive mastery of psychological tasks that hinges on a series of critical turning points. From birth to year one, trust or mistrust can be inculcated into the psyche of the individual as a result of his or her early experiences with others; from one to six, the turning point becomes one of developing autonomy as an individual, versus shame; from six to ten, initiative or guilt; from ten to fourteen, industry as opposed to inferiority; from fourteen to twenty, identity versus role confusion; from twenty to forty, intimacy or isolation; from forty to sixty-five, generativity or creativity, as opposed to stagnation; and from sixty-five until death, a strong sense of ego and integrity as opposed to overwhelming despair.[11]

Different analysts have developed variations on this theme, but the theory is essentially the same: An individual is faced with critical turning points in his or her life, and these occur at specific ages. Importantly, a person can become mired in the negative option of any given phase, and fail to move beyond that phase. Thus, for example, a person could fall into a pattern of isolation, rather than intimacy, in his or her twenties or thirties, and fail to develop as an adult from that point.

The adult psychologists agree that when people are in their twenties and thirties, the most overriding psychological task is that of achieving personal intimacy. It is during this phase that a person shifts from his or her dependency on parents, and to an intimacy with (or isolation from) mates and peers in the work environment and society.

The next major phase is what is known popularly as the "mid-life crisis." How intense that crisis is varies from individual to individual, but people experience at least a "mid-life transition," if not a dramatic crisis. Mid-life transition is a period occurring from as early as the late thirties, through as late as the early sixties, and women may experience more of a crisis during this phase than men.[12]

It is during mid-life that the individual chooses between such deeply set alternatives as looking at career options, resigning oneself to having attained all that one can attain professionally or personally, and accepting, or becoming embittered, over one's condition. George E. Vaillant refers to this period as one of determining whether an individual can "keep the meaning" of what his or her life or career has signified in reality, or becoming rigid and inflexible over a personal set of principles that may have grown hollow over time.[13]

Finally, an individual enters late adulthood, a period in which one reflects on what one's life has meant. These reflections focus on the development of a sense of integrity about what he or she stands for, as opposed to a sense of despair over what one has failed to accomplish.[14] One can, in sum, close one's life with serenity and contentment, or sadness and self-contempt.

Adult Development and the Public Organization

Manfred Kets de Vries and his colleagues conducted research that related the experience of Canadian executives in both the public and private sectors to adult life span development.[15] Kets de Vries found a strong correlation between high and low levels of satisfaction with the organization and one's work and specific phases of adult development.

The first phase, which Kets de Vries calls "reality shock," and which occurs during the twenties when one enters one's first "real job," is characterized by very low levels of satisfaction. This shock was attributable to unrealistic expectations, and the anxiety-inducing search for a mentor among the senior executives—a search which might or might not be successful.

Organizational mentors become exceptionally important in the development of individuals as adults within the organization. The mentor is typically eight to fifteen years older than the person being mentored, takes the younger employee under his or her wing, and represents wisdom and authority to that person. Few people have as many as three or four mentors, and, more commonly, fewer.[16]

In a comparison of the mentoring function in public and private organizations, it was found that public administrators were more likely than were their counterparts in the private sector to find a mentor outside of the organization in which they worked; often, the mentor of a young public administrator is a former professor. Public administrators also are less likely than private managers to find mentors at the top rungs of the organization, a condition that may reflect the relatively frequent turnover of top political executives. Both public and private administrators, however, found the influence of mentors on their career development to be "substantial."[17] Daniel Levinson, who studied executives extensively within the framework of adult psychology, found that at about the age of thirty-seven the individual leaves the protection of the mentor and takes full charge of himself or herself.[18]

Leaving the mentor (if one has been found), and overcoming reality shock and dissatisfaction with the job, is followed by a period of socialization in the organization and personal growth, which occurs in the thirties. It is during this phase that the manager invests a sense of self in the organization and in his or her career. Levinson calls this period one of "settling down," and Vaillant refers to it as a period of "career consolidation."[19]

Not every one, however, is able to settle down. Levinson found that 45 percent of the individuals he studied "had major difficulties" during the "settling down" period, and, as a result, they could not create the basis for even a moderately satisfactory life in middle age.[20] Vaillant determined that 10 percent of his sample remained "perpetual boys," and never entered the successive stages of adult maturation. A larger proportion of his subjects never passed beyond the stage of career consolidation (or Levinson's time of "settling down"), and grew stagnant.[21]

If one is capable of consolidating one's career and enters the late thirties through the mid-forties, job satisfaction takes a steep downward spiral. This is the most likely time that people are going to have a mid-life crisis, and consider the possibilities of new careers, new life-styles, and new spouses. Michael Maccoby has concluded that today's executives are less egocentric and narcissistic than were the leaders of the public and private sectors of the past. The newer generation's characteristics of relative tolerance, flexibility and openness appeared to be very important in weathering the mid-life transition, and moving on to a satisfying late adulthood.[22]

Job satisfaction typically rebounds during the late forties and fifties; Kets de Vries calls this period, "acceptance," a notion that echoes Vaillant's concept of "keeping the meaning" of one's life and personal principles.

The roller coaster of job satisfaction takes yet another dip in the mid-to-late fifties, and continues to decline, although not as rapidly, through the early sixties as the individual nears retirement. Oddly, it appears that, while job satisfaction continues to decline, the individual's satisfaction with his or her organization appears to bounce back toward the end of his or her career.

The implications of the psychology of adult development for public organizations are several.[23] Obviously, young people entering the public bureaucracy in their twenties, like all other young people entering the workforce, probably are going to experience a reality shock. Perhaps public organizations should be increasingly sensitive to this early phase of an individual's working life. Ironically, even though the individual is most vulnerable to "reality shock" when he or she first enters the public organization, the individual is also the most energetic and determined to succeed. This is the time to cultivate both organizational loyalty and individual ability by investing—in terms of responsibilities, training, and attention—in the new public administrator.

As those same public administrators enter their fifties, they, more often than not, will want to pass on their wisdom to the younger generation. This can be encouraged by top management, and perhaps should be. Both the new public administrators in their twenties, and the more mature public administrators in their fifties, apparently need to get in touch with each other—both for the benefit of them as individuals, and the organization in which they work. This matching up seems to be particularly needed in the public sector, where, as we have noted, finding mentors in the organization is more difficult than in the private sector.

The literature of adult development gives us a useful perspective on how people evolve throughout their organizational lives, and even how they evolve before they enter organizational life as young adults. So does another body of knowledge, if from an entirely different viewpoint, and that is the literary corpus of national culture.

MODELS OF CULTURAL BEHAVIOR

Although there is a vast literature on comparative and development public administration, which we mentioned in Chapter 2, relatively few theorists have considered the specific impact of *national culture* (or "the collective mental programming of people in an environment"[24]) on organizational behavior, but some who have deserve mention. In the following discussion, we review three major themes of national culture and organizations: Use of information, organizational failure, and management.

Culture and Organizational Intelligence

Harold Wilensky, for one, has considered how cultural variables relate to attitudes about organizational uses of information and patterns of bureaucratic secrecy.[25] In his view, modern totalitarian governments based on technology (*e.g.*, Stalin's Russia, Hitler's Germany) were and are the most fully organized to protect secrecy. Information pathologies attained their ultimate expression in both states: Huge sums were passed to "experts" of various kinds, antiintellectualism was rife, an immense intelligence-gathering apparatus was created, interagency sabotage was commonplace, and the general dysfunctions of bureaucracy were exaggerated. When these pathologies were combined with a dogma, such as proletarianism or racism, "grotesque intrigues," official paranoia, and spectacular intelligence failures (such as Hitler's strategy for the conduct of World War II) were the result.

Wilensky compares the administrative methods of developing radar employed by the British and Germans during World War II as an illustration of how differing sociopolitical cultures can affect organizations. Although the Germans may have had an earlier start than the British, they soon felt it necessary to bureaucratize their system of radar research by creating a Plenipotentiary for High Frequency Techniques. The Plenipotentiary established himself as a coordinator between a chain of new research laboratories that he had built and the Air Ministry. Abstract specifications of what the *Luftwaffe* wanted then were sent by the Ministry to the Plenipotentiary, who checked his list of available laboratories and mailed the data to the one needing work. Because of an absence of interaction between fliers and scientists, German radar development eventually ground to a halt. In contrast, the British effort was characterized by continuous discussions between members of the Royal Air Force and the Telecommunications Research Establishment. A feature of this relatively open-model approach was the frequent use of "Sunday Soviets," in which officials and experts of all ranks and designations discussed various aspects of radar development. Needless to add, it was the British use of radar that was instrumental in winning the Battle of Britain.[26]

Wilensky believes that the parliamentary democracies with traditions of aristocracy, such as Britain and France, fall midway between the pathologically secretive totalitarian nations and the publicity-hungry United States, which he feels has organizations that are the least constrained by secrecy. In the United States, news "leaks" are a common strategy of interagency rivalry, exposes of public figures are encouraged by the press, congressional investigations are favored, and the libel laws are loosely construed. In England, however, an administrator's first loyalty is to the Cabinet, and the Official Secrets Act is an effective cork on the leakage of secret information.

Unfortunately, in Wilensky's view, Americans display a love/hate syndrome for secrecy. Pressures for publicity provoke counterpressures for the reestablishment of "national security," and it is Wilensky's worry that the publicity consciousness of America's culture may strengthen the power of secrecy via a kind of rebound effect; that is, "Let's not go too far with this publicity stuff, because we may sell ourselves down the river to our enemies abroad." The various investigations of the Watergate affair provide an example of America's love/hate syndrome for secrecy, particularly when the intense publicity that surrounded them is contrasted to the political defense of the accused: That a cover-up of the Watergate break-in was necessary for the sake of national security.

Culture and Organizational Failure

Unlike Wilensky, Michel Crozier has focused his research less on the effects of national culture on the organization's relationship with its political environment, and more on the influences that culture has on the internal workings of the organization. Crozier's thesis is that each national culture has a unique effect on organizations operating in that culture, and this effect ultimately will constitute the primary pathology of the organizations. In France, as noted earlier, the culturally derived pathology is *bon plaisir*—that is, to quote Crozier, "it is considered better to restrict oneself and to remain free within the narrower limits one has fixed or even those one has had to accept."[27] Philippe d'Iribarne has extended this notion to the *honor* of each class in French society; the French accept their stratum in society (whether high or low), but insist on maintaining its dignity, of not straying from the proper confines of their own cadre.[28]

Russia, however, has quite an opposite cultural phenomenon that impinges on the workings of bureaucracy. This is the *blat*, which refers to an informal network of complicity entered into by middle managers as a means of assuring that the national production quotas set by the state are met. The *blat* is characterized by a high degree of mutual, almost familial, trust among middle managers. Middle managers are quite willing to enter into "illegal" deals with one another in order to fulfill the demands of "the plan," which rarely if ever provides the methods of its own success. As a result, hierarchy, suspicion, and control are emphasized by the top echelons of the Russian bureaucracy, but often the otherwise destructive consequences of these pathologies do little to undermine the functioning of the *blat*.

In extreme contrast to Russian organizations, American organizations are characterized by divisions of labor and due process of law. These twin cultural factors bring about organizational pathologies unique to American bureaucracies. Functional specialization (which is almost another way of saying professionalization) results in an abnormally high number of jurisdictional disputes within and among American organizations, while Americans' passion for due process of law produces a plethora of impersonal bureaucratic rules designed to protect the individual from injustices. Both cultural traits tend to magnify the role of lawyers, or any official who is in a position to interpret organizational rules, jurisdictions, and prerogatives, and this aspect often impedes change in American organizations.

British organizations, on the other hand, are permeated by a deference system emanating from their culture that makes the use of impersonal rules to assure compliance by subordinates unnecessary, since the authority of superordinates possesses greater legitimacy than in American organizations. In France, peer-group resistance to authority acts as a substitute for impersonal rules and due process of law.

In Crozier's view, American organizations, on the whole, tend to protect the rights of individuals more effectively, are better attuned to reality, are characterized by more cooperation, and are generally more open than French, Russian, or British organizations. But the existence of many centers of authority in American organizations, and the difficulties that must be surmounted in coordinating them, pose problems of change for American organizations. Although American organizations are likely more open to innovation than the French, British, and Russian, Crozier notes that "Willful individuals can block the intentions of whole communities for a long time; numerous routines develop around local positions of influence; the feeble are not protected so well against the strong; and generally, a large number of vicious circles will protect and reinforce local conservatism."[29]

These pathologies, like the bureaucratic dysfunctions of a differing nature in other countries, are the result of cultural factors unique to America that no organization can escape.

Culture and Managerial Behavior

National culture has a large impact not only on how organizations behave, but also on how managers manage. What has become increasingly clear is that the American lens of management theory, which has focused most of the international thinking about management around the globe in the twentieth century, may obscure more than it reveals about managerial behavior in countries other than the United States. Although American theories of management are often touted as "universal" in their applicability, they are, in fact, not. "Cultural values of the United States underlie and have fundamentally framed management research, thus organizational science with inappropriate universalism."[30]

Certainly the most systematic and massive attempt to categorize national cultures in ways that are potentially useful to managers is by Geert Hofstede, who for decades has been collecting data on management and national culture, much (but not all) of it based on the responses of the employees of an American-based multinational corporation in forty countries. Hofstede has identified five fundamental dimensions of national culture: power distance, uncertainty avoidance, individualism-collectivism, masculinity-femininity, and long-term–short-term orientation. Specific national cultures can be any combination

Table 5-2 Culture Dimensions for Eight Nations

Nation	Power Distance	Uncertainty Avoidance	Individualism-Collectivism	Masculinity-Femininity	Long-Term–Short-Term Orientation
Brazil	Small	Strong	Collectivist	Feminine	N.A.
China	Large	Medium	Collectivist	Midway	Long-term
France	Large	Strong	Individualist	Midway-to-Feminine	Short-term
Germany	Small	Medium	Individualist	Masculine	Midway
Japan	Medium	Strong	Midway	Masculine	Long-term
Russia	Large	Strong	Midway	Feminine	Short-term
West Africa	Large	Medium	Collectivist	Medium	Short-term
United States	Small	Weak	Individualist	Masculine	Short-term

Sources: Geert Hofstede, "Cultural Constraints in Management Theories," *Academy of Management Executive,* 7 (Winter 1993), p. 91, and Hofstede, "Motivation, Leadership and Organization: Do American Theories Apply Abroad?" *Organizational Dynamics,* 9 (Summer 1980), pp. 43-62.

of these.[31] Table 5–2, derived from Hofstede's work, identifies some selected countries along these five dimensions.

Power distance refers to "the extent to which a society accepts the fact that power in institutions and organizations is distributed unequally."[32] Societies characterized by "small" power distance believe, among other things, that inequality should be minimized, superiors should be accessible, all should have equal rights, and that a latent harmony exists between the powerful and the powerless; cultures with a "large" power distance believe that a social order rightly assures proper inequalities in society, superiors should be inaccessible, power should have privileges, and that latent conflict exists between the powerful and the powerless.

Uncertainty avoidance is the extent to which a culture feels threatened by ambiguity. Cultures with "weak" uncertainty avoidance are more accepting of uncertainty, live from day to day, have lower stress levels, believe time is free, accept dissent, are unthreatened by social deviations, are more risk prone, are not too nationalistic, are youth oriented, and are not enamored by a lot of rules. "Strong" uncertainty avoidance cultures perceive uncertainty to be a continuous threat, experience greater stress, believe time is money, promote consensus over dissent, consider deviance to be dangerous, are security conscious, are highly

nationalistic, are distrustful of the young, and like a lot of rules.

Individualism-collectivism refers to a continuum of cultures; at one extreme (individualism), society is seen as a loose grouping of people whose primary concern is in caring for themselves, while the opposite extreme (collectivism) reflects a tight social framework in which in-groups are distinguished from out-groups, and the in-group is expected to take care of the individual member in exchange for his or her total allegiance to it. In the individualist culture, identity is based on the individual, leadership is the ideal, and decisions are made by the individual. In collectivist cultures, personal identity is based on the social system, membership in the organization or in-group is the ideal, and decisions are made by the group.

The *masculinity-femininity* dimension, like individualism-collectivism, is a continuum ranging from a masculine pole in which assertiveness, performance, money, independence, ambition, machismo, and indifference to others are characteristic, to a feminine extreme in which nurturing, quality of life, people, the environment, interdependence, service, androgyny, and caring for others are the dominant values.

Finally, *long-term-short-term* orientation refers to a cultural direction relative to time. Nations with a long-term orientation are directed toward the future, and value thrift and persistence. Countries with a short-term orientation are more poised toward the past and present, and place premiums on respect for tradition and fulfilling social obligations.

Although there are numerous exceptions, countries tend to group along the foregoing cultural dimensions by language and geography. For example, the seven Latin American countries that Hofstede surveyed all are cultures that accept large inequalities of power relationships, strongly avoid uncertainty, and are collectivist. All the Asian countries that Hofstede studied are large power distance countries, collectivist, and have a long-term orientation. All ten English speaking countries, including those in Africa and Asia, are accepting of uncertainty and are masculine; and, except for those in Asia, all English-speaking countries are individualistic. All four Scandinavian nations are feminine.

The United States is a small power distance country (that is, its citizens value equality); a weak uncertainty avoidance nation (in fact, it is well below average, indicating high risk-taking propensities and tolerance for dissent, among other characteristics); is exceptionally individualistic as a society; is well above average as a masculine culture; and has a short-term orientation. These dimensions have fashioned a national culture that is uniquely American, and which, because of its uniqueness, should dampen the enthusiasm of Americans for interpreting managerial behavior in other countries by relying only on their own cultural perspective.

Consider, for example, A. H. Maslow's "hierarchy of human needs," described in Chapter 3, and which is absolutely central to mainstream organization theory, especially human relations and organization development. Maslow's theory, which culminates in the ultimate personal achievement, self-actualization, is predicated on the idea that certain, basic needs must be satisfied first, such as the need for security. Maslow's hierarchy is, at root, a theory of human motivation.

Hofstede's research indicates that Maslow's theory of motivation is less than universal and, in fact, is bound in the American cultural context. Self-actualization is a concept that can be supported only in a society that places a high premium on performance and achievement (or a society that is strongly individualistic and masculine, as

is the United States), and on a willingness to take risks so that achievements may be made (or a culture that has weak uncertainty avoidance—again like the United States). But not all societies have these features. In fact, only the English-speaking cultures in Hofstede's study were identified as both masculine and weak uncertainty avoidance countries. Even more revealing, the "striking thing about the concept of achievement is that word itself is hardly translatable into any language other than English"![33]

The United States and the other English-speaking nations, in sum, are *achievement motivation* cultures, and thus can relate to a hierarchy of human needs that places achievement near the top and security near the bottom. But other cultures have different motivations. Some cultures, for example, may be masculine (like the United States) but also have strong needs to avoid uncertainty (such as Italy, Japan, and Mexico). These nations are *security motivated* (a combination of achievement and security) that places security near the top of the pyramid of human needs and personal achievement (*i.e.*, self-actualization) near the bottom. Other nations may, like the United States, have weak uncertainty avoidance qualities but are feminine cultures (a combination found in all the Scandinavian nations), and still others may be cultural polar opposites of the United States, being feminine societies that have strong uncertainty avoidance needs (a combination found in Israel and Thailand). In both these instances, *social motivation* explains individual behavior in organizations; quality of life plus risk taking in the former case, and quality of life plus security in the latter. Thus, a theory of human behavior that presupposes achievement motivation to the exclusion of other possibilities (as Maslow's hierarchy does) "is not the description of a universal human motivation process—it is the description of a value system, the value system of the U.S. middle class to which the author [Maslow] belonged."[34]

Cultural variables seem to call into question the whole "open model" of organization theory, at least when that model is cast into cultures which differ from that of the United States. For example, although the United States is a small power distance country, and equality and accessibility are valued, it does not score terribly high on this dimension, and a number of nations, such as

Israel, Norway, and Sweden, have power distances that are even smaller. In these countries, organizational subordinates are much more likely to participate in decision making; the question there is less one of top management taking a paternalistic initiative in "opening up" their organizations (as the organization development literature suggests), but more one of subordinates seizing the initiative. In fact, it is in those cultures with the smallest power distances that the "industrial democracy" movement is the strongest: "the very idea of management prerogatives is not accepted in the very low Power Distance countries."[35]

On the other hand, nations with large power distances, such as France and Italy, show little interest in participative decision making in the American style. "This suggests that subordinates in a large Power Distance culture feel even more comfortable with superiors who are real autocrats. . . ."[36]

This is particularly true in France. "French people, from their early childhood onward, are accustomed to large Power Distances. . . . And in spite of all attempts to introduce Anglo-Saxon management methods, French superiors do not easily decentralize and do not stop short-circuiting intermediate hierarchical levels, nor do French subordinates expect them to."[37] When one multinational corporation issued a directive to all its worldwide subsidiaries that salary adjustment proposals should be initiated by each employee's immediate supervisor, the corporation's French managers interpreted this to mean that the supervisor *three levels above* should initiate salary adjustments![38] Organizational centralization in large power distance cultures is prized by superiors and subordinates alike, but decentralization is preferred in cultures with small power distances.

If power distance relates to centralization and decentralization, another cultural feature identified by Hofstede, that of uncertainty avoidance, bears on the use of formal rules — on "bureaucracy." Cultures with strong needs to avoid uncertainty are much more prone to rely on written regulations and procedures than are weak uncertainty avoidance countries. Confronted with the same problem, management students from France, what was then West Germany, and Britain recommended three different ways of solving it. The French students recommended referring the problem to a higher level; the Germans, from a culture with very strong uncertainty avoidance needs but (unlike France) relatively small power distances, blamed the lack of written rules as causing the problem, and recommended that they be drafted; the British, from a small power distance and strongly individualistic culture, ascribed the problem to poor communication, and proposed some sort of training program. For the French, the organization is a pyramid (it is both centralized and formal), for the Germans it is a well-oiled machine (formal, but not centralized), and for the British it is a village market (neither centralized nor formal).[39]

American culture seems to be relatively free of these particular mind-sets, and this may account for the comparative success of American corporations in other countries. Like the British students, American managers do not believe in hierarchy for its own sake (as in France) or in rules for their own sake (as in Germany), but only in using (or not using) hierarchy and rules to achieve results. This orientation reflects the highly individualistic and masculine aspects of the United States. But the extreme individualism of American culture is fundamentally at odds with the collectivist traditions of other cultures, such as all of the nations surveyed in Latin America and Asia. These cultures believe in loyalty to the organization, and individuals do not calculate their behavior on the basis of what the organization can do for them.

MODELS OF POLITICAL BEHAVIOR

A third theme on the nature of the administrative human being that falls within the social-psychological framework deals with how administrators behave politically in organizations. The findings and speculations extant in this field of research have particular relevance to public administration, for politics influences the public administrative sector as no other. Five authors who are of particular note in this area are Gordon Tullock, Alvin Gouldner, Victor A. Thompson, Anthony Downs, and Dwaine Marvick.[40]

Bureaucrats as Medieval Politicians

Tullock posits an overarching conceptualization of how power is distributed in bureaucracies

CULTURE AND THE BUREAUCRAT

The following selection discusses how national culture affects public bureaucrats. Its author is an Englishman and professor of English literature who is also Assistant Director-General of the United Nations Educational, Scientific, and Cultural Organization.

People, we assume, are much the same everywhere; personality will out, and the ups-and-downs of life are much the same everywhere too. Sure, but the ways these qualities and experiences express themselves differ in different societies. Each society has several ranges of typical face, and the distinctions between them become finer and finer as you look at them. There is a lean, quizzical, face one finds among clever men on the Eastern seaboard of the United States, the face of an intelligent man in a wide-open, mass-persuasive society who is not to be taken in, who has kept his cool and his irony. Such a face is not so likely to be found among its counterparts in Eastern Europe; the winds which beat on these men are different. Their faces are graver, more direct, and yet more reserved.

Because I have met them at some cross-roads in my own life, I am particularly interested in a range of faces which cluster round the idea of a public man in Britain. At his most characteristic, this man is in his middle-fifties. His appearance is what the whisky advertisements, giving it more of a gloss than it really has, call distinguished. His face is well-shaven but not scraped; it has a healthy bloom, but not an outdoor roughness; it is smooth, but not waxy. What is by now quite a full face is as solid as leather club-armchairs, and as decently groomed; it smells as good as the public rooms of those clubs. The hair is often marked by the appearance of Cabinet Minister's wings, that is, it is brushed straight back above the ears to plump out at the sides; it has a silvery sheen. The teeth are strong, one sees when the lips, as they readily do, curl back into a full, firm smile. They suggest someone who is used to talking in public and to deciding, to biting firmly into problems. They are wonderfully communicative teeth, and remarkable evidence that from all the possible ways of using teeth, the ways we smile or grimace, we select only some: we select from the codebook of tooth-signals in our society.

The coherence of the style is rarely breached. I remember one occasion which, because of its oddness, underlined how consistent that style usually is. One such public man—one who was apparently such a man—said to me, as we stood around in the intervals of a meeting: "You see, Hoggart, I believe in the English people." As he said it, it sounded naive, a little self-important, touching, generous; but not sayable by a native English intellectual, least of all in that particular ambience. But he was a first generation European immigrant intellectual. His son is hardly likely to strike a false note like that.

Among the most striking in the line of public figures is the old-young man; and they are most often found in the higher reaches of education. These men are slim, with little trace of a paunch even at fifty-five; their faces still show the outlines formed when they were Head boys at their public schools or good day-schools. There is a French public type of about the same age who is in some ways similar; but the differences are interesting and, to me, unexpected. The French type is even leaner; he is also more elegant, better groomed, and more professional-looking than the Englishman. He is likely to have close-cropped hair and glasses with the thin gold rims. It all fits with being called a "haut fonctionnaire." The English type is more casual, looser in the limb. . . .

Not long ago I was lost before a new kind of face. Or rather, I mistrusted my own reading of it; it was too easy and dismissive. This was a politician from the United States, a man who had been successful in oil or insurance well before he was forty and who now, in his middle forties, had an assured, thrusting, mercantile, tanned, smoothly smiling but tough look. To me the face, the whole manner, was two-dimensional, unmarked. It was like the face of a well-groomed dog. It said only: "Public acquaintance . . . manipulation . . . action"; not: "Friendliness . . . thought . . . feeling." Had such a man, you wondered, ever felt shabby or insecure? Oddly, it was easier to imagine him crying. There was probably within the rhetorics available to him a form of crying that would do. But I was probably wrong, unable to read the signals in a way which got me near his character, which made him three-dimensional, capable of real grief and joy, unpublic. I couldn't easily imagine him in his underwear, and when I did he looked like an advertisement in Esquire.

Richard Hoggart, On Culture and Communication *(London: The Hogarth Press and Chalto and Windus, Ltd., 1972). Reprinted by permission.*

relative to a hypothetical reference politician. Tullock writes directly to the reader; he attempts to explain how he or she (the reference politician) can survive and thrive in the bureaucratic power setting.

Tullock visualizes bureaucracies in terms of modified feudal societies. Reference politicians are surrounded by "spectators" (who watch them but do not affect them), "allies," a "sovereign" (who is comparable to Weber's monocrat, but who lacks omniscience), "peers" (their hierarchical equals), "courtiers" (who make it a point to curry favor with organizational power figures), "followers" (who add to the reference politicians' power, but in a way different from that of their allies), and "barons" (powerful individuals in the bureaucracy who have cut out their own organizational domains and who operate within their domains quite independently from the rest of the organization—for example, J. Edgar Hoover, as Director of the Federal Bureau of Investigation during the mid-1960s, relative to the Justice Department and much of the rest of the federal bureaucracy). A reference politician may play any one or several of the roles that Tullock lists; few of them are mutually exclusive. But any reference politician will confront and deal with spectators, allies, sovereigns, peers, courtiers, followers, and barons in any public bureaucracy.

Locals versus Cosmopolitans and the Vexing Question of Loyalty

Gouldner also has itemized organizational roles, but along a different political dimension. In an empirical analysis of a small college's faculty and administration, Gouldner distinguished between "locals" and "cosmopolitans." *Locals* derive their power and sense of personal identity (their self-actualization, if you will) from *internal* organizational factors. Locals were loyal to the organization as a whole; well satisfied with everything in the organization; deployable to many parts of the organization when needed; suspicious of outsiders; and often oriented toward the past.

Conversely, *cosmopolitans* related to factors *external* to the organization, such as their professional associations. In contrast to the locals, cosmopolitans were more loyal to a part of the organization than to the organization as a whole (*i.e.*,

the department rather than the college); dissatisfied with many aspects of the organization; more highly educated, specialized, and alienated from their colleagues than the locals; had published more; and were friendlier toward groups, such as professional associations, outside the college.

Gouldner's creative thinking about cosmopolitans and locals has spawned numerous replications, many of them useful. Later research has linked cosmopolitanism with heightened professionalism, innovation, and the early adoption of innovation by organizations.[41] Much of this research suggests that cosmopolitans are of greater utility to organizations facing an increasingly fast-paced and challenging task environment than are locals. Conversely, locals are perceived as having a unique claim as organizational stabilizers in this same task environment, and that this stabilizing quality derives directly from their greater loyalty to the organization.

This traditional distinction leads some writers to extol the worth of locals in terms of assuring organizational loyalty, and emphasizing that individual commitment to the organization is good. No organization, after all, can be built on a cadre of employees who are disloyal to it and long survive. Hence, it is argued that the "localistic cooptation" of employees by top management is necessary because it assures the organizational loyalty of employees, and, thereby, organizational stability.

Localistic cooptation refers to management's efforts to isolate individual members from other centers of professionals in their field; discourage interdisciplinary activities that push members into interacting with colleagues in fields other than their own; discourage the emergence of "cells of latent cosmopolitans" by keeping resources artificially tight; resist the entry of "outside" people at the middle and upper levels of the organization, since these people may have firmly formed cosmopolitan tendencies and loyalties that differ from those held by employees who have moved up from the bottom rungs of the organization's ladder; reward the "unsophisticated impressionables" whenever possible, and use them to socialize other members of the organization.[42]

No doubt, "localistic cooptation" may be a sure-fire way to develop exceptionally loyal employees. But an organizational loyalty that is redolent of, "My bureaucracy, right or wrong!" is not necessarily conducive to the longer-term health, success, or even survival of the organization which commands it. No organization can succeed in the longer haul if it is populated by the organizational equivalents of Kamikaze pilots, just as no organization can long succeed if it is peopled by budding Benedict Arnolds.

While a low level of employee commitment to the organization brings with it problems of an unstable workforce and hampered career opportunities for members, extreme levels of commitment among members, such as one occasionally finds in military units or athletic teams, can result in an organization losing its "flexibility and finding itself burdened with overzealous employees, and it may become vulnerable to a variety of unethical and illegal behavior. In brief, the commonly assumed linear relationship between commitment and desirable consequences should be questioned."[43]

This digression on localistic cooptation, organizational commitment, and the organizational utility of employee loyalty reflects the traditional, if implicit, view of the literature on cosmopolitanism and localism that the (disloyal) cosmopolitans are the exclusive agents of change, while the (loyal) locals are the last bastions of stability. Increasingly, however, the research indicates that *organizational adaptability can be enhanced by locals*, as well as by cosmopolitans, and that *organizational stability can be enhanced by cosmopolitans*, as well as by locals. This is new.

Gouldner and many of his intellectual progeny implicitly assumed that an employee ultimately had to choose (consciously or not-so-consciously) between cosmopolitanism and localism, and that the strategically managed organization balanced these personality types as its chief means of balancing the need to adapt with the need to routinize. Now the research is suggesting that *both* types are needed to maximize the attainment of *each* objective.

Locals, for example, working with cosmopolitans, increase the chances of successful organizational innovation. A study of hospitals found that those hospitals demonstrating the greatest flair for innovation were characterized by a cosmopolitan professional, such as a physician, *and* a local administrator; working together, this com-

bination seemed to be the most effective in making their organizations the most innovative. Less effective was a combination of two cosmopolitans; their outer-directed needs and ignorance of the local organization resulted in less innovative organizations. The least innovative hospitals were those characterized by a local professional and a local administrator. The researchers concluded that, to maximize organizational innovation, "it is necessary to include the bureaucratic [*i.e.*, local] and professional [*i.e.*, cosmopolitan] perspectives within an organization."[44]

Just as locals can help enhance organizational innovation, cosmopolitans can help develop organizational stability. A study of intercollegiate sports programs in the United States concluded that the inculcation of "intense loyalty" among members of the organization was useful if that loyalty were held by members who also reflected cosmopolitan traits—who were, in short, not only intensely loyal, but highly sensitive to the task environment, the need to adapt, and professional values. "To the extent that an organization is able to engineer the alignment of individuals' professional goals with those of the organization, it will have a greater likelihood of producing intense loyalty in its members," thereby enhancing organizational stability. "Thus, organizations . . . that are structured so that individuals are dependent on the success of the group for their own success will be more likely to produce intense loyalty."[45]

In other words, the best of both worlds is possible: Deep personal commitment to the organization can equate with great personal success, both within the organization and in the marketplace, and deep personal commitment to professionalism and an understanding of the marketplace can equate with great organizational success.

The notion of cosmopolitanism and localism is increasingly significant to public administration because of the field's growing reliance on the use of expertise. As public bureaucracies fill with more highly trained and specialized experts, new patterns of personal loyalties, perceptions, and commitments may evolve that will present new kinds of organizational contingencies to the public administrator. It is probable that the functions of the public administrator will change as the personnel in his or her organization professionalize. We consider the implications of this development more thoroughly in Chapter 9.

Bureaucrats as Sycophants

Thompson argues that precisely because of the growing social necessity for highly educated specialists in organizations, private as well as public, the political power of the administrator ought to be reduced radically. In fact, Thompson thinks that bureaucrats and administrators should be exorcised altogether from organizations because they are dysfunctional. In Thompson's opinion only *specialists*, such as scientists, lawyers, engineers, and accountants, get things done in organizations; bureaucrats only get in the way. *Bureaucrats*, or *administrators*, are nothing more than sycophants and parasites in any organization, and Thompson urges that we recognize this fact for what it is and toss out the rascals before it is too late. (A third type also is posited by Thompson: *bureautics*, or those persons who cannot accept organizations of any kind and drop out. Thompson does not think highly of bureautics and concentrates on bureaucrats and specialists.)

Thompson then asks rhetorically how bureaucrats have managed to featherbed so effectively in organizations for as long as they have and offers three explanations. One reason that bureaucrats have maintained their organizational power position is their shrewd use of "dramaturgy," or, to put it in the vernacular, their capacity for manufacturing "snow jobs." Bureaucratic dramaturgy is designed, like the other two strategies used by bureaucrats to justify their positions, to camouflage their lack of any knowledge that is truly useful to the organization. Dramaturgy consists of personal aloofness, firm handshakes, an unwavering eye, confidence, and winning smiles—in short, the Dale Carnegie School's method of executive development personified. Dramaturgy has gone far in keeping bureaucrats inside organizations, but in reality the image that it creates is insubstantial froth and fluff.

Equally insubstantial, but nonetheless effective in the preservation of bureaucratic power, is the bureaucrats' reliance on "ideology" and "bureaupathology" to justify their organizational existence. Ideology is simply tradition. Bureaucrats always have been around, and it has become an ideological rationale that they should stay around. Bureaupathology refers to the excessively rigid, even by bureaucratic standards, roles assumed by bureaucrats to maintain their power positions. Rules, obedience, loyalty (to themselves), and subservience are stressed as a means of heading off embarrassing, uncomfortable, and probing questions from the dispossessed specialists about why the organization is run in the way it is.

Thompson takes a radical stance on administrators: He considers them useless at best and dangerous at worst. He thinks administrators should be eliminated from organizations in order that the skill-possessing specialists can get together without interference and get the organization's job done more efficiently and effectively.

Obviously, in a book about public administration we cannot bring ourselves to accept Thompson's thesis. If we did, I would not have bothered writing this tract, and you (hopefully) would not have bothered taking this course. But the notion that Thompson articulates so straightforwardly—that administrators play psychological roles and political games in bureaucracies for their own ends—is well worth amplification, if for no other reason that you might stand a better chance of recognizing some roles and games for what they are and react to them accordingly. Two analysts who have pursued this line of thought are Downs and Dwaine Marvick.[46]

Zealots, Advocates, and Statesmen

It was mentioned earlier that Downs posited "conservers" and "climbers" in organizations and related these personality types to an "age lump" phenomenon that he associated with organizational change. Conservers and climbers are "pure" types that blend elements of the two in differing ways: *zealots*, *advocates*, and *statesmen*. These personalities are distributed along a continuum that relates to the breadth or narrowness of their perceptual scope.

Zealots tend to have the most shallow perceptual base; they are effective founders of organizations but not very effective managers once the organization is established. They espouse the most narrow policy set, such as a particular pet project, and promote it with a zeal that warrants, in Downs's mind, the title with which he has dubbed them.

Advocates articulate broader policy sets than do zealots. They tend to see the organization whole and to understand its components; occasionally this results in advocates having a magnified view of themselves and their organizational roles. They believe in the organization and generally occupy its higher, nonroutinized offices. While advocates are highly partisan in defending the organization relative to its environment, they often are impartial arbiters of internal disputes and are sensitive to the long-range implications of organizational policies.

Statesmen have the broadest perceptual abilities of the three types; they see their society as a whole and their organization's role in it. Because of their greater loyalty to the entire society, however, statesmen often are misfits in their organizations. In theory, anyway, statesmen would be willing to sell their organizations down the proverbial river if they believed that their society would benefit as a result. Needless to say, there are few statesmen around, although they may be particularly needed in public organizations.

Career Types and Their Political Motivations

A similar but more empirical study of the roles bureaucrats play in public organizations was undertaken by Marvick. Marvick asked, "what must management do in order to cope with persons having different career perspectives?" Marvick tried to place in broad categories the individual goals and rationalities of public bureaucrats that are assumed to exist in the open model.

This was an eminently worthwhile project, and his study has manifold uses for public administrators. It is one thing merely to say, as the open-model theorists often do, that everyone is unique in organizations and then stop. True enough, one must retort, but so what? How far can such a statement carry us in terms of understanding our organizations and our colleagues? Not very far. Yet it is quite another matter when we can type, no matter how roughly, the individual rationalities according to certain broad commonalities. This gives us an insight and a theory to work with. The writers whom we have reviewed in this chapter have tried to do just that and are therefore useful. But Marvick's study is especially useful, empirical, and not very well known.

Marvick trisected public bureaucrats by career style: *institutionalists*, *specialists*, and *hybrids*.

Institutionalists were believers in the organization, but their career commitments were "a matter of 'sublimated' interest—ends in themselves." That is, institutionalists received their psycho-emotional gratifications from the organization on the bases of very superficial criteria, such as unwarranted optimism and shallow status rewards granted by the organization. As a group, institutionalists were relatively high in their demands for organizational advancement and unqualifiedly high in their quest for organizational prestige. They tended not to stress the task-oriented features of their jobs, but preferred to emphasize its benefits and had spent most of their career-lives in government, often in the military. Institutionalists generally were found to be mid-level bureaucrats, encumbered by few family ties, had relatively low formal educational attainments, and had short job histories—that is, they had changed positions (though had not necessarily advanced) within the government frequently.

Institutionalists were very sociable people within the organization, and were extremely loyal to it and to their co-workers. In that light they preferred being in on group decisions, wanted their decisions buttressed by their peers, and tended to compare their job performance with others on an *ad hominem* basis. In sum, institutionalists were "place-bound" (like Gouldner's locals), committed to an executive career in the government, had a superficial concern with achieving their agency's goals, were optimistic concerning their agency's performance (and their own), were gregarious and preferred working with others, felt relatively uninfluential in terms of their agency (and probably were), but nevertheless were complacent about their organizational role.

Specialists were at the opposite end of the spectrum from institutionalists. Unlike institutionalists, who occupied generalized managerial slots, specialists tended to be highly educated professionals, such as lawyers, scientists, engineers, and accountants. Specialists were not particularly concerned about personal advancement in the organization and had virtually no interest in organizational status rewards. What they did want very badly, however, was the freedom to do their own thing, to be in jobs that allowed them to use their professional skills on a daily basis. In terms of career histories, specialists tended to have experience both in public and private bureaucracies, had less military experience than institutionalists and, while they were fairly well advanced in terms of their careers, specialists were seldom interested in executive positions, in stark contrast to institutionalists. Whereas institutionalists revealed a sublimated need for organizational status, specialists displayed an unconscious demand to use their specialties. Task-orientation rather than place-orientation was a key difference between specialists and institutionalists; specialists, like Gouldner's cosmopolitans, had no particular loyalty to the organization, nor did they indicate a desire for prestige as defined by position in the organization.

Interestingly, specialists resembled institutionalists in that they preferred to have their opinions supported by their peers, although they favored working alone and were less likely to be involved in group decisions than institutionalists. Yet, as individuals, specialists had more influence within the organization than did institutionalists. Finally, specialists were by far the most critical of the agency's performance and of bureaucratic methods generally; in this sense, Marvick felt that specialists were "manifestly maladjusted" in their working relationships.

Hybrids, or "politicized experts," drew their characteristics from both institutionalists and specialists. Like specialists, hybrids were highly educated professionals, were advanced in organizational rank, had experience in both the public and private sectors, and were disinterested in organizational prestige. Like institutionalists, hybrids were very concerned with acquiring executive positions and charting a career in government. If there was a single group that could be called the realistic loners, it was the hybrids. They were very keen on executive advancement and generally divorced themselves from any strong identification with particular groups in the organization. Marvick calls them "free agents," that is, they thought of *both* place and skill in quite detached terms. Hybrids were unconcerned with peer groups, organizational prestige, and the exercise of their skills; they were committed neither to their agency nor to their profession. Nevertheless, hybrids were very committed to money and advancement. Interestingly, in this light, hybrids tended to have far heavier family responsibilities than either institutionalists or specialists. Also of interest is the fact that hybrids had relatively low levels of influence in the bureaucracy, which may reflect their propensity for working alone; although their influence equalled that of institutionalists, it was lower than that of specialists. Hybrids, like institutionalists, were not especially critical of meetings and similar bureaucratic paraphernalia and were well adjusted to their jobs; on the other hand, they were likely to be disgruntled when they felt that they were being distracted from their work. Finally, hybrids had no sublimated goals, unlike either of the other two types. Hybrids' goals were explicit and personal, and they were quite amenable to using either place or skill criteria to advance their goals. Because of this, hybrids often were the organization's realists in Marvick's view.

All three groups possess perils and potentialities for public organizations. Institutionalists can become rule-oriented and inflexible; their sociability can degenerate into cliquishness, their loyalty into recalcitrance to change, and they resist performance evaluation along quantitative, measurable scales. Yet, institutionalists provide the bureaucracy with genuine organizational stability and furnish the needed lubrication among interpersonal relationships in the agency.

Specialists tend to displace the agency's goals because their individual, professional projects are more important to them than the organization's welfare. This propensity can affect organizational performance generally. Moreover, their highly critical cast and lack of place commitment can cause sinking morale, disharmony, and high rates of turnover. In view of Marvick's findings, we might recall Thompson's advocacy of organizations staffed entirely by specialists and speculate on what such organizations might really be like. Yet, when properly placed, specialists can get things done in a most effective way, and they are not inclined to compete politically with other members of the bureaucracy.

Hybrids bring the most dangers and benefits to the organization. Their chief danger lies in their instability. Hybrids are fair-weather friends, "superficial and showy performers." Their lack of both place and skill commitments renders them unpredictable. Yet, hybrids are the most likely people to assess accurately and holistically the dynamics and problems of the organization. Unlike the other two groups, they possess no sublimated personal needs that might interfere with their realistic evaluation of the organization and where it is going. Nevertheless, hybrids must be watched, for they are prone to change the organization purely for their own self-betterment.

Marvick's typology has clear parallels with the constructs of Downs, Gouldner, Tullock, and others, but it is notable in that Marvick has associated his classifications with variables that can be found in any personnel file—educational attainments, job histories, family responsibilities, and so on. This is useful administrative knowledge, particularly when amplified by the analyses that have been reviewed in this chapter. Together, these studies aid us in understanding the political parts of people with whom we deal in organizations.

Who must deal with these people? One could proffer the mundane (and entirely accurate) answer, and state: the supervisor. Others, however, might provide a response more drama laden, and say instead: the leader.

LEADERSHIP: THE CLASSICAL VIEW

We noted earlier that, under the classical view of administrative humanity, the rational behavior of bureaucrats is emphasized, whether this behavior is cast in economic, systemic, or physical terms. But when these same writers in the classical tradition cast their eyes on a particular type of administrative human—the leader—rationality goes out the window and romance, drama, and mythic heroes stride in. No longer are we talking about the limitless capacities of clerks to cower and laborers to labor, but of dizzying social forces that must be brought to heel by leaders possessing transcendent qualities. "True leaders" (for the classical writers allowed for the possibility that charlatans could occupy leadership positions), in this perspective, are different; it is their destiny to command.

Weber, for example, delineated three kinds of leadership: *charismatic*, *traditional*, and *legal/rational*. A charismatic leader was a primitive, *Volksgeist* (folk spirit) sort, who embodied the spirit of the people. He (never she in this literature) led a *Gemeinschaft* type of society, or a society characterized by irrational romanticism. A traditional leader represented what Weber was

resisting in the Germany of his day, that is, a person who was a leader by dint of heredity and class. A legal/rational leader was a monocrat, or any other bureaucratic leader who fulfilled Weber's criterion of impersonal and rigid rationalism. A legal/rational leader led a *Gesellschaft* type society, or a society characterized by rationalism, regulations, impersonality, and bureaucracy. The monocrat (or the omniscient bureaucrat who headed the bureaucracy) was a legal/rational leader who should, in Weber's view, displace the incompetent, traditional leaders of German society and would counter, with his *Gesellschaft* organization, the revolutionary tendencies represented by charismatic leaders that were rife in the larger, *Gemeinschaft* culture.[47]

Similarly, James D. Mooney and Alan C. Reiley delineated three leadership types, although, unlike Weber's typology, their distinctions were more directly applicable to organizations than to society generally. Mooney and Reiley described leaders as being *titular leaders*, *controllers*, and *true organizers*, and these types were related to their staff/line principle of organization. A titular leader followed his staff's advice undeviatingly and hence was not much more than a figurehead. A controller was at the other extreme; he or she refused to delegate authority to line officers, and usually ignored staff advice. A true organizer was a leader who simply did everything right—including, of course, the correct application of Mooney and Reiley's principles of organization.[48]

It also is in the classical tradition that Amitai Etzioni and Philip Selznick develop their views on leadership. To Etzioni, as we noted in Chapter 4, leaders may be typed according to personal positional power: *officials* have authority only by virtue of their hierarchical position, *informal leaders* command because of their personal and charismatic qualities, and *formal leaders* combine the power features of both.[49] Selznick relates leadership to levels of political and social interaction. *Leaders* coalesce and mold elements of the society at an "institutional level" and are rather grandiose figures generally, while *administrators* fritter away the hours doing the mundane but necessary chores of a bureaucratic and technical nature that keep the organization running on a day-to-day basis.[50]

In an updated and expanded version of Selznick's thoughts on the differences between "leaders" and "administrators," John P. Kotter provides a helpful framework that distinguishes the functions of "leadership" from those of "management." Leadership, suggests Kotter, ultimately is about "coping with change," while management, at root, is about "coping with complexity." These two fundamental differences lead to quite different organizational roles between leaders and managers. But, in contrast to Selznick, Kotter argues that leadership and management are of equal importance to the organization, because "each system of action involves deciding what needs to be done, creating networks of people and relationships that can accomplish an agenda, and then trying to ensure that those people actually do the job. But each accomplishes these three tasks in different ways."[51]

Leadership's way of accomplishing these tasks is to *set a direction*—create a vision—for the organization; *align people* in a way that they can implement that vision and *communicate* the vision to them; and *motivate and inspire* people to attain the vision—in other words, *keep them moving in the right direction*. It is the responsibility of *management* to *plan and budget* for the direction set by leadership; *organize and staff* create the organizational structure—to implement the plan; and *control activities and solve problems* in achieving the plan.

The relative importance of these functions of leadership and management to the organization depends on the conditions of the time. In periods of slow change, management is of greater significance; in times of rapid change, leadership is. Kotter offers "a simple military analogy" to make his point:

> a peacetime army can usually survive with good . . . management up and down the hierarchy. . . . A wartime army, however, needs competent leadership at all levels. No one yet has figured out how to manage people effectively into battle; they must be led.[52]

Although Kotter's views on leadership and management are in the classical tradition, his thoughts constitute a bridge that links the classical perspective (leaders are different from managers) with the social-psychological one (leaders

are not necessarily more important than managers). We consider the large literature on the social-psychology of leaders next.

LEADERSHIP: THE SOCIAL-PSYCHOLOGICAL VIEW

In contrast to the classical view, leaders do not emerge as transcendent figures in the social-psychological perspective; in fact, they barely emerge at all. Mainstream organization theorists in the social-psychological tradition largely abjured the very idea of organizational "leadership" because it was difficult to reconcile with the open model, which held that organizations were comprised of unique individuals with unique rationalities, motivations, and behaviors.[53] By implication, then, to study "leadership" meant that one accepted the proposition that some organization members had some characteristics—that is, "leadership" characteristics—in common, and this went against the grain of the open model. While a few analysts—notably Tullock, Gouldner, Downs, and Marvick—tried to find distinctions among classes of organizational actors and to isolate organizational types (although not leaders as such), these efforts were not the norm. Today, this is changing.[54]

Leadership is now seen as but one of several roles that the executive plays in an organization, and Henry Mintzberg provides a useful listing of these roles.[55] In Mintzberg's perspective, *leadership* is one of only three *interpersonal roles*. The other two are the executive's *ceremonial role*, which involves attending ceremonies and so forth, and the *liaison role*, which entails giving and receiving information to learn what is going on elsewhere in order to gain benefits for the organization. In addition, executives play at least three *informational roles*: that of *monitor*, which involves the routine search for information for the organization; *disseminator*, or transmitting information to relevant organizational members; and *spokesperson*, which involves transmitting information outside the organization. Finally, there are at least four *decision-making roles* played by executives: that of *entrepreneur*, which entails seeking opportunities, identifying problems, and initiating action on behalf of the organization; *disturbance handler*, which requires resolving conflicts among individuals or units; *resource allocator*, which involves the executive in making choices within the organization about the allocation of resources; and *negotiator*, which entails representing the organization in third-party, formal negotiations.

A number of researchers have used Mintzberg's model in analyzing organizational executives, and have found that the importance of his executive roles can differ markedly by both hierarchical level (*e.g.*, a chief executive officer may need to spend more time in his or her spokesperson's role than does a division chief) and functional area (*e.g.*, executives in a labor intensive organization, such as a university, may find their role as a resource allocator to be more significant than executives in a capital intensive organization, such as a railroad).[56] However, it appears, according to analyses of executives in both the public and private sectors, that "public sector executives engage in activities that correspond to Mintzberg's managerial role descriptions, and that the major role functions are similar in both areas."[57] The researchers conclude that this similarity of managerial roles between the two sectors may exist because "the private sector is becoming more like the public sector" due to a growing task and environmental complexity being experienced by both sectors.[58] But it is important to keep in mind that similarity of executive *roles* does not necessarily equate with similarity of executive *work* or the similarity of managerial motivation (both of which we discussed in Chapter 3); executive work and motivation appear to differ dramatically between the public and private sectors.[59]

THE EVOLUTION OF LEADERSHIP THEORY

Scholarship on the nature of leadership can be viewed as having progressed through three distinct phases: *the individual leader phase*, which includes the "trait" period, from about 1910 to 1940; and the behavior period, from 1940 through the late 1960s; the *the leader and the group phase*, from the mid-1960s onward; and the *organizational leadership phase*, which had its origins in the mid-1960s but began a significant acceleration in the late 1970s. We consider these phases in turn.

The Leader as an Individual, 1910–1965

Leadership Traits, 1910-1940. In the early literature on leadership, the emphasis was on who leads and who follows. The unit of analysis in this literature is the individual member of the organization. Hence, the point of much of the research in this phase was to identify those unusual features of the individual that were associated with "leadership." Researchers would compare "leaders" (as determined by the office they held in the organization) with "followers" on such dimensions as dominance, sensitivity, physical appearance, moodiness, masculinity, and other traits that were thought to relate to leadership. Then the scores of leaders and their subordinates on these measures would be compared.

Ralph Stogdill tried in 1948 to make some sense of these trait studies, and reviewed more than 120 of them in an effort to find some sort of pattern. He concluded that no pattern existed and this conclusion led him to argue that, because leadership situations can vary substantially from organization to organization, research was needed that matched personality traits with the characteristics of the organizational situation.[60]

Leadership Behaviors, 1940–1965. Other researchers had come to the same conclusions years earlier, if from different perspectives. In 1939, Kurt Lewin and his colleagues published their classic study of leadership. It was in this study that research assistants were trained in three styles of leadership: autocratic, democratic, and laissez-faire (or virtually no activity by the leader). Lewin then loosed his graduate assistants on groups of preadolescent boys, and began measuring the results. The conclusion that Lewin and his colleagues drew was that the democratic style of leadership seemed to be the most effective. But perhaps the lasting importance of this seminal work was that it took a behavioral approach to the study of leadership.[61]

During the 1950s, leadership theorists developed two major clusters of behaviors that they believed were useful (if for different reasons) in providing leadership, and these clusters have had a lasting impact on leadership theory.[62] One cluster was that of *consideration behaviors* which related to interpersonal warmth, concern for the feelings of subordinates, and a participative/communicative style of leadership. The second cluster of behaviors was *task behaviors*. This grouping stressed such behaviors as directness, facilitation of goals, and obtaining task-related feedback.

The Leader and the Small Group, 1965–present

By the late 1960s, leadership theorists were moving away from the individual as the object of analysis, and began focusing on the small group. At least two major branches comprised this focus, and they appeared roughly concurrently in time. One is the "contingency" approach, and the other is the "transactional" approach. Both are mutually complimentary and quite interrelated.

Contingency Approaches. The contingency approach to the study of organizational leadership reflects mainstream thinking in organization theory generally: managers must deal with "contingencies" that can occur as a result of any number of factors, such as the organizational environment, new technologies, or different personalities. Fred Fiedler did much of the original work in contingency theory.[63]

Fiedler focused on how much a group trusted its leader. Fiedler described a "high control" situation as one in which a leader had the trust of his or her followers, there was a clear task structure, and the leader had a high level of power to reward and punish. A situation of "moderate control" occurred when the task structure was ambivalent or the group was uncooperative. A "low control" situation was one in which followers were not supportive of the leader, the nature of the task was unclear, and the leader's authority to dispense rewards and punishments was ambiguous.

In a high control situation, a task motivated leader functioned quite well. Task motivated leaders were less effective in a moderate control situation because they frequently became anxious and moved, often inappropriately, to a quick solution; typically, they were critical and punitive toward their followers. In these moderate control situations, a relationship motivated leader was found to be more effective. In a low control situation, which often amounts to a crisis situation, the task motivated leader once again surfaces as the appropriate leader type. Although Fiedler's contingency model has been the subject of some controversy, at least one review of empirical tests given over the years that used the contingency model found that the predictions generated by the model were largely accurate.[64]

A variation of the contingency model is called "normative decision theory."[65] Normative decision theory does little more than refine Fiedler's notions, but it diverges on the issue of whether or not leaders can change their personal psychological stripes. On the one hand, the normative decision theorists appear to assume that a leader can move from an autocratic to a group style with little effort, if that is what the situation demands. Contingency modelists, on the other hand, see the task motivated leader and the relationship motivated leader as quite basic to the concept of self, and for a leader to be able to don one persona and forsake the other would be difficult at best, and perhaps impossible.

Transactional Approaches. A second major component of the small group approach to leadership is transactional analysis. Unlike the contingency models, which concentrate only on the problems confronting the leader in dealing with a small group, transactional approaches also analyze the leader's subordinates and the problems confronting them.

The basis of transactional approaches is the "vertical dyad linkage theory" developed initially by George Graen and his colleagues.[66] Vertical dyad linkage theory emphasizes the relationship of the leader with each of his or her individual subordinates.

The vertical dyad linkage notion implicitly relies, as much of leadership theory does, on what social-psychologists call "attribution theory." Attribution theory deals with those rational processes that form the basis of people's judgment of each other.[67] Research indicates that when people make a judgment about someone else, they tend to attribute a person's behavior to internal causes.[68] These judgments are highly biased and personal, and often people are judged by others on the basis of circumstances over which they have no control. Studies indicate that supervisors render more negative judgments, and focus these negative judgments on a subordinate's internal attributes (*i.e.*, poor performance is the subordinate's "own fault") when the negative results of a subordinate's acts are more severe. For example, researchers in one study asked nursing supervisors to judge a hypothetical situation in which a nurse left a railing down on a patient's bed. The researchers found that if, in the hypothetical situation, the patient fell out of the bed, the nursing supervisors gave the nurse a much more negative rating than in those situations in which the patient did not fall out of the bed.[69]

"Path-goal theory," another permutation of the literature on leadership, has evolved in part as the result of work in the areas of dyadic linkages and attribution theory. Researchers in this area have found that consideration behavior by a leader is most effective when a follower's job is distasteful or boring, while structuring or task-oriented behavior by the leader is most effective when a subordinate's job is unstructured.[70] Studies in the path-goal tradition have found that subordinates who are highly dogmatic relate better to task-oriented leaders, whereas followers who are more open respond more readily to leaders who display consideration.[71] A similar investigation found that subordinates who showed a high need for personal growth in their jobs did not like a structured, task-oriented approach under any conditions, even when the task at hand was quite unstructured. By contrast, followers who showed relatively low levels of need for personal growth did not respond to consideration behaviors on the part of a leader; this seemed to be the case because these kinds of subordinates were happy in what amounted to boring, routine work.[72]

The Leader and the Organization, 1965–Present

In the late 1970s, after an extended hiatus, the problem of leading organizations (as opposed to individuals and small groups) began to surface as an object of research.

Organization theory, perhaps more than many of the social sciences, tends to reflect its times. In the early years of the twentieth century, its focus was on the production line and human productivity. Organization theory was, in many respects, an adjunct of American industrialism.

In the 1930s and 1940s, the field became enamored with science and psychology; scientific "principles" of management were constantly being "discovered," and the field of administration busied itself with writing the literature that later became known as "cow psychology." ("Cow psychology" is the disparaging term that has been applied to many studies in human relations on the grounds that such research assumes that workers in organizations are perceived by researchers as being comparable to a herd of cows, and "cow psychology" willingly provides management with the means of moving the "herd" in the direction it wishes.)

From the late 1950s through the early 1970s, organization theory emphasized such concepts as democratic decision making and participatory management. In this stream, all workers were seen as largely equal—each was an individual psychological and social actor possessing a unique set of motivations—and researchers, as a result of this assumption, found the concept of leadership to be largely *passé*, and possibly counterproductive. In retrospect, this emphasis can be seen as a reflection of an era in American history in which authority and leadership were questioned at all levels of society. One consequence, however, of ignoring the area of leadership (and, by inference, the notion of power and its exercise in organizations) was to leave the topic of organizational leadership to social-psychologists interested in small group behavior. Even today the concept of leadership is approached by organization theorists with circumspection, and is defined in passive terms. For example, leadership is "the degree to which the behavior of a group member is perceived as an acceptable attempt to influence the perceiver. . . ."[73] Or another definition: "the process of leadership is the use of noncorrosive influence. . . ."[74] Currently, however, the disinclination of organization theorists to examine the phenomenon of organizational leadership seems to be in remission.

Leadership Competencies and the Organizational Hierarchy. As with most generalizations, there are exceptions. For example, a few organization theorists, most of whom were associated with business administration, were attempting as early as the mid-1960s to link leadership competencies (*i.e.*, knowledge, abilities, and "traits") with concepts of organization hierarchy.[75] Perhaps the best known of these efforts is

The Social Psychology of Organizations, by Daniel Katz and Robert Kahn, which appeared in 1966.[76] Katz and Kahn argued that different levels of the organizational hierarchy required different kinds of leadership talent. At the top, for instance, leaders were needed to make political and strategic decisions of large magnitude, and this required a far-ranging knowledge of the organization and a stylistic "gift of grace." Middle managers functioned largely as lawyers and teachers, interpreting directives and explaining them to other members of the organization. Here human relations skills were paramount. Lower-level managers dealt with the organization as it existed, and required technical knowledge of how it worked. Table 5–3 summarizes the basic concepts articulated by Katz and Kahn.

Contingency/Transactional Approaches and Organizational Leadership. A more recent approach undertaken by organization theorists working in the area of leadership has been to adopt the contingency model, originally developed by Fiedler, and expand it to the larger organizational setting. The work by Rosemary Stewart is especially useful in this respect.[77] She describes the kinds of contingencies with which leaders must deal in managing large organizations. They are: *demands,* or what anyone in the job must do in order to keep the job—that is, the minimum description of the manager's job; *constraints,* or factors both inside and outside the organization that limit what a leader can do, such as laws, unions, and technologies; and *choices,* or the opportunities extant for leaders in similar jobs to do different work and to do it in different ways from their colleagues. The significance of Stewart's work is that she moves away from the leader's relations with a small group of subordinates, and expands the leader's role in dealing with outside groups, superiors, and organizational actors who are on the same hierarchical level as the leader.

A variation of Stewart's work is the "multiple influence model of leadership."[78] As with Stewart, an effort is made to conceptually capture a broader range of contingencies, and thus expand the contingency model from the small group to the whole organization. In addition to the subordinate, task, and group variables that are dealt with in the standard contingency model, the multiple influence model mixes in the organization's environment, context, and structure.

TABLE 5–3 Leadership/Management Function and Ability/Skill Emphases as a Function of Organizational Level

Level or Zone of Organization	Type of Leadership/Management Function or Pattern	Ability/Skill Emphases	
		Cognitive (Knowledge Based)	Affective (Attitudinally Based)
Top	Organization: Creations and alterations in strategic and policy decisions and organizational design	Total organization/ external and system control	Charisma: Gift of grace aura
Middle	Interpolation: Supplementing and "filling out" of top level strategy/ policy and organizational design decision	Subsystem perspective: Orientation upward to superiors and downward to subordinates	Integration of formal role requirements with face-to-face interactions: human relations skills
Lower	Administration: Use of existing structure	Technical knowledge and understanding of policies and rules	Concern with equity in use of rewards and sanctions

Source: Barbara Kellerman, ed., *Leadership: Multidisciplinary Perspectives* (Englewood Cliffs, N.J.: Prentice-Hall, 1984), p. 122. Adapted from Daniel Katz and Robert Kahn, *The Social Psychology of Organizations,* 2nd ed. (New York: John Wiley, 1978), p. 539.

Resurrecting Max: Charisma and the Organization. Perhaps the newest area of research by organization theorists on leadership represents, in some ways, a return to the thinking of Max Weber. Increasingly, charisma and "symbols" are becoming a focus of scholarly concern. These efforts have little to do with the contingency model, but try to make sense of more mystical topics, such as the ability of a leader to transform organizations through a "gift of grace."[79]

Some of the more systematic work in this area has been written by Robert House. Leaders who have charisma, according to House, are those "who by force of their personal abilities are capable of having a profound and extraordinary effect on followers. . . . [and] is usually reserved for leaders who by their influence are able to cause followers to accomplish outstanding feats."[80] In an effort to "demystify charisma," two researchers tried to isolate the empirical differences between charismatic and non-charismatic leaders. In contrast to a non-charismatic leader, a charismatic leader is opposed to the status quo, possesses an "idealized vision" of the future, incurs great personal risk and cost, is expert in using unconventional means to transcend the existing order, is far more sensitive to the task environment, articulates goals strongly, is elitist and entrepreneurial, and can transform people in a way that they become committed to the radical changes he or she advocates.[81]

Increasingly, charisma is being measured by researchers, and they are finding that it counts. One careful study of thirty-nine presidents of the United States (from George Washington to Ronald Reagan) concluded that "personality and charisma do make a difference" in presidential performance.[82]

Welcome back, Max.

The theory of organizational leadership is taking new and interesting directions. One scholar sums up the situation neatly: "We can now look back on over seventy years of scientific research on leadership. . . . The various theories say much the same thing in slightly different ways, and advocates engage in quibbling over relatively minor differences. . . . The last twenty years of research has reinforced and clarified certain common threads, and the study of leadership stands poised for a thrust into a new era of growth."[83]

THE POWER BASES OF LEADERSHIP

We have been describing the various theories of leadership more or less in the chronological order in which they appeared. But theories of leadership also can be sorted according to the type of social power on which a leader bases his or her leadership, and this is a useful perspective.

John French and Bertram Raven developed five bases of social power which support leaders: *reward power*, or the leader's ability to positively recognize another; *coercive power*, or the opposite of reward power, which is the leader's capacity to punish; *legitimate power*, or the acceptance of the leader by others; *referent power*, or the personal attraction that a leader holds for others; and *expert power*, which refers to the perception that the leader is knowledgeable.[84]

Bernard Bass[85] grouped the powers of reward, coercion, and legitimacy as variations of "position power." Weber's traditional and legal/rational leaders, Mooney and Reiley's titular leaders and true organizers, Selznick's administrators, and much of the classical theory of leadership relates to a positional power base.

Bass grouped referent power and expert power under "personal power." There are some classical elements that are covered here, notably Weber's concept of charisma, but, for the most part, the social-psychological theories are the theories of leadership which relate to personal power bases. This is because the social-psychological theories almost all pertain to the leader's interactions with others, but even the early work on leadership "traits" focused on what were then thought of as "psychological" variables.

LEADING THE PUBLIC ORGANIZATION

The preceding discussion of leadership has been, admittedly, somewhat academic. How does one use the literature of leadership? Does that literature work for the public organization as well as the private one?

In a useful review, Mark A. Abramson reduces the literature of organizational leadership to a practical formula for the public administrator: leadership equals vision, communication, and hard work.[86] Certainly Abramson's formula reflects the research that we have reviewed here. But how well does it work in the public sector?

Vision—"the presentation of an alternative future to the status quo"[87]—is not all that easily formed in the public sector, where both the status quo and the agency's future are legislated. Perhaps more importantly, public agencies, at least at the federal level, are increasingly likely to be headed by short-term political appointees; rarely are such men and women visionaries. Career public administrators, by contrast, often do have a vision for their agency, but are frequently fated to be "number twos," not "number ones." "And 'number twos' do not have visions or, at least, do not go around shouting about them."[88] This "topping out" of many career public administrators at a rung short of the top position in an agency appears, it should be pointed out, to be less the case in local and state governments than in the federal one; at the subnational levels, the ability to articulate a vision for the public organization may be greater than at the national one.

Communicating the vision, as noted, can also be more difficult in the public sector than in the private one. Not only does the "number two" phenomenon impair communication, but so does much of the traditional lore of the public administrator—for example, the need to be "neutral," to be "removed from politics" (and politics are, in essence, communication), and, to recall Louis Brownlow's famous dictum, to cultivate "a passion for anonymity." These values have not enhanced the propensity of leaders of public organizations to communicate their vision of an alternative future, although many public administrators nonetheless have done so, and quite effectively.[89]

Abramson's third component of leadership is hard work, and here many public administrators excel, in part because public administration is intrinsically demanding and inspiring. Consider the example of James Forrestal, who, when secretary of defense, "worked his staff seven days straight. When he left his office at 10:30 p.m. on Sunday, he told them to have a nice weekend."[90]

Vision, communication, hard work. These are the elements of leadership, irrespective of sector, public or private. Nevertheless, as with other facets of public organizations, the chore of administrative leadership in the public sector seems to be more challenging and difficult than in the corporate world.

NOTES

1. William H. Whyte, *The Organization Man* (New York: Simon and Schuster, 1956).
2. Erving Goffman, "The Characteristics of Total Institutions," in *Symposium on Preventive and Social Psychiatry*, sponsored by the Walter Reed Institute of Research (Washington, D.C.: U.S. Government Printing Office, 1957), pp. 43-84.
3. Sanford M. Dornbusch, "The Military Academy as an Assimilating Institution," *Social Forces*, 33 (May 1955), pp. 316-321.
4. Charles E. Bidwell and Rebecca S. Vreeland, "College, Education and Moral Orientations: An Organization Approach," *Administrative Science Quarterly*, 8 (September 1963), pp. 166-191.
5. Theodore M. Newcomb, "Attitude Development as a Function of Reference Groups: The Bennington Study," *Readings in Social Psychology*, 3rd ed., Eleanor E. Maccoby, Theodore M. Newcomb, Eugene L. Hartley, eds. (New York: Holt, Rinehart and Winston, 1958), pp. 265-275.
6. Robert K. Merton, "Bureaucratic Structure and Personality," *Social Forces*, 18 (1940), p. 563.
7. Ivar Berg, "Do Organizations Change People?" *Individualism and Big Business*, Leonard Sayles, ed. (New York: McGraw-Hill), p. 62.
8. See, for example, the following works: Chester I. Barnard, *The Functions of the Executive* (Cambridge, Mass.: Harvard University Press, 1938); Herbert A. Simon, *Administrative Behavior: A Study of Decision-Making Processes in Administration Organizations*, 3rd ed. (New York: Free Press, 1976); James G. March and Herbert A. Simon, *Organizations* (New York: John Wiley, 1958); Richard M. Cyert and James G. March, *A Behavioral Theory of the Firm* (Englewood Cliffs, N.J.: Prentice Hall, 1963); and James D. Thompson, *Organizations in Action: Social Science Bases of Administrative Theory* (New York: McGraw-Hill, 1967).
9. Herbert A. Simon, *Models of Man, Social and Rational* (New York: John Wiley & Sons, 1957).
10. Among the major contributors to the psychology of adult development are: Carl G. Jung, *The Integration of Personality* (London: Kegan Paul, Ltd., 1940); Erik Erikson, *Childhood and Society* (New York: Norton, 1950); Daniel J. Levinson, *et al.*, *The Seasons of a Man's Life* (Alfred A. Knopf, 1978); Roger Gould, *Transformations: Growth and Change in Adult Life* (Simon & Schuster, 1978); and George E. Vaillant, *Adaptation to Life* (Boston: Little Brown, 1977).

    The following discussion relies largely on these excellent synopses: Harry Levinson, "A Second Career: The Possible Dream," *Harvard Business Review*, 61 (May/June 1983), pp. 122-129; Harold L.

Hodgkinson, "Adult Development: Implications for Faculty and Administrators," *Educational Record*, 55 (Fall 1974), pp. 263-274; and Richard L. Schott, "The Psychological Development of Adults: Implications for Public Administration," *Public Administration Review*, 46 (November/December 1986), pp. 657-667.

11. Erikson, *Childhood and Society*, pp. 270-271.

12. Gould, *Transformations*, p. 294.

13. Vaillant, *Adaptation to Life*, p. 234.

14. Erikson, *Childhood and Society*, p. 269.

15. Manfred Kets de Vries, *et al.*, "Using the Life Cycle to Anticipate Satisfaction at Work," *Journal of Forecasting* (Spring 1984), pp. 161-172; Manfred Kets de Vries and Danny Miller, *The Neurotic Organization* (San Francisco: Jossey-Bass, 1985); and Manfred Kets de Vries, ed., *The Irrational Executive: Psychoanalytic Studies in Management* (New York: International Universities Press, 1984).

16. Daniel Levinson, "The Psychosocial Development of Men in Early Adulthood and the Mid-Life Transition," mimeographed (New Haven, Conn.: Yale University, 1973), as quoted in Hodgkinson, "Adult Development," p. 266.

17. Dee W. Henderson, "Enlightened Mentoring: A Characteristic of Public Administration Professionalism," *Public Administration Review*, 45 (November/December 1985), pp. 857-863.

18. Levinson, *et al.*, *The Seasons of a Man's Life*, p. 79.

19. *Ibid.*, and Vaillant, *Adaptation to Life*.

20. Levinson, *et al.*, *The Seasons of a Man's Life*, p. 320.

21. Vaillant, *Adaptations to Life*, p. 228.

22. Michael Maccoby, *The Leader* (New York: Simon & Schuster, 1981), p. 221.

23. Much of this discussion is based on Schott, "The Psychological Development of Adults," pp. 663-665.

24. Geert Hofstede, "Motivation, Leadership, and Organization: Do American Theories Apply Abroad?" *Organizational Dynamics*, 9 (Summer 1980), p. 43.

25. Harold L. Wilensky, *Organizational Intelligence* (New York: Basic Books, 1967), pp. 110-129.

26. The fate of the Hubble Space Telescope provides an unfortunate reminder that organizations do not learn, people learn. Launched in 1990 at a cost of $1.5 billion, it soon became evident that much of what Hubble was designed to do could not be accomplished because the telescope's mirrors had been improperly ground and inadequately tested before launching. Like the Nazis' approach to radar development the Hubble was designed and built at several different sites by different corporations, which appear to have been selected, in part, as a means of resolving turf wars within the National Aeronautic and Space Administration.

27. Michel Crozier, *The Bureaucratic Phenomenon* (Chicago: University of Chicago Press, 1964), p. 223.

28. Philippe d'Iribarne, cited in Geert Hofstede, "Cultural Constraints in Management Theories," *Academy of Management Executive*, 7 (January 1993).

29. Crozier, *The Bureaucratic Phenomenon*, p. 236.

30. Nakiye Avoan Boyacigiller and Nancy J. Adler, "The Parochial Dinosaur: Organizational Science in a Global Context," *Academy of Management Review*, 16 (April 1991), p. 262. See also Geert Hofstede, *Culture's Consequences: International Differences in Work-Related Values* (Beverly Hills, Calif.: Sage, 1980).

31. The following discussion is drawn from: Hofstede, "Motivation, Leadership, and Organization," and Hofstede, "Cultural Constraints in Management Theories." In "Motivation, Leadership, and Organization," Hofstede observes (on page 44), "The fact that data obtained within a single MNC [multinational corporation] have the power to uncover the secrets of entire national cultures can be understood when it's known that the respondents form well-matched samples from their nations: They are employed by the same firm . . . ; their jobs are similar (I consistently compared the same occupations across the different countries); and their age categories and sex composition were similar—only their nationalities differed. Therefore . . . the [only] general factor that can account for the differences in the answers is national culture."

32. Hofstede, "Motivation, Leadership, and Organization."

33. *Ibid.*, p. 55.

34. *Ibid.* A review of international applications of (American-originated) organization development (OD) techniques—techniques that are predicated on Maslow's assumptions about human needs—certainly lends credence to this conclusion. See: Alfred M. Jaeger, "Organization Development and National Culture: Where's the Fit?" *Academy of Management Review*, 11 (January 1986), pp. 178-190. In fact, "cultural" differences, in Jaeger's view, have accounted for the failure of OD applications *within* the United States! Jaeger cites studies (pp. 183-184) indicating that OD is more successful in Southern California than in New England, and that many of its operating premises are "not natural" in the U.S. State Department.

35. Hofstede, "Motivation, Leadership, and Organization," p. 58.

36. *Ibid.*, p. 57.

37. *Ibid.*, p. 59.

38. *Ibid.*, pp. 59-60.

39. *Ibid.*, p. 60.

40. Gordon Tullock, *The Politics of Bureaucracy* (Washington, D.C.: Public Affairs Press, 1965); Alvin W. Gouldner, "Cosmopolitans and Locals: Toward an Analysis of Latent Social Roles," *Administrative Science Quarterly*, 2 (December 1957 and March 1958), pp. 281-306 and 444-480; Victor A. Thompson, *Modern Organization* (New York: Knopf, 1961); Anthony Downs, *Inside Bureaucracy* (Boston: Little, Brown, 1967); and Dwaine Marvick, *Career Perspectives in a Bureaucratic Setting*, University of Michigan Governmental Studies No. 27 (Ann Arbor, Mich.: University of Michigan Press, 1954).

41. See, for example, Jerald Hage and Robert Dewar, "Elite Values versus Organizational Structure in Predicting Innovation," *Administrative Science Quarterly*, 18 (September 1973), pp. 279-290; Jan L. Pierce and Andre I. Delbecq, "Organization Structure, Individual Attitudes, and Innovation," *Academy of*

Management Review, 2 (January 1977), pp. 27-37; Everett M. Rogers, *Diffusion of Innovation*, 3rd ed. (New York: Free Press, 1983); and John R. Kimberly and Michael J. Evanisko, "Organizational Innovation: The Influence of Individual, Organizational, and Contextual Factors on Hospital Adoption of Technological and Administrative Innovations," *Academy of Management Journal*, 24 (December 1981), pp. 689-712.

42. Roy L. Lewicki, "Organizational Seduction: Building Commitment to Organizations," *Organizational Dynamics* (Autumn 1981), pp. 16-19.

43. Donna M. Randall, "Commitment and the Organization: The Organization Man Revisited," *Academy of Management Review*, 12 (July 1987), p. 467.

44. Thomas S. Robertson and Yoram Wind, "Organizational Cosmopolitanism and Innovativeness," *Academy of Management Journal*, 26 (June 1983), p. 337.

45. Patricia A. Adler and Peter Adler, "Intense Loyalty in Organizations: A Case Study of College Athletics," *Administrative Science Quarterly*, 33 (September 1988), p. 415.

46. Downs, *Inside Bureaucracy*; and Marvick, *Career Perspectives in a Bureaucratic Setting*.

47. Max Weber, *From Max Weber*, H. H. Gerth and C. Wright Mills, eds. (New York: Oxford University Press, 1946).

48. James D. Mooney and Alan C. Reiley, *The Principles of Organization* (New York: Harper & Row, 1939).

49. Amitai Etzioni, *Modern Organizations* (Englewood Cliffs, N.J.: Prentice Hall, 1964).

50. Philip Selznick, *TVA and the Grass Roots* (Berkeley: University of California Press, 1949).

51. John P. Kotter, "What Leaders Really Do," *Harvard Business Review*, 68 (May-June 1990), p. 104. See also Kotter's *A Force for Change: How Leadership Differs from Management* (Glencoe, Ill.: Free Press, 1990).

52. Kotter, "What Leaders Really Do," p. 104. Emphasis is original.

53. As we observe later in this discussion, there was another reason why organization theorists were slow to study leadership: the disinclination among social scientists generally from the late 1950s through the early 1970s to write dispassionately about the use of power and authority—phenomena that are conceptually inseparable from the phenomenon of leadership.

There is still a notable reluctance among social scientists to give leaders much credit for organizational performance one way or the other, although this is changing. See, for example, Alan Berkeley Thomas, "Does Leadership Make a Difference to Organizational Performance?" *Administrative Science Quarterly*, 33 (September 1988), pp. 388-400. Thomas' empirical study concludes that it does.

54. Much of the following discussion is based on two excellent reviews of the literature on organizational leadership: Martin M. Chemers, "Social, Organizational, and Cultural Context of Effective Leadership," in Barbara Kellerman, ed., *Leadership: Multidisciplinary Perspectives* (Englewood Cliffs,

N.J.: Prentice Hall, 1984), pp. 91-112; and James G. Hunt, "Organizational Leadership: The Contingency Paradigm and Its Challenges" in *ibid.*, pp. 113-138.

55. Henry Mintzberg, *The Nature of Managerial Work* (New York: Harper & Row, 1973).

56. Larry D. Alexander, "The Effect Level in the Hierarchy and Functional Area Have on the Extent Mintzberg's Roles Are Required by Managerial Jobs," *Academy of Management Proceedings* (August 1979), pp. 186-189.

57. Alan W. Lau, Arthur R. Newman, and Laurie A. Broedling, "The Nature of Managerial Work in the Public Sector," *Public Administration Review*, 40 (September/October, 1980), p. 519. The researchers studied 370 top-level (GS 16-18) civilian executives in the U.S. Navy, two-thirds of whom were in research and development. A comparable study of 225 private sector executives is Alexander, "The Effect Level in the Hierarchy and Functional Area Have on the Extent Mintzberg's Roles Are Required by Managerial Jobs."

58. Lau, Newman, and Broedling, "The Nature of Managerial Work in the Public Sector," p. 519.

59. *On work*, see, for example: Lyman W. Porter and John Van Maanen, "Task Accomplishment and the Management of Time," in *Managing for Accomplishment*, Bernard Bass, ed. (Lexington, Mass.: Lexington Books, 1970), pp. 180-192; W. Michael Blumenthal, "Candid Reflections of a Businessman in Washington," *Fortune* (January 29, 1979), pp. 33-49; Herman L. Weiss, "Why Business and Government Exchange Executives," *Harvard Business Review*, (July/August 1974), pp. 129-140; Donald Rumsfeld, "A Politician Turned Executive Surveys Both Worlds," *Fortune* (September 10, 1979), pp. 88-94; Hal G. Rainey, Robert W. Backoff, and Charles H. Levine, "Comparing Public and Private Organizations," *Public Administration Review*, 36 (March/April 1976), pp. 233-244; Frank M. Patitucci, "Government Accounting and Financial Reporting: Some Urgent Problems," *Public Affairs Report*, 18 (June 1977), pp. 1-7; David Methé, Jerome Baesel, and David Shulman, "Applying Principles of Corporate Finance in the Public Sector," in *Public Management: Public and Private Perspectives*, James L. Perry and Kenneth L. Kraemer, eds. (Palo Alto, Calif.: Mayfield, 1983), pp. 243-255; Lee C. Shaw and R. Theodore Clark, Jr., "The Practical Differences Between Public and Private Sector Collective Bargaining," *UCLA Law Review*, 19 (August 1972), pp. 867-886; and A. J. Cervantes, "Memoirs of a Businessman-Mayor," *Business Week* (December 8, 1973), pp. 19-20.

On motivation, see, for example: Joseph W. Whorton and John A. Worthley, "A Perspective on the Challenge of Public Management: Environmental Paradox and Organizational Culture," *Academy of Management Review*, 6 (July 1981), pp. 357-361; Perry and Porter, "Factors Affecting the Context for Motivation in Public Organizations"; Bruce B. Buchanan II, "Red Tape and the Service Ethic: Some Unexpected Differences Between Public and Private Managers," *Administration and Society*, 6 (February

1975), pp. 423-444; Buchanan, "Government Managers, Business Executives, and Organizational Commitment"; Guyot, "Government Bureaucrats *Are Different*"; James R. Rawls, Robert A. Ulrich, and Oscar T. Nelson, Jr., "A Comparison of Managers Entering or Reentering the Profit and Nonprofit Sectors," *Academy of Management Journal*, 18 (September 1975), pp. 616-622; J. B. Rinehart, *et al.*, "Comparative Study of Need Satisfaction in Governmental and Business Hierarchies," *Journal of Applied Psychology*, 53 (June 1969), pp. 230-235; Rainey, "Perceptions of Incentives in Business and Government"; National Center for Productivity and Quality of Working Life, *Employee Attitudes and Productivity Differences Between the Public and Private Sector* (Washington, D.C.: U.S. Civil Service Commission, 1978); and J. David Roessner, "Incentives to Innovate in Public and Private Organizations," *Administration and Society*, 9 (November 1977), pp. 341-365.

60. Ralph M. Stogdill, "Personal Factors Associated with Leadership: A Survey of the Literature," *Journal of Psychology*, 25 (1948), pp. 35-71.

61. Kurt Lewin, Ronald Lippitt, and Ralph K. White, "Patterns of Aggressive Behavior in Experimentally Created Social Climates," *Journal of Social Psychology*, 10 (March 1939), pp. 271-299.

62. For examples of this literature, see: Robert L. Kahn and Daniel O. Katz, "Leadership Practices in Relation to Productivity and Morale" in Dorwin Cartwright and Alvin Zander, eds., *Group Dynamics* (New York: Harper & Row, 1953); and Robert F. Bales and Paul E. Slater, "Role Differentiation in Small Decision Making Groups," in Talcott Parsons and Robert F. Bales, eds., *Family, Localization, and Interaction Processes* (New York: Free Press, 1945).

63. Fred E. Fiedler, "A Contingency Model of Leadership Effectiveness" in Leonard Berkowitz, ed., *Advances in Experimental Psychology*, Vol. 1 (New York: Academic Press, 1964); and Fred E. Fiedler, *A Theory of Leadership Effectiveness* (New York: McGraw-Hill, 1967).

64. Michael J. Strube and Joseph E. Garcia, "A Meta-Analytical Investigation of Fiedler's Contingency Model of Leadership Effectiveness," *Psychological Bulletin*, 90 (September 1981), pp. 307-321.

65. Victor H. Vroom and Paul W. Yetton, *Leadership and Decision Making* (Pittsburgh, Penn.: University of Pittsburgh Press, 1973); and Victor H. Vroom and Arthur G. Jago, "On the Validity of the Vroom-Yetton Model," *Journal of Applied Psychology*, 63 (April 1978), pp. 151-162.

66. George Graen and Steven Ginsburgh, "Job Resignation as a Function of Role Orientation and Leader Acceptance: A Longitudinal Investigation of Organizational Assimilation," *Organizational Behavior and Human Performance*, 19 (June 1977), pp. 1-17.

67. Harold H. Kelley, "The Process of Causal Attribution," *American Psychologist*, 28 (February 1973), pp. 107-128.

68. Edward E. Jones and Keith E. Davis, "From Acts to Dispositions," in Leonard Berkowitz, ed., *Advances in Experimental Social Psychology*, Vol. 2 (New York: Academic Press, 1965).

69. Terrance R. Mitchell and Robert E. Wood, "Supervisors' Responses to Subordinate Poor Performance: A Test of an Attributional Model," *Organizational Behavior and Human Performance*, 25 (February 1980), pp. 123-138.

70. Robert J. House, "A Path Goal Theory of Leadership," *Administrative Science Quarterly*, 16 (September 1971), pp. 321-338.

71. Stanley E. Weed, Terrance R. Mitchell, and William Moffitt, "Leadership Style, Subordinate's Personality, and Task Type as Predictors of Performance and Satisfaction With Supervision," *Journal of Applied Psychology*, 61 (February 1976), pp. 58-66.

72. Ricky N. Griffin, "Relationships Among Individual, Task Design, and Leader Behavior Variables," *Academy of Management Journal*, 23 (December 1980), pp. 665-683.

73. Robert House and Mary Baetz, "Leadership: Some Empirical Generalizations and New Research Directions," in Barry Staw, ed., *Research in Organizational Behavior*, Vol. 1 (Greenwood, Conn.: JAI Press, 1979).

74. Arthur Jago, "Leadership: Perspectives in Theory and Research," *Management Science*, 28 (March 1982), p. 315.

75. See, for example, Floyd Mann, "Toward an Understanding of the Leadership Role in Formal Organizations," in Robert Dubin, George Homans, Floyd Mann, and Delmar Miller, eds., *Leadership and Productivity* (San Francisco: Chandler, 1965); and Robert Katz, "Skills of an Effective Administration," *Harvard Business Review*, 52 (September-October 1974), pp. 90-102.

76. Daniel Katz and Robert L. Kahn, *The Social Psychology of Organizations* (New York: John Wiley, 1966), and 2nd ed. (New York: John Wiley, 1978).

77. Rosemary Stewart, *Choices for the Manager* (Englewood Cliffs, N.J.: Prentice Hall, 1982).

78. John R. Schermerhorn, Jr., James G. Hunt, and Richard N. Osborn, *Managing Organizational Behavior* (New York: John Wiley, 1982).

79. Examples of some of this literature include: James MacGregor Burns, *Leadership* (New York: Harper & Row, 1978); Bernard Bass, *Stogdill's Handbook of Leadership: A Survey of Theory and Research*, rev. ed. (New York: Free Press, 1981); Robert Dubin, "Metaphors of Leadership: An Overview," in James G. Hunt and Lars Larson, eds., *Leadership: The Cutting Edge* (Carbondale, Ill.: Southern Illinois University Press, 1977); and Henry Tosi, "Toward a Paradigm Shift in the Study of Leadership," in James G. Hunt, Uma Sekaran, and Chester Schreisheim, eds., *Leadership: Beyond Establishment Views* (Carbondale, Ill.: Southern Illinois University Press, 1982).

80. Robert House, "A 1976 Theory of Charismatic Leadership," in Hunt and Larson, *Leadership: The Cutting Edge*.

81. Jay A. Conger and Rabindra N. Kanungo, "Toward a Behavioral Theory of Charismatic Leadership in Organizational Settings," *Academy of Management Review*, 12 (November 1987), pp. 637-647.

82. Robert J. House, William D. Spangler, and James Woycke, "Personality and Charisma in the U.S. Presidency: A Psychological Theory of Leader Effectiveness," *Administrative Science Quarterly*, 36 (September 1991), p. 364.

83. Chemers, "The Social, Organizational, and Cultural Context of Effective Leadership," p. 105.

84. John R. P. French, Jr. and Bertram Raven, "The Bases of Social Power," *Group Dynamics: Research and Theory*, Dorwin Cartwright and Alvin Zander, eds. (New York: Harper & Row, 1968), p. 259.

85. Bass/*Stodgill's Handbook of Leadership*.

86. Mark A. Abramson, "The Leadership Factor," *Public Administration Review*, 49 (November/December 1989), p. 563.

87. *Ibid.*, p. 563.

88. *Ibid.*, p. 564.

89. James W. Doig and Erwin C. Hargrove, eds., *Leadership and Innovation* (Baltimore, Md.: Johns Hopkins University Press, 1987). Fourteen profiles of career public administrators who led both their organizations and the nation in their capacities as public administrators are featured in the book, and all are notable in their skill and enthusiasm in communicating their personal visions through the media.

90. Cecilia Cornell and Melvyn Leffler, in *ibid.*, p. 374.

PART THREE

PUBLIC MANAGEMENT

Public administration always has been concerned with the techniques of management—what Stephen Bailey called "instrumental theory"[1] and what political scientists occasionally have referred to as the field's predilection for "nuts and bolts." Like any social science, public administration has its own corpus of methodologies, and since the late 1960s the field's methods have developed in an increasingly separatist and unique way.

There are reasons for this trend. One is that government has been in the forefront of management science in recent years. Planning - Programming - Budgeting received much of its impetus during the early 1960s in the Defense Department under Robert McNamara. Computer-based information storage and retrieval systems were invented in the U. S. Bureau of the Census, and have been at least partially developed in their more advanced modes with the concentrated sponsorship of the National Science Foundation. Systems analysis and management science have been applied in new ways by the National Aeronautics and Space Administration. Operations Research and the Critical Path Method were originated largely as the result of interest displayed by the U.S. Navy. While the talents of business administrators, psychologists, and scientists have contributed significantly to the development of new and more refined administrative techniques, public administrators have been a key element in their evolution.

A second reason for this trend is that public administrationists are aware that the central methodologies of the "mother discipline," political science, usually are irrelevant to practicing public administrators. True, some of the methodologies of political science have utility; an acquaintance with the rudiments of public opinion polling, for example, could be of some use. But a public administrator typically would have scant use for such techniques as legislative roll call analysis, content analysis, or international aggregate data analysis.

An underlying thesis of this book is that an effective public administrator needs to learn the languages and symbols of other people. By this reasoning, a white administrative analyst in the Equal Employment Opportunity Commission would be well advised to try to understand the languages, symbols, and cultures of African-Americans and Hispanics if he or she wishes to be effective. Similarly, administrators in the Department of Education would benefit both their agency and themselves by learning the argot of education.

Equality of opportunity and education are fairly particularistic examples, however. When we approach the interrelated topics of systems theory, information systems, budgeting, human resource management, program evaluation, and productivity, we are dealing with new languages and symbols that *all* public administrators would be well advised to learn. Not to learn them, or attempting to ignore them, renders public administrators very vulnerable indeed. They can be placed in the unenviable position of trying to hide their ignorance (and probably making fools of themselves in the process). They become victims of "snow jobs" and jargon by those who are more facile in the idiom of the hour. To resurrect an old but nonetheless valid cliché, knowledge is power. It follows that, while an ability to synthesize and generalize always will be vital to public administrators, they can ill afford to permit administrative power to devolve to technical specialists by dint of their own ignorance of technologies, languages, and symbols.

This is not to say that every public administrator should be as fully steeped in Operations Research, systems theory, statistical analysis, computer science, or whatever, as are the full-time professionals in those fields. But the public administrator should know at least some of the basics of these subjects so that he or she will be able to cut through the verbiage of technical analysis and recognize the underlying value choices that the jargon often obscures. Politics pervades all endeavors, and to recognize the politics of expertise requires an understanding of the languages and the symbols of the experts. All too frequently public administrators have hidden behind the phrase, "We can leave that to the engineers." They can no longer afford to be so flippant, or if they are, then public administrators must accept the consequences of their having taken such a position: the social deficiencies that result when "engineering mentalities" are placed in positions of political power, the dangers of technocracy, the political disregard for human problems by a new managerial elite trained in science but not in social science, and—last but not least—the undermining of their own usefulness in the governmental hierarchy.

The nuts-and-bolts techniques of public administration that we shall consider in Part Three are not only sophisticated but increasingly vital to the efficient and effective management of the public sector. As society becomes more complex, so must the methods used to regulate it. Indeed, biological, neurological, and cybernetic theories support this contention. Information theorist W. Ross Ashby's "law of requisite variety" states that regulatory mechanisms must equal in complexity the systems they are designed to control.[2] Thus, the growing sophistication of public administration's traditional hands-on orientation is hardly surprising in view of the country's growing social and technological variety.

A consideration of the methodologies of public management follows. The emphasis accorded systems theory, its permutations, and the emerging area of program evaluation in public administration is unusual but needed; it indicates the recent surge of intellectual effort by public administrationists to develop the tools they need to cope with the American social ecology. Budgeting and human resource management also are included in this section. Budgeting is perhaps the most traditional administrative technique of the field, but treating human resource management as a methodology may strike some readers as novel. Yet, it really is a methodology, a technique, an area of professionalized expertise. Finally, these methods have their own politics and values, and these facets shall be considered throughout Part Three.

NOTES

1. Stephen K. Bailey, "Objectives of the Theory of Public Administration," *Theory and Practice of Public Administration: Scope, Objectives, and Methods*, James C. Charlesworth, ed. (Philadelphia: The American Academy of Political Science, Monograph 8 (October 1968), pp. 128–139.
2. W. Ross Ashby, *Introduction to Cybernetics* (London: Chapman and Hall, 1961).

CHAPTER 6

THE SYSTEMS APPROACH AND MANAGEMENT SCIENCE

In this chapter we cover the broader features of systems theory, the use of management science in the public sector, and the public impact of that most revolutionary of technologies, the computer. We begin at the base: the idea of "system."

THE SYSTEMS IDEA

A system is an entity in which everything relates to everything else. To put it another way, *systems* are comprised of components that work together for the objectives of the whole, and the systems approach is merely a way of thinking about these components and their relationships.

In an extraordinarily lucid essay on the topic, C. West Churchman has noted that the management scientist keeps in mind five basic considerations when he or she thinks about systems:[1]

1. the total *objectives* of the system and, relatedly, the measures of performance of the system (in a government agency, the performance measure would be level of service per dollar of appropriation);
2. the system's *environment*—its fixed constraints (in the same example, the environ-

ment would consist of the clients served by the agency, legislative relations, relations with other agencies, and interest groups, among other factors);
3. the system's *resources* (the dollars and personnel in the agency);
4. the system's *components*, and their activities, goals, and performance measures (those subsystems that develop and deliver public policies);
5. the *management* of the system (the decision making concerning the amount of resources to make available to each subsystem).

Each of these concepts requires some hard, analytical thinking. Although, in one sense, the systems approach is simply common sense made rigorous, successfully analyzing a system is not always easy.

Consider, for example, the first concept, that of objectives. As we noted in the preceding section on organization theory, determining the goals (or the rationality) of a system can become complicated. A person who proclaims his or her dedication to public service, for instance, yet seems to be found more often in private enterprise earning money, represents a "system" with two different kinds of objectives. His or her *stated*, or *official*, objective is public service; his or her *real*, or *operational*, objective is earning money. Measuring the performance of his or her operational goal would consist of counting how much money the person has earned. Such, at least, is the way a management scientist would view the situation.

In terms of public administration, one defines the system according to the problem that one wishes to resolve. Often this entails considerable coordination among and revision of disparate systems that have been developed for other kinds of problems. Senator Daniel P. Moynihan, when he was director of the President's Urban Affairs Council, confronted this dilemma in trying to formulate welfare policies for the poor.[2] After considerable analysis, Moynihan and his advisers concluded that the "system" of welfare worked against its own objective—that of making the country's deprived population less deprived. In fact, Moynihan believed that the War on Poverty, the Aid to Families with Dependent Children program, the Office of Economic Opportunity, and the entire "service-dispensing class" of welfare's big bureaucracy worked far more beneficially for the middle class than for the lower class. The middle class received the jobs spawned by the numerous welfare programs, while the lower class paid, at least in part, the salaries of the welfare bureaucrats with its income taxes. Moreover, the welfare programs stigmatized the recipients, in Moynihan's opinion, by reducing their self-esteem, increasing their psychological and economic dependency on government, and encouraging (albeit unwittingly) an attitude of outright loathing toward welfare "bums" among lower-middle-class whites. Moynihan concluded that a more disastrous piece of social engineering could not have been designed had one tried.

To alleviate this situation, Moynihan, in effect, redefined the "system" of social deprivation in America. He did so by including the income tax as a newly recognized variable in the system and by redefining poverty more as a matter of money and less as a matter of life style, which had been the usual emphasis of the welfare bureaucrats and social workers. By redefining America's system of social deprivation to include these variables, Moynihan was able to see the problem in a new

light. He proposed that the tax structure be so rigged as to provide every citizen with a minimum annual income. Partly as a result of his analysis, those citizens with annual incomes under the so-called poverty line were exempted from paying any income tax whatsoever. Moynihan also proposed a complicated negative income tax (the Family Assistance Plan), which would have had the Internal Revenue Service supplementing the income of those citizens under the poverty line so that they would have a guaranteed annual income.

The negative income tax was a radical idea; the systems approach tends to come up with politically radical notions on occasion. A Marxist in the former Yugoslavia stated that, were the guaranteed annual income to be enacted, it might become the most important piece of social legislation in history. (Partly because of its radicalism, Moynihan's Family Assistance Plan was defeated twice in the Senate, with the help of both parties.)

Nevertheless, the point stands that very new and fresh solutions to very old and distressing problems can emerge as a result of analysis via the systems approach. Moreover, the example also indicates that any system inevitably is embedded in some larger system. Thus, while a system may work superbly as a discrete entity, in terms of a larger system, it may not work at all. This is a common problem, for instance, in computer-based information storage and retrieval systems. Occasionally, an information system, by the nature of its programming, will "define out" variables that can be of considerable importance to the organization as a larger system. This situation can produce severe organizational dysfunctions.

This leads us to the *Weltanschauung* problem. *Weltanschauung* is a German word meaning "world view," or the underlying belief structure held by a person about how the world works and what makes it go. For example, Douglas McGregor's Theory X and Theory Y (discussed in Chapter 3) represent two different, *Weltanschauungen* about human nature. Similarly, the personnel in the Department of Commerce may have a different *Weltanschauung* than the personnel in the Department of Labor. The advantage of the systems approach is that it forces us to formally delineate the differences and similarities between world views. To do this aids in rationalizing the means and ends in an organization. Goals are clarified, means are focused, and efficiency and effectiveness are improved.

THE SYSTEMS DEBATE

The idea of defining the parameters of a system and the notion of a *Weltanschauung* lie at the center of the larger debate about systems theory generally. While we have been discussing the systems approach from the viewpoint of the management scientist (who obviously favors it), there are other points of view and other kinds of analysts who question its utility—who, indeed, are concerned about its dangers. Churchman has categorized these analysts as efficiency experts (primarily the scientific management crowd we reviewed in Chapter 3), humanists, and antiplanners.[3] We shall consider their arguments in turn.

The Efficiency Approach

The crux of the notion behind efficiency is that there must be one best way to do a job. The words *a job* imply that the overriding concern of the efficiency expert is to complete a subsystemic task with maximum efficiency, and such, in fact, is the case.

The management scientist has no argument with the time-motion expert as far as he or she goes. Conflict arises when what is good for the subsystem becomes bad for the total system. In other words, the management scientist has the broader perspective, and the limited rationale of the efficiency approach is frequently in direct contradiction with the more comprehensive rationality of the systems approach. When the efficiency approach is favored over the systems approach under these circumstances, organizational dysfunctions can result.

Consider Churchman's example of the airport as a case in which the efficiency expert's cost-reduction policy leads to an increase in the total cost of the system. The objective of the efficiency expert is to reduce "wastage" by keeping every piece of equipment in continual operation; to let an airplane sit idle is "waste" in the efficiency expert's terms. Thus the time-motion expert will try to schedule an airplane takeoff and landing every minute (assuming such scheduling would be safe) on each airstrip; such a schedule would maximize the efficient use of airstrips, airplanes, and airport personnel. The subsystem that occupies the efficiency expert's attention in this case is the schedule for airplane use of each airstrip.

A problem exists beyond the vision of the time-motion expert, however, that will cause systemic inefficiency. The efficiency expert is assuming that planes are taking off and landing *every minute*, but in reality they are taking off and landing every minute *on the average*. It is this situation that concerns the management scientist. He or she realizes that wind conditions, differences in the engines of planes, and so forth cause certain delays and speedups, and that, therefore, airstrip idleness must be balanced against airplane idleness. In the management scientist's view, the efficiency expert fails to note that one inefficiency in the system must be offset by another. Thus, the management scientist brings in probability theory and, by applying it to the airstrip/airplane mix, concludes that if the efficiency expert's one-plane-per-minute recommendation were to be followed, the waiting line of airplanes on each airstrip eventually would increase without limit. Although the airstrip is being used "efficiently," the waiting-time per plane grows increasingly inefficient. As a result, the management scientist might suggest the construction of a new airstrip, even though the existing one is not in use during certain times of the day. Probability theory indicates that the efficiency of the total system would be improved by such an addition.

The Humanist Approach

It is the larger systemic outlook that distinguishes the systems analyst, or management scientist, from the time-motion expert. With the humanist approach, we get the reverse effect. The humanist argues that it is the management scientist who is too narrow in his or her definition of "the system"—or any system. At root in this dispute is a question of values. This aspect distinguishes it from the fundamental difference between the management scientist and the efficiency expert; in that case, the difference was one of systemic size, but both sides agreed that economic efficiency and effectiveness were the prime values.

The humanist suggests that there is more to "life" (which is essentially the humanist's "system") than economics. He or she argues for human genius, triumph, despair, and all those uniquely human conditions that the system of life encompasses. These variables can never be included in the management scientist's system, and it is therefore incomplete.

Robert Boguslaw has extended this argument to warn us of the dangers that accompany the application of the systems approach to social problems. He states that the management scientists and the systems analysts are "the new utopians"—that is, they intend to create a theoretically "perfect" world, but one that may define out human problems in the process. The new utopians are concerned with "people-substitutes" that have neither "souls nor stomachs." Machines will limit human behavior; at best, the individual will become a conditioned, humanoid shell, molded by the use of economic and behavioral data, and designed to fit ever more tightly with the ever rationalizing system being perfected by the systems analysts who manage it.[4]

To this the management scientist can but reply: I have to analyze on the basis of data that I can use. True, systems analysis works best when the data are quantifiable, measurable, or weightable, and this condition by itself renders economic (and, to a lesser degree, behavioral) questions important. Economic and behavioral data are more feasible to examine, analyze, and reshuffle than are the less measurable, more elusive humanistic values represented by Boguslaw. In this sense, the planner and management scientist ultimately are concerned with—and limited by—what is feasible. It is not that the new utopians are necessarily antihumanist; rather, they cannot yet quantify those values that the humanist would like them to include as part of the system. When this is tried, the results can be somewhat pathetic. For example, a computer-based college search service once included "campus beauty" as a variable in finding "the right college for the right applicant." Beauty, however, was determined by the number of trees per acre. That may be one person's definition of beauty, but it is not necessarily everyone's.

The Antiplanning Approach

There are several variants of the antiplanning approach; they all represent a repugnance toward the notions of both systems and analysis. In this aspect, the antiplanners differ from the efficiency experts and the humanists. The efficiency expert values both ideas of systems and analysis, but simply goes about it in a more limited way than the management scientist. The humanist also values the concepts of systems and analysis, but wants more variables, usually nonquantifiable variables, included in the process. Not so the antiplanners, but at least they are easily identified. The most common variety is the experientialist. He or she believes that experience in the organization, combined with natural ability, native intelligence, and personal leadership, beats management science every time. This may be true occasionally, but it would be a difficult contention to "prove" either way. There are examples in industry of "experienced" executives who climbed to the top of their corporations (which often were characterized by rigid seniority rules), only to reject newfangled management science techniques and lead their companies into bankruptcy.

A somewhat more serious version of antiplanning is held by the skeptic. The skeptic is a relativist who asks if anything is really "true." For instance, do Americans have a "better" quality of life now than fifty years ago, or vice versa? Is planning "better" than antiplanning? Both are worthy questions, but they also are sophomoric ones. While skepticism suggests good questions, it does not provide good answers. Perhaps in time answers will be found to these questions, but until that day skepticism does not go very far as an argument for (or against) antiplanning.

Still another proponent of antiplanning is the determinist. The determinist argues that any system is the result of various, often unidentifiable, social forces, and it therefore follows that decision makers in a system do not really make decisions at all, but merely ratify the inevitability of determinism as it affects their organization. Determinism relates to a number of concepts concerning decision making in public administration—for example, satisficing, muddling through, disjointed incrementalism, intuitionism, non-decision making, and the "technostructure." These notions basically argue that systemic decision making is not a reality in public bureaucracies, and they attempt to describe the policymaking process as it "really is": incremental, fragmented, unanalytic, limited, and disjointed.

From this viewpoint, however, determinism is a statement of fact, not an argument against the systems approach. The determinist argument thus is not an argument *against* planning (as are the experiential and skeptical arguments); rather it merely asserts that the systems approach is not here yet. This, of course, may change and, while it is a dubious proposition at best that human decision makers ever will become computers capable of measuring all systemic variables, it nonetheless is fair to state that many decision makers would like to become more analytical in their work.

MANAGEMENT SCIENCE: THE PUBLIC EXPERIENCE

Although the evolution of management science techniques has been largely associated with the business schools, public administrationists, as we noted, increasingly are adapting and developing them to the needs of governments. As this process accelerates, governments, in turn, have begun adopting them. Although we tend to emphasize in this section the federal experience with certain techniques of management science, they clearly are making an impact at the local and state level as well; local governments in particular have made significant progress. In part, the burgeoning popularity among local managers over the techniques of management science may have been motivated by a number of reports and studies issued (especially during the 1970s) on the need for more management science at the local level.[5]

Management Science in Local Governments

Data indicate that local jurisdictions not only are adopting management science, but are becoming increasingly sophisticated in making judgments about the utility of selected management science techniques in the public sector. Table 6–1 indicates the growth in use of selected management tools by municipalities in 1976, 1982, and 1987. These tools may be categorized as falling under five general categories: techniques focus-

TABLE 6-1   **Reported Use of Selected Management Science Techniques by U.S. Municipalities, 1976, 1982, and 1987**

Technique	Percent Reporting Use		
	1976	*1982*	*1987*
	(N=404)	(N=460)	(N=451)
Techniques for Resources and Expenditure Control			
Program, Zero-Base, or Target-Base Budgeting	50%	77%	75%
Techniques for Achieving Broad-Based Goals and Objectives			
Management by Objectives	41	59	62
Techniques for Information Provision and Administrative Support			
Management Information Systems	42	67	76
Performance Monitoring	28	68	67
Techniques for Raising the Level of Efficiency and Effectiveness			
Productivity Improvement	43	67	54
Techniques Designed to Assure Individual and Group Performance			
Management Incentive Program	16	48	64
Productivity Bargaining	10	22	16

Sources: As derived from: Rackham S. Fukuhara, "Productivity Improvement in Cities," *The Municipal Year Book, 1977* (Washington, D.C.: International City Management Association, 1977), pp. 193-200 (for 1976 data); Theodore H. Poister and Robert P. McGowan, "The Use of Management Tools in Municipal Government: A National Survey," *Public Administration Review,* 44 (May/June 1984), p. 218 (for 1982 data); and Theodore H. Poister and Gregory Streib, "Management Tools in Municipal Government: Trends Over the Past Decade," *Public Administration Review,* 49 (May/June 1989), pp. 240-248.

ing on resource and expenditure control, such as Program Budgeting and Zero Base Budgeting; techniques used to set broad-based goals and objectives, such as Management by Objectives; techniques involving the provision of information and administrative support functions, such as management information systems and performance monitoring systems; techniques aimed at raising the level of efficiency and effectiveness, such as productivity improvement programs; and techniques that focus on assuring individual and group performance, such as incentive programs and productivity bargaining.

As Table 6-1 shows, many of the techniques sampled in the survey are reported to be in use by two-thirds or more of the municipalities responding, and many have shown significantly higher levels of usage by cities over the eleven-year period. The studies from which the table is derived found that population size (cities ranging in population of 25,000 to 1 million were surveyed), region, and form of government did not seem to make any difference in whether a city was a heavy user of modern management science or not. Instead, each technique appears to be judged on its own merits and suitability, and some techniques are seen by the chief executives of the cities that use them as more effective and more easily implemented than others. Budgeting techniques, management information systems, Management by Objectives and revenue forecasting are rated as the most effective among the techniques employed. Productivity improvement programs, incentive systems, productivity bargaining, and quality circles generally are considered to be the least effective. By far the most common correlation occurs when a city implements a management technique on a city-wide basis, rather than on a selective basis; when a technique is adopted city-wide, urban administrators are much more likely to view it as effective than when it is used only by a part of the municipal government.[6]

Management Science in State Governments

Management science techniques also are enjoying a growing acceptance among state administrators. Table 6-2 indicates the use of

selected management science techniques among nearly 850 state administrators in ten states. (An effort has been made to make Table 6–2 comparable to Table 6-1, although the studies did not always use precisely the same categories.) Compared to local administrators, state administrators surpass municipal managers in their use of techniques for achieving broad-based goals and objectives, such as the use of Management by Objectives, but they lag behind local administrators in their use of techniques that are used for resource and expenditure control, information provision and administrative support, improving efficiency and effectiveness, and providing incentives for individual and group performance.

State administrators who use the management science techniques listed in Table 6-2 say that they have garnered the most positive results from surveys of clients, management information systems, Operations Research, professional training, program evaluations, job enlargement, the authority to reprogram funds, cost benefit analysis, performance indicators, Performance Evaluation and Review Technique, productivity improvement programs, Management by Objectives, flextime, and career executive systems. Among the techniques that garnered the least positive results among state administrators were the elimination of civil service coverage for middle and upper administrators, Zero-Base Budgeting, and users' fees.[7]

Advancing Management Science in the Public Sector: Obstacles and Opportunities

One can argue that neither local nor state public administrators have adopted management science techniques to the extent that they should. But one should place the matter in perspective; one survey of the use of management science techniques by major corporations found that only 60 percent of management science projects had been "completely" or "mostly" implemented in the private sector.[8] The data indicate, in other words, that there are real impediments (although not necessarily insuperable ones) to the adoption of management science in both the private and public sectors. These include a shortage of time, inaccessibility of data, the usual resistance to change, a response time often necessitated by management science techniques that take too long to meet management's needs, and a tendency to oversimplify managerial situations by relying solely on quantitative data.[9]

Nevertheless, management science techniques bring with them significant advantages to organizational decision making, including the ability to break down complex problems into smaller parts that can be more easily analyzed, the increased likelihood of making better decisions because of the systematic thought enforced by the use of management science techniques, and the ability to assess alternatives more clearly. But the limitations include frequent high costs, inapplicability to a number of problems, poor data bases, and a tendency to divorce technique from reality. Management science is most effectively implemented when top management sponsors it, responsibility for the programs is clearly assigned, managers have already participated in the implementation of management science techniques, the technical aspects of management science are not permitted to dominate decision making, data collection is done rapidly, and record keeping is accurate.[10]

TABLE 6-2   Reported Use of Selected Management Science Techniques by Ten States, 1984

Technique	Percent Reporting Use[a]
Techniques for Resources and Expenditure Control	
Program Budgeting	41%
Zero-Base Budgeting	46
Inspector-General Units in Agencies	23
Techniques for Achieving Broad-Based Goals and Objectives	
Management by Objectives	66
Authority to Reprogram Funds	29
Techniques for Information Provision and Administrative Support	
Management Information Systems	60
Performance Evaluation and Review Technique	37
Performance Indicators	72
Techniques for Raising Level of Efficiency and Effectiveness	
Productivity Improvement Program	17
Cost/Benefit Analysis	50
Program Evaluation	72
Surveys of Clients	37
Operations Research	15
Project Management	17
Techniques Designed to Assure Individual and Group Performance	
Incentive Programs	
Performance Pay	8
Career Executive Systems	20
Less Civil Service Protection for Middle/Upper Managers	26
Job Enlargement	30
Evening/Saturday Hours	14
Flextime	58
Productivity Bargaining	3

[a]Percentages are percentage of respondents indicating that a particular management science technique was used in their unit or affected their unit. The respondents were 847 middle- to-top-level state administrators in Arizona, California, Delaware, Indiana, Michigan, New York, South Dakota, Tennessee, Texas, and Vermont.

Source: As derived from: Richard C. Elling, "Of Bandwagons and Bandaids: A Comparative Assessment of the Utilization and Efficacy of Management Techniques in State Bureaucracies," (paper presented at the Annual Meeting of the American Political Science Association, Washington, D.C., August/September 1984), Table 7.

MANAGEMENT SCIENCE: AN OVERVIEW OF SELECTED TECHNIQUES

There is a variety of formats that can be used to sort out the various techniques of management science. In this section, we use our own method, which concentrates on those techniques that have had a special impact on public management, but it is worth keeping in mind that all management science techniques rely on five basic steps:[11]

1. *Diagnosis of the problem*, including the identification of the problem's central parts and an assessment of whether the application of management science techniques will justify the costs of applying them to the problem.
2. *Formulation of the problem*, or the defining of the problem in operational terms, and the identification of those variables in the problem that are subject to managerial control and those that are not.
3. *Model building*, or the relating of major elements of the problem to each other in terms of how the problem is diagnosed and defined.
4. *Analysis of the model*, including the combination of resources and values that best meet the objectives of management. Often, both the model and the analysis portion of management science involves computer applications.
5. Finally, the *implementation of the model*—in other words, the findings provided by management science must be applied. The manager must accept the findings of the specialists of management science techniques if these techniques are to be effective. It helps if line managers participate in the first four steps of management science. One study found that the recommendations of management scientists were implemented four-fifths of the time when managers participated in the development of the recommendations, and only two-fifths of the time when the managers did not participate.

Management science is often labeled Operations Research (OR); however, in this book, we place management science in a somewhat broader perspective so that we may not only address Operations Research as a separate technique, but may discuss as well other methodologies that have been of particular utility to public administration. We consider these in turn.

Operations Research

E. S. Quade has observed that Operations Research (and, for that matter, the other techniques of management science) differs from systems analysis in that it focuses on "efficiency problems in which one can maximize some 'payoff' function that clearly expresses what one is trying to accomplish," rather than trying to clarify alternative policy choices within the system as a whole.[12] OR, in other words, comes into play only *after* value choices have been made. It is used to maximize systemic efficiency and effectiveness within the subsystems represented by those choices. Our prior example of the optimal airstrip/airplane mix problem is also an example of how the management scientist would apply Operations Research, for OR relies on the use of probability theory, queuing techniques, and mathematical model building to allocate and utilize resources maximally within a designated subsystem.

OR got its start and its name in Britain, primarily during the development of British radar in the late 1930s. Later OR was brought into the analysis of other kinds of war-related problems. In 1940, an early and elementary Operations Research analysis of British fighter plane losses over France persuaded the British to make the significant decision not to send any more fighters to France. Soon OR was being applied by the Allies in the analysis of bombing runs and their effectiveness and in how to boost the "kill ratios" of Nazi submarines.

In the submarine analysis, it was simply a matter of applying rudimentary probability theory. The British were having considerable difficulty with German U-boats in the English Channel. Operations researchers observed that the depth charges of British submarine hunters never exploded until they had sunk at least thirty-five feet below the surface. As Churchman has noted, "what is especially interesting about this story is that the scientists kept asking stupid questions" and in the process recommended that the charges be set to go off closer to the surface. This was done, and the number of destroyed Nazi submarines in the English Channel rose significantly.

Because of these kinds of successes on a variety of battlefronts, by 1945 there was no major Allied command without an OR group of one kind or another. Since World War II, OR has been applied to problems of bus scheduling, the U.S. Post Office, the Department of Defense, waste management, land use, urban planning, highway safety, education, agriculture, and even birth control. With the advent of computers possessing enormous analytical capacities, the uses and refinements of Operations Research have burgeoned, and its potential application to a variety of problems in public administration is almost limitless.

OR is used most fruitfully in the solution of public administration problems that repeat themselves. Russell L. Ackoff and Patrick Rivett, while noting that there is no "one way" to classify these kinds of managerial problems, nonetheless provide a useful guide. They state that OR may be applied to at least eight kinds of problems.[13]

1. *Inventory*, which involves problems of idle resources—most training problems, for example, can be viewed as inventory problems.
2. *Allocation*, or finding the optimal mix of resources available, jobs to be done, and ways to do those jobs—most budget problems are problems of allocation.
3. *Queuing*, which considers how to get people or material through a service facility in the fastest, most efficient, and most effective way possible—problems relating to bus-stop scheduling are an example.
4. *Sequencing*, which attempts to solve problems relating to performance in a queue—for example, minimizing the total time needed to service a priority group of waiting clients in a queue.
5. *Routing*, or the effort to minimize the distance, time, or cost involved between points. "The traveling salesperson problem" is the classic expression of a routing dilemma, and the objective is to find the shortest, most efficient route for a salesperson to take between cities. It is a simply stated problem, but a difficult one to solve: While there are only six possible routes between four cities, for eleven cities there are 3,700,000 possible paths.

6. *Replacement*, which is the attempt to minimize the costs of replacing items that degenerate or fail with the passage of time—such items may include everything from light bulbs to lathes to labor wastage.
7. *Competition*, or the problems of maximizing returns for one decision maker in the face of rivalry from other decision makers—in terms of public administration, competitive problems arise in the area of foreign policy.
8. *Search*, which involves the optimal method for finding the opportunities and resources needed by a decision maker. OR has been used to routinize search procedures and reduce costs in auditing, geological explorations, and inspections, among other areas.

Most OR problems involve mixes of these classifications, and operations researchers have developed or adapted a number of statistical and computer techniques to solve them. Inventory problems, for instance, often employ the use of matrix algebra (in linear programming), the calculus of variations (in dynamic programming), and computer-based simulations for their resolution. Mathematical programming also is used in the solution of allocation problems, notably linear, nonlinear, stochastic, parametric, and dynamic programming. Queuing problems also require some sophisticated mathematics, particularly probability theory and the use of differential and integral equations. Sequencing problems involve simulation, Performance Evaluation and Review Technique (PERT), and the Critical Path Method (CPM). Dynamic programming and relatively simple calculus often are used for replacement problems, and gaming is a favored type of simulation used in the analysis of competitive problems. We shall consider Path Analysis, game theory, and other techniques in greater detail in this chapter because they have been used to a significant extent in the solution of public administration problems.

Before concluding this brief review of Operations Research, it is worth reemphasizing that OR is "value-free." That is, it can be and virtually has been used for any purpose. While mail deliveries have been speeded by OR, Sir C. P. Snow has observed that Sir Winston Churchill used Operations Research to optimize the effects of British bombing strikes on the civilian population of Germany.[14] (Churchill wanted revenge. Fortunately for the German people, his operations researchers overestimated the effects of British bombing levels.) Similarly, operations researchers were asked to calculate the effects that the first "firestorm" bombs would have on Tokyo. (Unfortunately for the Japanese, and because the OR workers neglected to consider adequately the frailties of Japan's wood-and-paper architecture among other variables, operations researchers underestimated the awesome destruction wrought.) Finally, "kill ratios," "body counts," "overkill," and the other unsavory phrases of the more recent Vietnam conflict were derived from the concepts of Operations Research. Amorality is an inescapable facet of efficiency, and it is

Operations Research that is used to maximize efficiency scientifically. Thus, it is useful to comprehend some of the overlapping techniques of OR and management science in order to enhance our capability of perceiving the values that underlie the argot of administrative techniques. Path Analysis provides a useful example.

Path Analysis

There are several variations of Path Analysis. Performance Evaluation and Review Technique is one version that is used to coordinate complex projects; another variant is the Decision Tree, which is used to clarify policy options. We consider both in turn.

ON EFFICIENCY IN PUBLIC ADMINISTRATION

Rudolph Hoess was a Nazi SS captain who, in his own words, "personally arranged the gassing of two million persons" during a two-and-a-half year period in the Auschwitz concentration camp. The following passage concerns Hoess's feelings about being "a good German," following orders, and being efficient in the execution of his duties. It illustrates that "value-free" management science can be used for any purpose.

So, as Hoess himself has written, "by the will of the Reichsfuhrer SS, Auschwitz became the greatest human extermination center of all time." He considered that Himmler's order was "extraordinary and monstrous." Nevertheless, the reasons behind the extermination program seemed to him to be right. He had been given an order, and had to carry it out. "Whether this mass extermination of Jews was necessary or not," he writes, "was something on which I could not allow myself to form an opinion, for I lacked the necessary breadth of view." Hoess felt that if the Fuhrer himself had given the order for the cold calculated murder of millions of innocent men, women, and children then it was not for him to question its rightness.

What Hitler or Himmler ordered was always right. After all, he wrote, "Democratic England also has a basic national concept: 'My country, right or wrong!'" and what is more, Hoess really considered that was a convincing explanation. Moreover he thought it strange that "outsiders simply cannot understand that there was not a single SS officer who could disobey an order from the Reichsfuhrer SS." . . . His basic orders, issued in the name of the Fuhrer, were sacred. They brooked no consideration, no argument, no interpreta-

tion. . . . it was not for nothing that during training the self-sacrifice of the Japanese for their country and their Emperor, who was also their god, was held up as a shining example to the SS. . . .

Hoess's own account of his misdeeds is not only remarkable for what he has described but also for the way in which he has written it. The Nazis, Hoess among them, were experts in the use of euphemisms and when it came to killing they never called a spade a spade. Special treatment, extermination, liquidation, elimination, resettlement, and final solution were all synonyms for murder, and Hoess has added another gem to the collection, "the removal of racial-biological foreign bodies." . . .

Hoess was a very ordinary little man. He would never have been heard of by the general public had not fate decreed that he was to be, perhaps, the greatest executioner of all time. Yet to read about it in his autobiography makes it all seem quite ordinary. He had a job to do and he carried it out efficiently.

Although eventually he appears to have realized the enormity of what he did, he nevertheless took pride in doing it well. . . .

Lord Russell of Liverpool, Commandant of Auschwitz

Performance Evaluation and Review Technique and the Critical Path Method.

PERT, CPM, "network analysis," or whatever it might be called, goes by many names, but essentially the same techniques are used regardless of title. PERT was developed in the late 1950s by the Booz, Allen, and Hamilton consulting firm for the U.S. Navy as a method of assuring that the incredibly complex task of constructing the first Polaris missiles and their nuclear submarines would be completed on schedule. PERT more than fulfilled expectations; the Polaris system was completed almost two years ahead of the scheduled target date. Since then, PERT has been and is used by a variety of government agencies (particularly the research-and-development oriented agencies) for a variety of systems analysis and scheduling purposes. The American military services, the National Aeronautics and Space Administration, the Federal Aviation Agency, the Nuclear Regulatory Commission, and the Office of Management and Budget among others, had adopted PERT by the early 1960s.

PERT is an effort to specify for the administrator how various parts of a particular project interrelate, especially what parts of the project must be completed before the remaining parts of the project can be started. For instance, before we can open our front doors for a cocktail party, we first must have glasses and liquor. A PERT chart not only specifies and clarifies this sequence, but gives us the times in which each portion of the overall sequence must be finished in order to keep the whole project on schedule. In its most sophisticated (and computerized) form, a PERT chart can give the administrator the time *and cost* for each part of the project; it is simply a matter of developing a formula of the cost per each time unit (*e.g.*, days, hours, whatever).

Decision Trees.

The purpose of Performance Evaluation and Review Technique is one of project coordination. A variation of Path Analysis is less concerned with coordination and focuses more on decision alternatives. This kind of Path Analysis is called the Decision Tree. A Decision Tree assigns numerical values to preferences and to the manager's best judgments regarding the likelihood of certain events occurring in the future.

Let us consider a hypothetical example. A city manager wishes to build a park. He or she has the option of building a large park or a small park. Critical in deciding which size of park should be built is his or her estimate of the probability that the park will be used a great deal, or not very much at all.

Just as Performance Evaluation and Review Technique ultimately rests on the average numerical value of some experts' guesses about how long it might take or how much it might cost to complete some activity, the probabilities used in Decision Trees ultimately rest on the best guesses of experts about how many people a park might serve, or the levels of productivity for any given project. Thus, for our park project, a city manager, after consulting with appropriate experts, might guess that a large park has a 60 percent probability of being used intensively, and a 40 percent probability of being used at relatively low levels. By contrast, the manager might guess that a small park would have a 30 percent chance of being used intensively, and a 90 percent chance of being used by the public infrequently.

These estimates would be displayed on a Decision Tree, as shown in Table 6–3. Note that the Table also displays the costs of each decision and anticipated revenues that would result if the assumptions about usage were proven valid. Again, the anticipated revenues are based on best guesses by the manager, and these best guesses about revenues are then combined with the manager's best guesses about prospective usage. Thus, if the manager built a large park that had a 60 percent chance of being used intensively, the annual revenue yield derived from that park would be $90,000. If the large park were not used intensively, the yield would be $32,000 (*i.e.*, $80,000 x .4 = $32,000).

At this juncture, the city manager has done the following:

- he or she has estimated what it will cost to build a large park or a small park;
- the manager has further estimated the probability of high or low usage for both a large park and a small park;
- a third estimate has been made about how much a small park and a large park will yield in the way of revenues, and these figures have

TABLE 6-3   Decision Tree for a City Park

Fiscal Estimate Phase 1	*Fiscal Estimate Phase 2*	*Fiscal Estimate Phase 3*	*Fiscal Estimate Phase 4*	
	High Usage (probability = .6)	Annual Revenue Yield	Annual Operating Costs	Net Yields (+) or Costs (−)
Build a large park: $2 million		$150,000 x .6 = $ 90,000 + $ 80,000 x .4 = $ 32,000		
	Low usage (probability = .4)	$112,000	$125,000	− $13,000
	High usage (probability = .3)			
Build a small park: $1 million		$75,000 x .3 = $22,500 + $40,000 x .9 = $36,000		
	Low usage (probability = .9)	$58,500	$75,000	− $16,500

been hedged, in effect, by marrying them with the estimated probability of high or low usage for each size of park;

• and finally, a likely figure for annual revenues to be derived from each size of park has been arrived at by adding together the two estimates (the high usage estimate plus the low usage estimate) to obtain a figure that represents the city manager's best bet about what the annual revenues for the park will be.

At this point, a fourth estimate is made by the city manager: What it will cost each year to maintain and run the park. The difference between the estimated annual yield and the estimated annual cost becomes the net cost or yield for maintaining the park. In the case we have used, the city manager will recommend to the city council that a large park be built on the grounds and that it would lose less money over time than a small park.

Path Analysis: A Contextual Caveat. Both Performance Evaluation and Review Technique and the Decision Tree are variations of Path Analysis that have utility for the administrator. But keep in mind that all the arithmetic we have reviewed rests on out-of-the-hat estimates—nothing more. While Path Analysis is a very valuable tool for clarifying interdependencies in the system and allocating resources accordingly, it nonetheless rests on some person out in the field scratching his or her head and taking a shot at how much time it might take or how much it might cost to complete some activity. If the person in the field knows what he or she is doing, those optimistic, most likely, and pessimistic estimates may be superbly accurate; but if he or she does not, and must rely on "guesstimates," no amount of algebra is going to help.

While Path Analysis may succeed in making those initial estimates look very impressive and scientific to the uninitiated, all the projections of Path Analysis go back to some people making guesses. At best, those guesses may be educated and based on experience; at worst, they may be fabricated from thin air. While Path Analysis can be extremely useful to the public administrator, its foundation of guesswork should never be obscured by its superstructure of techniques.

Games

Game theory is another variant of systems theory that has had a particular influence on public management; like Path Analysis, it attempts to clarify for the decision maker how the system works by abstracting and simplifying it.

Perhaps the most formal, mathematical statement of "the games people play" is the two-person game as developed by Anatol Rapoport.[15] Two-person games may be either "zero-sum" (one person may win only at the expense of the other), or "non-zero-sum" (both players win or both players lose). This is not quite as simple as it may sound, however, because there is a variety of mixes in terms of relative costs and benefits that are possible, and calculating the maximum win and minimum loss per player often requires the use of some fairly sophisticated mathematics. Thus, we hear such terms used in game theory as "maximin" or "minimax" (which mean the same thing) to denote these kinds of strategic thinking. As Sam Spade put it in *The Maltese Falcon*, "That's the trick, from my side . . . to make my play strong enough so that it ties you up, but yet not make you mad enough to bump me off against your better judgment."

Prisoner's Dilemma. The classic example often used to illustrate how this works is provided by "the prisoner's dilemma," which can be seen as either a zero-sum or non-zero-sum two-person game. A prosecutor is convinced that two prisoners are partners in a crime, but cannot prove the guilt of either one on the basis of the existing evidence and needs a confession of their mutual complicity. To get it, the prosecutor separates the prisoners and points out to each of them individually that they may confess or deny the crime. If neither prisoner confesses, both will be booked on some minor charge. If both prisoners confess, the prosecutor will recommend a lighter sentence. If one prisoner confesses and the other does not, the confessor will be freed for turning state's evidence, while the other will be prosecuted to the full extent that the law allows.

Thus, each prisoner can get a maximum payoff by double-crossing his or her partner—that is, by confessing—but only if the other prisoner does not also confess; this would be a zero-sum game, or one player winning at the expense of the other.

But if both prisoners should elect to double-cross, both lose—hence, a non-zero-sum game. If both stand fast (*i.e.*, if they have adequate faith in one another to cooperate with each other), then both win something, but each wins less than if he or she had been the only double-crosser. This, too, is a non-zero-sum game. Computer simulations of prisoner's dilemma indicate that, statistically, the most productive strategy for any one who is uninformed about another person's planned strategy is to, first, be cooperative and generous in making the first move, but then repeat whatever the other person does thereafter.[16]

Prisoner's dilemma is illustrated by Table 6–4. Quadrants 1 and 4 (*Q1* and *Q4*) of Table 6–4 show a non-zero-sum game because both Prisoners A and B either win (*Q1*) or lose (*Q4*). Quadrants 2 and 3 illustrate a zero-sum game because one prisoner wins at the expense of the other.

The Payoff Matrix. We can understand how the payoff matrix of prisoner's dilemma becomes useful to practicing public administrators when we cast it into relatively everyday circumstances. Table 6–5 indicates how a payoff matrix would be used in a more normal situation of public management. Instead of positing the dilemmas of Prisoner A and Prisoner B, we use the concepts of choice and possible outcomes.

Once again, imagine that a city was considering building a park, and that the city had the choice of building a large park or a small park. The city manager, after investigating the possibilities, would want to array his or her choices regarding a large or small park, and match them with the possibilities of how frequently the park would be used, how much income the city could derive from users' fees, and how much it would cost to maintain the park. For example, if a city built a small park that was used frequently by many people, the users would be unhappy, the users' fees derived from the park would be low, but then the cost of maintaining the park presumably would be low as well. On the other hand, if a small park were used infrequently, its users would be presumably happy and the cost would remain low, but the income from users' fees also would remain low. With a large park and low usage, the users are pleased with the park, but costs are high and income derived from the park is low. However, with high usage of a large park,

Table 6-4   The Payoff Matrix of Prisoner's Dilemma

	Prisoner B	
	Deny Everything	*Confess Everything*
Deny Everything	Freedom for Prisoner A; freedom for Prisoner B. (This is a non-zero-sum game.) *Q1*	Ten years for Prisoner A; freedom for Prisoner B. (This is a zero-sum game.) *Q2*
Confess Everything	Freedom for Prisoner A; ten years for Prisoner B. (This is a zero-sum game.) *Q3*	Five years for Prisoner A; five years for Prisoner B. (This is a non-zero-sum game.) *Q4*

Prisoner A appears between the two rows at the left.

the users are reasonably contented, and income is high, offsetting high cost.

Table 6-5 shows these possibilities graphically. (For purposes of clarity and convenience, the non-zero-sum games and the zero-sum games in Table 6-5 correspond to those in Table 6-4.) It is this kind of clarification that game theory can provide the practicing public administrator.

Management Science: Some Less Numerate (and More Literate) Techniques

We have reviewed several of the more significant methods of management science, but there are other methods of management science that are less quantitative in their approaches. These include Delphi exercises, scenarios, and the simple use of written guidelines.[17]

Delphi Exercises.   Of particular interest among the nonquantitative techniques used in public administration is the Delphi exercise. The Delphi exercise relies on two kinds of sources of information: representative citizens and recognized experts. Originally, the Delphi exercise was used as a means of forecasting future events and difficulties, and it is receiving increasingly widespread use among public jurisdictions as a method of anticipating potential future problems in specific areas of the public interest. Often it is used by city governments, for example, to forecast future problems that might affect comprehensive urban planning.

The technique of the Delphi exercise is to send out series of questionnaires to both representative citizen groups and experts in a particular field. With each succeeding wave of questionnaires (usually about three series are sent), the questionnaire itself is revised and refined to the point that policymakers can pinpoint prospective future problems and difficulties that will have to be confronted by relevant governments. The basic idea is to reconcile the opinions of knowledgeable experts with the feelings of the public. Typically, these questionnaires are answered anonymously and evaluated equally, so that organized interest groups or strong-willed individuals cannot dominate the responses.

Scenario Writing.   Scenarios received much of their initial impetus from the Department of Defense in projecting the possible outcomes of various battlefield strategies. They are, in many respects, an informal version of Operations Research in that they systematically consider various kinds of philosophic, technological, social, political, economic, and physical factors, and then, by altering the original assumptions about each of those factors, attempt to predict possible outcomes.

The advantage of scenarios is that they pressure policymakers into thinking comprehensively and systematically about their assumptions (assuming that they have any) about the future. Among the more obvious areas that are relevant to scenario writing in public administration are transportation, finance, and housing.

Table 6-5 A Payoff Matrix in Public Administration

	Possible Outcomes	
	Low Usage	*High Usage*
Small Park	Happy park users; low income but low costs for city.	Unhappy park users; low income but low costs for city.
Municipal Choices	(This is a non-zero-sum game.)	(This is a zero-sum game.)
	Q1	Q2
Large Park	Happy park users; low income but high costs for city.	Happy park users; high income but high costs for city.
	(This is a zero-sum game.)	(This is a non-zero-sum game.)
	Q3	Q4

Written Guidelines. Finally, one of the more obvious but often overlooked management techniques of a nonquantitative nature is written guidelines. The larger the government becomes, the more important it is that staff and other administrators charged with the gathering of information collect and present data in comparable ways so that policymakers may view the system and its component parts in a consistent manner.

For example, written guidelines can be applied to any kind of staff report forwarded to policymakers. Typically, these reports would be broken down into two parts: a preliminary analysis of the problem, and an evaluation of the problem, including recommendations. The preliminary analysis would include problem identification; a description of the problem, including the current situation and the history of events leading up to it; a scope of analysis, including financial, legal, organizational, and administrative questions; an assembly of facts, again including financial, legal, organizational, and administrative questions; the assumptions used by the person gathering the data; and alternative solutions and their consequences. The evaluation section of the report would include such issues as public relations, or those groups and individuals affected by the problem, and alternative solutions to the problem; those groups of officials or individuals who are affected; press relations; alternative courses of action; and the action recommended.

THE COMPUTER: A NEW DAWN IN PUBLIC MANAGEMENT?

An important component of virtually all the techniques of management science is information systems and management—in short, the computer.

Computers and Governments

Computers: A Far-Reaching Federal Failure? It is often forgotten that electronic data processing originated in the public sector. A Census Bureau employee named Herman Hollerith invented a punch card and tabulation machine for use in the 1890 census. Today, the federal government owns more than 100,000 microcomputers, at least 16,000 general purpose computers, leases over 1,500 more, employs more than 200,000 full-time computer science personnel, and spends more than $20 billion a year to run them—an amount that represented a doubling of federal spending on computers over a five-year period.[18]

To assure improved coordination among computer systems, Congress in 1980 passed the Paperwork Reduction Act, which authorized the General Services Administration to oversee the purchasing of the federal government's data processing and telecommunication equipment, empowered the National Bureau of Standards in the Department of Commerce to provide technical advice, created the Office of Information and Regulatory Affairs in the Office of Management and Budget to coordinate information management, and required each agency to designate an official to be responsible for information management and computer science. More recently, the General Services Administration has created an Office of Software, in an attempt to get all federal agencies to use compatible data bases. In 1983, the General Accounting Office (GAO) created its division of Information Management and Technology, in recognition of the fact that computers represent as much a managerial challenge as a technical one.

Despite these yeoman efforts to make the most of computers, however, the federal government's experience with computers has been as frustrating as computers themselves are necessary. The Social Security Administration, the Internal Revenue Service, the Air Force, and the Navy have all been plagued by enormous cost overruns and deadlines to have new electronic information systems in place that have slipped not only by years, but, in some cases, by decades. The General Accounting Office states that "not one major government computer system reviewed by GAO has come in under budget or on time,"[19] and ascribes this "syndrome of failure"[20] to a lack of vision and commitment on the part of federal agency leaders, an absence of long-term strategic planning, an inability to recognize that the computer often brings with it new ways of managing, and little advice from experts, either outside or inside the agencies. In the view of the GAO, these problems seem likely to expand, not recede.[21]

Computers: Gratifying at the Grassroots?
Computers also have made themselves felt among the grassroots governments. By the mid-1970s, at least 90 percent of cities and counties and all of the states were using computers in a systematic way.[22] Most of the local uses of computers revolve around the areas of finance, utilities, services, personnel records, administration office support, and law enforcement, although there are about 450 different computer applications at the city and county levels alone.[23]

Only 3 percent of American cities and counties do not have some sort of computer support (and 88 percent have their own in-house computer system, as opposed to having a joint use arrangement with other governments or privatizing their computer services).[24] Ninety-six percent of local governments use at least one central system; 73 percent employ microcomputers; 77 percent have used some sort of computer for five or more years; more than two-thirds have a technical staff dedicated solely to computing; 57 percent of local governments have a separate data processing department.[25]

On the average, the data processing budget as a percentage of the total operating budget of local governments is only slightly more than 1 percent.[26] This seemingly modest figure, however, is misleading; one survey of county governments in the United States found that 22 percent of all full-time county employees work in information technology or information services.[27]

Microcomputers clearly are the rage among America's local governments. In 1982 only 18 percent of local governments (and even fewer small local governments) used microcomputers; only three years later, this proportion had rocketed to about 84 percent.[28]

Fifty percent of local government managers are very satisfied with their central computer systems and 41 percent are very satisfied with their microcomputer systems. Indeed, only about 5 percent of local government managers are dissatisfied with their systems.[29]

The significant investment in computers by state and local governments seems to have (by and large) paid off in the long term, justifying the overall satisfaction of state and local administrators with their information systems. A survey of forty-six American cities which had committed to computers relatively early found that, between 1976 and 1988, these metropolises made major gains in the areas of fiscal control, cost avoidance, and improved relations with citizens. These gains were not immediately realized, however, and represented long-term payoffs over a period of years. On the other hand, it remained problematic whether computers would ever deliver comparable benefits in the areas of planning and managerial control.[30] Problems of quality of computer service had far less to do with technical and structural factors (*e.g.*, centralization versus decentralization of computer services), than with relations between municipal administrators who provided computer services and those who used them.[31]

These human-based problems of information service quality in American local governments lead directly to the question of adequate training of computer personnel. City and county administrators report that their most serious problem with their information systems is one of hiring experienced and competent technical staff and training problems.[32] Another survey exclusively of county administrators found the same frustration, yet determined that training was accorded the smallest single share in the budget of county information system offices (13 percent), and that trainers occupied the smallest proportion of positions in information system and technology jobs—fewer than 1 percent![33]

From Data to Decisions

Increasingly, the literature distinguishes between two basic types of information systems in public management. The first is the *management information system* (or MIS), which is "an interconnected set of procedures and mechanisms for data accumulation storage and retrieval, which is designed to convert organizational data into information appropriate for managerial decision making." Generally, a management information system summarizes data on such items as population, facilities, salaries, services provided, inventories, employees, and provides these data on demand to managers. By contrast, a *decision support system* (DSS) is "an interactive computer based system that is structured around analytic decision models on a specialized management data base directly accessible to managers, that can be used to assist management at all levels of an organization with decisions about *unstructured* and *nonroutinized* problems."[34]

The key distinction between a management information system and a decision support system is that the management information system is merely a data base to be used by managers, while a decision support system provides decision-making assistance for unstructured problems and the incorporation of modeling techniques that are directly accessible to the decision maker. In other words, a decision support system can be designed to assist in "what if" kinds of inquiry, such as projecting possible increases in transit costs.

Clearly, public agencies are moving increasingly toward the supplementation of management information systems with decision support systems. A survey of state agencies in Colorado found that 57 percent of the agencies indicated that they had a decision support system in place. In most cases, decision support systems are used primarily by middle managers, and most of these administrators were quite pleased with the usefulness provided by decision support systems.[35]

More innovative governments have combined both types of information systems and used them to deliver services more effectively and efficiently. Wichita Falls, Texas, for example, has aggregated and stored data for purposes of equalizing property taxes, and automated its purchase order processing through the application of computer techniques borrowed from both types of systems.[36] Fort Lauderdale, Florida, by borrowing the Census Bureau's geographic data and combining them with its own management information system, was able to equalize crew work loads and ensure more efficient refuse service in its sanitation department.[37] Tulsa, Oklahoma, created the Tulsa Regional Automated Criminal Information System, which allows police officers to call in to headquarters on a twenty-four-hour-a-day basis to collect such information as a briefing on a car or person, stolen vehicle information, and current warrants or arrest records.[38] Some cities have placed computer terminals in their firetrucks that display a map showing the fastest route to the fire, architectural drawings of the building on fire, and hazardous conditions in the building.

This last example is a type of geographic information system, or GIS, which has been called "the single hottest topic in computing that cuts across the federal, state, and local governments."[39] A survey of all county governments found that the installation of GIS was the "number-one priority investment for smaller counties."[40]

A *geographic information system* is a location-related computer program that combines data and, typically, maps for a variety of uses. Urban centers usually derive the greatest benefits from GIS, particularly in the areas of public works, code enforcement, and fire control. Geographic information systems produce superior-quality maps, promote data integration from a variety of governmental data bases, and increasingly are being used for streamlining economic development, planning, land use, zoning, reapportionment, solid waste collection, libraries, housing, and health policy development.[41]

These examples indicate the several uses to which computers may be put in the public sector. Kenneth Kraemer and his colleagues have categorized these uses on a scale ranging from basic to sophisticated.[42] At the bottom of Kraemer's pyramid of governmental uses of computers is the performance of routine and repetitive administrative tasks, such as payroll calculations and licensing chores. Here is where management information systems are all that is needed. At a higher level of sophistication is the use of computers for planning and control of internal management operations, such as scheduling, allocating, and monitoring traffic control and emergency vehicles. In this usage, there is an emphasis on rapid response capability. At the top of the pyramid is the use of computers for strategic planning and scheduling, involving such techniques as Performance Evaluation and Review Technique, which we covered earlier in this chapter; decision support systems come into play at this level.

The organizational and human implications of information management, the systems approach, and management science run deep, and "The Computer" symbolizes the threat of these techniques for many people. The concluding portion of this chapter will consider some of the ramifications of information systems technology for organizations and decision making.

TECHNOLOGY, THE PUBLIC BUREAUCRACY, AND THE PUBLIC

Herbert A. Simon has observed that popular views on the implications of computers and automation for human beings can be classified according to "economic" and "technological" dimensions, and by "conservative" and "radical" interpretations.[43] These are shown in Table 6–6.

Simon considers himself to be a technological radical and an economic conservative in his perceptions of computers and automation; that is, he foresees employment patterns similar to today's, and computers taking over the more mundane activities of humanity—in short, the best of both worlds. In this view, Simon argues that the computer will free people from the dispiriting and deadly routine chores that have burdened bureaucracies for too long and release the energies of human beings in more fulfilling enterprises. Notably, people no longer will have to be clerks and assembly-line workers; instead they can work in jobs involving face-to-face, human-to-human interaction. In Simon's view this will be a far more gratifying experience than is possible in the unautomated present. Already, in fact, computers (in the form of management information systems, noted earlier) have taken over the solving of "well-structured problems" (such as sending and collecting telephone bills), rapidly are usurping "ill-structured problems" (in the form of decision support systems), and slowly are developing heuristic problem-solving techniques for application to supervisory duties.

Moreover, Simon contends, the fears of a "technocracy" (or a ruling class possessing the skills demanded by a technologically advanced society) developing along with the expansion of computers are unfounded. As a technological radical, Simon argues that computers can be programmed to program themselves, thus preventing programmers and mathematicians from evolving into a powerful elite. He contends that as automation progresses, maintenance problems decrease.

TABLE 6-6   Views on the Human Implications of Computers and Automation

	Economic Dimension	*Technological Dimension*
Radical Perceptions	A "glut" of goods, widespread unemployment, the rise of a technocracy.	Computers can do anything that human beings can do, including thinking.
Conservative Perceptions	Rising production, full employment, with employment patterns similar to today's.	Computers can do only what human beings program them to do.

Similarly, full employment should accompany automation, and as an argument Simon offers an analogy: The horse disappeared because of automation (in the form of the automobile), but human beings did not; the horse corresponds to the machine, but humanity does not. Thus, technology will increase real wages and capital per worker. In brief, Simon urges that we recognize the enormous significance of the computer in forming human kind's image of itself. Galileo and Copernicus showed us that human beings are not at the center of the universe; Darwin enlightened us with the knowledge that humanity is not created by God, not especially endowed with soul and reason; Freud demonstrated that the individual person is not completely rational; and the computer will yield us the insight that the human race is not uniquely capable of thinking, learning, and manipulating its environment.

There is, of course, a less optimistic view concerning computers and automation. Boguslaw, Jean Meynaud, and Jacques Ellul,[44] among others, argue that technology will dehumanize humanity and possibly create economic chaos if carried to its automated extreme. Boguslaw phrases this view particularly succinctly. He suggests that "the automation revolution has *not* led to a world of happier and more vital people" because a basic tenet of the technological value structure is that work is stupid. This tenet goes against the grain of traditional Western (especially American) thought. "For example, fundamental to Max Weber's Protestant Ethic is the notion that hard labor—sweat-of-the-brow-type labor—is essentially a good and desirable thing." But the values of automation and technology contradict this historic value, and

> have turned Max Weber's ethic on its head to read, "Hard work is simply a temporarily unautomated task. It is a necessary evil until we get a piece of gear, or a computer large enough, or a program checked out well enough to do the job economically. Until then, you working stiffs can hang around—but, for the long run, we really don't either want or need you."[45]

This value dissonance, combined with the ongoing popular glamorization of science, quantitative techniques, and professionalism, work to provoke deep-set anxiety and alienation among workers and managers alike. Boguslaw wonders what the successor to the Protestant work ethic might be:

> Will the unspoken creed, which once could be verbalized as "I may not be a brain but I can always make a living with these hands; I am fundamentally the producer," be replaced by another, which when verbalized might say, "All these hands (or all this mind) can do is what some machine hasn't yet gotten around to doing. . . . I am the one, in effect, who is doing the exploiting—why not do it deliberately and systematically?"[46]

Simon and Boguslaw are sufficiently representative of the two poles of the computer/planning/automation/technology/humanism/organization/management debate. What is worth examining further at this juncture are the potential effects of the new technologies on the managerial echelons of organizations, particularly public organizations, and there are a few studies that have attempted to do this. In them, the investigative mission of the authors revolve around such questions as: Will middle management be displaced by machines? Will top management control all variables in the organization via computer technologies and management science, or will it, too, be displaced by automation? Will administrators generally be alienated by the new machinery, or will they become "true believers"? Will the authority relationships and controlling abilities of administrators be altered by the use of computers? It is these kinds of concerns that characterize the studies that we shall review briefly in terms of the computer's impact on authority and control, organizational structure, "dehumanization" and alienation, decision making, and the special case of government data banks and citizen privacy.

Authority and Control

A frequent premise of investigators is that computers facilitate the concentration and centralization of authority in organizations. Although empirical findings are mixed in this area, the bulk of the research tends to support the proposition but with some interesting variations.[47] A study by

Thomas L. Whisler of twenty-three large insurance companies indicated that where computers were introduced in the organization, decision-making loci tended to move upward in the hierarchy; indeed, the most commonly reported phenomenon in the study was the centralizing of control after the introduction of computers. Computers tended to displace clerks in the companies; it was estimated that without information technology, the companies would have required a 60 percent increase in their clerical staff, only a 9 percent hike in supervisory personnel, and a mere 2 percent increase in managerial jobs.[48] Simon's observations on the propensity of information systems to solve well-structured, ill-structured, and supervisory problems in an ascending order of rapidity and accuracy would seem to be substantiated by Whisler's research.

From another viewpoint, however, managers report a "decentralization" of authority attributable to computers, but only in the sense that managers are released from routine chores and are able to spend more time on authoritative decision making. In a study of fifty state employment agencies (plus Puerto Rico, the Virgin Islands, and Washington, D.C.), S. R. Klatzky observed a "cascade effect" in terms of authority as a result of computers. Computers created a "vacuum" of activity at the managerial levels by freeing these managers from many routine jobs; if top-level managers then *decided* to let their authority devolve after the introduction of information technology, the resulting "new" authority granted to each level of the hierarchy could be handled more effectively since computers had taken over routine tasks.[49] Thus, computers, together with a decision by top management to decentralize their authority, created a "cascade" of authority to lower levels that increased the mission effectiveness of the organization generally.

The cascade effect can also be seen in a study conducted by Donald R. Shaul of fifty-three middle managers and fourteen top managers in eight companies. Shaul found that after information technology had been adopted, 60 percent of the managers reported an increase in planning activities, a "high percentage" increased their directing activities, and a greater propensity by managers to relinquish certain kinds of authority was observed. Interestingly, two-thirds of the managers reported less need to bother with "controlling" subordinates because the computer kept an adequate check on misuse of budgetary funds and work time, while opportunities for engaging in coordination activities increased.[50]

Withington observes in this regard the phenomenon of "flickering authority" in organizations enabled by the advent of information technology. Because the computer frees all managers from a plethora of mundane duties and furnishes them with information that they can use more potently than ever before, they have more time to develop their ideas and more information to substantiate them, and authority thus becomes more accessible to all managers. In Withington's words, "The effect is that the authority for originating and testing ideas for change 'flickers' within the management structure of the organization. He who has the idea is the one who temporarily has the authority to proceed with its analysis. . . . "[51]

In a careful empirical analysis of nearly 1,500 employees in forty-two municipal governments, it was found that "greater employee control in the work place is attributed to the computer as the employee's role ascends the organizational hierarchy. This is the first empirical confirmation that computer technology enables the information elite to reap the greatest increases in control within organizations."[52]

The researchers in this study distinguished four role types of municipal professional service workers: managers (or top administrators who typically rely on summaries of information to make decisions), staff professionals (data analysts who advise managers), "street level bureaucrats" (line personnel who directly provide city services to citizens), and "desk top bureaucrats" (who are extensively involved in processing information). Table 6–7 indicates the findings of this study.

Staff professionals, for example, experienced less supervision of their work by others, more influence over others, and an increase in time pressure as a consequence of the introduction of computers. Staff professionals, in short, were the most likely to gain more organizational authority as the result of their understanding and use of electronic data processing. However, intensifying time pressures accompanied this expansion of their authority.

Managers also were able to increase their

TABLE 6-7 Summary of Findings about Relative Impacts of Computing on Control of Work

	Pervasiveness of Data-handling in Work [a]		
	High	*Low*	
			Actual Impacts [b]
Autonomy in the organization's hierarchy **High**	Staff Professionals	Managers	+ *Influence over others*
Low	Desk top bureaucrats	Street level bureaucrats	- *Influence over others*
Actual Impacts	− Supervision of work by others + Time pressure	++ Supervision of work by others − Time pressure	

[a]High means that data-handling tends to be direct, multi-modal, and continual: low means that data-handling tends to be indirect, use-oriented (relative to generation and manipulation), and intermittent.

[b]Impacts are those effects on control of work attributed to computers. The table indicates those roles which have experienced an impact in a significantly different pattern than the roles with which it is contrasted.

Source: Kenneth L. Kraemer and James N. Danziger, "Computers and Control in the Work Environment," Public Administration Review, 44 (January-February 1984), p. 39. Reprinted with permission from *Public Administration Review* © 1984 by The American Society for Public Administration, Washington, D.C. All rights reserved.

influence over others, but found themselves to be more closely supervised by others as well. However, time pressures on managers were reduced by the introduction of computers.

The desk top and street level bureaucrats lost their influence over others, but beyond that commonality, the impact of the computer on their working roles varied. The desk top bureaucrats found that their work was less supervised by others, but that time pressures increased, while street level bureaucrats (or those who dealt with people and clients on an on-going and continuous basis) found themselves to be more supervised by others, but also under fewer time constraints. As the table indicates, the computer affects the control of work in the work place on the basis of how pervasive data handling is in one's work, and the level of autonomy that one possesses in the organization's hierarchy.

Organizational Structure

If computers have an effect on the exercise of authority in organizations, they have an equal impact on hierarchical structure. Most analysts agree that information technology will pressure the hierarchical pyramid to "flatten," and this pressure would appear to be the result of increased organizational control made possible by computer technology.

Some three decades ago, John Pfiffner and Robert Presthus prophesied in their public administration textbook that the hierarchial pyramid would not so much flatten as a result of computer as spread into a "bell" shape. This, they believed, would occur because middle managers would be displaced by the new and evolving information technologies.[53]

Later research supports Pfiffner and Presthus' predictions. Rolf T. Wigand points out that a major function of middle managers is communication—transmitting orders from the top of the pyramid to the bottom, and providing feedback from the base to the peak. In large organizations, middle managers tend to evolve into an "organizational sponge," retaining and eventually squeezing upwards or downwards information that is provided them by the top or bottom of the hierarchy. The "sponge" effect, which is created by middle management, is an organizational pathology in that information is distorted, delayed, or withheld. Computers and new communication and information technologies can and are slicing through (and slicing out) the sponge of middle management, and the process is so gradual that often it is not noticed. But it does seem to be real; by the mid-1980s, unemployment among managers and administrators in non-farm industries occasionally was reaching levels that had not been attained since World War II.[54]

Changes in organizational structure resulting from information technology present difficulties for public administrators. A study by Marshall W. Meyer, using data gathered from 254 state, county, and city finance departments and comptrollers' offices, found that tensions arose between superordinates inexpert in information systems and subordinates proficient in computer science because electronic data processing requirements forced superordinates and subordinates to cooperate in ways not provided for by the traditional bureaucratic structure. If the organization was able to adapt to the use of information technology, Meyer found, horizontal interaction increased and the normal vertical interaction of the closed model decreased; if the organization was too stultified to change, administrative pathologies quickly surfaced.[55] In this light, Whisler noted a blurring of traditional line/staff distinctions in organizations; as a result of the introduction of information systems, staff members with computer skills gained new organizational prestige.[56]

With the advent of microcomputers, the research on the impact of computers on organizational structure has moved from a general consensus that computers tended to centralize organizations to a growing opinion among researchers that computers promote the decentralization of organizations.[57] Perhaps the best characterization of this research, however, is that computers centralize some decisions and decentralize others. As two researchers in the area note, computer "technology supports either arrangement; which arrangement is followed in any particular instance is a function of organizational history, management, and politics."[58]

"Dehumanization" and Alienation

If clerks are the bureaucrats most often displaced by automation, those clerks who remain frequently find that their jobs become rigidly routinized, and occasionally they are transformed into key punch operators. Such, at least, was the conclusion of Albert A. Blum in a study of information technology and white-collar workers.[59]

On the other hand, the promotion possibilities for those clerks remaining are about the same as they were prior to the introduction of information technology, and Whisler found that, while clerical responsibilities were not enlarged, salaries went up with the increased need for clerical precision.[60]

A survey of more than 2,000 secretaries conducted in twenty-one major American cities found unusually high levels of job satisfaction among secretaries concerning the use of office automation, particularly computers, especially as that satisfaction concerned microcomputers and word processors. Eighty-seven percent felt that office automation had had a positive effect on the secretarial profession, and more than nine out of ten stated that secretaries could produce a higher volume of work as a result of automation, and that office automation allowed secretaries to be more efficient. Significant majorities of secretaries stated that office automation had made their jobs more challenging, allowed them to spend more time on more responsible activities, had made their jobs more fulfilling, had increased their productivity, and in fact, had increased the managerial productivity of executives.[61]

Older bureaucrats occasionally experience a sense of alienation when information technology is introduced. Meyer's findings imply this, but a study by H. S. Rhee specifically noted the presence of conflict between older, bureaucratically oriented locals and younger, professionally oriented cosmopolitans over the automation issue.[62]

Generally speaking, research on the impact of computing on work life agrees that job performance improves and the work environment is enhanced by the introduction of computers.[63] In a massive study of 2,400 people whose jobs had been affected by computers, it was found that three-quarters of the respondents believed that computing had "provided them with a greater sense of accomplishment in their work."[64]

Computers and Decision Making

One of the more intriguing questions is how computers affect not only the quality of the working environment, but also the quality of the work output itself. One study concluded that mid-level managers actually appear to make *different kinds* of decisions depending upon whether or not they are computer literate! Mid-level managers familiar with computers tend to make their decisions on the basis of computer-provided information rather than on information furnished by other sources, such as books and journals. Often, however, the kind of information provided by computers differs from the information gleaned from other sources. While it is an open question whether the kinds of decisions resulting from the use of computer-based information are "better" or "worse" than decisions that are based on information from other sources, it nonetheless is of note "that when computers are involved, computer literate decision makers choose different information than computer novices and that the selection of computer information has an effect on the outcome of the decision."[65]

Generally, most investigators seem to agree that information technology does not affect top-level decision makers very much one way or another. Rodney H. Brady, after interviewing more than one hundred top managers and examining in detail the decision-making process in more than a dozen large companies, concluded that the computer has not had much impact on decision making at the top.[66] On the other hand, information technology has speeded the overall decision-making process in organizations by making more information more readily available to top managers. Rhee found that the concern over a computer-oriented technocratic elite eventually displacing top administrators was a view not shared by top administrators themselves; in fact, highest-level decision makers did not consider a technical background to be a prerequisite for their positions.[67] Whisler reported that the organizational centralization accompanying the introduction of computers tended to increase the responsiveness and power of the topmost echelon,[68] while Shaul concluded that middle managers, too, believed that their responsibilities and capabilities had increased after the advent of information technology.[69]

Still, one wonders. There have been reports in business magazines of "deskless offices" in the presidential stratum of "progressive" multinational corporations. In these poshest of quarters, there are no desks, only chairs, lounges, and coffee tables. The underlying assumption is that the top-most corporate decision makers should be only that; he or she should do no more than listen, confer, and decide; he or she should be relieved of anything resembling paperwork; the brain is all. Similarly, the growing "fetish of the clean desk" refers to the propensity of top-level administrators to have no more than one sheet of paper on their desks at any one time, and betokens an emphasis on "thought" and decision making rather than on "paper shuffling"; the presidents of private foundations seem to favor this clean desk affectation. Continuing this line of thinking, a major company once introduced a "water bed room" for use by its top-level executives (presumably on a one-at-a-time basis); the idea is that an executive floats, meditates, and ultimately decides about the grand issues facing the company.

Do these developments reflect anything other than a desire to make the decision-making process more effective and, probably, more pretentious? It seems possible, at least, that top executives may be trying to manipulate their images (their "dramaturgy," to recall Victor Thompson's term) in such a way as to distinguish their functions from the functions of the computer. The more they are unlike the computer, the less paper they handle, the more they "think," the more essential they become as human beings. This, of course, is only speculation, but the increasing obsequiousness displayed for the decision-making function in organizations may reflect a subliminal fear over the awesome, if as yet unrealized, cognitive powers of The Computer.

Data Banks, Privacy, and Public Policy

As with other administrators, computers and the many overlapping techniques of management science have had an impact on public administrators. Paul Armer observes that governmental use of information technology could facilitate interagency sharing of information, reduce expensive duplication of information systems, improve planning, upgrade auditing (thus increasing revenues), and bring about more responsive services to the public generally. In Armer's view, information systems will increase the pressures for the consolidation of national, state, and local government, starting only with the consolidation of files through information-sharing systems but ultimately consolidating and centralizing governmental authority as well: Cities will defer power to counties, counties to states, states to regions, and regions to the nation.[70]

Nevertheless, Armer desponds that governments are beset by factors that inhibit the optimal use of computer-based information storage and retrieval systems. Notable in this regard are the unfamiliarity of top-level government executives with information technology and management science, a lack of qualified personnel to perform the necessary kinds of systems analysis, the need to rewrite laws in order to permit the integration of files and information-sharing arrangements, a general lack of coordination among government agencies, the parochialism of many agencies, and finally, popular and official fears of invasions of privacy and of a *1984* variety of technocratic state. The dismal experience with information systems among some federal agencies, noted earlier, would seem to verify Armer's pessimism, although local governments' often innovative use of information technology counters his views to some degree.

Armer's final caveat regarding computers and government is worth additional examination; the computer-and-privacy/computer-and-policy issue is one unique to *public* administration. In 1977, in *Whalen* v. *Roe*, the Supreme Court recognized for the first time the constitutionally protected "zone of privacy" of the individual, a concept that involved the right of people to prevent others (such as a government agency or a private firm) from disclosing personal data to the public. Congress has recognized the value of individual privacy as well by its passage of the Fair Credit Reporting Act of 1970, the Privacy Act of 1974, the Right to Financial Privacy Act of 1978, and the Computer Matching and Privacy Protection Act of 1988. These laws have not been especially effective in preventing the accessing of private records, although the Privacy Act has been somewhat useful in restricting the distribution of data about citizens by federal agencies.

As late as the mid-1970s, concerns over government's misuse of personal data seemed somewhat overdrawn. A federal study conducted in 1975 found that nearly three-quarters of the personal data systems subject to the provisions of the Privacy Act were not even on computers and

were completely manual![71] By 1985, however, privacy concerns were intensifying. The Office of Technology Assessment reported that twelve cabinet departments and thirteen independent agencies maintained 539 record systems to which the Privacy Act applied, containing more than 3.5 billion records, or an average of fifteen files for every man, woman, and child in the United States.[72] Sixty percent of all these systems were fully computerized, and 78 percent of those systems that contained files on more than a half million people were computer based.[73] In fact, about eighty-five federal data bases contain some 288 million records on 114 million people.[74] Some forty states provide information to direct mail firms for a fee, using information provided by citizens when applying for a driver's license or registering a vehicle. And more than 15 million centrally stored records of individual arrest histories are available to at least 64,000 law enforcement agencies which employ more than 1 million officers who are authorized to request these records from the FBI's National Criminal Information Center.[75]

Of even graver concern is the accelerating trend among government data banks to "mix and match" information on individuals, and at least fifteen federal agencies engage in this practice.[76] Computer matching is the electronic comparison of two or more sets or systems of individual personal records. The federal government through such legislation as the Deficit Reduction Act of 1984, the Debt Collection Act of 1982, the Federal Managers Financial Integrity Act of 1982, the Paperwork Reduction Act of 1980, the Social Security Amendments of 1977, the Food Stamp Amendments of 1977 and 1980, and other laws, has encouraged computer matching as a means of detecting fraud and other criminal activity, abuse of the welfare system, and tax evasion, among other objectives. These new acts have resulted in the creation of such electronic dossiers as the Internal Revenue Service's Debtor Master File and the Medicaid Management Information System, among other federal systems that are extensively engaged in computer matching. It appears that the number of matches tripled from 1980 to 1984, and that more than 2 billion separate records were exchanged during those four years.[77] As one observer has noted, "No longer is information merely stored and retrieved by computer. Now, information is routinely collected on computer tapes, used within an agency in computer form, exchanged with and disclosed to regional offices or other agencies in computer form, manipulated and analyzed with sophisticated computer software, and archived on computer tapes. These disclosures and manipulations are currently performed for entire systems of records. . . ."[78]

The Computer Matching and Privacy Protection Act of 1988 was designed, despite its name, less to prohibit these kinds of exchanges among federal agencies and more to verify that information about individuals is accurate. It also requires that studies be conducted to determine if computer matching is worth the cost. But the law does not seriously impede computer matching.[79]

The worries of Americans over issues of personal privacy have grown as these trends have accelerated. In 1970, about 35 percent of Americans expressed themselves "concerned" over "threats to personal privacy"; by 1990, nearly[80] percent registered themselves as "concerned" or "very concerned" over these threats. Americans express considerably higher trust over the government's potential use of personal files than over how private firms may use them, but 71 percent of Americans agree that "consumers have lost all control over how personal information about them is circulated and used by companies."[80]

In a useful summary of the computer-and-privacy/computer-and-policy issue, Alan F. Westin has observed that there are at least five kinds of data bank systems emerging in American society: statistical systems for policy studies, executive systems for general administration, systems designed to centralize data gathered by other agencies, individual agency data-bank systems, and mixed public/private systems.[81] All these data-bank systems bring with them new problems of public policy. If we are to learn more about our citizenry in order to develop more responsive and effective public policies, where do we draw the line? At what point does the collection, storage, retrieval, and sharing of social information become an invasion of the citizen's privacy? Emerging from this fundamental dilemma of the government's use of computers are delicate political issues: Who will control this new technological capacity? Will new knowledge of old prob-

lems inspire brand-new problems in society (as may be the case with improved crime statistics, which have served to frighten many a formerly complacent citizen)? Where does the expertise and planning enabled by the computer end, and where does democratic participation by the public in public policymaking begin?

In any event, it seems unavoidable that new knowledge of problems will undermine the justifications of past government inaction in attempting to resolve those problems. Knowledge is pressure, with or without pressure groups, and the computer makes all of us, whether private citizen or public bureaucrat, more knowledgeable about government, society, and our problems. In short, computers, systems analysis, and management science may serve not merely to centralize the administration of government, but to widen the scope of government activities beyond anything yet envisioned.

NOTES

1. C. West Churchman, *The Systems Approach* (New York: Dell, 1968).
2. Daniel P. Moynihan, *Maximum Feasible Misunderstanding: Community Action and the War on Poverty* (New York: Free Press, 1969).
3. Churchman, *The Systems Approach.*
4. Robert Boguslaw, *The New Utopians: A Study of System Design and Social Change* (Englewood Cliffs, N.J.: Prentice Hall, 1965), pp. 1-28.
5. See, for example, Study Committee on Policy Management Assistance, Office of Management and Budget, *Strengthening Public Management in the Intergovernmental System* (Washington, D.C.: U.S. Government Printing Office, 1975); Advisory Commission on Intergovernmental Relations, *Improving Urban America: A Challenge to Federalism* (Washington, D.C.: U.S. Government Printing Office, 1976); Special Task Force on Intergovernmental Management, American Society for Public Administration, *Strengthening Intergovernmental Management: An Agenda for Reform* (Washington, D.C.: American Society for Public Administration, 1979); and Charles R. Warren and Leanne R. Aronson, "Sharing Management Capacity: Is There a Federal Responsibility?" *Public Administration Review,* 41 (May/June 1981), pp. 381-387.
6. Theodore H. Poister and Gregory Streib, "Management Tools in Municipal Government: Trends Over the Past Decade," *Public Administration Review,* 49 (May/June 1989), pp. 240-248. Poister and Streib surveyed 1,060 cities ranging from 25,000 to 1 million people in 1987-88, and received 451 usable

responses, or a response rate of 43 percent. For 1982, see: Theodore H. Poister and Robert P. McGowan, "The Use of Management Tools in Municipal Government: A National Survey," *Public Administration Review*, 44 (May/June 1984), p. 221; and "Municipal Management Capacity: Productivity Improvement and Strategies for Handling Fiscal Stress," *The Municipal Year Book*, 1984 (Washington, D.C.: International City Management Association, 1984), p. 208. Poister and McGowan surveyed 1,052 municipal jurisdictions with populations ranging from 25,000 to 1 million and received 460 usable responses or a response rate of 44 percent. The 1976 survey can be found in Rackham Fukuhara, "Productivity Improvement in Cities," *The Municipal Year Book, 1977* (Washington, D.C.: International City Management Association, 1977) pp. 193-200. Fukuhara surveyed cities of the same population range as the later surveys and obtained useable responses from 404 cities, or a response rate of 43 percent.

7. Richard C. Elling, "Of Bandwagons and Bandaids: A Comparative Assessment of the Utilization and Efficacy of Management Techniques in State Bureaucracies," paper presented at the Annual Meeting of the American Political Science Association, Washington, D.C., August-September 1984, Tables 13 and 14.

8. Efraim Turban, "A Sample Survey of Operations Research at the Corporate Level," *Operations Research*, 2 (May/June 1972), pp. 708-721.

9. C. Jackson Grayson, Jr., "Management Science and Business Practice," *Harvard Business Review*, 51 (July/August 1973), pp. 41-48.

10. Randall L. Schultz and Dennis P. Slevin, eds., *Implementing Operations Research/Management Science* (New York: Elsevier, 1975).

11. Lars Lonnstedt, "Factors Related to the Implementation of Operations Research Solutions," *Interfaces*, 5 (February 1975), p. 24.

12. E. S. Quade, "System Analysis Techniques for Planning- Programming-Budgeting," *Planning-Programming-Budgeting: A Systems Approach to Management*, Fremont J. Lyden and Ernest G. Miller, eds. (Chicago: Markham, 1972), p. 246.

13. Russell L. Ackoff and Patrick Rivett, *A Manager's Guide to Operations Research* (New York: John Wiley, 1963), pp. 21-34.

14. C. P. Snow, *Science and Government* (Cambridge, Mass.: Harvard University Press, 1961), pp. 47-53.

15. Anatol Rapoport, *Fights, Games, and Debates* (Ann Arbor: University of Michigan Press, 1960).

16. Roger Fisher and Scott Brown, *Getting Together: Building Relationships As We Negotiate* (New York: Penguin Books, 1988), p. 199.

17. The source of much of this discussion is David R. Morgan, *Managing Urban America*, 2nd ed. (Monterey, Calif.: Brooks/Cole, 1984), pp. 105-110.

18. Pete Earley, "Government Computer Network is Aging," *The Washington Post* (February 21, 1983); Kathryn Johnson, "Washington Catches Up To the Computer Age," *U.S. News and World Report* (April 2, 1984), pp. 27-28; Frank Reilly, "Information

Technology and Government Operations," *The G.A.O. Journal*, 5 (Spring 1989), p. 42; and Sam Overman, "When GAO Comes, Mind Your Bits and Bytes," *Government Executive* (September 1990), p. 30.

19. "Bringing Order to Government Information Systems," *Facing Facts: Comptroller General's 1989 Annual Report* (Washington, D.C.: U.S. General Accounting Office, 1990). p. 27.

20. Reilly, "Information Technology and Government Operations," p. 44

21. "Bringing Order to Government Information Systems," pp. 28-29. See also: D. Richard de Silva, "A Confederacy of Glitches," *Newsweek* (September 21, 1992), p. 29.

22. Rob Kling and Kenneth Kraemer, "Computing and Urban Services," in *Computers and Politics: High Technology in American Local Governments*, James N. Danziger, William Sutton, Rob Kling, and Kenneth Kraemer, eds. (New York: Columbia University Press, 1982), p. 200; and James N. Danziger, "Evaluating Computers: More Sophisticated EDP Uses," *Nation's Cities*, 13 (October 1975), pp. 31-32.

23. Among the major surveys of local government uses of computers are: Kenneth L. Kraemer, *Evaluation of Policy-Related Research in Municipal Information Systems* (Irvine, Calif.: Public Policy Research Organization, University of California at Irvine, 1975); Donald F. Norris and Vincent J. Webb, *Microcomputers, Baseline Data Report*, Vol. 15, No. 7 (Washington, D.C.: International City Management Association, July 1983); James N. Danziger, William Sutton, Rob Kling, and Kenneth L. Kraemer, eds. *Computers and Politics: High Technology in American Local Governments* (New York: Columbia University Press, 1982); Kenneth L. Kraemer, *et al.*, *Microcomputer Use and Policy, Baseline Data Report*, Vol. 17, No. 1 (Washington, D.C.: International City Management Association, 1985); John Scoggins, Thomas H. Tidrick, and Jill Auerback, "Computer Use in Local Government," *The Municipal Year Book, 1986* (Washington, D.C.: International City Management Association, 1986), pp. 33-45; Jeffrey L. Brudney, "Computers and Smaller Local Governments," *Public Productivity Review*, 12 (Winter 1988), pp. 179-192; and Alana Northrop, Kenneth L. Kraemer, Debora Dunkle, and John Leslie King, "Payoffs from Computerization: Lessons Over Time" *Public Administration Review*, 50 (September/October 1990), pp. 505-514. Patricia Fletcher, Stuart Bretschneider, Donald Marchand, Howard Rosenbaum, and John Carlo Bertot, *Managing Information Technology: Transforming County Governments* (Syracuse, N.Y.: School of Information Studies, Syracuse University, 1992). For a comparatively rare survey of state governments' management of computers, see: Sharon L. Caudle, "Managing Information Resources in State Government," *Public Administration Review*, 50 (September/October 1990), pp. 515-524.

24. Scoggins, Tidrick, and Auerback, "Computer Use in Local Government," p. 34.

25. *Ibid.*, pp. 34-35.

26. *Ibid.*

27. M. J. Richter, "Managing Information: The County Study," *Governing* (August 1992), p. 32. This is a report on the 1992 Syracuse University study cited earlier.

28. Scoggins, Tidrick, and Auerback, "Computer Use in Local Government," p. 40; and Donald F. Norris and Vincent J. Webb, "Microcomputers: A Survey of Local Government Use," *The Municipal Year Book, 1984* (Washington, D.C.: International City Management Association, 1984), p. 195.

29. Scoggins, Tidrick, and Auerback, "Computer Use in Local Government," p. 43.

30. Northrop, Kraemer, Dunkle, and King, "Payoffs from Computerization," p. 505.

31. James N. Danziger, Kenneth L. Kraemer, Debora E. Dunkle, and John Leslie King, "Enhancing the Quality of Computer Service: Technology, Structure, and People," *Public Administration Review*, 53 (March/April 1993), pp. 161-169.

32. Scoggins, Tidrick, Auerback, "Computer Use in Local Government," p. 43.

33. Richter, "Managing Information," p. 44.

34. All the quotations in this paragraph are from: James Senn, "Essential Principles of Information Systems Development," *MIS Quarterly*, 2 (June 1978), p. 17. Emphasis is original.

35. Robert P. McGowan and Gary A. Lombardo, "Decision Support Systems in State Government: Promises and Pitfalls," *Public Administration Review*, 46 (November 1986), pp. 581-582.

36. Gerald G. Fox, "Information Systems and Decision Making," *Public Management*, 53 (October 1971), pp. 9-11.

37. Robert H. Bubier, "Modern Refuse Vehicle Routing," *Public Management*, 55 (August 1973), pp. 10-12.

38. Carole H. Hicks, "The Broad Scope of Computer Usage in City Government," *Current Municipal Problems*, 7 (1980-1981), pp. 191-196.

39. Bruce Rocheleau, "Information Management in the Public Sector: Taming the Computer for Public Managers," *Public Administration Review*, 52 (July/August 1992), p. 399.

40. Richter, "Managing Information," p. 39.

41. William E. Huxhold, *An Introduction to Urban Geographic Information Systems* (New York: Oxford University Press, 1991).

42. Kenneth Kraemer, *et al*, *Integrated Municipal Information Systems: The Use of Computers in Local Government* (New York: Praeger, 1974), pp. 50-51.

43. Herbert A. Simon, *The Shape of Automation for Men and Management* (New York: Harper & Row, 1965).

44. Jean Meynaud, *Technocracy* (London: Faber and Faber, 1968). Jacques Ellul, *The Technological Society* (New York: Knopf, 1967).

45. Boguslaw, *The New Utopians*, p. 25.

46. *Ibid.*, p. 26

47. For reviews of this research, see: Kenneth L. Kraemer and John Leslie King, "Computing and Public Organizations," *Public Administration Review*, 46 (November 1986), pp. 488-496, but especially p. 492; and Rolf T. Wigand, "Integrated Communications and

48. Thomas L. Whisler, *The Impact of Computers on Organizations* (New York: Praeger, 1970).

49. S. R. Klatzky, "Automation, Size, and Locus of Decision-Making: The Cascade Effect," *Journal of Business*, 43 (April 1970), pp. 141-151.

50. Donald R. Shaul, "What's Really Ahead for Middle Management?" *Personnel*, 41 (November/December 1964), pp. 9-16.

51. Withington, *The Real Computer*, p. 203.

52. Kenneth L. Kraemer and James N. Danziger, "Computers and Control in the Work Environment," *Public Administration Review*, 44 (January/February 1984), p. 32.

53. John M. Pfiffner and Robert Presthus, *Public Administration*, 5th ed. (New York: Ronald Press, 1967), p. 247.

54. Rolf T. Wigand and U.S. Department of Labor statistics as cited in Kris Aaron, "Computers are Squeezing Out Many Middle Managers," *Scripp-Howard Business Journals* (December 1984), p. 2. But see also Wigand's "Integrated Communications and Work Efficiency," paper presented to the Munchner Kreis Congress in Integrated Telecommunications, Munich, West Germany, November 5-7, 1984, pp. 11-14.

55. Marshall W. Meyer, "Automation and Bureaucratic Structure," *American Journal of Sociology*, 74 (November 1968), pp. 256-264.

56. Whisler, *The Impact of Computers on Organizations.*

57. See, for example, Charles Myers, *The Impact of Computers on Management* (Cambridge, Mass.: MIT Press, 1967) for a view that computers tend to centralize management, in contrast to the perception that computers tend to decentralize management, as contained in, for example, Peter Blau, *et al.*, "Technology and Organization in Manufacturing," *Social Science Quarterly*, 21 (March 1976), pp. 20-40.

58. Kraemer and King "Computing and Public Organizations," p. 49.

59. Albert A. Blum, "White Collar Workers," *The Computer Impact*, Irene Taviss, ed. (Englewood Cliffs, N.J.: Prentice Hall, 1970).

60. Whisler, *The Impact of Computers on Organizations.*

61. Anne-Marie Schiro, "Secretaries' Poll on Computers," *New York Times* (March 14, 1983). The study is titled, "The Evolving Role of the Secretary in the Information Age," and was conducted by the Minolta Corporation in cooperation with the Professional Secretaries International Association.

62. H. A. Rhee, *Office Automation in Social Perspective* (Oxford: Basil Blackwell, 1968).

63. See, for example A. J. Jaffe and Joseph Froomkin, *Technology and Jobs: Automation and Perspective* (New York: Praeger, 1966); Russell Rumberger, "The Changing Skill Requirements of Jobs in the U.S. Economy," *Industrial and Labor Relations Review*, 34 (July 1981), pp. 578-590; and Jon Shepard, *Automation and Alienation: A Study of Office and Factory* (Cambridge, Mass.: MIT Press, 1971).

64. James N. Danziger and Kenneth L. Kraemer, *People*

and Computers (New York: Columbia University Press, 1986), p. 380.

65. Ralph F. Shangraw, Jr., "How Public Managers Use Information: An Experiment Examining Choices of Computer and Printed Information," *Public Administration Review*, 46 (November 1986), p. 514.

66. Rodney H. Brady, "Computers in Top Level Decision-Making," *Harvard Business Review*, 45 (July/August 1967), pp. 67-76.

67. Rhee, *Office Automation in Social Perspective*.

68. Whisler, *The Impact of Computers on Organizations*.

69. Shaul, "What's Really Ahead for Middle Management?"

70. Paul Armer, "Computer Applications in Government," in Taviss, *The Computer Impact*.

71. Office of the President, *Federal Personal Data Systems Subject to the Privacy Act of 1974: First Annual Report of the President, 1975* (Washington, D.C.: U.S. Government Printing Office, 1975), pp. 4-6. Nevertheless, the remaining systems were fully or partially computerized, and contained more than 80 percent of the total individual records owned by the federal government.

72. These figures are for 1982, when the federal government's computerized files on individuals were last counted. See: Robert S. Boyd, "An Eagle's Eye," *Savannah News-Press* (July 22 1990). No doubt, there are more such files now.

73. U.S. Congress, Office of Technology Assessment, *Federal Government Information Technology: Electronic Record Systems and Individual Privacy*, OTA-CIT-296 (Washington, D.C.: U.S. Government Printing Office, 1986), p. 22.

74. Anne R. Field, "'Big Brother, Inc.' May be Closer Than You Thought," *Business Week* (February 9, 1987), p. 27.

75. *Ibid.*

76. *Ibid.*; and Priscilla M. Regan, "Privacy, Government Information, and Technology," *Public Administration Review*, 46 (November/December 1986), p. 631.

77. Field, "'Big Brother, Inc.' May be Closer Than You Thought," p. 28; and Regan, "Privacy, Government Information, and Technology," p. 631. New controls, however, are being introduced; from 1984 to 1989, when Congress stopped the practice, the Social Security Administration provided private credit bureaus with verification of citizens' Social Security numbers. See: Boyd, "An Eagle's Eye."

78. Regan, "Privacy, Government Information, and Technology," p. 630.

79. Jeffrey Rothfeder, *Privacy for Sale: How Computerization Has Made Everyone's Private Life an Open Secret* (New York: Simon & Schuster, 1992), p. 146.

80. Harris Polls conducted in 1970, 1977, 1978, 1983, and 1990, as cited in Boyd, "An Eagle's Eye." Unless noted otherwise, all figures in the paragraph are for 1990.

81. Alan F. Westin, " Civil Liberty and Computerized Data Systems," *Computers, Communications and the Public Interest*, Martin Greenberger, ed. (Baltimore, Md.: Johns Hopkins, 1971), pp. 151-168; and "Information Systems and Political Decision-Making," in Taviss, *The Computer Impact*, pp. 130-144.

CHAPTER 7

PUBLIC PROGRAM EVALUATION AND PRODUCTIVITY

Planted in a lush landscape of large political change and reared in reformist roots, the methods of public program evaluation and the productivity movement sprouted into the Saguaro cactus of public management: tough, prickly, and dry.

Today, public program evaluation and productivity constitute the primary and highly interrelated answers by public administrators to those Americans who question the efficacy and efficiency of "Big Government," and who promote its attendant tax revolts. In this chapter, we review these answers in terms of their political and intellectual evolution, their impact on governments, and their permutations, processes, and problems.

Public program evaluation, also known as evaluation research, is the "hands on" component of productivity. Perhaps the most useful definition of *public program evaluation* is provided by the U.S. General Accounting Office (GAO): "program evaluation is a way of bringing to public decision makers the available knowledge about a problem, about the relative effectiveness of past strategies for addressing or reducing that problem, and about the observed effectiveness of particular programs."[1] Program evaluation

increasingly is concerned "with both information on the outcomes of programs and judgments regarding the desirability or value of programs."[2] In other words, a program evaluation is becoming a major means of determining whether governmental policies are continued or discontinued.

Productivity is the larger environment in which the evaluations of public programs are conducted, and can be defined as those governmental activities that concern themselves with the improvement of economy, efficiency, and effectiveness in the implementation of public programs.[3] This environment is less than tidy. One review of the literature on productivity concluded, quite accurately, that "the amazing thing about public productivity research is [that] different clusters of researchers investigate the same problems in different ways . . . the majority of researchers in one cluster are not aware, let alone familiar with, the studies of the other clusters ...all these differences put researchers into intellectual ghettos." [4]

Concerns over academic ghettoization aside, practical attempts to estimate what the public may gain from improved governmental productivity reach impressive conclusions. The General

Accounting Office has stated that for every 5 percent increase in federal productivity, the federal government would save $4.5 billion dollars. The Joint Economic Committee has contended that a 10 percent increase in the productivity of the federal government could reduce federal expenses by $8 billion, yet maintain present levels of service. The President's Private Sector Survey on Cost Control (popularly known as the Grace Commission after its chair, J. Peter Grace) has estimated that, if its suggestions were implemented, the federal government could save $424.4 billion over three years.[5]

There is less research concerning the amount of dollars that state and local governments might save by using the techniques of public program evaluation, but a national survey of chief administrative officers of American cities found that 61 percent of the respondents felt that, on balance, "the positive payoffs of the performance measures used in their jurisdictions were worth the cost and organizational strain of collecting these data. Less that one percent felt that it was not."[6] The larger the municipality, the stronger this correlation was likely to be.

THE EVOLUTION OF PUBLIC PROGRAM EVALUATION AND PRODUCTIVITY

Public program evaluation and productivity sprang from relatively simple, moralistic concerns, and waxed to complex economic concepts. We treat the evolution of public program evaluation and productivity in four phases, emphasizing, in turn, efficiency, budgeting, management, and privatization. Table 7-1 is an effort to illustrate how public program evaluation and the productivity movement have evolved over time in the United States, and the reader may wish to refer to it as this discussion proceeds.[7]

Table 7-1   The Evolution of Public Program Evaluation and Productivity

Feature	Efficiency (1900-1940)	Budgeting (1940-1970)	Management (1970-1980)	Privatization (1980-Present)
Motivation	"Better" government.	Control expenses.	Efficiency and effectiveness.	Reduce deficit, taxes, and government expenses.
Dominant Level of Government	Local, federal by 1930s.	Low involvement at all levels.	Federal, state, and local.	Federal
Initiators: Productivity Movement	Citizens, business people, scholars, and experts.	Budget-oriented public administrators	Elected officials, followed by public administrators and academics.	Citizens and businesspeople.
Initiators: Program Evaluation Techniques	Time motion studies. Bureau of Municipal Research. New Deal Administration. National Committee on Municipal Standards.	Great Society administrators; Organization Development pioneers.	Urban Institute, universities.	Business community, universities, conservative think tanks.
Political Environment / Working Assumptions	Politics is separate from administration; efficiency equates with better government; better government equates with the elimination of corruption.	Comprehensive productivity is not explicit as a goal, and is subsumed under budgetary innovations.	Public and private sectors place a high premium on productivity.	Private sector can improve the public sector's productivity.

The Efficiency Phase, 1900–1940

The movement to develop techniques of public program evaluation and to focus public resources on higher levels of productivity in government began at the municipal level. Public program evaluation and productivity were very much a part of the government "reform movement" that swept the United States during the early twentieth century, and many of the contributors to some of the first thinking about public administration that we reviewed in Chapter 2, particularly those associated with Paradigm 1 (the Politics/ Administration Dichotomy) and Paradigm 2 (the Principles of Public Administration) were contributors to the productivity movement as well.

The motivation of these reformers (who were business people, academics, and civic-minded citizens) was to create "better" government, which meant more efficient government, which, in turn, meant corruption-free government. The founding in 1906 of the Bureau of Municipal Research in New York City, which conducted a variety of studies on how to make municipal government more efficient, symbolized the reform movement. The National Committee on Municipal Standards, formed in 1928, was another major contributor in the development of ways of measuring the efficiency of government services. Many of these techniques were borrowed from Frederick Taylor and his time motion studies, which we described in Chapter 2. These early efforts at the municipal level found their way to the federal level as well. As early as 1912, the federal government created the Commission on Economy and Efficiency, although sustained federal interest in productivity and program evaluation began in the 1930s under the New Deal of Franklin Delano Roosevelt. The President's Committee on Administrative Management, noted in Chapter 2, which published its impressive report in 1937, is testimony to federal involvement in productivity efforts during this period.

The Budgeting Phase, 1940–1970

By 1940, the motivation to improve governmental productivity was a result less of a crusade to quash corruption and more of a wish to control expenses. Because expenditure control was the primary motivation underlying productivity, governmental interest in public program evaluation and a comprehensive approach to public productivity took a seat far to the rear of public administrators' fascination with new budgeting techniques. We consider these techniques in the following chapter, but our point here is that relatively little overt activity was occurring in program evaluation, and there was minimal interest in a comprehensive approach to productivity.

Nevertheless, some groundwork for later developments was being laid. The early pioneers of organization development, reviewed in Chapter 3, originated some of the basic theoretical precepts of program evaluation.[8] With the inauguration of Lyndon Baines Johnson's Great Society legislation in the 1960s, social scientists rediscovered poverty, education, and similar domestic issues, and LBJ's Office of Economic Opportunity (later retitled as the Community Services Administration in 1975 and ultimately eliminated in 1981) was especially aggressive in encouraging an evaluation research component in its various projects. The Elementary and Secondary Education Act of 1965 did much to promote program evaluation in education.

The Management Phase, 1970–1980

By 1970, people in the public administration community were beginning to wonder what had happened to program evaluation and productivity. In 1971, a leading public administrationist asked, as the title of an editorial in the field's leading journal, "Why Does Public Administration Ignore Evaluation?" and even four years later this author could accurately observe that "the practice of evaluation in public administration remains in its formative stages."[9]

The renewal of program evaluation and productivity was led by elected politicians. In 1970, Senator William Proxmire noted to the Comptroller General (who heads the GAO) that it was "distressing that we have no real measures of the efficiency of the federal sector," and the Comptroller General shortly appointed a taskforce that led to the creation, by President Richard Nixon in 1970, of the National Commission on Productivity, which eventually evolved into the National Center for Productivity and Quality of Working Life. Although the emphasis of the

Commission, and later the Center, was on productivity in the private sector, both organizations had a public component.

The National Center for Productivity and Quality of Working Life folded in 1978, and its public sector functions were transferred to a new group called the Center for Productive Public Management, which later became the National Center for Public Productivity. The Center serves today as a national clearinghouse for public productivity studies at all levels of government.

During this phase, the federal government aggressively tried to integrate a productivity focus and program evaluations into the management of its own agencies. Congress, through its passage of the Congressional Budget and Impoundment Control Act of 1974, directed the General Accounting Office to "develop and recommend to Congress methods of reviewing and evaluation of Government programs."[10] Today, this charge is the mission of the GAO's Division of Program Evaluation and Methodology.[11] In 1978, Congress passed the important Inspector General Act, considered later in this chapter. In 1979, the federal Office of Personnel Management created its Productivity Resource Center, which distributes information on ways of enhancing the effectiveness of public employees. Other agencies also added specific program evaluation components. So the federal government, largely due to the personal interests (if, perhaps, differing motives) in public management of Presidents Nixon and Jimmy Carter, took significant steps during the 1970s in incorporating program evaluation and a comprehensive approach to productivity in its delivery of public policies.

At the state level, the governors of Wisconsin and Washington led the way during this management-oriented phase in focusing their governments on program evaluation and productivity, and these states often are cited as exemplary in this regard. However, by the end of the decade, both governors were out of office, and the program evaluation and productivity efforts that they initiated in those states withered in their absence.

Local governments enthusiastically rediscovered program evaluation and productivity, and, as with the federal and state governments, were led in this rediscovery by elected officials. John Lindsay, and his successor, Abraham Beame, both were mayors of New York City who placed

a great emphasis on increasing municipal productivity—at least until 1975, when New York's financial crisis resulted in the slashing of resources supporting those programs. The Urban Institute, working in coordination with the National Center for Productivity and the Quality of Working Life and various urban professional associations, provided much of the research on new techniques of public program evaluation and productivity during this management oriented-phase.

The Privatization Phase, 1980-Present

The values of the management phase continue today, although they flourish most vigorously at the local level. With the election of Ronald Reagan as president in 1980, however, a new aspect was added to the ongoing development of public program evaluation and productivity. This new aspect was *privatization*, or the contracting out of government services to private companies, and its impact was felt mostly, but not exclusively, at the federal level. Privatization is a large and somewhat complicated phenomenon, and we devote Chapter 11 to it. But its effects on public program evaluation and productivity can be reviewed here.

The motivation underlying the privatization phase was to reduce the dramatically growing federal deficit—a growth that began in the early 1980s—to reduce taxes, and to reduce government expenses. Its leaders were concerned citizens and the private sector. The public appeared to be convinced during the 1980s that business could deliver a number of government programs more efficiently and effectively than could governments themselves, whereas the private sector stood to benefit from potentially lucrative contracts with governments to deliver those services. These factors, combined with the ideological orientations of a conservative presidency, resulted in a major effort by the federal government to privatize many public functions in the belief that such privatization would make government more productive.

This effort took several forms. For example, "Reform 88" was an attempt by the President's Council on Management Improvement, begun in 1982, to integrate productivity goals with the basic processes of government, and "to make the bureaucracy perform like a corporation."[12] In 1983, the Office of Management and Budget rewrote its OMB Circular A-76 on "Performance of Commercial Activities," with the goal of improving productivity by relying more heavily on the private sector to deliver specific government services. In 1984, the President's Private Sector Survey on Cost Control (the Grace Commission) released 2,478 recommendations on 784 separate aspects of federal management in the form of forty-seven reports toting up to more than 12,000 pages, bound in thirty-eight volumes. Unlike earlier reports on federal administration, the Grace Commission's massive report was not only the largest ever, but also unique in its reliance on the private sector (some 2,000 volunteers donated by 859 corporations and other private organizations had written the report) for making recommendations that evidenced an unambiguous tilt against the continuance of many federal programs and policies, and a clear preference for hiring private companies to deliver a wide array of federal services.

With the inauguration of Bill Clinton as president in 1993, the efforts to privatize the federal government appeared to be leveling, and may decelerate, although much of this deceleration may result from a reduction of federal programs in an effort to control the soaring federal deficit. In addition, the ideology of the private sector being inherently more effective and efficient than the public sector no longer prevails in the White House, and this, too, likely will diminish the federal privatization effort.

The state and local governments never took to contracting out public services in the same fashion that the federal government did in the 1980s and early 1990s, but continued to adopt on an increasingly broader basis new techniques of program evaluation and productivity over time. By the 1990s, at least at the local level, these programs were well in place in many jurisdictions.

PROGRAM EVALUATION, PRODUCTIVITY, AND AMERICAN GOVERNMENTS

Today, the techniques of public program evaluation and the productivity movement are felt at every level of American government, but at some levels more forcefully than others. We consider these in turn.

Federal Forward—Slowly

A 1970 study of federal evaluation practices concluded that "the whole federal machinery for making policy and budget decisions suffers from a crucial weakness; it lacks a comprehensive system for measuring program effectiveness."[13] By the mid-1970s, this condition was changing, and, as we have noted, a variety of federal agencies have now embraced program evaluation and productivity programs.

In 1987, at the apex of Washington's fascination with privatization, the General Accounting Office concluded that, despite a significant decline between 1980 and 1984 in the level of federal resources available for program evaluation research, the number of program evaluations produced by federal agencies remained about the same as in earlier years, "suggesting continued executive branch interest in obtaining evaluation information."[14]

Congress has been supportive of federal administrators' continuing interest in program evaluation. In 1990, Congress passed the Federal Managers Financial Integrity Act, requiring agencies to report (for the first time!) to the Office of Management and Budget (OMB) their financial and programmatic problems, and their progress (or lack thereof) in rectifying them. This law quickly showed itself to be very helpful in improving federal management.

In what could be a very significant long-term development for federal program evaluation, President Bill Clinton in 1993 signed into law the Government Performance and Results Act, which requires the Office of Management and Budget to designate pilot projects in performance measurement and goal setting in ten agencies. OMB and the General Accounting Office are to report on these projects in 1997, to be followed by Congressional mandating of five-year strategic planning and annual performance reporting for all federal agencies. The legislation appears to be intelligently conceived, allowing more managerial flexibility than is usual for Congress, and it moves federal administrators away from the tradition of reporting on their compliance with procedures and toward reporting on their achievement of measurable results. The Government Performance and Results Act of 1993 "represents a major effort by Congress to focus on the efficiency and effectiveness of federal programs."[15]

Congress also in the 1990s has beefed up the federal budget for general management improvement. But, despite good intentions, the view of most well-informed observers is that federal evaluation programs are not well developed. As the Deputy Director for Management at OMB has noted, "On a scale of 10," the federal government's ability to measure performance is "about at a 2."[16]

Nevertheless, there seems to be a renewed enthusiasm for productivity improvement in federal circles, and this enthusiasm could move the government in Washington a few more points up the performance evaluation scale.

Starting and Stopping in the States

A survey of the states conducted in 1972 ascertained that only half of the forty-two responding state governments had a full-time program analyst in at least one agency.[17] State respondents showed a strong desire to learn more about program evaluation and productivity, and to implement it more widely. Even so, a federal study conducted in 1978 indicated that state governments needed more evaluation research, but faced significant problems in acquiring it.[18] A 1980 survey of state governments found that, while most states still did not have comprehensive, formal productivity improvement programs, there remained considerable interest in program evaluation.[19] Another poll discovered that by the mid 1980s legislatures in thirty-five states had expanded existing agencies or had created new ones charged with the evaluation of program effectiveness and efficiency.[20]

Table 7-2 shows some of the results of a twenty-year survey of all state governments. As it indicates, the states report a steadily increasing reliance on effectiveness and productivity measures in managing state agencies.

Another study of all fifty states indicated that, while much remained to be done in the way of program evaluation and productivity, progress had been made. Ten states had centralized—that is, they were responsible for improving produc-

tivity in all state agencies—productivity improvement programs. Most of these operations were located in the state budget office or the department of administration, and focused on upgrading technology, particularly as it pertained to computers, and employee motivation systems, such as merit pay and performance appraisals. Nevertheless, the overall assessment of state centralized productivity improvement efforts was one of a "lack of stability . . . an 'up-and-down' pattern."[21] The states' long-term commitment to system-wide productivity enhancement is, in short, unclear.

Local Leadership: Productivity and Progress

Of all levels of government, local governments seem to have made the most significant progress in introducing public program evaluations and productivity improvements. In part, this progress is attributable to the early interest of local governments in enhancing productivity, but their success

Table 7-2   States' Use of Effectiveness and Productivity Analysis, 1970–1990

State Agency	1970	1990
Central budget office conducts:		
Effectiveness analysis	18%	66%
Productivity Analysis	31	94
Other central staff organizations conduct:		
Effectiveness analysis	2	28
Productivity analysis	8	30
Most major agencies conduct:		
Effectiveness analysis	14	45
Productivity analysis	20	49
Legislature conducts:		
Effectiveness analysis	14	51
Productivity analysis	51	16

Effectiveness was defined in the survey as measures which "define and quantify the ultimate effects of government activities on society or the environment."

Productivity was defined in the survey as measures which "define and quantify the goods or services being produced."

Source: As derived from: Robert D. Lee, Jr., "Developments in State Budgeting: Trends of Two Decades," *Public Administration Review*, 51 (May/June 1991), p. 257, Table 6.

also relates to the fact that local governments tend to be responsible for a larger proportion of public programs that can be more readily measured—for example, sanitation, public safety—than are the federal and state governments.

As with the federal and state governments, the base line of recent progress for local governments dates to the early 1970s. A national survey of all cities and counties with more than 50,000 people conducted in 1971 found that only 38 percent of the responding governments had some form of program evaluation unit in even one agency or more.[22] Since then, this condition has changed dramatically. In 1976, a survey of local governments found that 64 percent were using program evaluations to improve productivity. Almost half of the cities had organized special staffs to evaluate productivity in their governments and to identify better methods to improve the delivery of services.[23] A 1987 survey that was designed to replicate the 1976 survey found that 80 percent of local governments were using evaluation research and productivity improvement measures—a "significant increase" over the less than two-thirds of the municipalities which were using program evaluations eleven years earlier. The wider the scope of the program evaluation effort, the more satisfied local officials were with it. In those cities that used program evaluations and productivity improvement techniques on a city wide basis (rather than just in selected departments), 49 percent of local officials concluded that the program evaluation was a "very effective" management tool.[24]

Even though localities deliver many public services that are relatively easily measured, it still is not an easy task for any local government to adopt the techniques of performance evaluation and increase productivity; one exhaustive review of the literature identified no fewer than thirty-seven barriers to increasing productivity in local governments, ranging from the lack of political appeal inherent in the techniques themselves to various "performance myths," such as the presumed advantages of certain, expensive police practices.[25] Those local governments that are most successful in adopting productivity improvement measures are those which have a participative management style in city government, relatively high levels of privatization, a local emphasis on economic development, department heads who have college educations, a comparatively low reliance on intergovernmental sources of revenue,[26] and extensive civil service reforms in city governments, such as the decentralization of decision-making authority concerning personnel, the creation of a senior executive service, and the elimination of veterans' preference in hiring and promoting.[27]

Local governments favor the use of *workload measures* (or measures of the amount of work performed or service provided, such as trash collected) in adopting the techniques of performance evaluation. Other performance measures, such as *unit costs* (i.e., the dollar cost per unit of workload, such as the cost of collecting a bag of trash), *effectiveness measures* (or the extent to which objectives are achieved, such as the containment of the number of burglaries), and *citizen satisfaction measures* (or the determination of the extent to which program clients feel that their needs are met, such as conducting citizen surveys) are used considerably less by local governments. Workload-related information, however, can be generated comparatively easily, and is useful, too.[28]

Whatever the level, governments' commitment to program evaluation and productivity seems to associate with governments that are interested in improving all kinds of management, and this government interest appears to stem from an underlying disaffection among citizens with what they deem to be the disappointing results of public programs. As Francis G. Caro notes,

> there is every reason for dissatisfaction with the current state of intervention on problems of health, economic security, education, housing—indeed on the entire range of social disorders. . . . Neither the rhetoric of politicians nor the pleas of do-gooders of various persuasions are sufficient to guide program development. Similarly, neither the theories of academicians nor the exaggerated statements of efficacy by practitioners are adequate bases for the support and expansion of various human service activities. Evaluation research, not a new but nevertheless an increasingly robust enterprise, can have a major impact on social problems.[29]

PUBLIC PROGRAM EVALUATION: PURPOSES AND PERMUTATIONS

Public program evaluation and productivity may be inspired by a taxpaying citizenry disaffected with the efficiency and effectiveness of governments, as Caro suggests, but there are other purposes as well, and there are many kinds of program evaluations that have been developed to deal with these varying purposes—not the least of which are, on occasion, political as well as economic.

The Purposes of Public Program Evaluation

The emphasis that current definitions of public program evaluation place on the effectiveness of programmatic outcomes (and on the desirability of even having those programs as social policy in the first place) leads us to ponder the real purposes of program evaluation. At one level, program evaluation allows policymakers to confront the problem of resource allocation. Policymakers obviously must choose among competing social objectives and among competing ways of achieving those objectives; moreover, these choices must give full consideration to the somewhat abstruse principles of justice, equity, and political reality. Thus, certain social questions can be raised that public program evaluation often can clarify.[30] These policy queries include: What is the appropriate level of achieving a particular objective? Are there choices for reaching that level? What resources will be required to attain the program objective? Are there obstacles to the implementation of a particular alternative, and what would be the costs of attempting to overcome the obstacles? And finally, are there equity considerations connected with the leading alternative?

If resource allocation questions were the only purpose underlying public program evaluation, they would provide more than adequate justification for conducting it, but there is a deeper motivation initiating program evaluations, a motivation that is more political than economic. As one analyst notes, "evaluation research can be invoked for a variety of purposes, not only as a means of improving programs. Sometimes evalu-

ation is undertaken to justify or endorse an on-going program and sometimes to investigate or audit the program in order to lay blame for failure, abolish it, change its leadership, or curtail its activities."[31] The purpose of public program evaluation, in other words, is dependent on the motivations of those who initiate the evaluation.

Kinds of Public Program Evaluation

Nowhere is the intellectual ghettoization of public program evaluation and productivity more evident than in researchers' efforts to describe various types of evaluation research. The types that we describe here are all in current use, although, fortunately, there is an emerging coherence of thought about types of program evaluation, as represented by the typology offered by the Evaluation Research Society.

Early, but Still Current, Typologies.   Among the most basic distinctions in the literature of evaluation research is that made between summative and formative research.[32] *Summative evaluation* is designed to assess a program's result after the program has been well established. *Formative evaluation* is meant to improve a program while it is still on-going and fluid.

These very basic distinctions have since been refined, and a variety of taxonomies have been developed by specialists in public program evaluation. For example, the now-defunct Community Services Administration distinguished between *program impact evaluation*, which assesses the impact and effectiveness of a program; *program strategy evaluation*, which evaluates the program's strategies that are the most effective in delivering services; and, finally, *program monitoring*, which assesses the individual project in order to determine operational efficiency.[33] The Urban Institute modified these distinctions formulated by the Community Services Administration to include *project ranking*, which is an effort to rank the *relative* achievements of local projects.[34]

Conversely, the RAND corporation developed a somewhat different series of distinctions for the Department of Health, Education and Welfare (now the Departments of Education and Health and Human Services). It separated evaluation from compliance control and capability building. *Compliance control* is defined as "monitoring for compliance with legislative intent and administrative regulations," while *capability building* is attained through efforts to make a program more subject to evaluation techniques, including "increasing state and local decision makers' ability to carry out their own evaluations."[35]

One of the more useful categorizations of the evaluation literature is that devised by Orville F. Poland, in which the schemata of effectiveness evaluation, efficiency evaluation, and eclectic evaluation is offered.[36] *Effectiveness evaluation* uses controlled experiments to determine how well programmatic goals have been achieved. *Efficiency evaluation* uses cost effectiveness approaches to determine what the cost of the goals being achieved are. *Eclectic evaluation* analyzes a program's secondary criteria, such as its inputs, outputs, and processes, in an effort to identify programs needing greater attention; it can lead to a better understanding of how the program really works.

The Typology of the Evaluation Research Society. Given the various efforts at categorizing kinds of program evaluation (and there are many more than we have mentioned in this chapter), perhaps the most straightforward approach is that offered by the Evaluation Research Society, which has listed six types of program evaluations that are conducted on a routine basis.[37] We shall review these kinds of program evaluation with an emphasis on identifying what sorts of information these evaluative approaches produce for the public administrator.[38]

Front-end analysis is evaluation research that is conducted before a decision is made to engage in a new program. Generally, it addresses policy formulation problems, often relying on the findings of prior evaluations, in an effort to estimate how feasible the program might be and its possible effects.

The kinds of information that front-end analyses produce are data relating to planning, and which can be used to provide a rational approach to a program and its later evaluation. Front-end analysis also measures ongoing problems and the progress of programs that have been conducted in the past. An example of a front-end analysis is the General Accounting Office's study of teenage pregnancy that was provided to Congress before legislation was introduced proposing service programs for pregnant teenagers.[39]

A second kind of evaluation research is evaluability assessment. Evaluability assessment is employed to answer questions of policy formulation and implementation. The policy assumptions underlying a program are compared to what the program says it is supposed to do (*i.e.*, its stated objectives), and an effort is made to assess the reasonableness of those assumptions and the probability that the program is able to attain its objectives. Evaluability assessment describes the characteristics of how the program is being implemented, and it is helpful in determining the practicality and utility of undertaking a later full-scale evaluation of the effectiveness of the program; if it is determined that a full-scale evaluation of the program would be in order, evaluability assessment typically provides the basis for such a large-scale evaluation. Fundamentally, evaluability assessment is retrospective in nature, and involves questions of accountability.

More than any other type of public program evaluation, evaluability assessment provides the public administrator with information about the implementation and management of a public program. An example of an evaluability assessment is Bruce Buchanan's effort to assess whether the Senior Executive Service of the federal government has met its goals.[40]

Process evaluation is a kind of program evaluation that can either be used by itself or in combination with some other kind of evaluation research. Like evaluability assessment, it employs a retrospective view of programs. The goal of process evaluation is to describe and assess the processes of discrete program activities, such as management, strategic planning, operations, costs, and the details of the implementation process. A process evaluation can be very helpful in determining the effects of a particular program on its clientele group.

In sum, the process evaluation not only can enlighten questions of policy implementation, but also can be useful, especially when used in tandem with effectiveness evaluations (to be discussed next), in answering questions of accountability. Thus, the primary type of information that the process evaluation provides a public administrator is knowledge about the implementation and management of a program (which evaluability assessments also do), and about the effectiveness of the way in which the program is being implemented and managed (like the effectiveness evaluation does). Examples of a process evaluation are those studies that focus on how innovations in the public sector are circulated and become routinized among governments.[41]

The *effectiveness*, or *impact evaluation*, is perhaps the most appreciated by top agency executives and legislators, principally because it focuses on whether or not a public program is doing what it is supposed to be doing. Like process evaluations, an effectiveness evaluation is retrospective. In its effort to determine how well a program has been doing, it must face up to the very real problem of showing that changes observed in a particular problem area can be attributable to the impact of the program, rather than to the trends in the environment over which the program has no control. As a consequence of making this difficult distinction, effectiveness evaluations must be designed in such a way that an understanding can be obtained from the evaluation about what conditions might have been—or would have been—if the program had not been present. As Eleanor Chelinsky observes, "This, of course, is the quintessential accountability question."[42] Effectiveness evaluations, however, also are needed to address questions of implementation, since it is at the level of execution of a policy where the impact of that policy may or may not be made.

Effectiveness evaluations provide the public administrator with information regarding the impact of the program, its implementation, and its management; it also measures ongoing problems inherent in the program and the progress of the program. An example of a well-known effectiveness evaluation is the Kansas City Police Department's study about the effectiveness of police patrols in preventing crime; this evaluation found that there were no statistically significant differences in crime rates, citizen attitudes, the reported number of crimes, citizen behavior, or even in the rate of traffic accidents among areas where no police patrols were sent out, and police responded only to specific calls for help; areas where patrols were maintained at previous levels; and areas where patrols were doubled or tripled in size.[43]

A fifth kind of program evaluation is *program and problem monitoring*. Rather than using a single shot or retrospective approach, program and problem monitoring is continuous, and its purpose is to provide information on problems, or, at least, to track problems, both long-term and short-term, in a variety of areas simultaneously. Program and problem monitoring attempts to focus on how the problem may have changed over time, whether or not the program is continuing to comply with public policy, how service delivery methods may have altered over time, and so forth. Program and problem monitoring can be used not only to address policy formulation and policy implementation questions, but accountability questions as well. Its unique value is that it enables administrators to follow the evolution of problems, and the impact of a program on those problems, over time. Frequently, program and problem monitoring relies on time-series analysis, data systems, and forms to be filled out by public administrators who work far down the line from those public administrators who demand and use the forms.

The types of information that program and problem monitoring provides public administrators typically focuses on planning and designing a program and its evaluation, implementing and managing the program, justifying and demonstrating program effectiveness, and, of course, most obviously, measuring on-going problems and program progress. Program and problem monitoring is capable of furnishing all these kinds of information standing alone, and not in conjunction with any other type of program evaluation. An example of a program and problem monitoring evaluation is the General Accounting Office's study of the effectiveness of the Comprehensive Employment and Training Act Program, which employed three different sets of monitoring data: data on characteristics of the participants (which addressed how well the program was targeted); financial data (which addressed how much the program was costing); and, status reports (which addressed the mix of services and how many participants were being actually placed in jobs). All these sets of data were provided by local public administrators to federal public administrators on a quarterly or yearly basis.[44]

Program and problem monitoring is one of the more favored types of public program evaluations among local governments. Local governments use it because, as we noted earlier, workload measures of performance can be easily incorporated into program monitoring, and local governments use workload measures more than any other type of performance measure. Increasingly, the federal government is using program and performance monitoring as well.[45]

Finally, *meta-evaluation*, or *evaluation synthesis*, constitutes our sixth form of public program evaluation. Meta-evaluation re-analyzes findings from a number of previous evaluations (but occasionally from just one evaluation) to find out what has been learned in the past about a public policy. Meta-evaluation is the most comprehensive, and obviously retrospective, approach to evaluation research in that it synthesizes a number of findings for purposes of determining program effectiveness and what may be known about a given problem area. It is highly flexible, and can provide public administrators with information about all the major questions of public policy: Is the policy accountable? Is it effective? And what more about the policy area needs to be known?

Evaluation synthesis provides the public administrator with information on planning and evaluating programs, justifying the effectiveness of the program's implementation and management, and demonstrating the effectiveness of a program. An example of an evaluation synthesis is the General Accounting Office's study of drinking age laws and their effects on highway safety.[46]

These six kinds of program evaluation constitute, in the words of one authority in the field, "the everyday repertoire of program evaluation."[47] As we noted earlier, these approaches are certainly not the only ways to classify program evaluations, but "it would be fair to say that they represent widespread agreement in the field with regard to common practice in program evaluation, and that they are relevant, in various degrees, to the needs of public administrators."[48]

THE EVALUATION PROCESS

As noted, the process of evaluation is far from simple, and Figure 7-1 illustrates this process. The chart shows four basic fundamentals of the evaluation process: ascertaining decision makers' needs; defining the nature and scope of the problem; determining valid objectives; and specifying comprehensive measures.[49] Let us consider these in turn.

Four Fundamentals of Public Program Evaluation

To determine a decision maker's needs, we first must ask what *the decision maker's perceptions of the problem* are. Is he or she dissatisfied with the effectiveness or the results of the program—or with the lack of a program—to meet a particular social mission? How will the information brought out by a program evaluation be used? When is the final report needed?

Defining the nature and scope of the problem also is important, and it is vital that the people who are to use the results of the study (in other words, the decision makers themselves) understand the nature and scope of the issues at stake at least as thoroughly as the people responsible for conducting the study. This means that all persons involved in the evaluation should be aware of the study's origin, review legislative hearings and reports associated with the topic, be informed about the history of the program designed to deal with the problem, and examine together the past analyses and evaluations of the issue. The General Accounting Office has noted that "there is often a trade-off between the breadth of a study and the precision of the results."[50]

Determining valid objectives is a third area of importance. To the extent possible, a statement of objectives should include a complete understanding of the intended benefits. It should include how many of those benefits are expected to be attained, identify possible recipients of adverse consequences or unintended benefits that cannot be avoided, include important qualitative features (although measuring qualitative attainments is hardly an easy task), and finally, account for multiple objectives that may conflict with each other or, conversely, be in support of one another. As

FIGURE 7-1   The Process of Program Evaluation

Source: U.S. General Accounting Office, *Evaluation and Analysis to Support Decision Making* (Washington, D.C.: U.S., Government Printing Office, 1976), p.8.

the GAO again notes in this regard, "the importance of taking such a comprehensive view of objectives cannot be overstated. Oversimplified statements (1) will not capture all essential aspects of the effects intended, and (2) may contain implied conflicting consequences for groups other than the intended beneficiaries (e.g., to eliminate hunger or to achieve energy sufficiency)."[51]

The final area of importance is specifying *comprehensive measures*. It should include quantifying the extent to which the program's goals are met—in other words, effectiveness measures. These comprehensive measures should involve capturing qualitative aspects of the consequences, or those *intangible measures*; quantifying to the degree possible unintended consequences, or *side effect measures*; and quantifying as much as possible the differences of impact on the beneficiaries and the bearers of the cost, or what are known as *distribution measures*.

Conducting a Public Program Evaluation

Once these fundamentals of the evaluation process are established, certain basic steps must

be taken to successfully execute a program evaluation.[52] Among the first is *preparing a detailed study plan*. The plan should include a clear statement of the problem and a careful listing of built-in constraints and assumptions to be used in evaluating the problem. It should state the methods to be used and elaborate the resources to be committed in the study. It should include a report schedule, specified procedures for amending the study plan, and finally, a time frame for completing the major components of the study, including a final deadline.

Next, *a study team should be selected, lines of communication established, and appropriate methods to conduct the study determined*. We shall return to the problem of method later, but suffice it to note here that in selecting appropriate methods the following criteria should be used: *level of validity* (how much confidence can a program manager have in the results of the study?); *relevance* (will the results be useful to decision makers?); *significance* (will the study results show the program manager substantially more than can be deducted from direct observation?); *efficiency* (does the value of the study exceed the cost?); and finally, *timeliness* (will the analytical information be available in time to meet program objectives and legislative schedules?).

All evaluation plans should *specify procedures for using the results.* In other words, the evaluation's results must be communicated if they are to have any effect, and this means specifying the nature of the reports and to whom they are to be made; communicating those reports with clarity and with conciseness; and following up. The follow-up should include interpreting the report to decision makers, responding to questions that have not been answered by the report, and generally helping decision makers develop a logical reaction to the report.

THREE INNOVATIONS: THE BOTTOM LINE, THE INSPECTOR GENERAL, AND TOTAL QUALITY

These basics of conducting a program evaluation are fundamental, and are used in many contexts, including relatively new ones. We consider next three of the more interesting and, perhaps, modish innovations in the evolving area of public program evaluation and productivity: Data Envelopment Analysis, which is uniquely useful in quantifying what "efficiency" means in the public sector; the federal experience with Inspectors General, an office focusing on the evaluation of fiscal management programs; and Total Quality Management, a philosophy and set of techniques born in industry that is having a growing influence among those who are trying to increase productivity in government.

Data Envelopment Analysis: Finding the Bottom Line in Public Management

One of the great potential utilities of program evaluation is that it may enable us to determine what the "bottom line" in public administration is. The private sector long has had "bottom line" measurements available to it, specifically the profit margin. But the nonprofit sector does not, and researchers in the field of program evaluation slowly are developing measurement techniques that enable them to determine their level of efficiency in the delivery of public services.

Efficiency is a term that can have several

implications. As Roger B. Parks points out, "efficiency" often has meaning beyond the phrase of "the biggest bang for the buck." Such a definition does not necessarily take into account how many resources it takes to conduct a program, nor the corresponding potential prices of policy outputs. Nor does such a definition include other measures that might be attached to the value of the outputs produced by a public agency, such as the degree of importance that citizens and clients might attach to those outputs.

We are not considering these refined definitions here. Instead, we are talking in terms of what the field of program evaluation commonly calls "technical efficiency," or the attempt to maximize the difference between all benefits from all costs in an operation.[53]

Data Envelopment Analysis is an unusually useful technique being used to measure technical efficiency—the "bottom line"—of the public sector.[54] In its simplest terms, *Data Envelopment Analysis* establishes measurable outputs for a particular "decision making unit," such as a government agency or a corporation. For example, a police department (a "decision-making unit") would have certain obvious kinds of outputs, such as number of suspects arrested, number of officers assigned to patrol, and so forth. These outputs are then divided by pertinent inputs. In the case of the police department, the pertinent input would be the department's budget. This procedure is then done for a number of police departments and the results are compared. Those departments that do not measure up to the average performance (as determined by specific measures) of the other police departments are thus made aware that they are not performing at their potential efficiency.

In an effort to be fair, other factors are mixed into these measures of efficiency, such as environmental factors over which the decision-making unit may have no control. In the case of the police department, for example, such factors may include the percent of population below the poverty line, since poor populations often are afflicted with higher crime rates. In this fashion, the productivity and efficiency of decision-making units can be compared on the basis of "fairness"; in other words, police departments that are working in high crime areas, or in areas with large percentages of their populations below the poverty line, are compared only with those police departments that are working in areas afflicted by similar levels of crime and impoverishment. Or, if these kinds of comparisons are not possible (which is not uncommon), then those police departments that are in tougher areas than are other departments are granted advantages— "weights" along specific measurement areas— that are designed to render them comparable to their peers.

Data Envelopment Analysis has been applied with some success to school districts and police departments.[55] One study of police departments which analyzed data from a set of 469 municipal police agencies concluded, by using Data Envelopment Analysis, that some factors relating to police department efficiency were more controllable than were others. Among those factors not at all amenable to control were the proportion of citizens living below the poverty level and the age of the police department itself. Factors more subject to control were those of utilization of resources, organizational structure, and personnel policies. The study found that the allocation of resources to the patrol division was associated with somewhat higher levels of efficiency among the more efficient police departments, although this relationship was not a strong one. However, the relative bureaucratization of the police department (*i.e.*, several more hierarchical layers than the average) did associate strongly with lower levels of efficiency. Among personnel policies, unionization of the police force had a negative association with efficiency, while police departments that were unburdened with civil service and educational requirements showed a bimodal pattern; departments without civil service or educational requirements were more likely to be found in the lowest and highest quartiles of the efficiency distribution of the study.[56]

Our point is not to delve into the details of what makes some police departments more efficient than others, but rather to convey a flavor of how Data Envelopment Analysis can work. Data Envelopment Analysis may be as close to any of the program evaluation methodologies that we have in deriving measures of technical efficiency for the public sector. It is a methodology that likely could be used with benefit more widely than it is.

The Inspector General: An Experiment in Evaluating Federal Fiscal Programs

Perhaps the public programs most worthy of continuing evaluation are those dealing with government finance, since it is these programs that underwrite the delivery of all other public policies. Increasingly, the federal government has been a leader in the innovative evaluation of its financial management, notably in its appointment of Inspectors General (I.G.'s) throughout the federal bureaucracy.[57]

Inspectors General are charged with exposing waste, fraud, and abuse in federal agencies, and to help federal administrators eliminate these problems. (In this charge, I.G.'s represent a return to the precepts of the efficiency phase of public program evaluation and productivity.) They have had a largely positive, if somewhat controversial, impact on the productivity of the federal government.

The appointment of Inspectors General can be traced to the 1960s by a few agencies acting on their own volition, but their formal institution began with the Inspector General Act of 1978, which was amended and broadened in 1988; currently, there are about sixty I.G. offices in as many federal agencies.[58] The Inspectors General in the fourteen cabinet departments alone employ over 84,000 people.[59]

The twenty-seven Inspectors General responsible for the largest federal agencies are nominated by the president and confirmed by the Senate; the remaining thirty-four I.G.'s are appointed by agency heads without Senate confirmation. Uniquely, Inspectors General report to both the heads of the agencies to which they are assigned *and* to Congress; moreover, they are the only presidential appointees who may communicate directly to Congress without clearance from the Office of Management and Budget — a clear indication of their power in government.

The I.G.'s have been aggressive and successful, and more than 38,000 federal employees, contractors, and others have been successfully prosecuted for corruption over a ten-year period as a consequence of investigations by Inspectors General. I.G.'s may recover for the federal government as much as $750 million a year in fines and penalties imposed on companies and individuals by the courts, and save it $23 billion a year in retrieving questionable charges by contractors and by recommending ways to expend agency funds more astutely.[60]

At least two problems have surfaced in the federal government's experience with Inspectors General. One is the opportunity of I.G.'s to be high handed with federal agency administrators. For example, the Inspector General of the Agency for International Development was quoted in *The Washington Post* as allegedly stating (he denied it) that the Agency had "a crime rate higher than downtown Detroit."[61] Inspectors General are viewed by some federal administrators as more interested in exposing problems than in helping to rectify them, and often as unimaginative squelchers of new managerial approaches as well.

Second, when an I.G. does report waste, fraud, and abuse to Congress, Congress sometimes yawns. For example, when widespread corruption was exposed in the Department of Housing and Urban Development in 1989, Congress was outraged at being kept in the dark—until it became clear that the Department's I.G. had been reporting these problems to Congress (as well as to the Department and OMB) since 1985. Congress's studied ignoring of bad news is, of course, not new. During the 1980s, the brewing crisis in the nation's savings and loan associations was made plain to Congress in many ways before Congress accepted the fact that the government's largest financial scandal in history was well underway.[62]

Despite these problems of communication, however, the I.G. experiment has been a productive one, and stands as an important federal contribution to the productivity of the public sector. Congress has recognized the value of Inspectors General, and in 1991 passed the Chief Financial Officers Act, which places chief financial officers in the twenty-three largest federal agencies. These officers report directly to the I.G.'s of those agencies. Clearly, the Act will strengthen the role of the Inspector General over time.

Total Quality Management: Industry's Model for Public Productivity?

Total Quality Management (TQM) is a philosophy of administration, a set of principles, and a series of quantitive techniques that are designed to continuously improve, and, if necessary, transform the processes of the organization from top to bottom so that customers are fully satisfied with the organization's products, performance, procedures, and people. TQM is currently a hugely influential phenomenon in both public and private management. It originated in the corporate world, and, increasingly, it is gaining adherents in the world of government as a major means of improving productivity.

Total Quality Management was born in the brains of Americans, and quickly adopted by Japanese. Walter A. Shewhart, a scientist at Bell Laboratories, devised a technique for measuring variance in production lines in the 1920s that he dubbed "statistical process control"; the U.S. War Department used Shewhart's methods for converting industry to defense purposes during World War II, and hired Shewhart's student, W. Edwards Deming, to help it do it. The government was so impressed with Deming that they classified his methods as military secrets.

The military used Shewhart's and Deming's techniques of quality control—and Deming himself—in rebuilding the Japanese industrial base during the American occupation of that country. During this period, Deming toured Japan giving lectures on quality control, and by 1953 the Japanese were sufficiently convinced of the utility of Deming's views that they established the nation's "Deming Award" for industrial quality.

It was also in the 1950s that the U.S. Government sent Joseph M. Juran to Japan to improve industrial quality. Juran's ideas are perhaps more suitable to public management than are Deming's because they are more human-based. It was Juran who introduced the ideas of defining quality as customer satisfaction, and "getting it right the first time" as a cornerstone of efficiency.

In contrast to Japan, American industry largely ignored Deming's and Juran's increasingly trenchant criticism of its problems over the ensuing thirty years. By the 1990s both men had become the reigning "gurus" of TQM in American industry.

TQM: Governments' Tentative Response.
By the 1980s, American industry was discovering Total Quality Management with a vengeance

born of declining market shares, and the private sector's enthusiasm—which occasionally bordered on the manic—for TQM had an inevitable impact on the public sector. The U.S. Department of Commerce introduced in 1987 its "Malcolm Baldrige National Quality Award," a clone of Japan's Deming Award, and in 1988 the federal government created the Federal Quality Institute, which is charged with promoting a quality-based approach to governing throughout the bureaucracy by rotating federal executives through it; there is now a federal Quality Improvement Prototype Award for federal agencies.

These efforts are doubtless wholesome, and they appear to have had an effect. According to the General Accounting Office, 68 percent of the federal government's 2,800 installations are using TQM methods to improve services, although only 18 percent of these offices can report long-term benefits from these efforts, and only 13 percent of their employees are involved in them.[63] The Internal Revenue Service and the Department of Defense are among the most aggressive federal agencies in their pursuit of "total quality."

State and local governments have felt the influence of TQM, too. Nevertheless, the permeation of new productivity approaches, such as TQM, in these governments is dependent to some degree on the commitment of the chief executive, who may or may not remain in office long enough for Total Quality Management to "transform" the government in the manner that its advocates envision. This appears to have been the experience of Minnesota and Michigan in the 1980s, when both states had governors who were implementing TQM variants, but who were unseated in 1990, and much of their states' TQM programs with them. Local governments, particularly those with council-manager forms of government, seem more successful with TQM than states: Austin, Dallas, Fort Collins, Madison, New York, Palm Beach County, Phoenix, St. Paul, San Luis Obispo, and Sunnyvale, California, are among the localities that have performance-sensitive, TQM-type plans in place that are evidently working well.

TQM: Appropriate for the Public Sector?
Despite its many proponents, Total Quality Management is no panacea for the productivity

problems of organizations, whether public or private. Even corporations, for which TQM was originally designed and exclusively meant, have had mixed experiences with it. Florida Power and Light, which won Japan's Deming Award for its successful and extensive use of TQM, discarded it when its top management changed in 1992; winners of the Baldrige Award—General Motors, IBM, Xerox, and Westinghouse—have all shown deteriorating performance after receiving the award, and one, the Wallace Company, filed for bankruptcy soon after winning the Baldrige Award in 1990.[64]

Table 7–3 lists what have come to be known as the fourteen "commandments" of Total Quality Management, and, in a gunshot way, assesses the prospective practicality and utility of each commandment for government. Table 7-3 has some limited use in conveying a sense of how TQM might improve public productivity (and how it might be misapplied to government as well) but, more broadly, it is important to understand that TQM addresses only some of the problems faced by democracies in enhancing their governments' productivity, and some problems it addresses not at all.

Total Quality Management could be a very effective management tool in refocusing governments' mission as servants of the citizenry by concentrating the resources of public administration on the governmental processes that can be enhanced to deliver higher quality services; by encouraging the decentralization of bureaucratic authority; by stressing the prevention of problems (as opposed to solving them later); and by helping public administrators understand that most problems (Deming says 85 percent) result from faulty systems, not faulty people. But TQM simply fails to address those problems of productivity that are unique to the public sector, notably the fact that governments are monopolies; that they lack the internal organizational authority possessed by their counterparts in the private sector; that they must develop substitutes for profit to measure their productivity; and that different government agencies often are charged by legislatures with vastly different government missions.[65]

Even those features of Total Quality Management that are adaptable, at least in principle, to government face obstacles that seldom are present in corporations. Perhaps the most serious one

TABLE 7-3   The "Commandments" of Total Quality Management (TQM) and Their Applicability to Government

The Fourteen "Commandments of TQM"	Their Applicability to Government
1. Establish constancy of purpose.	Questionable: The changing political environment and short lead times in government work against constancy.
2. Improve systems always and forever.	Applicable: Rebuild agencies around delivering quality services to citizen-clients.
3. Eliminate numerical goals.	Inapplicable: The public sector's challenge is to develop numerical measures of performance.
4. Eliminate fear.	Applicable: Civil service rules largely assure personal security.
5. Establish leadership: "Don't boss —coach."	Applicable: A coaching style of leadership is attainable in both public and private organizations.
6. Consider quality, not just low cost, in accepting bids.	Questionable: Most governments mandate that only lowest bids be accepted, but this could be changed.
7. Break down departmental barriers.	Applicable, but difficult: Differing, sometimes opposing goals of some agencies in larger governments inhibit break down.
8. Institute on-the-job training.	Applicable: Agency directors typically cut training budgets first, but this attribute could be reversed.
9. Eliminate annual ratings of employees.	Applicable, but difficult: Some civil service rules protecting job security would likely have to be changed.
10. Establish employee education and self-improvement programs.	Applicable, but difficult: Civic culture could question such programs as "boondoggling."
11. Eliminate slogans and exhortations.	Applicable, but irrelevant: Governments have few, if any, slogans or exhortations.
12. Stop depending on mass inspections.	Applicable, but irrelevant: Governments use few mass inspections beyond the military services.
13. Adopt the TQM philosophy.	Applicable: At least for those "commandments" that can be adapted to the public sector; moreover, public employees want to improve governmental performance.
14. Use top management to drive transformation.	Applicable, but difficult: Brief tenures and high turnovers of top administrators in many governments (e.g., cabinet secretaries, city managers) inhibit role of top management.

is the high turnover of top public executives, which actively undermines at least two of TQM's "commandments": constancy of purpose, and top management driving the "transformation" of the organization. Consider the example of Hillsborough County, Florida, which had been a leader in implementing Total Quality Management in government. When a newly elected board of county commissioners took office, it promptly eliminated TQM and fired the county's top management. "TQM was a factor in the firing; the board saw the new management style as a threat to its power."[66] Even when Total Quality Management is not viewed as threatening by elected officials, they nonetheless understand that it garners them few, if any, political returns (a generalization that can be applied, perhaps, to efforts by elected officials to improve the whole of public administration as well).

It also is worth noting that the political environment in which governments must function is volatile (as Hillsborough County illustrates), and this works against the long-term implementation by governments of not only TQM, but any concentrated effort to improve governmental systems over time. And Total Quality Management requires time; it took, after all, thirty years before the Japanese saw returns on their initial adoption of Deming's and Juran's theories. It may be that the long-term orientation of Asian cultures, noted in Chapter 5, in contrast to the short-term orientation of American culture, has made TQM a more viable option for Japanese organizations than for American ones. It is of interest in this respect that state universities, whose "ivory tower" qualities are often criticized, but which do give them relative stability and a longer-term perspective than most public agencies, are among the public sector's most enthusiastic adopters of TQM.

These systemic difficulties aside, there is a raft of more technical questions that render the adoption of Total Quality Management by governments challenging. These questions include the well-known problem of developing performance measures: including and involving all employees (those in unions, too) in the designing of new, TQM-based processes; finding new ways to acquire consumer feedback; matching budgeting decisions with quality improvement efforts; refocusing human resource systems (including the pervasive annual evaluations of each employee's performance) along TQM criteria; defining who is the "customer"[66] in agencies that deliver broadly conceived public programs; and inserting long-term thinking into the short-term culture of the American public sector.[67] Though "technical," perhaps, these tasks are not trivial.

The relevance of Total Quality Management to public program evaluation and productivity is not universal—but much of TQM is relevant to public management, and, once the special strengths that it can bring to government are sorted out and understood more fully, TQM can be a powerful tool in improving public productivity. At root, TQM's strengths for the public sector may reside more in the "philosophy" of Total Quality Management, and less in its "commandments" and techniques, for TQM pressures management to think in terms of defining quality in client-based terms; of seeing the larger picture; of improving processes (and, if necessary, discarding poor processes in favor of creating whole new approaches); of empowering employees; of long-term strategic planning; and of never being content with the *status quo*. No organization can improve its performance and productivity unless its people identify with and promote these somewhat philosophic notions, and Total Quality Management has the unique ability to draw this kind of managerial thinking to the forefront. Because of this ability, TQM likely will not fade from the public management scene as just one more administrative fad.

PUBLIC PROGRAM EVALUATION AND PRODUCTIVITY RESEARCH: THREE PROBLEMS

Data Envelopment Analysis, Inspectors General, and Total Quality Management are all innovative approaches to public program evaluation and productivity. But collecting and sifting the data on which to base evaluative decisions—in other words, research—is and will be an ever-present chore in public program evaluation and productivity, whether the approach is new, inventive, and radical or old, standard, and mundane. In this section, we review three problems of evaluation research: scientific and technical, administrative and political, and ethical and moral.

Note that in this discussion, we tend to use the term "evaluation research" rather than "public program evaluation." Although the terms are, as we have stated, generally interchangeable in the literature, we use the phrase "evaluation research" here because we like its connotation of gathering and culling data, in contrast to making evaluations of public programs based on the data, and the three problems that we will be reviewing here are primarily problems of data gathering.

The data underlying the assessment of a public program, or *evaluation research*, differ from basic research. Evaluation research is a form of applied, or "action research," because it may, wittingly or unwittingly, contribute to social action. Evaluation research, like basic research, is concerned with theory and experimental design, but its chief purpose is to evaluate comprehensively a particular activity, and to meet an agency's deadline in the process.

Scientific and Technical Problems in Evaluation Research

Henry Riecken has given us a succinct and pointed statement about the scientific and technical pitfalls associated with evaluation research: "The central scientific problems in evaluation are (a) the segregation of treatment effects per se from random variation on the one hand and from systematic biasing through uncontrolled factors that are extraneous to treatment on the other hand, and (b) the reliable measurement of these effects."[68] Let us consider his points in turn.

Problems of Validity and Measurement. The first part of the problem, as Riecken phrases it, deals essentially with the question of validity.[69] Evaluation researchers can use a number of methods to assure validity—selecting the appropriate experimental methods, using a nonrandom comparison group method, comparing similar programs using time series analysis, and similar approaches.

The other portion of Riecken's dilemma is that of measurement. Before a program evaluator can measure anything, however, he or she must identify the objectives of the program in a way that permits valid measuring. Such an identification of program goals includes the content of the objective (in other words, what is to be changed by the program), the target of the program, the time frame within which the change is expected to occur, the number of objectives if there are more than one, and finally, the extent of the expected effect.

Once objectives are so defined, then distinctions can be made between immediate, intermediate, and ultimate objectives, and measurements can be developed accordingly. One type of measurement, for example, is input measurement: What are the resources allocated by an agency for a particular program relative to the services actually received by the clients of that program? In this case, the resources would be the inputs. Original and secondary data also need to be measured. As Caro observes, "identification of variables is, of course, only a first step in the measurement process. Evaluators are often confronted with serious obstacles in seeking the valid, reliable, and sensitive measures they need," going on to note that agency records often are seriously deficient and the evaluator must collect his or her own original and secondary data; such data collection "may add enormously to the cost of evaluation."[70]

Caro also notes that the subjects of the evaluation (*e.g.*, public administrators) may try to redirect their behavior in an effort to affect the evaluation's outcome, and that detecting this attempt becomes particularly difficult when evaluative criteria and data are incomplete. An example of the evaluative problems posed by incomplete data is provided by higher education. Who has not heard of the "publish or perish" dictum in universities and not wondered if the number of a professor's publications actually has anything to do with his or her teaching abilities? Relatedly, do grades indicate the real level of learning by a student?

Finally, there is the measurement problem of occasionally trying to measure the unmeasurable—a problem more common in the public sector than in the private one. Assigning a monetary worth to a human life is an example. Early cost-benefit analyses conducted by government based the value of a human life on a person's projected earning power—a calculus that strikes some as a bit cold blooded. Still, determining the value of a human life is difficult to sidestep in many program evaluations, notably those in health, safety, defense, crime, transportation, the environment, and many other areas of basic governmental functions; the conclusion is inexorably, if reluctantly, drawn that, whether or not life can be measured, it nonetheless must be assigned some dollar value in many program evaluations, if the evaluations are to be useful.

Federal officials are doing precisely this, but without coherence. The U.S. Department of

Agriculture low-balls a human life at $1.1 million; the Office of Management and Budget pegs a life at $1 million to $2 million; and the Consumer Product Safety Commission agrees that a life tops out at $2 million. The Occupational Safety and Health Administration measures a really good human life at $3.5 million (and a poor one at a baseline of $2 million); the Nuclear Regulatory Commission says each and every life is worth $5 million (its figure, interestingly, is based on the hazard pay for fighter pilots in the Korean Conflict), while the Environmental Protection Agency says a life can be worth as much as $8 million—or as little as $1.6 million.[71]

Problems of Research Design. A final major problem of a scientific and technical nature in evaluation research is that of dealing with program research design. The design problem can be broken down and understood in terms of the components of controlled interaction between program practitioners, interaction between recipients of the program, and the fact that many programs are both diffuse and unstable.

Achieving control over the variables in a program for purposes of evaluating that program is unusually difficult in an action setting. When a control group (that is, a group of clients who are excluded from receiving the benefits of a particular experimental program designed to improve services) is set aside for purposes of comparing it with an experimental group (a group of clients who do receive the benefits of a particular program innovation), there is often a great deal of social and political pressure to provide the benefits of that experiment to both groups. Thus, both the program's administrators and the program's clients are reluctant to withhold services from a particular group that might benefit from those services, even though the evaluation might be ruined by doing so. Relatedly, self-selection is a problem in a program evaluation in an action setting; "it is difficult to refuse service to those who seek it and provide service to those who resist it."[72]

In short, action settings simply inhibit evaluators from using a well-controlled experimental design. However, one of the real problems in developing a research design for program evaluation is more political than social; hidden motives on the part of the evaluator can interfere with accurate measurement. For example, private consultants, who must make a living by securing contracts from public agencies, may promise too much in writing their research design. Among the more vivid examples of this is provided by a program evaluation attempted by the Office of Economic Opportunity in 1972, in which 120 drug treatment centers in six cities were evaluated in a study involving interviews with 9,000 present and former drug abusers. The purpose of the study was to assess client characteristics and behavior, the delivery system, the relationship of the project to the communities themselves, and the program's cost-effectiveness. All of this was to be accomplished in thirteen months. After seven months of rather grotesque trial and error, the project was abandoned. During that time, the program evaluators (a private consulting firm) had collected data on nine treatment centers and 1,270 clients at a cost of more than $2 million.[73]

Avoiding such fiascoes as the Office of Economic Opportunity's abortive attempt to evaluate drug abuse treatment programs can be enhanced by asking certain basic questions about the research design itself.[74] Is the research design explicit about important constraints in the study? Does it use standard evaluation procedures as much as possible? Have the evaluators adjusted expectations to known data reliability and availability? Does the evaluation rely on opinions as measures only if the program is intended to change opinions? Does it mandate a clear separation between the results of the data collection and analysis and the evaluators' judgments and beliefs? Does it specify at least one acceptable measure of accomplishment? Does it keep the questions relatively few in number? Does it establish priorities? And does the design require as few formal reports from the evaluators as possible, depending instead on frequent and informal contacts? While such questions may seem elementary, the sad fact is that they are rarely asked in many research designs.

Administrative and Political Problems in Evaluation Research

A second major problem in conducting evaluation research, apart from the scientific and technical ones, are the administrative and political difficulties to be surmounted in conducting an evaluation. Riecken observes that "in comparison with the vast amount of scholarly examination of the design and measurement features of evaluation, the matter of day-to-day execution of these tasks has received scant attention," noting further that political realities complicate evaluation management because evaluation "is always undertaken in a context of decisions about the use of resources and, accordingly, has implications for the acquisition, distribution and loss of social or political power."[75]

Who Are the Evaluators? To understand the administrative and political implications of evaluation research, we must first know who the evaluators are. Program evaluators play many social roles, and the roles they assume affect the ways they discharge their responsibilities. In his excellent study of policy analysts in the federal government, Arnold Meltsner identified four separate roles played by program evaluators: the entrepreneur, who has excellent analytical and political skills; the politician, who has reasonable political skills but who is less impressive in intellectual analysis; the technician, who has good analytical skills but is apolitical; and finally what Meltsner calls the pretender, who is weak both analytically and politically.[76]

Similarly, K. A. Archebald has observed three roles: academics, or evaluation researchers who typically are funded by grant monies and conduct a study with minimal contact with the program's clients; clinicians, who respond only to their own interpersonal dynamic and who treat (quite paternally) the client as a patient who needs help to cure a sickness; and strategizers, who use the management consultant approach and who work with clients as if they were colleagues. Archebald contends that in an evaluation that blends all three evaluator roles, it is the program's clients who often have the ultimate responsibility for decisions regarding research and their consequences.[77]

Administrators Against Evaluators? Because of the social and political roles that program evaluators frequently play, tensions can develop between the evaluators and the line managers of an agency. As a result, it is unfortunately not unusual for conflict to erupt between the program managers and the program's evaluators, whom the managers may see as self-anointed prophets passing judgment on the managers' efforts to solve real and long-standing social problems. Mutual perceptions aside, evaluators often do have different perspectives, purposes, and values from the on-line practitioners. Conflict can occur if the practitioners feel themselves threatened—and objective analysis in and of itself, irrespective who is conducting it, often can be perceived as such a threat. Often, however, tensions between evaluators and managers result simply from the evaluators' failure to make a clear distinction between the administrative and personal qualities of the managers and the actual effectiveness of the treatment they happen to be using. In any event, there is an unusually rich empirical literature on the interplay of political and administrative forces extant among managers and evaluators.[78]

As a result of these problems, most experts in the field of evaluation agree that the evaluation of a program ought to be commissioned and sponsored by the highest level in an organization that has program responsibility and, on balance, evaluation that is conducted by an external agency or by a third-party consultant probably is preferable.[79] By commissioning an evaluation by the upper-most level of an organization and by using outside evaluators, some of the natural strains between practitioners and researchers are avoided. Notably such an approach can avoid those tensions that emanate from such diverse values as *specificity versus generality* (researchers are more likely to be interested in long-term problem solving, while practitioners are more likely to be concerned with solving immediate problems); *status quo versus change* (practicing administrators, on the one hand, may attempt to conceal badly managed programs and to resist any change that they perceive as being potentially disruptive, while academic evaluators, on the other hand, often claim a superior knowledge of human affairs that predispose them to dramatize the inadequacy of the administrators); and finally, *academic knowledge versus practical experience* (because the evaluator is, in fact, usually an academic, the practitioner views him or her as having no "real-world" experience in or awareness of such practical problems as limited budgets and personnel resources).[80]

While the general thrust of the evaluation literature tends to favor the use of outside consultants, arguments can be made for either inside or outside evaluators. Contentions favoring the use of outside consultants include: They are more objective; they are more likely to question the basic premises of the organization; they would be more effective mediators because of their objectivity; and they are more likely to devote their time more fully to the research problem at hand. Still, insiders have certain advantages, too, including a more detailed knowledge of the organization, and the probability that they are in a better position to be able to do continuing, long-term program evaluation.[81]

Ethical and Moral Problems In Evaluation Research

Finally, evaluators should be cognizant of some basic ethical and moral problems associated with the conduct of evaluation research. Principal among these are problems involving privacy, confidentiality, and informed consent.

The issues of privacy and confidentiality are not unique to evaluation research, but they do assume a somewhat different tenor in this context. In program evaluation projects, *privacy* refers to the state of the individual; *confidentiality* refers to a state of information. Thus, privacy becomes a matter between the evaluator and the respondent. It hinges on the degree to which the evaluator's questions, in and of themselves, are perceived by the respondent to be prying or embarrassing. Hence, privacy is not a matter of *who* knows the answer, but of whether certain kinds of knowledge are known to *anyone* other than the respondent. The test of an invasion of privacy is to ask if the respondent will voluntarily furnish answers under conditions that appear to appropriately restrict the use of those answers.

Confidentiality refers to the question of whether an investigator's promise of confidentiality to a respondent is either sufficient or even necessary. The evaluator's promise, no matter how solemnly given, may not be sufficient because, under certain legal situations, the investigator must yield the information he or she has collected or go to jail. The legal fact of the matter is that social science research records are not protected under statutory law as a privileged com-

munication, as are the records of lawyers and physicians.

Central to the ethical issues of privacy and confidentiality is the problem of *informed consent*, which refers to whether or not a respondent understands what he or she is consenting to. Such an understanding, of course, is particularly important in cases of human experimentation, but it also has a bearing on program evaluation studies. As Riecken observes, "lawyers have questioned the legality as well as the ethicality of experimental design and random assignment of participants to treatment for purposes of program evaluation. The grounds for such questioning include the issues of informed consent, equal protection, and the statutory (or other) authority of the agency to conduct experimental evaluations."[82]

DOES PUBLIC PROGRAM EVALUATION MATTER?

We have reviewed a number of difficulties regarding public program evaluation, but we have not asked what Republicans in the White House used to call the "big enchilada"—that is, is public program evaluation used by anyone? Carol H. Weiss observes in this connection that, "there is a pervasive sense that government officials do not pay much attention to the research their money is buying. The consensus seems to be that most research studies bounce off the policy process without making much of a dent in the course of events. Support for this notion surfaces in many quarters—among social scientists, executive branch officials, and members of Congress."[83]

Examples to support Weiss's assessment are plentiful, and perhaps the most notorious instance of program managers resisting program evaluation has occurred over the years in elementary and secondary education. Because the education establishment in the United States is a highly decentralized one, local educators have successfully resisted attempts to evaluate such basic programs as whether or not pupils are learning to read. Under Title I of the Elementary and Secondary Education Act of 1965, for example, the U.S. Office of Education (now the Department of Education) requested achievement test data from

A NOTE OF GRACE AND A CASE OF REALITY

In the field of public administration, ideology can become mixed with reality, and this is particularly true in the areas of program evaluation and productivity. An example of ideology being mistaken for reality is provided in the following synopsis of the final report of the President's Private Sector Survey on Cost Control (the Grace Commission). An example of public management being conducted effectively and without ideological bias is furnished by the following case study conducted by the American Productivity Center on the City of Phoenix, Arizona.

The Grace Commission's report was publicly accepted in 1984 by the president as his program for reducing the federal deficit. The Commission argued a commonly held ideology that by applying "solid business management" to the public sector, enormous savings could be realized. However, as the analysis that follows points out, there are anomalies in applying the unadapted techniques of business to the public interest.

Reality, rather than ideology, is more apparent in the case study of the City of Phoenix that follows. Phoenix is known as a "star" city among public administrators, and is one of the most effective and efficient urban governments in the country. The city has been able to attain this stature by constantly testing what management techniques work and what do not, and monitoring the performance of the programs that it conducts. Empiricism replaces ideology.

Unlike the nominal predecessors of the Grace Commission (which, in many ways, were not at all its predecessors, since they were significantly smaller in both scope and number of participants), the Brownlow Commission, the two Hoover Commissions, the Ash Council, and the Carter Reorganization Project were comprised largely of analysts from many walks of life, but who were inside government or who knew a great deal about it. Not so with the Grace Commission. The Executive Committee of the President's Private Sector Survey on Cost Control consisted of 161 members, virtually all of whom were executives in the business world. About a fourth headed firms listed in the Fortune 500, but also represented were about a third of the top fifty commercial banks in the country, the nation's three largest insurance firms, and other members of similar backgrounds. Only seven of these 161 members of the Executive Committee were from occupations that were not businesses, such as representatives from universities, labor, and the Heritage Foundation.

The reports themselves are unusually difficult to read. None is indexed; they are long; and the writing style is arid. Some parts of the reports are actually censored.

The analyses are of mixed quality. An example of a constructive analysis is a study of correspondence control in the Department of Health and Human Services, which found that it took fifty-eight days to answer a letter in the Office of the Secretary, compared to eighteen days at the Pentagon, and nine at a Prudential

Insurance office. An example of a poor analysis is the report's criticism of the Department of Energy on the grounds that its span of control is considerably narrower than that of the federal government as a whole. What is not mentioned in this critique, however, is the fact that the Department uses 90 percent of its budget allocations to contract out its programs, and greater control is often required.

Recommendations for achieving savings meet a similarly mixed fate. For example, the final report argues for cheaper packaging of ammunition for the military, but ignores prospective damage in shipping that would offset such savings. The report also urges that 7,000 small post offices and almost two-thirds of Social Security district and branch offices be closed in order to save money. No doubt savings would accrue, but at what cost in services? The question of government's obligation to provide services is not addressed in this instance, and is rarely addressed throughout the report.

The final report also contains some serious misrepresentations. First, the Commission grossly exaggerates the savings it claims would be achieved (nearly half a trillion dollars over three years) if its recommendations were followed. But as the Commission states in the fine print, its projected savings are of a "planning" quality and not of a "budget" quality, despite the fact that the proposed savings are presented in the context of the growing national debt. Similarly, the figures presented by the Commission refer not to mere savings but to revenue increases and accelerations in cash flow that the report contends will result if its recommendations were implemented; yet, faster revenue collections and slower disbursements are not true "savings," but merely bookkeeping artifices. Most importantly, however, the potential savings claimed by the Commission really are only estimates, and not well-grounded projections. Many of the recommendations by the Commission are of a sort that their financial implications simply are not measurable, even speculatively.

A second type of misrepresentation by the Grace Commission occurs in the context of its claim that its objective was not to change policy, but merely to improve efficiency in the federal government. Yet, as the General Accounting Office observed, "policy-oriented issues make up a large portion of the Commission's total estimated savings." For example, the report advocates repeal of the Davis-Bacon Act, the Walsh-Healey Act, and the Service Contracts Act; it urges the Environmental Protection Agency to propose new block grant programs to replace categorical grants for environmental assistance; it proposes that the sale or lease of public range lands in ten Western states be reevaluated; it supports increased production of plutonium and tritium in three nuclear facilities; it suggests that the State Department push for a new voting system in the United Nations that is weighted for relative budgetary contributions to the U.N.; and it urges that the president be granted an item veto power. While such measures may result in greater savings by the federal government, they clearly are policy changes as well, and the Commission had a duty to say so that it did not fulfill.

Many of the proposals of the Grace Commission display a business-oriented prejudice that is not identified in the report for what it is. Most obvious in this regard is the Commission's commitment to a privatization philosophy. As in the report of the second Hoover Commission (reviewed in Chapter 11), it is urged that far more contracts be granted to the private sector to conduct and implement public programs. Among other federal operations slated for privatization by the Grace Commission are the Military Commissary System, the Strategic Petroleum Reserve, hydroelectric power plants, space shuttle launching services, electronic data processing for the Social Security System, Coast Guard Search and Rescue Operations, patient care in small military hospitals, operation of the Army's personnel and payroll system, and municipal waste water treatment. Many of these and other suggestions would result in extraordinary profits for certain industries.

A similar bias is found in the Grace Commission's

clear preference for deregulation, including the deregulation of nuclear power plants. The Commission also recommends that more user charges be levied. However, user charges should be put on a really paying basis, not merely offsetting the full costs of providing a service, but charging what the market will bear and making a profit! Now *that* is private enterprise!

The Commission also made allegations and proposals that seem purposely designed to undermine morale in the federal service. J. Peter Grace, the Chair of the Commission, for example, continually insisted throughout the Commission's deliberations that "government is run horribly," despite the fact that many of the reports provided by his own Commission stated otherwise. In fact, the Commission admitted that top federal executives were inadequately paid compared to their counterparts in the private sector, and suggested raises ranging from 20 to 30 percent. But at the lower levels of the federal bureaucracy, arguments were made by the Commission to significantly reduce pay; in making its case, no reference was made to the recommendation by the Advisory Committee on Federal Pay that overall federal salaries need to be raised by nearly 22 percent to catch up to private sector. The Commission also urged significant decreases in the size of the federal work force, but with little analysis to support such cuts.

Finally, many of the managerial innovations urged by the Grace Commission were not all that novel; in fact, the General Accounting Office has stated that about half of the proposals suggested by the Commission already had been recommended by the GAO but had not been adopted. On the other hand, the Office of Management and Budget reported a year after the release of the Grace Commission's report that 879 (or 35 percent) of the Commission's 2,478 recommendations had been enacted by the Reagan Administration, at a three-year cost savings of $111,882,000.

In sum, the President's Private Sector Survey on Cost Control has some pluses and it has some minuses. But unlike its predecessors, not only is the report of the Grace Commission far more sweeping in its scope and in its recommendations, its members were far less representative of people who understand government, and who comprehend the obligation mandated by society for government to provide services.

Sources: Derived from: Charles T. Goodsell, "The Grace Commission: Seeking Efficiency for the Whole People?" Public Administration Review, 44 (May/June 1984), p. 197; U.S. General Accounting Office, Com pendium of GAO's Views on the Cost Saving Proposals of the Grace Commission. Vol. I—Summary of Findings. Vol. II—Individual Issue Analyses. GAO/OCG-85-1. (Washington, D.C.: U.S. Government Printing Office, February 19, 1985); and Office of Management and Budget, Management of the United States Government (Washington, D.C.: U.S. Government Printing Office, 1985).

The City of Phoenix is the ninth largest city in the country and employs about 10,000 people. It is one of the nation's fastest growing cities and, in part as a result of that growth, the city initiated a comprehensive plan to improve productivity in the early 1970s. At first, Phoenix tried a centralized approach that had an industrial engineering orientation, but this tack eventually proved to be so cumbersome that it was phased out. But the initiation of this system did begin what observers called a "cultural change" in the attitudes of both managers and their employees.

In 1977, another kind of approach was begun. A Citizens Productivity Advisory Committee was appointed to advise the city on how to improve municipal productivity, and as a result of its recommendations, a major effort was made to make departments more accountable and employees more participatory in decision making. Problem solving work groups were established in every area of the city's business, and the results have been successful. An annual survey of city employees shows increased employee involvement in decision making for every year that the program has been in operation.

A similar effort was made to decentralize management. The director of management and budget assigned twelve to fifteen of his staff members to operating departments to monitor productivity projects that departments undertake each year. By integrating these analysts into the operating departments, they become a part of the team of that department rather than being perceived as outside "graders."

The city also created a Value Management Resource Office, which combined the training and development staff with the operations analysis staff. This Office functions as a team of internal consultants who use both industrial engineering and behavioral science methods to improve productivity. Included in its functions are surveys of employees and clients, work load distribution analyses, the development of work output measures, the diagnosis of problems, work group development, management consultation, conflict resolution, customized training, work flow and scheduling, productivity train-

ing, and decision making assistance. The Office provides some thirty formal training programs for city workers affecting about 800 employees each year.

Phoenix city government places a high value on training and education. It offers tuition reimbursement to any of its employees, provided that employees take courses that relate to their employment.

The city also has initiated a "pay for performance" compensation system that in effect is a modified Management by Objectives system. The system requires all departments to establish a plan for achieving their objectives and to list productivity improvement goals within a particular time frame. When these goals are achieved, salaries are adjusted with increases based on inflation rates plus merit increases that are closely tied to the attainment of objectives.

Among the most innovative approaches that Phoenix has taken is the application of competitive bidding procedures not only for private companies but for its own city agencies as well. Thus, not only do private corporations bid for a city contract, but so do other city agencies, a process that has resulted in saving the city about $3 million a year. The city has found in the area of garbage collection, for example, that some routes can be conducted less expensively by private contractors, but not other routes, which it handles itself. According to one city official, "We learn from losing a bid. We are more than willing to go after other departments . . . if their charges caused our bid to be too high! It's a team effort to cut costs. In theory, unless our city government is inherently inefficient, we should win the bids."

Other innovations introduced by Phoenix include a computerized dispatch system for the fire department, rather than a radio dispatch system, which has greatly improved response rates and information available for units at the scene, including computer displays of such items as floor plans, the presence of handicapped or elderly residents, the location of dangerous substances, and a variety of other information.

The city also promotes the use of fees for service, or user charges, but without cutting into basic services. For example, there is a standard monthly fee for garbage pickups, but citizens may obtain more frequent service for an additional fee. The water department uses a similar plan by charging a higher fee per gallon as consumption increases beyond a baseline point. This emphasis on fee for services has forced all departments to contain costs.

The city's employee suggestion program also was significantly upgraded. As a result, program participation increased from 100 employees to 1,000, and documented productivity savings went up from $20,000 per year to more than $1,000,000 a year. The city has won a number of awards from the National Association of Suggestion Systems.

The city also uses management retreats in which city management meets off site to share information and experiences twice a year, and has created a Citizens' Assistance Office to help residents resolve problems relating to city services.

Phoenix has one of the lowest tax bases in the nation and one of the highest service levels. So productive is the city that the Japanese government invited Phoenix's city manager to Tokyo to advise it on how to increase productivity. In an age when Americans are asking the Japanese how to manage, that is a kudo of no mean significance.

Sources: As derived from Case Study 38, American Productivity Center; Randy Fitzgerald, *"We* Can *Lower Local Taxes,"* Readers' Digest; *Michael DeCourey Hines, "Cash-Strapped Cities Turn to Companies to Do What Government Once Did,"* The New York Times *(May 14, 1991) and personal conversations with Phoenix managers.*

---

local school officials; the data were wanted both by Congress (which sought such data as a means of reforming education) and federal executives (who wanted the data as a management tool). Local school officials, however, thought these federal attempts at rather rudimentary program evaluation to be threatening and, although student scores on national tests declined steadily between 1963 and 1982 (and have risen and fallen modestly since then), local educators still have successfully resisted efforts by the federal government to find out more about student achievement in the nation.[84]

The example of public education indicates in broad strokes the basic problems to be overcome in getting governments to use program evaluations. At one level the reasons why program evaluations are used less frequently by policymakers than they might be are fairly straightforward. Often the research cannot produce results early enough to be employed in short-term policy decisions. The evaluator, is after all, often only an advisor, and policymakers are under no particular obligation to accept the evaluator's recommendations. Disagreements between evaluators and practitioners contribute to the fact that the evaluation is not used; occasionally, for instance, administrators will claim that the "real goals" of the project were not accurately measured.[85]

At a deeper level, however, a lack of use of evaluation by policymakers stems from the different perceptions between practitioners and evaluators reviewed earlier. Evaluators generally tend to place the most importance on a study, and sometimes the demand for an evaluation is a sig-

nal that a program is in trouble. Adding to this problem is the fact that scarce staff may have to be reallocated to compile data (which may not be wanted by top administrators in the first place), leading to complaints by staff that they have less time, as a consequence, to carry out their assigned responsibilities. Thomas V. Bonoma suggests that the prior relationships between the evaluator and administrators whose program is being evaluated largely determine the nature of the evaluation that is subsequently conducted, the level of resistance to initiating changes recommended by the evaluation, and the strategies to be used by evaluators in overcoming bureaucratic resistance to their findings. Bonoma ranks these strategies for overcoming administrative resistance to organizational changes that are recommended by evaluation research along a continuum ranging from coercion and inducement, to rational persuasion, and finally to "consensual cooperation."[86]

Although the often-observed resistance of government executives to initiating recommended changes may be frustrating to the evaluators, it nonetheless should be recognized that the very act of program evaluation often serves a purpose that is both important and underrecognized by social scientists. Weiss calls this hidden purpose "the enlightenment function," citing as evidence for its existence three major studies on the uses of evaluation research that indicate, in Weiss's words, that "some other process is at work."[87] This process, according to Weiss, is not the conventional wisdom of the social researcher, which holds that, "to the extent that he departs from the goals and assumptions adhered to by policymakers, his research will be irrelevant to the 'real world' and will go unheeded. [Therefore, for maximum research utility,] the researcher should accept the fundamental goals, priorities, and political constraints of the key decision-making group. He should be sensitive to feasibilities and stay within the narrow range of low cost, low change policy alternatives."[88]

Weiss argues that this perception by the evaluation researcher is both cynical and naive. The real utility of public program evaluation, according to Weiss, is that it is a form of social criticism and should be viewed by social scientists as such. "The enlightenment function" of evaluation research is based on assumptions that are quite at odds with the conventional wisdom of the social scientists. The enlightenment model,

> does not consider value consensus a prerequisite for useful research. . . . it implies that research need not necessarily be geared to the operating feasibilities of today, but that research provides the intellectual background of concepts, orientations, and empirical generalizations that inform policy. As new concepts and data emerge, their gradual cumulative effect can be to change the conventions policymakers abide by and to reorder the goals and priorities of the practical policy world.[89]

The enlightenment model posited by Weiss is perhaps the most succinct and useful view of the role that public program evaluation plays in public administration. Although not rigorously scientific, it does appeal to the basic precepts of how knowledge is used. In this view, public program evaluation sensitizes policymakers. It opens new options that, over time, they are more likely to adopt because of the background data provided by an evaluation research project. Evaluation research may not be used as immediately and radically as the evaluation researcher might wish, but in the long run program evaluations are employed by policymakers, and perhaps on a broader plane than evaluation researchers realize.

In many ways, the current intellectual revival of public program evaluation and productivity among public administrationists represents a return to the golden era of public administration in the 1930s, when the "principles of public administration" paradigm was dominant. Fortu-

nately, public program evaluation and productivity have sidestepped the intellectual pitfalls of the "principles" period and have simultaneously provided the field of public administration with much of its long-needed scholarly focus. Like the "principles" of yore, public program evaluation and productivity are a major means of demonstrating the legitimacy of government. Government has no profit margin by which it can demonstrate to the taxpayers a reason for existing. Instead, government must demonstrate more difficult concepts to justify itself, such as efficiency, effectiveness, and social worth in carrying out its programs. Public program evaluation and productivity, in their sophisticated but deeply rooted appeal to Western beliefs in the scientific method, may provide one such means of demonstration and, as such, will become increasingly important components of public management in an age when government consumes more economic resources than ever before in history.

In their effort to demonstrate the efficient and effective use of public funds, public program evaluation and research provides a graceful introduction to our next chapter on the public budget and how to use it.

NOTES

1. Eleanor Chelinsky, "Evaluating Public Programs," in James L. Perry, ed., *Handbook of Public Administration* (San Francisco: Jossey-Bass, 1989) p. 259.
2. Francis G. Caro, "Evaluation Research: An Overview," *Readings in Evaluation Research*, Francis G. Caro, ed. (New York: Russell Sage Foundation, 1971), p. 2.
3. Geert Bouckaert, "The History of the Productivity Movement," *Public Productivity and Management Review*, XIV (Fall 1990), p. 53.
4. *Ibid.*, p. 83.
5. C. Dineen, "Productivity Improvement: It's Our Turn," *The Bureaucrat* 14 (Winter 1985), pp. 10-14.
6. Robert P. McGowan and Theodore H. Poister, "The Impact of Productivity Measurement Systems on Municipal Performance," paper prepared for delivery at the 1984 Annual Conference of the American Political Science Association in Washington, D.C., August/September, 1984, pp. 12-13.
7. This discussion is based largely on Geert Bouckaert's fine review, "The History of the Productivity Movement," pp. 53-89, cited in Note 3.
8. See, for example, Kurt Lewin, *Resolving Social Conflicts* (New York: Harper & Row, 1948); Ronald

Lippitt, *Studies in Experimentally Created Autocratic and Democratic Groups*, University of Iowa Studies: Studies in Children's Welfare, Vol. 16, No.3, pp. 45-198, 1940; and Leon Festinger and Harold Kelley, *Changing Attitudes through Social Contact* (Ann Arbor: University of Michigan Press, 1951).

9. Orville F. Poland, "Why Does Public Administration Ignore Evaluation?" *Public Administration Review*, 31 (March/April 1971), p. 201, and Nicholas Henry, *Public Administration and Public Affairs* (Englewood Cliffs, N.J.: Prentice Hall, 1975), p. 222.

10. For a description see: U.S. General Accounting Office, *Evaluation and Analysis to Support Decision-Making*, PAD-75-9, (Washington, D.C.: U.S. Government Printing Office, 1976), pp. 1-2.

11. For a description see: Susan Salasin and Laurence Kivens, "Fostering Federal Program Evaluation: Current OMB Initiatives," *Evaluation*, 2 (July/August 1975), pp. 37-41.

12. Graeme Browning, "Quest for Quality," *National Journal* (December 21, 1991), p. 1496.

13. Joseph S. Wholey, et al, *Federal Evaluation Policy: Analyzing the Effects of Public Programs* (Washington, D.C.: Urban Institute, 1970), p. 23.

14. U.S. General Accounting Office, *Federal Evaluation: Fewer Units, Reduced Resources, Different Studies From 1980*, GAO/PEMD-87-9 (Washington, D.C.: U.S. Government Printing Office, 1987), p. 1.

15. John Mercer, "The Government Performance and Results Act," *The Public Manager*, 21 (Winter 1992), p. 17.

16. Frank Hodsoll, as quoted in: Charles F. Bingman, "Installing the M-Team," *Government Executive*, (January 1992), p. 25.

17. Unpublished report conducted by the Council of State Governments and the Urban Institute, 1972; cited in Harry P. Hatry, et al., *Practical Program Evaluation for State and Local Government Officials* (Washington, D.C.: Urban Institute, 1973), p. 17.

18. U.S. General Accounting Office, *State and Local Productivity Improvement: What Is the Federal Role?* (Washington, D.C.: U.S. Government Publishing Office, 1978). The report said much the same for local governments, too.

19. James E. Jarrett, "Productivity," *The Book of the States, 1982-83* (Lexington, Ky.: Council of State Governments, 1982), pp. 296-301.

20. Judith R. Brown, "Legislative Program Evaluation: Refining A Legislative Service and a Profession," *Public Administration Review*, 44 (May/June 1984), p. 258.

21. Theodore H. Poister, *et al.*, "Centralized Productivity Improvement Efforts in State Government," *Public Productivity Review*, 9 (Spring 1985), p. 18.

22. Richard E. Winnie, "Local Government Budgeting, Program Planning, and Evaluation," *Urban Data Services Report* 4, No. 5 (International City Management Association, May 1972).

23. Rackham S. Fukuhara, "Productivity Improvement in Cities," *Municipal Year Book*, 1977 (Washington, D.C.: International City Management Association, 1977), pp. 196-197. All cities between 25,000 and one

million people were surveyed. The response rate was 43 percent.

24. Theodore H. Poister and Gregory Streib, "Management Tools in Municipal Government: Trends Over the Past Decade," *Public Administration Review*, 49 (May/June 1989), pp. 242, 245. All cities with populations of 25,000 to one million were surveyed. The response rate was 42 percent.

25. David N. Ammons, "Common Barriers to Productivity Improvement in Local Government," *Public Productivity Review*, 9 (Winter 1985), pp. 293-310.

26. David H. Foly and William Lyons, "The Measurement of Municipal Service Quality and Productivity," *Public Productivity Review*, 10 (Winter 1986), pp. 21-33.

27. Jonathan P. West, "City Government Productivity and Civil Service Reforms," *Public Productivity Review*, 10 (Fall 1986), pp. 45-59.

28. Theodore H. Poister and Robert P. McGowan, "The Contribution of Local Productivity Improvement Efforts in a Period of Fiscal Stress," *Public Productivity Review*, 8 (Winter 1984), pp. 386-394. All cities with populations of 25,000 to one million were surveyed in 1982. The response rate was 44 percent.

29. Caro, "Evaluation Research," p. 1.

30. See U.S. General Accounting Office, *Evaluation and Analysis to Support Decision-Making*, pp. 4-5.

31. Henry W. Riecken, "Principal Components of the Evaluation Process," *Professional Psychology*, 8 (November 1977), p. 395.

32. Michael Scriven, "The Methodology of Evaluation," *Perspectives on Curriculum Evaluation* (Chicago: Rand-McNally, 1967), p. 43.

33. See Wholey, et al., *Federal Evaluation Policy*, p. 62.

34. *Ibid.*, pp. 24-26.

35. R. A. Levine and A. T. Williams, Jr., *Making Evaluation Effective: A Guide*, R-788-HEW ICMUO (Santa Monica, Calif.: RAND Corp., 1971).

36. Orville F. Poland, "Program Evaluation and Administrative Theory," *Public Administration Review*, 34 (July/August 1974), pp. 333-334.

37. Evaluation Research Society Standards Committee, "Evaluation Research Society Standards for Program Evaluation," as published in P.H. Rossi, ed., *Standards for Evaluation Practice* (San Francisco: Jossey-Bass, 1982).

38. Much of the following discussion is based on Chelinsky, "Evaluating Public Programs," pp. 266-272.

39. U.S. General Accounting Office, *Teenage Pregnancy: 500,000 Births a Year But Few Tested Programs*. GAO/PEMD-86-16BR. (Washington, D.C.: U.S. General Accounting Office, 1986).

40. Bruce B. Buchanan II, "The Senior Executive Service: How Can We Tell If it Works?" *Public Administration Review*, 41 (May/June 1981), pp. 349-358.

41. See, for example, Robert K. Yin, "Life Histories of Innovations: How New Practices Become Routinized," *Public Administration Review*, 41 (January/February 1981), pp. 21-28.

42. Chelinsky, "Evaluating Public Programs," p. 268.

43. George Kelling, et al., *The Kansas City Preventive Patrol Experiment: Summary Report* (Washington, D.C.: The Police Foundation, 1974).

44. U.S. General Accounting Office, *CETA Programs for Disadvantaged Adults—What Do We Know About Their Enrollees, Services, and Effectiveness?* GAO/IPE-82-2 (Washington, D.C.: U.S. General Accounting Office, 1982).

45. Joseph S. Wholey and Harry P. Hatry, "The Case of Performance Monitoring," *Public Administration Review*, 52 (November/December 1992), pp. 604-610.

46. U.S. General Accounting Office, *Drinking-Age Laws: An Evaluation Synthesis of Their Impact on Highway Safety*. GAO/PEMD-87-10. (Washington, D.C.: U.S. General Accounting Office, 1987).

47. Chelinsky, "Evaluating Public Programs," p. 269.

48. *Ibid.*

49. U.S. General Accounting Office, *Evaluation and Analysis to Support Decision-Making*, p. 11.

50. *Ibid.*, p. 13.

51. *Ibid.*, p. 14.

52. The section on conducting a program evaluation is drawn from *ibid.*, pp. 17-41.

53. Roger B. Parks, "Technical Efficiency of Public Decision Making Units," *Policy Studies Journal*, 12 (December 1983), p. 337.

54. A. Charnes, W. W. Cooper, and E. Rhodes, "Measuring the Efficiency of Decision Making Units," *European Journal of Operational Research*, 2 (September 1978), pp. 429-444.

55. See for example Authella M. Bessent and E. Wailand Bessent, "Determining the Comparative Efficiency of Schools through Data Envelopment Analysis," *Educational Administration Quarterly*, 16 (Spring 1980), pp. 57-75; A. Charnes, W. W. Cooper, and E. Rhodes, "Evaluating Programs and Managerial Efficiency: An Application of Data Envelopment Analysis to Program Follow Through," *Management Science*, 27 (June 1981), pp. 668-697; Roger B. Parks, "Metropolitan Structure and Performance: Compositional and Relational Effects," Paper prepared for the NATO Advanced Research Workshop on Analytical Models and Institutional Design in Federal and Unitary States, Erasmus University, Rotterdam, The Netherlands, June 1983; and Parks, "Technical Efficiency of Public Decision Making Units.".

56. Parks, "Technical Efficiency of Public Decision Making Units," p. 344.

57. For a thorough review of the federal government's experience with Inspectors General, see: Paul C. Light, *Monitoring Government: Inspectors General and the Search for Accountability* (Washington, D.C.: Brookings Institution, 1993).

58. Dana Priest, "Panel Inspects Inspectors General," Washington Post, May 27, 1992.

59. Tom Shoop, "The IG Enigma," *Government Executive* (January 1992), p. 31.

60. These figures pertain to 1990, according to the President's Council on Integrity and Efficiency, as cited in *ibid.*, p. 40.

61. Quoted in Shoop, "The IG Enigma," p. 39.

62. Sheila Kaplan, "Oversight Unseen," *Legal Times* (February 10, 1992), p. 20.

63. U.S. General Accounting Office, as cited in John Hillikirk, "Uncle Sam Begins Push for Quality," *USA Today*, September 9, 1992. Figures are for 1992.

64. Albert C. Hyde, "The Proverbs of Total Quality Management: Recharting the Path to Quality Improvement in the Public Sector," *Public Productivity and Management Review*, 16 (Fall 1992), p. 30.

65. This paragraph is drawn, very loosely, from: David Osborne, "Why Total Quality Management Is Only Half a Loaf," *Governing* (August 1992), p. 65

66. Jonathan Walters, "The Cult of Total Quality," *Governing* (May 1992), p. 40.

67. This discussion is based, more or less, on: Hyde, "The Proverbs of Total Quality Management," pp. 31-35; Michael Milakovich, "Total Quality Management for Public Sector Productivity Improvement," *Public Productivity and Management Review*, 14 (Fall 1990), pp. 23-34; and James W. Swiss, "Adapting Total Quality Management (TQM) to Government," *Public Administration Review*, 52 (July/August 1992), pp. 356-361.

68. Riecken, "Principal Components of the Evaluation Process," p. 398.

69. Much of this discussion is based on: U.S. General Accounting Office, *Evaluation and Analysis to Support Decision-Making*, pp. 17-20, and Edward Suchman, "A Model for Research and Evaluation on Rehabilitation," *Sociology and Rehabilitation*, Marvin Sussman, ed. (Washington, D.C.: Vocational Rehabilitation Administration, 1965), pp. 64-65

70. Caro, "Evaluation Research," p. 22.

71. Christopher Scanlan, "U.S. Measures Human Value, A Life-and-Death Calculation," *Philadelphia Inquirer* (September 2, 1990). Figures are for 1990.

72. Caro, "Evaluation Research," p. 24. Much of this discussion is drawn from *ibid.*, pp. 23-27.

73. H. Donald Messer, "Drug Abuse Treatment: An Evaluation That Wasn't," *Program Evaluation at HEW: Research Versus Reality. Part 1: Health*, James G. Abert, ed. (New York: Marcel Dekker, 1979), pp. 113-168.

74. The following paragraph is drawn from Donald R. Wideman, "Writing a Better RFP: Ten Hints for Obtaining More Successful Evaluation Studies," *Public Administration Review*, 37 (November/December 1977), pp. 714-717.

75. Riecken, "Principal Components of the Evaluation Process," pp. 401-402, 405.

76. Arnold J. Meltsner, *Policy Analysis in the Bureaucracy* (Berkeley: University of California Press, 1976), Chapter 2.

77. K. A. Archebald, "Alternative Orientations to Social Science Utilization," Social Science Informant, 9 (April 1970), pp. 7-35.

78. A good review of this literature, as well as some original research on the subject, is: John G. Heilman and David L. Martin, "On the Organizational Theory of Evaluation: Economic and Political Constraints and the Choice of an Evaluation Agent," *Administration*

and Society, 18 (November 1986), pp. 315-333

79. Riecken, "Principal Components of the Evaluation Process," p. 405
80. Caro, "Evaluation Research," pp. 13-15
81. *Ibid.*, p. 17
82. Riecken, "Principal Components of the Evaluation Process," p. 408
83. Carol H. Weiss, "Research for Policy's Sake: The Enlightenment Function of Social Research," Policy Analysis, 3 (Fall, 1977), p. 532
84. M. McLaughlin, *Evaluation and Reform: The Elementary and Secondary Education Act of 1965*, Title I, Report R-1292-RC (Santa Monica, Calif.: RAND Corporation, 1974)
85. Caro, "Evaluation Research," pp. 12-13
86. Thomas V. Bonoma, "Overcoming Resistance to Change Recommended for Operating Programs," *Professional Psychology*, 8 (November 1977), pp. 451-463
87. Weiss, "Research for Policy's Sake," p. 535
88. *Ibid.*, p. 544
89. *Ibid.*

CHAPTER 8

THE PUBLIC BUDGET: CONCEPTS AND PROCESSES

Budgets are beyond dollars. They are choices, policies, and philosophies, and the ways in which budgets are made reflect the choices, policies, and philosophies of governments. Aaron Wildavsky writes that the "budget is the life blood of the government. . . . If we substitute the words 'what the government ought to do' for the words 'ought to be in the budget,'" the centrality of the budget to governance itself becomes clearer.[1]

Of the many variants of systems theory that have been applied to problems of public administration, budgetary concepts have had the longest and most pronounced impact on the field. Like the other techniques reviewed in the preceding chapters, the budget represents a technique of administrative control that has been extended conceptually from a negative to a positive (and increasingly political) function.

In this chapter, we shall trace the evolution of budgetary concepts in government. We shall also consider the impact, or lack of it, of budgeting concepts on various levels of American government, and the political significance of the budgetary process.

A HISTORY OF BUDGETARY CONCEPTS

The centrality of the budget to governance is why it is important to understand the evolvement of budgetary thinking by public officials.[2] Briefly, the development of the budget can be categorized into six periods: (1) traditional, or Line-Item Budgeting, with its control orientation; (2) Performance Budgeting (sometimes called Program Budgeting), with its management orientation; (3) Planning-Programming-Budgeting, sometimes called Planning-Programming-Budgeting System, with its economic planning orientation; (4) Management-by-Objectives, with its emphasis on budgetary decentralization; (5) Zero-Base Budgeting, with its stress on ranking program priorities; and (6) Top-Down Budgeting/Target Base Budgeting, with its centralizing and legislative overtones. As with our other reviews of how various concepts evolve in public administration, the time periods associated with each of these phases is not as neat as we indicate; some levels of government, for example, continue to develop one concept of budgeting while other levels move on to new concepts—or regress to old ones.

In each of these six thrusts, the idea of what a budget is, could be, or should be, has assumed a different cast. Nevertheless, the essential meaning of the word "budget" has remained unaltered. To borrow Wildavsky's definition, a *budget* is "a series of goals with price tags attached."[3] There are, of course, other and lengthier definitions of budget, but Wildavsky's pithy one-liner has the blessed advantage of being unmysterious, accurate, and short, so we shall rely on it.

Line-Item Budgeting (1921–1939)

Most people know what a budget looks like. Each line on a sheet of paper has an item (for example, pencils, 112) on the left side followed by a cost ($5.00) on the right side; hence, the traditional budget acquired its descriptive title of "line-item," or "objects-of-expenditure." A *Line-Item Budget* is simply the allocation of resources according to the cost of each object of expenditure.

Of course, all governments have always had some form of line-item budget. From the days of the ancient courts of Egypt, Babylon, and China, something was needed to keep track of expenses. But in American public administration, the refinement of the Line-Item Budget was a product of national political and reformist pressures of the early twentieth century, which we have mentioned in previous chapters. One such pressure was the drive to establish a consolidated "executive budget." The value behind this drive was one of ousting financial corruption in government, and the way to accomplish this goal was to consolidate public financial management bureaus under the chief executive.

This thrust related to a second pressure, which was the administrative integration movement. The proponents of administrative integration advocated the functional consolidation of agencies, the abandonment of various independent boards, the enhancement of the chief executive's appointive and removal powers, and the short ballot, among similar reforms designed to assure efficiency and coordination in government.

The third pressure was the desire of political reformers to build in administrative honesty by restricting the discretionary powers held by public administrators. Thus, innovations such as competitive bidding for contracts, centralized

purchasing, standardized accounting procedures, and expenditure audits emerged. All related directly to the notion that the budget was a useful device for controlling public administrators (if in a purely negative way) and ensuring morality in government. Among other results of these forces, the Budget and Accounting Act of 1921 was enacted. This act centralized federal budget formation in the Bureau of the Budget, and established the General Accounting Office (GAO) as the congressional check on federal expenditures.

The Line-Item Budget rapidly became associated with governmental honesty, efficiency, and less propitiously, inflexibility. In 1923 Charles G. Dawes, as first director of the Bureau of the Budget (now the Office of Management and Budget), wrote: "The Bureau of the Budget is concerned only with the humbler and routine business of government. . . . it is concerned with no question of policy, save that of economy and efficiency."[4] As a result of these very limited objectives, the Line-Item Budget emphasized such factors as skilled accountancy, the objects needed to run an office or program and their costs, incremental policymaking throughout government, dispersed responsibility for management and planning, and a fiduciary role for the budget agency. Technical definitions of items were stressed (for example, pencils, 112, with l/2-inch erasers, wood, No. 2 grade lead, 6" x 1/4"), and the use of such phrases as "watch-dog of the treasury" and "balanced budget" were common, indicating the mentality of this control-oriented stage of budgetary thought.

Line-Item Budgeting will always be with us, and necessarily so; fundamentally, budgets must tell us how much each item costs, and the Line-Item Budget does this. But, as we shall see, the absence of abstraction inherent in, and the simplicity of, the Line-Item Budget do not render it suitable for larger purposes, and it is best used at the lower levels of the organization. Occasionally, this is not fully appreciated by executives, and when it is not, use of the Line-Item Budget can result "in micro-management at the macro level."[5]

The Line-Item Budget covers *inputs* only, meaning that it deals only with what it took to make a project continue—floppy discs, desks, and secretaries. Consider two examples, paperclips and parks. Under a Line-Item Budget, the only policy-related questions that a public administrator would be channeled into asking are: (1) How many paperclips do we need and what will they cost? or (2) How many parks do we have and what will it cost to maintain them? We shall refer again to paperclips and parks as examples of how each successive concept of the budget changed the policy-related questions that pertained to them. The point is that the budget represents a way of thinking about, measuring, and evaluating public policy.

Performance Budgeting (1940–1960)

Although lone voices were heard throughout the 1920s and 1930s advocating a budget attuned to government performance as well as objects of expenditure, the meaningful shift to this kind of thinking came with President Franklin D. Roosevelt's New Deal. A number of historical factors influenced this movement. One was the firm establishment of the control techniques advocated by the line-item budgeteers. With the setting up of accurate accounting, purchasing, and personnel practices, budgeting as a concept was released from many of its traditional watchdog duties. Second, the government was expanding enormously, and there emerged a corresponding need to centralize and coordinate managerial activities more effectively. The budget provided the obvious salient tool for systematically coordinating government management. Third, government was increasingly perceived as an institution that delivered benefits, and the budget in turn was seen as a means by which the appropriate managerial delivery systems could be measured.

With the New Deal, these factors congealed. Between 1932 and 1940 federal spending more than doubled. The President's Committee on Administrative Management recommended (in the form of Luther Gulick's and Lyndall Urwick's oft-mentioned report of 1937) that the Bureau of the Budget shed its control orientation in favor of a managerial emphasis, and that the Bureau be used to coordinate federal administration under presidential leadership. In 1939, the Bureau of the Budget was transferred from the Treasury Department to the newly founded Executive Office of the President. The Bureau's staff was increased by a factor of ten, it developed new methods of statistical coordination and budgetary apportionment, and it increasingly drew its personnel from the ranks of public administration rather than from accounting. Executive Order 8248 officially expressed the new managerial role of the Bureau of the Budget: "to keep the President informed of the progress of activities by agencies of the Government with respect to work proposed, work actually initiated, and work completed, together with the relative timing of work between the several agencies of the Government; all to the end that the work programs of the several agencies of the executive branch of Government may be coordinated and that the monies appropriated by the Congress may be expended in the most economical manner possible to prevent overlapping and duplication of effort."[6]

The managerial orientation of the budget was strengthened by the preeminence of administrative management in public administration and, to a degree, by scientific management in business administration. This general emphasis was known as "Operations and Management," and government bureaucracies, particularly the Bureau of the Budget, became preoccupied with originating measures of work performance and performance standards. In 1949 the Hoover Commission's report gave this thrust the name by which we know it: Performance Budgeting. Prior to 1949 Performance Budgeting was called "Functional" or "Activity Budgeting." Although the federal government had in fact been practicing Performance Budgeting, largely under the aegis of Harold D. Smith, director of the Bureau of the Budget (1939-1946), the Hoover Commission more or less clinched its worth by dramatizing the problems that the government faced under Line-Item Budgeting. The Commission observed that the federal budget for fiscal year (FY) 1949-1950 was 1625 pages long with approximately 1.5 million words and questioned its utility as a document that facilitated more coordinated and effective public management.[7] In 1950 President Harry S. Truman sent Congress the first full-fledged federal Performance Budget.

Performance Budgeting is "budgeting that links performance levels with specific budget amounts."[8] It covers more administrative activities than had the traditional line-item budget. Now *outputs* as well as *inputs* were considered.

Budget officers saw their mission not only as one of precise and controlled accounting, but the development of activity classifications, the description of an agency's program and its performance, and the exploration of various kinds of work/cost measurements. Administrative, as opposed to accounting, skills were stressed, activities of the agency were given precedence over the purchase of items required to run the office, management responsibility became newly centralized, although planning responsibility remained dispersed, policymaking remained incremental, and the role of the budget agency evolved from a fiduciary to an efficiency function.

What did this new role of the budget signify for our original examples of paperclips and parks? Under a Line-Item Budget, an administrator asked only input-related questions: How much will it cost next year to assure an adequate supply of paperclips for the office? How much will it cost next year to assume adequate maintenance of the parks for the public? Under a Performance Budget, an administrator was pushed into asking not only input-related questions but output-related questions as well: How many papers will be clipped? How many people will be served by the parks? In other words, the *performance* of the objects of expenditure became important and, as a result of output-related queries, we might anticipate administrative studies to be generated that would survey the average number of papers clipped per paperclip, or the average number of persons visiting each park. In short, how did paperclips and parks perform?

Among the more lasting impacts of the Performance Budgeting phase on American governments was its displacement of (but not to the exclusion of) budgeting by objects of expenditure (*e.g.*, "pencils, 112") with budgeting by programs (*e.g.*, "accounting program"). This practice (accelerated by the succession of Planning-Programming-Budgeting in the 1960s, considered next) is now pervasive in the public sector, and, in fact, Performance Budgeting occasionally is called "Program Budgeting" in governmental circles, indicating at least one longer-term impact that its use during the 1940s and 1950s has had on public budgeting. As we see later, however, some elements of Performance Budgeting, which are more basic than arranging budgets by programs

rather than by objects of expenditure, are being rediscovered by governments, so the effect of Performance Budgeting on public finance may be more lasting than we presently appreciate.

Planning-Programming-Budgeting (1961–1970)

While Performance Budgeting represented a step forward in budgetary theory, it did not delve into the deeper levels of government. Unquestionably, Performance Budgeting made a significant contribution in attempting to devise measurements of an agency's effectiveness, and this was to the public's good. But, as one New York state legislator exclaimed after looking over his state's performance budget, "Who the hell cares how much a pound of laundry costs?"[9] Such data represent needed knowledge, to be sure, but ultimately the more important issue is: How should funds be allocated among various programs? Which programs are the most important? After this issue is resolved, then we can begin evaluations of a program's performance.

There were other problems with Performance Budgeting. It was becoming increasingly subjective. The description of various programs that accompanied an agency's budget to the legislature were beginning to serve a justificatory function for each agency. Performance Budgeting (like Line-Item Budgeting) tended to increase the purview and costs of an agency's programs incrementally. This "keep-on-truckin" attitude impaired the articulation of the single essential question of planning: Why? Why do we need this or that program? Instead, Performance Budgeting merely stated: We've got the program, so let's do it efficiently.

These concerns eventually led to the displacement of Performance Budgeting concepts in government by Planning-Programming-Budgeting (PPB). PPB-related notions had their origins in industry. As early as 1924, General Motors Corporation was using variants of PPB, and during World War II the Controlled Materials Plan of the War Production Board relied on PPB concepts. By the 1950s the U.S. Air Force's RAND Corporation began applying systems analysis to the evaluation of weapons systems and recommended the institution of "program packages" as budgeting units in Air Force planning. The Air Force rejected the idea, but later found it expeditious to retrench when Robert McNamara became Secretary of Defense in 1960.

McNamara had been trained as an executive in the confines of Ford Motor Company. The Defense establishment that he entered was beset by almost cut-throat competition between the services, each of which was vying for control of as many new weapons systems as it could acquire. Each service viewed its particular programs not only as vital to the defense of the nation, but also as essentially the nation's only defense. Hence, each service defined the country's defense issues in ways that suited their peculiar capabilities. Combined with the competitive milieu of the Pentagon, this viewpoint produced a situation in which the Air Force was preparing for a brief, nuclear war (which would be air-centered), and the Army was girding for a long, conventional war (which would be ground-centered). Thus, it was contended in 1961 before the Senate Subcommittee on National Security and International Operations that because "the land and tactical air force were being planned for different kinds of war, they were not ready to fight either."

McNamara and his "whiz kids" (a not entirely affectionate appellation given the McNamara team by the military) shook up the services. They felt the services were autonomous to a possibly dangerous point of inefficiency and uncoordination. McNamara's method for reestablishing central control of the military services was systems analysis, and the primary expression of this analysis was PPB. By 1964, PPB was (and still is) standard operating procedure in the Defense Department. President Lyndon B. Johnson was sufficiently impressed that in 1965 he ordered PPB to be applied throughout the federal government. By 1967 the Bureau of the Budget had instructed the use of PPB in twenty-one agencies, with a final goal of thirty-six agencies.

What is PPB? What precisely is PPB? Taking its component concepts one by one, *planning* is the defining and choice of operational goals of the organization and the choice of methods and means to be used to achieve those goals over a specified time period. *Programming* is the scheduling and implementation of the particular projects designed to fulfill an organization's goals in the most favorable, efficient, and effective way possible. *Budgeting* is the price estimate attached to each goal, plan, program, and project. By way of example, one official goal of the United States government is the attainment of the people's welfare. When this goal is made operational, a variety of subgoals result. One such *operational goal* is the achievement of a certain minimum income level for every American family. One *plan* for achieving this operational goal is unemployment assistance. A *program* is distributing welfare checks. A *project* is the setting up and managing of the various welfare bureaucracies in the United States.

Beyond simple definitions, however, PPB represents a systemization of political choice in the format of budget formulation. PPB is an effort to render decision making by public administrators as rational as possible. PPB represents a rapprochement between budgeting and planning. Specifically, *Planning-Programming-Budgeting* is an effort to integrate budgetary formulation with Keynesian economic concepts (that is, it attempts to consider the effects of government spending on the national economy); to develop and use new information sources and technologies to bring more objective and quantitative analysis to public policymaking; and to integrate systems-wide planning with budgeting.

PPB is associated with budget officers who have skills in economic analysis, as well as in accountancy and administration. The purposes of various programs become the chief concern, as opposed to their objects of expenditure or activities. Decision making becomes less incremental and more systemic throughout the bureaucracy. Management responsibility grows more supervisory in nature, while planning responsibility becomes increasingly centralized. Finally, the budgetary agency is seen more than ever before as a policymaking body—a far cry from Dawes's statement in 1923 about the Budget Bureau being concerned with the "humbler and routine business of government."

Another way of phrasing the preceding paragraph is to say that PPB is concerned not only with inputs and outputs but also with effects and alternatives. How does this broadened conceptual scope of the budget affect the questions that we have been asking about our original examples of paperclips and parks? With inputs, you recall, we ask only: How much will a year's supply of paperclips or a year's program of park maintenance cost? With outputs, we must ask: How many papers will our paperclips clip, or how many people will visit the parks?

With effects and alternatives, however, our budget-related questions become considerably more sophisticated and penetrating. For example, in order to determine the effects of our paperclips, we must ask: What effect do the clipped papers have on the agency and its mission? Does paperclipping them facilitate the achievement of agency goals? Does the process expedite anything, or should paperclips be abandoned as an item in the budget? How do we measure the effects of the paperclips program on agency goals? After determining paperclips' effect on the accomplishment of the agency's mission, we then must ask about alternatives. Should we use staples instead? Is there an optimal paperclip/staple mix? Do other alternatives exist?

Parks present a similar dilemma. When we ask about the effects of parks, we also must ask: What are parks really meant to do? The answer, of course, is that the purpose of parks is to provide recreation to the public—to allow citizens to "re-create." Yet, we soon discover that recreation is not much of an answer, particularly when we try to measure the effects of the parks program. It is no longer enough to count visitors per day to each park—that is, to measure the parks' performance, or output. Now we must ascertain whether or not each visitor is "re-creating" in the park—whether he or she is having fun. That chore is not only difficult, but it may be impossible. For instance, we may discover that after midnight the park is visited entirely by muggers, rapists, and victims—not an entirely unwarranted assumption, given urban crime patterns. Under these conditions, we may assume that only half of the park's visitors from midnight to four in the morning—the muggers and rapists—are having fun and it is not even good, clean fun. The other half of the park's twelve-to-four A.M. population—the victims—presumably are not.

This kind of thinking, which is enabled by PPB, also forces us to consider more systemic questions about parks. We may find out that the recreation function of a city affects other urban functions, such as crime control. If it is discovered that parks correlate positively with crime, we may wish to reconsider the utility of parks in light of the total urban system. At the very least, the role that parks play in the larger urban system will be clarified by asking questions about the effects of parks, and planning for public policy presumably will be made more precise, responsive, and rigorous.

Finally, we can consider alternatives to parks. Would public libraries provide more opportunities for re-creating among the citizenry, and should monies allocated for parks be used instead for libraries? Might not many neighborhood miniparks provide more effective recreation than a few superparks? These and other alternatives would come up for evaluation under a PPB budget.

PPB in Government. PPB met with mixed welcomes in various American governments. Despite President Johnson's executive order in 1965 that PPB be adopted by virtually all federal agencies, there was substantial resistance to its implementation in many agencies, including the Bureau of the Budget.[10] Much of this recalcitrance stemmed from the need for new information that the use of PPB required. A number of agencies simply had neither the information nor the ability to acquire it, and they fell back on generating largely useless reports as a means of bureaucratic compensation. This early emphasis by topside on procedures fostered some resentment concerning PPB in the minds of many federal administrators, and the implementation of PPB concepts was not aided by the Johnson administration's premature insistence for unavailable data. Nevertheless, there was some progress. Five of the sixteen agencies surveyed were receiving substantial support from above in developing genuine PPB systems, and one was in the process of beginning development.

What ultimately buried Planning-Programming-Budgeting in most federal agencies (the Department of Defense was and remains a noteworthy exception), however, was its own tendency to analytically overkill. Elmer Staats, then director of the Bureau of the Budget, reported a conversation with the Secretary of Agriculture (and Agriculture, ironically, was one of those five agencies that reported substantial progress in implementing PPB) that went as follows: "Elmer, I have a stack of PPBS papers on my desk about four feet high. What am I supposed to do with them?"[11]

State and local governments had mixed reactions regarding PPB.[12] By 1968, twenty-eight states and sixty local governments reported that they were in the process of implementing PPB and 155 additional localities were considering its adoption. Once state and local officials decided that they liked PPB, however, other obstacles prevented its adoption. The principal hurdles were lack of local resources or lack of authority. Also in 1968, seventy-three local governments reported that they had decided against using PPB largely for those reasons. New York and California, both early proponents of the notion, ultimately abandoned it.

With Richard Nixon's election as president in 1968, the federal government moved steadily away from the policy-planning orientation of PPB. In the late 1960s, for example, then Secretary of Defense Melvin Laird spoke of instituting "participatory budgeting" in the Department of Defense. By this he meant that the admirals and generals would be able to participate more fully in budget formation, although participatory budgeting was seen by many outside critics as an attempt (ultimately unsuccessful) to dismantle the well-controlled and highly centralized PPB system established in the Pentagon by Robert McNamara.

Also during this period, President Nixon revamped (for virtually the first time since its founding in 1939) the Executive Office of the President in accordance with the recommendations of the President's Advisory Council on Executive Reorganization (the Ash Council). A Domestic Council was established as a new unit that in effect undercut the programmatic and planning responsibilities of the Bureau of the Budget. In 1970, the Bureau was retitled the Office of Management and Budget (OMB), indicating its new, managerial orientation. According to former President Nixon, "The Domestic Council will be primarily concerned with *what* we do"—that is, with policy and planning; "the Office of Management and Budget will be primarily concerned with how we do it and how *well* we do it"—that is, with management and effectiveness.[13]

In 1971 a memorandum to all federal agencies from OMB concerning their budget preparations

stated, "Agencies are no longer required to submit with their budget submissions the multi-year program and financing plans, program memoranda and special analytical studies . . . or the schedules . . . that require information classified according to their program and appropriation structures." Allen Schick has written that "by these words, PPB became an unthing."[14]

Management-by-Objectives (1970–1976)

With the abandonment of Program-Planning-Budgeting by the federal government (with the notable exception of the Defense Department) and by many state and local governments in the late 1960s, budgeteers turned to a new concept of budgeting (or, more precisely, to a variant of budgeting): Management-by-Objectives. Management-by-Objectives got its start in the private sector, and in 1954, Peter Drucker wrote a book titled *The Practice of Management*, which generally is thought to be the first major expression of the MBO concept.[15]

Management-by-Objectives may be defined as "a process whereby organizational goals and objectives are set through the participation of organizational members in terms of results expected."[16] Management-by-Objectives encourages "self-management" and decentralization, advocates an integrated approach to total management, stresses the concept of communication and feedback, encourages organization development and change, and emphasizes policy research and the support of top management. MBO, in short, is an attempt to set objectives, track the progress of the appropriate program, and evaluate its results. Through this process, an organization decentralizes by operationalizing its objectives and letting the individual managers most concerned with the appropriate aspects of the program achieve those objectives in the most effective fashion possible.

We have seen how PPB was concerned with inputs, outputs, effects, and alternatives as a budgetary posture. By contrast, MBO is in many ways a return to the world of Performance Budgeting. MBO is concerned with inputs, outputs, and effects, but not necessarily with alternatives. It deals primarily with agency performance and the effectiveness of governmental programs, but when it comes to forcing policymakers to ask what else—or what "other"—might government do to accomplish a particular social mission, MBO appears to be at somewhat of a loss. MBO has a managerial orientation that stresses, in terms of personnel skills, something called "common sense." It is concerned paramountly with program effectiveness, and its policymaking style is decentralized. In terms of planning—and very much *unlike* PPB—MBO is comprehensive in one sense (*i.e.*, it sets operational goals centrally), but it allocates the implementation of that comprehensive planning responsibility to on-line managers. Thus, the budgetary agency becomes concerned chiefly with program effectiveness and efficiency, much in the style of Program Budgeting of the 1950s.

In relating MBO to our previous examples of paperclips and parks, we do not ask what the alternatives to paperclips and parks might be in accomplishing the mission of the agency. Instead, we merely ask: How effective are paperclips in achieving the agency's mission? How effective are parks in achieving society's objectives? We do not ask, however, what alternatives there are to paperclips or to parks.

The advantages of an MBO system are obvious. It gives those people closest to the problem some latitude in dealing with that problem and simultaneously measures their performance according to criteria developed by policymakers at the highest level. An MBO system that works should permit individual initiative and innovation, but Management-by-Objectives is no administrative panacea and, like any other quantitatively based system, MBO can be used to obscure efficient and effective management as well as to enhance it.

Even so, MBO has been used in a number of governmental contexts, and it is perhaps somewhat surprising, given MBO's emphasis on decentralization and on subordinates' implementing policy, that the federal government embraced Management-by-Objectives in a big way under the Nixon administration—an administration, as we noted in Chapter 1, not known for its trust of bureaucrats beyond the immediate confines of the White House. In explaining the introduction of MBO to the federal government by the Nixon White House, observers cannot avoid noting that "the attitude of the Nixon top management was

one of low trust and contempt towards civil service."[17] It was, however, partly because of this distrust of civil servants that Nixon introduced MBO to government through the Office of Management and Budget, which he had staffed with officials who were closely associated with the business community.

Many federal administrators, as we noted, were becoming disillusioned with Program-Planning-Budgeting in the early 1970s, particularly because of what one observer called PPB's "unfortunate association with a passion for uniformity and detail,"[18] and MBO looked like a flexible alternative. In 1975 the Office of Management and Budget issued Circular A-11, which required the submission of agency objectives with the fiscal year budget estimates. This, in effect, was a new budgetary format, and OMB was implementing an MBO concept. Soon afterwards, President Gerald Ford endorsed MBO, and the notion rapidly was adopted by a number of federal agencies.

As implemented in its short duration in the federal government, MBO emphasized productivity measurement, program evaluation, and the effort to establish social indicators of program effectiveness. As Jerry McCaffery points out, "In theory, the decision flow is opposite—PPB down and MBO up. The outstanding difference seems to lie in PPB's ability to compare programs across departmental lines. But PPB's weakness was its lack of flexibility, whereas MBO has great flexibility in system design and application."[19] It was this flexibility, in contrast to PPB's alleged inflexibility, that made MBO attractive to many federal administrators under Nixon.

By 1976, MBO's last year of preeminence in the federal government, 41 percent of American cities reported that they were using it; six years later, 59 percent of these municipalities had adopted it, and, according to later surveys, its use has essentially leveled off since then. By the mid-eighties, two-thirds of 847 top- and mid-level state administrators responding to a survey conducted in ten representative states said that they were using Management-by-Objectives or that their units had been affected by it.[20]

There is a significant body of empirical research on the results of applying Management-by-Objectives in the public sector that, when casually perused, is inconclusive in drawing conclusions about MBO's usefulness. This ambivalence is apparent mainly because the researchers themselves often reject each others' methodologies on the basis of their own unfounded assumptions. However, in an unusually thorough and important analysis of thirty major investigations of governments' experience with Management-by-Objectives, which focused on their methodological approaches, it was found that, in every one of the thirty studies, productivity and performance gains resulted from MBO, and were accurately and legitimately reported; when top management was strongly committed to Management-by-Objectives, "MBO programs result in large productivity gain."[21] Large indeed—an average of 58 percent gains in productivity in those studies where percentage gains were estimated.

Zero-Base Budgeting and Sunset Legislation (1976–1980)

Although President Ford had warmly embraced Management-by-Objectives, a new face in the White House brought in a new budgeting concept. The new face was Jimmy Carter, a nonestablishmentarian fresh from Georgia who had had a good experience with a concept called Zero-Base Budgeting (ZBB) when he was governor. Indeed, Carter was the first elected executive to introduce ZBB to the public sector. Carter, as governor of Georgia, contended that ZBB was instrumental in making his government more cost-effective, noting, "The services provided by Georgia's state government are now greatly improved and every tax dollar is being stretched farther than ever before. There has not been a general statewide tax increase during my term. In fact there has been a substantial reduction in the ad valorem tax."[22]

Peter Pyhrr, perhaps the proponent most often associated with Zero-Base Budgeting, has stated that ZBB forced some major reallocations of resources in Georgia under the aegis of Jimmy Carter. Notably, as governor, Carter allegedly was able to reduce agency budget requests anywhere from 1 percent to 15 percent by using ZBB, while the corresponding program reduction within each agency ranged from no change whatever to the total elimination of the agency itself.[23]

Zero-Base Budgeting is the allocation of resources to agencies on the basis of those agencies periodically reevaluating the need for all of the programs for which the agency is responsible, and justifying the continuance or termination of each program in the agency budget proposal. In other words, an agency reassesses what it is doing from top to bottom—from a hypothetical "zero base."

In practice, ZBB employs two steps. The first step is the development of "decision packages" for each agency with each package containing a summary analysis of each program within the agency. These packages are ranked by the agency head in accordance with his or her perception of overall agency priorities. The second step requires that each decision package be evaluated by top management to determine whether it is justified for further funding. Programs that are considered ineffective or to have outgrown their usefulness are discarded, modified, or combined in other agencies. In short, ZBB asks, what would we do with this agency's funds if they were not already committed? To determine such options, practitioners of ZBB identify each decision unit, analyze each decision unit within a decision package, evaluate and rank all decision packages to develop the appropriations request, and finally prepare a detailed operating budget that reflects those decision packages approved in the budget appropriations.

When President Carter came to Washington, Zero-Base Budgeting came with him; as one high ranking officer in the Office of Management and Budget noted, "Never has any management fad so completely taken over this town."[24] By mid-1977, OMB had issued its Bulletin No. 77-9, stating that agencies had to rank their decision packages and submit the required documents in support of those packages. This bulletin was, in effect, the beginning of Zero-Base Budgeting in the federal government. Schick, an astute observer of the federal budgetary scene, noted that, with the introduction of ZBB to Washington, agency heads were notably speedy to adopt the concept. To quote Schick,

> ZBB was introduced quickly and painlessly because it did not alter the rules of evidence for budgeting or the structure for budget choices. There is not a single bit of budgetary

data unique to ZBB. . . . Agency after agency accommodated ZBB to its existing budgetary framework. If an agency had a program budget, it selected programs as decision units; if its budget still was oriented to organizational lines, these became its ZBB categories.[25]

Schick points out that the key to the acceptance of ZBB by the bureaucrats in Washington rested with the notion of decision units and how to rank those decision units in terms of establishing priorities for budgetary choices. Because of this, an agency head was given an unusual opportunity to define what a decision unit is, and in effect, to fool around with how that decision unit is ranked with other units.

In 1981, the Office of Management and Budget officially terminated ZBB. But by that time, its popularity had extended to the grassroots governments: As many as half the states are using elements of it,[26] and about 35 percent of the nation's cities.[27]

Does Zero-Base Budgeting work? One review of empirical research on the experiences of federal, state, and local governments with ZBB concluded that it works within narrow limits and certain circumstances.[28] Specifically;

- Zero-Base Budgeting is by no means as radical as its name implies; programs virtually never are cut to zero. Typically, government agencies submit their "cut back" decision packages at levels ranging from 75 to 90 percent of last year's budgets.
- ZBB is useful for comparing programs and assisting decision makers in deciding which ones they want to spend more on and which ones they want to spend less on. ZBB cannot (as was often touted in the seventies) identify issues, set objectives, or determine alternative ways of conducting programs.
- ZBB can coexist on reasonably friendly terms with other budgetary concepts and processes. It adapts easily. In this sense, ZBB is a marginal and incremental budgetary tool, one not central to budgeting and management in the way that PPB is.
- Program managers clearly feel that they participate more in the budgetary process, and communication among all levels of the govern-

ment bureaucracy is enhanced when ZBB is introduced. These are perhaps the most conclusive findings of the research.
- However, unless ZBB is introduced carefully, program managers can become parochial in their use of it and fail to see larger issues.
- Paperwork increases with ZBB, but its expansion appears to be controllable. Not all observers agree with this conclusion, however, and at least one authority contends that ZBB "became mired in mammoth amounts of paperwork, probably even more so" than PPB.[29]
- Zero-Base Budgeting does not seem to reduce government spending by the federal and state governments, where expenditures are largely obligated by formula-based public programs, but most local administrators believe ZBB to be quite useful in holding down costs.

So what impact would Zero-Base Budgeting have on an agency's use of paperclips or a city's parks program? For one, a great many more public managers would be talking about both topics as the decision-making process progressed; ZBB pushes participation at all levels, and this is likely to the good. But the inputs, outputs, and effects of paperclips and parks would be incidental considerations; decision makers would be concentrating on alternatives. At the agency level, for example, the head of the Office of Paper Fastening Technologies would be deciding between paperclips, staples, tape, or glue, but at the top level a city manager might be choosing between purchasing more paperclips or closing more parks. These decisions would be formulated as decision packages and cast in terms of the agency's or government's broadly defined program or purpose. Ultimately paperclips and parks would be rank-ordered in terms of their relative usefulness to the government's overall mission.

Sunset, Sunrise

Because Zero-Base Budgeting overtly considers, at least, in theory, the termination of public programs, ZBB is closely associated with "sunset legislation." A *sunset law* provides that, unless the legislature specifically acts otherwise, public programs or agencies are disbanded after a set period of time, for example, five to ten years. Programs and agencies are reviewed periodically by the legislature under this threat of termination, with the idea that overlapping jurisdictions and inefficient programs can be eliminated or possibly reworked.

The federal government has been considering such legislation since the mid-1970s, and Colorado became the first state to enact sunset legislation in 1976; by 1981, thirty-six states had passed sunset laws, although none have been adopted since then.

The results have been mixed. It has been learned that citizen participation in reviewing agencies and programs generally is sparse; sunset laws work most effectively when used in tandem with more orthodox oversight mechanisms, such as program evaluations; lobbyists can and do protect programs from being terminated; and, while peripheral boards and commissions are far more likely to be "sunsetted" than are entrenched agencies, it "appears that the termination component of Sunset has met with a modicum of success."[30] Sunset legislation has often led to the reorganizating, splitting, and merging of state agencies and boards, and at least sixteen states have enacted "sunrise" regulations, which are designed to legislatively review proposals for the founding of new state agencies—at least some of which, it has been discovered, are "sunsetted" agencies trying to rise again.

It has not been demonstrated conclusively that sunset laws save money, and in 1983, Arkansas repealed its sunset law, and six states followed; another half-dozen states have suspended their laws, beginning in 1979. Twenty-three states retain sunset legislation on their books. Typically, the states most likely to "sunset" sunset laws are those with low levels of legislative professionalism (*i.e.*, their legislatures are composed of part-time legislators, have few staffers, etc.).

Nevertheless, "where legislators are committed and the legislative institution has sufficient capacity to manage the process effectively, Sunset continues to serve as a useful catalyst for oversight."[31] This legislative enhancement of oversight may be sunset's real usefulness. "The beauty of sunset is not so much that you can get rid of something. The beauty is the chance to take an objective look at an agency and make needed changes."[32]

The Emergence of the "Uncontrollables"

Both the MBO and ZBB approaches represented reactions by public administrators to the relatively rigid, systemic, and centralized approaches that were attempted under PPB. They also were predicated on the assumption—as were their predecessors, Line-Item Budgeting and Performance Budgeting, as well as PPB—that the federal budget was determined each year by the president and Congress. But there was a growing and discomfiting realization among public officials that this was less and less the case.

By 1981, when Ronald Reagan took office, the federal budgetary process no longer was driven by congressional or presidential initiatives, but by formulas, debt payments, and previous obligations. As one observer has noted, "The federal budget is driven by formulas. The figures for budgetary allocations still march across the pages of the budget document and each ranks by function and by agency, to all appearances the result of conscious annual decision. But in reality, a large proportion are derived from the operation of legislative formulas which automatically determine their amount."[33]

Some of these formulas are tied to the growth or shrinkage of a particular type of population, and government payments to individuals grow or shrink automatically as the number of recipients who are eligible increases or decreases; an example is unemployment insurance. Other formulas are based on the economy and are indexed for inflation; an example is Social Security.

Irrespective of the formula used, these programs are called entitlements on the logic that a person meeting the qualifications of an entitlement program is "entitled" to its payments by right. Most entitlement programs are based on economic formulas and are linked to inflation. Of the federal government's sixteen major entitlement programs, eight are tied to the consumer price index and another three are partially indexed. Together, entitlements (or "payments to individuals") add up to massive transfers of federal revenues. About four in every ten American households receive some kind of cash benefit from the federal government, a figure that includes in part one-third of American households which receive some sort of in-kind benefit, such as health care, food stamps, and school lunches.[34]

The entitlement programs constitute the bulk—more than half—of a class of federal expenditures that federal policymakers call "relatively uncontrollable outlays," to use the official term. The "uncontrollables" comprise more than three-quarters (over 76 percent) of all federal spending.[35] The term itself identifies what federal officials believe to be part of their problem: People no longer control the budget; uncontrollable obligations do.

Besides payments to individuals (the "entitlements" based on formulas), which amount to 42 percent of all federal budget outlays, uncontrollables include interest on the national debt, which is a product of levels of deficit spending and current interest rates, farm price supports, contractual and similar obligations entered into by the government during the previous year, and a variety of open-ended programs and fixed costs. After payments to individuals and prior contractual obligations, interest on the debt comprises the largest portion of all federal budget outlays: nearly 15 percent.

Federal administrators have ample reason to view the budget as increasingly uncontrollable and less subject to human policymaking. In 1970, uncontrollables accounted for less than 62 percent of total federal outlays. This is an impressive proportion. Today, impressive has ballooned to gigantic, and uncontrollable outlays account for more than three-quarters of all federal spending.

State and local governments have their own version of "uncontrollables." Health care costs, notably Medicaid (a federal health care program for the poor, the costs of which are shared by the states), corrections, and the public schools are the leading programs at the subnational levels that are consuming ever-larger slices of the state and local revenues. By and large, these programs are driven by demographics, and as poverty, crime, and youth increase, so are state and local budgets less and less "controlled" by public officials.[36]

The Emergence of Serious Public Debt—and Deficit

Just as federal policymakers grew hemmed in by uncontrollable outlays, which effectively limited their options in making policy to perhaps a fourth of the federal budget,[37] another inhuman phenomenon was narrowing the range of human choice, too: the federal debt. In 1981, the federal debt stood at less than $786 billion; by 1992, it was over $3.2 *trillion*, accounting, as we have noted, for 15 percent of all federal expenditures in the form of interest payments. (In 1981, this figure was 10 percent.) More grimly, the proportion of this debt as a percentage of the Gross Domestic Product (GDP)—in other words, the national economy—grew from 26 percent in 1981 to 50 percent in 1992.[38]

Debt is the total amount of money that the government owes. *Deficit* is the amount of money that the government spends above the amount that it collects each year, and it is the federal deficit, which increased radically in the 1980s, that has contributed alarmingly to the burgeoning national debt. Between 1981 and 1992, federal deficit spending doubled from $155 billion, or over 3 percent of the Gross Domestic Product, to $290 billion, or nearly 5 percent of the GDP. Should present trends continue, the deficit could account for a fifth of the national economy by 2020.[39]

In an effort to regain control over deficit spending, Congress passed the Budget Enforcement Act of 1990. The Act controlled discretionary spending through the congressional appropriations process (with the notable exception of Defense), and prohibited the expansion of entitlement expenditures; despite its success in trimming deficit spending by $500 billion over five years, the deficit nonetheless grew to record levels, essentially because it failed to control the burgeoning costs of existing entitlement programs.

State and local debt has risen, too, from 16 percent of personal income in 1982 to 19 percent in 1989.[40] But, unlike the federal condition, deficit spending is not the problem that it is at the national level, in part because no state (with the exceptions of Connecticut and Vermont) permits deficit spending. Many of these prohibitions on deficits are written into the states' constitutions, and are not easily circumvented.

"The deficit" has become a political rallying cry that, in 1992, was largely responsible for an independent candidate capturing 19 percent of the national vote for president, much of it in the form of write-in ballots. There is no doubt that growing public concern over a growing federal deficit will work against spending on new programs by national policymakers.

Top-Down Budgeting/Target Base Budgeting (1981–Present)

These stark and unpleasant realities of public finance have had a radical impact on government budgeting at all levels. The budgetary targets for agencies increasingly arc centralized in the executive branch, particularly in the offices of the elected chief executive and the budget director, while implementation of budget expenditures are increasingly decentralized to agencies. We call this redistribution of budgetary power "Top-Down Budgeting," which is also known as "Target Base Budgeting" in state and local governments.

Top-Down Budgeting is a method of allocating public revenues to agencies in which agency spending limits (and, often, agency goals, too) are set by the chief executive officer of the government, while agency heads are permitted to attain their goals in the manner that they deem to be most effective within these centrally set spending limits, and are expected to demonstrate progress in the achievement of agency goals in next year's budget request; increasingly, agencies are provided with budgetary incentives by chief executive officers to attain their goals.

Top-Down Budgeting has not been overtly, and even theatrically, introduced to government, as were, for example, Planning-Programming-Budgeting and Zero-Base Budgeting. As one observer put it, "There has not been a major drive to install a new [budget] system since President Carter promulgated the Zero-Base Budgeting system. . . ." Nevertheless, although budgeting systems "no longer get much attention, each system

has had a lasting effect. Their legacies continue to influence budget practices."[41]

This is particularly true with Top-Down Budgeting (which has elements of Performance Budgeting, PPB, MBO, and ZBB), but there also seem to be additional dimensions that are growing from the grassroots bureaucrats at all levels of government. The Pentagon is proposing "mission budgeting." Local governments are experimenting with "entrepreneurial budgeting." State governments are introducing "executive guidance" to their budget-making procedures on a large scale, and public administrators are emphasizing "budgeting for results."[42]

State and local governments have been especially progressive in introducing incentives to agencies to attain goals, notably by allowing agency heads greater flexibility in the use of their agency's funds, and, more importantly, "profit sharing," which permits an agency to keep the funds (or a large proportion thereof) that it saves for the agency's use in following fiscal years. Profit sharing, among other advantages, eliminates the widespread motivation of agency heads to spend all of their yearly allocations by the close of the fiscal year in an attempt to "prove" to their superiors that they really need bigger budgets.

Despite its emphasis on decentralizing the management of funds to agency heads, Top-Down Budgeting clearly empowers the central administration to set expenditure and programmatic goals; therefore, it is a complete reversal of the traditional budgetary process in government, which is "bottom-up." In other words, in a traditional budget-making process, agencies send their spending requests upward toward the budget director and the elected chief executive. These requests are filtered through a series of discussions and hearings, and planning ceilings for each agency are established under the general guidance of the director of the budget. Ultimately the chief executive approves or disapproves of the director's recommendations, and agency heads may appeal the recommendations of the director. While this system is still more or less in place, it is largely pro forma, particularly in the federal government. The real system of budgeting now is from the top downward.

Top-Down Budgeting: The Reagan Revolution

Top-Down Budgeting was reinforced during the Reagan administration by the implementation of OMB Director David Stockman's (who served as director from 1981 through 1985) drive to deal with the total budget (aside from Defense, which President Reagan decreed was to be left virtually entirely to the Pentagon). In a radical departure from previous approaches to the budget, which amounted to incremental decisions on discretionary programs, Stockman succeeded in putting on the bargaining table the entire federal domestic budget including entitlements, indexed benefit programs, and all the other supposedly "uncontrollable" expenditures that had never been seriously questioned in prior budget making.

A second phenomenon that reinforced top-down budgeting was the constant need to adjust the overwhelming problem of federal deficit spending. In an effort to control the deficit, the director of OMB was forced to look far beyond the prospects of "trimming fat" in government programs and to begin cutting out muscle and bone. Because it would be highly unlikely for an agency director to take such an approach to his or her own programs, only the White House and its Office of Management and Budget could reasonably be expected to make such deep cuts. As one expert on the budget process has asked, "How does one convince administrators to collect information that might help others, but can only harm them?"[43]

To aid the president in controlling his own bureaucracy required that the executive branch deal more openly with Congress. In the past, administrations had left the defense of particular programs and the budget requests associated with them to the agency directors. With the advent of the Reagan administration, this was changed overnight. Now OMB was accorded the responsibility of defending the administration's budget proposals at each congressional subcommittee and committee hearing. Ultimately this required that the Office of Management and Budget develop statements about what the president's desired budgetary outcome was for every committee and subcommittee, since it was only at these levels that decisions were really made about the ultimate shape of the federal budget.

To present a coherent budgetary document to Congress meant that OMB had to reformat the budget into terms that Congress could comprehend as policy changes. On a technical level, this meant that OMB budgetary proposals had to be transliterated from the traditional accounting categories used by the executive branch into statistical analyses that Congress (and other legislatures) uses to make budget decisions. Operationally, budgeting for legislative advantage meant that the top personnel of the Office of Management and Budget had to maintain a continuous presence in Congress at the subcommittee and committee levels. Politically, it meant that the director of the Office of Management and Budget and the director's top assistants had to be willing to argue against any changes proposed by Congress in the budget document submitted by OMB, and to show how such changes would affect domestic spending.

This new encouragement of Congressional understanding of the budget required OMB to make some major internal changes. Among them was the development of a new budgeting document published by OMB that is considerably more sophisticated as an advocacy paper than previous publications by the Office of Management and Budget. Stockman also created a legislative liaison staff and appointed "bill trackers" whose primary function was to attend every hearing of a congressional committee or subcommittee and report on what occurred. Prior to 1981, no such staff existed in OMB.

Most significantly, however, Stockman set up the Central Budget Management System as the focus of his management of the budget process. The Central Budget Management System is a computer program that tracks budgetary decision making in Congress and projects the implications of alternative decisions along a wide range of dimensions. It allows OMB to break down the president's budget into congressional committee and subcommittee allocations, into functional categories, into agency budgets, into comparisons with previous resolutions or the previous year's budget, and to calculate the cost of existing policy under a variety of definitions. It allows OMB to keep track on a daily basis all budget decisions being made at all levels, from that of a budget examiner to the White House, in terms of budget authority outlays or any other category. The

Central Budget Management System allows the director to have a "rudder in his head showing him the general and detailed shape of the budget he wants."[44]

Stockman concluded that he needed something like the Central Budget Management System early in 1981 when he discovered that the ways that congressional analysts prepared budget estimates and the ways his OMB analysts prepared budget estimates resulted in billion dollar differences between the estimates. Thus, television news stories were treating the nation to the spectacle of the director of OMB appearing before congressional committees using a hand calculator to arrive at new budget estimates in an effort to reconcile OMB figures with congressional ones.

The Central Budget Management System was designed to change this, and it has. Increasingly, OMB is speaking the language of the congressional budget process and the Central Budget Management System is at the heart of its newfound ability to deal with Congress.

The Techniques and Traits of Top-Down Budgeting at the Grassroots

The quiet revolution in government budgeting brought about by a top-down approach takes several forms. The features that we shall review here are the emergence of Target Base Budgeting, which is essentially a particular type of Top-Down Budgeting that is increasingly favored in the states; the reappearance of Performance Budgeting concepts; and the development of "cutback management," which is how governments are implementing the new and grim fiscal realities of the public sector. Each of these facets of Top-Down Budgeting has had a particularly heavy impact on state and local governments.

Target Base Budgeting. State and local governments have invented their own variants of Top-Down Budgeting, and these techniques are becoming increasingly codified and formal. Perhaps the best known is Target Base Budgeting (TBB), or Target Budgeting. *Target Base Budgeting* is a resource allocation procedure which sets limits on the budgets that departments may request. Those limits, or "targets," are established by the chief executive and the budget

director. Usually a second part of the budget request also is present, which are those departmental fund requests that are not part of the target, but which the department still needs; almost always, these requests are ranked by priority.

Target Base Budgeting is driven by revenues, and in this respect TBB is an unusually realistic budget system. Whether the revenue base is determined by economic conditions beyond the control of policymakers, or by conscious political choices, such as tax caps, is irrelevant: Budgeting targets will have a much better likelihood of reflecting available revenues because the chief executive is setting the targets.

There are a number of elements of Zero-Base Budgeting present in Target Base Budgeting, and most of them work to the advantage of TBB as an easily implemented budget system. These elements include a premium on prioritization; agency budget requests based on service levels, whether current or desired; or a requirement by the chief executive that the agency propose a budget that is supportive of new government policies. "Target base budgeting is a version of zero-base budgeting without a lot of the extra work. Instead of examining all programs or providing alternative scenarios with multiple budgets, target budgeting is based on one figure. . . ."[45] Because it gives greater reign to agency heads in attaining goals, TBB also relates well with Management-by-Objectives, and, because it also centralizes goal setting, TBB also relates well to the new governmental emphasis on performance measures and strategic planning.

Some analysts contend that many federal agencies have used TBB by other names for as long as forty years,[46] and certainly there is no doubt that the new federal favor for Top-Down Budgeting is a loosely constructed type of Target Base Budgeting. Although there are no definitive figures on the use of TBB in local governments, it appears that some cities have been using it since the early 1980s, notably Rochester, Tampa, Phoenix, and Cincinnati.[47]

State governments are especially enthusiastic about Target Base Budgeting and procedures that promote executive guidance of departmental budget requests. One study of all fifty state budget systems conducted over two decades concludes that, "The days of agencies having the freedom to request budgets in whatever amounts they see fit are gone, and in their stead are various control mechanisms or types of ceilings that must be observed when requesting funds."[48]

In 1970, 59 percent of governors suggested no ceiling for budget requests of any kind to their departments, only 16 percent recommended "policy ceilings," or instructions which encouraged or discouraged the growth of certain types of departmental programs, and no governor specified a dollar level ceiling in agency requests. By 1990, only 11 percent of the governors still had no ceiling of any kind, 60 percent were using policy ceilings, and 45 percent specified agency budget targets in dollars.[49]

No doubt, this resurgence of the governors in the budgetary systems of the states has been assisted by a growing professionalism in state budget offices. Forty-five percent of state budget staffs have at least a master's degree (1990), compared to 18 percent twenty years earlier, and between 1975 and 1990, the average size of state budget offices ballooned from twenty-nine to forty-seven, But more and more highly educated budgeteers have had the inevitable effect of strengthening the role of central management in the formulation of state budgets.[50] Top-Down Budgeting is entrenched and here to stay in the states.

Performance Measures: A Renewal of Performance Budgeting. We noted in the preceding chapter that there is a renewed interest in the federal government with the development of program performance measures, and nowhere is this interest more evident than in the enactment of the Government Performance and Results Act in 1993, which charts a cautious, multi-year plan for ultimately re-introducing Performance Budgeting to the federal government. Soon after the Act's passage, in fact, the General Accounting Office, in an effort to learn more about how Performance Budgeting could be introduced to the federal government, conducted a careful analysis of the twelve states "regarded as leaders in performance budgeting." The GAO found that, while these states were indeed doing some impressive work in the on-going development of performance measures, and that these efforts were very useful in establishing state priorities, strengthening management, and dealing with budget cuts, performance measuring had yet to be wed to budget-

ing—in fact, the two did not even date. Obstacles to the nuptials included an inability of state officials to agree over what were meaningful performance measures, and dissimilar reporting and accounting structures among state agencies—in other words, very basic problems. Performance measures had "not attained sufficient credibility to influence resource allocation decisions. Instead . . . resource allocations continue to be driven, for the most part, by traditional budgeting practices."[51]

These findings should not be all that discouraging, however, because, at root, they say little more than that, in the highly politicized world of making state budgets, policy makers are still unprepared to rely too dependently on formulas and measurements. Within this culture of caution, the evidence indicates that state governments are increasingly responsive to what program evaluations and performance measures can show them about the policies they implement, and are inclined toward using performance measures in budget formulation; it is just that state officials remain reluctant to place all of their states' budget-making eggs in a basket woven of still-evolving performance measures that they are unprepared to fully trust. This caution is not necessarily an indictment of the states as governments which reject management in favor of politics (which may have been the unspoken standard of the GAO in conducting its study); one may interpret it, as we do, as a slow coming around by the states to a possible implementation of true Performance Budgeting. Should this occur, Performance Budgeting likely will be conducted in the larger context of Target Base Budgeting.

Table 8–1 illustrates this possible "coming around" by the states. It shows that state agencies increasingly—and even dramatically—are providing performance and productivity information in making their annual budget requests, and, more than ever before, legislatures, governors, and their budget officers are demanding performance data to make their allocation decisions.

There are few definitive data at the local level concerning Performance Budgeting, but it seems likely that it may be in more extensive use in local governments than in either federal or state governments. Local jurisdictions, because they are smaller and implement a high proportion of readily measurable programs, logically would find

TABLE 8-1 **The Growing Use of Program Productivity Information in State Budget Systems**

Type of Information	1970	1990
Agency includes productivity estimates in its budget requests.	24%	86%
Most or some agencies include productivity measures in the budget documents.	45	77
Central budget office conducts productivity analysis.	31	94
Executive budget decisions are based on productivity analysis to a substantial degree or to some degree.	51	100
Legislative decisions are based on productivity analysis to a substantial degree or to some degree.	44	94

Productivity was defined in the survey as measures which "define and quantify the goods or services being produced."

Source: As derived from, Robert D. Lee, Jr., "Developments in State Budgeting: Trends of Two Decades," *Public Administration Review*, 51 (May/June 1991), pp. 254–261, Tables 3, 5, 6, and 7.

Performance Budgeting relatively accessible and useful. We do know that more than two-thirds of American municipalities report that they use "performance monitoring" techniques, and over half have productivity improvement programs.[52]

One analysis of municipal budget reforms concluded that performance-based approaches probably were widespread in American cities: "They are not just used as a window dressing; they are used by programmatic managers and politicians to solve problems. Moreover, budget reforms turn out not to always be cabooses behind political reform; sometimes they head the train."[53]

Cutback Management: Responding to the Reality of Red Ink. Unlike the federal government, which can and does engage in deficit spending, state and local governments must, by law, balance the books. The 1990s are an era of reduced revenues—a "decade of red ink," to borrow one description—for the public sector, and state, but particularly local, governments have developed systematic ways of responding to these new realities. These methods are called "cutback

management," and they are very much a part of the package of Top-Down Budgeting. *Cutback management* is the collection of techniques that have been developed by practicing public administrators to reduce or eliminate public programs when confronted by fiscal constraints.[54] These techniques of cutback management include short-term and long-term approaches. Short-term cutback management includes hiring freezes, unilateral budget cuts, reducing temporary employees, deferring maintenance, and postponing equipment purchases.

A *hiring freeze* simply means that no one new is hired, and relies on a process of natural attrition (*i.e.*, employees retiring or leaving the agency voluntarily for other jobs) to effect cost savings. There are a number of disadvantages to hiring freezes, notably that they are likely to hurt minorities and women first, since they often are disproportionately represented among the "last hired, first fired" employees of public agencies. Hiring freezes also can disadvantage some units of government more than others if, for whatever reason, they lose more employees to attrition than do other units, and yet, like those other units, still are not allowed to hire replacements. One remedy to these problems is to permit the hiring of one person for every three lost by attrition until an established level is reached.

"Across-the-board" budget cuts constitute another short-term method of cutback management, and this approach has the advantage of relieving the senior public administrator of considerable stress, since it is, essentially, mindless: A 10 percent cut in the budgets of all units may be an easy decision for the chief executive to make, but it is insensitive to the varying needs and services of those units. Typically, unilateral budget cuts harm those agencies that have a high proportion of skilled workers providing sophisticated services, while they do not have a major impact on agencies which deliver a routine service that simply can be slowed down to accommodate a budget cut.

Reducing temporary employees, deferring maintenance, and postponing equipment purchases also are relatively stressless decisions for the senior public administrator to make when implementing cutbacks, and, also like hiring freezes and unilateral budget cuts, have the advantage of buying time for the longer haul. Ultimately, these techniques are short-term approaches. To actually reduce expenditures permanently requires more thought.

Longer-term approaches to reducing expenditures over time can be accomplished by examining alternative delivery systems, achieving direct cost savings, and setting programmatic priorities and eliminating those programs that appear on the bottom of the priority list.

There are at least four ways of delivering public programs, often with the same level of service, but at a reduced level of cost. These include contracting with volunteer groups (as is done extensively by local governments and certain state and federal agencies, such as the U.S. Forest Service); using part-time and lower-cost personnel; privatizing services; and eliminating duplication of services through inter-agency agreements with other governments.

Using part-time personnel is reasonably self-evident as a cost saving delivery system for public programs; volunteerism (or "co-production"), privatization, and intergovernmental agreements, however, are sufficiently complex that we devote Chapters 11 and 12 to discussions of these alternative systems of implementation.

Direct cost savings often can be achieved by reorganizing services to eliminate duplication. This can be done through intergovernmental agreements, as mentioned earlier, or by consolidating governments themselves. This latter approach, however, is rarely popular with the public; fewer than thirty city-county consolidations, for example, have taken place since the first one in 1805.[55] In addition, using a lower-cost employee, such as student interns and temporary service personnel who typically do not demand a high level of benefits, can result in direct cost savings as well.

Finally, priority setting can result in the elimination of low-priority programs and their expenses in an agency. Nevertheless, how those priorities, low and otherwise, are determined by agency administrators can be a painful process that requires sophistication and sensitivity to reduce the conflict that is inherent in making such choices. Practicing public administrators, particularly at the local level, seem to agree that the following steps should be taken in determining program priorities when faced with cutbacks:

- Be sure that all interested parties are informed of the need for cutbacks, and solicit their views on those cutbacks.
- Determine the criteria for how priorities should be set. While these criteria should be determined by the chief executive, the views of other employees in the agency should be carefully considered, and if possible, implemented.
- Establish a preliminary and tentative priority list based on the explicit criteria that have been developed for priority setting.
- Attempt to build some public consensus through various meetings and hearings to develop a final priority list.
- Insure that various elected officials and other pertinent decision makers approve of the priority list.
- Understand that there will never be complete agreement in the priority setting process, but keep trying to explain why the priorities have been set in the manner that they have to the public at large and to agency employees.
- Public executives faced with cutting public programs should remain calm, professional, honest, open, and unflappable in the process of setting priorities. Cutback management is, above all, a process of conflict reduction.

The New Realities of Top-Down Budgeting

We consider here some new realities in government that have resulted from Top-Down Budgeting. Some are good, others more questionable; some are more evident at the national level, others are more prominent at the subnational levels.[56]

Reinstatement of the Chief Elected Executive in Budgetary Policy. Perhaps most importantly, the elected chief executive has been reinstated in the budgetary (and policymaking) process in a major way. At the federal level, the transformation of the Office of Management and Budget under David Stockman had worked to place the president in a better position than ever before to make policy for the whole of government. In the states, the techniques of Target Base Budgeting and their widespread use by governors have made the governors far more powerful actors in state budget formulation.

Empowerment of the Executive Budget Agency. At the federal level, the executive budget process, the budget's presentation to Congress, and ensuing negotiations over the budget between the two branches are now centralized as never before, and likely will remain so. It is now the Office of Management and Budget, particularly the top echelons of that Office, that deal directly with the committees and subcommittees of Congress where the real budgetary decisions are made. "No president or budget director is likely to want to go back to the days when the president's proposal was largely left to the tender mercies of the spending agencies and the committee system."[57]

This centralization of the executive budget process and the consequent empowerment of the executive budget agency may be the most enduring change in the practice of government wrought by Reagan. "The first Reagan year witnessed the striking and sudden emergence of OMB to the posture of principal executive leader, short of the president himself, in policymaking and politics."[58]

This posture has continued. Observers have noted how the four public administrators who hold "the unheralded title of associate director for programs in the Office of Management and Budget, a name worthy of a dutiful bean counter. . . .[wield] power that outstrips that of most Cabinet secretaries."[59] "Aside from Cabinet officers and perhaps one or two people on the West Wing [of the White House] staff, they are arguably the most powerful people on the civilian side of the government."[60]

A similar phenomenon is happening in the states. A study of the state budget offices in three midwestern states concluded that, "Budget offices and their staffs do indeed appear to exercise significant influence in state policy making," and that this influence was increasing over time.[61]

Development of a Common Language of the Budget. At least at the federal level, Top-Down Budgeting has provided both the executive branch and Congress with a new and more coherent way of looking at things. OMB and Congress increasingly speak in the same language when it comes to the budget. Budget packages are now being voted on by members of Congress who have an improved knowledge over what the implications of their votes might be. This is by no means the result only of actions by David Stockman and OMB, but it is also a consequence of the impact that the Congressional Budget Office, established in 1974, has had upon members of Congress.

By the close of the Reagan era, it was clear that this common language was in place: "the Budget Summit Agreement of 1987 embodied a vocabulary and set of principles that would not just have been unacceptable in 1981, but more importantly, unrecognizable."[62]

A Shift from Allocative/Incremental Budgeting to Economic Forecasting. Economic assumptions and the formulas by which federal dollars are disbursed under certain entitlement programs have changed the budget process from one of annual allocations and incrementalism to one in which economic assumptions and entitlement formulas are emphasized. Increasingly, federal budgets are developed on the basis of economic projections. Originally, these projections and estimates were meant to guide policy, but, in the words of one Washington lobbyist, "revenue estimating has become policy."[63]

This federal trend (it is considerably less present among states and localities) started well before the advent of Top-Down Budgeting (which clearly accelerated it), when Congress passed the Congressional Budget and Impoundment Act of 1974; the Act required that all bills passed by committees be accompanied with cost estimates. The Budget Enforcement Act of 1990 made this mandate more stringent by stipulating that all new federal spending proposals be linked either to new taxes or to new budget cuts.

Just how accurate these estimates are is highly debatable. One analyst at the National Research Council, which studied the accuracy of these influential estimates, concluded that, "We don't know if they're good, so-so, or terrible."[64]

Despite these serious flaws, economic estimates are heavily relied on in making budgets.

But, in making them, very small adjustments in the assumptions underlying economic projections can result in huge budgetary differences. "For example, $1 billion can be 'saved' . . . by lowering the forecasts of interest rates starting October 1 . . . by less than one-half of one percentage point. No one can forecast interest rates with anything remotely resembling that degree of accuracy, and few would notice such a change. Faced with the choice of 'saving' $1 billion by cutting Social Security or by a minute change in economic assumptions, it is little wonder that the latter looks so tempting."[65] Estimates about economic growth yield even more dramatic differences than projections of interest rates, and an "increase of 1 percentage point in real growth [would lower] the deficit by $19 billion . . . according to a 'rule of thumb' by the Congressional Budget Office."[66]

Intensification of Conflict. As a result of these dynamics, the budget process increasingly becomes a conflict over whose assumptions will be used in developing the budget. Analysts from the Congressional Budget Office use one set of assumptions in developing their economic projections, while analysts from the Office of Management and Budget use their own. These assumptions can be radically different, or even if not radically different, can nonetheless result in radical differences in the ultimate budget figures. While the new era of Top-Down Budgeting has brought about an increased ability of the executive and legislative branches to communicate with each other, it has not resulted in a system in which both branches are using the same basic assumptions about the future, and the differences in economic projections coming from the White House and Congress have been, on occasion, vast.[67]

Certainly under the Reagan administration, the prospect for conflict over these assumptions was magnified. The White House wanted to cut domestic spending while Congress, by and large, wished to protect it. Thus, the effort to cut budgets did not result in "decrementalism, an incrementalism in reverse with similar attributes. Rather it heightened conflict and destabilized the budget process, placing strain on institutions, so that new rules began to emerge, even though these may not have been wholly satisfactory to participants. These rules related to the base for cuts, veracity of the cuts, and a new vocabulary of budget cutting."[68]

As a consequence of these new rules, an absence of real deadlines in the budgetary process and continuity of the budget cycle are now facts of federal life. The traditional budgetary timetable no longer holds, and "continuing resolutions" on the budget and special sessions of Congress called each year (in an effort to assure that federal employees are paid on time) are now the rule. The underlying reasons for these changes reflect the continuing need to adjust assumptions about the economy and the budget's impact on it as the fiscal year progresses, as well as heightened and continuous conflict over the budget between the president and Congress.

Top-Down Budgeting for Paperclips and Parks

What about our ongoing examples of paperclips and parks? Top-Down Budgeting would push budgeteers into taking a perspective that is highly political and goal-specific. In the administrations of Reagan and George Bush, that goal was to balance the budget by (with the exception of Defense) cutting the volume of expenditures so, for the moment, let us use that goal of cutting expenditures in discussing paperclips and parks.

Under Top-Down Budgeting, budgeteers would ask: If paperclips and parks were deleted from the budget, whose oxen would be gored? By how much would the total budget be reduced? Alternatives to paperclips and parks are not really considered, since the overriding objective is to cut spending. Similarly, outputs are incidental; it really does not matter what a public program is doing, since the budgeteers are prepared to cut whatever program that the legislature will allow. Inputs and effects, by contrast, are very much present. But only *goal-related* (in this case, economic) inputs and *goal-related* effects seriously interest the budgeteers. How much money are we spending on paperclips and parks? What will be the effect on the deficit if we eliminate them? Paperclips and parks are not differentiated in any way by budgeteers using Top-Down Budgeting other than on the basis of the amount of money they consume—or, more broadly, how they affect the achievement of the overall goal. In all likelihood, budgeteers would prefer to cut parks rather than paperclips from their budgets on the grounds that parks are more costly, and they would be quite pleased to eliminate both programs if the legislature would let them.

One fact emerges very clearly in Top-Down Budgeting: Budgeteers and executive policymakers know their overriding goal and budget exclusively for that goal. As Top-Down Budgeting was practiced in Reagan's Washington, this goal was economic: Cut the non-Defense budget. But in theory, other goals are equally possible. For example, the goal of the executive branch might be to provide more and better parks. In this case, all other programs, such as paperclips, would be slashed by as much as the legislature would permit, and all savings and revenues would be redirected toward parks.

The point is that for the first time, budgeteers in the central budget office (such as OMB) of a government can deal with the budget as a whole and use it to advance whatever goal they are pursuing. Top-Down Budgeting appears to have succeeded, at least in relative terms, where Programming-Planning-Budgeting failed. The concept *really is* systemic and centralized; control by the top of the bureaucracy of its lower echelons *really has* been achieved.

In summary, each budgetary form not only forces the bureaucrat to ask increasingly basic questions about the agency's programs, but each form connotes different patterns and functions for the whole of government as well. The principal features of and differences between the Line-Item, Performance, Planning- Programming-Budgeting, Management-by-Objectives, Zero-Base Budgeting, and Top-Down Budgeting concepts are summarized in Table 8-2.

THE BUDGETARY PROCESS: STRATEGIES FOR BUDGETARY SUCCESS

Irrespective of what budgetary notion is in vogue, it is important to realize that the essence of the budgetary process is political. Wildavsky, Richard F. Fenno, Jr., and Jesse Burkhead, among others, have addressed what it means for a budgeteer to be a politician in securing an agency's funding, and a review of some of their thinking on the topic is worthwhile.[69] Although they broach the federal budgetary process almost exclusively, the same basic rules apply to state and local governments as well. Politics requires the use of strategies and the politics of the budgetary process is no exception. As Wildavsky observes in his classic essay on the topic:

What really counts in helping an agency get the appropriations it desires? Long service in Washington has convinced high agency officials that some things count a great deal and others only a little. Although they are well aware of the desirability of having technical data to support their requests, budget officials commonly derogate the importance of the formal aspects of their work as a means of securing appropriations. . . . But, as several informants put it in almost identical words, "It's not what's in your estimates but how good a politician you are that matters."[70]

To be a good budgetary politician requires the use of "ubiquitous" and "contingent" strategies.[71] We consider these in turn.

Ubiquitous Strategies

Ubiquitous strategies are pervasive and used on a continuing basis by an agency; their purpose is to build confidence in the agency among the public, and to add to its clientele. There are at least three types of ubiquitous strategies.

Find, Serve, and Use a Clientele for the Services You Perform.   The thought here is that an agency, when threatened, mobilizes its clientele. A case in point is the former Office of Economic Opportunity (OEO). When the Office was budgetarily emasculated under the Nixon administration, various organizations representing the poor rose to its defense, fighting a remarkable rearguard action in the courts in an effort to preserve OEO. Although OEO can be faulted on other strategy counts, the Office unquestionably had found and used a clientele. A number of observers felt that OEO had politicized and organized "the forgotten fifth" in the United States to a point at which the poor were better equipped to fend for themselves when it came to passing and implementing federal legislation, with or without OEO.

TABLE 8-2 Some Differences Among Budgetary Concepts

Feature	Line-Item (1921-1939)	Performance (1939-1959)	PPB (1960-1969)	MBO (1970-1976)	ZBB (1977-1980)	Top-Down Budgeting (1981-present)
Basic orientation	Control	Management	Planning	Management	Decision making	Control and attainment of a single, systemwide goal
Scope	Inputs	Inputs and outputs	Inputs, outputs, effects, and alternatives	Inputs, outputs, and effects	Alternatives	Goal-specific inputs and goal-specific effects
Personnel skills	Accounting	Management	Economics and planning	Managerial "common sense"	Management and planning	Political, coordinative, and knowledge relevant to the systemwide goal
Critical information	Objects of expenditures	Activities of agency	Purposes of agency	Program effectiveness	Purpose of program or agency	Does program or agency further the systemwide goal?
Policymaking style	Incremental	Incremental	Systemic	Decentralized	Incremental and participatory	Systemic and aggressive
Planning responsibility	Largely absent	Dispersed	Central	Comprehensive, but allocated	Decentralized	Centralized
Role of the budget agency	Fiscal propriety	Efficiency	Policy	Program effectiveness and efficiency	Policy prioritization	Attainment of a single systemwide goal

Establish Confidence in the Mind of the Reviewer That You Can Carry Out the Complicated Program (Which He or She Seldom Understands) Efficiently and Effectively. Here, the key notion is that if legislators believe in your abilities, you can get just about anything you want. Exemplary in this regard is the National Science Foundation (NSF), founded in 1950. An early fear held by a number of citizens was that NSF would become an all-powerful "science czar" of the United States. Through the strategic use of a low administrative profile, academic trappings, and capitalizing on a popular romanticism concerning science, the Foundation not only eliminated this worry but eventually was operating in a budgetary environment that permitted an awesome degree of latitude: Science could (and should) be funded solely for the sake of science, and fellow scientists were deciding who among them should be awarded NSF grants.

The Foundation's premise—that science should be funded according to what happened to interest scientists rather than for the achievement of larger social goals—ultimately (in the late 1960s) came under some hard questioning in Congress. But for many years NSF enjoyed an impressive degree of budgetary success despite a virtual absence of accountability in terms of what it did with the money.

Attempt to Capitalize on the Fragmentary Budgetary Review Process. A notable example of this strategy is provided by the Air Force. Throughout most of the 1950s, the Air Force practiced "phased buying." This meant that the Air Force bought parts for a larger number of weapons than its appropriations request indicated it intended to purchase. As a result, Congress and the president were left with little choice but to authorize the purchase of the remaining parts if

A FOUNDER ON THE DEFICIT

Most informed observers agree that the burgeoning national debt and the uncontrolled deficit of federal spending that is expanding so rapidly are the results less of economics, and more of inadequate political will. The nation's first Secretary of the Treasury, Alexander Hamilton, made this very point some two centuries ago, noting that, when the burdens of public debt grow too heavy on the citizenry, "convulsions & revolutions . . . are a Natural offspring."

To extinguish a Debt which exists and to avoid contracting more ideas are almost always favored by a public feeling and opinion; but to pay Taxes for one of the other purpose, which are the only means of avoiding the evil, is always more or less unpopular. These contradictions are in human nature. And the lot of a Country would be enviable indeed, in which there were not always men ready to turn them to the account of their own popularity or to make other sinister account.

Hence it is no uncommon spectacle to see the same men Clamouring for Occasions of expense, when they happen to be in unison with the present humour of the community, whether well or ill directed, declaiming against a Public Debt, and for the reduction of it as an *abstract thesis*, yet vehement against any plan of taxation which is proposed to discharge old debts, or to avoid new by defraying the expence of exigencies as they emerge.

The consequence is, that the Public Debt swells, 'till its magnitude becomes enormous, and the Burthens of the people gradually increase 'till their weight becomes intolerable. Of such a state of things great disorders in the whole political economy, convulsions & revolutions of Government are a Natural offspring.

[My previous report] suggests the idea of "*incorporating as a fundamental maxim* in the SYSTEM of PUBLIC CREDIT of the United States, *that the creation of Debt should always be accompanied with the means of extinguishment*—that this is the true secret for rendering public credit immortal, and that it is difficult to conceive a situation in which there may not be an adherence to the Maxim" and it expresses an unfeigned solicitude that this may be attempted by the United States.

Alexander Hamilton, Secretary of the Treasury,
"Report on a Plan for the Further Support of Public Credit," January 16, 1795

any of the weapons were to be useful. For many years, this questionable use of the fragmentary review process worked handsomely, but in 1957, after a public furor arose, Secretary of Defense Charles Wilson ended the practice. In effect, however, "phased buying" continues under a new guise, which is the research and development contract. The Defense Department argues (with some reason) that productive research cannot be scheduled rigidly by the calendar, so R&D projects are extended (often reluctantly) year after year by Congress, on the logic that there is little choice if the research is to pay off.

Contingent Strategies

Contingent strategies are more tactical than are ubiquitous strategies, and are designed to capitalize on unusual opportunities perceived by the agency that might defend of expand its base. As with ubiquitous strategies, there are three types.

Guard against Cuts in the Old Programs. There are a number of ways for an agency to do this; a favorite strategy is to cut the most popular program that the agency has, on the logic that citizen complaints will get back to congressmen more speedily. Thus, the National Institutes of Health have been known to start a dental research program by cutting heart, cancer, and mental health research in its proposed budget. Because of constituent pressure, Congress restored these funds and approved the whole package.

Attempt to Inch Ahead with Old Programs. It is always easier to get new appropriations if they are made to look like old programs. A favored device for accomplishing this is the numbers game. The National Institutes of Health, for example, long have engaged in this strategy by reducing the number of its research grants ("Look! We're economizing!"), but increasing their size (thus inching ahead).

Adding New Programs.   The final contingent strategy used by budgetary officers is the incremental addition of new programs. Because the new and novel often are distrusted by those empowered to distribute money, every effort is made in the agency to make its new program look

as old as possible. Variants of this strategy include the contention that the new program is only temporary, that it is exceedingly small and thus hardly worth examination, that it is merely a logical continuation of an old program, that it is an attempt to reduce some sort of backlog in the agency, and that it will save money.

On the other hand, an agency occasionally will try to make the program look as new and "with-it" as possible. This variant also has its uses. A favored strategy is christening the new program with an inspiring title—for example, the "War on Poverty," "Polaris," "Titan," and "Mission 66" (which was a park improvement program). Salesmanship is not neglected; members of Congress, on occasion, have been irritated by the use of a "Peter Rabbit" presentation—simple graphs, fancy brochures, and lots and lots of pictures. Salesmanship often is used in conjunction with the recognition of some new crisis. Witness the effects of such drama-ridden salesmanship on a member of one appropriations committee:

> A week ago, Mr. Chairman, after this hearing about cancer, I went home and checked all the little skin flecks and felt for bumps and bruises. I lay awake that night and could have convinced myself I had cancer. And then more recently I lay awake listening to my heart after hearing the heart trouble talk. . . . And here I am listening to all this mental health talk . . . and I wonder what I am going to dream about tonight.[72]

If the foregoing strategy review sounds cynical, it is. To be cynical, however, is not necessarily to be scrofulous. Bureaucrats-as-politicians are capable of using cynical means for the sake of noble ends, and this phenomenon is well exemplified by the budgetary process.

An alternative always is possible, however. Cynical means can be used to attain cynical ends. As an administrative technique, the budget has its own combination of means and ends, methods and values. The ways in which these variables are interrelated by administrators are in essence political and affect programs and people.

So it is, too, with another management technique, human resource management. Like budgeting, public personnel administration is draped with the trappings of professionalism, technology, and expertise, but it is also a system of values and politics. We consider this subject in the next chapter.

NOTES

1. Aaron Wildavsky, "'Political Implications of Budget Reform:' A Retrospective," *Public Administration Review*, 52 (November/December 1992), p. 595.
2. Much of this discussion is based on: Bertram M. Gross, "The New Systems Budgeting," *Public Administration Review*, 29 (March/April 1969), pp. 113–137; and Allen Schick, "The Road to PPB: The Stages of Budget Reform" *Public Administration Review*, 26 (December 1966), pp. 243-258.
3. Aaron Wildavsky, *The Politics of the Budgetary Process*, 2nd ed. (Boston: Little, Brown, 1974), p. 4.
4. Charles G. Dawes, *The First Year of the Budget of the United States* (Washington, D.C.: U.S. Government Printing Office, 1923), p. ii, as cited in Schick, "The Road to PPB."
5. Verne B. Lewis, "Reflections on Budget Systems," *Public Budgeting and Finance*, 8 (Spring 1988), p. 7.
6. Executive Order 8248, as quoted in Schick, "The Road to PPB," p. 250.
7. Commission on Organization of the Executive Branch of Government, *Budgeting and Accounting* (Washington, D.C.: U.S. Government Printing Office, 1949), p. 8.
8. U. S. General Accounting Office, *Performance Budgeting: State Experiences and Applications for the Federal Government*. GAO/AFMD – 93 – 41 (Washington, D.C.: GAO, February 1993), p. 1.
9. Quoted in Allen Schick, *Budget Innovation in the States* (Washington, D.C.: Brookings Institution, 1971), p. 127.
10. Edwin L. Harper, Fred A. Kramer and Andrew M. Rouse, *Implementation and Use of PPB in Sixteen Federal Agencies* (Washington, D.C.: U.S. Bureau of the Budget, April 1969).
11. Orville Freeman, quoted in Lewis, "Reflections on Budget Systems," p. 11.
12. This paragraph is drawn from: Harry P. Hatry, *Status of PPBS in Local and State Governments in the United States* (Washington, D.C.: Urban Institute, 1974).
13. Reorganization Message of President Richard M. Nixon to Congress, March 12, 1970. Quoted in Allen Schick, "A Death in the Bureaucracy: The Demise of Federal PPB," *Public Administration Review*, 33 (March/April 1973), p. 151.
14. Ibid., p. 146.
15. Peter Drucker, *The Practice of Management* (New York: Harper & Row, 1954).
16. Jong S. Jun, "Management by Objectives and the Public Sector, Introduction," *Public Administration Review*, 36 (January/February 1976), p. 3.
17. Frank P. Sherwood and William J. Page, Jr., "MBO and Public Management," *Public Administration Review*, 36 (January/February 1976), p. 5.
18. Chester A. Newland, "Policy/Program Objectives and Federal Management: The Search for Government Effectiveness," *Public Administration Review*, 36 (January/February 1976), p. 20.
19. Jerry L. McCaffery, "MBO and the Budgetary Process," *Public Administration Review*, 36 (January/February 1976), p. 35.
20. See: Rackham S. Fukuhara, "Productivity Improvement in Cities," *The Municipal Year Book, 1977* (Washington, D.C.: International City Management Association, 1977), pp. 193-200 (for 1976 figure); Theodore H. Poister and Robert P. McGowan, "The Use of Management Tools in Municipal Government: A National Survey," *Public Administration Review*, 44 (May/June 1984), p. 218 (for 1982 figure); Theodore H. Poister and Gregory Streib, "Management Tools in Municipal Government: Trends Over the Past Decade," *Public Administration Review*, 49 (May/June 1989), p. 242 (in 1987, 62 percent of cities used MBO); and Richard C. Elling, "Of Bandwagons and Bandaids: A Comparative Assessment of the Utilization and Efficacy of Management Techniques and Strategies in State Bureaucracies," paper presented at the 1984 Annual Meeting of the American Political Science Association, Washington, D.C., August-September 1984 (for 1984 figure). The municipal surveys sampled all cities of 25,000 to one million people. Four hundred-four cities responded in 1976, 460 responded in 1982, and 451 in 1987. The state survey had a response rate of 40 percent (or 847 administrators) and included Arizona, California, Delaware, Indiana, Michigan, New York, South Dakota, Tennessee, Texas, and Vermont.
21. Robert Rodgers and John E. Hunter, "A Foundation of Good Management Practice in Government: Management by Objectives," *Public Administration Review*, 52 (January/February 1992), p. 34.
22. Jimmy Carter, "Planning a Budget from Zero," *Innovations in State Government* (Washington, D.C.: National Governors Conference, 1974), p. 42.
23. Peter A. Pyhrr, "The Zero Base Approach to Government Budgeting," *Public Administration Review*, 37 (January/February 1977), p. 7. It is probable, however, that Pyhrr is overstating the case, especially since Georgia was also undergoing a governmental reorganization. See also: Thomas P. Lauth, "Zero-Base Budgeting in Georgia State Government: Myth and Reality," *Public Administration Review*, 38 (September/October 1978), pp. 420-430.
24. Quoted in: Donald F. Haider, "Zero Base: Federal Style," *Public Administration Review*, 37 (July/August 1977), p. 401.
25. Allen Schick, "The Road from ZBB," *Public Administration Review*, 38 (March/April 1978), p. 178.
26. Allen Schick, *Zero-Base 80: The Status of Zero-Base Budgeting in the States* (Washington, D.C.: National Association of State Budget Officers and The Urban Institute, 1979); and Elling, "Of Bandwagons and

Bandaids," Table 7.

27. Poister and Streib, "Management Tools in Municipal Government," p. 244.

28. Frank D. Draper and Bernard T. Pitsvada, "ZBB—Looking Back After Ten Years," *Public Administration Review*, 41 (January/February 1981), pp. 76-83. The principal studies of ZBB's use in the public sector are: Schick, *Zero-Base 80* (which focuses on state governments); Perry Moore, "Zero-Base Budgeting in American Cities," *Public Administration Review*, 40 (May/June 1980), pp. 253-258; and, for the federal experience, Frank D. Draper and Bernard T. Pitsvada, *A First Year's Assessment of ZBB in the Federal Government—Another View* (Arlington, Va.: Association of Government Accountants, 1978); Frank D. Draper and Bernard T. Pitsvada, "Congress and Executive Branch Budget Reform: The House Appropriations Committee and Zero-Base Budgeting," *International Journal of Public Administration*, Vol. 2, No. 3 (1980), pp. 331-374; Comptroller General of the United States, *Streamlining Zero-Base Budgeting Will Benefit Decision-Making*, PAD 79-74, (Washington, D.C.: General Accounting Office, 1979); and Comptroller General of the United States, *Budget Formulation: Many Approaches But Some Improvements Are Needed*, PAD 80-31, Report to the House Committee on Government Operations (Washington, D.C.: General Accounting Office, 1980).

29. Harry P. Hatry, "The Alphabet Soup Approach: You'll Love It!" *Public Manager*, 21 (Winter 1992-1993), p. 9.

30. Richard C. Kearney, "Sunset: A Survey and Analysis of the State Experience," *Public Administration Review*, 50 (January/February 1990), p. 53.

31. *Ibid.*, p. 56.

32. Brad Mallon, quoted in Charles Mahtesian, "Why the Sun Rarely Sets on State Bureaucracy," *Governing* (June 1992), p. 25.

33. Naomi Caiden, "The New Rules of the Federal Budget Game," *Public Administration Review*, 44 (March/April 1984), p. 110.

34. Robert J. Lampman, "Secondary Consumer Income: Interfamily Transfer Flows, 1950-1978," Mimeograph 1983, Table 3.3.

35. U.S. Bureau of the Census, *Statistical Abstract of the United States*, 1990 (Washington, D.C.: U.S. Government Printing Office, 1990), Table 502, p. 313. Unless noted otherwise, the following discussion on uncontrollables is drawn from this source, and all figures are for Fiscal Year 1989.

36. Penelope Lemov, "The Decade of Red Ink," *Governing* (August 1992), pp. 22-26.

37. It all depends, of course, on how one calculates the numbers, but clearly the amount of discretionary spending available to federal policymakers is in decline. The General Accounting Office says that it has fallen from 45 percent in 1981 to 40 percent in 1991. See: U. S. General Accounting Office, *Budget Issues*. Transition Series, GAO/OCG-93-1TR. (Washington, D.C.: General Accounting Office, December 1992), p. 20.

38. *Ibid.*, p. 12.

39. *Ibid.*, pp. 4, 14. Figures are for the federal "unified deficit."

40. Roy Bahl and William Duncombe, "State and Local Debt Burdens in the 1980s: A Study in Contrasts," *Public Administration Review*, 53 (January/February 1993), p. 34.

41. Lewis, "Reflections on Budget Systems," p. 4.

42. Dan A. Cothran, "Entrepreneurial Budgeting: *An Emerging Reform*?" Public Administration Review, 55 (September/October 1993) pp. 445-454.

43. Aaron Wildavsky, *Speaking Truth to Power* (Boston: Little, Brown, 1979), p. 212. In light of the self-evident truth implicit in Wildavsky's question, it is odd how frequently public administrators engage in asking each other to recommend cuts in their own programs, and this practice seems to be particularly favored in state universities. For an intriguing case study of the perils of "bottom-up" budgeting, see: Edward Foster, "Planning at the University of Minnesota," *Planning for Higher Education*, 18, No. 2 (1989-90), pp. 25-38.

44. Unnamed official in the Central Budget Management System, Office of Management and Budget, as quoted by Hugh Heclo, "Executive Budget Making," paper presented to the Urban Institute's Conference on the Federal Budget Policy in the 1980s (Washington, D.C.: September 29-30, 1983), p. 35.

45. Irene S. Rubin, "Budgeting for Our Times: Target Base Budgeting," *Public Budgeting and Finance*, 11 (Fall 1991), p. 6.

46. Lewis, "Reflections on Budget Systems," p. 15.

47. Rubin, "Budgeting for Our Times," p. 6.

48. Robert D. Lee, Jr. "The Use of Executive Guidance in State Budget Preparation," *Public Budgeting and Finance*, 12 (Fall 1992), pp. 29-30.

49. *Ibid.*, p. 22.

50. Robert D. Lee, Jr. "Budget Office Personnel and State Budgeting Processes," *Public Budgeting and Finance*, 11 (Fall 1991), pp. 70, 72.

51. U. S. General Accounting Office, *Performance Budgeting*, p. 1.

52. Poister and Streib, "Management Tools in Municipal Government," pp. 240-248. See also Table 6-1.

53. Irene S. Rubin, "Budget Reform and Political Reform: Conclusions from Six Cities," *Public Administration Review*, 52 (September/October 1992), p. 465.

54. Much of this discussion is based on the chapter by Frank Sackton, "Financing Public Programs Under Fiscal Constraints," in Robert E. Cleary and Nicholas Henry, eds., *Managing Public Programs: Balancing Politics, Administration, and Public Needs* (San Francisco: Jossey-Bass, 1989), pp. 147-166. Among the better examples of the cutback management literature are: Charles H. Levine and Irene Rubin, eds., *Fiscal Stress and Public Policy* (Beverly Hills, Calif.: Sage, 1980); E.K. Kellar, ed., *Managing With Less* (Washington, D.C.: International City Management Association, 1979); G.W. Wynn, ed., *Learning from Abroad—Cutback Management: A Trinational Perspective* (New Brunswick, N.J.: Transaction Books, 1983); and Charles H. Levine, Irene S. Rubin, and G. Wolohojian, *The Politics of Retrenchment: How Local Governments Manage*

Fiscal Stress (Beverly Hills, Calif.: Sage, 1981).

55. National Association of Counties and International City-Management Association, "Consolidated County-Type Governments in the United States," mimeo, 1980; Joel C. Miller and Richard L. Forstall, "Annexations and Corporate Changes: 1970-79 and 1980-83," *Municipal Year Book*, 1984 (Washington, D.C.: International City Management Association, 1984), p. 101; and Joel Miller, "Annexations and Boundary Changes in the 1980s and 1990-1991," *Municipal Year Book, 1993* (Washington, D.C.: International City Management Association, 1993), p. 108. By 1991, twenty-seven city-county consolidations of any consequence had occurred.

56. The primary sources for the following discussion are: Caiden, "The New Rules of the Federal Budget Game," pp. 110-115; and Heclo, "Executive Budget Making," pp. 40-46.

57. Heclo, "Executive Budget Making," p. 43.

58. Frederick C. Mosher and Max O. Stephenson, Jr., "The Office of Management and Budget in a Changing Scene," *Public Budgeting and Finance*, 2 (Winter 1982), p. 28.

59. Steven Mufson, "'PADs' Wise to Ways of Power," *Washington Post* (April 25, 1990).

60. Fred Khedouri, quoted in *ibid.*

61. James J. Gosling, "The State Budget Office and Policy Making," *Public Budgeting and Finance*, 7 (Spring 1987), p. 67. The three states were Iowa, Minnesota, and Wisconsin.

62. David G. Mathiason, "The Evolution of the Office of Management and Budget Under President Reagan," *Public Budgeting and Finance*, 8 (Autumn 1988), p. 14.

63. Mark Bloomfield, quoted in Albert B. Crenshaw, "Putting Their Best Guess Forward," *Washington Post* (May 23, 1993). Emphasis is original.

64. Constance F. Citro, quoted in Julie Kosterlitz, "Educated Guesswork," *National Journal* (October 5, 1991), p. 952. The NRC study was conducted in 1988.

65. Rudolph Penner, "Budget Assumptions and Budget Outcomes," *The AEI Economist* (August 1981), reprinted in the Committee for a Responsible Federal Budget, *Symposium on the Congressional Budget Act and Process—How Can They be Improved?* (Washington, D.C.: Committee for a Responsible Federal Budget: January 12-13, 1982), p. 4.

66. Stephen E. Nordlinger, "U.S. Economic Seers Often Miss the Mark," *Baltimore Sun* (February 8, 1987).

67. For summaries, see: *ibid.*; Paul Blustein, "The Outlook," *Wall Street Journal* (April 27, 1987); and Johnathan Rauch, "CBO's Wishful Thinking," *National Journal* (March 7, 1987), pp.1069-1078.

68. Caiden, "The New Rules of the Federal Budget Game," p. 115.

69. Wildavsky, *The Politics of the Budgetary Process*; Richard F. Fenno, Jr., *The Power of the Purse: Appropriations Politics in Congress* (Boston: Little, Brown, 1966); and Jesse Burkhead, *Government Budgeting* (New York: John Wiley, 1956).

70. Wildavsky, *The Politics of the Budgetary Process*, p. 64.

71. The following discussion of budgetary strategy is drawn from *ibid.*, pp. 63-127.

72. Quoted in *ibid.*, p. 120.

CHAPTER 9

MANAGING HUMAN RESOURCES IN THE PUBLIC SECTOR

It is our purpose in this chapter to review four public personnel systems, to trace the development of the profession of human resource management in the public sector, to sketch the nuts and bolts of public personnel administration, and to consider some value dilemmas in the field. The traditional field of public personnel administration has expanded its conceptual boundaries and increasingly is called "human resource management"; *public human resource management* is the administration of and policymaking for people and positions in government. It long has been a mainstay in the field of public administration; its scholars traditionally have seen themselves as grappling with "people problems" and wrestling with the stuff of politics and the public interest. In recent years, however, the basic intellectual premises of human resource management have undergone some serious questioning in the public sector, and human resource management has been buffeted by new developments in the public merit systems. Many public administrationists now favor dealing with "people problems" within the conceptual framework of organization theory, and the whole notion of "merit" has received new and bizarre meanings,

at least in the opinion of some human resource managers and academicians. While this chapter does not represent an attempt to "straighten things out" in the field, we shall consider some of the difficulties and challenges confronting public personnel administration.

There are at least four broad types of personnel systems functioning concurrently in American government: the political executive system, the general civil service, professional career systems, and the collective system of unionized public employees.[1] Often, every one of these personnel systems can be found within the same agency.

The four public personnel systems represent fundamental value differences in the practice of public human resource management, and, throughout this chapter, we shall stress the kinds of values represented by proponents of each of these systems.

THE POLITICAL EXECUTIVE SYSTEM

Political executives are those public officials appointed to an office without tenure, who have significant policymaking powers, and who are outside the civil service system. They have been called "the true nexus between politics and administration."[2] There are about 2,500 political executive positions (*i.e.*, presidentially appointed) in the federal government,[3] and uncounted thousands at the state and local levels. Contrast this number to the roughly 100 political appointees available to each of the prime ministers of Britain, France, and Germany.[4] We shall focus our discussion on the federal experience with political executives, ending with a review of what we know (which is comparatively little) about political executives in state and local governments.

The number of political executives in the United States "is not fixed and varies depending on who does the counting and how positions are defined. . . . What is important is the *trend* toward more political appointees for each presidential administration. The direction of this trend is not in dispute."[5] That direction, of course, is toward the appointment of greater numbers of public administrators who hold their positions, at least in the federal government, because presidents have put them there. Today's 2,500 presidential appointees are quite an increase from the 200 or so available to Franklin Delano Roosevelt.

An Increase of Intellect and a Decrease of Partisanship

As a group of men and women in the public employ, political executives exhibit certain systemic tendencies. Most notably, perhaps, is the growing emphasis on intellect—partisan political experience seems to be of declining importance in the selection process. This is not to imply that partisan sympathies and willingness to be a "team player" are not vital considerations in the appointment process, but it appears to be increasingly recognized that, in the words of President John F. Kennedy, "you can't beat brains." At the assistant secretary and deputy agency administrator level, 90 percent of the assistant secretary and deputy agency administrators in the Kennedy administration were college graduates, a figure that has risen with every administration since that of Franklin D. Roosevelt.[6] The federal administrative level just below that of assistant secretary has more formal education than their counterparts in the military, civil service, and Foreign Service.[7] Education in the social sciences is increasingly represented among political executives, while the ratio of lawyers in this group (at least in the lower echelons) is only about 25 percent and declining. One analysis found that only 30 percent of "politically" appointed assistant secretaries were appointed on the basis of a particular specialization, and the remainder because of "general experience."[8]

At the cabinet level, educations in law dominate. Nearly half of the secretarial and deputy secretarial appointments from 1952 to 1980 had law degrees; the next highest field of study represented at this level was economics.[9] Still, law in the longer view is declining as the predominantly represented field at the top of the federal hierarchy; during the nineteenth century, lawyers (a profession virtually synonymous with politics at that time) held around 90 percent of the cabinet-level appointments.[10]

There also is a declining emphasis on partisanship in the political executive personnel system. One indication of this is that even when a presidential appointee is a member of the president's party, this common political loyalty appears to account for very little in securing the appointment. An intensive study of assistant secretaries found that a mere 10 percent were appointed primarily by dint of "service to party."[11] Another analysis found that, between 1960 and 1978, the proportion of top-level presidential appointees who were affiliated with the president's party never exceeded 70 percent, and dipped as low as 56 percent.[12] Contrast this percentage with the 90 percent of the government's top echelon appointees who were Democrats or closely affiliated with the president's party in Franklin Roosevelt's administration.[13] As we observed in Chapter 1, however, there was a significant reemphasis on assuring the ideological loyalty of presidential appointees during the administration of Ronald Reagan.

"A Government of Strangers"?

If partisanship is in decline in making presidential appointments, the tradition of appointing political executives who have little knowledge of the federal machinery is flourishing. The median tenure of political appointees between 1932 and 1966 (excluding those appointees whose tenure was fixed by law) was two years.[14] Later research (aptly entitled, *A Government of Strangers*) found that the average tenure of an undersecretary or assistant secretary was even less—fewer than twenty-two months.[15] It appears that even these brief tenures of political appointees are getting briefer over time,[16] and that the higher political executives rise, the likelier they are to leave quickly. One analysis found that, throughout the federal government, the average tenure of the political appointees in the Senior Executive Service (SES) was about eighteen months in one position, and even briefer in the higher positions: "Governmentwide, fully one-third of the political appointees in the SES change jobs or leave government every year."[17]

After reviewing these data, the question becomes obvious: How can a government of strangers—or, more to the point, ignoramuses in the ways of federal management—intelligently administer the national government of the world's largest and most complex democracy?

The Rise of the White House "Loyalty Tests"

Both partisan fealty and governmental experience are qualifications of diminishing import in the political executive system. But loyalty to the occupant of the White House (including, it appears, loyalty to the president's ideology) is another matter, and it is clear that recent presidents have placed considerable stock in controlling the appointment of political executives.

This is new. When assistant secretaries were analyzed in 1965, it was found that the appointment of these men and women was "a highly centralized and personalized process revolving around the respective department and agency heads," and when a rare difference of opinion arose between the secretary and the White House staff over a candidate, "the secretary generally won."[18]

This condition had begun to alter as early as the 1950s, but President Reagan culminated the reversal and rendered White House control over the political executive system complete. To quote the Director of the Presidential Personnel Office under Reagan: "We handled all the appointments: boards, commissions, Schedule C's, ambassador-

ships, judgeships. . . . If you are going to run the government, you've got to control the people that come into it."[19] The number of career service positions in top federal management circles declined under Reagan, while the number of political appointments rose,[20] and, in this sense, the federal government was "politicized."

No one can dispute the desirability of a democratically elected chief executive to establish his or her control over the policymaking and policy-executing apparatus of the executive branch, and appointing loyalists in key positions is an important means of establishing this control. But there are problems. For one, establishing the kind of pervasive, centralized control over the political appointee system exemplified by the Reagan White House is simply very difficult to achieve. One former Presidential Personnel Assistant, who was notorious for his belief in the necessity of the president's controlling the appointment process, later admitted, "If you try to do everything, I'm not so sure you can succeed. It's an awfully difficult job just to handle the *presidential* appointees. . . . if you try to do too much, you may be diluted to the point where you're not as effective."[21]

A Question of Quality

It is at least arguable that attempts to centralize all 2,500 presidential appointments in the White House, as was done in the Reagan Administration, can result in some appointees of questionable quality. A survey of members of the Senior Executive Service (which is comprised of the top 7,000 federal administrators) found that 93 percent of the career members of the SES believed that their fellow careerists made decisions about grants, contracts, and loans based on merit, but only 55 percent of the career executives felt that political appointees in the Senior Executive Service made these same decisions based on merit; careerists rated political appointees lower than their fellow careerists in the SES on a wide variety of administrative skills.[22]

An image of unprofessionalism and dubious competence is, perhaps, one consequence of attempting to centralize presidential appointments. But a more serious result is corruption. Because of some of Reagan's appointees, the "sleaze factor" in his administration became a recurrent target of the press, and perhaps with some reason. During Reagan's two terms as president (1981–1989), 7,462 federal officials were prosecuted—that is, were indicted, convicted (3,226), or awaiting trial—for public corruption. Compare this figure to the total number of prosecutions of federal officials for public corruption during the preceding eight years (1972–1980): 1,694. About four-and-a-half times more federal officials were prosecuted and convicted for corruption during the eight years of the Reagan Administration than were prosecuted and convicted during the preceding eight years![23] Whether these prosecutions and convictions for corruption can be attributed to the way presidential appointments were made by the Reagan White House is impossible to judge (the argument could be advanced, after all, that more convictions for federal corruption in the Reagan Administration are attributable to Reagan's prosecutorial zeal), but there did seem to be some substance to the press's charge of "sleaze" among some of Reagan's top administrators.

Perhaps more fundamentally, it is unclear that White House dominance of the Reagan stripe over the political executive system was needed to achieve competent bureaucratic responsiveness to presidential policy. A survey of all presidential appointees who served between 1964 and 1984 found that they believed strongly in both the competence and responsiveness of the career civil service; depending upon the administration, 92 percent to 77 percent of the presidential appointees stated that career federal employees were competent or very competent, and 89 percent to 78 percent said they were responsive or very responsive.[24] Similar views seem to be held by White House staffers, who typically are the most keen to establish presidential control over the standing bureaucracy, and the "evidence is overwhelming that experienced political appointees, regardless of administration, party, or ideology, believe that career executives are both competent and responsive."[25]

Political Executives at the Grassroots

In contrast to developments over the past three decades at the federal level, the political executive system of public personnel administration at the state level is tilting more in favor of career administrators. Research consistently indicates that the quality and professional career orientation of upper-echelon state administrators, including gubernatorial appointees, has been increasing steadily for at least the past thirty years.[26]

Without doubt, the decline of political appointees in the states will accelerate. In 1990, the U.S. Supreme Court decided, in a five-to-four decision in *Rutan* v. *Illinois Republican Party*, that party affiliation could not play a part in the hiring, promoting, or transferring of most of Illinois' 60,000 gubernatorial appointees. The governor of Illinois was shocked, saying the decision "turns politics on its head."[27]

Other states that traditionally have had large numbers of political appointees—Indiana, Massachusetts, New York, North Carolina, Pennsylvania, and West Virginia—have taken steps to reduce the power of partisan politics in their personnel systems as a direct consequence of *Rutan*. As one observer notes, "Nobody wants to be sued. They tend to pay attention to a major decision like this."[28] Of course, the *Rutan* decision does not affect those states (and there are many, mostly in the West) that have never had a significant number of patronage jobs, and by no means can all political appointees be accurately described as "political executives"; most are of humbler station.

What is true for the states is even more in evidence among local governments, where reformist pressures have their roots. Today, almost a fourth of American counties and over two-thirds of American cities have professional chief administrative officers, who, in over 31 percent of cities, have the sole authority to appoint department heads in municipal governments. In fact, mayors may appoint department heads in only 26 percent of the nation's cities; the remaining cities and towns appoint department heads by using a combination of the mayor and chief administrative officer (7 percent), or some other method (36 percent).[29]

Unlike the federal government, the grassroots governments, it seems, are increasingly comfortable with a human resource management system that accords significant policymaking authority to career civil servants, and at the expense of political appointees.

THE DEVELOPMENT OF AMERICAN HUMAN RESOURCE MANAGEMENT IN THE PUBLIC SECTOR

The evolution of American human resource administration can be divided into seven phases: the guardian period of a relatively high sense of administrative ethics; the period of unmitigated "spoils"; the reform period; the scientific management period with its concern for efficiency; the administrative management period with its emphasis on political executives versus career executives; the professional period that witnessed a huge influx in government of highly educated and socialized personnel from a wide spectrum of differing professional backgrounds; and our present period of professional public administration, which weds the values of professionalism and management in the public service. None of these periods, of course, is as discrete in time and as clear-cut in definition as the following review may imply.

Phase 1: The Guardian Period, 1789–1829

Mosher calls the guardian period "government by gentlemen,"[30] and it corresponds principally to George Washington's influential administration as president. Washington set the moral tone of the early federal bureaucracy by appointing men to office who were reputed to be persons of character as well as competence. Character was synonymous with merit, and merit during the administrations of Washington, John Adams, and Thomas Jefferson meant a respected family background, a high degree of formal education, and substantial loyalty to the president—in short, being a member of the establishment. Sidney H. Aronson's statistical analysis of the early public service in the United States shows that it was of a highly elitist nature, with roughly 65 percent of the highest level appointees being drawn from the landed gentry, merchant, and professional classes.[31]

Moreover, the early public service was highly political. While ability and integrity were valued, it did not hurt to be a "team player." Aronson's analysis indicates that of the eighty-seven major

political appointments made by Adams, sixty were new appointments. In other words, more than two-thirds of Washington's original appointments to top-level positions were tossed out by the new administration. Similarly, of the ninety-two top appointments made by Jefferson, seventy-three were original appointments; stated another way, four-fifths of Jefferson's top administrators were team players.[32] So, while the guardian period may have been government by gentlemen, they were nonetheless political gentlemen. Nevertheless, the notions of character, ethical conduct, and public trust commanded considerable respect in making appointments to the public service during the first half-century of the American experiment.

Phase 2: The Spoils Period, 1829–1883

With the inauguration of Andrew Jackson as president in 1829, the United States government was put on a paying basis. That is, the government (and the taxpayers) paid the party that won. The period acquired its name from a remark made in 1832, attributed to Senator William L. Marcy of New York: American politicians "see nothing wrong in the rule that to the victor belong the spoils of the enemy."[33] The rationale underlying the spoils system was that if presidents were to emerge, like Jackson, from the class that earned its own living, then politics had to be made to pay. And history indicates that it did.

While Jackson symbolizes the ascension of the spoils system in the public bureaucracy, a more accurate assessment is that Jackson simply fostered the democratization of the public service. The percentage of top administrators appointed by his predecessor, John Quincy Adams, that Jackson removed so that he could appoint his own people to top posts was very similar to that of Jefferson; for Jefferson, approximately 80 percent were original appointments, and for Jackson the figure was closer to 90 percent.[34] Nevertheless, Jackson likely started the process of making the public service a system redolent of bribes and graft. Power was transferred from one group (the gentry) to another (political parties), but never to the people as a whole.

Phase 3: The Reform Period, 1883–1906

The corrupt excesses of the spoils system during this period eventually resulted in a reform movement determined to rid government of those bureaucrats who owed their office to no more than party hackwork. From 1865 to 1883, a small group of intellectual idealists agitated for thoroughgoing reform of the entire public personnel system. Notable in this respect were George William Curtis, Carl Schurz, Richard Henry Dana, and Thomas Jenckes. Largely as a result of their efforts, the New York Civil Service Reform Association, the nation's first, was founded in 1877. In 1881 thirteen associations modeled after the New York group merged to form the National Civil Service Reform League, now known as the National Civil Service League. British concepts of merit in the public service were of considerable interest to the civil service reform movement, and Dorman B. Eaton's report to President Rutherford B. Hayes (1877–1881) on the English civil service (published as a book in 1879) enhanced their influence.[35] The assassination of President James A. Garfield by a mentally ill, dissatisfied office-seeker in 1881 effectively assured national legislation of civil service reform. In 1883 Congress passed the Civil Service Act (the Pendleton Act), which created a bipartisan Civil Service Commission (which was replaced in 1978 by the Office of Personnel Management and the Merit Systems Protection Board) responsible to the president and charged with the duty of filling government positions by a process of open, competitive examinations.

Although the Civil Service Act had been influenced by the British system of public service (notably the principles of competitive examinations and a "neutral" civil service free from partisan pressures), the Senate inserted some major provisos into the Act that were uniquely American in character. One such clause was that the Senators required civil service examinations to be "practical in character." While talented essayists of an academic sort might be nice to have floating around in the federal bureaucracy, it was far more important that the bureaucrat be able to do his or her job. This requisite provided the basis for a detailed system of position classification several years later; to be able to administer "practical" entrance tests, one first had to know what the job was all about.

Second, the Senate omitted the requirement that an applicant could enter the federal service only at the lowest grade. This permitted an "open" civil service with "lateral entry" as a possibility for all administrators (for example, a GS-13 level official in the Commerce Department could execute a "lateral arabesque" into a GS-13 position in the Transportation Department if he or she so desired).

Third, no special tracks were laid between the public service and the universities, unlike Great Britain. Indeed, initially it was preferred that the service be as highly "democratic" in character as possible. Only in 1905 did the Civil Service Commission first observe that "the greatest defect in the Federal Service is the lack of opportunity for ambitious, well-educated young men," and only in the 1930s was a major effort begun to upgrade the educational level of the national bureaucracy.[36]

Finally, the Pendleton Act set up no special "administrative class," no "permanent undersecretaries," contrary to the practice in Britain and Western Europe generally. Thus, the idea of political neutrality was not upheld at the potential expense of social responsiveness; instead the top bureaucratic echelon was occupied by *political* executives.

The crusade for reform of the public service had three dominant characteristics. First, the reform movement had been negative. That is, the reformists wanted to do away with the spoils system and its attendant evils. Second, the movement had been highly moral in tone. In Frederick Mosher's words, "it associated what we now refer to as personnel administration with morality, with a connotation of 'goodness' vs. 'badness,' quite apart from the purposes for which people were employed or the nature of the responsibilities they would carry."[37]

Third, and not too emphatically, the reform movement had been concerned with efficiency in government, and the reformers believed that the merit system would help assure "more efficient" (*i.e.*, less corrupt) practices. These characteristics, combined with the antielitist sympathies of the Civil Service Act itself, acted to create what

Mosher has called a period of "government by the good";[38] ethics and egalitarianism were prized. Managerial effectiveness, however, was an incidental consideration at best.

There were two lasting effects that this phase of moral rectitude had. The first was its influence on the study of public administration. Only four years after the passage of the Pendleton Act, Woodrow Wilson wrote his seminal essay on "The Study of Administration" (recall Chapter 2). The moral tone of Wilson's article reflected the mental set of the reform period, and it has been a continuing undercurrent in the study of public administration. Wilson, an ardent reformer and later a president of the Civil Service Reform League, facilitated the expansion of an ethical sense of public duty beyond the conceptual confines of the civil service and into the entire intellectual terrain of public administration. Relatedly, the old politics/administration dichotomy, long favored as an academic focus in the field of public administration, received much of its initial legitimacy and acceptance as a result of the thinking that dominated the reform period of public personnel administration. "Politics" was "bad" in the civil service, and "administration" was "good." Frank Goodnow's *Politics and Administration*, published in 1900, both reflected and strengthened the prevalent intellectual view that administration not only was different from politics, but also was somehow better.

The second effect of the reform period related more to the practice of public administration: The continuing independence of the Civil Service Commission was fostered, and its use as a model in the reform of state and local governments was encouraged. The Commission evolved into a buffer against political pressure brought on by both Congress and the president. In this development during the reform period, not only was morality increasingly identified with public personnel administration, but also public personnel administration as a field gradually was disassociated from the substantive and managerial functions of government. To put it far too crassly but clearly: The bureaucrats responsible for getting a job done and the bureaucrats responsible for keeping government moral became increasingly distinct entities.

Phase 4: The Scientific Management Period, 1906–1937

Increasingly, the academic field of public administration was being influenced by developments in business administration, which then was dominated by the time-motion, scientific management school represented by Frederick Taylor and Frank and Lillian Gilbreth (recall Chapter 3). The ultimate value of this period was efficiency—in other words, doing the job with the least resources. The values, concepts, and structure of the civil service were most compatible with the notion of efficiency. During the reform period, efficiency had been associated with morality and lack of corruption. Efficiency also was "neutral," another traditional value of the civil service and public personnel administration. Thus, a somewhat inconsistent but soothing amalgam of beliefs emerged that packed goodness, merit, morality, neutrality, efficiency, and science into one conceptual lump. Of these values, efficiency came to represent the best of the rest, a value "more equal" than the others—what "good" public personnel administration was all about.

The drive for scientific management in government began at the local level, largely because American government was concentrated at this level at the beginning of the twentieth century. In 1902, aside from the national defense budget, nearly 75 percent of public expenditures were at the local level. Moreover, because the functions of local governments at that time were mostly to provide routine, physical services (*e.g.*, garbage collection, fire protection, water supplies, and so forth), local government tasks often were receptive to improved efficiency via the techniques of scientific management. Scientific management generated a concern in governments for such topics as planning, specialization, quantitative measurements, standardization, and the discovery of the "one best way" to perform a duty. Instrumental in inaugurating the scientific management period of public personnel administration was the founding in 1906 of the New York Bureau of Municipal Research. Mentioned in the preceding two chapters, the Bureau was the prototype of numerous bureaus that later sprang up in cities throughout the country, most of them endowed with philanthropic funds and offering gratis their not-always-appreciated services to local officials.

The municipal bureaus provided the linkage between the techniques and values of scientific management and the public sector. Their staffs were enthusiastic developers of quantitatively oriented and detailed job descriptions, productivity measurements, training programs, examinations keyed to job-related abilities, and efficiency ratings. Science and technique were stressed, particularly in the field of testing applicants for employment qualifications.

There were some notable effects of the scientific management period in human resource management, both intellectual and practical. The intellectual effect was to strengthen the politics/administration dichotomy, already popular as a partial result of the reform period, in the study of public administration. Public personnel administration was where the quantitative action was in public administration, and "hard-nosed" public administration largely meant the application of scientific management for the sake of governmental efficiency.

The practical effects of the scientific management period were to widen the scope of the merit system in the federal government and to aid in the development of the city manager profession in the United States. Because of the considerable effort expended on the development of job descriptions, tests, and measurements, the informational basis for position classification was broadened significantly. Once a thoroughgoing system of position classification was capable of being implemented, it was only a matter of time for the civil service system to extend its control of the public personnel system. This it did. Although civil service regulations applied to less than 46 percent of the federal government's nonmilitary employees in 1900, by 1930 almost 80 percent of these employees were under its auspices. Much of this expansion can be attributed to the focus of the civil service system on the position as opposed to the person, and the success of scientific management in rendering many public positions quantifiable, measurable, and susceptible to classification.

During the scientific management period, the city manager profession received its initial impetus. The justification of the city manager idea

reflected the politics/administration dichotomy in public administration as it was enhanced by scientific management: The city manager would administer the policy formed by the city council in an expert, scientific, and efficient fashion. The first genuine city manager plan was adopted in the United States in 1914, and the early literature on the topic almost exclusively related to the notion of the "professional manager," removed from, unresponsive to, and, indeed, contemptuous of local politics. Proposals were even made during this period to have for each state a manager, who would be an administrative counterweight to the political/policymaking governor.

Phase 5: The Administrative Management Period, 1937–1955

The advent of the New Deal in 1932 brought with it a new view of the role of government: The public sphere should be active, aggressive, and positive in the rectification of public problems. This attitude was reflected in public personnel administration. "Management" became the new goal of public personnel administration, and although it never displaced efficiency as a major value of the public service, the concept of management waxed and worked in tandem with efficiency.

The objective of management implied that there was something more to public personnel administration than mere efficiency. In reality—and more broadly—the traditional politics/administration dichotomy that had provided the essence of the field's focus was being questioned. Increasingly, people in the public service were perceived as having a political and policymaking role as well as an administrative function, and "management" served as a convenient code word with which to express this new dimension.

The benchmark for the advent of the administrative management period is the report of President Roosevelt's Committee on Administrative Management (known as the Brownlow Committee) in 1937.[39] The clear thrust of the Brownlow Committee's report was one of centralizing the powers and responsibilities of the president: Agency functions should be consolidated, lines of authority and communication should be clarified, and the president's administrative authority should be enhanced. Although the Committee favored extension of the civil service system "upward, outward, and downward," it nonetheless was critical of the Civil Service Commission's past attitudes as encouraging a narrow, specialized, and technically oriented breed of public bureaucrat. Generalism, too, was a clear value of the Brownlow Committee. Not only did the Committee's predilection for generalist public administrators challenge the civil service system's long-standing emphasis on the position as the basis for personnel administration, but it blurred the distinction between politics and administration that dominated the whole of public administration as well. Although the Committee rationalized the politics/administration dichotomy as valid, it hardly dwelled on it, and considered far more thoroughly those "positions which are actually policy-determining. . . ." A series of executive orders beginning in 1938 on public personnel administration (notably Roosevelt's order of that year requiring the establishment of professionally staffed personnel offices in each major agency), the Social Security Act Amendments of 1939, the first Hoover Commission (1949), and the development of "little Hoover commissions" in the states extended and amplified the values of the administrative management period as represented by the Brownlow Committee throughout the federal and state structures: Public personnel administration was part of the general managerial function (just like budgeting, planning, organizing, reporting, coordinating, and so forth), and the goal of human resource management in the public sector was to enhance the effectiveness of public management.

With Dwight D. Eisenhower's election as president in 1952, the comfortable separation between politics and administration that had served Democratic appointees to the federal service for so long as a rationalization of their personal policy preferences suddenly received a stark challenge. During the preceding twenty years of Democratic rule, the federal government had burgeoned to many times its size under Herbert Hoover. Few seasoned Republicans were available for duty in the new regime as a result of their long isolation from the federal bureaucracy, and many positions (and the Democrats in them) that entailed major policymaking powers were protected by civil service regulations (thus aggra-

vating Republicans). At the same time many New Deal public administrators felt themselves threatened by a rising tide of McCarthyism that they associated with the Republican party. The problems of transition were severely exacerbated and highlighted the quintessential dilemma: how to render a theoretically neutral public service responsive to the political and policy preferences of a fundamentally new administration. As a result of this problem, a second Hoover Commission was created in 1953. Its report two years later included the first thorough analysis of the relations between political appointees and career administrators.[40]

The second Hoover Commission revitalized the faltering politics/ administration dichotomy, which was by then under intellectual attack. It assumed that the distinction was valid, but that it should be made more operational, in terms of government personnel, than it was. Thus, the Commission recommended that no more than 800 presidentially appointed political executives should fill top public positions and went on to propose a new upper-echelon administrative class of approximately 3,000 persons to be called the "senior civil service." These officials would be politically neutral career types and, significantly, transferrable from one post to another. For both groups, the abilities of the person would outweigh the requisites of the position. The proposal for a professional senior civil service in the tradition of Western Europe died a quiet death in the late 1950s (although it resurrected in 1978 in the form of the Senior Executive Service), but the idea that public administrators could and should be transferrable from agency to agency lived on and prospered by practice.

In terms of its overall impact, the administrative management period integrated public personnel administration with other administrative functions under the value/rubric of "management." Administrative management was perceived as an area of research and learning that was a needed profession for good government regardless of the specialty of any particular agency. Thus, the period witnessed the development of personnel directors in each agency who were responsible to (and a part of) the centralized managements of the agencies themselves. This intraagency personnel function was an effective agency counterforce to the quasi-autonomous

Civil Service Commission; it proved especially useful as a means of hiring, promoting, demoting, and firing people on the basis of management's evaluation of their individual talents, but which personnel administrators were in no position to recognize or appreciate.

Phase 6: The Professional Period, 1955–1970 and the Professional Career System

The idea of rendering public human resources more responsive and helpful to government managers did not fade away after the issuance of the report of the second Hoover Commission in 1955. Indeed, it strengthened over time. But another value was entering the milieu of public personnel administration by the mid-fifties: professionalism.

In a way, the stress that the second Hoover Commission placed on the differences and relationships between political executives and the career civil service signaled a recognition of the growing professionalism in government. The community of public personnel administration thought it knew who the political executives were—they were the principal administrative appointees of the elected chief executives—but who the career civil servants were was an increasingly problematic—and often frustrating—question. More and more, the career civil service was filling with highly educated professionals in a wide variety of fields.

The public human resource management community was never terribly sensitive about the implications of the entry of lawyers, scientists, physicians, statisticians, and other professionals into the public bureaucracy. But their impact on public personnel administration was nonetheless real.

Professional Career Systems and Their Rise in Public Bureaucracies. The various professional career systems of the public service are made up of white-collar personnel, generally professionals and paraprofessionals, who are tenured in a de facto (*i.e.*, in actuality) if not always in a de jure (*i.e.*, in a legal) sense. The system's principal feature is the emphasis that is placed on the *person*, rather than on the position, as in the civil service system. In a career system an individual's

career is administered in a planned manner; he or she is expected to advance upward through several hierarchical positions in which he or she can use his or her professional expertise in increasingly responsible and effective ways. Professional career systems place high value on the concepts of "professionalism," "specialization," and "expertise," and their rise in the public service has had a profound and disquieting impact on the more traditional civil service system.

A *profession* may be defined as an easily identifiable and specialized occupation, normally requiring at least four years of college education, which offers a lifetime career to the persons in it. Professions are beset by status problems. They attempt to maintain their public visibility, yet they prefer accomplishing this task with dignity. (Surgeons, for example, seldom offer "cut-rate" prices to potential clients.) Professions try to achieve status by refining their work content; the body of knowledge and expertise that must be learned (along with the manifold modes of acceptable behavior) in order to be "professional" grows with each passing year and becomes increasingly academic in character. Hence, professions and being professional are identified closely with the university and the professional association—institutions well removed from the usual circles of government. In this light, professionals also prefer autonomy, the right to do their own thing in their own way. Finally, and stemming fairly logically from the values of status, education, expertise, specialization, and autonomy already mentioned, professionals do not like politics. Nor, for that matter, do they like bureaucracy. This aversion is reasonable enough, given the historical struggles of many professions (*e.g.*, the city manager, the social worker, the librarian) to develop a corpus of knowledge and skill purged of detrimental influences from nonscientific, emotional, and ignorant outside sources. Put bluntly, however, professionals who choose the public service often must overcome their antipathy for its two major features: politics and administration.

The entrance of professionals into the public service is accelerating and its impact is deepening.[41] Nearly 40 percent of all "professional, technical and kindred" (to borrow the Census Bureau's terminology) civilian workers in the United States are employed by a government, a figure that has remained stable since 1970.[42] Eighty percent of the federal workforce is white collar as opposed to blue collar (up from 70 percent in 1968), 55 percent of all federal civilian workers have some college training, at least 30 percent have a baccalaureate degree, and 16 percent have completed some post-graduate work.[43]

Not included in these figures are the engineers, scientists, and other professionals who are technically working for private industry, but whose salaries are paid by government contracts and grants. We do not know how many of these people there are, but it has been estimated that at least 3 million employees in the private sector are employed through contracts and grants let by the federal government alone.[44]

About a third of all government employees are engaged in some kind of professional or technical pursuit, a figure that is three times their proportion in the private sector. Professional, technical and kindred public employees account for more than a fifth of all federal civilian employees, 39 percent of all state employees, and 42 percent of all local employees. More state and local personnel than federal workers are designated professional, technical, and kindred employees, primarily because more than half of state and local personnel are educators. But even when educators are deleted from these statistics, the percentage of professional, technical, and kindred personnel in government at all levels is still more than 21 percent, almost double the comparable percentage in the private sector.[45]

Who are these professionals? The federal government tends to favor the use of professionally trained military officers, Foreign Service officers, foresters, and scientists from virtually all the disciplines, while state and local governments employ social workers, psychiatrists, educators, and professors; all American governments hire engineers, public health physicians, lawyers, and computer specialists. Additionally, new, exclusively (or almost so) governmental professions are making an impact via vastly improved or totally new programs in higher education: Examples are police, tax assessors, penologists, employment security officers, public health paraprofessionals, park recreation specialists, purchasing experts, urban planners, librarians, environmental scientists, and, of course, graduates of public administration programs.

Although the Brownlow Committee report and the reports of the two Hoover Commissions barely considered professions other than that of administrative management, within ten years after publication of the second Hoover Commission's Report it was apparent that government managers were becoming concerned over the need for them; the 1962 analysis by the Municipal Manpower Commission concentrated entirely on "APT" personnel, an acronym for administrative, professional, and technical.[46] Similarly, studies of diplomatic personnel, public health personnel, and urban governance personnel all reflect an overriding awareness of the new role of the professional specialist in government. Yet, public personnel administration as a field has been curiously slow in recognizing the implications of professionalism. As Mosher has stated, few specialists "have recognized them—few even of the authors of books about public personnel administration."[47]

The Impact of Professionalism. While the effects of professionals on public personnel administration may be profound, precisely what those effects are and the patterns they may take are open to speculation. We have already considered the impact of professionals on organizations in Chapter 4, but the more general significance of professionalism on the public bureaucracy is worth some discussion in its own right.

Perhaps the most striking feature of professionals in the public service is the direct challenge that they pose to the traditional values of the civil service system. Professionals make up the emergent and increasingly competitive career system, which is characterized by its focus on the person rather than the position. These foci are fundamentally at odds. The civil service system is egalitarian by tradition, whereas the career system is elitist; what one does in a job is of paramount importance in the civil service system, whereas how one does it is of major significance in the career system; neutral and autonomous control of the entire public personnel system is valued by the civil service system, while planned and autonomous control of the individual professional is the concern of the career system. Although the merit system technically controls more than 90 percent of the federal employees in the public service, pressures from the various career systems throughout the government in fact have weakened the hold of the traditional, position-centered system on the careers of many professionals. Indeed, the Office of Personnel Management officially has excepted approximately ninety different professions from its purview. What appears to be happening is the evolution of new operational definitions of what "merit" means, and these definitions reflect the value differences between professionalism and traditional public personnel administration.

In addition to the rivalry that the career systems pose to the civil service system, there are at least three other effects that professionals have on the public service: the growing influence of professional elites inside government agencies, the growing influence of private professional associations on government, and the indirect but growing influence of universities on the personnel policies of public agencies.

Professional elitism appears to be an expanding source of conflict in some agencies. Research conducted among government agencies in California by Frederick Mosher and Keith Axtell indicates that the more established and recognized a profession is in society, and the scarcer the professionals available to a particular agency for hire, the more probable that the professional elite in question will exercise real and effective control over agency policies, standards, actions, and its entire personnel system, irrespective of the de jure control over personnel practices supposedly exercised by the civil service system. Mosher and Axtell found this to be the case regardless of governmental level—whether national, state, or local.[48]

A variation of the conflict that professionalism can bring to government is that of conflict between professional groups. City attorneys and city managers, for example, long have been at odds over their respective roles and responsibilities in municipal governance: Is the attorney a member of the "management team," or a "watchdog of the public trust," who happens to be paid a salary by the management team? Such conflicts can have a deleterious effect on governmental efficiency, effectiveness, and responsiveness.[49]

Professional societies are increasingly exercising considerable power in public affairs; the intimate connection between them and public personnel career systems enhances this power.

Studies indicating this growing and discomfiting influence by the professionals in government, mostly by political scientists, are too numerous to list, and the variations and subtleties that their influence can assume are limitless. It will suffice to note that the control professions possess over a particular sliver of knowledge enables these private professional associations to have considerable input vis-à-vis those public decisions made in their sphere of expertise. Studies of the decision process in regulatory agencies, the politics of professional licensing procedures in the states, the raw power and generously funded political activity of some "apolitical" professional societies, such as the American Medical Association, indicate the gravity of this problem not only for public personnel administration but for the public generally.[50]

Finally, the universities, those accreditors and sanctifiers of established and emerging professions, exercise an oblique influence on the dynamics of public personnel administration. Increasingly, academic standards (*e.g.*, university attended, grades, and faculty references) count more heavily in getting into the public service than does the traditional, position-centered entrance examination; more often than not, governments defer to universities the responsibilities for filtering applicants to administrative positions. The sheepskin is becoming the symbol of merit, and the more sheepskins the more meritorious the applicant.

The Dilemmas of Management and Professionalism

Professional, technical, and kindred employees attained their present share—almost 40 percent—of all public sector jobs in 1970, so we have selected that year as the closing date of the professional period in human resource management in the public sector. Yet, as with the field's administrative management phase (1932-1955), its impact on public personnel administration continues unabated. Together, Phases 5 and 6 pose grave dilemmas for the public human resource management community.

Mosher has pointed out that the two overriding values of public personnel administration for the future will be those of "professionalism" and "management." Together these two realities raise questions that have yet to be resolved by the American civil service: What is the relationship between the political executive service and the career service? What are the limits of loyalty that a public servant accords a leader, who is either elected by the people or appointed by elected officials of the people's government, when that public servant's superior issues directives that offend his or her interests or principles?[51]

We do not pretend to answer these eminently serious queries here, but clearly the rise of both the administrative management period and the professional period of public personnel administration has forced us to phrase these questions in tones more discomfiting than ever before. Both phases have contributed to the idea of the "professional public administrator," who blends the values of both "management" and "professionalism" in his or her public occupation.

Phase 7: Professional Public Administration, 1970–Present

The emergence of public personnel administration's seventh and current phase is in many ways its most interesting. Its appearance implies a rejection of the entire civil service system, as one of the four public personnel systems that we listed earlier. The concept of building a personnel system around the *position*—which is the rockbed of the civil service system—is simply not present; instead, the professional public administration period builds its edifice on the *person*.

In this sense, the professional public administration phase reflects the values of the professional career system, which is also predicated on developing the person in his or her career. But Phase 7 accepts few other elements of either the professional career system or the professional period of public personnel administration. Unlike the professional phase, the professional public administration phase accepts, indeed welcomes, both "politics" (as in *public*) and "bureaucracy" (as in *administration*) as the defining and entirely legitimate keystones of the *profession* of public administration. This is new.

The recognition by the field of public personnel administration of the role of the professional public administrator can be traced back to the Brownlow Committee of 1937. But at least an equally reasonable case can be made for a benchmark date of 1970 because it was in this year that the National Association of Schools of Public Affairs and Administration was founded, marking a critical point in the evolution of any profession—a commitment to it by the academic community—and it was in 1970 that the National Civil Service League released its sixth Model Public Personnel Administration Law.

The Model Public Personnel Administration Law of 1970. The formulation of the Model Public Personnel Administration Law of 1970 by the National Civil Service League is important because it reflected the consensus of opinion in the community of scholars and practitioners involved in public personnel administration. By contrast, the Brownlow Committee was comprised of scholars and practitioners who had their intellectual and professional roots largely in management and political science. The Model Public Personnel Administration Law of 1970 is significant, therefore, because it reflected "a sea change in the views of the cognoscenti about what the public service should be and how it should be governed."[52]

The Model Public Personnel Administration Law of 1970 replaced the League's previous model law of 1953, and it was a radically different document from all of its five predecessors. Rather than emphasizing the protection of the civil service against partisan patronage and similar transgressions, the 1970 Law reflected the values of the Brownlow Committee of 1937: Personnel directors should be appointed and removable by the executive; citizen advisory boards should replace the civil service commissions; a career civil service should be encouraged; and the interchange of public administrators among different departments should be facilitated. It went beyond the Brownlow Committee's report by advocating the recognition of public employee unions and collective bargaining, relaxing restrictions on political activities by civil servants, and advocating equality of opportunity. But the Model Law's basic thrust remained the same as that of the Brownlow Committee: "Personnel administration must be regarded as a part of management, not a protector against it."[53]

The National Civil Service League's Model Public Personnel Administration Law of 1970 has not had a particularly noticeable impact on the federal government, but it has had a major effect on state and local governments. A survey of all state and local personnel systems taken in the mid-1970s found that 63 percent reported that they were greatly influenced by the Model Law in reformulating their personnel policies and regulations, and that, five years after its publication, 55 percent of state and local governments had taken steps to make their personnel directors more responsive to executive leadership.[54]

Watergate.   But if the public personnel administration community in state and local jurisdictions was for the first time passionately embracing the importance of "public management," the nation was beginning to have quite a different reaction to the behavior of federal public managers. After an extended crucible that seared the nation, President Richard M. Nixon became, in 1975, the only president of the United States to resign from office. Nixon's resignation was the result of excesses and abuses of power that had been conducted almost entirely by elected office holders and officers whom Nixon had appointed. Much of these excesses revolved around the Nixon White House's efforts to circumvent the federal civil service. Among the more notorious examples of this was the so-called "Malek Manual," named after Fred Malek, a top White House official, who encouraged the appointing of high-level federal executives on the basis of partisan politics.[55]

Even though the line civil service was essentially uninvolved in Watergate, the public bureaucracy did not fare well in the public mind. As Mosher put it, "However justified or unjustified they may have been, the effects of Watergate unquestionably were to tarnish the reputation of the public service in general. . . . It cannot be said that many leaders or other representatives of the career services were out blowing whistles or otherwise resisting the transgressions that were being pursued. And the U.S. Civil Service Commission, which had been set up in part as a watchdog of the integrity of the civil service system, did not attack, or growl, or even bark until the affair had ridden most of its course. . . . Watergate generated doubts in the nation as a whole . . . about the public service as a whole, both career and noncareer."[56]

Watergate implied that human resource managers were not protecting the career civil service from presidential excesses. The "merit principle" was not being applied by those charged with applying it (*i.e.*, the Civil Service Commission) to promote and protect "good government" and all that phrase connoted for the traditional, merit-based values of public personnel administration.

The Civil Service Reform Act of 1978.   But if public personnel administrators were notably weak-kneed when it came to protecting the merit principle from dilution by the White House, they seemed positively ferocious in using it to harass federal managers who were trying to administer their public programs. One survey of top-level civil servants found that half of the senior executives in the federal government and 60 percent of federal managers believed that they did not have enough authority to hire competent people when they were needed, and 40 percent of federal senior executives and 55 percent of federal managers did not believe that they had enough authority to promote people.[57] These public administrators appeared to attribute at least some of the reasons for their lack of managerial authority to the heavy hands of the personnel administrators and federal rules that were based on the values of the reform period of public personnel administration.

Because the Civil Service Commission seemed not to be doing its job when it should have been, and doing it all too avidly when it should not have been, pressures were generated for far-reaching changes in the personnel practices of the federal government. In his 1978 State of the Union address, President Jimmy Carter said that reform of the civil service was "absolutely vital."[58] And the director of the U.S. Civil Service Commission backed him up with report after consternating report about the lack of control and authority held by federal administrators.[59]

As a consequence of these initiatives, there ensued a hugely ambitious and deep-reaching study of public personnel administration involving more than 1,500 practitioners, scholars, organizations, and other sundry experts. Ultimately the Civil Service Reform Act of 1978 was enacted, thus replacing the Pendleton Act which had been civil service policy for the United States for ninety-five years.

The Civil Service Reform Act replaced the Civil Service Commission with a three-member, bipartisan Merit Systems Protection Board that is in charge of adjudications and employee appeals, and which has its own special counsel to investigate allegations that federal personnel and related laws have been violated. It also established an Office of Personnel Management that advises the president on personnel matters and coordinates the government's personnel programs. The director of the Office of Personnel Management and his or her deputy are appointed and may be removed by the president. An independent Federal Labor Relations Authority was also established to oversee, investigate, promulgate, and enforce rules regarding federal labor relations programs.

The Act also was the first legislation to list merit system principles and prohibited personnel practices. It simplified and strengthened due process for employees, strengthened minority recruitment programs, and authorized the expenditure of funds for research and development in the field of human resource management.

Importantly, the Act states that authority and responsibility for managing people should be vested insofar as practicable in those supervisors who are responsible for programs, as opposed to centralized personnel agencies; decentralization is a clear value of the Civil Service Reform Act.

Federal administrators in the super grades and comparable pay levels are eligible under the legislation to join the Senior Executive Service. Out of the roughly 7,000 persons who were originally eligible, almost 99 percent joined the Senior Executive Service and this level of participation has remained stable. Noncareer officials (*i.e.*, presidential appointments) may comprise no more than 10 percent of the Senior Executive Service, and 45 percent of the Service's positions must be reserved for career personnel.

The Senior Executive Service was designed to improve federal management by creating what amounted to a professional administrative class in the European tradition. Senior executives may be assigned, reassigned or removed on the basis of their ability or performance. Contrary to traditional civil service concepts, rank in the Senior Executive Service is invested in the person as opposed to in the position; members of the Service carry individual rank and therefore may be assigned to those areas in which their talents are most needed. Senior Executives are eligible for 20 percent bonuses each year for good performance; however, they also may be retired early and against their will.

Figure 9-1 illustrates the new organization of federal human resource management that resulted from the Civil Service Reform Act of 1978. Clearly, the essential idea of the Act was "management." As Mosher has stated, "The main thrust of the Carter reforms, repeated in virtually all the speeches and arguments of their supporters, was management. . . . Here was the culminating event of 'government by managers,' espoused four decades earlier by the Brownlow Committee."[60] As a small but revealing indication of this change in perspective, the Office of Personnel Management (formerly the U.S. Civil Service Commission), in the year following the passage of the Act abandoned the name and content of its house organ, the *Civil Service Journal*, and retitled it *Management*.

Professional Public Administration at the Grassroots. The reforms in the federal civil service made their mark on subnational personnel systems. Within a year after the implementation of the Civil Service Reform Act, jurisdictions in thirty-two states initiated changes that reflected the management-emphatic thinking underlying the new federal policies. By 1980, local governments in twenty states had begun experimenting with merit pay and performance appraisal systems. Perhaps as many as 30 percent of state and local governments have implemented new performance evaluation and innovation systems for their public employees since the Civil Service Reform Act was passed.[61]

State governments were, in some ways, well ahead of the federal government in recognizing the desirability of bringing personnel administration and public management closer together. In 1963, California became the first of fourteen states to create an executive personnel system, preceding the federal government's decision to found its Senior Executive Service by fifteen years. In fact, four states, all justly renowned for the professionalism of their administrative structures, had executive personnel systems in place

FIGURE 9-1   Federal Government-wide Organization for Personnel Management

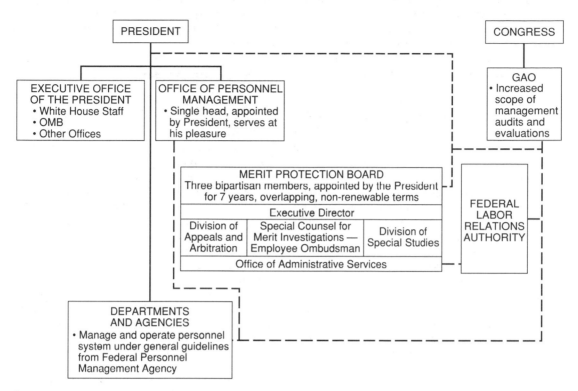

Source: Final Staff Report, Personnel Management Project, (Washington, D.C.: Government Printing Office, 1977), p.244.

before 1978, although federal initiatives clearly affected the decisions of many other state governments to establish their own executive personnel systems after that year. These state systems typically do not cover more than 1 percent of a state's employees, and, as with the federal experience, it is unclear how effective state executive personnel systems have been in both improving public management and developing a cadre of talented top careerists in public administration.[62]

Quite aside, however, from the impact on state and local jurisdictions of the Model Public Personnel Administration Law of 1970, or the Civil Service Reform Act of 1978, or the independent initiatives of the states themselves, it is clear that these governments are encouraging the idea of professional public management. A careful study of state agency heads that has been conducted periodically since 1964 indicates a deepening commitment to professional public management in the states.[63]

One indication is that their educational levels have gone steadily and dramatically up. In 1964, more than a third of state agency heads had not completed college, and 15 percent had not attended college. Forty percent held a graduate degree. By 1988, however, only 7 percent had not completed college, only 2 percent had not attended college, and 56 percent had earned their graduate degree, mostly in management and public administration.

A second indication of a deepening professionalism is that more state agency heads have chosen state public administration as a career. One measure of this commitment is the fact that state agency heads are entering the state service at an earlier age and pursuing long-term careers in it. In 1964, 35 percent of state agency heads held their first position in state government before they were thirty years old, and their median age when they first entered state government was thirty-three. Twenty-four years later, this percentage had nearly doubled, and two-thirds of the top state administrators had entered state public service before they were thirty.

Comparable data exist at the local level. We noted earlier that more than 67 percent of cities and over 23 percent of counties have chief administrative officers, and it may safely be assumed that virtually all of these executives are professionally attuned and have college degrees. Data available from the 41 percent of American cities and towns which use the council-manager plan[64] indicate high and rising levels of educational attainment among these urban professionals. Over half have master's degrees, and there is a growing and significant trend among city managers to complete degrees in management or public administration, at the expense of the traditional preparation of engineering; over three-fourths of the degrees held by city managers are in these fields.[65] The increasing commitment to higher education and to education in management, public administration, and government—along with its attendant and on-going linkages with the universities—indicate a growing professionalism among America's local public managers that parallels what is occurring at the state level.

THE CIVIL SERVICE SYSTEM: ORGANIZATION AND DYNAMICS

We have been discussing in rather broad strokes the underlying values and philosophies of public personnel administration that have emerged at various periods over the course of its evolution. Some of these values and philosophies have resulted in the traditional civil service system, and some have been responses to that system. We consider the organization and dynamics of the civil service system here.

The general *civil service system* is comprised of those white-collar, generally nonprofessional, career personnel who have tenure and who are administered according to traditional civil service practices; its overriding characteristic is the emphasis that is placed on the *position*: its description of duties, responsibilities, requirements, and qualifications. As a public personnel system, the civil service has been the historic

locus of public administration and, of course, public personnel administration. Paramountly the civil service system values the notions of "neutrality," "merit," and being removed from "politics."

The Scope of "Merit"

The federal "merit system," which normally is taken to mean the general civil service system including general merit and special merit personnel systems (*e.g.*, the Public Health Service, Foreign Service, Federal Bureau of Investigation), encompasses almost 94 percent of all federal employees.[66] This is quite an increase from the merit system's coverage in 1884, after the passage of the Civil Service Act, when the merit system covered not much more than one in every ten federal employees.

Among the fifty states, thirty-six now have comprehensive merit systems, a trend that appears to be accelerating (in 1958 only twenty-three states could make this claim), and the remaining states have some form of a more limited merit system. The Social Security Act Amendments of 1939, which mandated the use of state merit systems in state agencies that managed federally assisted programs in health, welfare, employment security and civil defense, and the Intergovernmental Personnel Act of 1970 (that was effectively curtailed in the early 1980s), which initiated a program of grants to inaugurate and improve merit systems in states and localities, were instrumental in the development of merit-based personnel systems in state governments.

Merit systems are prevalent in American cities and towns as well. Excluding education, civil service protection covers an estimated 95 percent of municipal employees.[67] Only in county governments has the merit system been accepted with relative reluctance. It is estimated that it covers less than 10 percent of the nation's county employees, although some very populous states, notably California, New York, and New Jersey, all require merit systems in their counties.

Although these figures are open to interpretation, and the various merit systems themselves are vulnerable to circumvention, the scope and expansion of the general civil service system in American government is impressive.

The Profession of Human Resource Management

The professional public personnel administrators who are hired to manage these merit systems focus their energies on several major activities: job analysis, human resource planning, performance appraisal, selection, employee development, discipline and dismissal, counseling, labor relations, communications, research and evaluation, wage and salary administration, benefits and services, and the political rights and constraints of public employees.[68] Some 272,000 people are employed in personnel work in both the public and private sectors in the United States, and of these 30 percent (about 81,000) work in the public sector. The number of employees in personnel has grown about 5 percent every year since 1970.[69]

Public personnel administrators are a reasonably well-educated group. Various studies indicate that 85 to 97 percent of human resource administrators in state and local governments have a bachelors degree or higher, and the educational levels of these public personnel managers appear to be higher than those in the federal government.[70] Human resource managers in the private sector tend to major more frequently in areas that are clearly useful to their professional expertise than do those in the public sector;[71] however, public personnel administrators appear to have a high job satisfaction, and most perceive their jobs as being a long-term professional career.[72]

The Civil Service Structure

The civil service has at least three defining characteristics: the *position classification system*, which directly affects *compensation*, and *training*, which can change with one's position classification.

The Position Classification System. The basis of the civil service, irrespective of governmental level, is the position classification system. Public personnel classification techniques received their impetus during the scientific management period of public personnel administration.

In 1923, as a result of increasingly vocal dissatisfaction over the lack of rigor in federal personnel classification policies and an on-going belief in the "equal work for equal pay" ideology, Congress passed the Classification Act, which established the Personnel Classification Board to group public positions into rational classes on the bases of comparable duties, responsibilities, and skills of each function. A new and more comprehensive Classification Act was enacted in 1949.

All state governments, and virtually all local governments now have a position classification system. Most cities and counties use a single classification system for all employees, although many (like the federal government) use different classification plans for different kinds of employees, such as clerks, trades people, professionals, and executives. The smaller the jurisdiction, the more likely there will be multiple classification systems.[73]

The Salary Structure. The Classification Acts provide the foundation for the salary structure of the federal government. At present there are four major pay systems in the federal government for civilian employees: the General Schedule (which applies to almost half of the federal civilian personnel), the wage board system, the postal field service system (these two are the lowest paying systems), and various remaining pay systems of limited scope, such as that of the Foreign Service. The General Schedule (GS) has eighteen levels, each level having a number of steps within it.

The salaries of most top federal executives (*e.g.*, Cabinet members, agency heads, undersecretaries, assistant secretaries, bureau chiefs, and members of independent commissions) are regulated under the procedures of the Federal Salary Reform Act of 1962 and the Federal Executive Salary Act of 1964. The Pay Comparability Act of 1970 delegated authority to the president to set salaries for General Schedule and Foreign Service employees; the president is assisted in this function by the director of the Office of Personnel Management, the director of the Office of Management and Budget, the Federal Employees Pay Council, and his Advisory Committee on Federal Pay. Their advice to the president is based on annual reports from the Bureau of Labor Statistics, which is charged with maintaining federal rates of pay that are comparable to those of private industry, a policy that was established by the Federal Salary Reform Act of 1962. The far-reaching Federal Employees Pay Comparability Act of 1990, the first significant reform of the federal salary structure in twenty years, is considered later in this discussion.

In an effort to attract executives for those top federal positions not covered by the Federal Salary Reform Act, in 1967 Congress established the Commission on Executive, Legislative, and Judicial Salaries, which recommends salary levels to the president for executive-level personnel in all three branches. The president has more discretionary authority in determining salary rates for these officials than he does for those administrators covered under the General Schedule and Foreign Service systems.

In part because of presidential recalcitrance, the salary situation for federal administrators was, by the early 1990s, reaching critical conditions. The purchasing power for top federal administrators had, depending on the study, fallen by 30 to 40 percent over some fifteen years, whereas the purchasing power of executives in the private sector had burgeoned by nearly 70 percent over the same period.[74] At the lower end of the scale, for clerical and technical federal workers, the story was much the same.[75] In light of the dramatically diminishing purchasing power of federal employees, it is perhaps not surprising that a survey conducted by the Merit Systems Protection Board found that frustrations over compensation and advancement were the major reasons given by 71 percent of the federal employees who left the civil service for the private sector—where they earned, on the average, 25 percent higher salaries![76]

To retain talented people in government, the Commission on Executive, Legislative and Judicial Salaries recommended that the salaries of many officials, particularly administrators, be nearly doubled.[77] In keeping with presidential tradition, however, President Reagan discounted the Commission and recommended to Congress a pay raise for these officials that ranged from about 2 percent to 16 percent (the high figure being for members of Congress).[78]

This situation did not (and still does not) pertain to the same degree in many state and local governments. Typically, average salaries for state employees are slightly ahead of those in the private sector, and salaries in local governments are less so, but still quite comparable.[79] As a respected British publication put it, "The secretaries of state and defense . . . are paid less than the city manager of Phoenix, Arizona, and the director of higher education in Georgia."[80]

In 1990, Congress took a significant step toward rectifying the problem of federal pay by enacting the Federal Employees Pay Comparability Act. The Act represented a new federal pay system, and implemented two major reforms: large pay hikes for top federal administrators, and the setting of federal salaries by locality.

As part of his agreement with Congress, President George Bush in 1990 increased the salaries of the Senior Executive Service by 22 percent, and the pay of the sub-Cabinet officers by 29 percent. This dramatic increase was accomplished by an executive order, and brought the salaries of top federal executives closer to their counterparts in the private sector.

The Federal Employees Pay Comparability Act also sets federal pay by a position's comparability with the private sector and by locality (*e.g.*, a federal worker in San Francisco is paid more than one employed in the same job in Statesboro, Georgia). In 1992 and 1993, federal employees were guaranteed an annual raise of up to 5 percent based on the Employment Cost Index, which measures the alterations in private local labor market salaries and wages. In 1994, the Act continued this procedure in modified form, but also added for federal workers in high-cost cities a locality-based raise of 20 percent of the total federal-private sector pay gap. From 1995 through 2005, the remaining differential will be closed by 10 percent in each of these ten years, although the president regains his broad authority to lower or raise salaries regardless of these benchmarks.

To accomplish this complex task, Congress established the Federal Salary Council, comprised of three experts in labor relations and six representatives of employee organizations, all appointed by the president. The Council is charged with setting geographic boundaries for federal pay regions and, in cooperation with the Bureau of Labor Statistics, conducting pay surveys of non-federal employers.

The Federal Employees Pay Comparability Act of 1990 is breakthrough legislation that immediately reinvigorated the federal service. In 1989, only 11 percent of the members of the Senior Executive Service responded to a survey that they were satisfied with their salaries; by 1991, 78 percent of SES members said they were satisfied with their salaries, and the number of top federal managers who were concerned about the image of the federal civil service had declined by 14 percent.[81]

Training Bureaucrats. A variety of in-service executive training programs are offered to public administrators, particularly at the federal level. In-service training is a relatively new development in public bureaucracies; most of it, in fact, emerged when the Government Employees Training Act was enacted in 1958. The Act required federal agencies to provide training for their personnel, using both public and private facilities. As a further stimulus President Lyndon B. Johnson issued Executive Order 11348 in 1967, which encouraged the U.S. Civil Service Commission to work more actively with agency heads to develop in-service personnel training programs. Johnson's Executive Order resulted in the creation of the Commission's Bureau of Training and Regional Training Centers nationwide and, a year later, Johnson followed this up with the inauguration of the Federal Executive Institute in Charlottesville, Virginia. The Institute is designed for the enrichment of supergrade federal administrators, and similar centers have been established in California, Colorado, New York, and Tennessee for mid-range administrators, grades 13 through 15.

As the result of a presidential memorandum in 1969, a provision in the Equal Employment Opportunity Act of 1972, the Labor Department's Public Service Careers Program, and the activity of the Office of Training and Development of the Office of Personnel Management, all federal agencies have begun to develop in-service training programs designed to encourage the upward mobility of lower-echelon as well as mid-level personnel, with special emphasis to assuring the advancement opportunities of minority groups. About 200,000 federal managers participate in these programs each year. Nevertheless, when

fiscal push comes to budgetary shove, it appears that federal administrators are prone to focus on agency training programs when they need to cut budgets, and to cut them back more than other programs.[82]

In-service training programs in the states and cities are less developed than in the federal bureaucracy. California is an exception, and has its own Executive Institute for state administrators; many large cities also have in-house training programs of high quality.

Traditionally, however, most training programs for state and local administrators are conducted by universities particularly those with institutes of government or public administration, or well-established continuing education programs that are well connected with the public administration faculty. Federal officials also participate in university-based training programs, however, and there are a number of university training programs that limit participation to executives working in a specific level of government—federal, state, or local.[83] Most of these training efforts concentrate on state and local administrators.

One survey found that about four-fifths of city and county managers and state executive and legislative officials report that they have used university-based institutes for training, research, technical assistance, analysis, and education, and rank the services provided by these institutes as "moderately high," and comparable to services furnished by the private sector; state and local administrators give their highest marks to university-based training programs of all types of services offered by universities.[84]

Labor Force Demographics and the Public Employer: New Realities

The population characteristics of the American labor pool have shifted vastly since the 1960s, and these shifts have had an unavoidable impact on government as an employer. Briefly, these changing demographics have rendered the nation's workforce smaller, older, less qualified, more feminine, and more ethnically diverse.[85] We consider the effects on government of more women and minorities in the labor force later in this chapter, but we consider here the implications of an older, smaller, and less-qualified labor supply.

The "Baby Boom" that made itself felt in the sixties became, by the mid-eighties, a "Baby Bust" insofar as entrants into the workforce were concerned. By 1995, the number of workers aged eighteen to twenty-four had dropped by nearly six million people from 1984 levels, and will not begin to rebound until 2000.[86] By 2000, there will be nearly 82 million baby boomers between the ages of thirty-five and fifty-five—the modal age of those who manage—but only about two-thirds of that number (or about some 56 million baby busters) will range between the ages of twenty and thirty-five—the modal age of those who are managed. One possible outcome of this new and odd generational ratio is that large organizations will have only a third of the managerial positions and half of the management levels by 2010 that they had in 1990.[87]

With every passing year, the demand of employers, in both the private and public sectors, for increasingly better educated and trained employees accelerates, and, in this sense at least, the supply of qualified workers decreases. For example, one survey of twenty-one large corporations in a representative array of industries found that close to three-fourths of the firms reported that they had raised the levels of numeracy, literacy, and cognition needed by employees over the last five years, and 71 percent, as a consequence, perceived an "overall reduction in candidates with necessary skills."[88] Similarly, federal employees believe the quality of new recruits to the federal workforce is in steep decline. Extensive surveys of federal workers at all levels taken by the Merit Systems Protection Board have found that between 41 and 61 percent of all federal supervisors believed that the quality of all applicants had worsened, and that the decline was accelerating.[89] And they may be right. Although almost half of the entering employees of the federal government have college diplomas in specifically useful fields, less than 3 percent have any training in political science or public affairs, and are "largely untutored in the most basic structural, procedural, and institutional knowledge of government."[90]

Size, age, and education are and will be three vital variables of the workforce with which governments must deal in luring new and able public administrators to their ranks.

The Civil Service Dynamic

Facing these and other new realities is the machinery of public personnel systems. We consider these machinations next, in the forms of governmental practices in hiring, promoting, demoting, and firing the people who practice public administration.

Getting a Job in Government. Between 1955 and 1974, the federal government gained most of its new recruits to the civil service through the Federal Service Entrance Examination, its first "universal" instrument for selecting college graduates for entry into the management positions of the federal government, and which tested general verbal and quantitative skills. In 1974, this was replaced with the Professional and Administrative Career Examination, which tested not only general competencies, but attempted to gauge the professional training of applicants. Blacks failed this examination in substantially greater numbers than did whites, and in 1981 the Office of Personnel Management signed a consent decree in which it agreed to eliminate its use.

Between 1981 and 1990, the finding of an entry-level administrative position in the federal government was, as the director of the Office of Personnel Management phrased it, "intellectually confusing, procedurally nightmarish, inaccessible to students and very difficult to explain."[91] Applicants were hired at the individual agency level on the bases of college grade-point averages, references, interviews, or highly specialized written tests developed for specific jobs, such as "Tax Technician" and "Customs Inspector"; between 5,000 and 6,000 federal hires a year were made in these ways, including about 200 graduates per year of Master of Public Administration programs who are brought into the federal government via the Presidential Management Internship Program (begun in 1977), which channels the top MPA graduates from campuses around the country to federal positions.

Ironically, it was unclear at best that these methods were resulting in a more representative or talented federal service.[92] What was clear, however, was that a mishmash of federal job application procedures was helping reduce the talent pool available to government; a 1988 survey of college placement officials and deans found that, in their opinion, most students did not see the government as their first choice of an employer.[93]

In 1987, a U.S. district court judge demanded that the federal government develop a replacement examination, and in 1990, the Office of Personnel Management introduced a new "universal" test for selecting applicants for entry-level management positions in the federal government, called the Administrative Careers with America examination. Although its initial impact was modest (only 85,000 people took it when it was first introduced), it is anticipated that from 300,000 to 500,000 people will take the examination each year. Some 5,000 applicants are hired for positions in 118 different occupations via the new examination. The courts will monitor the results of these tests until the mid-1990s to determine whether they are non-discriminatory.

Administrative Careers with America was pretested in France and Spain, as well as in the United States, and is a written examination. Although the test continues to assess language reasoning and quantitative abilities, it contains a new "biodata test" (a common examination in private industry), called "Individual Achievement Records," which focuses on determining experience, skills, achievements, and how applicants have played the hand that life has dealt them; blacks and whites score comparably on the Individual Achievement Records.

The federal experience with using (or not using) written tests has not been emulated at the state and local levels, where the courts have not really questioned the use of written examinations to determine entry into the public service.[94] We discuss this in greater detail later in the chapter.

Aside from scoring well on tests, how does one get a job in government? According to merit principles, all one should have to do is possess the proper educational and professional credentials and fill out an application. But more is involved, particularly when a personal interview is required. Employers in government (and presum-

ably in private enterprise as well) often seem to prefer hiring someone who is professionally less able and personally more amiable. Consider the following passage from Frank J. Thompson's study of personnel politics in Oakland: "The attitudes of the statistical service officer show how important amiability can be. He would rather hire a mediocre programmer who is easygoing and pleasant, than a very able one who is abrasive—who 'makes waves and stirs up trouble.' On one occasion, he served on an oral board, which was interviewing a young lady. In terms of the applicant's computer knowledge, she was clearly superior to all the other applicants. But he and the other board members felt that she was too 'aggressive and dynamic.' There was too much 'hostility' in her replies and, consequently, they flunked her."[95]

So much for merit principles in hiring. Some evidence suggests that the test-based merit system does not work even when judged by its own standards. In a study of the New York City civil service, which had roughly 250,000 out of a total of 400,000 employees who were considered "competitive class" employees (that is, they were hired and advanced on the basis of competitive tests), it was found that the "merit" system discriminated *against those applicants who are most qualified according to its own standards.* Candidates with low passing grades are actually *more* likely to be hired than those with high passing grades! Furthermore, this perverse result seems to hold true for all skill levels."[96] How so? The investigators found that the city had a lengthy waiting period between the date that an applicant took the examination and the date of hire—a median of seven months—and that, during this period, the best qualified were skimmed off by other employers. Conclusion: "New York City's civil service system functions as an inverse merit system (something the public at large has cynically assumed for years)."[97]

Being Promotable and Being Promoted.

Once inside the civil service, many public administrators find that seniority counts when it comes to being promoted. In his analysis of the U.S. Civil Service Commission (now the Office of Personnel Management) Ivar Berg found that when "age and length of service are considered together, as a surrogate measure of experience [and as a genuine measure of seniority], the combination becomes the strongest factor in accounting for the promotion rates of the highest level, the GS 11-14 category. . . ."[98]

The considerable advantages of seniority are a fact of life in virtually any organization, but the efforts made in the field of public personnel administration to reward ability rather than more time-in-grade are worth a brief observance. The Office of Personnel Management first required formal promotion plans from federal agencies in 1959, and since 1969 the Office has been notably more aggressive in trying to minimize the detrimental effects of the seniority factor by emphasizing intraagency ranking procedures based on job-related standards and by broadening the scope of promotional searches within the agency. State and local governments are more prone to rely on written tests as a basis for promotion than are federal agencies.

Being Demotable and Being Demoted. Service ratings are a device favored for determining not only promotions but also pay increases, decreases, demotions, and dismissals. The first Hoover Commission initially proposed the use of service ratings in government;[99] often they amount to little more than adjectival descriptions (e.g., excellent, average, poor) by a supervisor of his or her employee. There are two principal kinds of service ratings, "trait rating" and "performance rating." Trait rating attempts to evaluate such personality features as industry, intelligence, tact, and courtesy, while performance rating tries to judge how effectively the employee is fulfilling the duties of his or her position.

The federal government and most states and localities use performance ratings. At the federal level, at least, precious few of these employee ratings are used to demote or dismiss employees. More than four-fifths of federal employees receive above average grades (*i.e.*, "Exceeds," "Fully Successful," and "Outstanding") from their supervisors, and only one in 500 employees is rated "Unacceptable." But rating inflation is hardly unique to the public sector (it plagues corporations, too), and, in the federal government's case, public employee unions and members of Congress representing districts around Wash-

ington derailed plans to limit the percentages of federal managers who were allowed to be included in each rating category—a policy that would have forced a wider distribution of performance ratings.[100]

Getting Out of a Job in Government. The ways in which administration affects the lives of those in it are usually most dramatically visible when demotions and dismissals are being processed. Dismissal, of course, means being fired for cause. It does not refer to those employees who are (to use the current parlance) "riffed"—a derivative of the phrase "reductions in force"; these government workers often are the victims of economizing measures but who do not necessarily have low service ratings.[101]

Blowing whistles. But this is not always the case, and talented administrators occasionally are fired for reasons other than riffing or low service ratings. An incident that dramatized this phenomenon began in 1969 when A. Ernest Fitzgerald, a GS-17 Deputy for Management Systems in the Office of the Assistant Secretary of the U.S. Air Force, was effectively fired by the Air Force for his candid testimony before Congress on a $2 billion cost overrun incurred by the C-5A cargo transport plane development project—testimony that did not rest easily with the Pentagon brass.[102] Ultimately, it took thirteen years in court before Fitzgerald won full reinstatement in 1982.[103]

Fitzgerald is among the better known examples of a courageous (some would say crazy) class of public employee called "whistleblowers" because they "blow the whistle" on their agencies for engaging in shoddy, incompetent, or corrupt practices. At least 8,500 incidents of whistleblowing have been documented, and the practice appears to be growing.[104]

The "typical" whistleblower is a white, forty-seven year-old, well-educated family man who has been in his organization seven years.[105] About half are well-placed administrators or professionals who have considerable autonomy within the organization, although they do not appear to concentrate at any particular hierarchical level or share common career histories.[106] "The overwhelming majority of whistleblowers contacted are apparently uninterested in regulating their behavior to conform to particular situations. . . . because they rely on their own attitudes and beliefs, which include a strong endorsement of universal moral standards as a guide."[107]

A strong sense of self is needed. Surveys of whistleblowers report that, after they blow the whistle, over four-fifths experience some sort of physical or emotional deterioration (over a fourth sought medical or psychiatric counseling), and that they were hounded by their superiors; over half say they were harassed by their peers at work, were transferred to another agency, experienced disruptions in their family lives, and became mired in personally costly proceedings for over two years (a fourth said these expenses were the worst consequence of their whistleblowing);[108] 59 percent of federal whistleblowers in one study had lost their jobs.[109]

Federal whistleblowers discovered to their dismay that the Merit Systems Protection Board, the Office of Special Counsel, and "all executive branch organizations of the United States government whose official responsibilities include handling complaints of waste, fraud, and abuse" were (in their opinion) the least helpful to them,[110] even though the Civil Service Reform Act of 1978 is designed to encourage whistleblowing and to protect federal whistleblowers. In the view of Congress, the Act had failed in these respects, so Congress passed two new laws intended to further encourage and protect whistleblowers: the False Claims Act of 1986, and the Whistleblowers Protection Act of 1989.

The False Claims Act promotes whistleblowing by private citizens (including public employees) on government contractors who may be misusing federal funds by allowing the whistleblower to collect up to 25 percent of any money recovered by the government. The legislation has been most successful; federal recoveries had more than quintupled to over a quarter billion dollars only four years after the Act's passage. The record amount collected by a whistleblower to date was by an auditor in the Defense Contract Audit Agency, who was awarded $7.5 million in 1992.[111]

The Whistleblower Protection Act separated the Office of Special Counsel from the Merit System Protection Board, and established it as an independent agency with the charge of protecting federal whistleblowers. It, too, seems to work.

Within its first year of operation, there were more allegations of reprisals made by whistleblowers which were upheld by administrative law judges than were upheld in the ten years before the Act was passed![112]

Despite this important legislation, whistleblowers had best be prepared for a long, hard haul. But there is a bright side: Most would do it again. In one survey, 81 percent said they would do it all over again, and 87 percent stated that they would blow the whistle again if presented with a similar situation in the future.[113] As one federal whistleblower put it, "Finding honesty within myself was more powerful than I expected."[114]

Does whistleblowing work? Yes, more or less. Although the after-the fact rationalization of an act that brought immense personal pain likely enters into the respondents' replies in some fashion, 51 percent of the whistleblowers in one survey nonetheless reported that their actions resulted in some form of external investigation, and 62 percent stated that they saw evidence of change within their organizations.[115]

Dealing with incompetents. Whistle blowing, however, is one matter, and incompetence is another; rightly or wrongly, the procedures that must be followed to dismiss genuine incompetents can be time-consuming and costly. The appeals procedure can be wearing for everyone involved, and due process of law must be observed so stringently that a class of lawyers that specializes in defending public employees fired from government has emerged.

Because firing a clearly incompetent public employee can take a notoriously long time, it is perhaps not too surprising that one of the major arguments that has emerged against civil service systems is that they provide a sinecure for life to public bureaucrats. Because their jobs cannot be threatened, they are responsible and responsive to no one. Nevertheless, it is unclear how firmly ensconced in their positions public bureaucrats really are. O. Glenn Stahl contends that, although it is difficult to compare the proportionate number of dismissals between the public and private sectors because of different data bases, it nonetheless appears that "there is every reason to believe that the annual rate of removal, ranging from a little less than one to about one and a half percent of public jurisdictions in the United States as a whole, is exceeded, if at all, in certain categories of private employment, such as a few areas of manufacturing."[116] In other words, according to Stahl, the proportionate numbers of people fired in both private enterprise and in government are about the same.

If these figures are accurate, then it is surprising that the rate of dismissal in the public sector is as high as it is, considering how inordinately difficult it is to fire a public employee. In California, for example, a teacher may demand a hearing upon receiving notice of dismissal and the school board, unless it rescinds its action, must file a complaint in Superior Court requesting the court to make an inquiry and to determine if the basis of dismissal is supportable. Then court-appointed referees hold hearings and report back to the court. A trial is held by the court itself, and a decision is made on whether the board may, in fact, dismiss the teacher. In effect, any contested dismissal of a California teacher brings the judiciary into the act. Stahl contends that this is "perhaps the most extreme instance of abridgement of executive power in American school administration."[117]

But even reaching the point of firing a public employee is difficult and it is much more difficult to adjudge an employee's performance in some types of jobs than it is in others. Thompson has observed that the standards used in local government to evaluate performance can themselves be unclear, and the visibility of a subordinate to his or her supervisor can vary from agency to agency. For example, it is relatively clear whether or not a secretary is producing typing quickly and accurately, and a secretary is relatively visible to his or her supervisor. But in police departments, patrol officers are not very visible to their supervisors, nor is their standard of performance a particularly clear one.[118]

To compensate for these problems of assessing personnel in agencies where employees are relatively on their own, supervisors develop complicated performance forms and rating systems. Some observers contend that these forms seldom follow function, and to presume that the form is actually evaluating the performance of an employee is likely to be wrong. Nevertheless, bureaucrats are not spending their time ritualistically filling out useless pieces of paper. As Herbert Kaufman has stated in his classic study of *The Forest Ranger*, the forms actually are used to prevent problems from arising and to justify to outsiders a disciplinary action or decision to remove an employee. A record is kept by the forms, although the forms are seldom read by the supervisor when they are received.[119]

The employee, once dismissed or demoted, has extensive rights of appeal, and the example in California is an excellent illustration of how far this appeal can go—and how precipitously. Employees who are fired often attempt to bring in outsiders and to apply public pressure to be reinstated. The ploy of expanding the scope of conflict between the employee and the employer, either in the courts or with the public, is a classic one in public employment circles. In Oakland, while dismissals of the Oakland workforce averaged less than 1 percent a year, almost two-thirds of those fired were on probation and therefore had no right of appeal to the city's civil service commission; however, at least one-third of those persons who were dismissed as regular, nonprobationary employees appealed their dismissal to the commission.[120] In short, a supervisor likely can expect problems if he or she fires someone in the public bureaucracy, but, if care is taken, the employee's basic rights are observed, and records are kept, then the dismissal of an incompetent worker can be accomplished.

In any case, the public workforce, as a whole, seems placid. If the federal example is any indicator, not only are precious few government employees given low performance assessments, but most want to stay in government. An analysis of the "quit rates" in the federal civil service over a twelve-year period concluded that, "Despite declines in federal pay relative to the private sector, quit rates in federal white-collar employment have been remarkably stable . . . and remain as, or lower than, those in most private firms." Although there were some detected propensities among experienced federal administrators, and perhaps among the college educated, to leave the federal government, the research found that, "Civil service retention rates should benefit from demographics" until the next century, "until the leading edge of the baby boom begins to reach retirement age."[121]

Regardless of the internal dynamics of govern-

RIFFED

Beginning in the early 1980s, the federal government began to "rif" public administrators. "Rif" is an abbreviation of "reduction in force." There are many ways to rif employees. Here is how it happened to one.

Aside from the personal anguish he and his family are experiencing, the example of Burke Walsh illuminates a critical public question: the working of the federal government. It underscores one of the Reagan administration's blackest marks, the mindless wholesale destruction of the career public service, one I believe will cause damage to the country for years to come.

Two weeks before Christmas, Burke was informed he would be dismissed from his federal government job, effective New Year's Eve.

He was a victim of a sweeping government reduction in force—or RIF, in Washington parlance—sharply cutting back the Labor Department's Employment and Training Administration, the so-called CETA program. In particular, the information office in which he was working was being drastically reduced in size. He, and others, were out.

The dismissal meant more than the loss of his $50,000, Grade 15 government job, with all the obvious hardship for his family, the children's education, the mortgage payments and the rest. It meant the end of a government career for which he had been recruited, and in which he had performed well.

And, Burke quickly found out, it also meant a severe problem he had not anticipated. Including his Army time, he has 17 years of government service, three years shy of qualifying for a pension. Yet, under the present system, he will not be eligible for any pension payments for nine more years when he reaches the age of 62.

What's more, he has found the government is singularly unconcerned about what happens to the career people it is dismissing, for no fault of their own.

"To my knowledge," he says, "there is absolutely no real assistance that you get once you are dismissed. No official representative of the government has ever contacted me. There has never been any official prescription of jobs or availabilities afforded me from the government for placement. There is no effort by the government to help me find jobs in private industry or in government. There's no government-wide policy to help someone in my circumstances, and that is the truth.

"As far as my department is concerned, there was no review of my situation taking into consideration the length and effectiveness of my service. No one ever really reviewed to see what kind of work I had done. I fitted into a slot that was official and I was dismissed. I had no recourse as far as that dismissal was concerned. There was no consideration of the fact that I was what in the government is called a five-point veteran. My wartime service in Korea did me no service at all. There was no panel that I could go to and say, 'Look, I've been here for 17 years counting my service time. Maybe you'd like to take a look at this thing and ask whether you really intend to dismiss senior officials in their fifties. But this was not done for me, and it was not done for anyone as far as I know. . . .

"There's a perhaps unnecessary but pervading embarrassment that attends this situation," he says. "There's an embarrassment that you personally feel. There's an embarrassment that you feel with your peers and your family. You know they're feeling an embarrassment for you that you try to avoid as far as your dealings with them are concerned.

"You're embarrassed for yourself, and you're embarrassed for them. You can't avoid the feeling that the people around you have the feeling that there was some inadequacy on your part that led to your dismissal. You failed somehow. You failed them, and you failed yourself. All at a point in your career when you can't expect to have to come to grips with failure. You've done all the right things, made all the right moves. You've driven yourself to this point in a career—a career, not a job—and someone comes along and says you've done nothing wrong, but now you're out. And people look at you and they're embarrassed for you, and you are for yourself. It's a two-way street, and it's the damnedest two-way street you've ever been on.

"I've talked to people on the phone about this. I've talked to them face to face and, Haynes, this is the God's honest truth, I've had at least three or four people say to me, 'I could not take it.' They come just short of saying, 'Burke, I don't know how you haven't put a bullet in your head.'"

Burke is a proud man, and he remains proud of what the government has been and should be.

"I come from a family that's been in Washington

for 135 years," he says. "They came here from Ireland, through Philadelphia. My great-grandfather was the maitre d' in the Willard Hotel during the Civil War. He was a Confederate, a friend of Jubal Early. Used to go out in the weeds and talk to him. That's the last time that we had a subversive in the family that I know of. All of our family have been—well, we've got our military heroes. My grandfather and his group of Emmett guardsmen charged up San Juan Hill with Teddy Roosevelt. Literally did. One of the few people that actually got to shoot a Spaniard during the Spanish-American War. He went on to the Philippines. My father was in naval intelligence, so I have all kinds of Washington credentials, and rather honorable ones, I would think.

"I have a background that gives a sense of government. I didn't work for Ronald Reagan or Jimmy Carter or anyone else. From the day I came in, I felt that I had an obligation to the United States government. And if you want to know the truth, I feel the United States government has let me down, because I never broke faith with them. I was encouraged to come in. They asked me. I joined the government as a career station in life, not to get rich. I must confess, I joined it for the security of government, plus the fact I was told my talents would enhance government.

"As I've said to you before, there is waste in government. There's no question about it. But the way waste has been addressed is abysmal. It's ridiculous. Two administrations in a row have run against the government worker. What they've done is contribute to what they're trying to undo. The danger is that the kind of milieu we're developing now in the government could be translated into a much larger hurt for this nation.

"We've got to stop picking on the government. First of all, *we* created the government service. This nation created it. It's like the separation of church and state. It's an abiding thing there. It's part of the United States. It's like the Army and the Defense Department which are held in such reverence. It's there. It's part of what makes this whole thing go. Yet we've attacked it like it's a bastard child. If we don't stop this we'll be killing ourselves." . . .

A day will come, if it isn't already here, when the United States will need its most capable citizens to serve. How can the government possibly expect to attract such people when it, and its highest leaders, treat them so miserably?

To ask the question is to answer it.

Haynes Johnson, "Waste in Government: Wasting the Civil Servant,"
*(*The Washington Post*, March 28, 1982).*

---

ment personnel systems, it is clear that some very basic concepts of the "merit" system are being challenged by various social developments. These include the issues of affirmative action, unionism, and collective bargaining. We consider these issues in turn.

RACE, SEX, AND JOBS: THE CHALLENGE OF AFFIRMATIVE ACTION

One of the myths of American democracy is that jobs, especially public jobs, are open to all. They are not. Prejudice is still with us and working against both women and members of minority groups. Women, for example, have been disqualified from public jobs (such as fire fighting and police work) on the basis of physical "qualifications" that may not be necessary to do the work.

Similarly, increasingly more rigorous requirements concerning formal education work against those minorities who already are disadvantaged in society since, as a group, they are less likely to have attained as much formal education as whites; yet few people seriously argue that a high school diploma ever made its recipient intelligent or a quick learner. This argument is persuasive and as a result the public bureaucracy has witnessed the rise of "affirmative action." *Affirmative action* is a policy that argues for the hiring of members of disadvantaged groups on the grounds that government positions should be open to as many people as possible.

The Federal Impact

Affirmative action is a highly sensitive issue in public administration today. The federal government favors hiring members of deprived groups and consequently has implemented affirmative action policies that have had and are having a profound effect on the national employment picture. The major legislation in this area is the Civil Rights Act of 1964, which paved the way for the more specific efforts that followed. These included tougher executive orders by the president; prohibitions of discrimination in agencies and by private contractors on the federal payroll; more positive antidiscrimination policies by local, state, and federal civil service commissions; and some significant court decisions.

An especially important law, the Equal Employment Opportunity Act of 1972, brought for the first time state and local governments under the provisions of the Civil Rights Act. The Act also provides the first statutory grounds for the federal government's equal employment opportunity programs. The Act prohibits discrimination based on race, religion, sex, and national origin and directly affects some 3 million federal and 13 million state and local government employees. The U.S. Equal Employment Opportunity Commission (EEOC), which the Act established, may investigate charges of employment discrimination in state and local governments and, if no conciliation is achieved, the U.S. Department of Justice may bring suit against the alleged offender. On top of that, the person in question may also initiate his or her own private litigation.

In 1990, Congress enacted the Americans with Disabilities Act, which, for the first time, defined the disabled as a group entitled to basic civil rights. The law covers the physically impaired and people with learning disabilities, and prohibits discrimination against the disabled in employment and accommodations.

This kind of federal legislation, plus significant court cases, have made state and local governments and private employers extremely aware of the demands of minority groups, women, and the disabled.

The Quota Question

These realities in national policy bring us quickly to the question of quotas. *Quotas* in public personnel administration refer to the argument that the traditional entry and promotion qualifications of the civil service, such as high test scores, should be reduced or waived for the disadvantaged until the number of women and minority group members working in government at all ranks at least equals their proportion of the population at large. In brief, each group, such as African-Americans, would have a quota, or a percentage, of the public jobs allotted to it which equals its percentage in the state's or city's population. If a city, for instance, had 10 percent blacks in its population, it would then follow that blacks should be allocated 10 percent of the jobs available in city hall.

Pressure generated for the establishment of quota systems in state and local governments has met with some success. For example, a federal district court ordered that one black be hired for every newly hired white until the all-white Alabama State Police Force was 25 percent black, a figure corresponding to the percentage of blacks in Alabama according to the 1970 census. In one other case, while the federal court denied the legitimacy of an outright quota system, it nonetheless ordered the Minneapolis Fire Department to hire at least one minority applicant for every two whites in its next sixty openings. A federal court ordered the San Francisco Civil Service Department to establish two separate lists of candidates for entry-level positions and promotions, one for minorities and one for nonminorities, and to hire three minority candidates for every two nonminority candidates until the number of minority police officers was brought up to at least 30 percent of the total.[122] There are other examples.

Perhaps the most definitive early court ruling on quotas *per se* was given in the case of *Bratton v. Detroit*, although one must use "definitive" in this instance with circumspection. In the early seventies, the Detroit police department originated an affirmative action plan mandating that black and white officers were to be promoted in equal numbers until 1990, or until half of the officer corps was black at every rank and level. Whites initiated a class action suit contending that such a quota violated their civil rights. The federal District Court in 1980 denied this contention out of hand, but in 1983 the U.S. court of appeals did not; the appellate court had problems with the Detroit plan because it not only benefitted officers who had suffered from illegal discrimination in the past (*i.e.*, blacks), but also those who had *not* endured past discrimination (*i.e.*, whites), since the plan guaranteed that for every one black officer promoted, a white officer would be promoted as well. Hence, the appellate court remanded the plan back to the district court for further consideration. Even though the court of appeals had done this, the U.S. Justice Department petitioned the Supreme Court to hear the case, which the Court denied in 1984.

The upshot of this less-than-satisfying legal chronology is that the judiciary seems to have ruled that racially based quota systems are acceptable if prior discrimination has created a need for them, and whether the plan devised to implement quotas is "reasonable." Reasonableness is present if the plan does not stigmatize whites and sets specific goals. Factors to be considered in determining whether a plan to fill racial quotas is reasonable include whether the affirmative action program is the only solution; whether it is temporary; whether it relates to its stated objective; and whether it avoids infringing unnecessarily on the interests of whites.[123]

In 1986, the U.S. Supreme Court did render some rulings on quotas in a series of three cases: *Wygant* v. *Jackson Board of Education*, *Local 93 of the International Association of Firefighters* v. *City of Cleveland*, and *Local 28 of the Sheet Metal Workers* v. *Equal Employment Opportunity Commission*. Although these decisions were characterized by close votes and numerous separately written opinions, the broadly sustained principle that appears to have been stated by the Court is that limited, carefully conceived plans designed to reduce the effects of prior discrimination may take race into account. Further, plans to implement quota systems that are meant to benefit minorities may also benefit persons who were not actual victims of discrimination.[124]

While plans to implement quota systems may, as a side effect, benefit persons who were not actually victims of discrimination, they can also harm, inevitably, persons who were neither victims nor perpetuators of discrimination; this harm is, under certain circumstances, tolerable to the judiciary. In *United States* v. *Paradise*, the Supreme Court held in 1987 that quota plans which diffused the burden of implementation over many people were acceptable, although if the burden were to be borne by particular individuals, the quota plan might not be acceptable.

In *Paradise*, the federal district court had ruled that the Alabama Department of Public Safety had been unduly slow and discriminatory in promoting African-Americans, and ordered the Department to implement a one-black-for-one-white promotion quota. The U.S. Department of Justice joined Alabama in appealing the decision, claiming that the equal protection clause of the Fourteenth Amendment had been violated by the district court.

The Supreme Court upheld the district court, and did so unanimously in terms of finding the Alabama Department of Public Safety guilty of "pervasive, systematic, and obstinate discriminatory exclusion of blacks." But it upheld by only a five-to-four vote the district court's one-for-one quota plan, and much of the division centered on how intense the negative impact of the plan would be on innocent white officers applying for promotions. Justice Lewis Powell, Jr., wrote for the majority that, "Unlike layoff requirements, the promotion requirement at issue in this case does not 'impose the entire burden of achieving racial equality on particular individuals,' and it does not disrupt seriously the lives of innocent individuals." In sum, the *Paradise* decision reinforced the idea that "race-conscious relief" must be "narrowly tailored to the problem it is supposed to solve."[125]

Also in 1987, the Supreme Court added an interesting fillip to the concept of quotas. In *St. Francis College* v. *Al-Khazraji*, the Court held unanimously that Arabs, Jews and other ethnic groups no longer could be counted as whites in discrimination suits. The Court cited a federal statute enacted in 1866 that banned racial discrimination in making its rulings, and, in so doing, instantly made into minorities people who were previously categorized as whites by the courts. Justice Byron R. White, in writing the full Court's opinion, said that the 1866 law was "intended to protect from discrimination identifiable classes of persons who are subjected to intentional discrimination solely because of their ancestry or ethnic characteristics," and not merely former slaves.

Perhaps the greatest beneficiaries, at least in terms of numbers, are the nation's 20 million Hispanics, who generally were classified as whites by the judiciary prior to the *St. Francis College* decision. But the decision potentially applies to any ethnic group—Russians, Iranians, Liberians, Chinese, Poles, Italians, Norwegians, and Anglo-Saxons, among many, many others.

In 1989, the Supreme Court decided a series of five cases that, overall, made "more arduous a demonstration of discrimination," but which made "easier a challenge to affirmative action." [126] The principal decisions revolved around three of them.

One was *Ward's Cove Packing Company* v. *Antonio*, which reversed the long-standing judicial doctrine of "disparate impact." *Disparate impact* is an employment practice which results (whether unintentionally or not) in reducing the numbers of minorities or women in an organization or in the higher-paying positions in it; when disparate impact is shown, the burden of proof is on the employer to demonstrate that discrimination did not occur. In *Ward's Cove*, the Supreme Court held otherwise, and said that the burden of proof was on the complainant to demonstrate discrimination.

The second major decision was *Patterson* v. *McLean Credit Union*. In this case, the Court took the interesting position that harassment or intentional discrimination of employees which was based on race, sex, religion, national origin, or disability was legal—at least to the point that the victim of such harassment or discrimination could not sue for damages under the auspices of a federal law enacted in 1866.

Finally, in *Martin* v. *Wilks*, the Court held that new, white fire fighters employed by the Birmingham, Alabama, fire department could sue the department and challenge old court orders regarding past discriminatory employment practices on the basis that the new fire fighters had not been employed by the department when the original suits had been filed. This ruling made the permanency of standing court orders on ending employment discrimination in governments and companies problematic at best.

Nineteen eighty-nine was not a good year for affirmative action in the Supreme Court. But the impact of all of the Court's decisions of 1989 could be reversed by national legislation, and, in 1991, Congress did so with the Civil Rights Act of that year. The Civil Rights Act of 1991 clearly placed the burden of proof on the employer to show nondiscrimination when a disparate impact on minorities and women was evident; rejected absolutely the Court's position in *Patterson*, and in doing so clarified the 1866 law; and forbade people from suing to reopen old employment discrimination cases as long as they had had "actual notice" of the judicial decree and a reasonable opportunity to object to it before they were employed, or if their interests had been "adequately represented" in the decree.

The Supreme Court's efforts to undermine affirmative action in 1989, and the president's attempts in 1990 to support some of the Court's efforts by battling the Civil Rights Act of 1991, were overturned by a determined Congress. Such is the elegance, at least on occasion, of the Constitution's division of powers.

Tests: Problems of Validity and Bias

We have been reviewing the judiciary's evolving thinking about how personnel practices can result in discrimination (intended or otherwise) in agencies and companies, and one such practice that has come under special scrutiny is that of testing applicants to determine their suitability for particular jobs. The courts have focused especially on the problems of whether tests actually test for job qualifications that are really needed to do the job in question, and whether tests are biased against minority applicants.

The Validity Question. A landmark court case that has had a major impact on public personnel practices was the 1971 U.S. Supreme Court case *Griggs* v. *Duke Power Company*. On the face of it, the *Griggs* decision had nothing whatever to do with governments. The Court ruled that the Civil Rights Act banned discriminatory employment practices against blacks in a private company. Nevertheless, this decision has had considerable relevance for public personnel administration because it effectively bars those employment practices (notably intelligence tests and minimum education requirements) that operate to exclude members of disadvantaged groups when those practices cannot be shown to relate to job performance. The ruling did not demand the institution of flat quota systems in the employment of minority group members, nor did it preclude the use of tests in performance measurements. It did require that any such device actually indicate levels of employee performance and individual potential objectively.

The Supreme Court's decision in *Griggs* leads us directly to the issue of test validity. *Test validity* means: Do the several kinds of tests administered by the public bureaucracy for determining entry and promotion really indicate how well qualified an employee is for a job? Test validity is determined by comparing "successful" employees with their scores on tests that are thought to be job-related. High job performance should correlate with high test scores.

The Cultural Bias Question.

The growing controversy over test validity relates to another problem of public personnel examinations, that of cultural bias in testing. *Cultural bias* refers to the tendency of those highly educated people who write examinations to unwittingly slant the phrasing and nuances of their test questions in a way that reflects their own culture. Thus, people taking an examination who are not members of the dominant culture (*i.e.*, who are not white) are unfairly handicapped in their chances to score as well as those examinees who have been reared in the prevailing culture. After investigating the phenomenon of cultural bias in testing, the California State Personnel Board concluded that "written tests were more of a barrier to employment of minorities than any other phase of the selection process." Accordingly, the board instituted greater use of nonverbal aptitude tests, tried to root out culturally biased language in written examinations, and placed more members of minority groups on oral examination boards.[127]

Reflecting this concern over cultural bias in testing is a spate of court cases. In 1975, a federal court held (in *David* v. *Washington*) that the fact that African-American applicants failed a written test given to all applicants to a local police force at a rate of more than four times that of whites was adequate evidence to prove that the examination had a "racially disproportionate" impact, and that blacks were therefore being discriminated against in police force hiring.

A second significant case is that of *Albemarle Paper Company* v. *Moody*, which was decided by the Supreme Court in 1975. In its decision, the Court stated that back pay could be awarded to an employee who had been denied a promotion as a

consequence of discriminatory testing procedures, even though the employer was not intentionally discriminating. The decision also held that a promotion system based on supervisory ratings was questionable because subjective human judgments were involved. The case reified the importance of developing valid testing procedures for promotions and other personnel decisions.

In 1982, the Supreme Court again addressed the problem of cultural bias in testing in the public service in the case of *State of Connecticut, et al.* v. *Winnie Teal Adele*. Black state employees who had been serving as provisional welfare eligibility supervisors in Connecticut had failed a written examination. The passing rate for blacks was approximately two-thirds of that for white applicants. But the State of Connecticut argued that it had promoted more minorities than it had promoted whites, and so the "bottom line" was not discriminatory against African-Americans or other minorities. Thus, the use of the test that had discriminatory effects was irrelevant, since more blacks nonetheless were being promoted than whites.

The Court disagreed with the state's arguments, and held that merely because the "bottom line" was that more African-Americans were being promoted than whites, the state still could not allow racial discrimination against those black employees who were failing a test that was itself discriminatory. The Court held quite clearly that cultural bias in testing is against the law.

Written Tests: Still in Extensive Use.

The problems of validity and cultural bias in personnel testing have cast doubt as to the use of tests to measure job-related ability as a means of controlling entry and promotion in public personnel administration. As we have noted, the federal government was barred by the courts for a decade from using a common written test for entry into the federal service because of problems of cultural bias. On the other hand, local governments continue to use written tests extensively; Nearly 95 percent of the personnel departments of large cities (more than 100,000 people) report that they rely, at least in part, on a written examination for entry into certain kinds of positions.[128] Most examinations test performance skills and job knowledge, but aptitude tests are used in 44 percent of all cities and counties with populations greater than 50,000; 42 percent of these local governments test writing skills, and nearly a fifth administer intelligence tests[129]—examinations of a kind that would seem to require at least validation under the principles enumerated by the courts in the *Griggs* decision and in later cases. Nevertheless, only 35 percent of the cities report that they have offered fewer written tests since 1972 (the year following the *Griggs* ruling), and 62 percent say they have offered the same or more written examinations since 1972![130] Yet, when asked what are the principal obstacles that impede minorities from being hired by local governments, local managers consistently identify "test results" as the single greatest disqualifier, followed by educational requirements.[131]

It appears that the grassroots governments remain committed to the written entry examination, and that the judiciary has not seriously challenged these governments (in contrast to the federal government) in their continued reliance on written tests. Fortunately, state and local governments have taken the problem of cultural bias and sex discrimination in testing fairly seriously. A survey conducted by the National Civil Service League of every major state and local public personnel system (outside of education) in 1970 indicated that only 54 percent of them validated any tests in any way regardless of type—written, oral, or whatever.[132] But a second survey taken about five years later by the National Civil Service League found that 87 percent had initiated test validation procedures.[133]

Women's Work? The Bona Fide Occupational Qualification, Comparable Worth, and Sexual Harassment

At least three issues are present in government's attempts to end discrimination in employment that are of special relevance to women, although none of them is necessarily the sole preserve of women: the bona fide occupational qualification, comparable worth, and sexual harassment.

The Bona Fide Occupational Qualification Question. Our first issue relates to test validity,

and concerns qualifications for jobs that are based on sex. For example, laws stating that women may not lift more than thirty pounds of weight on a job may prohibit perfectly qualified women from being considered for a position. These kinds of qualifications are referred to as "protective labor laws" on the logic that they are designed to "protect" women from being in jobs that are too strenuous for them.

In 1963 and 1964, federal legislation designed to eliminate sex discrimination was enacted and quickly came into conflict with a number of state protective laws. This legislation was the Equal Pay Act of 1963, and Title VII of the Civil Rights Act of 1964.

The Equal Pay Act was an amendment to the Fair Labor Standards Act of 1938 and was later extended in 1968. The Act was helpful in eliminating artificial qualifications that prevent women from being considered for certain jobs.

Title VII of the Civil Rights Act made it unlawful to discriminate on the basis of sex as well as race. However, Title VII does allow an employer to discriminate on the basis of sex if such discrimination constitutes a "bona fide occupational qualification reasonably necessary to the formal operation of that particular business or enterprise."

Two major cases in 1968 and 1969 took issue with what a bona fide occupational qualification amounted to when applied to women. In 1968, the Supreme Court upheld in *Rosenfeld* v. *Southern Pacific Company* that certain weight-lifting limitations for women established by California were not valid. In 1969, in *Weeks* v. *Southern Bell Telephone and Telegraph Company*, the Court of Appeals held that "an employer has the burden of proving that he had reasonable cause to believe . . . that all or substantially all women would be unable to perform safely and efficiently the duties of the job involved." This was the argument used to permit Weeks, a woman, to become a "switchman" thus voiding a thirty-pound weight-lifting limit for women established by the state. In effect, both cases held that certain state protective labor laws could not be used to deny women a job or promotion, and the burden of proof regarding the fairness of the bona fide occupational disqualification is on the employer, rather than on the employee.

The Curious Question of Comparable Worth.
"Comparable worth" is a somewhat newer wrinkle in the fabric of affirmative action than is the bona fide occupational qualification. *Comparable worth* means that employees should be paid the same rate of pay for performing tasks that involve roughly the same levels of importance, knowledge, stress, skills, and responsibilities, even though the tasks themselves may be quite different. For example, a secretary may be performing a task that compares favorably to that of a highway repair worker in terms of its importance to society, the knowledge and skills it requires, the mental demands it makes, the stress it induces, and its level of responsibility.

As a practical matter, comparable worth is being used to pressure employers to pay women as much as men. American women, on the average, earn about a third less than men.[134] Although this differential is significantly narrower in the public sector, as we detail later, the difference nonetheless remains dramatic for public employees, too.

It is important to keep in mind that the unit of analysis used in comparable worth is not individual positions, such as a secretary, but whole position classifications, such as all secretaries. Comparable worth as a concept relies on comparing different job classifications; when one job classification is judged to be of comparable worth to another job classification (for example, if what secretaries do is deemed to be comparable to what highway repair workers do), then both classifications must be paid at a comparable rate.

Questions of comparable worth are especially likely to rise when an entire position category is dominated by women, as secretarial and clerical categories usually are. These female-dominated classes are compared to job categories of comparable worth that are dominated by men, and if the female-dominated job class is found to be paid less than the male-dominated class, it is assumed that the pay differential is attributable to systematic discrimination against women, and all employees in that class (including men) must be paid at a rate comparable to that of the male-dominated class.

Comparable worth relies on the idea that the social value of occupations can be compared, and this can be a tricky business. For example, are the musicians in a city's symphony orchestra worth "more" to society than the workers in the municipal waterworks? The contributions of the musicians may elevate and inspire our souls, but we need potable water. Because the theory of comparable worth leads to these kinds of questions, the chair of the U.S. Commission on Civil Rights (a man) called the concept "the looniest idea since Looney Tunes came on the screen,"[135] and the Director of the U.S. Office of Personnel Management (a woman), in testifying against comparable worth in Congress, stated that pressures for its adoption were "perplexing at best."[136] Women's rights groups immediately took sharp issue with both officials.

Perplexing or not, comparable worth is making headway among the grassroots governments.[137] At least thirty states have established various kinds of commissions to study and make recommendations to their legislatures about adjusting state government salaries for purposes of achieving comparable worth between male- and female-dominated jobs. Four states have gone farther. Minnesota, New Mexico, and Washington adopted comparable worth plans in 1983, and began the process of raising the salaries of numerous female-dominated job classes; Iowa initiated its comparable worth adjustments in 1984. Also in 1984, Minnesota extended its comparable worth policy to all employees in its 1,600 local governments, and today about a tenth of all cities and counties in the nation have enacted comparable worth policies.[138]

Much of the interest in comparable worth associates with the case of *American Federation of State, County, and Municipal Employees (AFSCME)* v. *State of Washington.* A federal district court ruled in 1983 that Washington's state government had violated Title VII of the Civil Rights Act by discriminating against its employees on the basis of sex (despite the fact that the state already had initiated its own comparable worth plan), and ordered Washington to award back pay to 15,500 employees in female-dominated position classifications and to speed up the implementation of the state's comparable worth plan.

But the judiciary appears to be ambivalent on the issue of comparable worth. In 1984, the Ninth Circuit Court of Appeals upheld the decision of the lower court by ruling in *Spaulding* v. *University of Washington* that the University was not in violation of Title VII, even though it paid its nursing faculty (who are mostly women) less than faculty in male-dominated departments.

Most significant was the decision rendered in 1985 by the same court in the appeal by Washington State over the case it had lost in 1983, *American Federation of State, County and Municipal Employees (AFSCME)* v. *State of Washington.* The Ninth Circuit Court of Appeals overruled the lower court and held that Washington did not have to award back pay to 15,500 employees in position classifications dominated by women. "Neither law nor logic deems the free market a suspect enterprise," said the court, adding that the Civil Rights Act did not obligate Washington "to eliminate an economic inequality which it did not create." Women's rights groups reacted to the decision immediately, vociferously, and hostilely.

Ultimately, the case was settled out of court, and Washington State agreed to set new pay levels for some 60,000 state employees, at a cost of $570 million, in an effort to bring women's salaries in line with those of men. The effect of this decision was to provide "the nation's biggest test so far of paying women the same as men who have different but equally demanding jobs."[139]

What are the early test results? On the one hand, Washington State has been most successful in equalizing the pay of its male and female employees: from a 20 percent gap in 1986 to a 5 percent one by 1990. On the other hand, job segregation by gender does not seem to have dissipated; because of the cost of the program, the pay for some state positions had slipped by as much as 30 percent in comparison with comparable positions in the private sector; pay compression (*i.e.*, the reduced distance between the wage levels of higher and lower ranks) had intensified; and men may be leaving Washington State government at a rate greater than before the state's efforts to establish comparable pay.[140]

In light of these preliminary findings in Washington State's experience with comparable worth, it is perhaps not surprising that other states, like the courts, are approaching comparable worth with caution.

Although four states have taken the initiative in introducing comparable worth plans, another four (Colorado, Florida, Missouri, and Nebraska) have explicitly rejected comparable worth. In 1989, a federal judge dismissed a lawsuit filed on behalf of 60,000 female employees of California who wanted pay equity with their male counterparts. On the other hand, the people seem to be for it—perhaps by as much as three to one.[141]

Whether comparable worth is "looney," progressive, or merely "perplexing," it will be an issue for some time to come.

The New Meaning of Sex at Work. Clearly not looney but perhaps as perplexing is another personnel policy that has a particular (but not exclusive) applicability to women: sexual harassment. The federal government, at least two-thirds of the states (only eight states clearly fail to address this issue),[142] and almost 90 percent of local governments have policies prohibiting sexual harassment.[143]

Sexual harassment is a workingplace environment, comment or act made or permitted by a superior in the workplace which is interpreted by a subordinate to have sexual overtones, and causes discomfort in, or is offensive to, the subordinate. Sexual harassment can range from the contemptible (*e.g.*, a superior demanding sexual favors from a subordinate as the price of continued employment) to the boorish (*e.g.*, a pattern of vulgar jokes by a peer). Whether or not a superior personally commits an act of sexual harassment is almost irrelevant; if the superior knowingly permits it, then he or she, and the organization in which the harassment occurred, are liable.

This liability took on new meaning in 1992, when the U.S. Supreme Court decided the case of *Franklin* v. *Gwinnett County Public Schools.* Christine Franklin was a high school student in Gwinnett County, Georgia, who had been sexually harassed by one of her teachers. Franklin sued her high school under Title IX of the Civil Rights Act, which bars discrimination "on the basis of sex" in schools receiving federal funds, on the grounds that school officials knew of the harassment and failed to stop it. A federal trial judge dismissed her suit, holding that Title IX does not authorize monetary awards for damage, and this view was upheld by a federal court of appeals. Franklin appealed to the Supreme Court, which reversed the rulings of both lower courts. To the argument (which had prevailed until the Court's decision in *Franklin*) that money damages should not be paid in sex discrimination cases (although restitution of back pay and lawyers' fees had been allowable), Justice Byron White replied that, "This position conflicts with logic." How, he asked, could a student, with no back pay to recover, be made whole without the award of money damages?

The significance of *Franklin* is that is paved the way for employees who have been victims of sexual harassment to sue their employers for damages. As a consequence, it is singularly unwise for employers to tolerate sexual harassment.

The "Reverse Discrimination" Dilemma

These ambivalent attitudes and new public policies over the whole spectrum of affirmative action have resulted in the accusation of "reverse discrimination," a charge usually leveled by organizations composed largely of white males. White police officers in Dayton, Ohio, for example, sued that city in 1973 charging racial discrimination in promotions.

The earliest well-known reverse discrimination case was that of *DeFunis* v. *Odegaard*, which involved a white male who applied to the University of Washington Law School in 1971. His application was rejected by the law school and he filed a suit contending that the school's admission procedure had admitted minority applicants with test scores and grades lower than his. A trial court ordered him admitted in 1971, the decision was appealed by the University of Washington Law School, was overturned, and DeFunis then appealed his case to the U.S. Supreme Court, which adjudged his case moot in 1974.

The most famous reverse discrimination case, however, is *Regents of the University of California* v. *Bakke*, in which Allan Bakke, a white male, was denied admission to the University of California's Medical School at Davis because that institution had set aside a portion (16 percent) of each entering class for blacks and other "approved minorities." In 1977, the California Supreme Court upheld a lower court's ruling, and with it Bakke's position, by refusing to endorse racial quotas, arguing that doing so "would call for the sacrifice of principle for the sake of dubious expediency," going on to note

that people should "be judged on the basis of individual merit alone." Both the lower court and the California Supreme Court, in deciding against the university, had ruled that the university had violated the Civil Rights Act of 1964 and, significantly, the Fourteenth Amendment of the Constitution, which forbids states to "deny to any person . . . the equal protection of the laws." The University of California appealed to the U.S. Supreme Court, which agreed to hear the case.

In 1978 the Supreme Court, in a five-to-four decision, ruled against the university, thus upholding the California Supreme Court. But the Court's ruling was not clear-cut. Justice Powell, writing the Court's main opinion, stated that the medical school had gone too far in considering race as a criterion for admission, but Powell also said (if rather vaguely) that affirmative action programs could properly be a factor in admitting students. Powell stated that, "Preferring members of any one group for no reason other than race or ethnic origin is discrimination for its own sake," holding that such discrimination, as expressed by rigid racial quotas, was in violation of the Fourteenth Amendment and thus was unconstitutional.

Importantly, each of the remaining four justices in the majority wrote their own separate opinions, and none of them took Powell's position that quotas were unconstitutional. Instead, they held that Bakke should have been admitted to the University of California medical school on the basis of the Civil Rights Act of 1964. Justice John Paul Stevens stated, in words reflecting this tack, that the act prohibited "in unmistakable terms . . . the exclusion of individuals from federally funded programs because of their race."

The distinction between ruling racial quotas unconstitutional (as Powell did) or illegal (as the other four justices did) is significant. If the majority had held that the University of California had violated the Constitution, then affirmative action programs across the country would likely have faced dismantling. Fortunately for these programs, however, all the nine justices agreed that affirmative action programs *per se* were neither unconstitutional nor illegal, and that being from a minority group could "be deemed a 'plus' in a particular applicant's file," to quote Justice Powell, although it would "not insulate the individual from comparison with all other candidates. . . ."

Justice Thurgood Marshall, the Court's only African-American, wrote the dissenting opinion, stating that "If we are ever to become a fully integrated society, one in which the color of a person's skin will not determine the opportunities available to him or her, we must be willing to open those doors" that have been shut to blacks in the past.

The *Bakke* decision, although limited to education admissions policies, had obvious ramifications for affirmative action programs in all sectors and for that reason was greeted with demonstrations across the country calling for its overturn.

A year following the *Bakke* ruling, the Supreme Court heard a second case that came to be known as the "blue-collar *Bakke*" decision. In *Weber* v. *Kaiser Aluminum and Steel Corporation and United Steel Workers Union*, Brian Weber, a white lab technician, charged that both his employer and his union were discriminating against whites by mandating that a joint union and company training program for skilled craft jobs must have half of its available positions filled by whites and the other half filled by blacks. Weber had been denied entrance into the program, even though he had more seniority than two African-Americans who were admitted. The Court, in a five-to-two decision, held that Kaiser as well as other employers could consider race as one of many factors in hiring and promotion policies. The Court argued that Title VII of the Civil Rights Act had been passed for the purpose of improving the economic status of blacks, and so a voluntary program in the private sector that gave special preferences to African-Americans was not in violation of the statute.

In 1984, the Supreme Court altered the direction of its moderately pro-affirmative-action decisions in the area of reverse discrimination by overturning two lower courts and ruling in a six-to-three opinion that layoffs based on seniority did not violate Title VII of the Civil Rights Act. *Firefighters Local Union No. 1784, et al.* v. *Carl W. Stotts, et al.* involved the City of Memphis's decision in 1981 to lay off fire fighters on the basis of seniority (*i.e.*, last hired, first fired), a standard practice among unionized workers, and a resultant temporary restraining order by a federal District Court forbidding the city to lay off any black fire fighters in the process. The reason-

ing of the District Court in issuing its order was that Memphis had entered earlier into a consent decree, approved by the District Court in 1980, which held in part that the city would try to attain a goal of a fire department that was 20 percent black. In the District Court's view, to lay off fire fighters by seniority would not only violate the consent decree, but would disproportionately affect blacks, who had been hired later than whites. Thus, the city was ordered by the District Court to lay off whites who had more seniority than blacks. This ruling was upheld by the U.S. Court of Appeals.

The Supreme Court took a different perspective, however, and stated that "there was no finding that any of the blacks protected from layoffs had been a victim of discrimination and no award of competitive seniority to any of them." Hence, the Civil Rights Act had not been violated by Memphis's decision to lay off its fire fighters on the basis of seniority because the intent of Congress in the Act is to "provide make-whole relief only to those who have been victims of illegal discrimination." In other words, black fire fighters in Memphis, according to the Court, had not been discriminated against in the past, and therefore a policy of last hired, first fired was an appropriate way to decide who was going to be laid off.

The likely effect of this decision is to make it more difficult for minorities and women to keep their jobs in unionized government agencies and industries because minorities and women tend to have less seniority than do white males. The Court's opinion—an important one for blue-collar public employees—was not greeted with favor by the nation's civil rights groups.

But in 1987, the Supreme Court made amends. In *Johnson* v. *Transportation Agency, Santa Clara County*, the Court held in a six-to-three decision that higher test scores, more job-related experience, and the judgment of a personnel examining board could be ignored in making a promotion in favor of promoting on the basis of sex, even when there was no history of discrimination.

Diane Joyce and Paul Johnson were among seven qualified finalists who applied for the position of road dispatcher in the Transportation Agency of Santa Clara County, California. Johnson scored higher on the civil service test than

Joyce (75 versus 73), and had more experience and the recommendation of the examination board as the best qualified applicant. The Agency's director nonetheless awarded the promotion to Joyce because all 238 of the agency's skilled crafts workers were men when the Agency's affirmative action plan had been adopted nine years earlier by the Santa Clara Transit District Board of Supervisors, and the plan had targeted 36 percent of these positions for women. Johnson sued, contending that his rights had been violated under Title VII of the Civil Rights Act.

In deciding against Johnson, the Court cited the *Weber* case as precedent and noted, in its majority opinion written by Justice William J. Brennan, Jr., that the Transportation Agency had rightly based its decision to promote Joyce on "a multitude of practical, realistic factors," and that the Agency "earmarks no positions for anyone; sex is but one of several factors that may be taken into account. . . . the agency has no intention of establishing a work force whose permanent composition is dictated by rigid numerical standards."

Writing for the minority, Justice Antonin Scalia retorted that, with this decision, "Ever so subtly . . . we effectively replace the goal of a discrimination-free society with the quite incompatible goal of proportionate representation by race and sex in the workplace. . . . Today's decision does more . . . than merely extend [*Weber*] to public actors. . . . After today's decision the failure to engage in reverse discrimination is economic folly and arguably a breach of duty to shareholders or taxpayers. . . . A statute [the Civil Rights Act] designed to establish a color-blind and gender-blind workplace has thus been converted into a powerful engine of racism and sexism. . . . The only losers in the process are the Johnsons of the country. . . . The irony is that these individuals—predominantly unknown, unaffluent, unorganized—suffer this injustice at the hands of a court fond of thinking itself the champion of the politically impotent."

Regardless of how reverse discrimination suits will be decided in the courtroom, it is clear that the problem is both real and divisive, not only for public administrators, but also for the citizenry. A review of public opinion polls on the topic concluded that "Americans are sensitive to the distinction between *compensatory action* and *prefer-*

ential treatment" in the hiring and promotion of minorities and women.[144] In other words, vast majorities of whites in various surveys conducted from 1972 on respond that they approve of such actions as government job training programs for minorities, but draw the line in suspending normal merit standards as a means of hiring and promoting minorities. Indeed, African-Americans and women also respond in this way; in a Gallup poll, for example, blacks endorsed promoting minorities on the basis of "ability" over "preferential treatment" by 64 to 27 percent, and 71 percent of the women respondents favored the same distinction.[145]

Nevertheless, whose ox is getting gored remains a valid political principle, and the discrimination issue is no exception. College faculty members, for example, heavily favor using affirmative action criteria in deciding the admission of undergraduates to college (62 percent), but are not nearly so positively disposed toward the notion when it comes to deciding their own careers; less than 35 percent of the nation's professors favor giving preferential treatment to women and minority applicants for faculty positions.[146]

In responding to the dilemma of reverse discrimination, some state and local governments seem to have gone overboard—perhaps in part because of the wiliness of their employees.[147] For example, in 1977 fifty-three San Francisco police officers claiming that they were Native Americans were hauled before the Equal Opportunity Commission, and all were officially reclassified as white.

In Los Angeles, a city long under federal pressure to desegregate its schools, both white and minority teachers began claiming they were of a different race in order to avoid being sent to another school district as part of the school board's efforts to attain faculties in each school that were at least 30 percent minorities. To counter this ploy Los Angeles established "ethnic review committees" that investigated "ethnic discrepancies" among teachers.

In New York, both teachers and pupils are "visually confirmed" by the board of education for racial identification purposes—and the subsequent assignment to a school.

If all this sounds a bit like springtime in Hitler's Germany, it is. Racial certification, regardless of motivation, is unpalatable to most Americans. Nevertheless, racial review boards may be a standard component in the state and local governments of the future as public employees of all races try to "pass" for the sake of enhancing their work location and promotion prospects.

The Grassroots Politics of Affirmative Action

Most jobs in government—some 13 million—are offered by the state and local levels, and it is at those levels where most of the political action is in terms of getting more minorities and women into public positions. But with time, the nature of this action has changed, and apparently for the better.

The Early Years: The Oakland Experience. How governments used to respond to the then ill-understood question of affirmative action has been detailed in Thompson's case study of Oakland. [148] In 1969, spokespersons for minority job hunters challenged Oakland's personnel director over his policies concerning affirmative action. The challenge came as the result of a report in 1969 issued by the U.S. Commission on Civil Rights, which observed that Oakland was the only major jurisdiction among seven metropolitan areas studied in which the three main minority groups were substantially underrepresented in the city's job rosters; with a minority population of almost 50 percent in Oakland, only 15 percent of city hall employees were black, and fewer than 2 percent were Hispanic or Asian-Americans.

Oakland's minority leaders focused on two strategies: They attempted to "bang Oakland officials over the head" with its own dismal record of minority employment, and they also tried to involve themselves in the recruitment structures of the city. A major target of the minorities was the police force: Minority leaders felt that its written tests were culturally biased, and a suit was duly filed. Minorities also pressured for a Citizens' Advisory Committee for the force, which was resisted by the police chief and the personnel director, who saw it as a front for a community control board.

Oakland city officials were quick to construct their own version of a domino theory on affirmative action; that is, if one department "fell" to minority pressure, then all the departments would become more susceptible to affirmative action demands. Although Oakland officials had the legal and actual power to flatly deny the demands of minorities, they elected not to be so direct and thus avoid an image of unresponsiveness. Delay was a major tactic in this strategy. Because recruitment authority in Oakland's city hall was widely dispersed, officials had great deal of opportunity to pass the buck. One frustrated minority spokesman compared the bureaucracy of Oakland to a "monolithic multi-headed hydra—when we approach one head, it always tells us that the other head is responsible." Or, as another minority member stated, "In Oakland the buck never stops."[149]

City officials marshalled a variety of tactics designed to justify their own positions and throw the blame on the minorities. For example, the personnel director warned that, "The city was responsible to the taxpayer and can't afford to hire people not capable of doing their jobs."[150]

To be fair, not all of Oakland's officials were so recalcitrant on the issue. Some procedures were changed to encourage minority applicants, and the use of oral examinations was expanded to facilitate the entrance of minorities into city government. Thompson concluded that, in the face of demands from minorities to expand minority representation in the city, a personnel director generally would put more pressure on those city departments that have hired few minorities, have made little effort to recruit them, have jobs that require simple skills (at least in the opinion of the personnel director), and that have a substantial number of open slots. Despite these patterns, however, the lack of official enthusiasm for attracting minorities (not to mention women) to Oakland's municipal labor force seemed patent.

How representative Oakland was of how the grassroots governments responded to the inaugural years of affirmative action cannot be known, but it seems reasonable to conclude that Oakland's response was not unique.

Auguries of Improvement. By the mid-Seventies, there were signs that, rather than fighting a guerrilla action against minorities and women entering public service, the bureaucratic establishment was beginning to lead their charge, and this change of sides seemed particularly evident in local governments, including Oakland's. For example, a survey of more than 2,000 city managers conducted in 1974 found that only 46 percent of these cities had begun action plans for meeting affirmative action goals for women, but that in more than four-fifths of these cases the city manager had started the plan on his or her own initiative, and in barely half of these initiatives did the manager have the support of the city council. For minorities, the figures were comparable: Fifty-five percent of the cities had begun action plans for getting more minorities into local government, but the city manager had started over four-fifths of these plans on his or her own initiative, and had the backing of the city council only 56 percent of the time. "While managers and chief administrators exhibit no strong personal commitment to [affirmative action] goals, they are *far and away* the principal initiators of affirmative action in their governments."[151]

By the 1980s, the use of affirmative action plans among local governments was considerably more universal and, if the research conducted in the early 1970s is any indication, this dramatically widening use was attributable more to the urban bureaucracy and less to the local political leadership.

The Triumph of the Bureaucrats?   By 1989, a national survey found that over two-thirds of cities and counties had government-wide affirmative action policies, and more than half reported that their line departments incorporated affirmative action plans into their operations. Over 95 percent of these local policies covered minorities, nine out of ten included women, and well over three-quarters addressed the disabled (before the passage of the American with Disabilities Act, so it is likely this figure will rise). Although there were suggestions in the data that the number of local governments with affirmative action policies had decreased since the mid-eighties, localities had initiated a number of positive measures to recruit minorities and women (the research noted that "it is probable, based on the responses . . . that a number of cities and counties have self-imposed hiring quotas"), and about two-thirds of the cities and counties reported that the Equal Employment Opportunity Commission had received no complaints about them over the last two years.[152]

These numbers imply real public progress, and, as noted, this progress seems to be attributable to the public bureaucrats. More than 55 percent of city managers believe that government should intervene on behalf of women, more than 60 percent think that a woman should be hired if male applicants are only equally well qualified, and nearly four-fifths oppose expressions of sexism.[153] Only 6 percent of city personnel directors are opposed to quotas (a major point of controversy) for women and minorities.[154]

Even in the federal government, where, with the impact of the conservative administration of Ronald Reagan from 1981 to 1989, alarms were raised about continued federal commitment to equality of opportunity,[155] it appears that federal administrators did not lose their long-standing dedication to affirmative action. Even at the height of the Reagan Administration, nearly half of the personnel directors in large cities perceived federal agencies to be supportive of aggressive affirmative action policies; only 9 percent reported "perceptions of federal activity in tune with well publicized Reagan Administration policies, namely deemphasis on affirmative action. . . ."[156]

In short, it would appear from the data that it is less the elected representatives of the people who are champions of affirmative action, and more those symbols of the system, the bureaucrats.

The Effects of the Efforts

Attitudes and perceptions are one thing; accomplishment is another. At the federal level, the efforts to bring minorities and women into government have, by at least one measure, been largely successful. In 1967, not quite 19 percent of all federal full-time employees were from minority groups in a population in which less than 17 percent are minorities. By 1990, this figure had risen to 27 percent. Of these, 17 percent were African-American (whose proportion of the total American population is not quite 12 percent) and 5 percent were Hispanic (who number more than 6 percent of the total population). These are encouraging figures. But as Table 9-1 notes, minorities are far more fully represented on the bottom rungs of the federal career ladder than they are at the top. Forty-two percent of the bottom four rungs of the General Schedule (the federal pay system that includes some three-fourths

TABLE 9-1 Full-Time Employment of Minorities in the Federal Government by Level and Pay System, 1980 and 1990

	1980			1990		
Pay System	*All Minority Groups[a]*	*Black*	*Hispanic*	*All Minority Groups[a]*	*Black*	*Hispanic*
All Pay Systems, Total	24%	17%	4%	27%	17%	5%
General Schedule and Equivalent Systems, Total (77% of federal employees)	24	15	4	26	16	5
GS 1-4 ($10,581-$18,947)	33	24	5	42	29	7
GS 5-8 ($16,305-$20,081)	26	20	4	33	23	6
GS 9-12 ($24,705-$46,571)	15	9	3	21	12	5
GS 13-15 ($42,601-$76,982)	9	5	2	13	6	3
Executive Total	7	5	Fewer than 50	8	5	2
Wage Pay Systems (17% of federal employees)	30	21	6	34	20	7
Other Pay Systems (5% of federal employees)	15	9	2	21	10	4

[a] Includes American Indians, Alaska Natives, Asian Americans, and Pacific Islanders not shown separately. In 1988 there were 2,125,100 full-time employees in the executive branch. Employees of federal corporations, such as the U.S. Postal Service, are not included. Percentages have been rounded, and may not total 100 percent.

Sources: Derived from: U.S. Bureau of the Census, *Statistical Abstract of the United States*, 1992 (Washington, D.C.: U.S. Government Printing Office, 1992), p. 333, Table 522, and *1982-83*, p. 269, Table 460.

of all federal full-time employees, both white collar and blue collar, excluding the U.S. Postal Service), are from minority groups. By contrast, only 8 percent of the very top rungs of the same Schedule are occupied by minority groups.

A somewhat different configuration is evident for women in the federal employ. Women comprise 51 percent of the American population, 45 percent of its labor force, and 48 percent of the full-time white-collar employees who work in the federal government. In 1970, 33 percent of the federal white-collar work force were women. As Table 9-2 shows, the great bulk of women who work in the federal government are secretaries or clerks. Three-quarters of women working for the federal government under the General Schedule and equivalent pay systems are found in the lowest grades, 1 through 6. Only 9 percent of the top federal executive force are women. However, women seem to be moving up the federal ladder. In 1970, only a bit more than 1 percent of the two top grades in the federal pay system were occupied by women, and in 1980, 4 percent were.

Similar patterns can be found at the state and local levels. Table 9-3 displays a number of interesting data. Over a fourth of full-time state and local employees (excluding educators) are from minority groups, but as with the federal government, most minorities are found at the bottom rungs of the state and local employment ladders. However, it should be noted that state and local governments are substantially ahead of their federal counterpart in that significantly greater proportions of minorities are at the top of the state and local employment ladder. Fifteen percent of minorities, for example, are officials and administrators in state and local governments, and 22 percent are professionals of other kinds. These are the two most highly paid categories of the eight categories shown in the table.

Progress in minority hiring and promotion is relatively dramatic among the grassroots governments. Although both African-American and Hispanic employees of state and local governments still were paid, on the average, 9 percent less than whites in 1990, in the nation as a whole minorities earned from 22 (blacks) to 29 percent (Hispanics) less than whites.[157] Also of signifi-

TABLE 9-2 Full-Time White-Collar Civilian Employment of Women in the Federal Government, by Level and Pay System, 1970, 1980, and 1989

Pay System	1970	1980	1989
Total Employment	33%	39%	48%[a]
General Schedule and Equivalent Systems, Total (72% of full-time white-collar employees)	40	45	49
GS 1-6 ($10,581-$23,628)	72	74	76
GS 7-10 ($21,195-$35,369)	33	46	54
GS 11-12 ($29,891-$46,571)	10	19	33
GS 13-15 ($42,601-$76,982)	3	8	17
GS 16-18 ($69,451-78,200)	1	4	9
Postal Pay System (27% of full-time white-collar employees)	N.A.	27	36
Other Pay Systems (2% of full-time white-collar employees)	46	36	40

[a] Data are for 1987. In 1989, there were 2,203,000 full-time white-collar employees in the federal government. Percentages have been rounded and may not total 100 percent.

Source: U.S. Bureau of the Census, *Statistical Abstract of the United States, 1992* (Washington, D.C.: U.S. Government Printing Office, 1992), p. 330, Table 515.

cance is the fact that only 9 percent of officials and administrators, and only 16 percent of professionals, were members of minority groups in 1980.[158]

Table 9-3 also displays data for women. As it shows, 43 percent of all state and local employees (again excluding educators) are women. As with the federal government, most women employees in state and local governments tend to be found on the lower rungs of the ladder, particularly in the paraprofessional and administrative support categories. However, unlike the federal government, a significantly greater number of women are found in the upper rungs of the occupational ladder. Thirty-one percent are officials or administrators in states and localities, and fully half are professionals, a share larger than the percentage of women working for state and local governments at all levels.

It is in the area of salaries that genuine disparities are evident. On the average, women working in state and local governments earn 20 percent less than their male colleagues, although this is a narrower wage gap than what women earn relative to men in the nation as a whole, where the difference is 30 percent. Women, however, con-

tinue to climb the ladder in state and local governments. In 1980, women were less represented at the administrative (23 percent of officials and administrators were women) and professional levels (44 percent) than they were a decade later.[159]

Overall, state and local governments appear to be the institutional vanguard in giving minorities and women a better opportunity in American society. Not only are the grassroots governments generally ahead of their federal counterpart in promoting women and minorities to the top rungs of the public career ladder, but they seem to be ahead of the private sector, too. An extensive analysis of data from the Equal Employment Opportunity Commission[160] concluded that there were proportionately fewer white males, more blacks, and more women working at the technical, professional, and managerial echelons of state and local governments than there were in these positions in the corporate world. (Another study found that less than 3 percent of the executives in over 6,500 top positions in the *Fortune* 500 companies were women, compared to 9 percent in the federal government, and 31 percent in state and local governments.[161]) Only Hispanics

TABLE 9-3 **Full-Time Employment and Occupation (excluding Education) in State and Local Governments by Sex and Minority Groups, 1990**

Percent Employed	Total	Officials/ Administrators	Professionals	Technicians	Protective Service	Paraprofessionals	Administrative Support	Skilled Craft	Service/ Maintenance
Women	43%	31%	50%	41%	13%	72%	87%	4%	21%
Minority Groups									
Total	27[a]	15	22	24	23	38	30	23	42
Black	18	10	13	15	16	31	20	15	31
Hispanic	6	3	4	6	6	5	8	7	9

[a] Includes other minority groups not shown separately. In 1990, state and local government employed 5,374,000 people full-time, excluding education. Percentages have been rounded.

Source: As derived from U. S. Bureau of the Census, *Statistical Abstract of the United States, 1992* (Washington, D.C.: U. S. Government Printing Office, 1992), p. 305, Table 483.

were relatively disadvantaged in state and local governments on this dimension in comparison to the business sector.

However, both African-American men and Hispanic men were paid more in high-level positions in state and local governments than they were in comparable positions in the private sector; in fact, black and Hispanic males in government were paid more than white males in government! Black women and Hispanic women working in government not only were paid more than their counterparts in the for-profit sector (although less than men of all races), but, like minority men in government, minority women in government earned higher salaries than white women in comparable positions in the private sector. "In the aggregate, state and local governments are doing considerably better than the private sector in living up to the challenge of attaining sexual and racial-ethnic employment equity...by the relative standard of private sector performance, the record established by state and local governments has been quite impressive."[162]

A Demographic Solution?

In light of the effort that has been expended by governments to provide more opportunities for minorities and women, it is ironic that the future looks far fairer for these populations, but not entirely because of those efforts. Demographics may effect more "affirmative action" in the governmental (and corporate) workplace than affirmative action policies have yet done.

The number of jobs held by white males in the United States has been in steady decline since the mid-1970s. In 1976, nearly 49 percent of all jobs were held by white men, but, according to the U.S. Department of Labor, by 2000, only 39 percent of the nation's jobs will be held by white males.[163] Women, African-Americans, and Hispanics will take and are taking their place.

This loss of white males in the workforce is due to the fact that the country's supply of young white men is shrinking by about 2 percent a year.[164] Young women, African-Americans, and Hispanics are replacing them; 68 percent of new workers in the 1990s are women and minorities.[165] Women are expected to continue to enter the work force at a much faster rate than men (between 1950 and 1990, the number of women

in the labor pool exploded by 200 percent, while men increased by only 55 percent) through 2005; minorities will continue their growth, too (with the largest increases among Asians and Hispanics), and likely will constitute 27 percent of the work force by the same year (up from 21 percent in 1990).[166]

When we add these demographic changes to what appears to be a propensity among both women and minorities to enter the public sector at a more rapid rate than the private sector (and for good reason—they tend to be promoted faster in the public sector), then it is possible that we may look forward to governments staffed far more by women, African-Americans, Hispanics, and Asian-Americans than they are now, and that there will be more women and minorities working in government relative to corporate America in the future as well.[167]

These demographic trends do not, of course, guarantee equality of opportunity to advance up the organizational ladder; but they do increase, and dramatically so, the entry of women and minorities into agencies and companies. Between these realities of the labor pool and continued efforts by governments and corporations to increase talent and representation at all levels of employment, equality of opportunity may be enhanced.

BLUE-COLLAR BUREAUCRATS: THE COLLECTIVE SYSTEM

Our fourth and final public personnel system is the *collective system*, and it refers primarily to blue-collar workers (with influxes of white-collar workers from the civil service and career personnel systems) whose jobs are administered via agreements between management and organized workers.

The Scope of the Collective System

The unionization of public employees is a relatively new and occasionally discomfiting phenomenon in public administration. Nearly 17 percent of all union members are public employees; more than 6 percent of all union members work for the federal government, and more than 10 percent have jobs in state and local governments.[168]

About 37 percent of all government workers belong to unions, a figure that has stayed the same since the early eighties; 43 percent of all government workers, however, are represented by unions; a number that declined slightly over the decade.[169]

Sixty percent of all federal employees are represented by about 100 unions or similar organizations, a figure that has remained constant since 1981.[170] The number of federal employees who are dues paying members of unions, however, is considerably lower. It is estimated that only about 30 to 35 percent of federal employees actually belong to unions.[171]

Over 40 percent of all full-time state and local employees are members of unions: 31 percent of state employees, and 42 percent of local employees.[172] Fire fighters have long led the list as the most heavily organized of public employees, followed by teachers and police. These and other occupational groups are represented by nearly 34,000 bargaining units.[173]

The major unions of government workers are the National Education Association with nearly 1.7 million members; the American Federation of State, County and Municipal Employees (AFSCME) with 1.2 million members; and the American Federation of Teachers with more than 570,000 members. The National Federation of Federal Employees represents more than 150,000 federal workers, but only 45,000 pay dues; the National Treasury Employees Union represents 120,000 federal employees, of whom only 65,000 pay dues; the American Federation of Government Employees represents more than 700,000 federal workers, although only 150,000 are dues paying members; the Postal Workers Union and the National Association of Letter Carriers represents more than 830,000 employees of the U.S. Postal Services, but have only 228,000 and 210,000 members, respectively; the Fraternal Order of Police has more than 150,000 members; and the International Association of Fire Fighters has approximately 150,000 members.[174]

A number of unions more commonly associated with the private sector also bargain for public employees. For example, about one-third of the one million members of the AFL-CIO's Service Employees International Union is comprised of public workers, and it is the AFL-CIO,

in effect, that is representing these workers to government mediators.

Efforts to organize public employees are not new, and early attempts at organizing go back to the 1830s. In fact, the National Education Association was founded in 1857, roughly thirty years before the birth of the American Federation of Labor. And in the 1800s, public employees had good reason to organize. Police and fire fighters, for example, who are among the most heavily unionized public employees today, traditionally have tolerated among the worst working conditions. In 1907, the New York Health Department condemned thirty of the city's eighty-five police stations as uninhabitable, and the police worked from seventy-three to ninety-eight hours a week. Fire fighters, who commonly were paid low salaries, worked twenty-one hours *a day* and had only one day off in eight.[175]

Despite such conditions, there was considerable resistance to the unionization of public employees, mostly for ideological reasons, but also for economic ones. As merit systems developed in state and local governments, job security became more assured and working conditions did improve. There were (and are) also a spate of state and local laws forbidding or discouraging any kind of union activity by government workers (the constitutionality of which is at least questionable). White-collar workers, as a class, had never really identified with unionization and, finally, there was a considerable weight of public opinion against the notion of government workers being allowed to disrupt vital public services by resorting to the strike.

Securing the Right to Collective Bargaining

Although federal employees had secured the right to organize in 1912 with the passage of the Lloyd-La Follette Act, the rights to negotiate collectively and to strike were resisted until the 1960s, and the initial indications that attitudes were shifting on these issues came not from Washington but from state and local governments. In 1959, Wisconsin passed the first law requiring its local governments to bargain collectively.

State and local governments are only beginning to approach sophistication in their collective bargaining with organized employees. Generally, state and local policies on government negotiations with organized employees are of two types. The *collective bargaining* approach permits decisions on salaries, hours, and working conditions to be made jointly between employee and employer representatives. The *meet-and-confer* tack says only that both sides must meet and confer over these issues, but that management has the final decision.

Judging by their written policies, the great majority of states and localities prefer the collective bargaining approach. Forty-two states have a labor-relations policy, and thirty-six states and the District of Columbia use collective bargaining as their primary method of dealing with labor unions; only three states have specified the usage of meet-and-confer bargaining. [176] Of the 13,342 local jurisdictions that have a labor relations policy (or 16 percent of all local governments), 88 percent use collective bargaining in dealing with employees. [177]

State and local governments are becoming increasingly innovative in bargaining with their employees. Englewood, Colorado, for example, has passed a city ordinance that stipulates that impartial fact-finders' recommendations will be put on the ballot with the best offer of the union and management alongside it; then Englewood lets the voters decide the issues. Englewood reflects the increasing use of "goldfish-bowl bargaining," or "sunshine bargaining," in which the public is being brought increasingly into the negotiation process, a process that traditionally, particularly in the private sector, has gone on behind closed doors. In this way the public's right to know is protected, and the bargaining is opened up at a time when the public's knowledge can affect the outcome of the negotiation process.[178] About a dozen states have enacted sunshine bargaining statutes.[179]

Federal activity in the field of collective bargaining is marked by President John F. Kennedy's Executive Order 10988 of 1962. The order stated that certain conditions of employment could be bargained for collectively between agency managements and employees; wages, hours, and fringe benefits, however, were excluded because these topics were subject to regulations of the various agencies and the Civil Service Commission.

Employee representatives found these limitations restrictive, and, in 1969, President Richard Nixon issued Executive Order 11491 in response to growing discontent. This order attempted to rectify a plethora of negotiating problems that had emerged since 1962: multiple labor representatives competing to bargain with management, the absence of third-party machinery, the abuse of power by some agency heads in determining bargaining units, exclusive agents, and unfair employment practices. These latter decision-making areas were transferred from the agency heads to the Assistant Secretary of Labor for Labor-Management Relations, and appeals from the Assistant Secretary's decision could be made to the Federal Labor Relations Council. A Federal Service Impasse Panel, empowered to resolve bargaining impasses, also was created by the order.

Within a few months of the issuance of Executive Order 11491, the first major strike by federal employees occurred. In March 1970, about 200,000 postal workers staged an unprecedented walkout. For the first time, federal representatives bargained on salaries (subsequently ratified by Congress), and later Congress legislated the right of postal employees to bargain collectively for wages. This incident, in the eyes of many observers, rendered Executive Order 11491 obsolete, and as a result Executive Order 11616 appeared in 1971, amending minor portions of the previous order. Collective negotiations on salaries and fringe benefits remained off-limits, however, and labor representatives did not consider Executive Order 11616 to be a substantial improvement.

In 1978, President Jimmy Carter's Reorganization Plan No. 2 created the Federal Labor Relations Authority as an independent agency. The new Authority (whose functions were enacted into law later in 1978 with the passage of the Civil Service Reform Act) took over the responsibilities of the Federal Labor Relations Council, and its creation represented an attempt to clarify the role of organized labor in government. As formalized by the Civil Service Reform Act, federal employees had the right to join unions, but strikes and slowdowns were prohibited. Federal agencies which issue government-wide directives that affect all federal employees now must consult with labor representatives before major directives are issued.

Although the federal government has made some progressive moves in recognizing organized labor, it also has shown itself to be increasingly tough in dealing with unions. In the same year that the Civil Service Reform Act was enacted, President Carter signed Public Law 95-610, which prohibits union organization of the armed forces and punishes any member of the armed forces who might join a military labor organization. Existing unions that try to enlist soldiers and sailors for the purpose of organizing them into a collective bargaining unit also are subject to stiff penalties.

In 1981, the Federal Labor Relations Authority showed that it meant business when it was dealing with organized federal workers when it decertified—that is, no longer recognized a union as the official representative of its members—the Professional Association of Air Traffic Controllers (PATCO). In effect, this act by the Federal Labor Relations Authority eliminated the union and deprived virtually all of its members of their jobs.

How Powerful Are Public Unions?

Forty-three percent of all public employees are covered by collective bargaining agreements.[180] Unlike labor-management negotiations in the private sector, neither labor nor management in the public sector is bargaining about its own money. Public labor unions demand tax monies for wages that may or may not be in the public till, and public administrators negotiate with tax monies that likewise may not be in the public till. The person who pays is the taxpayer.

When we combine this reality with unions that have become increasingly sophisticated in their bargaining skills and financial research abilities (several public sector unions now devote full-time professional staffs who do nothing but analyze state and local budgets[181]), it is not too surprising that public laborers made considerable financial gains in their negotiations with public management, particularly in the 1970s, although the gains of public employee unions have been in decline in recent years. Increasingly, public managers are resisting the views expressed some years ago by the pension specialist of the American Federation of State, County, and Municipal Employees who, when queried where

the money for higher pensions for his members would be coming from, replied, "That's the government's problem. Just because there is a pinch for money, it's no excuse to make the employees do without."[182]

Unions of public employees have been a factor in raising salaries, health benefits, and pensions of government workers, and these costs to public budgets are relatively apparent; they are (with a few notable exceptions), in the view of most informed observers, not really responsible for the fiscal stress of governments (even big city governments) in the nineties.

What is less known are the costs of nonwage areas that unions negotiate with governments, such as the regulation of hours, caseload ceilings (for social workers and nurses, for example), arrangements for paraprofessionals, assignment and transfer provisions, standards for entry, promotions and reductions in force, professional development provisions, and other areas that have nothing to do with compensation but which are nonetheless expensive to conduct. Once careful review of the literature found "no studies" on the effects of "working conditions, job security, and professional provisions on public budgets."[183]

When public workers grow sufficiently dissatisfied with their conditions, and feel that they have the clout to change them, they go on strike—or at least engage in work slowdowns. "Blue flu" (meaning a police slow down), "red rash" (fire fighters), and "Human Error Day" (when municipal workers in San Diego misplaced everything from files to phone calls) are variants of these slowdowns.

Strikes, stoppages, and slowdowns will always be with us, regardless of whether or not there are laws permitting or prohibiting strikes by public employees. (Only nine states directly protect the public employee's right to strike, although even these place restrictions on that right.[184]) Nonetheless, the emotional issue of the public employees' right to strike runs deep. One viewpoint holds that a strike by public employees amounts to an act of insurrection because such strikes are directed against the people themselves; the opposing view contends that the right of government workers to strike is a basic freedom protected under the Constitution. To deny public employees a right granted to workers in private corporations is to treat public personnel as second-class citizens. The courts thus far have held that there is no constitutional right of public workers to strike, but neither has the judiciary prohibited the enactment of laws permitting government employees to strike.

It used to be that sanitation workers were the most frequent public employees to walk the picket lines, but more recently it has been teachers who are more inclined to strike. Strikes and work stoppages by public employees peaked in 1979 at 536, and both the number of strikes and stoppages and the length of their duration have been in remission since. The number of strikes and work stoppages by state and local employees has been fewer than thirty a year since 1986.[185]

The dramatic downturn in strikes and stoppages among public workers is attributable both to tighter times in governments and to a public disaffection with public unions. Some of this disaffection has been brought on by the unions themselves. Some observers point to 1979, the peak year for strikes by public employees, as the year when the citizenry turned on unions of government workers; it was in 1979 that New Orleans police struck just prior to Mardi Gras, effectively canceling the holiday, and cost the business community millions.

These kinds of stunning gaffes in public relations—like strikes themselves—rarely happen anymore. Increasingly, public administrators and public workers are cooperating to successfully balance the budget and protect union jobs in the process.

So how powerful are public unions? More powerful when they work with public employers than when they work against them.

Unions versus Merit: The Basic Differences

The future of collective bargaining, unionization, and the right to strike bode ill for the traditional merit standards of the civil service personnel system. At root, there are two differences between the "collective system" and the "civil service system." One difference concerns the notion of sovereignty. The civil service system holds that a public position is a privilege, not a right, and that each public servant is obliged to uphold the public trust accorded to him or her by a paternalistic government. Conversely, the collective system holds that employees are on an equal footing with employers, and that they have a right to use their collective powers as a means of improving their conditions of employment. The civil service system sees this contention as a threat to the sovereignty of the state. At the same time the collective system views the traditions of the civil service as redolent of worker exploitation.

The second difference concerns the concept of individualism. The American civil service system long has valued the ideal that the individual worker be judged for a position on the basis of his or her unique merits for performing the duties of a particular job; the collective system argues that the identity of the individual should be absorbed in a collective effort to better the conditions of all workers. Hence, the relations of the individual with his or her government employer are replaced by a new set of relations that exists between the government employer and a collective "class" of employees.

Among the conflicts that result from these fundamental differences between the two systems over sovereignty and individualism are disputes over employee participation and rights (equal treatment versus union shop); recruitment (competitive tests versus union membership); promotion (performance versus seniority); position classification and pay (objective analysis versus negotiation); working conditions (determination by legislatures and management versus settlement by negotiations); and grievances (determination by civil service commissioners versus union representation to third party arbitrators). Like the other systems of human resource management, the collective system has real differences with the traditional values of the civil service, and these differences are reflected in the administration of government itself.

DOES HUMAN RESOURCE MANAGEMENT HAVE A FUTURE?

The problems reviewed here are complex and massive. Public personnel administration, like any other form of public administration, has large dollops of politics as part and parcel of it. The historic efforts of "good government" reformers to rid public personnel systems of "politics" have traditionally been based on the introduction of "merit principles" in the management of the public bureaucracy. Merit principles, as they normally have been understood, are now under considerable attack. The efforts to include more minorities and women in government, the drive to bring more professionals into government (who often do not identify with the public service in the same sense that traditional personnel specialists have related to it), the reality of unionism and collective bargaining, and the drive to overhaul the civil service all lead one to wonder what "merit" in public human resource management really means.

Concerns such as these inevitably lead one to speculate on the continuing role of the personnel function in government. One of the unique aspects of the public sector is that important system-wide missions are sometimes superimposed upon the public bureaucracy that have nothing to do with the day-to-day implementation and management of programs and policies, but which do reflect strongly held social values. Not only are government bureaucracies supposed to administer legislatively enacted public policies for all the people, but they are also directed by legislatures to "clean up their own houses" in certain areas, such as kicking out the party hacks (*i.e.*, instating the "merit principle"), or eliminating discrimination on the basis of race, sex, or disability (*i.e.*, the implementation of affirmative action).

(It is of note that legislatures—certainly Congress—rarely if ever apply these same "house cleaning" rules to themselves. Congress, for example, has never permitted its personnel practices to be subject to the Office of Personnel Management or any other civil service agency, and it has never applied affirmative action standards or veterans' preference policies to its own treatment of employees. Among the many other of its own laws from which Congress has exempted itself are virtually all of the laws pertaining to human resource management, such as the Equal Pay Act of 1963, the Civil Rights Acts of 1964 and 1990, the Age Discrimination Act of 1967, the Occupational Safety and Health Act of 1970, the Equal Employment Opportunity Act of 1972, the Ethics in Government Act of 1978, and the Americans with Disabilities Act of 1990.)

To achieve these social missions, the legislature, or the bureaucracy itself, typically creates a new agency to bring the other agencies into line. In 1883, the U.S. Civil Service Commission was set up to assure that incompetents were not hired by all the other federal agencies. Various agencies were established by Congress in 1964 and 1972, such as the U.S. Civil Rights Commission and the Equal Employment Opportunity Commission, and existing agencies gained new powers to assure that minorities, women, and the disabled were fairly represented in the government bureaucracy. In 1978, Congress established the Senior Executive Service and the Office of Personnel Management to disburse something called "management" throughout the federal structure.

These are all desirable objectives. But when they are met—or when they come into conflict with new social missions—perhaps it is time to reconsider the duties and activities of the various organizations that were created to implement them.

An example of this may be the "merit principle." The principle has been implemented. Party hacks (in part because political parties are in decline) seldom are found in the federal bureaucracy, and in fewer states and local ones. Although there are some exceptions, the rampant spoils system of the last century is no longer with us. More importantly, the implementation of the "merit principle" has come into conflict with new social missions, notably affirmative action and management improvement in government.[186]

As a consequence, the traditional functions of human resource management in the public sector seem a little obsolete. Job classification and analysis—a basic tenet of public personnel administration—is an example. Agency administrators typically must bargain with human resource managers about how high or low a position should be ranked in the agency hierarchy, and what kinds of qualifications prospective applicants should have. Often agency heads, who are interested in effective management, and personnel administrators, who want uniformity in the classification system, find themselves at odds. Moreover, human resource managers may not comprehend the wide-ranging professional and administrative needs of the more general public manager. An allegedly true example of this concerns the state agency administrator who asked the state personnel department to find job applicants who understood the management technique of "path analysis"; the personnel department responded that, since the agency was not responsible for forestry programs, a knowledge of path analysis for the position was not required.

We are not arguing for the abolition of government personnel departments. But we do suggest that their uses have changed. Perhaps such traditional activities of public personnel administration as job classification and analysis, human resource planning, performance appraisal, selection, discipline, and dismissal should be turned over to agency administrators. Placing the control of these functions directly in the hands of the agency heads should strengthen public management. It is still desirable, however, that other traditional activities of public personnel administration be retained in one or more separate staff units, such as departments of human resources, on the grounds that they are less directly critical to the management function or can be handled more effectively by a central agency; these activities include training, employee development, labor relations, research, and the administration of wages, salaries, benefits, and services. Of particular importance is employee development and training, an activity that government personnel departments have not emphasized in the past.

Human resource management in the public sector does have a future. Nevertheless, it is a future that will require some adaptation.

NOTES

1. The following discussion is drawn largely from Frederick C. Mosher, *Democracy and the Public Service*, 2nd ed. (New York: Oxford University Press, 1982), pp. 110-216.
2. Frederick C. Mosher, *Democracy and the Public Service* (New York: Oxford University Press, 1968), p. 166. Unless noted otherwise, all references to this work are to the second (1982) edition.
3. In 1992, there were 2,435 political appointment positions in the federal government. See: U. S. General Accounting Office, as cited in Mike Causey, "Jobs in Balance," *Washington Post* (July 15, 1992). For more details, James P. Pfiffner, "Political Appointees and Career Executives: The Democracy-Bureaucracy Nexus in the Third Century," *Public Administration Review*, 47 (January/February 1987), p. 58; and Patricia W. Ingraham, "Building Bridges or Burning Them? The President, the Appointees and the Bureaucracy," *Public Administration Review*, 47 (September/October 1987), p. 427.
4. Pfiffner, "Political Appointees and Career Executives," p. 57.
5. *Ibid.*, p. 58. Emphasis is original.
6. Dean E. Mann with Jameson W. Doig, *The Assistant Secretaries: Problems and Processes of Appointment* (Washington, D.C.: Brookings Institution, 1965).
7. Lloyd W. Warner, *et al., The American Federal Executive* (New Haven, Conn.: Yale University Press, 1963).
8. Mann and Doig, *The Assistant Secretaries*. But see also Thomas P. Murphy, Donald E. Nuechterlein, and Ronald J. Stupak, *Inside the Bureaucracy: The View from the Assistant Secretary's Desk* (Boulder, Colo.: Westview, 1978); and Hugh Heclo, *A Government of Strangers: Executive Politics in Washington* (Washington, D.C.: Brookings Institution, 1977). Both of these more recent works tend to support the earlier study.
9. Steven E. Rhoads, "Economists and Policy Analysis," *Public Administration Review*, 38 (January/February 1978), p. 113.
10. Mosher, *Democracy and the Public Service*, p. 179.
11. Mann and Doig, *The Assistant Secretaries*, p. 120.
12. Roger G. Brown, "Party and Bureaucracy: The Presidents Since JFK," paper prepared for the 1981 Annual Meeting of the American Political Science Association, New York: September 3-6, 1981, Tables 1-10. This analysis included all cabinet, subcabinet, policymaking officials, judges, and ambassadors. The percentage of appointees who were members of the president's party that were appointed by Kennedy was 70 percent, Johnson 56 percent, Nixon 70 percent, Ford 61 percent, and Carter 61 percent. The Carter appointees cover only 1977 and 1978. After 1978 information on partisan affiliation became unavailable on a systemic basis.
13. David T. Stanley, Dean E. Mann, and Jameson W. Doig, *Men Who Govern* (Washington, D.C.: Brookings Institution, 1967), p. 24.
14. *Ibid.*
15. Heclo, *A Government of Strangers.*
16. C. Brauer, "Tenure, Turnover, and Postgovernment Employment Trends of Presidential Appointees," in G. Calvin Mac Kenzie, ed., *The In-and-Outers* (Baltimore, Md.: Johns Hopkins University Press, 1987), pp. 1-29.
17. Ingraham, "Building Bridges or Burning Them?" p. 429.
18. Mann and Doig, *The Assistant Secretaries*, pp. 99, 165.
19. Pendleton James, quoted in Pfiffner, "Political Appointees and Career Executives," p. 59.
20. Judith Havemann, "Top Federal Jobs 'Politicized,'" *Washington Post* (August 6, 1987).
21. Fred Malek, Presidential Personnel Assistant in the Nixon Administration, quoted in *ibid.*, pp. 63-64.
22. U. S. General Accounting Office, *Senior Executive Service: Opinions About the Federal Work Environment*, GAO/GGO-92-63 (Washington, D.C.: General Accounting Office, May 1992).
23. As derived from: U.S. Bureau of the Census, *Sta-*

tistical Abstract of the United States, 1986 (Washington, D.C.: U.S. Government Printing Office, 1985), Table 301, p. 175; and U.S. Bureau of the Census, *Statistical Abstract of the United States, 1992* (Washington, D.C.: U.S. Government Printing Office, 1992), Table 324, p. 195.

24. National Academy of Public Administration, *Leadership in Jeopardy: The Fraying of the Presidential Appointments System* (Washington, D.C.: National Academy of Public Administration, 1985), p. 67. The high figures in both categories were provided by presidential appointees in the Johnson Administration; the low figures were given by those in the Reagan Administration. The response rate was 56 percent.

25. Pfiffner, "Political Appointees and Career Executives," p. 61.

26. See, for example, Deborah D. Roberts, "A New Breed of Public Executive: Top Level Exempt Managers in State Government," *Review of Public Personnel Administration*, 8 (Spring 1988), pp. 20-36, and Deil S. Wright, Jae-Won Yoo, and Jennifer Cohen, "The Evolving Profile of State Administrators," *Journal of State Government*, 64 (January-March 1991), pp. 30-38.

27. James R. Thompson, as quoted in Jeffrey L. Katz, "The Slow Death of Political Patronage," *Governing* (April 1991), p. 58.

28. Stephen Allred, as quoted in *ibid.*, p. 62.

29. Tari Renner and Victor S. De Santis, "Contemporary Patterns and Trends in Municipal Government Structures," *Municipal Year Book, 1993* (Washington, D.C.: International City Management Association, 1993), p. 63. More than 67 percent of cities in the survey of all U. S. cities and towns employed a chief administrative officer, who reports directly to the mayor or council. The figure for counties with administrators is derived from "Introduction" in *ibid.*, Table 3, p. xiv.

30. See Mosher, *Democracy and the Public Service*, p. 58.

31. Sidney H. Aronson, *Status and Kinship in the Higher Civil Service* (Cambridge, Mass.: Harvard University Press, 1964), p. 61.

32. *Ibid.*

33. Quoted in Leonard D. White, *The Jacksonians* (New York: Macmillan, 1954), p. 320.

34. Mosher, *Democracy and the Public Service*, pp. 66-72.

35. *Ibid.*, p. 67.

36. U.S. Civil Service Commission, *22nd Report* (Washington, D.C.: U.S. Government Printing Office, 1905), quoted in *ibid.*, p. 69.

37. *Ibid.*, p. 68.

38. *Ibid.*, p. 66.

39. Committee on Administrative Management (Louis Brownlow, Chair), *Personnel Administration in the Federal Service* (Washington, D.C.: U.S. Government Printing Office, 1937).

40. Commission on Organization of the Executive Branch of the Government, *Personnel and Civil Service* (Washington, D.C.: U.S. Government Printing Office, 1955).

41. The bulk of the following discussion is drawn from Frederick C. Mosher and Richard J. Stillman II, "Introduction to Symposium on the Professions in Government," *Public Administration Review*, 37 (November/December 1977), pp. 631-632; and Mosher, *Democracy and the Public Service*, pp. 110-142.

42. Mosher, *Democracy and the Public Service*, p. 113.

43. Terry Newell, "The Future and Federal Training," *Public Personnel Management*, 17 (Fall 1988), p. 264, and Beverly A. Cigler, "Public Administration and the Paradox of Professionalism," *Public Administration Review*, 50 (November/December 1990), p. 637. Figures are for 1983 and 1985.

44. Barbara Blumenthal, "Uncle Sam's Invisible Army of Employees," *National Journal* (May 5, 1979), p. 732.

45. Frederick C. Mosher, "Professions in Public Service," *Public Administration Review*, 38 (March/April 1978), p. 147; and Mosher, *Democracy and the Public Service*, p. 113.

46. Municipal Manpower Commission, *Governmental Manpower for Tomorrow's Cities* (New York: McGraw-Hill, 1962).

47. Mosher, *Democracy and the Public Service*, first (1968) edition, p. 124.

48. Frederick C. Mosher and Keith Axtell, unpublished studies cited in Mosher, *Democracy and the Public Service*, pp. 136-137. But see also the first (1968) edition, p. 127.

49. Doyle W. Buckwalter and J. Ivan Legler, "City Managers and City Attorneys: Associates or Adversaries?" *Public Administration Review*, 47 (September/October 1987), pp. 393-403.

50. See, for example, Corinne Lathrop Gilb, *Hidden Hierarchies: The Professions and Government* (New York: Harper & Row, 1956); Jethro K. Lieberman, *The Tyranny of the Experts: How Professionals Are Closing the Open Society* (New York: Walker, 1970); Guy Benveniste, *The Politics of Expertise*, 2nd ed. (San Francisco: Boyd & Fraser, 1977); and Stephen L. Esquith, "Toward a Theory of Professional Power," paper presented at the 1985 Annual Meeting of the American Political Science Association, New Orleans, August 29-September 1, 1985.

51. Mosher, *Democracy and the Public Service*, pp. 104-105.

52. *Ibid.*, p. 103.

53. *Ibid.*

54. Jean J. Couturier, "The Quiet Revolution in Public Personnel Laws," *Public Personnel Management* (May/June 1976), pp. 150-159. Three hundred thirty-eight public personnel systems responded to the survey.

55. "The 'Malek Manual'" is published in *The Bureaucrat*, 4 (January 1976), pp. 429-508. One reviewer has said it "stands as the best guide as to how the federal civil service works, as well as a monument to concerted attempts to achieve political control over large sections of the federal bureaucracy." See: H. Brinton Milward, "Politics, Personnel, and Public Policy," *Public Administration Review*, 38 (July/August 1978), p. 395.

56. Mosher, *Democracy and the Public Service*, pp. 104-105.

57. Office of Personnel Management, *Federal Employee Attitudes, Phase I: Base Line Survey, 1979, Government-Wide Report* (Washington, D.C.: U.S. Government Printing Office, 1979), p. 25.

58. Jimmy Carter, State of the Union message, January 19, 1978.

59. A good example is Alan K. Campbell, "Civil Service Reform: A New Commitment," *Public Administration Review*, 38 (March/April 1978), especially pages 101-102.

60. Mosher, *Democracy and the Public Service*, p. 107.

61. Office of Personnel Management, *Civil Service Reform: A Report on the First Year* (Washington, D.C.: U.S. Government Printing Office, 1980); Nolan J. Argyle, "Civil Service Reform: The State and Local Response," *Public Personnel Management* (Spring 1982), pp. 157-164; and Dennis L. Dresang, "Diffusion of Civil Service Reform," *Review of Public Personnel Administration*, 2 (Spring 1982), pp. 35-47.

62. See, for example, Roberts, "A New Breed of Public Executive"; Frank P. Sherwood and Lee J. Breyer, "Executive Personnel Systems in the States," *Public Administration Review*, 47 (September/October 1987), pp. 410-416; H.O. Waldly and Annie Mary Hartsfield, "The Senior Management Service in the States," *Review of Public Personnel Administration*, 4 (Spring 1984), pp. 28-39; and A. Finkle, H. Hall, and S. Min, "Senior Executive Service: The State of the Art," *Public Personnel Management*, 10 (Fall 1981), pp. 299-312.

63. The following paragraphs are drawn from Wright, Yoo, and Cohen, "The Evolving Profile of State Administrators," pp. 30-38.

64. As derived from Table 2, *Municipal Year Book, 1993*, p. xii.

65. Heywood T. Sanders, "Government Structure in American Cities," *Municipal Year Book, 1979* (Washington, D.C.: International City Management Association, 1979), pp. 102, 104; Richard J. Stillman II, "Local Public Management in Transition: A Report on the Current State of the Profession," *Municipal Year Book, 1982* (Washington, D.C.: International City Management Association, 1982), p. 163; Allan Klevit, "City Councils and Their Function in Local Government," *Municipal Year Book, 1972* (Washington, D.C.: International City Management Association, 1972), pp. 15-19; and Raymond Bancroft, *America's Mayors and Councilmen: Their Problems and Frustrations* (Washington, D.C.: National League of Cities, 1974).

66. O. Glenn Stahl, *Public Personnel Administration*, 8th ed. (New York: Harper & Row, 1983), p. 42. Figure is for 1980.

67. *Ibid.*, p. 43; and Andrew W. Boessel, "Local Personnel Management," *Municipal Year Book, 1974* (Washington, D.C.: International City Management Association, 1974), pp. 92-93.

68. Dennis L. Dresang, *Public Personnel Management and Public Policy* (Boston: Little, Brown, 1984), p. 4.

69. Steven W. Hays and T. Zane Reeves, *Personnel Management in the Public Sector* (Boston: Allyn & Bacon, 1984), p. 87. Figures are for 1980. These figures are somewhat misleading in that perhaps 40 to 50 percent of cities and counties lack full-time personnel directors; typically, other functionaries, such as city and county managers or department heads add the duties of personnel director to those that they already have. See: Office of Personnel Management as cited in *ibid.*

70. For a synopsis of surveys of the personal characteristics of human resource managers in the public sector, see: Steven W. Hays and Richard C. Kearney, "State Personnel Directors and the Dilemmas of Workforce 2000: A Survey," *Public Administration Review*, 52 (July/August 1992), p. 383.

71. Myron D. Fottler and Norman A. Townsend, "Characteristics of Public and Private Personnel Directors," *Public Personnel Management*, 6 (July/August 1977), p. 252.

72. *Ibid.*, and American Society of Personnel Administrators, *The Personnel Executive's Job* (Englewood Cliffs, N.J.: Prentice Hall, 1977).

73. N. Joseph Cayer, "Local Government Personnel Structure and Policies," *Municipal Year Book, 1991* (Washington, D.C.: International City Management Association, 1991) p. 9.

74. Commission on Executive, Legislative, and Judicial Salaries, *High Quality Leadership: Our Government's Most Precious Asset* (Washington, D.C.: Commission on Executive, Legislative, and Judicial Salaries, 1987), and Task Force on the Senior Executive Service, Twentieth Century Fund, *The Government's Managers* (New York: Priority Press Publications, 1987). See also: Task Force on Pay and Compensation, *Report of the Task Force on Pay and Compensation to the National Commission on the Public Service* (Washington, D.C.: National Commission on the Public Service, 1989). The Task Force found (p. 206) that "From 1970 to 1987, the cost of living as measured by the Consumer Price Index increased by 183 percentage points; pay for white-collar workers in the private sector increased 165 points, and pay for federal white-collar work increased 124 points."

75. U.S. General Accounting Office, as cited in Bennett Minton, "GAO Study Confirms Pay Gap," *Federal Times* (June 11, 1990). Data available for 1988 were analyzed. Private employees in sixty-three metropolitan areas were paid more than federal employees 90 percent of the time, and by significant margins.

76. Merit Systems Protection Board, *Why Are Employees Leaving the Federal Government? Results of an Exit Survey* (Washington, D.C.: U. S. Government Printing Office, May 1990). The reason cited most frequently for resigning after pay and advancement was organizational management concerns, with 17 percent—a distant second.

77. Jeanne Saddler, "Panel Recommends Large Pay Increase for U.S. Officials," *Wall Street Journal* (December 16, 1986).

78. "Even Bureaucrats Deserve a Raise," *Business Week* (January 26, 1987), p. 26.

79. U. S. Bureau of Labor Statistics, as cited in Jeffrey L. Katz, "Government Perks?" *Washington Times* (December 20, 1991).

80. "Federal Pay: Better at the Top," *The Economist* (January 10, 1987), p. 35.

81. U. S. Merit Systems Protection Board, *Working for America: A Federal Employment Survey* (Washington, D.C.: U. S. Government Printing Office, June 1990), and U. S. General Accounting Office, *Senior Executive Service.*

82. U.S. General Accounting Office, *Training Budgets: Agency Budget Reductions in Response to the Balanced Budget Act* (Washington, D.C.: U.S. General Accounting Office, 1986), p. 2. The GAO's analysis of fifty-six federal agencies in Fiscal Year 1986 found that forty-two of them cut training budgets in an effort to comply with the Deficit Control Act (*i.e.,* the Gramm-Rudman-Hollings balanced budget act), and that thirty of the agencies cut their training budgets by 10 percent or more, even though the Act required a reduction of only 4.3 percent.

83. Charles J. Spindler, "University-Based Public Sector Management Development and Training," *Public Productivity and Management Review*, 14 (Summer 1992), p. 447.

84. Joseph W. Whorton, Jr., Frank K. Gibson, and Delmer D. Dunn, "The Culture of University Public Service: A National Survey of the Perspectives of Users and Providers," *Public Administration Review*, 46 (January/February 1986), pp. 39-40. Seventy-nine percent of local administrators and 80 percent of state administrators reported using universities for assistance of some sort at least once over the last three years. Two-hundred forty local executives responded (a 55 percent response rate), and 198 state officials in all states (a 66 percent response rate). See also: James D. Slack, "Information, Training, and Assistance Needs of Municipal Governments," *Public Administration Review*, 50 (July/August 1990), p. 453. Sixty-eight percent of 500 mayors and city managers who received Slack's questionnaire responded. Forty-nine percent of the respondents said that they had been contacted by universities regarding training services.

85. Gary W. Loveman and John J. Gabarro, "The Managerial Implications of Changing Work Force Demographics: A Scoping Survey," *Human Resource Management*, 30 (Spring 1991), pp. 7-29.

86. Human Technology, Inc., *The Future Environment for Federal Workforce Training and Development: An Analysis of Long-Term Trends and Their Impacts*, report to the U.S. Office of Personnel Management, (McLean, Va.: Human Technology, 1986), p. 9.

87. WEFA Group and Forecasting International, as cited in Kerry Pechter, "Office Memos: Some Predictions about the Workplace of the Future," *Wall Street Journal* (June 4, 1990).

88. Loveman and Gabarro, "The Managerial Implications of Changing Work Force Demographics," p. 15.

89. See: Merit Systems Protection Board, *Working For America.* The Merit Systems Protection Board surveyed 15,939 federal workers at all levels in 1990. A comparable survey by the Board conducted in 1986 also found large numbers of federal supervisors who believed that the quality of applicants had declined. See: U. S. Merit Systems Protection Board, *Merit Principles Survey, 1986* (Washington, D.C.: U. S. Government Printing Office, 1986).

90. Larry M. Lane and James E. Wolf, *The Human Resource Crisis in the Public Sector: Rebuilding the Capacity to Govern* (New York: Quorum Books, 1990), p. 77.

91. Constance Horner, as quoted in Judith Havemann, "New Federal Job Exams Set for June," *Washington Post* (April 22, 1990).

92. Carolyn Ban and Patricia W. Ingraham, "Retaining Quality Federal Employees: Life After PACE," *Public Administration Review*, 48 (May/June 1988), pp. 708-725.

93. U. S. Merit Systems Protection Board, *Attracting Quality Graduates to the Federal Government: A View of College Recruiting* (Washington, D.C.: U. S. Government Printing Office, 1988).

94. Lana Stein, "Merit Systems and Political Influence: The Case of Local Government," *Public Administration Review*, 47 (May/June 1987), p. 267; and Couturier, "The Quiet Revolution in Public Personnel Laws."

95. Frank J. Thompson, *Personnel Policy in the City: The Politics of Jobs in Oakland* (Berkeley: University of California Press, 1975), p. 106.

96. E. S. Savas and Sigmund G. Ginsburg, "The Civil Service: A Meritless System?" *The Public Interest*, 32 (Summer 1973), p. 76. Emphasis is in original.

97. *Ibid.*, p. 77.

98. Ivar Berg, with the assistance of Sherry Gorelick, *Education and Jobs: The Great Training Robbery* (Boston: Beacon Press, 1977), p. 107.

99. Commission on Organization of the Executive Branch of the Government, *Personnel Management: A Report to the Congress* (Washington, D.C.: U.S. Government Printing Office, 1949).

100. U. S. General Accounting Office, as cited in Frank Greve, "Federal Bureaucrats Are Getting High Marks, But Grading Is Suspect," *Philadelphia Inquirer* (March 10, 1992).

101. For a thoughtful statement on federal "riffing," see: U.S. Merit Systems Protection Board, *The RIF System in the Federal Government: Is It Working and What Can Be Done to Improve It?* (Washington, D.C.: U.S. Office of Merit Systems Reviews and Studies, 1983).

102. For a description of the Fitzgerald episode, see Barbara Newman, "The Cost of Courage," and A. Ernest Fitzgerald, "Fitzgerald on Fitzhugh," in *Blowing the Whistle: Dissent in the Public Interest*, Charles Peters and Taylor Branch, eds. (New York: Praeger, 1972), pp. 195-206 and 207-221.

103. N. R. Kleinfield, "The Whistle Blowers' Morning After," *New York Times* (January 19, 1986).

104. *Ibid.*

105. Unpublished study by Karen L. Soeken and Donald L. Soeken "A Survey of Whistleblowers: Their Stressors and Coping Strategies," 1987, as reported in: Clyde H. Farnsworth, "Survey of Whistle Blowers Finds Retaliation but Few Regrets," *New York Times*

(February 27, 1987). Other surveys show essentially the same personal characteristics.

106. Philip H. Jos, Mark E. Tompkins, and Steven W. Hays, "In Praise of Difficult People: A Portrait of the Committed Whistleblower," *Public Administration Review*, 49 (November/December 1989), p. 556.

107. *Ibid.*, p. 557. See also: Marcia P. Miceli, Bonnie L. Roach, and Janet P. Near, "The Motivations of Anonymous Whistleblowers: The Case of Federal Employees," *Public Personnel Management*, 17 (Fall 1988), pp. 281-296.

108. This is a compilation of data obtained from: Soeken and Soeken, "A Survey of Whistleblowers." Soeken and Soeken sent questionnaires to 233 individuals and obtained a response rate of 40 percent, 60 percent of whom were federal employees. (A comparable, though more anecdotal, survey of fifty-five whistle-blowers was conducted by Myron Peretz Glazer and Penina Migdal Glazer, *The Whistleblowers: Exposing Corruption in Government and Industry* [New York: Basic Books, 1989].) And Jos, Tompkins, and Hays, "In Praise of Difficult People," pp. 552-561. Questionnaires were sent to 329 whistleblowers, and a response rate of 56 percent was obtained, 80 percent of whom were public employees. A particularly thorough bibliography of whistleblowing appears on pp. 560-561 of the article.

109. Jos, Tompkins, and Hays, "In Praise of Difficult People," p. 555.

110. *Ibid.*

111. Daniel B. Moskowitz, "Windfalls for Whistle-Blowers Trouble Government, Companies," *Washington Post* (October 7, 1991), and Richard W. Stevenson, "U. S. Judge Orders $7.5 Million Award to Whistleblower," *New York Times* (July 7, 1992).

112. Philip H. Jos, "The Nature and Limits of the Whistleblower's Contribution to Administrative Responsibility," *American Review of Public Administration*, 21 (June 1991), p. 106.

113. Jos, Tompkins, and Hays, "In Praise of Difficult People," p. 555.

114. Quoted in Farnsworth, "Survey of Whistle Blowers Finds Retaliation but Few Regrets."

115. Jos, Tompkins, and Hays, "In Praise of Difficult People," p. 555.

116. O. Glenn Stahl, *Public Personnel Administration*, 7th ed. (New York: Harper & Row, 1976), p. 309. All other references to Stahl are to the eighth edition of this work.

117. Stahl, *Public Personnel Administration*, p. 158.

118. Thompson, *Personnel Policy in the City*, p. 142-143.

119. Herbert Kaufman, *The Forest Ranger* (Baltimore, Md.: Johns Hopkins University Press, 1960), p. 158.

120. Thompson, *Personnel Policy in the City*, p. 156.

121. Gregory B. Lewis, "Turnover and the Quiet Crisis in the Federal Service," *Public Administrative Review*, 51 (March/April 1991), p. 154. The years analyzed were 1976 through 1988.

122. Charles S. Rhyne, "The Letter of the Law," *Public Management*, 57 (November 1975), pp. 9-11.

123. John M. Capozzola, "Affirmative Action Alive and

Well Under Courts' Strict Scrutiny," *National Civic Review*, 75 (November/December 1986), pp. 355-357.

124. *Ibid.*, p. 355.

125. John Nalbandian, "The U.S. Supreme Court's 'Consensus' on Affirmative Action," *Public Administration Review*, 49 (January/February 1989), p. 39.

126. Evelina R. Moulder, "Affirmative Action in Local Government," *Municipal Year Book, 1991* (Washington, D.C.: International City Management Association, 1991), p. 47.

127. Vernon R. Taylor, "Cultural Bias in Testing: An Action Program," *Public Personnel Review*, 29 (July 1968), p. 170.

128. Stein, "Merit Systems and Political Influence," p. 267. Police positions are the highest scorer in this regard, with nearly 97 percent of large cities reporting that they use written tests for determining hires in the police field, followed by positions in fire departments and clerical jobs; the lowest use of written examinations (15 percent) is for positions as sanitation workers. About 45 percent of the cities use written tests for entry-level professional positions. Stein sent questionnaires to personnel departments in 172 cities with 100,000 people or more, and obtained a response rate of 86 percent. Data are for 1986.

129. "Local Government Recruitment and Selection Practices," *Municipal Year Book, 1986* (Washington, D.C.: International Management Association, 1986), p. 47. Questionnaires were mailed to 850 cities and counties with 50,000 people or more. The response rate was 41 percent. Data are for 1984 and 1985.

130. Stein, "Merit Systems and Political Influence," p. 267.

131. Moulder, "Affirmative Action in Local Government," p. 51, and Evelina R. Moulder, "Affirmative Action: The Role Local Governments Are Playing," *Municipal Year Book, 1986* (Washington, D.C: International Management Association, 1986), p. 26.

132. Jean Couturier, "Court Attacks on Testing: Death Knell or Salvation for the Civil Service System," *Good Government*, 88 (Winter 1971), p. 12.

133. Couturier, "The Quiet Revolution in Public Personnel Laws."

134. As derived from data presented in: U.S. Bureau of the Census, *Statistical Abstract of the United States, 1992*, p. 412, Table 654. Datum is for 1991, and is for women twenty-five years of age and older.

135. Clarence M. Pendleton, Jr., quoted in: Associated Press, "Rights Panel Chief Scoffs at Idea of Comparable Pay for Women," *New York Times* (November 17, 1984).

136. Constance Horner, quoted in Mike Causey, "Comparable Worth Plans," *Washington Post* (April 22, 1987).

137. The following discussion is drawn from: Keon S. Chi, "Comparable Worth: Implications of the Washington Case," *State Government*, 57, No. 2 (1984), pp. 34-45; and Keon S. Chi, "Comparable Worth in State Governments," *State Government News*, 27 (November 1984), pp. 4-6.

138. Cayer, "Local Government Personnel Structure and

Policies," p. 9. Almost 10 percent of cities and nearly 12 percent of counties have comparable worth policies.

139. Peter T. Kilborn, "Wage Gaps Between Sexes Is Cut In Test, but at a Price," *New York Times* (May 31, 1990).

140. *Ibid.*, and U. S. General Accounting Office, *Pay Equity: Washington State's Efforts to Address Comparable Worth*, GAO/GGO-92-87BR (Washington, D.C.: General Accounting Office, July 1992).

141. James E. Campbell and Gregory B. Lewis, "Public Support for Comparable Worth in Georgia," *Public Administration Review*, 46 (September/October 1986), pp. 432-437; and Mark A. Emmert, "Public Opinion of Comparable Worth: Some Preliminary Findings," *Review of Public Personnel Administration*, 6 (Fall 1985), pp. 69-75.

142. Cynthia S. Ross and Robert E. England, "State Governments' Sexual Harassment Policy Initiatives," *Public Administration Review*, 47 (May/June 1987), p. 261. Data are for 1985.

143. Cayer, "Local Government Personnel Structure and Policies," p. 12. Over 87 percent of cities and over 88 percent of counties have policies forbidding sexual harassment.

144. Seymour Martin Lipset and William Schneider, "An Emerging National Consensus," *The New Republic* (October 15, 1977), p. 8. Emphasis is in original.

145. *Ibid.*, p. 9. See also Lindsey Gruson, "Survey Finds 73% Oppose Racial Quotas in Hiring," *New York Times* (September 25, 1983).

146. Lipset and Schneider, "An Emerging National Consensus," p. 9. Figures are for 1975.

147. The following examples of "reverse passing" are in: "Disadvantaged Groups, Individual Rights," *The New Republic* (October 15, 1977), p. 7; and Eliot Marshall, "Race Certification," in *ibid.*, p. 19.

148. Thompson, *Personnel Policy in the City*, pp. 112-130.

149. *Ibid.*, p. 120.

150. *Ibid.*, p. 136.

151. Robert J. Huntley and Robert J. McDonald, "Urban Managers: Organizational Preferences, Managerial Styles, and Social Policy Roles," *Municipal Year Book, 1975* (Washington, D.C.: International City Management Association, 1975), p. 157. Emphasis has been added.

152. Moulder, "Affirmative Action in Local Government," pp. 47-52. The quotation is on p. 51. Questionnaires were sent to all cities of 10,000 population or more, and all counties with 25,000 people or more; the response rate was 36 percent. For 1984 data, see: Moulder, "Affirmative Action," p. 25-26. For 1974 data, see: Huntley and McDonald, "Urban Managers," p. 154.

153. James D. Slack, "Affirmative Action and City Managers: Attitudes Toward Recruitment of Women," *Public Administration Review*, 47 (March/April 1987) pp. 202-203. Two-hundred ninety city managers responded to the survey. Data are for 1985.

154. Stein, "Merit Systems and Political Influence," p. 270.

155. See, for example, Slack, "Affirmative Action and City Managers," p. 204.

156. Stein, "Merit Systems and Political Influence," p. 270. Data are for 1986.

157. As derived from: U. S. Bureau of the Census, *Statistical Abstract of the United States, 1992*, p. 412, Table 654.

158. As derived from: U.S. Bureau of the Census, *Statistical Abstract of the United States, 1982-83* (Washington, D.C.: U.S. Government Printing Office, 1982), p. 305, Table 504.

159. *Ibid.*

160. Nelson C. Dometrius and Lee Sigelman, "Assessing Progress Toward Affirmative Action Goals in State and Local Governments: A New Benchmark," *Public Administration Review*, 44 (May/June 1984), pp. 241-246. Data are for 1980.

161. Feminist Majority Foundation, as cited in "Study: Women Hold Only 3 Percent of Corporate Jobs" *Savannah News Press* (August 26, 1991) for *Fortune* 500 data; Table 9-1 for federal data; and Center for Women in Government, State University of New York at Albany, as cited in "Few Women Found in Top Public Jobs" *New York Times* (January 3, 1992), for state and local data. The Center's study, based on EEOC data, covered department heads, division chiefs, deputies, and examiners, and its findings were remarkably parallel to the figure in Table 9-3, which shows that 31 percent of "officials/administrators" were women.

162. Dometrius and Sigelman, "Assessing Progress Toward Affirmative Action Goals in State and Local Government," pp. 244-245.

163. U.S. Department of Labor, as cited in Robert A. Rankin, "Changing Demographics May Make Affirmative Action Moot in 1990s," *Philadelphia Inquirer* (July 1, 1990).

164. Audrey Freedman, quoted in *ibid.*

165. U.S. Department of Labor, as cited in *ibid.* See also: Hudson Institute, *Workforce 2000* (Indianapolis, Ind.: Hudson Institute, 1987).

166. Rosslyn S. Klaman, *The Changing Workforce: Demographic Issues Facing Employers*, GAO/T-GGO-92-61 (Washington, D.C.: General Accounting Office, July 29, 1992), pp.1-7.

167. *Ibid.* But see also: Audrey J. Cohen, "Predictors of Public and Private Employment for Business College Graduates," *Public Personnel Management*, 22 (Spring 1992), pp. 167-186. This and other research suggests that minority college graduates are considerably more favorably disposed toward working in the public sector than are white college graduates.

168. U.S. Bureau of the Census, *Statistical Abstract of the United States, 1982-83*, p. 410, Table 683. Figures are for 1978.

169. U.S. Bureau of the Census, *Statistical Abstract of the United States, 1992*, p. 422, Table 672. Figure is for 1991.

170. Judith Havemann, "Federal Relations Marred by Increasing Strife," *Washington Post* (May 31, 1987),

and Katherine C. Naff, "Labor Management Relations and Privatization: A Federal Perspective," *Public Administration Review*, 51 (January/February 1991), p. 24.

171. James W. Singer, "The Limited Power of Federal Worker Unions," *National Journal*, 10 (September 30, 1978), pp. 1547-1551.

172. Jonathan Walters, "The Chastening of the Public Employees," *Governing* (January 1993), p. 28. Figures are for 1991.

173. U. S. Bureau of the Census, *Statistical Abstract of the United States, 1986*, p. 425, Table 714. Figure is for 1982.

174. *Ibid.*, p. 423, Table 712; U.S. Bureau of the Census, *Statistical Abstract of the United States, 1992*, p. 421, Table 670; and Havemann, "Federal Labor Relations Marred by Increasing Strife."

175. Hugh O'Neill, "The Growth of Municipal Employee Unions," in Robert H. Connery and William V. Farr, eds. *Unionization of Municipal Employees* (New York: Academy of Political Science, 1970), p. 4.

176. John Thomas Delaney and Raymond D. Horton, "Managing Relations with Organized Employees," in James L. Perry, ed., *Handbook of Public Administration* (San Francisco: Jossey-Bass, 1989), p. 439, for collective bargaining figures, and David A. Dilts, William J. Walsh, and Constanza Hagmann, "State Labor-Management Relations Legislation: Adaptive Modeling," *Journal of Collective Negotiations in the Public Sector*, 22, No. 1, (1993), p. 80, for meet-and-confer figure.

177. U.S. Bureau of the Census, *Statistical Abstract of the United States, 1986*, p. 298, Table 487. Figures are for 1982.

178. Sam Zagoria, "Attitudes Harden in Governmental Labor Relations," *ASPA News and Views*, 26 (December 1976), pp. 1, 21, and 22.

179. Marvin J. Levine, "The Status of State 'Sunshine Bargaining' Laws," *Labor Law Journal* (November 1980), p. 713.

180. Delaney and Horton, "Managing Relations with Organized Employees," p. 439.

181. Llewellyn M. Toulmin, "The Treasure Hunt: Budget Search Behavior by Public Employee Unions," *Public Administration Review*, 48 (March/April 1988), pp. 620-630.

182. Quoted in Sterling Spero and John M. Capozzola, *The Urban Community and Its Unionized Bureaucracy* (New York: Dunellen, 1973), p. 218.

183. Anthony H. Pascal, "The Hidden Costs of Collective Bargaining in Local Government," *Taxing and Spending*, 2 (Spring 1980), as reprinted in Barry Bozeman and Jeffrey Straussman, eds., *New Directions in Public Administration* (Monterey, Calif.: Brooks/Cole, 1984), p. 259.

184. Dilts, Walsh, and Hagmann, "State and Labor-Management Relations Legislation," p. 84.

185. Walters, "The Chastening of the Public Employees," p. 29.

186. An example of this conflict is provided by O. Glenn Stahl, a distinguished scholar and practitioner of public personnel administration who is as staunch a defender of the merit principle in American government as one is likely to find. Stahl writes that a policy of affirmative action "discourages achievement and puts a premium on that attitude that effort is unnecessary to win a job—neither of which conditions bodes any good for the quality of American life. . . . We cannot expect a miraculous transformation [of the civil service system] overnight." See: O. Glenn Stahl, "A Fair Look at Fair Employment," *Public Employment Practices Bulletin*, 1971. The *Bulletin* was published by the International Personnel Management Association.

PART FOUR

IMPLEMENTATION

In the fourth and final part of *Public Administration and Public Affairs*, we explain how to get things done. Although we touched upon certain concepts of implementation in Chapter 4, notably in our discussion of administration in public organizations, in Part Four we take a broader view. Hence, we begin with a very general approach to implementation and close the book on some very specific—even personal—notes on the execution of decisions in the public sector.

The broadest of all treatments to the problem of implementation is the chapter which begins Part Four, "Approaches to Public Policy and Its Implementation." There is a large literature of public policy, and its various schools have varying objectives. From there we move to governments' relations with private corporations, public corporations, and "third-sector," or nonprofit, organizations, and how governments use these entities (and occasionally are used by them) to implement public policy. The rise of privatization, in the forms of government contracting and government corporations, is a relatively little known area of the administrative state, but is nonetheless one of extreme importance, and one of growing significance over time. In the following chapter we consider governments' relations with each other, and discuss how agreements among governments are used to conduct the public's business. Finally, and perhaps most importantly, we focus on the specific area of ethical decision making in the formulation of public policies.

Implementation is the execution and delivery of public policies. It is perhaps the most "hands-on" facet of public administration, but the subject of implementation is surprisingly, and justifiably, theoretical and often abstract. This is both an irony and a paradox in the study of the implementation of public policy about which the reader should be aware.

CHAPTER 10

APPROACHES TO PUBLIC POLICY AND ITS IMPLEMENTATION

The area of public policy, like the field of public administration itself, has had an ambivalent intellectual evolution. Public policy exists in both political science and public administration, but in different guises. Whatever its form, however, public policy is what public administrators execute, and it provides a fitting introduction to this section on implementation.

THE EVOLUTION OF PUBLIC POLICY ANALYSIS: PUBLIC ADMINISTRATION VERSUS POLITICAL SCIENCE

Occurring concurrently with the evolution of "self-aware" public administration was the development of the subfield of "public policy" within political science departments. And the subfield emerged for many of the same reasons that motivated public administration to secede from political science, particularly the concern shared by some political scientists that their field was far more concerned with science than politics. One of the early contributors to the public policy subfield, Austin Ranney, put it well: "At least since 1945 most American political scientists have

focused their professional attention mainly on the *processes* by which public policies are made and have shown relatively little concern with their *contents*."[1] Ranney and his colleagues took issue with this emphasis, and believed that a more substantive approach was needed. From its beginnings, in short, public policy has been an effort to "apply" political science to public affairs; its inherent sympathies with the "practical" field of public administration are real, and many of those scholars who identify with the public policy subfield find themselves in a twilight zone between political science and public administration.

Perhaps the first formal recognition by political scientists of the importance of public policy was a small meeting held in 1965 under the auspices of the Committee on Governmental and Legal Processes of the Social Science Research Council. Out of this meeting emerged "a consensus that the most timely and urgent question . . . is: What professional expertise and obligations, if any, have political scientists to study, evaluate, and make recommendations about the contents of public policy?"[2] Two Committee-sponsored conferences on the question followed in 1966 and 1967. Also in 1967, the American Political

Science Association's Annual Conference featured its first panel on public policy; in 1970, the Association granted public policy its first section at its annual conference. By the 1980s, around 150 papers on public policy analysis were being delivered at the annual meeting, and now public policy presentations are routine in political science circles.

Public policy was even more popular among political scientists than the proliferating presentations of papers on the topic indicate. During this period, for example, the Policy Studies Organization was founded (in 1972), and it provided additional outlets for political scientists interested in public policy—within a decade of its creation, the Organization had more than 2,000 members. The Policy Studies Organization's membership appears to be dominated by political scientists—more than two-thirds are political scientists.[3]

The Policy Studies Organization, of course, is not the only association of scholars with an interest in public policy. The Association for Public Policy Analysis and Management, the American Institute for Decision Sciences, and the Public Choice Society are examples of others, and there are more. But most of these groups have an intellectual cast that is distinctly economic or operations research in nature.

An important component of the public policy subfield is comparative, or cross-national, public policy. The specialization began to emerge in the early 1970s, and in 1975 a book on the topic received a major award from the American Political Science Association,[4] marking the establishment of the subfield. More than a quarter of the public policy papers presented at the annual conferences of the American Political Science Association are in the comparative area.[5]

Public policy as a subfield can be viewed as bisecting along two, increasingly distinct, intellectual branches. One is the substantive branch. The dominant mode of public policy as a subfield of political science has always been and continues to be substantive issues—what Ranney called "contents," and what Herbert Simon, years earlier, called "prescribing for public policy" (recall Chapter 2). Roughly half of the papers presented at the American Political Science Association's annual conferences in any given year deal with substance, such as the environment, welfare, edu-

cation, or energy. Paramountly, the substantive branch of public policy means a paper, article, book, or course on "The Politics of" some current issue.

The other, less leafy but nonetheless supple branch of public policy, is the theoretical branch. There are, of course, many ways in which this literature may be categorized, and we use our own approach in this chapter.

The "problem" of public policy as a subfield of political science is what it symbolizes for both political science and public administration.

First, political scientists and public administrationists seem to have different definitions of what they are doing in the subfield and why. Those public policy researchers who identify primarily with political science seem to be those who, by and large, work in the subfield's substantive branch ("The Politics of" something), while those who identify with public administration seem to be found more frequently in its theoretical branch, and are more concerned with problems of research design, public choice, strategic planning, implementation, organization, program evaluation, efficiency, effectiveness, productivity, and those kinds of public policy questions that are only incidentally related to matters of substance and content. The differences in these two approaches parallel the differences that the field of public administration has with political science: Public administrationists have always preferred studying questions of public policy that relate to "knowledgeable action" as opposed to an "intellectualized understanding" of public issues.

Of these two approaches to the study of public policy, the future seems fairer for that preferred by public administrationists. While there will always be both room and need for each tack, the substantive one has a deadly deficiency in the longer haul: It is, by dint of its structure, essentially atheoretical. One cannot "build" theory on the basis of ultimately transitory public events. True, there will "always" be public policies for health, energy, environment, welfare, or whatever, but how does understanding these issues as discrete phenomena get us very far in understanding the process of public policy—its formulation, execution, and on-going revision—so that we can develop ideas that enable us to make more responsive policies in *all* policy areas and deliver policies more effectively? Individual studies of individual public issues often yield us an appreciation of the issues involved, and this is important and useful; but aside from their utility as case histories, these studies by themselves cannot really address the larger theoretical questions, the answers to which can, one hopes, be of use to public decision makers regardless of the policy arena in which they are making policies.

A more worrisome aspect of political science's preference for the substantive approach to policy studies is that its intellectual evolution will parallel the experience of comparative public administration in that it will try to do too much, and ends up, to requote Robert T. Golembiewski on the dilemma of comparative public administration, creating "a self-imposed failure experience . . . an unattainable goal."[6] Certainly this dreary prospect at least seems possible when we appreciate the number of public policies extant, all of them fairly panting to be analyzed, and the problem is especially evident in the area of comparative public policy. The literature of comparative public policy is heavily substantive,[7] but as one specialist points out, the specialty has yet to develop a "guiding theory" of its own to focus research.[8]

A second problem of public policy analysis in its political science mode is that it smacks of an effort by political scientists to fill the vacuum created by the departure of public administration—a last gasp, croaked in the general direction of "hands-on" political science and, of course, "relevance." In this fashion, political science, symbolically at least, retains public administration without admitting it. The fact that the explosive growth of the public policy subfield correlates remarkably in time (*i.e.*, the 1970s) with the secession of public administration lends some credence to this notion.

There is nothing sinister in this effort to reestablish within political science a concern with what is "applied" and "relevant" under a new guise called public policy, but if this is the motivation, then it seems unlikely to succeed. Public policy in its substantive mode may not be, as we have noted, a vehicle ready for long journeys. It is no replacement for public administration. An understanding of education policy, for example, is no substitute for an understanding of human resource management, public budgeting and finance, organization theory, intergovernmental administration, program evaluation and the several other interrelated areas that comprise the public administration field.

OUR APPROACH TO THE LITERATURE OF PUBLIC POLICY: PROCESS VERSUS OUTPUT

We review the literature of public policy that relates to public administration in this chapter because it provides a logical introduction to our section on implementation. We bisect the literature into two broad streams. The first is the attempt to analyze the *process* of public policy making and implementation; it endeavors to be descriptive rather than prescriptive in tone. In terms of models of public policy, the elite/mass, group, systems, institutionalist, neo-institutionalist, and organized anarchy models would fall crudely under the rubric of processually oriented, descriptive literature on public policy making.

The second stream attempts to analyze the *outputs* and *effects* of public policy and is more prescriptive than descriptive. A related tangent is the effort to prescribe ways to improve the content of public policy by improving the way public policy is made. Using these schemata the incremental, rational, and strategic planning models of public policymaking represent this thrust.

In reviewing briefly both the processual and the output-oriented thrusts of public policy analysis, our purpose is simply that: to review. One ought to be aware of public policy analysis as a literature. Public policy is a broad field whose principal utility is one of clarification about how the public policymaking and implementation processes work.

MODELS OF PUBLIC POLICYMAKING AND IMPLEMENTATION AS A PROCESS

Attempts to understand the process of public policy making and implementation can be categorized along six emphases: elitism, groups, systems, institutionalist, neoinstitutionalist, and organized anarchy. We consider each in turn.

The Elite/Mass Model

Of these half-dozen approaches, the emphasis represented by the elite/mass model may be among the most germane to public administrators. Increasingly, public administrators appear to be perceived less as "servants of the people" and more as "the establishment."

In cursory form, the elite/mass model contends that a policymaking/policy-executing elite is able to act in an environment characterized by apathy and information distortion and thereby governs a largely passive mass. Policy flows downward from the elite to the mass. Society is divided according to those who have power and those who do not. Elites share common values that differentiate them from the mass, and prevailing public policies reflect elite values, which may be summed up as: Preserve the status quo. Finally, elites have higher incomes, more education, and more status than the mass. Perhaps the classic expression of elite theory can be found in C. Wright Mills's *The Power Elite*.[9]

A diagrammatic version of elite theory that relates it to public administration is found in Figure 10-1.

The Group Model

A second model of public policy is the group model. In these days of questionable campaign contributions and powerful vested interests, the notion of pressure groups and lobbies also has relevance. Another way of describing the group model is the "hydraulic thesis," in which the polity is conceived of as being a system of forces and pressures acting and reacting to one another in the formulation of public policy. An exemplary work that represents the group model is Arthur F. Bentley's *The Process of Government*.[10]

Normally, the group model is associated with the legislature rather than the bureaucracy, but it also has long been recognized by scholars that the "neutral" executive branch of government is buffeted by pressure groups, too. The numerous studies by political scientists on federal regulatory agencies, for example, all point to the same conclusion: The agency ultimately is "captured" by the group that it is meant to regulate, and its administrators grow increasingly unable to distinguish between policies that are beneficial to the interests of the public and policies that are beneficial to the interests of the groups being regulated. What is good for the group is good for the nation, in the eyes of the regulators.[11] Figure 10-2 illustrates the group model.

Bureaucracies, particularly in regulatory agencies, seldom encounter the countervailing pressures illustrated in Figure 10-2. In other words, Interest Group A might be the drug manufacturers, the Policymakers might be the Food and Drug Administration, and Interest Group B might be the unorganized public. This situation might be diagrammed more accurately by Figure 10-3.

FIGURE 10-1 **The Elite/Mass Model of Public Policy Making and Implementation**

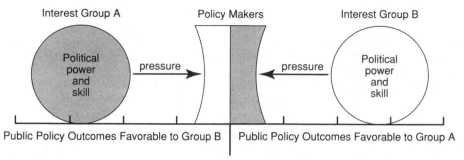

FIGURE 10-2   The Group Model of Public Policy Making and Implementation: I

The Systems Model

A third emphasis in the processual public-policy literature is the systems model. The systems model relies on concepts of information theory (*e.g.*, feedback, input, output) and conceives of the process as being essentially cyclical.

The systems model is concerned with such questions as: What are the significant variables and patterns in the public policymaking system? What constitutes the "black box" of the actual policymaking process? What are the inputs, "withinputs," outputs, and feedback of the process? A representative author of this literary stream is David Easton, particularly his *The Political System*.[12] The emphasis is diagrammed in Figure 10-4.

The Institutionalist Model

We include in the public-policymaking-as-a-process literature the traditional institutionalist model. The institutionalist model focuses on the organization chart of government; it describes the arrangements and official duties of bureaus and departments, but customarily it has ignored the linkages between them. Constitutional provisions, administrative and common law, and similar legalities are the objects of greatest interest; the behavioral connections between a department and the public policy emanating from it are of scant concern. Carl J. Friedrich's *Constitutional Government and Democracy* is a representative work.[13] Illustratively, an institutionalist model would look like the diagram in Figure 10-5.

With the onrush of the "behavioral revolution" in political science, institutional studies of the policy process were swept aside in favor of studies that relied more heavily on the group, systems, and elite/mass models, in about that order of emphasis. Yet the institutionalist model had a use, and it may experience a resurgence of favor in the future. New intergovernmental patterns and executive reorganization plans, among the other

FIGURE 10-3   The Group Model of Public Policy Making and Implementation: II

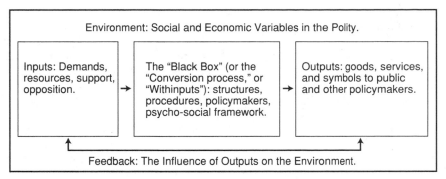

FIGURE 10-4   The Systems Model of Public Policy Making and Implementation

actual and potential rearrangements of the government bureaucracy, necessitate a renewed understanding of how the structure of government works before the public policymaking process can be analyzed fully.

The Neo-Institutionalist Model

Despite a possible reemergence of traditional institutionalist theory, however, a recent stream of public policy literature has surfaced that might best be described as neo-institutionalism, and it rests on a considerably more sophisticated analytical plane. Theodore J. Lowi, Randall B. Ripley, Grace Franklin, Robert Salisbury, John Heinz, Dean Schooler, Jr., and Michael Hayes number among its major contributors, and they attempt to categorize public policies according to policymaking subsystems.[14] For example, Lowi classifies policies by four "arenas of power": redistributive, distributive, constituent, and regulative.

In a *redistributive* arena of power, for instance, power is "redistributed" throughout the polity on a fundamental scale. Redistributive policies tend to be highly ideological and emotionally charged for particular groups, involving a fight between the "haves" and "have-nots," but having low partisan visibility. Usually these battles are centered in the bureaucracy. Lowi, in fact, considers redistributive policies to be concerned with "not use of property but property itself, not equal treatment but equal possession, not behavior but being," and believes, because of the secrecy enshrouding the redistributive policy process, that the policy process which takes place primarily in the government bureaucracy has received the least study by social scientists.[15]

Lowi's remaining policy arenas are less far-reaching in scope. A *distributive policy* is one in which benefits are made directly to individuals, but there are really no particularly visible costs associated with the policy. For example, various policies

FIGURE 10-5   The Institutionalist Model of Public Policy Making and Implementation

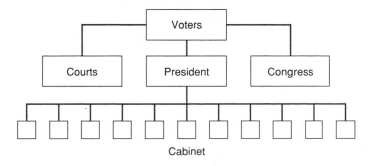

Cabinet

conducted by such agencies as the Weather Bureau and the Corps of Engineers implement distributive policies.

Regulative policies differ from distributive policies in that they are far more likely to be identified with costs to particular groups. Such agencies as the Federal Communications Commission and the Federal Aviation Administration are empowered to punish the violators of federal regulations, and their sanctions are both apparent and real.

A *constituent policy* is one that affects the people as political actors directly, such as a reapportionment statute. But constituent policies do not single out individuals for either punishments or rewards, and tend to reallocate political and economic values through the social structure itself.

Table 10-1 diagrams the neo-institutionalist approach to public policymaking. As it indicates, the neo-institutionalist approach is predicated on two dimensions: the probability of coercion and the target of coercion. The *probability of coercion*

may be remote or immediate. In the regulative policy arena, for example, the possibility of coercion is quite immediate because violators of federal regulations may be punished. Moreover, violators of federal regulations may be punished as individuals; a company violating the Sherman Antitrust Act, for example, will be punished as an individual company. Thus, we come to the *target of coercion*, which may be individual or systemic. In constituent and redistributive policy arenas, the government attempts to manipulate the conduct of the system itself through, for example, changes in the federal reserve discount rate, which can have a huge impact on the level of investments in the national economy. Yet these kinds of policies do not single out individuals as targets for coercion.

Lowi argues that from these policy arenas, which are determined by the target and probability of government coercion, emerge certain identifiable types of political behavior.[16] For example, distributive policies are more likely to

TABLE 10-1   Neo-Institutionalist Model of Public Policymaking and Implementation

		TARGET OF GOVERNMENT COERCION	
		Conduct of individual	*Conduct of system*
PROBABILITY OF GOVERNMENT COERCION	*Remote*	*Distributive* policy arena. e.g., agricultural subsidies *political behaviors and characteristics:* decentralized disaggregated local partisan/electoral logrolling legislatively centered	*Constituent* policy arena, e.g., reapportionment of legislature *political behaviors and characteristics:* centralized systemic national ideological partisan/electoral logrolling legislatively centered
	Immediate	*Regulative* policy arena, e.g., elimination of fraudulent advertising *political behaviors and characteristics:* decentralized disaggregated local special interests bargaining among groups bureaucratically centered	*Redistributive* policy arena, e.g., progressive income tax *political behaviors and characteristics:* centralized systemic national ideological special interests bargaining among groups bureaucratically centered

combine electoral and decentralizing political tendencies, while, as we have noted, redistributive policies tend to have low partisan visibility and to be highly centralized. Table 10-1 also lists some of the political behaviors associated with each policy arena.

The neo-institutionalists, in sum, are concerned chiefly with political institutions, but with an eye toward generating theoretical predictions about how policy types relate to the branches of government, to the polity generally, and to the typologies of political behaviors associated with each policy arena.

The Organized Anarchy Model

A final major model of public policymaking as a process is provided by John W. Kingdon.[17] Kingdon studied the agenda setting and policymaking process in two major fields, health and transportation, from 1976 through 1979. Over the four years, he conducted nearly 250 personal and detailed interviews. Kingdon applied to his empirical data the theoretical construct (with some slight variations) concerning "organized anarchies" developed by Michael Cohen, James March, and Johan Olsen in 1972, and which was described in Chapter 4.

Kingdon observed three "streams" that flowed largely independently of one another and which constituted the policymaking process. The first of these is the *problems stream*, which involves focusing the public's and policymakers' attention on a particular social problem, defining the problem, and either applying a new public policy to the resolution of the problem or letting the problem fade from sight. Getting attention for the problem may be accomplished by a number of processes, including the routine monitoring of social data; the occurrence of certain "focusing events," such as a powerful symbol like Proposition 13 in California which called national attention to the accelerating "tax revolt"; and the feedback from existing programs that can be obtained through such devices as congressional casework or the ongoing administration of public programs. Problems typically are defined in terms of *values*, such as conservative or liberal orientations; *comparisons*, such as the United States versus Libya; or *categories*—for example, is public transit for the disabled a "transportation" problem

or a "civil rights" problem? Categorizing the problem becomes quite significant in how the problem is resolved.

The second stream is the *political stream*. It is in the political stream that the *governmental agenda*—in other words, the list of issues or problems to be resolved—is formed. This formulation occurs as the result of the interaction of major forces, such as the "national mood," the perspective and clout of organized interests, and the dynamics of government itself, including personnel turnover, the settling of jurisdictional disputes among agencies and branches, and so forth. The primary participants in the formulation of the governmental agenda are what Kingdon calls the "visible cluster," or those participants who are most readily seen on the public stage. They include the administration, including high-level political appointees and the president's staff; members of Congress; the media; interest groups; those actors associated with elections, parties, and campaigns; and general public opinion. A consensus is achieved by bargaining among these participants, and at some point a "bandwagon" or "tilt" effect occurs that is a consequence of an intensifying desire by the participants to be "dealt in" on the policy resolution and not to be excluded.

The third stream is the *policy stream*. It is in the policy stream that the *decision agenda* or "alternative specification" is formulated. The decision agenda is the list of alternatives from which a public policy may be selected by policymakers to resolve a problem. Here the major forces are not political, but intellectual and personal. Ideas and the role of the "policy entrepreneur," or the person who holds a deep and long-abiding commitment to a particular policy change, are paramount. The major participants in the formulation of the decision agenda are what Kingdon calls the "hidden cluster." These include career public administrators; academics; researchers and consultants; congressional staffers; the Office of Management and Budget; and interest groups (interest groups, in Kingdon's analysis, are significant actors in both the visible and hidden clusters).

The policy stream moves from the formulation of a decision agenda to a "softening-up phase" in which "trial balloons" are released and a variety of suggestions are made both publicly and privately about how to resolve a particular problem. These ideas survive according to the criteria of whether they are technically feasible; whether they are acceptable to broad social values; and what future constraints—such as budgetary limitations and the prospects of political acceptance and public acquiescence—are anticipated by the actors in the policy stream. Unlike the political stream, consensus (or the "short list" of policy alternatives) is developed not by a bargaining process, but by the use of persuasion and rational argumentation among the participants in the policy stream. As in the political stream, however, a "bandwagon" or "tilt" effect occurs, and this happens when problems can be connected with alternative solutions and the solutions themselves are not perceived as being "too new" or radical.

When these three streams—problem, politics and policy—meet, a public policy can result. Kingdon calls these occasions "windows." Windows open because of a change of administration, changes in Congress, a shift in the national mood, or when a pressing public problem emerges. When the window opens that results in a restructuring of the *governmental* agenda, it could be solely the result of occurrences in either the problem stream or the political stream. But for a window to open that results in a restructuring of the *decision* agenda requires the joining of all three streams is required. In this latter case, the role of the policy entrepreneur is critical, and entrepreneurs must have legitimacy, connections, and persistence to be successful.

In many ways, Kingdon's analysis provides us with the single most satisfactory explanation of policymaking as a process. Although his analysis has limitations, it nonetheless is comprehensive, systemic, and empirical. This is a rare combination in the literature of public policy as a process, and it should not be dismissed lightly. Figure 10-6 is a simplified diagram of Kingdon's organized anarchy model of public policymaking.

MODELS OF PUBLIC POLICYMAKING AND IMPLEMENTATION AS AN OUTPUT

Our second major thrust of public policy analysis tends to stress the policy itself. In this stream, analysts appear to be more normative and prescriptive, and less "value-free" and descriptive. They are more concerned with how to improve the content of public policies themselves and how to improve the ways in which public policies are made, with the objective of forming better policies.

In the past there were only two models, incrementalism and rationalism. The former attempts to describe how the public policymaking process "really works" and what is good or bad about it; the latter explains how the process of incrementalism could or should work and offers suggestions toward this end. Thus, the incrementalist and rationalist models really are two poles of the same continuum; that is, they are both concerned with the "black box" of policymaking. More recently, "strategic planning" has emerged as an approach that occupies a place on the continuum mid-way between incrementalism and rationalism.

It is worth keeping in mind that neither the incrementalist nor the rationalist model of public policymaking is a particularly accurate description of the process of public policy formation. In his careful empirical analysis of the agenda setting and policymaking process, Kingdon found that there were "as many nonincremental as incremental changes" in the policy processes that he studied.[18] What Kingdon meant by this, however, was that some policies were changed or implemented very gradually and slowly over time, while others, after festering for years in the bowels of policymaking institutions, hit the public agenda virtually overnight and were rapidly put in place. But Kingdon's use of the term "nonincremental" does not mean that the policymaking process is rational. It merely means that the policymaking process can be quick. Hence, while public policy may not necessarily be made incrementally, neither is it necessarily made rationally.

The Incrementalist Model

In many ways, the incrementalist model of public policy already has been considered in Part Two on organization theory. "Satisficing," organizational "drift," "bounded rationality," and "limited cognition," among other terms of the literature of model synthesis in organization theory, reflect the basic idea of the incrementalist paradigm.

The various writings of Charles E. Lindblom are associated most closely with incrementalism and, in fact, it was he who is as responsible as

FIGURE 10-6 The Organized Anarchy Model of Public Policy Making and Implemenation

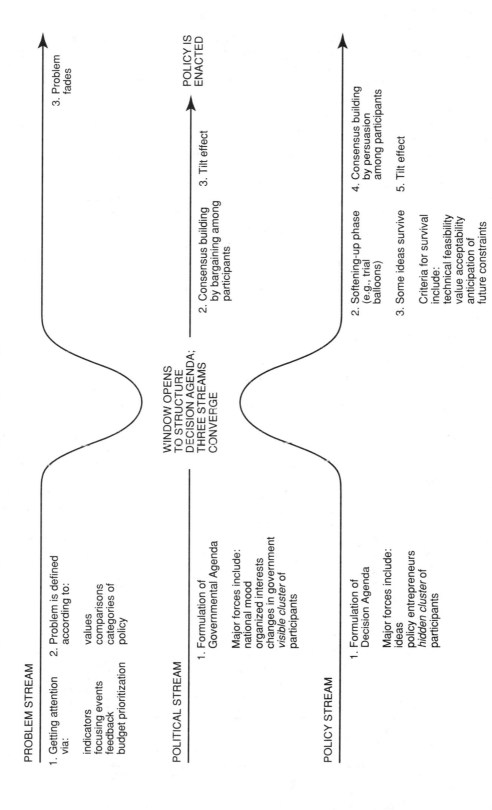

PROBLEM STREAM

1. Getting attention via:

   indicators
   focusing events
   feedback
   budget prioritization

2. Problem is defined according to:

   values
   comparisons
   categories of policy

3. Problem fades

POLITICAL STREAM

1. Formulation of Governmental Agenda

   Major forces include:
   national mood
   organized interests
   changes in government
   visible cluster of participants

2. Consensus building by bargaining among participants

3. Tilt effect

POLICY IS ENACTED

POLICY STREAM

1. Formulation of Decision Agenda

   Major forces include:
   ideas
   policy entrepreneurs
   hidden cluster of participants

2. Softening-up phase (e.g., trial balloons)

3. Some ideas survive

   Criteria for survival include:
   technical feasibility
   value acceptability
   anticipation of future constraints

4. Consensus building by persuasion among participants

5. Tilt effect

WINDOW OPENS TO STRUCTURE DECISION AGENDA; THREE STREAMS CONVERGE anyone for the notion's name, *disjointed incrementalism*, as a description of the policymaking process.[19] *Disjointed*, in this context, means that analysis and evaluation of conditions and alternative responses to perceived conditions occur throughout society, while *incrementalism* means that only a limited selection of policy alternatives are provided to policymakers, and that each one of these alternatives represents only an infinitesimal change in the status quo.

Before Lindblom made the incrementalist idea more academically legitimate (and pompous) by dubbing it "disjointed incrementalism," he called the concept "muddling through."[20] Muddling through, as a term, not only is a more colorful description of the policymaking process, but is also clearer and self-explanatory.

Basically, the incrementalist model posits a conservative tendency in administrative decision making; new public policies are seen as being variations on the past. The public policymaker is perceived as a person who does not have the brains, time, and money to fashion truly different policies; he or she accepts the policies of the past as satisficing and legitimate. There are also certain "sunk costs" in existing policies that probably would be impossible to retrieve if a radically new course were taken, and this discourages innovative action from the standpoint of political economy. And because social goals are devilishly difficult to operationalize, an incremental approach is certainly an easier row to hoe than a rational, systemic approach would be. Finally, incrementalist policies are nearly always more politically expedient than are rationalist policies that necessitate fundamental redistributions of social values. As one scholar of political feasibility put it, "what is most feasible is incremen-

tal."[21] In short, there are reasons (*rational* reasons, given the nature of the political system) for the prevalence of the incrementalist model. An illustration of the incrementalist model is shown in Figure 10-7.

The Rationalist Model

Rationalism attempts to be the opposite of incrementalism. As an intellectual endeavor, rationalism tries to learn *all* the value preferences extant in a society, assign each value a relative weight, discover all the policy alternatives available, know all the consequences of each alternative, calculate how the selection of any one policy will affect the remaining alternatives in terms of opportunity costs, and ultimately select that policy alternative that is the most efficient in terms of the costs and benefits of social values. Whether or not these goals can be realized, the point is that the rational model works toward their achievement, and toward the reduction of incrementalism.

Much of the rationalist model deals with the construction of public policies that assure better public policies. Yehezkel Dror (as good a representative as any of the rationalist modelists) calls this concern "metapolicy," that is, policy for policymaking procedures.[22] In this emphasis the rationalist model dwells on the optimal organization of the government structure that will assure undistorted information flow, the accuracy of feedback data, and the proper weighing of social variables.

Diagrammed, the rationalist model renders public policy formation into a linear flow chart, reminiscent of Operations Research, path analysis, and the related computer programming tech-

FIGURE 10-7 The Incrementalist Model of Public Policymaking and Implementation

Incremental variations on an agency's policies.

1988 1989 1990 1991 1992 1993 1994 1995

PUBLIC ADMINISTRATION AND THE POLICY PROCESS

The following passage attempts to "place" the role of the public bureaucracy in the policymaking process. As it indicates, to so "place" the bureaucracy may necessitate a basic reconsideration of traditional democratic theory.

It is remarkable how unappreciated the significance of the bureaucracy is among America's political thinkers. It is evident from reading *The Federalist* that the country's most original contributors to the world's political literature did not anticipate the rise of the public bureaucracy, much less its institutional dominance in the public policymaking process, nor the fact that by the middle of the 20th century there would be more Americans earning their livelihoods by working for it than there were Americans living when the Constitution was written. Less understandably, our current generation of political thinkers . . . also have failed to appreciate the importance of the public bureaucracy, despite its awesome magnitude, its growing administrative reliance on the techniques of social science, and its financial support of their own academic research. . . .

Is there a reason behind the disregard for and disinterest in the public bureaucracy that is exhibited by the bulk of modern political thinkers? One can conjure several possibilities, including that of rampant stupidity, but . . . I shall offer only one hypothesis. It is: The bureaucracy, as a public policymaking institution in a technological society, is antithetical to the pluralist paradigm of the democratic process originally conceived by James Madison and perpetrated by most of his intellectual progeny. . . . More pointedly, the Madisonian notion that the interests of the public will be best served in a democracy by the policy of compromise emerging from the contentions of interest groups (which "represent" those "publics" affected by the policy resolution) is of dubious validity in a techno-bureaucratic state. In brief, two overwhelming factors of modern culture—technology and bureaucracy—undermine what one political scientist has described as the "hydraulic theory" of the democratic process. The hydraulic thesis constitutes the basis of the pluralist paradigm shared by mainstream political scientists, and it is apparent, given the short shrift accorded the public bureaucracy, public administration, and technology assessment by political scientists as objects of study, that few scholars interested in politics are capable of denying interest-group pluralism as an apologia for how the public interest is achieved in a democracy.

Perhaps the hydraulic thesis still "works" (*i.e.*, interest group compromises are indeed in the public interest) in legislative and adjudicative policy settings, and perhaps its "provability" in these settings accounts for why political scientists much prefer studying voting behavior, legislative committees, lobbyists, and the judicial process in contrast to "bureaucratic politics." But in order to "work," the hydraulic thesis by necessity rests on at least three implicit assumptions concerning the political processes: that (1) all publics affected by a particular policy question are aware that its resolution will affect them, (2) all affected publics have a reasonable understanding of the policy question, and (3) if the affected publics are unaware of the policy question, it is only a matter of time before they find out about it and join in the policymaking fray in order to protect their interest.

These assumptions, combined with some strictly enforced rules of the game, such as freedom of the press, provided a rational foundation on which the hydraulic thesis could be constructed as an explanation of the policymaking process in a democracy—at least in the 18th century. Yet, in the 20th century, the interlaced forces of bureaucracy and technology deny these assumptions. For its part, bureaucracy denies assumptions #1 and #3. The well-documented penchant of bureaucrats for secrecy, and the mounting evidence that neither bureaucrats nor the citizenry always act on their "most rational" self-interest undercut the premises that people *know*, that people are *informed*, of what matters, and that they will act on what matters.

Technology denies assumption #2. Technology, or what is perceived by the people as being science "applied" for the rectification of their problems, is not simple. Technology is complicated, and it becomes more complicated when, as public bureaucrats are wont to do, technology is cast into the context of systems analysis in an effort to inhibit the proliferation of its socially dysfunctional side effects. Technology and its social assessment, by their very complexity, deny understanding to the people of what their problems are. Such concepts as "technocracy," "professionalism," "politics of expertise," "technipol," "systems politics," "noetic authority," and "participatory technology" represent intellectual efforts to address the enormous political problems of bureaucracy and technology not considered in the Madisonian pluralist paradigm—nor, for that matter, in the Constitution that Madison largely wrote. Yet, if democratic political processes are to be retained under the Constitution, bureaucracy and technology must be integrated into its framework, for the twin factors may be, in their essence, antithetical to democratic values.

Nicholas Henry, "Bureaucracy, Technology, and Knowledge Management,"
Public Administration Review, *35 (November/December 1975), pp. 572-573*

niques of the systems approach and information theory, as Figure 10-8 demonstrates. While Figure 10-8 may remind one of the systems model (Figure 10-4), the rationalist model actually deals only with the "black box" of the systems model. (So, for that matter, does Figure 10-7, the incrementalist model.) That is, the rationalist model articulates how public policy should be formed within government, or how the elements of the conversion process that change environmental inputs into environmental outputs should be arranged optimally. This is what makes the rationalist model so useful to public administration because, in one sense at least, making policy better is what the field ultimately tries to do.

Public Choice and Political Economy. A significant variation of the rationalist model is the literature dealing with public choice and political economy. The public choice literature has been of growing importance to public administration since at least 1963, when a small collection of scholars met to discuss, in their words, "developments in the 'no-name' field of public administration."[23] Since then, public choice and political economy are the terms most frequently used in describing this literature.

Public choice offers a variety of intellectual directions. Besides its overarching emphasis on the rationalist model as a policymaking tool, public choice is concerned with the nature of public goods and services (Otto Eckstein, Robert L. Bish, L. L. Wade, and R. L. Curry, Jr.[24] would be representative of this literary emphasis), the relationships between formal decision making structures and human propensities for individual action (*e.g.*, Gordon Tullock, Anthony Downs[25]) and for collective action (*e.g.*, Mancur Olson[26]), the requisites of constitutional government and corresponding patterns of collective action (*e.g.*, James M. Buchanan and Gordon Tullock[27]), and the interstices between producers, performance, consumer interests, and the provision of public goods and services (*e.g.*, Garrett Hardin, Joseph J. Seneca[28]).

Using the concepts of political economy, we can assess public policy in new ways. Consider, for example, the problems of air pollution, the energy crisis, the role of the automobile, which accounts for roughly 60 percent of the air pollutants in the United States, and almost 40 percent

of its fuel consumption. Rather than passing a flatly stated law that says little more than "Thou shalt not pollute nor use too much gas," a political economist would likely turn instead to the tax structure. He or she would reason that if a particular citizen chose to buy a Cadillac rather than a Honda, the general citizenry should not have to bear the common costs of that citizen's choice (*i.e.*, the extra pollutants emitted and fuel consumed by the Cadillac), but neither should all the other citizens be denied the Cadillacs if they really want them. Thus, a special tax should be established that taxes cars according to the pollutants they emit and the energy resources they consume; the more pollutants and gas, the higher the tax. In this method, the individual citizen still can buy a Cadillac, but the costs of the purchase to the general citizenry will be offset by the special tax that the owner is forced to pay by using that tax for pollution abatement and energy research programs. Such is the nature of assessment in the public choice literature.

On a more sophisticated plane, public choice is concerned with "Pareto optimality," a concept originally developed by the economist Vilfredo Pareto. Or, more exactly (and because optimality is supremely difficult to achieve in any context), public choice concerns "Pareto improvements," and the notions of trade-offs and externalities. A *Pareto improvement* is "a change in economic organization that makes everyone better off—or, more precisely, that makes one or more members of society better off without making anyone worse off."[29]

Pareto optimality may be illustrated with reference to public choice in graphic form. Figure 10-9 posits a hypothetical social value ("X") relative to the accomplishment of all other social values. The *indifference curve* refers to the combination of values about which society is indifferent (at least up to a point); the *value achievement curve* indicates the optimal combination of values that it is possible for government to encourage given limited resources. The point of optimal achievement of Value X and optimal achievement of all other social values constitutes the point of Pareto optimality. The closer that society gets to the point of Pareto optimality is considered a Pareto improvement.

Figure 10-9 also illustrates what the public choice writers mean by "trade-offs." A *trade-off*

FIGURE 10-8   The Rationalist Model of Public Policy Making and Implementation

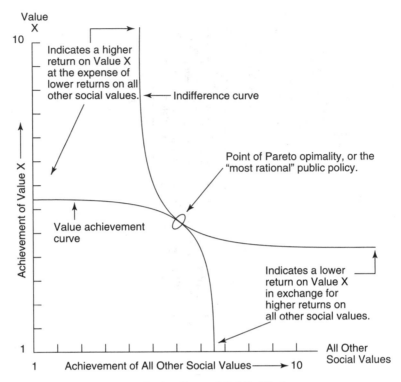

Value
X

10

Indicates a higher
return on Value X
at the expense of
lower returns on all
other social values. ←——— Indifference curve

Achievement of Value X ——→

Point of Pareto opimality, or the
"most rational" public policy.

Value achievement
curve

Indicates a lower
return on Value X
in exchange for
higher returns on
all other social values.

1

1   Achievement of All Other Social Values ——→ 10

All Other
Social Values

FIGURE 10-9   Pareto Optimality and Public Choice

refers to what value is being traded (and the social costs and benefits incurred in such a trade) for what other value. In other words, every time Value X is achieved more fully, all other values are correspondingly reduced in achievement; the benefits gained by increasing resource input into Value X must decrease resource input into all other values.

A related term common to the public choice literature is "externality," or "spillover effect." When a public policy in one sphere of social action affects other spheres of social action, the manner in which the other sphere is affected is called an *externality*; that is, the effects of a public policy in one sphere "spill over" into other spheres. Externalities may be positive or negative, intended or unintended. For example, a positive, intended spillover effect of reducing corporate taxes might be to raise employment levels. A negative, unintended externality of the same public policy might be to reduce the financial

resources available to the government for welfare programs.

Public and Private Goods and Services. Vincent Ostrom, Elinor Ostrom, and E. S. Savas, among others, have contributed yet another important variation of the rationalist model that stems largely from the public choice school.[30] This school of public choice theory deals with what kinds of goods and services should be delivered by government, and what kinds should be delivered by the private sector. To make this distinction, two concepts are employed: exclusion and consumption.

Exclusion refers to the degree of control that both the buyer and seller have over a particular commodity; in other words, how easy is it to exclude users or owners from using or owning a particular good or service? Most goods are like a bag of groceries; for a buyer to walk out of a supermarket with a bag of groceries requires that both the buyer and seller agree to a price. In this case (which is the most common one in the real world), the seller exercises a high level of exclusionary control.

But other goods and services are not so easily controlled. For example, a lighthouse has a very low level of exclusivity. All ships within sight of the lighthouse can benefit from its service. Exclusion, in short, is a matter of economics rather than choice. Some goods and services can be excluded from the marketplace more readily than others.

The second major point used by public choice theorists in this stream of literature is that of *consumption*. Some goods and services may be consumed, or used, *jointly* (that is, simultaneously) by many consumers without being diminished in either quality or quantity, while other goods and services are available only for *individual* rather than joint consumption. An example of joint consumption would be a television broadcast. All viewers may "consume" a television program "jointly" without the program being diminished in either quality or quantity. A fish and a haircut provide examples of individual consumption of a good and a service. Once they are consumed by an individual, no one else has access to them.

Using the notions of exclusion and consumption, we can begin to classify goods and services according to certain kinds of "pure forms." Savas lists these as being private goods, toll goods, common-pool goods, and collective goods.[31]

Private goods and services are pure, individually consumed goods and services for which exclusion is completely feasible. There is no problem of supply. The marketplace provides private goods readily, and this supply is based on consumer demand. Government's role in the supply of private goods and services is largely limited to assuring their safety (such as in building inspections), honest representation (such as weights and measures), and so forth.

Toll goods and services are pure, jointly consumed goods and services for which exclusion is completely feasible. As with private goods, toll goods can be supplied easily by the marketplace, and excluding consumers from using them is entirely practicable. But unlike private goods, consumption of toll goods is joint rather than individual. This is because many toll goods are natural monopolies, which means that as the number of users increases, the cost per user decreases. Examples include cable television, electric power, and water supplies. In the case of toll goods, government action may be required to assure that monopolies are created and granted in the first place and then regulated so that proprietors do not exploit their monopolistic privileges unfairly.

Common-pool goods and services are pure, individually consumed goods and services for which exclusion is not feasible. In the case of common-pool goods we do have supply problems, and this differentiates common-pool goods from both private goods and toll goods. There is neither a requirement to pay for common-pool goods nor any means to prevent their consumption; they are, in the short term, "free."

Common-pool goods bring us to the problem of what Garrett Hardin called the "tragedy of the commons"—that which belongs to everyone belongs to no one, and the problem of common-pool goods is that they can be easily squandered to the point of exhaustion. An example would be the clean air supply. Until government imposed regulations on the emission of air pollutants, the air was a "free good," at least from the perspective of the industrialist who could use it as a vast dumping bin for pollutants. The air was, in this sense, a "commons." Government has a much larger role in the administration of common-pool goods than it does in private and toll goods because it makes sense for government to regulate common-pool goods so that they are not destroyed by over-consumption.

Finally, there are *collective* or *public goods and services*, which are pure, jointly consumed goods and services for which exclusion is not feasible. The marketplace cannot supply these goods because they are used simultaneously by many people, and no one can be excluded from consuming them. Individuals have an economic incentive to exploit collective goods without paying for them, and to thus become what public choice theorists call "free riders." National defense, broadcast television, and police protection provide examples of collective goods.

Collective goods differ from common-pool goods on the basis of consumption. Common-pool goods are individually consumed (and, because of this, may be completely consumed), while collective goods are jointly consumed with-

TABLE 10-2   Goods and Services According to the Criteria of Exclusion and Consumption

		Consumption/Use	
		Individual Use	*Joint Use*
Exclusion	*Feasible*	*Private Goods and Services* (a bag of groceries, a haircut, a meal in a restaurant)	*Toll Goods and Services* (cable television, telephone service, theaters, libraries, electric power)
	Unfeasible	*Common-Pool Goods and Services* (water in a public well, fish in the ocean, air to breathe)	*Collective or Public Goods and Services* (peace and security, public safety, pollution control, weather forecasts, public television, and radio)

out diminishing the quality or quantity of the goods and services themselves.

It is in the area of collective goods that government has the greatest responsibility for management regulation. When we realize that such basic services as police protection is considered a collective good in this construct, the importance of government intervention in the marketplace seems obvious.

Table 10-2 provides examples of goods and services along the four typologies that we have discussed.

Savas argues that private goods "have been undergoing reclassification as common-pool goods, and toll goods have been subsidized or provided free so that they resemble collective goods," and provides as evidence of his argument dramatic increases in federal expenditures for such public policy areas as health, education, income maintenance, and housing, all of which were predominantly private goods and toll goods until the government, in effect, reclassified them by entering the marketplace. He urges that we reconsider the role of government in providing private and toll goods and services, and offers a variety of alternative institutional arrangements for the delivery of these goods and services. These include direct government service, intergovernmental agreements, contracts with the private sector, franchises (or the awarding of a monopoly to a private firm to supply a particular service, and which usually entails the firm's regulation by a government agency), grants (or a subsidy given directly by the government to a producer, and which can include tax subsidies),

vouchers (which, unlike grants, do not subsidize a producer, but instead subsidize the consumer and permit consumers to exercise a relatively free choice in the marketplace—food stamps are an example of the voucher system), marketplace mechanisms, voluntary service, and self-service. (The final three arrangements are self-explanatory and do not involve the public sector.)

Table 10-3 lists these alternative arrangements for the delivery of goods and services and categorizes them by the most appropriate and efficient means for their delivery. As one can see, this construct (which has a certain theoretical elegance) would work to the reduction of government's role in the provision of a variety of goods and services that government presently provides. Beyond this aspect, however, understanding how means of delivery might match most logically with type of service could result in more sophisticated and effective delivery systems for public services.[32]

Technology Assessment.   A final variant of the rationalist model, like public goods and services, also relies on concepts developed in the public choice school, notably the idea of externalities. Technology assessment is an effort to evaluate new technologies in light of their spillover effects throughout society. Thus, public policies for new technologies become the objects of analysis. A variant of technology assessment is technological forecasting, which is the attempt to predict what effects very new technologies might have on society. For instance, medicine may be viewed as a technology that, in its success in

TABLE 10-3   Types of Goods and Services and Institutional Arrangements for Their Delivery

Arrangement	Private Goods	Toll Goods	Collective Goods	Common-Pool Goods
Government service		x	x	x
Intergovern-mental agreement		x	x	x
Contract		x	x	x
Franchise		x		
Grant	x	x		x
Voucher	x	x		x
Market	x	x		
Voluntary		x	x	x
Self-Service	x			

Source: E. S. Savas, *Privatizing the Public Sector: How to Shrink Government* (Chatham, N.J.: Chatham House, 1982), p. 77.

extending life, has been more responsible than any other factor for the population explosion.

Consider another example, one perhaps more modest but also more germane to most readers: the copying machine. Photocopiers have lived up to all the original hopes that were held for them. As an information technology, photocopiers have facilitated research, record keeping, and decision making. They have probably reduced the inclination of patrons to vandalize volumes in libraries. They have eased the process of education throughout society and have made life far more convenient for innumerable people who handle paper as part of their jobs. They may even have contributed to more responsive policymaking in public organizations because they speed the information flow in the bureaucracy. They have made some people a lot of money. But the photocopier also has brought with it certain unintended externalities. Roughly 30 billion photocopies are made every year in the United States, and empirical research indicates that approximately 60 percent of these copies may be of materials protected by copyright.

Some questions inevitably come to the fore: If photocopies were unavailable, would sales of copyrighted books and periodicals rise? Is popular use of photocopying technologies cutting into the royalty payments of authors and publishers? And if so, are royalties being reduced to a point sufficient to undermine the financial incentive of authors to write and of publishers to risk capital to publish? Ultimately, have these machines contributed to a less creative society? Or will they? Is the incentive to develop new ideas in science, social science, and literature decreased by the emerging photocopier/copyright relationship, or is there more incentive because of the added convenience provided by photocopiers in transmitting new ideas? Although there are many opinions, many of them heated, among authors, publishers, librarians, and educators, the impact of the technology of photocopying on society has yet to be adequately assessed.[33]

Presumably, a more rigorous system of technology assessment and technological forecasting by the government could aid in achieving a more rationally planned society. As a significant step in this direction, Congress passed a bill in 1973 establishing an Office of Technology Assessment with a mission of advising Congress on matters of technology assessment. The Office is seen by some observers as representing a congressional effort to offset the almost total monopoly of scientific and technical information held by the executive branch.

Regardless of how the Office of Technology Assessment performs, the function of technology assessment remains a new and important aspect of public policy analysis generally and of the rationalist model particularly. Many agencies of government can use it in evaluating their programs. So *technology assessment* actually has a rather broad meaning: "A systematic planning and forecasting process that delineates options and costs, encompassing economics as well as environmental and social considerations that are both external and internal to the program and/or product in question, with special focus on technology-related 'bad' as well as 'good' effects."[34]

With this definition in mind, look at Figure 10-10, which illustrates the elements of technology assessment.

THE DEFICIENCIES OF INCREMENTALISM AND RATIONALISM

Both incrementalism and rationalism are attempts to improve the outputs of public policies, to make the contents of public policy "better." But in their efforts to do this, neither the incrementalists nor the rationalists have been particularly willing to work together.

Criticisms of the Rationalist Model

Incrementalists have criticized the rationalists on a variety of grounds. For example, they point to the fact that there is often a wide gap between planning and implementation, and it is undeniable that many plans have been written only to collect dust on many shelves, even though these plans had cost considerable sums of time and money to develop.[35]

Another problem is that rationalists often ignore the role of the entrepreneur. To be implemented and to work, a plan must be more than computer runs and printouts; a plan requires people and leadership to make ideas happen. Technical competence is not the same as leadership. Kingdon, for example, has shown how critical the "policy entrepreneur" is in both developing and implementing public policies in the federal government.[36]

A third criticism is that the rationalists are far too mechanical in their approach to what is in reality a complex form of life—the administrative organization. Organizations are less like machines and more like organisms, the criticism continues, and this fact has not been recognized by the rationalists. As a consequence, the rationalists typically ignore the "human factor," and this diminishes the utility of the plans that they develop. As

FIGURE 10-10   Technology Assessment in Public Administration one critic has noted, "This is an era of ecology...we can no longer profitably discuss our world and its future in simple linear terms . . . for the evidence all around us is of multi-dimensional, complex actions."[37]

A fourth criticism of the rationalists' approach is that the predictions it makes often are wrong, or it fails to make predictions when there appears to be ample evidence warranting certain predictions. The rationalists have a less than terrific record as forecasters of future events.[38]

Finally, it has been alleged that the effort to "gin up" large-scale comprehensive planning programs ends up spending more than the plans ultimately save their investors or the taxpayers. "In most states, it is very probable that the new costs of data manipulation have been met largely by reducing the support of the activities which are measured."[39] Planning in the comprehensive, rationalist mode, in short, costs more than it saves. (Or so say its critics; practicing public administrators, as we see later in this discussion, would appear to disagree with this criticism.)

Criticism of the Incrementalist Model

These are not untoward criticisms of the rationalists' approach. However, the incrementalists also have their critics. "Muddling through" has been described as "a form of tiptoeing naked and buttocks-first into history;"[40] examples of such mindless incrementalism include the American experience in Vietnam, which was entered into by increments.

A major criticism of the incrementalist model is that it is based on a bargaining concept. Unfortunately, bargaining tends to be far more successful in making policy when resources are relatively unlimited and there is something extra to divide up among the participants. In times of scarcity, however, other methods (usually rational methods) must be found to make hard choices.

A second criticism of incrementalism is what has been called "the beagle fallacy," or the fact that beagles have a superb sense of smell but very limited eyesight and often will miss a rabbit that is directly in front of them but downwind.[41] Incrementalists tend to downplay the use of models, including computer models, that provide clear information and delineate alternatives.

Models, when well done, can provide precise knowledge about interrelationships and in a way that no other approach can do. Incrementalism often results in the obscuring of interrelationships because, as a bargaining concept, the real objectives of participants often are deliberately hidden by the participants themselves. In this criticism, incrementalists are viewed as skilled players in a poker game, but none of them has been told that the objective of the other players is to win money.

A third criticism of incrementalism is that the incrementalists are singularly deficient in imagination. They have no vision and dislike imagining alternative solutions. Only what is, is real to the incrementalists. As one critic has put it, "Like beautifully muscled illiterates, incrementalists . . . have overdeveloped powers of political calculation and underdeveloped powers of social imagination."[42] Related to this charge is the concern that incrementalists are so wrapped up in political gamesmanship, they actually become anti-intellectual in their approach to the solution of social problems.

Finally, incrementalism is an inherently conservative approach. Drastic and far-reaching changes are eschewed in favor of minor adjustments. As change becomes more rapid and more endemic in America's technobureaucracy, the innate conservatism of incrementalism becomes less responsive and more counterproductive.

These are the main criticisms that the incrementalists and the rationalists allege about each other. But criticisms, no matter how accurate, are not always constructive. As Amitai Etzioni put it, "What is needed . . . is a strategy that is less exacting than the rationalistic one, but not as constricting in its perspective as the incrementalist approach; not as utopian as rationalism, but not as conservative as incrementalism; not so unrealistic a model that it cannot be followed, but not one that legitimizes myopic self-oriented, noninnovative decision making."[43]

THE STRATEGIC PLANNING MODEL

This "third approach" suggested by Etzioni has since acquired the title of "strategic planning," or, less frequently, "strategic decision making" or "strategic management,"and it is an eminently useful concept in that it attempts to combine the strongest features of incrementalism and rationalism, yet avoid their pitfalls. Strategic planning emerged largely in the world of business, and its birthplace is not too surprising when we realize that corporations have grown more competitive, more oriented toward long-term growth, politically regulated, and increasingly aware of the psycho-emotional needs of their employees. Yet they must also cope with fiscal reality, deficits, ecologists, religious groups, and other environmental pressures that force corporations into a bargaining mode. Hence, strategic planning recognizes that "organizations have *both* localized, short-term, and bottom-line demands and all-organization, long-term, and investment-strategies-for-the-future demands. They must live with the familiar today, yet also must be forever looking out for how to live in a very different tomorrow."[44]

Strategic planning is an attempt to recognize this reality. Alfred Chandler, Jr., first called attention to the practical emergence of strategic planning in major American corporations in 1962.[45] Since that time, however, strategic planning has made an impact on public agencies, and there is, according to some scholars, "ample evidence of the practical importance of the strategic management function in public organizations," despite the unique problems of "external factors" in government with which strategic planners in the public sector must deal.[46]

Strategic planning is neither the personal vision of the chief executive officer nor a collection of unrelated plans drawn up by department heads. Strategic planning is done by the top line officers of the organization, from the chief executive officer through the upper levels of middle management. It is not done by planners. As one planning official wrote, "First we ask: who is leading the planning? If it is a planner . . . we are in trouble."[47]

The strategic plan does not substitute numbers for important intangibles, such as human emotions, but it does use computers and quantification to illuminate choices. It attempts to go beyond a simple surrender by the organization to environmental conditions, and in this sense it is by no means a way of eliminating risks. What a strategic plan does is place line decision makers in an active rather than in a passive position about the future of their organization. It incorporates an outward-looking, proactive focus that is sensitive to environmental changes, but does not assume that the organization is necessarily a victim of changes in its task environment. "The aim of strategic planning is to place the unit in a distinctive position relative to its environment."[48]

Strategic planning concentrates on decisions rather than on extensive documentation, analyses, and forecasts. In this sense, it attempts to free itself of the constraints alleged by critics of the rationalist model to the effect that rationalist approaches cost more than they save, and have no particular bearing on decision making in an organization. Because it is decision-oriented, strategic planning blends economic and rational analyses, political values, and the psychology of the participants in the organization. To do this requires that strategic planning be highly participatory and tolerant of controversy. One city, which has received awards for its strategic planning efforts, is notable for its aggressiveness in involving its citizens in the planning process.[49] This participatory aspect of strategic planning leads strategic planners to concentrate on the fate of the whole organization above all other concerns; the fate of subunits in the organization are clearly secondary to this overriding value.

In these ways, strategic planning is an attempt to reconcile the rationalist and incrementalist approaches to the problem of public policy formulation. Figure 10-11 represents an attempt to synthesize the main features of strategic planning.

STRATEGIC PLANNING: THE PUBLIC EXPERIENCE

Strategic planning is making real inroads among governments. Three-fourths of American cities with a council-manager form of government reported in 1990 that they were in the beginning stages or had reached advanced levels in "strategic decision making," and over two-thirds considered the technique to be "very valuable" (28 percent said it was "somewhat valuable").[50] These are significant hikes from only three years earlier, when 60 percent of all cities (regardless of governmental form) surveyed were using strategic planning (at least in some departments), and only 38 percent found it to be "very effective."[51]

The states also are using strategic planning,

FIGURE 10-11   The Strategic-Planning Model of Public Policy Making and Implementation

although how extensively is unknown; one survey of all of New York State's agencies, however, found that over four-fifths of the respondents were engaged in strategic planning.[52] Congressional passage of the Government Performance and Results Act of 1993 presages the possibility of government-wide strategic planning at the federal level in the next century.

Although strategic planning has been described as "a hearty, public-sector perennial,"[53] there is relatively little empirical research about how strategic planning is used in the public sector.[54] Nevertheless, it is clear that strategic planning in its public mode is of more limited use in the public sector than it is in the private one. The "pervasive vagueness" of agency missions; environmental constraints in the form of interest groups, media, and other forces that render "bold moves" by public sector executives "almost completely impossible"; the uniquely omnipresent need to be sensitive to how a policy will be perceived, not just what it will do; arbitrary time constraints, such as budget and election cycles, that can rush or delay strategic decisions in ways that they no longer are strategic; and coalitions which are usually prone to disintegrate prior to the complete implementation of a strategic plan—all these and more limit the use of strategic planning in the public sector.[55]

Some observers have gone so far as to suggest that public administrators are so boxed in by their task environments that it is legitimate to define public strategic planning in some agencies as a bunker mentality, which is, essentially, little more than an implicit agreement among public administrators to "hunker down" and protect their organization against external threats,[56] or, at best, a way of competing with other public organizations for resources.[57]

But if one is to define *strategic planning* as it is generally understood, that is, "a disciplined effort to produce fundamental decisions and actions that define what an organization . . . is, what it does, and why it does it," then, "whatever the merits of strategic planning in the abstract, normal expectations have to be that most efforts to produce fundamental decisions and actions in government through strategic planning will not succeed."[58] Of course, such a statement must be placed in context; any process that is meant to force basic change in any organization, whether public or private, is unlikely to succeed more frequently than it fails.

Nevertheless, the use of strategic planning in the public sector potentially can produce beneficial results on a routine basis, as well as wreak fundamental organizational change on an intermittent one. At the very least, public strategic planning articulates implicit organizational objectives and issues, ranks them by priority, and communicates these objectives and issues to members of the organization. At root, public strategic planning is a method of making the decision premises (which we discussed in Chapter 4) of public administrators more uniform, and, because of this, strategic planning enhances the likelihood of improved organizational coordination and effectiveness. This is wholly good, but there is a lurking peril in that, by openly identifying and legitimizing specific organizational goals, morale can suffer if the public organization fails to attain those goals—typically because of declining budgets. As we discussed in Part Two, the uniqueness of the public organization is its vulnerability to its task environment, and this vulnerability wars against the unilateral utility and use of strategic planning. In the context of the public sector, strategic planning tends to over-promise (or, at least, raise expectations), and, if promises are unkept, disappointment and malaise can seep through the organization.

As a consequence of this peril of public strategic planning, public administrators may not only approach it cautiously, but, should they opt to take the plunge and attempt to channel the energies of their agency into developing a strategic plan, they may also appear to confront more obstacles than their counterparts in the private sector. An analysis of six local governments and two units of a county government in Minnesota found that a government or public agency is the most likely to succeed in initiating and completing a strategic plan if it has a "powerful process sponsor" (*i.e.*, one or [typically] more major figures who endorse the idea of strategic planning, even if tepidly), a strong "process champion" (a skilled administrator who knows what he or she is doing and believes in strategic planning); an agency-wide expectation of disruptions and delays; a willingness to be flexible about what, precisely, a strategic plan really is; an ability of administrators to derive satisfaction and a sense of progress at particular points in time during the plan's initiation; and a capacity to build and use different arguments in evaluating the plan.[59]

Initiating strategic planning seems to require considerable administrative effort in any context, but particularly so in public organizations. Moreover, its form in the public sector differs from its form in the private one. In the Minnesota research, it was concluded that, "governmental strategic planning probably should be judged by different standards than private-sector, corporate strategic planning"; none of the governments and agencies "was able to follow the linear, sequential planning models of the business policy textbooks, and none was able to prepare a public-sector equivalent of the slick corporate strategic plan."[60]

While messy, however, public strategic planning is not necessarily ineffective. If a public organization can complete a strategic plan, then it has been able to identify issues, prioritize them, and formulate ways of—that is strategies for—dealing with them. But just how effective public strategic plans are—that is, do they measurably facilitate public administrators in achieving their goals and resolving issues?—is not clear; one review of the literature concluded that "no careful study of the effectiveness of governmental strategic planning has been done", although it is known that those public administrators who develop and complete strategic plans believe that their efforts are worthwhile.[61] One survey found that urban officials gave high marks to strategic planning in terms of enabling their governments to solve major organizational problems, improving performance, dealing with change, maintaining control, establishing priorities, and similar benefits.[62]

Perhaps the assessment of the successful effort by the U. S. Food and Drug Administration (FDA) to develop "an orderly, analytical vision of the future" (which comes awfully close to being a strategic plan) phrases the utility of public strategic planning best: "The bad news" is that the FDA's initiative produced "only modest increases in rationality under particular circumstances, [but] the good news is that increases of any size are so rare that any success is newsworthy"; the bad news is that the effort "is likely to be resource intensive and fraught with hazards. . . . The good news is that the results of the process are likely to have valuable anticipated and unanticipated uses."[63]

Strategic planning is a means of implementing public policy, and, as such, is one of the "approaches to public policy and its implementation" that we have reviewed in this chapter. Implementation is the subject of this final section of this book, and concerns the question of how things get done, or, more specifically, how policies are delivered to the public. Aside from the techniques of public management themselves, which we explained in Part Three, public policies are implemented through grants and contracts with other governments, organizations, and private firms. We consider these methods in the next two chapters.

NOTES

1. Austin Ranney, "The Study of Policy Content: A Framework for Choice," *Political Science and Public Policy*, Austin Ranney, ed. (Chicago: Markham, 1968), p. 3. Emphases are original.

2. Austin Ranney, "Preface," in *ibid.*, p. vii.

3. Susan B. Hansen, "Public Policy Analysis: Some Recent Developments and Current Problems," *Political Science: The State of the Discipline*, Ada W. Finifter, ed. (Washington, D.C.: American Political Science Association, 1983), p. 239. In 1979, 68 percent of the members of the Policy Studies Organization were political scientists, although this figure may include academics who identify with public administration as well.

4. The book was Arnold J. Heidenheimer, Hugh Heclo, and Carolyn Teich Adams, *Comparative Public Policy: The Politics of Social Choice in Europe and America* (New York: St. Martin's, 1975).

5. Hansen, "Public Policy Analysis," p. 219. In 1982, 27 percent of the public policy papers took a comparative approach.

6. Robert T. Golembiewski, *Public Administration as a Developing Discipline, Part I: Perspectives on Past and Present* (New York: Marcel Dekker, 1977), p. 147.

7. Bibliographies dramatizing this point include: B. Guy Peters, "Comparative Public Policy (A Bibliography)," *Policy Studies Review*, 1 (August 1981), pp. 183-197; and Douglas E. Ashford, Peter J. Katzenstein, and T. J. Pempel, eds. *Comparative Public Policy: A Cross-National Bibliography* (Beverly Hills, Calif.: Sage, 1978).

8. Elliot J. Feldman, "Comparative Public Policy: Field or Method?" *Comparative Politics*, 10 (1978), pp. 287-305.

9. C. Wright Mills, *The Power Elite* (New York: Oxford University Press, 1956).

10. Arthur F. Bentley, *The Process of Government* (Bloomington, Ind.: Principia Press, 1949). First published in 1908.

11. For a good review of how this works, see: Louis M. Kohlmeier, *The Regulators: Watchdog Agencies and the Public Interest* (New York: Harper & Row, 1969). For an explanation of why it works this way, see: Murray Edelman, *The Symbolic Uses of Politics* (Urbana, Ill.: University of Illinois Press, 1964).

12. David Easton, *The Political System* (New York: Alfred A. Knopf, 1953).

13. Carl J. Friedrich, *Constitutional Government and Democracy* (Boston: Little, Brown, 1941).

14. See, for example, Theodore J. Lowi, "Decision-Making versus Policy-Making: Towards an Antidote for Technocracy," *Public Administration Review*, 30 (May/June 1970), pp. 134-139; Theodore J. Lowi, "Four Systems of Politics, Policy, and Choice," *Public Administration Review*, 32 (July/August 1972), pp. 298-310; Randall B. Ripley, "Introduction: The Politics of Public Policy," *Public Policies and their Politics: An Introduction to the Techniques of Government Control*, Randall B. Ripley, ed. (New York: Norton, 1966), pp. i-xv; Randall Ripley and Grace Franklin, *Congress, the Bureaucracy, and Public Policy*, 2nd ed. (Homewood, Ill.: Dorsey, 1980); Randall Ripley and Grace Franklin, *Bureaucracy and Policy Implementation* (Homewood, Ill.: 1982); Robert Salisbury and John Heinz, "A Theory of Policy Analysis and Some Preliminary Applications," *Policy Analysis in Political Science*, Ira Sharkansky, ed. (Chicago: Markham, 1970), pp. 39-60; Dean Schooler, Jr., *Science, Scientists, and Public Policy* (New York: Free Press, 1971); and Michael Hayes, "The Semi-Sovereign Pressure Groups: A Critique Theory and an Alternative Typology," *Journal of Politics*, 40 (February 1978), pp. 134-161.

15. Theodore J. Lowi, "American Business, Public Policy, Case Studies, and Political Science," *World Politics*, 16 (July 1964), p. 691. But see also: Theodore J. Lowi, "Population Policies and the American Political System," *Political Science and Population Studies*, Richard L. Clinton, William S. Flash, and R. Kenneth Godwin, eds. (Lexington, Mass.: D.C. Heath, 1972), pp. 25-53. For an attempt at integrating some of the contributors to this literature, see: Leonard Champney, "Public Goods and Policy Types," *Public Administration Review*, 48 (November/December 1988), pp. 988-994.

16. Lowi, "Population Policies and the American Political System," pp. 29-33.

17. John W. Kingdon, *Agendas, Alternatives, and Public Policies* (Boston: Little, Brown, 1984).

18. *Ibid.*, p. 85.

19. Charles E. Lindblom, *The Policy Making Process* (Englewood Cliffs, N.J.: Prentice Hall, 1968).

20. Charles E. Lindblom, "The Science of Muddling Through," *Public Administration Review*, 19 (Spring 1959), pp. 79-88.

21. Ralph K. Huitt, "Political Feasibility," in *Political Science and Public Policy*.

22. Yehezkel Dror, *Public Policy Making Reexamined* (San Francisco: Chandler, 1968), p. 8.

23. Vincent Ostrom and Elinor Ostrom, "Public Choice: A Different Approach to the Study of Public Administration," *Public Administration Review*, 31 (March/April 1971), p. 203.

24. See: Otto Eckstein, *Public Finance*, 2nd ed. (Englewood Cliffs, N.J.: Prentice Hall, 1967); Robert L. Bish, *The Public Economy of Metropolitan Areas* (Chicago: Markham, 1971); and L. L. Wade and R. L.

Curry, Jr., *A Logic of Public Policy: Aspects of Political Economy* (Belmont, Calif.: Wadsworth, 1970).

25. Gordon Tullock, *The Politics of Bureaucracy* (Washington, D.C.: Public Affairs Press, 1965); and Anthony Downs, *An Economic Theory of Democracy* (New York: Harper & Row, 1957).

26. Mancur Olson, *The Logic of Collective Action* (Cambridge, Mass.: Harvard University Press, 1965).

27. James M. Buchanan and Gordon Tullock, *The Calculus of Consent: Logical Foundations of Constitutional Democracy* (Ann Arbor: University of Michigan Press, 1962).

28. Garrett Hardin, "The Tragedy of the Commons," *Science*, 162 (December 13, 1968), pp. 1243-1248; and Joseph J. Seneca, "The Welfare Effects of Zero Pricing of Public Goods," *Public Choice*, 7 (Spring 1970), pp. 101-110.

29. E. J. Mishan, *Economics for Social Decisions: Elements of Cost-Benefit Analysis* (New York: Praeger, 1972), p. 14.

30. Vincent Ostrom and Elinor Ostrom, "Public Goods and Public Choices," in *Alternatives for Delivering Public Services*, E. S. Savas, ed. (Boulder, Colo.: Westview Press, 1977), p. 7-14; and E. S. Savas, *Privatizing the Public Sector: How to Shrink Government* (Chatham, N.J.: Chatham House Publishers, 1982). See also Hardin, "The Tragedy of the Commons" and Seneca, "The Welfare Effects of Zero Pricing of Public Goods."

31. Savas, *Privatizing the Public Sector*, p. 33. Much of the following discussion is drawn from Savas, pp. 29-52.

32. A good, practical case for this (and for Table 10-3) is made in: Harry P. Hatry, *A Review of Private Approaches for Delivery of Public Services* (Washington, D.C.: The Urban Institute Press, 1983).

33. For additional information on this complex topic that uses the perspective of technology assessment, see Nicholas Henry, *Copyright/Information Technology/Public Policy*, Volumes I and II (New York: Marcel Dekker, 1975 and 1976); and Nicholas Henry, ed. *Copyright, Congress, and Technology: The Public Record*, Volumes I, II, III, IV, and V (Phoenix, Ariz.: Oryx, 1978, 1979, and 1980).

34. Gabor Strasser, "Technology Assessment: A Fad or a New Way of Life?" *Science Policy Review*, 5, 1 (1971), p. 7.

35. See, for example, David Clark, "In Consideration of Goal-Free Planning: The Failure of Traditional Planning Systems in Education," *Educational Administration Quarterly*, 17 (Summer 1981), pp. 42-60.

36. Kingdon, *Agendas, Politics, and Public Policies*. But see also Joseph Schumpeter, "The Creative Response in Economic History," *The Journal of Economic History*, 7 (November 7, 1947), pp. 149-159.

37. Derek Viray, *Planning and Education* (London: Routledge and Kegan Paul, 1972), p. 4.

38. For examples of critiques of the forecasting weaknesses of the rationalists models, see Paul and Benjamin Ward, *What's Wrong with Economics?*

(New York: Basic Books, 1972); Seymour Martin Lipset, "The Limits to Futurology in Social Science Analysis," in Seymour Martin Lipset, ed., *The Third Century: America as a Post Industrial Society* (New York: Cooper Institution Press, 1979), pp. 3-18; and William Ascher, "Forecasting Potential of Complex Models," *Policy Sciences*, 13 (May 1981), pp. 247-267.

39. Emerson Shuck, "The New Planning and the Old Fragmentism," *The Journal of Higher Education*, 48 (September/October 1977), pp. 494-602.

40. George Keller, *Academic Strategy: The Management Revolution in Higher Education* (Baltimore, Md.: The Johns Hopkins University Press, 1983), p. 111.

41. Harold Enarson, "The Art of Planning," *Educational Record*, 56 (Summer 1975), p. 173.

42. Keller, *Academic Strategy*, p. 113.

43. Amitai Etzioni, *The Active Society* (Glencoe, IL: Free Press, 1968), p. 283. See also: Amitai Etzioni, "Mixed Scanning: A Third Approach to Decision Making," *Public Administration Review*, 27 (December 1967), pp. 385-392.

44. Keller, *Academic Strategy*, p. 116.

45. Alfred Chandler, Jr., *Strategy and Structure: Chapters in the History of the Industrial Enterprise* (Cambridge, Mass.: Massachusetts Institute of Technology Press, 1962). Other seminal contributions to the literature of strategic planning include: H. Igor Ansoff, *Corporate Strategy* (McGraw-Hill, 1965); Kenneth Andrews, *The Concept of Corporate-City Strategy*, rev. ed. (New York: Dow Jones-Irwin, 1980); Daniel Bell, "Twelve Modes of Prediction," *Daedalus*, 93 (Summer 1964), pp. 845-880; Henry Mintzberg, "Packets of Strategy Formulation," *Management Science*, 24 (May 1978), pp. 934-948; and James Bryan Quinn, "Strategic Change: Logical Incrementalism," *Sloan Management Review*, 20 (Fall 1978), pp. 7-21.

46. Barton Wechsler and Robert W. Backoff, "Policy Making and Administration in State Agencies: Strategic Management Approaches," *Public Administration Review*, 46 (July/August 1986), p. 326.

47. Michael Aiken and Jerald Hage, "The Organic Organization and Innovation," *Sociology*, 5 (January 1971), p. 80.

48. Richard Cyert, as quoted in Keller, *Academic Strategy*, p. 147.

49. Craig M. Wheeland, "Citywide Strategic Planning: An Evaluation of Rock Hill's Empowering the Vision," *Public Administration Review*, 53 (January/February 1993), pp. 65-72. The city is Rock Hill, South Carolina.

50. Gregory Streib, "Strategic Decision Making in Council-Manager Governments: A Status Report," *Municipal Year Book, 1991* (Washington, D.C.: International City Management Association, 1991), pp. 14-23.

51. Theodore H. Poister and Gregory Streib, "Management Tools in Municipal Government: Trends Over the Past Decade," *Public Administration Review*, 49 (May/June 1989), pp. 244-245.

52. Paul Meising and David F. Anderson, "The Size and Scope of Strategic Planning in State Agencies: The

New York Experience," *American Review of Public Administration*, 21 (June 1991), pp. 119-137.

53. Gerald J. Miller, "Unique Public-Sector Strategies," *Public Productivity and Management Review*, 13 (Winter 1989), p. 133.

54. *Ibid.*, p. 139. Among the more empirical attempts to analyze the use of strategic planning in the public sector are: Barry Bozeman, "Strategic Public Management and Productivity: A Fire House Theory," *State Government*, 61 (Winter 1983), pp. 2-7; John M. Bryson, *Strategic Planning for Public and Nonprofit Organizations: A Guide to Strengthening and Sustaining Organizational Achievement* (San Francisco: Jossey-Bass, 1988); John M. Bryson and William D. Roering, "Initiation of Strategic Planning by Governments," *Public Administration Review*, 48 (November/December 1988), pp. 995-1004; J. M. Stevens, "Strategic Public Management and Productivity Improvement: A Symposium," *Public Productivity Review*, 8 (Winter 1984), entire issue; J. M. Stevens and Robert P. McGowan, "Managerial Strategies in Municipal Government Organizations," *Academy of Management Journal*, 26 (September 1983), pp. 527-534; and Wechsler and Backoff, "Policy Making and Administration in State Agencies," pp. 321-327. Two good overviews of strategic planning in the public sector are: Jack Koteen, *Strategic Management in Public and Nonprofit Organizations* (New York: Praeger, 1991), and Jack Rabin, Gerald J. Miller, and W. Bartley

Hildreth, eds., *Handbook of Strategic Management* (New York: Marcel Dekker, 1989).

55. Miller, "Unique Public-Sector Strategies," pp. 137-138.

56. Wechsler and Backoff, "Policymaking and Administration in State Agencies," pp. 321-327.

57. James E. Skok, "Toward a Definition of Strategic Management for the Public Sector," *American Review of Public Administration*, 19 (June 1989), pp. 133-147.

58. Bryson and Roering, "Initiation of Strategic Planning by Governments," p. 995.

59. *Ibid.*, pp. 995-1004.. See also: Wechsler and Backoff, "Policymaking and Administration of State Agencies," pp. 321-327. Wechsler and Backoff found a similar set of eight variables in their study of Ohio state agencies.

60. Bryson and Roering, "Initiation of Strategic Planning by Governments," p. 1002. For another treatment of the limitations of strategic planning in the public sector, see: Arie Halachmi, "Strategic Planning and Management? Not Necessarily," *Public Productivity Review*, 10 (Winter 1986), pp. 35-50.

61. Bryson and Roering, "Initiation of Strategic Planning by Governments," p. 1003.

62. Strieb, "Strategic Decision Making in Council-Manager Governments," p. 18.

63. Gerald L. Barkdoll, "Scoping Versus Coping: Developing a Comprehensive Agency Vision," *Public Administration Review*, 52 (July/August 1992), p. 337.

CHAPTER 11

PRIVATIZATION: GOVERNMENT CONTRACTING AND THE PUBLIC AUTHORITY

In this chapter, we examine a facet of public administration that most books ignore: how and why governments implement public programs by hiring the private sector to do the work for them. "Privatization" is not easily defined. In some countries, for example, privatization refers to governments selling off commercial enterprises that had been state monopolies, a connection not normally made in the United States. In this chapter, *privatization* is the government's use of the private sector (both for-profit and not-for-profit) to deliver public policies and improve the content and implementation of public programs. This definition covers quite a bit of terrain, and it is meant to: from the contracting by governments with private providers for goods and services, to hiring consultants, to working with nonprofit organizations in the delivery of government services, to the creation and management of government corporations.

The heavy use by American governments of the private and quasi-private sectors to implement public policies is a phenomenon peculiar to the United States. It relates to some deep, underlying belief sets that may be unique to the American political culture. In the United States, there exists a pervasive myth that "business is better"—that private enterprise is more efficient and effective in getting the job done than is "the incredible bulk" of government. Although this is an unproven thesis, it nonetheless remains as a deeply held belief. One empirical analysis of contracting out by local governments, for example, concluded that, "To the extent that cost reduction is a motivation [for contracting out services to be delivered by private companies], the decision makers I studied made the more costly choice [of contracting out], evidently relying on the unexamined assumption of private sector efficiency."[1]

This "unexamined assumption" that business is inherently more efficient than government—an assumption held by many public administrators themselves—can be traced to the earliest American thinking about public administration as a profession: from Woodrow Wilson's characterization of it as "a field of business" (recall Chapter 2) in his founding essay of 1887, to the municipal research bureaus of the early twentieth century (mentioned in preceding chapters), which "were not supported by the broad public . . . [but typically] by a small number of wealthy business people. . . . It is not surprising in this context that the staff of research bureaus gave deference in their publications to the wonders of business efficiency, regardless of the accuracy of the claim."[2]

PUBLIC ADMINISTRATION AND AMERICAN ORTHODOXY

The myth that private enterprise can conduct public programs more efficiently and effectively than can government has supported the expansion of government contracting with private companies (especially at the federal level) and the rise of government corporations (almost entirely at the subnational level) as two of the three primary means of implementing public programs. (The third is the system of intergovernmental administration, considered in the next chapter.) The business administration literature reflects this popular belief-set.

Orthodox management theory strongly contends that the freer a manager is from public accountability, the more effective manager he or she will be. Thus, we hear arguments voiced for "privatizing" public agencies in order to make them more effective deliverers of public services; more often than not, for example, city garbage often is collected by private companies contracted by local governments. The principal points that proponents of standard administrative theory make in supporting their claims revolve around freedom from civil service systems, governmental pay scales, any kind of overview by a central budget administration, and governmental regulations on purchasing, contracting, and price setting practices. While these same proponents often argue strongly for just these kind of controls on government agencies, they feel they are not appropriate, and indeed detrimental, to the effectiveness of private management and government corporations.[3]

These orthodoxies have had a profound affect at all levels of government. They have worked to encourage policymakers to abjure public administrators in favor of using private administrators to implement public programs. But the federal government and the state and local governments have faced very different constraints in accommodating the deeply ingrained cultural value of "businesslike" government.

Coping at the Federal Level

The federal government, to cope with the exigencies of the Depression and later of World War II, had established a plentitude of federal government corporations. By 1945, there were sixty-three wholly owned federal corporations, thirty-eight partly owned ones, nineteen federal credit agencies, and hundreds of military-owned businesses. By 1953, Washington was "the largest electric power producer in the country, the largest insurer, the largest lender and the largest borrower, the largest landlord and the largest tenant, the largest holder of grazing land and timberland, the largest owner of grain, the largest warehouse operator, the largest shipowner, and the largest truck fleet operator."[4]

Such public enterprise did not rest easily with corporate America. The U.S. Chamber of Commerce, investor-owned utilities, and the National Association of Manufacturers, among other special interests launched a concerted lobbying drive to induce the feds to evict themselves out of "competition" with the private sector. This effort coincided with a conservative presidency, McCarthyism, and the Cold War—all of which served to keep "leftist" counterarguments muted. Moreover, the prestigious reports of the first and second "Hoover Commissions" in 1949 and 1955 on the management of the federal government were extremely useful to the foes of public enterprise. Former President Herbert Hoover, no friend of liberal thought, headed the commissions, which, with no evidence whatever, concluded that "the genius of the private enterprise system" led to its "initiative, ingenuity, inventiveness, and unparalleled productivity," while "the normal rigidities that are part of government, obviously" mitigated against the flowering of these attitudes in "government business enterprises."[5]

These professions of conservative faith did not fly in Congress, but they soared in Dwight Eisenhower's White House. Through a series of executive orders, most of the federal government's public authorities were reorganized or dismantled; although estimates vary, there are by one count only eighteen government corporations owned entirely by the feds.[6] Examples include the Tennessee Valley Authority, the Communications Satellite Corporation, the Corporation for Public Broadcasting, and the Export-Import Bank.

The view that the private sector somehow "can do it better" still prevails. Consider the argument expressed by a conservative member of the House of Representatives; "I do not believe government has any business being in business. I see no reason why it should compete with the private sector in providing goods and services. In those instances where the costs to the government will be less when a good or service is obtained by contract, that ought to be the course followed."[7] Hence, if the special business interests loath government corporations, they nonetheless adore government money, and these same interests have pushed for the "privatization" of government on the grounds that "business can do it better." To accommodate this mind- set, the federal government began contracting out its programs with a vengeance, and federal contract costs now exceed the federal payroll.[8]

Coping at the Grassroots

State and local governments are faced with precisely the same conservative mind-set as Washington, but are forced to find a different tactic to steer around it. State and local officials have found that they have to circumvent conservative mentalities by using the government corporation, because the privatization option is less available to them. Saddled with moribund constitutional limitations on public debt (only a third of the state constitutions were written in this century) and cumbersome financing procedures (for instance, in stark contrast to the situation at the federal level, only two states, Connecticut and Vermont, are not required by their constitutions to balance their budgets each year), yet whipped by demands for additional public services, state and local governments discovered (with federal encouragement) the manifold fiscal loopholes provided by the government corporation.

Moreover, unions of organized public employees are relatively stronger at the grassroots than in Washington; more than 40 percent of all state and local employees are members of unions. Organized labor can and does exert considerable pressure against state and local administrators not to "contract away" the jobs of public employees to the private sector; often, such restrictions are written into state civil service statutes.

One survey of sanitation services in all cities in the United States with 10,000 people or more found that the presence of unionized municipal sanitation employees had a clear and adverse impact on the cities' decision to contract these services with the private sector. Privatized sanitation services were much less likely to be present in cities where sanitation workers were organized, although they were more likely to be found in unionized cities where the relations between unions and management had a history of tension and contention. While the study concluded that the opposition of unions to privatization is "rational," in that unionization declined in those cities where privatization was implemented, privatization "did not necessarily lead to high unemployment among displaced workers" for several reasons, not the least of which was that former municipal workers often were hired by the private firm winning the contract.[9]

As a result of these conditions, "many scholars have suggested that there are between 10,000 to 12,000"[10] government corporations chartered by subnational governments, the bulk of which were founded after 1950. But no one really knows, and the estimates range, somewhat astonishingly, from 5,000 to 18,000.

In short, government administrators at the federal, state and local levels have found two different maneuvers that they can use to steer their ways around conservative belief systems. At the federal level, this method is the government contract awarded to the private entrepreneur. At the state and local levels, it is the public authority chartered, but not managed, by the government. All government levels, however, use some of both.

THE POLITICS OF PRIVATIZATION: MOTIVATIONS TO CONTRACT

Government's choice to provide public services by contracting with private corporations can bring with it several advantages, most of which relate to political flexibility. Political debts can be paid off, the size of governments can, at least on paper, be reduced, and genuine and responsible political responsiveness can, on occasion, be attained by maneuvering around a cumbersome public bureaucracy. These motivations, it should be stressed, hold true for public administrators at all levels of government, not just federal administrators, although the federal government remains the public sector's primary "privatizer." Let us consider some of these incentives in turn.[11]

- Contracting out, as opposed to using government personnel, permits the government to experiment with policies and new delivery systems. The government can always terminate a contract if the experiment fails, with little or no objection by an affected public.
- The desirability of using the private sector, rather than their own agencies, to try out new policies and delivery mechanisms, appears to be highly valued among public administrators. One survey of sixteen cities across the United States that privatized, or were seriously considering privatizing, federally mandated improvements in wastewater treatment works, found that these cities did so, in part, because they had "innovative managerial and institutional strengths."[12]
- Privatizing permits the government to hire specialists and people of unusual talent, without paying as much attention to such "affirmative action" items as sex, ethnicity, or veteran's status that can affect government hiring.
- Contracting out permits government agencies to benefit from, and have their services enhanced by, the existence of voluntary or charitable organizations that already may be doing what the government wishes to do. We discuss this aspect later in the chapter.
- Certain short-term savings often can be realized. For example, civil service rules on pay scales and fringe benefits may be skirted by using contractors who pay only minimum wages to their employees, and by leasing rather than purchasing new buildings, since the resultant government budget will show only the annual cost of the rent, as opposed to the expense of a capital project.

But the realization of long-term savings is considerably less clear. One analysis of financial data covering a nine-year period for 100 cities in Massachusetts that had contracted out their property tax assessments (a relatively popular function for local governments to privatize) found that "the private sector does not have a claim to cost savings in this instance. . . . Policymakers may do well to view contracting out as a temporary solution to technical infeasibility and should reevaluate their positions at the termination of contracts."[13]

The personnel working for government can be expanded through contracts, even though the official size of the civil service remains the same or is actually reduced. This final point is especially pertinent when we consider the burgeoning pension programs for government employees at all levels. The actual cost of the pension programs to taxpayers is not completely known, but it is known that at least some of these programs are unusually (and perhaps unrealistically) generous.

Finally, more political risks often can be borne by government when privatization is used. The government becomes a less visible, less direct actor when public policies are privatized.

Empirical studies indicate that risk avoidance, particularly the avoidance of political risks, is a major motivation in exercising the privatization option among public administrators. The survey of sixteen cities dealing with the implementation of improvements in wastewater treatment plants, mentioned earlier, found that overcoming "resistance to the attendant political and economic risks" was a large consideration in making the decision to privatize.[14]

The decision by policymakers to contract out the implementation of their policies to private entrepreneurs is, in short, at least as much a political decision as it is a managerial and financial one. As we discuss later in this chapter, political considerations also appear to play a prominent role in the decisions made by public officials to create government corporations for the delivery of public services.

THE PRIVATIZATION OF FEDERAL POLICY

Nearly a fifth of all federal expenditures—about $200 billion—flow to private interests through contracts. Nearly four-fifths of this amount goes to private businesses in the United States; most of the remainder involves purchases of goods and services by the Department of Defense in foreign countries; and a small amount, about 3 percent of these dollars, goes to American educational and nonprofit institutions.[15]

How these "de-federalized" funds are spent, and on what, is not easily ascertained. Slightly more than half of the government's contract dollars are expended on supplies and equipment; more than a third goes to construction and other services, such as leasing arrangements and management consultants; and 14 percent is allocated to research and development.[16] The federal government directly supports about half of the entire national R&D effort through a combination of grants and contracts.[17]

It has been estimated that there are some 3 million "indirect" federal employees in the private sector (about the same number of "direct" federal civilian employees) working for the government under contracts with corporations and other organizations.[18] The federal government lets, on the average, about 17 million contracts a year to private enterprise.[19]

Even in an age of an alleged "peace dividend," the Department of Defense remains Washington's biggest business. Three-quarters of all the federal government's expenditures on procurement contracts go to Defense. Eighty percent of the federal funds contracted to business and nearly 30 percent of the funds going to educational and nonprofit institutions are Defense dollars. The bulk of Defense contracts is spent on supplies and equipment.[20]

The Department of Defense, like the whole of the federal government, spends most of its contract funds on *procurement contracts*, or contracts for goods as opposed to services. Despite the fact that Washington's procurement enterprise is so vast, however, the federal government still may be competing with private enterprise. One federal study found that some 400,000 of the government's 3 million civilian employees are operating 12,000 businesses whose products probably could be provided by private companies.[21]

Federal Policies for Privatization

Federal policies dealing with contracting out can be traced back to 1955, when the Bureau of the Budget (now the Office of Management and Budget, or OMB) issued Bureau of the Budget Bulletin Number 55-4, which was a directive to the effect that government would rely on the private sector for commercial goods and services so that it would not be competing with business. In 1966, the Bureau altered this philosophy with what is now OMB Circular A-76 (expanded in 1979 and 1983). OMB Circular A-76 remains the federal government's core policy on contracting, and says that it is appropriate for the government to compete with private enterprise if the taxpayer benefits from that competition by greater governmental efficiency. OMB Circular A-76 states that it is the government's policy "to rely on competitive private enterprise to supply the commercial and industrial products and services it needs," although as the directive reluctantly notes, the government should perform those duties that "are inherently governmental in nature, being . . . intimately related to the public interest."

Although OMB Circular A-76 stipulates that rigorous cost comparisons between in-house executions and contracting out should be done for any given project, such comparisons rarely are made, largely because there are virtually no resources for doing so. The Office of Management and Budget, located within the Office of the President, and the General Accounting Office (GAO), which reports directly to Congress, are the two major federal agencies charged with assuring contract compliance and the efficiency and effectiveness of government programs generally. Yet the OMB has only one understaffed unit within it, the Office of Federal Procurement Policy, created in 1974, that deals with contracting services. Relatedly, the GAO has found the management of contracting to be less than tight on a number of grounds, but it has not really taken a hard look at the overall problem.

OMB Circular A-76 is amplified somewhat by OMB Circular A-120, issued in 1980, and which addresses consultants hired by the government. The Circular prohibits the use of consultants in "performing work of a policy, decisionmaking, or managerial nature, which is the direct responsibility of agency officials."

OMB Circular A-120 dovetails with OMB Circular A-76 in its prohibition of using consultants to perform work that should be the responsibility of public administrators. OMB Circular A-76 defines a *governmental function* as one "which is so intimately related to the public interest as to mandate administration by government employees." It is the view of the General Accounting Office that OMB Circular A-76 "appears to allow all functions not governmental in nature to be contracted out."[22] Within this very broad parameter, individual federal managers may decide on their own to contract out; Title VII of the Civil Service Reform Act of 1978 authorizes federal administrators to "make determinations with respect to contracting out."

Republican administrations promoted this kind of privatization with fervor in the 1980s and early 1990s. In 1987, President Ronald Reagan issued Executive Order 12615 which "renewed pressure on federal agencies [to contract out their functions] by reducing their budgets in *anticipation* of savings expected to result" from this privatization.[23] In 1992, President George Bush issued an Executive Order encouraging state and local governments to sell their assets—such as waste water treatment facilities, public housing, bridges, and roads—to private bidders in an effort to balance their budgets and "increase efficiency."[24]

The Process of Federal Privatization

The federal contracting system is one of inordinate complexity. In the procurement area, there are some 4,000 separate legislative provisions instructing bureaucrats how to contract. These laws are interpreted by 887 sets of regulations that the bureaucracy has imposed upon itself. These regulations add up to 64,600 pages, about a third of which are changed every year. Some 150,000 federal employees who handle contracts and who deal with tens of thousands of private businesses and 485 separate federal procurement offices in the process, must keep abreast of these changes.[25] In the Defense Department alone, there are 25,000 auditors and inspectors who check up on procurement regulations that exceed 30,000 pages. These regulations are issued by seventy-nine different Pentagon offices, which must report to fifty-five congressional subcommittees and twenty-nine congressional committees.[26]

The 150,000 federal contracting officers who must deal with the welter of regulations regarding privatization have an influence beyond their nominal station. Phillip J. Cooper notes that "the interaction of companies with federal contracting officers results in the adoption by firms of a set of prices and conditions for doing business with the federal government which are then applied to state and local activities. The negotiations with federal contracting officers . . . constitute *de facto* preemption of local negotiating efforts."[27]

Integration: Public Agency meets Private Organization. Cooper has described the contractual administrative process as an "integration-operation-separation model." The integration phase is, in Cooper's words, "politically overloaded . . . the concept that the contracting officer's primary purpose is to acquire a contract that promises the highest quality at the lowest price is misleading if not false . . . the primary task of the contracting officer is to balance political demands and supports with budgetary restrictions and governmental needs."[28]

Accordingly, firms are sought by the federal government in one of two ways: the "contract negotiation process" or the "advertised bid process." Although advertised bidding for virtually all contracts is required under federal law, notably by the Armed Services Procurement Act of 1949, by "the calculations of most authors and government reports, approximately 85 percent of contract expenditures" are never let for bid.[29]

All government contracts, whether they already have been awarded or not, are listed in the official government publication, *Commerce Business Daily*. More than 30,000 copies are distributed every day, five days a week. Although two-thirds of these contracts already have been awarded (or virtually so) without competitive bidding, much of the remaining third appear to have been quietly let by federal officials under the table to favored contractors, and advertising them in *Commerce Business Daily* is strictly *pro forma*. The editor of the *Daily* has noted several "scams" that agencies use to avoid competitive bidding, such as miscoding a contract in the advertisement so that potential bidders can never find it ("That happens pretty often"); mentioning a particular firm in the ad itself ("That's a pretty clear tipoff that there's not going to be any competition"); and mandating absurdly brief deadlines for bids. The Beltway bandits consider the process a joke; according to one, "Anybody who believes you read the [*Commerce Business*

Daily] and get your contracts is out of it. You'd starve."[30]

Negotiated contracts, obviously, constitute the vast bulk of federal contracts, at least as measured by dollars expended. These are of two types. The first is the *negotiated competitive contract*, in which a group of firms are involved in direct negotiations, or some advertising is actually indulged in and negotiations are initiated with the most interesting prospects. The other version is the *sole source contract*, in which the contracting officer selects whatever firm or organization that he or she believes capable of meeting the terms of the contract. Regardless of whether the contract was negotiated or bid upon, the contracting officer's decisions are virtually never overturned on appeals made by disappointed rivals. "Once integrated into the public sector, firms tend to remain there."[31]

Operation: A New Intimacy between Agency and Organization. The "operation phase" follows integration, in which the contractor is legally bound to the government, and this phase often involves an interesting intimacy between contractor and agency. Both sides "play games." Private companies tend to deflate their cost estimates to secure the contract. But it is a practice in which public agencies are complicit: "One of the things that we have got to stop doing in our contracting is playing games—the government and the contractor. . . . We know that if we tell the [Department of Defense] . . . how much something is really going to cost, they may scrub it. And they know that if they tell the Congress how much it's really going to cost the Congress may scrub it. So you start in with both sides knowing that it is going to cost more."[32]

The revolving door. Another aspect of the operation phase is the well-publicized "revolving door." When federal officials retire or resign from government, especially if they were in jobs that involve agency contracts with the private sector, they frequently end up as highly-salaried executives in the company with which they dealt as a federal administrator. One investigation by the Federal Pay Commission found that when top federal employees left government for private industry, their salaries went up, on the average,

by almost 75 to 100 percent. The longer one was in government service, the more lucrative one's opportunities outside of it.[33]

About a quarter of all military officers who retire at the rank of major or above go to work for defense contractors.[34] One study found that, of those military retirees who did go to work for defense firms, 28 percent had taken jobs that related directly to work that they had been doing while in active service.[35] The country's top eight defense contractors alone hired 1,455 military officers who retired in the 1970s. These "retirees" appear to do very well in their second careers. A minimum retainer for services in the defense industry is $30,000 a year, plus expenses, and consultants who once held important positions in the Pentagon commonly commanded $100,000 a year from each company that purchased their services.[36]

Moreover, it is not uncommon for public officials to start careers in government, leave for industry, return to government, and so on and so on. This is the "revolving door" phenomenon so often decried by the press. As one former contract officer at the Department of Energy, which spends nearly nine-tenths of its budget (about $11 billion) on contracts with private companies, has noted, "People at DOE bounce back and forth between government and industry just like Ping-Pong balls."[37] There have been cases recorded of old friends monitoring the contract compliance of each other. First, one works for the agency letting the contract, and the other works for the company receiving it; later, the roles are reversed, as one leaves the agency to work in the same company, and the other returns as a consultant to the agency to monitor the contracts that the agency awards to the company! And so the revolving door goes.[38]

It is not surprising that many public officials who administer contractual relationships with private companies see these contractors as prospective employers; objectivity, consequently, can become blurred. One major general in the Air Force, for example, who accepted a job just before retiring to a consultant firm that had just been awarded a $97,303 noncompetitive bid by him, was directed by the firm to manage the contract that he had just awarded it. He did, and a year later the contract was renewed by the Air Force for another $99,774.[39]

This kind of relationship between government and business is not isolated. A report on contracting practices in the Pentagon issued by the General Accounting Office found not only that more than four-fifths of its contracts had been awarded without competitive bidding, but also that more than half of these went to former high-level Pentagon executives. Almost three-quarters of the contracts awarded to former Defense officials were awarded without competition. Indeed, more than half of all contracts awarded by the Pentagon, competitive or otherwise, went to former Pentagon employees. Significantly, 40 percent of the contracts awarded by the Defense Department were originally suggested by the contractor instead of by the Department, a figure which appears to be about double that of civilian agencies.[40]

Even more disturbing, another investigation by the General Accounting Office concluded that about a third of 5,100 former high- and mid-level Pentagon employees who had retired three to four years earlier had gone to work for contractors whom they had dealt with as federal officials, had worked on the same project in both their federal and post-federal careers, or had been responsible in the Pentagon for Defense contracts that subsequently supported their private employment. "The public could perceive," reported the GAO, that these former public administrators "may not have acted in the best interest of the government because they viewed a defense contractor as a potential employer."[41]

Revolving foreign agents. The Pentagon, as the government's largest contractor by far, is logically the agency which has the greatest opportunity to engage in practices that smack of revolving doors. But the activity is by no means restricted to the Defense Department. Of the 5,650 former senior-level federal officials who left the government's employ between 1986 and 1991, eighty-two registered as exceedingly well compensated foreign agents—that is, lobbyists for foreign countries: two Senators, one Congressman, seven White House officials, thirty-three senior Congressional staffers, and thirty-nine top administrators of federal agencies.[42]

It should be noted that there may have been many more than eighty-two former high officials who retired over six years from federal service to lobby for foreign competitors. These eighty-two people were known to be foreign agents because they registered as lobbyists in compliance with the Foreign Agents Registration Act of 1938, which requires representatives of overseas firms and governments to identify themselves as such. Yet only 775 foreign agents have registered, and it is commonly thought that there are, in reality, thousands of lobbyists in Washington working for special interests abroad. Similarly, fewer than 6,000 lobbyists for American interests have identified themselves under the Lobbying Registration Act of 1946, even though educated estimates of the number of full-time lobbyists in Washington run to 80,000.[43] Our point is that there may be many more former federal officials working as lobbyists for special interests, both foreign and domestic, than is known.

Nevertheless, when the revolving door rotates recently retired federal officials to the employ of foreign interests, a particular concern arises that goes far beyond that of questionable ethics. One member of Congress characterized this syndrome as "an enormous problem that threatens our national security . . . former U. S. government officials are representing a foreign company and using their inside knowledge and high-level contacts to make a case for a foreign competitor."[44]

Although there are numerous federal statutes banning conflicts of interest between former federal employees and private companies, few, if any, work. Former public officials, depending on the circumstances, can be prohibited from representing private interests to their former agencies for a year after their departure to a lifetime, and penalties for violating these laws can be as much as two years in jail and $10,000 in fines. The Ethics Reform Act of 1989 actually prohibits former federal executives from lobbying not merely their former agencies, but even in their area of expertise, for a year following their departure from the government. But failure to enforce these statutes generally relates to what "representation" in such instances really means, and concomitant difficulties in proving representation.

At least, those are the legal difficulties. The more substantive difficulty may be that federal officials are loathe to imperil the prospects of a second and very lucrative career, regardless of the implications for the public interest and (in the case of foreign agents) the nation's global competitiveness. In noting that many of her congressional colleagues resist reforming the phenomenon of the revolving door, one Congresswoman observed that, "It's because there's a lot of money involved."[45]

Separation: The Unfulfilled Act. The final phase in the contracting cycle is that of separation, or how the government terminates contractors and resolves disputes.

Neither termination nor dispute resolution are simple acts, since agencies typically accept goods and services from contractors over a prolonged period of time. Moreover, terminating a contract often has adverse implications for the public contracting officer as well as for the contractor: often, a contract cancellation "drastically disrupts careers of those associated with it, including government administrators, private contractors, and scientists and engineers. . . . [It] hurts regional economies. What causes pain locally triggers congressional rescue activity."[46]

Bringing Congress into the act is in the interest of neither the agency nor the firm, but especially not of the agency. Thus, "government contractual relationships may be more like treaties than contracts in that often no real separation occurs. Certain obligations, which are in most cases politically rather than legally enforced, remain."[47]

Two Models of Contracting: The Case of Procurement

The treaty-like nature of federal contracting and procurement procedures relates to two very different perspectives on government's relationship with industry. These opposing world views have been called the "formal model" of contracting and procurement and the "joint management model."[48]

The formal model envisions that the relationships within the Federal Contract Procurement System and, for that matter, the "military-industrial complex" itself, as discrete, highly task-specific arrangements among parties that are entirely independent of one another. Buyers are wholly separate from sellers. "The steam behind the . . . [formal model] comes from a number of sources:

ideologies about the American free enterprise economy and anxieties about creeping socialism; desires to contract fairly; apprehensions about a nefarious military-industrial complex; fears of the political-moral dangers of anything other than arms-length government-industrial dealings; pragmatic hopes for a market-compelled efficiencies and economy; and optimistic expectations that, bolstered by sophisticated systems analysis and management science devices, market-based fixed price arrangements can be contrived that will solve many vexing procedural and managerial problems in the [Federal Contract Procurement System] . . . simply by making them go away."[49]

By contrast, the joint management model emphasizes cooperative problem solving between the public and private sectors and shared managerial tasks. The joint management model assumes that no mechanistic formal model strategy "can be competent to dynamic undertakings such as [research and development] or modern complex system acquisition. . . . in sharp contrast with the [formal model], the basic feature of the cooperative [joint management model] is a more or less even, although perhaps fluctuating, distribution of power between the participating actors and organizations"—in other words, the government buyer and the private seller.[50]

The Formal Model: Major Contractual Types. Among the contractual forms that are used under the formal model are *fixed price contracts*, which state that a private company will deliver whatever service or product is written into the contract on a predetermined date for a price that will not vary, regardless of unanticipated circumstances that may or may not arise prior to the delivery date.[51]

Another form of contract that falls under the category of the formal model is called total package procurement. Total package procurement amounts to a set of somewhat artificial devices designed to simulate a competitive market situation. Under *total package procurement*, contractors are invited to bid on a single package that runs from development, through production, to eventual operational support of a project. The idea was to encourage competition, reduce the length of contract negotiations, and to enhance the possibility of more frequent fixed price contracting. Total package procurement was abolished in the early 1970s after it was attempted on such fiascoes as the C-5A cargo plane and several other projects that ended in gross cost overruns.

A third version of the formal model is the incentive contract. *Incentive contracts* attempt to encourage contractors to increase the quality of their performance by permitting them to share in any monetary gains that may derive from improvements that they are able to attain in a particular project. For example, if a project is delivered ahead of schedule, the incentive contract would provide a bonus to the contractor on the logic that, by being ahead of schedule, the contractor saved the government money. In practice, incentive contracts rarely work because it is so difficult to project in any reasonable amount of detail what it will take to effect a contractor's day-to-day decisions and what specific improvements must be obtained. According to some authorities, the assumptions implicit in an incentive contract are, in fact, so complex that they have essentially failed as a method of implementing the formal model, the essence of which is the fixed price contract.[52]

Fixed price contracts, total package procurement, and incentive contracts are the major forms of contracting reflecting the values of the formal model, but the kinds of contracts used under the joint management model display an entirely different belief system, one, as we stated earlier, that assumes a close working relationship between the contractor and the government.

The Joint Management Model: Major Contractual Types.

The major type of contract used by the joint management model is the cost-plus contract. *A cost-plus contract* underwrites the contractor's risks by assuring that the government will cover all costs accrued by the contractor in developing a project and then adds an additional amount as the contractor's profit.[53]

There are at least two kinds of cost-plus contracts. One is the *cost plus fixed fee contract*, which provides for reimbursement of the contractor along with payment of a fee negotiated as a percentage of estimated costs of performance that has been established prior to undertaking the work. The cost plus fixed fee contract succeeded the now illegal *cost plus percentage of cost contract*, which based fees charged by the contractor

on actual costs. This type of contract was eliminated because it encouraged contractors to be as costly as possible, since their profits were based on costs they incurred. A second type of cost-plus contract is the cost plus award fee contract. *Cost plus award fee contracts* permit payments of a fee to a contractor on the basis of after-the-fact evaluations of performance by government officials. Both cost plus fixed fee contracts and cost plus award fee contracts have been criticized on the grounds that they lead to cost overruns or are highly subjective because awards are determined by government administrators.[54]

Contracting and Weltanschauungen.

The world views of the formal and joint management models of procurement and contracting are polar opposites. The formal model sees the public and private sectors as separate, perhaps adversarial, entities. It also assumes that everyone understands what the job is, and how it is to be done.

The joint management model does not distinguish between the public and private sectors; "a buyer actively participates in a seller's operational decisions and one can hardly tell the players except from the logo on their coveralls."[55] Also in contrast to the formal model, the joint management model often assumes—at least in R&D contracting—that no one really understands what the job is and how it is to be done. This is sensible. Research and development projects are, by definition, projects that explore the unexplored, so much of "the job" to be done always is unknown. And R&D projects are an important component in federal contracting: More than 70 percent of all federal R&D spending is contracted out to private enterprise, and Washington supports more than half of all research and development in the nation.[56]

The joint management model is less acceptable politically than the formal model. It assumes that the world, including the federal government and private corporations, is interdependent, while the formal model does not recognize interdependency.

Both models have relevance. Government hostility to the private sector implied by the formal model may be justified when we learn of inordinately lax cost controls exercised by the government over private contractors, and what appears to be extraordinary avarice evidenced by contractors. The hammer, for example, falls somewhat short of what we think of as a cutting-edge technology. Yet the Pentagon has been charged by its contractors and has paid them more than $350 for a hammer that can be purchased in a hardware store for $7.00. Incidents such as these are not isolated. Can we really accept the trusting premises of the joint management model in light of these occurrences?

It is also apparent, however, that we often do not know what is entailed in fulfilling a procurement contract, and in this sense the assumptions of the joint management model are accurate. The space shuttle and the stealth aircraft for example, represent R&D contracts that could never be conducted (at least not honestly) on the basis of a fixed-price contract. How does one fix the price of making an idea into a reality? But one can fix the price of a reality that is known, common, and routine, such as collecting garbage, manufacturing bullets, or buying hammers, and these more mundane kinds of government contracting often seem to be overlooked by critics of the formal model, who tend to stress the complexities of the world of research and development in their arguments.

FEDERAL CONTRACTING: A CRITIQUE

Irrespective of the contracting model employed, it may be that neither the manpower nor the will to assure compliance by outside contractors exists at the federal level. Hence, we witness an absence of any kind of central record keeping by governments concerning their contractors; a lack of program integration; no kind of central control over service quality, prices charged to clients, and cost overruns; a rather insidious irresponsibility developing among government bureaucrats who are charged with monitoring and arranging contracts; and units charged with controlling compliance, but which cannot, because they have overloaded working schedules already.[57] The Department of Defense, the largest single contractor in government, has itself observed that "accurate information on the nature and extent of contract studies within the Department is difficult and often impossible to obtain. . . . there is no effective control of contract studies within the Department."[58]

Conspiracy or Chaos?

Statements by federal contract officers in other departments on research and consulting contractors perhaps are more colorful:[59]

The bottom line on contracts—pure paper studies. . . . The public gets . . . maybe 10 percent of their money's worth.

Of one $250,000 study, described as "an unintelligible pile of papers," a federal administrator said, "Nothing was received and we paid thousands for it. It really is a lot of gobbledygook. . . . As a taxpayer, I'm sick."

We're so busy trying to shovel money out the door, we don't have time to see what happens to it after it leaves. All the money could be stolen and I wouldn't know it. . . . The place is a madhouse.

The waste, and the opportunities, are also recognized by the more enlightened contractors. A board member of the Institute of Management Consultants observes: "It's a game. . . . Government comes to us and wants help in identifying their problems, but they don't seem to be able to use the material. They could spend much less and get more for it."[60]

"It looks like a conspiracy, but really it's chaos."[61] So stated one of the nation's leading experts on governing-by-contracting, and likely he is accurate. Nevertheless, conspiracy can capitalize on chaos more readily than on order, and the milieu of federal contracting is more of the former than the latter.

Government and Business: Selected Cases

The examples are almost endless, but consider several instances of the relationships between government and business working together in the public interest.

Contracting in Conflicts of Interest. Monsanto Research Corporation, an arm of Monsanto Chemical Company, was awarded a $5.8 million contract by the Environmental Protection Agency (EPA) to measure the environmental dangers of various chemicals, including acrylonitrile.

Monsanto is the nation's fourth largest producer of chemicals, and the world's largest manufacturer of acrylonitrile, a chemical used extensively in industry. Its wholly owned subsidiary, Monsanto Research, reported to the EPA that acrylonitrile was not hazardous to the environment, although an EPA official stated, "Quite frankly, I don't see how they reached that conclusion. . . . It was not reasonable based on the data we have. . . . Our conclusion is that acrylonitrile is one of the biggest sources of hydrocarbons in the petrochemical industry. It is a major polluter."[62]

Similarly, Exxon Research and Engineering Corporation, a branch of Exxon Oil Company, the world's largest oil producer, was hired by EPA to write the Agency's environmental regulations for off-shore oil drilling. On the very day the EPA signed the $965,000 contract with Exxon, the Company discharged almost half a million gallons of polluted water into the sea near Alaska's Prudhoe Bay—a gross violation of EPA standards for which Exxon was later fined $100,000. When Exxon Research and Engineering Corporation sent its report to the Environmental Protection Agency, the Agency's contract officers labeled it "shallow" and self-serving. Exxon had concluded that off-shore oil drilling did not pose any serious pollution problems. According to one EPA official, "There was a lot of p. r. [public relations] nonsense in a technical report extolling their environmental awareness."[63]

Contracting in Corporate Incompetence. Conflicts of interest are one thing, incompetence another. Consider two additional cases. One occurred when the Stanford Research Institute (SRI) was hired by the U.S. Office of Education (now the Department of Education) to evaluate the progress of children enrolled in its Headstart Program. When the report from Stanford Research Institute finally arrived, six months late, at the Office of Education, it was judged, with considerable reason, to be unacceptable. The director of the Headstart Evaluation Branch of the Office of Education "found not only that the work was poor, but that SRI had plagiarized, from among all possible sources, her own work."[64] She went on to note that one section of the report was "lifted almost word for word from my 1969 paper. . . . can't your staff think for itself?"[65]

Despite what amounted to unequivocal proof that the Stanford Research Institute had no personnel qualified to undertake an evaluation of the Headstart and, later, the Followthrough Programs for the Office of Education, SRI's contracts were continued. Ultimately, the Stanford Research Institute was involved in an Office of Education contract amounting to more than $13 million; the Institute's "fee," by which was meant profit, for this project was $857,000.

Consider another example, the experience of the federal government when it undertook the largest job evaluation project ever attempted through a private contractor. When Congress created the U.S. Postal Corporation out of the old Postal Service in 1969, a remaining problem was the job status of the Postal Corporation's 750,000 employees. Reviewing and recategorizing the work of these employees amounted to a huge project in public personnel administration, yet the decision to let the contract in 1970 ultimately devolved to one man, whose background largely was in private business. He contacted a small number of corporations, but eventually awarded the contract to Westinghouse Corporation, which had bid $3 million—a bid that was $300,000 higher than the next highest bid, and a million dollars higher than the average bid of the four other bidders.

Cost and quality do not always correlate, and Washington's experience with Westinghouse shows that incompetence can come highly priced. By way of indication, the team of fifty self-designated experts that Westinghouse assembled to conduct a sophisticated study of human resource management included a sales manager of soft drink vending equipment, and a nuclear safety engineer.[66] According to Congress, not one member of this team had "specific and direct job evaluation experience."[67] In fact, so uncertain was Westinghouse over its own abilities in this area, that it hired Fry Consultants to actually train its own people so that they could conduct the study!

Westinghouse was so grossly unqualified to conduct a personnel study that its ineptness eventually resulted in the most detailed congressional investigation into a consultant contract ever undertaken. Among other problems, the House Post Office and Civil Service Committee concluded that not only had the contract been awarded to a firm that had absolutely no experience or ability in the field for which it was hired, and had made by far the highest bid to conduct the study, but also that there were no criteria in existence by which *any* contractors were selected! This applied not only to the Postal Corporation, but apparently to the whole of the federal government as well.[68]

Contracting in Complexity. All too frequently, the complexities that emerge from the interface between contractor and government make worthwhile public programs distressingly vulnerable. One of the sadder examples of the public's loss resulting from an arrogant press, understandably frustrated contractors, an ignorant Congress, and timid bureaucrats concerns a $3.4 million, five-year contract awarded in 1975 by the National Institute on Drug Abuse to Medical Research Applications, Inc. The firm was to collect clinical data on LAAM, a German drug reputed to be more effective than methadone for treating heroin addicts, and to develop it for widespread use. By 1979, the research (involving 6,000 addicts) was essentially completed, "and the work was found to be very good."[69] But columnist Jack Anderson was attacking the Institute (and Congress) as a wanton wastrel of taxpayers' dollars, citing the LAAM research contract as but one example. Consequently, the House Subcommittee on Health and the Environment questioned the Institute's management of the contract. Soon, according to the federal project officer in charge of the contract, Institute "people were saying, 'If we do this wrong, Anderson will write an article about us.'... Everybody was afraid."[70] When the nearly completed research project came up for renewal of its contract, the Institute withdrew its funding. Because of this termination, Medical Research Applications boxed up some 400,000 pages of first-rate data that it had amassed, and stored them—as was its legal right under its contract with the Institute.

The research, a critical part of a larger, $10 million research effort on LAAM sponsored by the Institute, has never been used, either by the government or the contractor; both sides need the other's data if LAAM is to be used in the United States to relieve heroin addiction. Both sides agree on one thing, however: Misguided politics

prevailed. A federal official familiar with the episode stated, "It was the government bureaucracy that botched it up. It was politics. The thing is, the contractor did a very good job."[71]

TO PRIVATIZE OR NOT TO PRIVATIZE: QUESTIONS OF EFFICIENCY, POLICY, AND CORRUPTION

Should government privatize or not? Was the Office of Education less or more competent than the Stanford Research Institute in managing the Headstart and Followthrough evaluations? True, Stanford Research Institute did not chalk up an admirable record in the process but, on the other hand, neither did the Office of Education by letting the contracts in the first place and further, not terminating them when its administrators found that the evaluations were being conducted with inordinate slovenliness. Was the Westinghouse Electric Corporation less or more competent than the Postal Corporation in conducting the personnel reclassification study? Competency is difficult to ascribe to either party.

In the following discussions we consider the three most significant issues of federal competency in the management of privatization: efficiency, policy, and corruption.

The Efficiency Question

Although we have deliberately steered shy of arguing the obverse of the conventional wisdom (*i.e.*, that business is more efficient than government) by contending that government is innately more efficient than private enterprise, it does appear that government agencies may be able to execute some of their policies less expensively than private contractors are doing. One estimate, for example, placed the cost of personnel working under federal grants and contracts at *seven times* the cost of full-time federal personnel.[72]

It has been only comparatively recently that the federal government has taken any sort of genuine interest in empirically determining, rather than ideologically justifying, the assumption that "business is better." Consider the fate, for example, of OMB Circular A-49, which was issued by the then Bureau of the Budget in 1959. It urges government agencies to evaluate and maintain evaluations of the work of consulting contractors. The Circular has been virtually forgotten by federal officials, although it is still on the OMB's list of active regulations. One study found that OMB had assigned not one of its employees to be responsible for its administration; "OMB Circular A-49 washes out in the files after 1962."[73] Although there are signs of improvement, so lax has the federal government been in following up on the performance of contractors that even debarred and suspended firms can still receive federal contracts. One investigation by the Senate uncovered instances of companies that had been suspended by federal agencies for fraud nonetheless were acquiring contracts from other agencies.[74]

Beginning in the late 1970s, Congress and federal administrators began to take a renewed interest in the question of whether private companies really could supply federal needs more efficiently than public agencies. The first indication of this questioning was a congressional exempting of certain governmental functions from the provisions of OMB Circular A-76 during the 1970s. In 1979, Circular A-76 was altered, for the first time, so that detailed work statements would be used to evaluate just how well federal work was done by private contractors; a second major change was introduced in 1983, and agencies were directed to determine the most efficient way to complete a project in-house before comparing costs to have it done in the private sector.

In 1987, two new policies were introduced that indicated a further federal effort to get a handle on whether cost savings were actually being realized under OMB Circular A-76. One was Executive Order 12615, mentioned earlier, which essentially directed the Office of Management and Budget to conduct more rigorous and regular analyses of the savings acquired by contracting out under the provisions of Circular A-76, with OMB picking up those savings at the agencies' expense, and the other was the Commercial Activities Contracting Act of 1987, which focused on assuring the reliability and accuracy of reported savings accrued via contracting out.

Despite these and other efforts, however, the assessment of whether privatizing federal projects actually saves money is still undone. The cost studies ordered by Executive Order 12615 have been barely undertaken at all; methodologi-

cal disputes abound, and so "a hard accounting of money saved and where it went is lacking";[75] and nineteen of twenty-one federal agencies surveyed believed that the goals of OMB Circular A-76 were unrealistic.[76] The chair of the Senate Budget Committee wrote the director of the Office of Management and Budget in 1990 that, "The pursuit of the [federal privatization] program by the Reagan administration seems to have been built around the dubious ideological objective of 'privatization' without serious regard for efficiencies achieved or money wasted."[77]

The Policy Question

Compounding the already extraordinary difficulties involved in determining "privatized" governmental efficiency are the problems unique to managing public programs in a political world. Paramountly, these problems occur when "advice" from private interests waxes into policy executed by public administrators. The General Accounting Office has called Congress' attention to this fundamental dilemma in formal reports dating from 1961. As one of them put it, "Federal agencies have used contractors . . . to perform work that should be done by Federal employees because it involves basic management decisions. Although contractors may not be making final decisions, we are concerned about the extent to which contractors are influencing agencies' control of Federal policies and programs. . . . it is sometimes difficult to tell where 'advice' stops and 'performance' begins."[78] Or, as a top official of GAO put it more pithily, "We've seen situations where an agency contracts out so much of its data gathering and policy analysis that it thinks it has control, but the consultant is, in effect, making the decision."[79]

The power that private interests have over public policy "makers" in the bureaucracy can be traced to their control of information. For example, the Institute for Government Research, founded in the early part of the century (in 1926 it merged with the Robert Brookings Graduate School and the Institute for Economics to form the Brookings Institution), was instrumental in drafting the Budget and Accounting Act of 1921, which provided not only the first guidelines for writing an annual, coherent budget for the federal government, but created the Bureau of the Budget (now called the Office of Management and Budget) and the General Accounting Office—the two most important fiscal agencies in Washington. In fact, President Warren G. Harding in 1921 asked the Institute for Government Research to actually *write* the federal budget! This was a rather incredible delegation of power by a government to a private body. "If there is any task that is supposed to be an official and nondelegable executive function, it is the preparation of the budget."[80]

Nevertheless, comparable activities occur today. In the 1970s, for example, the Federal Power Commission and the Department of the Interior requested, at the height of the Arab oil embargo, the American Gas Association to make the official estimates on national gas reserves. So sensitive was this information that the government permitted the natural gas industry to withhold data from the public in making its official estimates.[81]

Contracting for Federal Services: Problems of Public Probity.

lmost $50 billion—about a fourth—of what the federal government expends through contracts with the private sector are for "services." *A service contract* is a contract for professional and administrative support services, often in the form of hiring consultants. Between 1979 (the first year for which records wcrc kept) and 1989, the federal tab for service contracts more than doubled.[82]

This doubling in contracting for services with the private sector appears to be attributable to a combination of burgeoning rates of federal expenditures (indicating that federal managers have more to manage), and a declining rate in the federal hiring of more managers. Whereas federal budget outlays increased by 127 percent over ten years, and federal contracts for services almost kept pace by growing by 113 percent, federal personnel expenditures increased by only 73 percent.[83]

The upsurge in federal service contracts is significant because it is the service contract that melds the public's interest with the special interest in the most intimate, and perhaps inimicable, ways. Private interests may be guiding and forming public policies and engaging in government activities in ways that are inappropriate, and which run counter to the general welfare; a review by the General Accounting Office of contracts for consultants' services in four major federal agencies found that over a fifth of the contracts appeared to involve "inherently governmental functions."[84]

Contracts and Consultants.

The General Accounting Office's analysis of consulting contracts leads us to the federal government's extensive use of private consultants and "think tanks" in the implementation—and often formulation—of national public policies. This is an area of considerable bureaucratic murk, and the GAO has stated that it is unable to determine how much the federal government spends on consultants.[85] A consultant's professional trade association estimates that consultants' services cost all their contractors some $30 billion a year (almost a third of what wages and benefits cost the federal government), and the Office of Management and Budget states that over 52,000 private companies furnish the federal government with the expertise and advise of their employees.[86]

Private consultants often are among the most ardent in their arguments that private management somehow is more efficient than public management. For example, consultants were called into the state of Connecticut to analyze methods of solid waste disposal. Their report was notably ideological in its view that private business could handle the problems of solid waste disposal far more effectively and efficiently than could government. "The apparent assumption of the consultants was that inefficiency is inevitable in government agencies, even when those agencies are headed by businessmen (and, conversely, that efficiency is standard in authorities, even when they are headed by politicians)."[87] Similarly, when the Arthus D. Little, Inc., consultants analyzed postal services for the U.S. government in 1968, its report concluded, with essentially no evidence whatever, that an independent postal service would be a more "businesslike" operation, and therefore could provide less costly service, than would a public agency. When the reorganization of the postal service was accomplished in 1971, converting it from a public agency to a public corporation, the effect was to "substitute business patronage for political patronage."[88]

Who are these consultants? No one has a definitive list, but they include economists, social scientists, education specialists, management consultants, operations researchers, transportation consultants, and urban affairs consultants. These operations range from the infinitesimal (the so-called "boutiques" that are highly specialized and come and go) to the very large, such as Westinghouse and General Electric. The Washington-based consultants (almost 20,000 of them, working in more than 1,300 firms, by one count)[89] are known as the "Beltway bandits" because many of them are located near the Beltway Road that circles through the suburbs of Washington, and they have their own lobby in the capitol, the Professional Services Council.

Among the more intriguing recipients of federal consulting contracts are the think tanks that the Department of Defense has itself established to receive its contracts. Known as Federally Funded Research and Development Centers (FFRDCs), or Federal Contract Research Centers (a more dated title), these organizations were created by the Pentagon after World War II, and arc contracted by the Defense Department to develop weapons systems and other Defense programs. There are eleven FFRDCs—Rand Corporation, Mitre Corporation, and the Massachusetts Institute of Technology's Lincoln Laboratories number among them—employing 8,500 people, and which do a $1.5 billion annual business with the Pentagon. Ironically, these consulting centers often hire their own consultants to fulfill their federal contracts.[90]

Although the FFRDCs are big operations, their legality is unclear. The Government Corporation Control Act of 1945 seems to prohibit, in rather firm phrases, the creation of government corporations (which these Centers are) without the approval of Congress. Nevertheless, neither Congress nor the Comptroller General have been especially enthusiastic in their enforcement of the Act as it applies to Federally Funded Research and Development Centers, which have been established unilaterally by the executive branch.[91]

Other nonprofit research and consulting organizations are nominally the results of efforts by private industry, but often with substantial government encouragement as opposed to outright creation. One survey, conducted by the National Science Foundation, found 159 nonprofit research organizations of this kind. Nearly two-thirds of their research contracts came from the federal government, with the four largest of these organizations receiving a third of the total federal dollars contracted with the group; the eight largest took half of the federal contracts.[92] These include Stanford Research Institute, founded in 1946 by Stanford University; Battelle, founded by Gordon Battelle in 1923; the Brookings Institution (1926); the National Bureau of Economic Research (founded in 1920 by private economists, who developed such concepts as the Gross National Product); the Committee for Economic Development, and a number of others.

Consultants to the federal government operate in somewhat of a netherworld, and prefer it that way. It was only in 1990 that federal regulations appeared which required consultants who contracted or subcontracted with federal agencies to disclose their other public and private clients with whom they have worked over the past year. This requirement was issued because of a growing ethical problem: Consultants were promoting their other clients for government contracts with federal agencies with which they were consulting. One member of Congress has estimated that 70 percent of all the information released by the federal government is "tainted" by dint of having been formulated by consultants who could have a conflict of interest.[93] Presumably, federal administrators, as a result of the regulations of 1990, will at least be in a position to know when the consultants whom they have hire are "working both sides of the street." The public, however, will not be in the same position to know, since the disclosure forms are not available to the public.

It is also unclear if these regulations will work. "Washington's army of consultants has generally accepted the new rules without much more than grumbling—an indication that the regulations are not expected to significantly affect the way consultants go about their business.[94] Nevertheless, the Beltway bandits and their colleagues across the country are so ensconced in the Washington way of doing business that even their most fervent critics agree that the federal government would "stop" in the unlikely event that their services were suddenly and unilaterally terminated.[95]

The Corruption Question

Finally, and all too frequently, basic honesty can be as difficult to identify as either efficiency or appropriate policymaking in the federal contracting culture. The examples of fraud and corruption, particularly in the area of defense contracting, are becoming almost legion. Between 1983 and 1990, twenty-five of the hundred largest contractors for the Pentagon were found guilty of procurement fraud, some of them more than once.[96] "Operation Ill Wind," begun covertly in the mid-1980s by the U.S. Justice Department (it became public only in 1988), had, by 1990, convicted 39 corporate executives, government officials, corporations, and consultants who had contracts with the Defense Department for procurement fraud, with a total of 100 convictions ultimately anticipated.[97]

"Fraud," it should be noted, does not mean the inadvertent failure to dot the proverbial "i" in a procurement contract. In the case of Operation Ill Wind, for example, it meant that the thirty-nine convictions (as of 1990) led to the recovery of more than $24 million in fines and forfeitures. Fraud means bribing public administrators to obtain inside, often secret, information for purposes of bid-rigging; falsifying weapons test results; failing to conduct specifically contracted tests, and then lying about it; grossly overcharging the government with padded accounts; and hiding the bad news about grotesque cost overruns long after such overruns should have been reported.

Why does fraud continue unabated? Because, with few exceptions, the federal government keeps coming back for more.[98] Not one of the twenty-five major corporations convicted of procurement fraud was barred from further contract work with the federal government. For example, Northrup Corporation in 1990 pleaded guilty to falsifying test results on missile and aircraft components; the Pentagon "debarred" (that is, suspended) the division of Northrup which had been responsible for falsifying the results, but the other divisions of Northrup, notably one that supplied a component for the Marine Corps' Harrier jet, were permitted to continue their defense contracts and bid for new ones. Some companies are not even an inconvenienced as Northrup was. In 1990, Emerson Electric Company pleaded guilty to no fewer than four felony counts for over-charging the government for electronics components, but remained on the government's approved list of contractors. The list goes on.

The reason why the federal government keeps contracting with proven felons relates, in the view of some, to a contracting culture in the federal bureaucracy, particularly in the Pentagon, that places scant value on acquiring one's money's worth. As a former procurement officer for the U.S. Air Force put it, "It doesn't matter if you screw everything up, as long as you keep the dollars flowing."[99] When this entrenched bureaucratic culture (which places a premium on hiding the bad news, whether it is corruption or cost overruns, for the sake of assuring an unimpeded flow of federal allocations from Congress) is combined with the daunting political difficulties of separating, even in the face of criminal convictions, contractor from agency (which, as we discussed earlier, are conjoined more by "treaty" than by contract), then the vast dimensions of the problem become clearer. Corruption in contracting will never be controlled as long as careers depend more on maintaining that flow of federal dollars than managing it.

Just how deeply this culture penetrates can be judged by the brief history of the Pentagon's position of Under Secretary of Defense for acquisition—a position created as a civilian "procurement czar" by Congress in 1986 as a means of cleaning up the contracting situation in the Department of Defense. Within the space of its first four years of existence, the position's first three occupants failed to bring any control to procurement, and each resigned under pressure.

We stated earlier the effectiveness, efficiency, and the proper role of the private sector in the public's business are difficult to demonstrate empirically one way or the other. But this empirical difficulty does not extend to demonstrating the existence of widespread corruption, which can be and has been proven in court, nor to the federal government's lethargy in responding to that corruption.

PRIVATIZING AT THE GRASSROOTS

Local governments in the United States contract out more than a billion dollars a year in local services, and almost four-fifths of local administrators believe that "privatization will represent a primary tool to provide local government services and facilities in the next decade."[100] Local governments privatize in three principal ways: by selling off assets, by privatizing facilities, and (by far the most used) by contracting out local services.

Selling Out

One analysis concluded that the states and localities could gain nearly $227 billion if they simply sold off enterprises that are (in the opinion of the analysts) more appropriately owned and managed by the private sector. These enterprises include airports, electric and gas utilities, highways and bridges, parking facilities, ports, water works, wastewater plants, and others.[101] Selling assets, however, is not a favored form of privatization in the United States, and one survey found that only 24 percent of cities and counties had done so over a five-year period, and only 21 percent planned to sell governmental assets over the next two years (at an estimated return of $3 billion). Most local governments sell assets in the form of vacant land or obsolete facilities, and the primary motivation to do so is not to improve government services, but to balance budgets.[102]

Privatizing Facilities

A second form of privatization used by local governments is the construction or acquisition of facilities, such as sewage-treatment plants, by private companies, which then own and operate the facilities for the government. Over 32 percent of cities and counties had privatized facilities between 1982 and 1987, and over 38 percent planned to do so. Local governments which do privatize facilities favor privatizing roads, bridges, tunnels, street lights, wastewater, sewers, and solid waste treatment facilities, among others. In contrast to privatizing by selling off assets, the improvement of local services appears to be a principal motivator in the privatization of facilities: Capital-cost savings and a "lack of expertise" in managing the facilities are the most common reasons given by local officials for privatizing facilities.[103]

Contracting Out Local Services

By far the most common form of privatization at the local level is contracting with private organizations (both for-profit and not-for-profit) and other governments to deliver public services. Nearly 99 percent of cities and counties had contracted out services over a five-year period in the 1980s, and 96 percent planned to continue the practice.[104] Table 11-1 lists the major services contracted out by cities and counties; garbage collection and disposal, vehicle towing, and the maintenance of buildings and grounds typically lead the pack in most surveys.

Not all contracts entered into by state and local governments are with private firms. Local governments in particular contract with other governments and other nonprofit organizations, such as neighborhood associations, as well, and this important point sometimes is overlooked when contracting is considered at the grassroots.

With the exception of some minor delivery mechanisms, the methods by which local governments deliver services have not fluctuated significantly in recent years in terms of some methods being preferred over others. Over 28 percent of municipal services are delivered to citizens, either totally or partially, via contracts, and the mode clearly preferred by urban governments is to deliver these services directly—nearly 60 percent of city services are delivered by city government employees, and the remaining 11 percent of local services are delivered by franchises, vouchers, subsidies, tax incentives, volunteers, and other methods.[105]

Nevertheless, contracting with private companies, as a proportion of all local contracting, is gaining favor among local administrators. Of twenty-three services contracted out by cities and counties over ten years, contracting to private companies increased in all but four. These increases occurred primarily at the expense of intergovernmental service contracting by local governments.[106]

Contracting with the Third Sector

As we have noted, government contracting includes contracting not only with for-profit corporations but nonprofit organizations as well—organizations such as social service agencies, cul-

TABLE 11-1   Major Services Contracted Out by Cities and Counties over Five Years, 1982–1987

Service	Percentage Contracted
Solid Waste Collection or Disposal	60%
Vehicle Towing or Storage	45
Building of Grounds Maintenance and Services	45
Administration (*e.g.*, legal, accounting, payroll)	36
Traffic Signal or Street Lighting Services	32
Data Processing	31
Streets and Roads (including snow removal)	30
Fleet or Vehicle Maintenance	20
Recreation, Parks, Convention Halls, Stadiums, or Cultural Facilities	18
Transit or Transportation	17
Hospitals, Health Care, or Emergency Services	16
Elderly or Handicapped	12
Airports	10
Utilities	10
Public Safety or Corrections	7
Parking Lots or Garages	7
Housing or Shelters	4
Child Care or Day Care	4

Source: As derived from Irwin T. David, "Privatization in America," *Municipal Year Book, 1988* (Washington, D. C.: International City Management Association, 1988), p. 48, Figure 5/3.

tural groups, neighborhood associations, health organizations, and so forth, that are not government agencies. Cities and counties particularly favor contracting with nonprofit organizations, in contrast to for-profit organizations, for such services as emergency medical care, cemetery maintenance, paratransit systems, and the great majority of services that are usually included in the categories of health and human services and parks and recreation.[107]

We are only beginning to learn about the contractual and fiscal connections between the public sector and the *third sector*, or *independent sector*, as nonprofit, charitable, and voluntary organizations are sometimes called. There may be as many as three million third-sector organizations in the United States.[108]

The Urban Institute has made some important contributions to our understanding of how governments work with third-sector organizations. In a careful empirical examination of 3,411 local nonprofit human service organizations in twelve representative metropolitan areas and four rural areas, the Urban Institute discovered that governments are unusually and surprisingly hefty supporters of supposedly independent, nonprofit human service organizations. More than 38 percent of the revenues of these organizations comes from governments![109]

Because of "pass through" arrangements (*e.g.*, federal monies to subnational governments that ultimately are used to fund contracts with nonprofit service organizations), identifying the level of government (*i.e.*, federal, state, or local) and each level's proportionate contribution via contracts to these agencies can be extremely difficult to ascertain. However, it appears that most of the funds which are used to support contracts with nonprofit human services organizations are federal funds that Washington has transferred as grants-in-aid to state and local governments, while almost all of the contracting agents who negotiate contracts with these organizations are state and local officials. One study found that over half of all federal funds used for social services are now passed through state and local governments to nonprofit organizations, compared to almost no federal funds earmarked for social services that were transferred to nonprofits in 1960.[110] Governments, and government funds, are major actors in these "charitable" activities.

In fact, as the suppliers of 38 percent of the budgets of nonprofit human services organizations, governments are *the* major actors; the next largest source of revenues for nonprofit human services organizations is fees, dues, and charges to clients and members of the organizations themselves (less than 30 percent), followed by private and direct giving by individuals (nearly 12 percent), miscellaneous projects such as bake sales (6 percent), United Way (more than 5 percent), income from endowments and investments (less than 5 percent), foundation grants (less than 4 percent), corporate gifts (3 percent), and other sources contributing less than 2 percent. Total *private* giving to nonprofit human services organizations (which Americans typically perceive to be private charities) amounts to only 21 percent of their revenues, compared to the 38 percent of their income that is obtained from government contracts![111]

Just as governments support these nonprofit organizations with public funds, so do nonprofit organizations support governments by delivering human services. Forty-two percent of *all* public spending for health care (excluding hospitals), social services, housing and community development, employment and training, and arts and culture is spent in the form of government contracts with private, nonprofit groups![112]

Another 19 percent of government's human service delivery dollars is contracted with private, for-profit organizations. In other words, an impressive 61 percent of public expenditures for human services is channeled to private-sector organizations, both nonprofit and for-profit, that are responsible for implementing these programs! The remaining 39 percent of human services are delivered directly by government agencies. The largest single deliverer of publicly-financed human services, however, remains the nonprofit sector: "It is this government-nonprofit partnership that forms the core of human service delivery systems in the United States."[113]

This little known bond between the public sector and the third sector is surprisingly strong. An analysis of state agencies in New York which had contracted with nonprofit organizations to deliver services found that there was a high level of interdependence between the agencies and the organizations in obtaining resources for both. "Public-sector agencies and nonprofit sector agencies reported virtually identical resource dependence on each other."[114]

The third sector is, in sum, a significant player in the "privatization" of public policy delivery.

Beyond Contracting: Volunteers in Government

With all companies in the private sector and most organizations in the third sector, governments sign contracts because money is changing hands. But governments are less likely to enter into contracts when they are beneficiaries of volunteers from the private sector or the third sector, and these happy arrangements are becoming increasingly important in the implementation of public programs. These arrangements generally are called "coproduction."

Coproduction is the participation by volunteers in the delivery of government services. At least 20 percent,[115] and perhaps 40 percent, of American adults do volunteer work, valued at $170 billion, and the percentage is rising.[116] Many of these volunteers contribute their energies to government-related functions, such as schools (over 15 percent), civic organizations (over 13 percent), hospitals (over 10 percent), and welfare organizations (nearly 10 percent).[117] An estimated 10 million Americans volunteer for service in neighborhood crime watch groups,[118] and about 70 percent of cities and counties report that they use volunteers in delivering public programs.[119] Between 1982 and 1988, the number of urban services delivered by volunteers doubled, to about 4 percent of all municipal services.[120]

In the spirit, perhaps, of no good deed going unpunished, volunteers are not free. They cost, both in terms of time devoted to managing volunteers by public administrators and the corresponding expenses of devoting that time to them. Whereas volunteers can make possible governmental accomplishments that would not be possible without them,[121] there are limits to their benefits. Consider the example of volunteer fire fighters.

Perhaps the most extensive use of volunteers by American governments is that of volunteer fire fighters; there are over 25,000 volunteer fire departments and over a million volunteer fire fighters, comprising four-fifths of America's total fire fighting force and covering three-fourths of the United States. [122] Yet, one study of municipal fire departments in New York State found that, when the annual costs of recruiting, training, and managing volunteer fire fighters exceeded a relatively small sum ($800 per fire fighter), "the use of volunteers should be reconsidered" because it is more cost-effective to start adding full-time paid professionals.[123]

A More Manageable Task?

State and local governments appear to have a reasonably firm, if occasionally tenuous, grip on their private contractors. One reason why is that, despite its growing popularity among the grassroots governments, privatization nonetheless remains relatively restricted in its use at these levels, and so the supervisory chore is more manageable than at the federal level. A review of the literature on the topic concluded that subnational contracting of all types with private firms was "limited," and that privatizing public services by local governments ran a distant third to governments providing the services themselves or via intergovernmental agreements.[124]

Additionally, public controls over certain categories of contracting are relatively thorough at the subnational levels. Virtually all state and local governments have detailed regulations governing construction contracts with private builders; they maintain sizable building inspection operations and central purchasing units that are normally responsible and well-run. Moreover, state and local governments have considerable experience in using the contract (in the form of letting franchises, leases, concessions, and arranging sales) as a device that actually makes money for governments rather than as a mechanism for spending it.

Third, competitive bidding, while not as common a practice as it perhaps should be, seems to be used frequently by subnational governments. One national study found that 64 percent of cities and counties let contracts to the lowest bidder, and another 11 percent let contracts to the lowest bidder in a format in which governments preselected a group of qualified bidders; less than 22 percent of local governments selected contractors on the basis of "sole service procurement,"[125] in contrast to the estimated 85 percent of all contracts that are negotiated with a single company by federal agencies.

Finally, oversight of a company's performance by state and local officials, while less than systematic, at least seems to be a matter of concern. One survey found a surprising propensity among these officials to take "the fairly dramatic step" of changing from private supplier to public provider, or vice versa, indicating an interest by state and local governments in determining whether the private sphere or the public one was the more efficient deliverer of services.[126]

Privatization: Government Opinion, Business Opinion, and Public Opinion

What do local officials themselves think about the contracting option? Table 11-2 indicates these opinions. By and large, local officials think that they get both efficient and effective service by privatization, although there are some substantial minority opinions to the contrary. One national survey found that, among those local administrators whose governments had contracted with private service deliverers, nearly three-quarters had done so because they perceived cost savings to be an advantage.[127]

Nevertheless, the same poll found that, whereas local officials believed privatization to be a significant method in the delivery of local services for some time to come, there was little indication of a future upsurge in privatization among local governments: "About the same number have used privatization before or plan to use it in

TABLE 11-2 **Local Public Administrators' Opinions on Contracting Out Local Services**

Statement	Responses (N = 225)
Contracting out costs *less* than government provision	43%
Contracting out costs *the same* as government provision	13
Contracting out costs *more* than government provision	27
No answer	17
Total	100
Contracting out results in quality *poorer* than government provision	7
Contracting out results in quality *the same* as government provision	32
Contracting out results in quality *better* than government provision	32
No answer	29
Total	100

Source: Patricia S. Florestano and Stephen B. Gordon, "A Survey of City and County Use of Private Contracting," *The Urban Interest*, 3 (Spring 1981), p. 25.

the future."[128] Most local public administrators hesitate to privatize because they fear losing control of public programs (51 percent), employee and union resistance (47 percent), "politics" (42 percent), and a "lack of belief" in the benefits of privatization (38 percent).[129]

The prudent approach that local officials have taken to dealing with the private sector is reflected by the private sector itself, but in a quite different way: Businesspeople express irritation over the business practices of governments.

A survey of almost 3,000 companies that county governments maintained on file uncovered a "generally negative attitude" among the firms when it came to dealing with government. The major frustrations encountered by businesses concerned slow payment by governments of bills due (by far the top frustration); difficulty in communicating with their customers; bid specifications that were either too restrictive or too general; excessive paperwork; confusion over who was responsible for making the purchasing decisions; and "competition from other firms" which pushed "prices too low for the firm to com-

pete"—certainly a "negative" in the minds of the nearly 29 percent of the business executives who objected to governments pushing for rock-bottom prices, but perhaps not a negative in the minds of taxpayers.[130] Table 11-3 indicates the opinions of business executives about dealing with governments, and shows that most of them have low opinions about the quality and fairness of government purchasing practices.

It is entirely possible that local government officials would be more enthusiastic about privatization than they are if their citizens were more trusting of the privatization option. However, the people are notably leery about turning over the delivery of public services to private corporations. Asked in a national survey whether they thought local government or private enterprise could deliver six selected services more efficiently, only one (hospitals) was identified by Americans as a service that private vendors could provide more efficiently than local government— and then by the notably slender margin of 1 percent. Although more highly educated respondents

TABLE 11-3 **Opinions of Business Executives About Doing Business with Governments**

Area of Concern	Opinion		No Opinion
	Poor	Good	
Ability of government purchasing practices to attract first-rate vendors to compete for contracts	52%	35%	13%
Ability of government purchasing practices to produce quality goods and services at lowest cost	60	30	10
Fairness and impartiality of government purchasing practices	49	34	17

Source: As derived from: Susan A. MacManus, "Why Businesses Are Reluctant to Sell to Governments," *Public Administration Review*, 51 (July/August 1991), p. 329.

The number of firms responding to the survey was 3,282. Percentages have been rounded. The actual questions asked began with the phrase, "Businesses like mine generally believe...", and respondents gave a "yes" ("good" in Table 11-4), or "no" ("poor") response.

**TABLE 11-4   Popular Preferences About Local Service Deliverers, Public or Private, for Selected
Services, 1985**

Preferred Deliverer	Parking Facilities	Street Maintenance	Hospitals	Parks and Swimming Pools	Garbage Collection	Ambulance Services
Private Companies	42%	21%	46%	25%	41%	41%
Local Government	48	73	45	68	53	52
Don't Know	10	6	9	7	6	7

Source: Advisory Committee on Intergovernmental Relations, *Changing Public Attitudes on Government and Taxes,* 1985
(Washington, D. C.: U. S. Government Printing Office, 1985), pp. 25-29.

evidenced a greater faith in corporate America as
an efficient deliverer of local services (college
graduates picked private enterprise as a superior
provider of three of the six services), the point
nonetheless stands that, in one of the globe's
major bastions of capitalism, government generally is more trusted than corporations to deliver
public programs efficiently. Table 11-4 provides
details of the survey.

GOVERNMENT CONTRACTING: WHAT MUST BE DONE?

The relatively high concern displayed by local
administrators in measuring and comparing the
costs of services provided by the public and private sectors points to the fundamental dilemma
of government contracting: American governments have no instrument, no established procedures, for assuring that the public's business is
conducted efficiently, effectively, and without
undue influence by private interests. We are not
arguing that government can be conducted more
efficiently through public agencies, or through
government corporations (considered next), or
through private business. What we are suggesting is that improved means be established to
determine which of these and possibly other
devices conduct which projects most effectively
and efficiently.

How can we make these determinations? At
least three steps seem warranted. One is to establish within the chief executive offices of all levels
of government (*i.e.*, the president, the governors,
the mayors, and other local chief executives) an
authority for government contractors that would
have the power of advising the chief executives

on matters concerning government contracting,
categorize government contractors according to
function and performance, establish performance
auditing criteria, assist government contractors in
efficiently conducting their business, establish
annual reports on the activities of contractors,
verify the reports that are made to governments
by contractors, have the authority of establishing
and terminating government contracts as well as
settling disputes, and working with the public
prosecutors.[131] Some central figure who has both
access to the chief executives of American governments and values the growing need for more
managerial flexibility and authority in dealing
with contractors is needed to adequately control
the public's business.

A second step that must be taken is the reedu-
cation and intellectual upgrading of the more than
150,000 federal bureaucrats, and uncounted state
and local administrators, who manage the vast
and complex contracts and grants processes of
American governments. An indication of the low
levels of education held by these federal officials
is the fact that the federal procurement and contracting work force has, on the average, a high
school diploma plus three months of college education.[132] Education is a major means in bringing
the margins of the state under some degree of
control for purposes of knowledgeable action.

Finally, it is important to professionalize contract management as a field, and the need for this
professionalization seems particularly acute at the
federal level. In addition to infusing more formally educated administrators into the practice of
contract management, steps should be taken to
assure that contract managers can be promoted to
higher ranks as contract managers, and that, in a
field where one is expected to deal as a peer with

executives who travel in their own Gulfstream jets—executives who, moreover, may be tempted to attempt bribery as a cost-cutting ploy—contract managers be paid more than they currently are.

The lack of a professional corps of contract managers is indicated by the brief spells that federal contract managers are assigned to crucial projects. Despite the fact that no fewer than six special commissions since World War II have recommended that the tenure of program managers assigned to major weapons projects be lengthened, and legislation which was enacted in 1984 requiring that such administrators remain at their post for at least four years, the average time that these contract managers spend on a weapons acquisition project actually decreased from twenty-five months in 1984 to twenty-one months in 1990![133] According to one observer, "the services broke the law 89 percent of the time."[134]

Why? In part because it does not pay a military careerist to devote a lot of time to contract management, beyond getting one's "ticket punched" as quickly as possible in the field, and moving on. In 1990, the Pentagon initiated a new policy that established a separate career path for acquisition specialists designed to offset this pattern, and in 1991 Congress established the Defense Acquisition University as a procurement equivalent to the prestigious National War College. Both are steps in the right direction of working against the Pentagon's contracting culture, which gives little credence to protecting public funds from the predations of private contractors.

THE GOVERNMENT CORPORATION

As we observed at the beginning of this chapter, the reluctance of local officials, in contrast to federal administrators, to privatize extensively is rooted in certain political realities, notably the relatively vibrant unions of state and local employees that do not want to see their jobs "contracted away," and antiquated fiscal requirements that are often cemented into state constitutions. Nevertheless, state and local governments have borne the brunt of public demands for greater services over the last few decades and have, as a result, been forced to find ways to accommodate those demands. The answer that most states and local jurisdictions have found is the creation of the public corporation, a mysterious, veiled, and secretive entity that functions of the fringes of the public domain.

The *government corporation*, also known as the *special authority* or *public authority*, is an independent, legislatively created monopoly empowered to build, maintain, and manage public services. Such services include hospitals, bridges, university dormitories, tunnels, roads, senior citizen centers, public housing, seaports, mental health facilities, airports, pollution control programs, water and sewage plants, electrical power utilities, and a variety of other projects. Occasionally, special authorities have been established by governments to conduct relatively exotic public policies, such as thoroughbred horse breeding, foreign trade, radio stations, television networks, and railroads.

These special authorities have been created by all levels of government, but especially by state and local governments, and only until comparatively recently have they really been scrutinized as a species of quasi-government that flourishes on the margin of the state. The building public skepticism about public authorities stems from a plethora of new perceptions about their (heretofore) vaunted effectiveness and efficiency as implementers of public policy, their expanding number, and their burgeoning debt—for which the taxpayer ultimately is responsible.

Fiscal Power

The developing economic power of government corporations is both impressive and often overlooked. Public authorities employ 3 percent of the national labor force and account for 15 percent of the nation's fixed investment. They control four-fifths of the local public transportation systems, three-quarters of the country's water systems, and a fourth of its electrical plants and railways. The Port Authority of New York and New Jersey, one of the larger government corporations, has more debt than thirty-nine states combined, and more operating revenues than all but nine of the nation's biggest cities![135] They spend more than $14 billion a year on operations and invest more dollars (about $10 billion annually) in new capital facilities than all state and municipal governments combined![136]

As we noted earlier, experts differ widely on just how many public authorities there are, but they tend to gravitate to an estimated 10,000 to 12,000 government corporations functioning in the United States, although there may be considerably fewer or considerably more; of these, perhaps sixty, and possibly closer to twenty (depending on one's definition), are federal corporation[137] Although there are relatively few federal corporations, compared to the thousands of state and local ones, many of them, such as the U.S. Postal Service, with more than 800,000 employees and an annual budget surpassing $40 billion,[138] have a hugh fiscal impact on the nation. One class of federal corporation, the "government-sponsored enterprise," which boasts a total of only seven organizations, nonetheless controls almost a trillion dollars in obligations and mortgage-backed securities, an amount that is growing rapidly![139]

Despite such heavy-hitting federal corporations, the vast bulk of government corporations function at the state and local levels. New York and Pennsylvania are the major states that use the public authority and, between them, have developed the two basic models for setting them up. In New York, public authorities are individually chartered by the state legislature. In Pennsylvania, however, local governments (cities, counties, towns, and special districts) can create government corporations through a number of different devices, and with little or no interference from the state. Most states, more than two-thirds, use the Pennsylvania approach; in fact, only New York and Maine require that the state legislature enact specific legislation to establish each government corporation.

Public authorities support themselves by borrowing money in the nations's money markets, by grants from their sponsoring governments, and by charging user fees to customers who use the facilities they build—such as toll charges levied on toll road drivers. Most of their budgets, however, are borrowed, and special authorities have been consuming increasingly vast amounts of borrowed money.

Most of us have heard about these public authorities in the context of "tax exempt municipal bonds." In fact, government corporations are able to raise more money for investment than either all-state or all-municipal governments pre-cisely because bond buyers do not have to pay income taxes on the interest that bonds generate. Public authorities are the largest single category of borrowers in the tax-exempt municipal bond market and borrow more money than all state and local governments combined! "This corporate investment exerts a massive influence on the patterns of development in the nation, an influence that is largely insulated from public debate."[140]

Debt and the Government Corporation: No Guarantees

The rapid growth of the government corporation's fiscal role in the national economy is beginning to dwarf the very state and local governments that gave them birth. By 1979, fully half of all the long-term debts (which comprise over 95 percent of all state and local debts) incurred by state and local governments had been incurred by public authorities (up from 28 percent in 1955).[141] Currently, public authorities account for over 54 percent of all state and local long-term debt.[142]

This debt is "nonguaranteed" by state and local governments. In other words, public authorities are not technically obligated to pay off creditors in the event that the enterprises to which those creditors loaned money default. Non-guaranteed debt has risen dramatically. In 1950, 80 percent of long-term debt in the states was full faith and credit—that is, guaranteed to be repaid. By 1989, this ration had almost reversed, and 75 percent of state debt was *non*guaranteed debt![143] For local governments, the trend was quite comparable.[144]

Nonguaranteed debts occur because most state and local governments are saddled with archaic constitutional clauses and statutes that place artificially low ceilings on how much debt a state or locality may incur, or which require inordinately cumbersome procedures to borrow funds, and because these governments genuinely need the money to meet fundamental public needs, such as public health and safety. To raise this money, and to circumvent their own policy restrictions on borrowing (which, in many instances, have remained unchanged since the last century), subnational governments resorted to creating public authorities.

But these governments have additional fiscal

"WHOOPS!"

A recent incident illuminates the growing economic role that government corporations are playing in the nation.

The Washington Public Power Supply System (WPPSS), known as "Whoops!" to some critics, is a consortium of twenty-three public utilities in Washington State and eighty-eight additional public utilities in the Northwest. Created in 1957 by nineteen public utility districts and four Washington cities to construct a small hydroelectric project, WPPSS bumped along for years as a typical government corporation, thriving with ease in a monopolistic market. Then, in the early 1970s, after reading that demand for electricity in the Northwest was expected to increase by 7 percent a year for the foreseeable future, the directors of WPPSS decided to build three nuclear power generators, and later expanded the project to five.

By 1983, as a result of borrowing to finance the five plants, "Whoops" was more than $8.3 billion in debt. Like governments, government corporations such as WPPSS are free to raise revenues by selling "municipal" (even though they are not municipalities) bonds in the bond market. Investors in municipal bonds—nearly 90 percent of whom are private citizens—find municipal bonds attractive because the interest that the bonds earn is not subject to the income tax; they are tax free. And, at a 12.5 percent interest rate for some of its bond issues, the WPPSS consortium was selling a lot of bonds. In fact, WPPSS was the largest issuer of tax-exempt municipal bonds ever!

WPPSS was issuing a particular type of long-term municipal bond, the revenue bond, to underwrite its nuclear plants. *Revenue bonds* repay their buyers through fees collected from users of the project that they finance; in the case of "Whoops," for example, the bonds' purchasers would be paid back in the form of tax-exempt interest with the profits WPPSS made on selling electricity generated by its new nuclear facilities.

The other kind of municipal bond is the general obligation bond. *General obligation bonds* are backed by the full faith and credit of the government that issues them. In other words, a government is legally compelled to raise taxes, if necessary, to meet its "general obligations." For this reason, all issues of general obligation bonds must be first approved in a referendum by the voters. Not so, however, with revenue bonds, and that is why governments (and government corporations) increasingly like them. In the face of tax

revolts at the grassroots, state and local governments have been squeezed into issuing more and more revenue bonds. In 1970, 34 percent of all long-term tax-exempt bonds were revenue bonds; by 1983, 75 percent of these issues were revenue bonds, a percentage that remained constant until the end of the decade. In 1990, 68 percent of long term bonds issued by local governments were revenue bonds.

Governments feel constrained to issue revenue bonds to meet basic service demands, but also to finance projects that may not be so basic. State and localities now issue revenue bonds to underwrite all kinds of "private uses," such as building factories, housing, and buying pollution control equipment that would not have been contemplated before the tax revolt. The reasoning behind this maneuver is that the government is enhancing the public interest by making more jobs available, "leveraging in" private-sector dollars to strengthen the tax base, assuring public health, or whatever. But while revenue bonds may be in the best interest of a local jurisdiction's citizenry, they may not be in the best interest of their investors, who can lose their investments if the jurisdiction defaults.

In 1983, WPPSS defaulted. It was not a small default. In fact, it was an all-time national record: $2.25 billion was defaulted on revenue bonds that had been issued for plants 4 and 5, a sum that amounted to 2.4 percent of all municipal debt in the United States at the time.

What happens when a public authority, or a government, defaults? It does not necessarily declare bankruptcy and go out of business (as WPPSS did not); it merely declines to pay its investors—about 100,000 individual investors in the case of the "Whoops" default, such as the retired Tulsa policeman who had invested $45,000 in plants 4 and 5. In fact, more than half of the investors in plants 4 and 5 were retirees, and nearly nine out of ten of these retirees were counting on their investments in WPPSS for a significant portion of their retirement income. Although the bond issuer must sell the holdings it has acquired under the bond issue and turn over the proceeds to its investors, these returns typically amount to pennies on the dollar. Who, for example, would be in the market for two partially constructed nuclear plants and the roads leading to them?

Another effect of default, but especially the largest

municipal bond default in the nation's history, is that it hurts others besides investors. The governor of Washington released a study concluding that the WPPSS default would cost the state 20,000 jobs.

Finally, the viability, competence, and ethics of the bond market, Wall Street, and government come under question. In the case of WPPSS, perhaps with reason. Even after the board of WPPSS was well aware that the Northwest's projected electricity consumption rate was never likely to attain a growth rate of 7 percent a year, and in fact was increasing by closer to one percent annually, plants 4 and 5 were begun anyway. Because "Whoops" wanted to spread the wealth (and reap the resultant political support), forty-five to sixty-five contractors were employed on each job site, where nine to ten were the norm, resulting in a sixfold hike in the System's original cost estimates.

"Wall Street was intimately involved every step of the way, and kept the spigot wide open until belated investor skepticism forced it closed," according to *Business Week* magazine. An open fiscal spigot apparently was irresistible to the small-town businessmen who largely made up the WPPSS board. According to

their own chairman of the board, the WPPSS directors "had unlimited money. That was the worst of it." As one director put it, "Whenever cash was low, we'd just toddle down to Wall Street."

Wall Street was so pleased to sell the increasingly questionable "Whoops" bonds (pleased, possibly, to the point of "bond dumping" WPPSS issues on unsuspecting investors), that the Securities and Exchange Commission (SEC) launched an investigation similar to the one that it conducted in 1977 of New York banks, after the City had nearly defaulted in 1975. The SEC's 1,000-page report in that case alleged that in 1975 the six banks sold $4 billion in City bonds when they knew a possible default was imminent, and simultaneously dumped their own New York City bonds before the roof fell in.

The Washington Public Power Supply System expresses many of the dilemmas of government corporations. They are controlled neither by public institutions nor economic competition, yet they are increasingly important political and fiscal forces. *Caveat emptor.*

The preceding discussion is drawn from: "The Fallout from 'Whoops,'" Business Week *(July 11, 1983), pp. 80-87; James Bennett and Thomas DiLorenzo, "Utility Bond's Default: Iceberg's Tip?"* Washington Times *(October 26, 1983); "Learning from Whoops,"* The Wall Street Journal *(July 27, 1983); "WPPSS Default Investigated,"* Washington Post *(November 30, 1983); Andy Logan, "Around City Hall,"* The New Yorker *(January 23, 1978), pp. 98-103; and Carrie Dolan, "Several WPPSS Issues Still Unresolved,"* The Wall Street Journal *(October 24, 1985).*

motivations, too, when they create public authorities, and these relate largely to those financial and political motives underlying the decisions by public officials to privatize public policy via contracting with private companies. One study of 133 cities in Illinois with populations of 5,000 or more found that, "very little shows that officials use enterprises (*i.e.*, municipal corporations) to get around high tax levels. The data are clear that these cities do not use enterprise funds to offer additional services when tax revenues decline.... most Illinois cities do not create enterprise funds to expand services at all, but they use them to deliver traditional services."[145] Another analysis of twenty-one cities in South Carolina that had created municipal electric corporations concluded that these enterprises not only raised revenues for these cities, but were used to subsidize local property taxes; "public avoidance" of resolving hard

fiscal questions, and "fiscal illusion" in hiding the realities of municipal finance were cornerstone concepts in the creation of these municipal authorities.[146]

So it is fairly apparent that subnational governments have formed government corporations as their chief means not of expanding public services, but merely of coping with a citizenry that is, at one and the same time, both service-demanding and tax-resistant. Since the debts of government corporations, however, are nominally not backed by the governments that established them, they can legally borrow as much as they like. As a result, much of the nonguaranteed debt of state and local governments has been incurred by the government corporations that they have founded.

Precisely how free of the mounting debts that are being incurred by special authorities these governments really are is debatable. Should a public authority default, the courts could well find that the government which created it nonetheless owes its creditors—and, in fact, the courts have so ruled in such cases.[147] Moreover, many government corporations are empowered by their creators to issue "moral obligation bonds," which means that, although a state or locality may not technically be responsible for an authority's debts, it nonetheless has a legally recognized "moral obligation" to back them. In short, it appears that if the typical government corporation goes bust, it is the taxpayer who ultimately may pay its "nonguaranteed" debt.

The Evolution of the Government Corporation

Fiscally speaking (and, for that matter, politically speaking, too), the relationship of government corporations to the subnational governments is not merely one of the tail wagging the proverbial dog, but of figuring out which end of this moving and shaking mass is the tail and which is the dog! This disturbing situation is in part the result of fiscal experimentation by the federal, state and local governments over the past two centuries.

The first government corporations were banks chartered by the states; the federal government often held significant portions of the stock of these banks. Later in the nineteenth century, when all companies in nearly all the states were required to have a special state charter to set up business, a relationship frequently would develop between individual legislators and corporate interests to expedite the applications of business charters. Over time, these relationships reached such an intimacy that major scandals erupted in many states, and both states and municipalities often would default on their debts because their governments had invested in questionable business projects that had gone under. These defaults occurred well into the 1920s, and often involved investments of public funds in real estate developments.

As a consequence of these statewide and local defaults on debt, and also as a result of the public administration reform movement that was sweeping the nation around the turn of the century, virtually all state constitutions still have archaic pro-

hibitions not only on debt, but against lending or granting state or local money or credit to individuals or firms as well, and these clauses have inhibited the development of public ownership and investment in private corporations. As an alternative, state and local constitutions and statutes have encouraged the development of the publicly chartered, quasi-governmental public authority because its revenue bond method of financing allows states and localities to at least indirectly fund capital projects that are sometimes needed desperately.

The federal government is the single entity most responsible for the proliferation of subnational special authorities and their deepening debt. More than any other single factor, federal tax laws shaped the evolution of the public corporation at the state and local levels, although there is no constitutional reason why, for example, state and municipal bonds should be exempt from the federal income tax. In 1913 the Sixteenth Amendment permitted Congress to collect taxes on income, and specified that Congress may do so "from whatever source derived"—including, obviously, income from municipal bonds. In addition to its tax exempt status, the municipal bond market is, remarkably, the only major securities market that is free from oversight by the federal Securities and Exchange Commission, thus permitting greater flexibility in competing for investors.

Federal involvement in the development of public authorities can be traced to the federal government's purchase of the Panama Railroad Company in 1904. Its involvement intensified during World War I, when Washington set up a number of federal corporations to assist in the war effort: Shipping, housing, sugar and grain marketing, and finance were the major areas of federal involvement during this period. Most of these special authorities were disbanded after the armistice, but, with the Depression, Washington took a renewed interest in the concept. One of Herbert Hoover's last acts as president was the creation of the Reconstruction Finance Corporation in 1932, a federal authority that financed the establishment of numerous state and local government corporations designed to put men and women back to work on capital improvement projects.

It was Franklin Delano Roosevelt, however,

who saw in the government corporation a unique opportunity to circumvent antiquated state limitations on debt while still funneling obviously needed capital into the economy, and it was the Roosevelt administration that set up the system we have today of "nonguaranteed" public authority debt. Roosevelt's approach was twofold: He encouraged the use of nonguaranteed debt, and promoted the creation of public authorities by states and communities.

Roosevelt's Public Works Administration strongly encouraged the use of nonguaranteed debt by state and local governments, and its effectiveness was striking. Between 1931 and 1936, the number of states permitting nonguaranteed debt rose from thirty-one to forty. Today, all states allow its use, and over 70 percent of all state and local debt is nonguaranteed.[148]

Roosevelt's successes in the area of government corporations, however, were even more dramatic. FDR drafted "model legislation" for state and local governments to follow in creating government corporations; wrote a personal letter to all the nation's governors in 1934, urging that they back his model code and modify their state's laws on debt; and channeled large slices of the federal budget into the Reconstruction Finance Corporation (in 1933 alone, this single government corporation accounted for more than half of *all* federal outlays) and Roosevelt's own Public Works Administration, the two principal federal corporations that bought the revenue bonds of the state and local government corporations which flourished under Washington's guidance.[149]

These policies brought quick results. By 1948, forty-one of the forty-eight states had adopted variants of FDR's model legislation, and twenty-five states authorized their local governments to set up government corporations entirely by local initiative. Continuing federal encouragement (such as various grant programs) and federal tax shelters for certain kinds of investments (such as housing projects) have resulted in more subnational government corporations, although direct federal involvement in their development has not matched that of the thirties and forties.[150]

By the end of World War II, public authorities across the country stood at the head of a number of crossroads. The public authorities created during the 1930s were, for the most part, intended by the federal agencies that funded their creation to be "self-liquidating" corporations; that is, once their capital costs were paid off through the use of user charges (such as bridge tolls), the authorities themselves could go out of business and turn their functions over to state or local governments. Such, at least, was one option that the authorities had. Another alternative was that user charges could be continued, and the revenues could be deposited in state and local general funds. Finally, government corporations could keep the user charges flowing into their corporate treasuries and use those revenues to finance new projects. If they took this final route, public authorities would no longer be required to ask governments for tax funds.

The managers of special authorities, for the most part, chose the final route. Even though FDR's bureaucracy for financing subnational government corporations was dismantled during the 1950s (the federal Rehabilitation Finance Corporation, created in 1932, was perhaps the major backer of state and local special authorities throughout the 1930s and was abolished in 1954), state and local corporations that the feds had originally underwritten lived on and prospered in their monopolistic marketplaces.

Managing the Government Corporation

State and local public authorities are headed by boards of directors, typically of three members or more who serve without compensation, and who are appointed by elected officials, usually the mayor, governor, or legislative body. Directors tend to have business and professional backgrounds, and almost always have fixed terms; often, they are reappointed.[151]

Day-to-day management—and the real power[152]—rests with the executive director of the public authority.[153] In over four-fifths of government corporations, executive directors are appointed by their boards, and the remainder are appointed by the chief executive officer or legislature of the government which chartered the corporation. The typical authority executive is a well-educated, white, forty-eight-year-old man, although more women are authority executives than one might expect (at least in comparison to city managers): a fourth are women, and the bulk of these are in housing authorities. The mean number of employees supervised by executive directors is modest—eleven—although some manage very significant numbers of employees, up to 6,000. It appears that the employees of public authorities may be paid at a higher rate than employees of any other type of government[154] (although, technically, public authorities are not governments, but most are also special districts, which are a type of local government).

There are a number of clues in the personal histories of authority directors that point to their relative autonomy as public officials, and that of the government corporations which they manage. For one, authority executives have significantly longer average tenures in office than do city managers (almost eight years, compared to over five for city managers),[155] but lower levels of education (18 percent of authority executives have not completed college, compared to 12 percent of city managers),[156] indicating a relatively high premium being placed on stability and experience in authority management (38 percent were employed by a public authority prior to being appointed as the executive director of one).

Compared to city managers, authority executives seem to feel a markedly lesser need to understand challenges emanating from their external environments, perhaps because they face, in fact, fewer and less demanding challenges. One study found that, "in a fundamental difference, the city managers gave a higher ranking to skills in bargaining and political analysis than did the authority directors. . . . In contrast to city managers, authority executives deal with fewer competing demands and expectations."[157]

A Surfeit of Freedom

Although fewer demands and expectations doubtless are a factor in the relative serenity of the lives of the executive directors of public authorities, they also are an indicator of the fact that political control over a public authority is a supremely difficult achievement. The government corporation is, in theory, responsible to those who appoint its board members, and normally this is the governor or mayor. Although political patronage often dominates the initial appointments of members of the boards of directors of public authorities, the staggered terms of board membership inhibit any kind of effective political control by the elected chief executive.

The supervision of government corporations typically is assigned to an executive agency or several executive agencies of the state or local government. But very few states and localities have emulated the kinds of relatively rigorous controls exercised over federal public corporations, principally through the Government Corporation Control Act of 1945. In most state governments, no single department even maintains an accurate listing of active public corporations, who their officers are, and even what their addresses might be. In fact, the Securities Industries Association has no more information than do state governments on the financial transactions of government corporations.[158]

State legislatures and city councils also have very limited control, if any, over their own public authorities. Although the statutes that establish public authorities can be and frequently are very specific and detailed, once the authority is established, legislative control often becomes a mockery. Legislators ritualistically carp that they have very little control over their own bureaucracies, much less the independent public authority, and even "sunset legislation," which we described in Chapter 8, has not been effective in implementing any kind of thorough legislative review of the government corporations. Thus, while elected bodies may have a rather impressive array of sanctions with which to threaten public corporations, they do not have any realistic means of enforcing those sanctions.

This problem is compounded by the intergovernmental system that exists in almost all states for establishing public authorities, and which permits counties and municipalities to create public corporations essentially on their own, and often these local charters are vague and unstandardized.[159]

Suing government corporations in court also has not provided consistent public control over government corporations. Although the courts have chipped away, on occasion, at the more arbitrary actions of certain public corporations, this process has been piecemeal at best, and the judiciary has not produced any guidelines of consequence for the control of public authorities.

An Absence of Control

These realities have contributed to an independence of economic and political action that any company executive or elected politician would envy. Public authorities, although chartered by governments, are rarely controlled by them. The career-oriented professional managers of government corporations are casually supervised by politically appointed boards that do not spend an inordinate amount of time at such chores. Tax-exempt bond holders have less interest in scrutinizing the day-to-day activities of the government corporation than, perhaps, do the stockholders of private corporations. As long as the public corporation meets the minimum revenue producing requirements, its management does not have to show increasing profits, dividends, or stock prices. Marketplace competition for most public corporations is minimal because they operate in monopolistic economic conditions and revenues, as a consequence, rarely decrease. Moreover, management of public corporations can operate at a much higher level of secrecy than can private firms, which must report their finances to the Securities and Exchange Commission.

In short, the managers of the public corporations have all the powers and autonomy of management that are shared by their counterparts in the private corporation, and which the on-line, government bureaucrat does not have; yet, the manager of the public corporation does not have to be responsive or responsible to the stockholders, bondholders, boards of directors, or even the public. As a result of this uniquely independent position in the marketplaces of both commerce and politics, public authorities have waxed more powerful at the expense of the subnational governments that chartered them.

Inadequate political controls over public authorities have contributed to their narrowness of view in formulating policy—an approach that "defines out" the less lucrative, people-oriented projects and "defines in" capital projects that often can disrupt the polities in which they reside, or, at the very least, not attempt to alleviate the more pressing and interrelated public problems of the area.

A relative absence of political accountability has led to certain behavioral commonalities among special authorities, such as to build (and to borrow to build) with minimum delay; to choose projects that are more conducive to garnering profits than providing public service; to rarely innovate in their approaches to alleviating public problems; and to stress physical rather than social objectives.[160]

These corporate tendencies, which are shared by most public authorities across the country, tend to reinforce one another, and comprise the ultimate policy biases of government corporations. "The successes of public authorities have, in fact, motivated much of the criticism of them. Critics on the left seek a more purposeful, dynamic, and democratically controlled public sector. Those on the right seek to reduce the scope of government enterprise, or at least check its growth, and to limit its activities to those that aid private endeavors, . . . public authorities have withstood such assaults practically unscathed and continue to claim rights of independent management."[161]

Another Perspective: The Benefits of "Large Powers"

If government corporations are "practically unscathed," it does not bother all observers. Not everyone agrees that government corporations are unaccountable, loose cannons, rolling on the economic and political decks of the nation. Indeed, they are extraordinarily useful. Jameson W. Doig, for example, suggests that public authorities are precisely what Woodrow Wilson had in mind when he wrote his essay on administration a century ago.[162] Government corporations, because they do possess what Wilson called "large powers," and because they do separate "politics" from "administration" more than most public entities, attract large people to their employ—the David Lilienthals and Robert Moses. Additionally, they attract and retain more specialized but talented professionals, such as planners and engineers, because they are insulated from the tides of electoral politics. Such drawing power by governments, even by quasi-governments, is not to be dismissed lightly.

Moreover, unlike government agencies, special authorities possess a distinctive ability to conduct long-term planning that often is absent in the public sector, and in part because of this ability, accountability for the actions of public authorities is not all that absent. In one sense, for example, those government corporations that span several local jurisdictions comprise a far more visible and coherent focus for concerned citizens than do a batch of "mini-govs," all trying to deal with the same problem in their separate, fragmented ways. The concept of "professionalism" itself, which is a deeply imbued value among personnel in public authorities, also provides a brake on the emergence of projects that would seriously violate the public interest as well as professional standards. But, as Doig points out, when all is said and done, problems of accountability persist. Nevertheless, these problems must be balanced with the public's need to get things done.

If the states and localities seem to have avoided the worst excesses of Washington in privatizing public policies by contracting them out, it is equally possible that they, as an alternative, may have created some excesses of their own in the form of government corporations. These man-made organisms, originally developed as the corporate progeny of their parent governments, clearly have a political life—and a will—of their own.

THE NEW YORK EXPERIENCE: MOSES VERSUS ROCKY

Consider, in this regard, the experience of New York, both city and state. Nowhere have potentialities and pitfalls of the government corporation—and its high political drama—been illustrated more vividly than in New York, particularly the rise of Robert Moses and his Triborough "empire," and Moses' ultimate conquest by the late Governor Nelson A. Rockefeller, who was unique in his own use (and abuse) of the government corporation. Few, if any, examples can furnish as rich a study of what the special authority means in American politics than New York's experiences with it.

Moses: Master Builder or Massive Destroyer?

The late Robert Moses held an unbelievable quantum of power in New York State for forty-four years (1924-1968) and in New York City for thirty-four years (1934-1968). It is not hyperbolic to dub him America's greatest builder. He changed the face of New York by raising and spending $27 billion (in 1968 dollars) for public works.

Through shore line projects, he added 15,000 acres to the city and changed its physical configuration. With one exception (East River Drive), Moses built every major expressway in the metropolitan region. Nine enormous bridges link the island city of New York; Moses built seven of them. Lincoln Center, the New York Coliseum; the campuses of Pratt Institute and Fordham and Long Island universities; the headquarters of the United Nations; 416 miles of landscaped parkways; Jones Beach; more than 1,000 apartment buildings housing more people than live in Minneapolis; 658 playgrounds; 673 baseball diamonds; 288 tennis courts—all these and more are his. Beyond the city, Moses built huge power dams on the St. Lawrence and at Niagara, Massens, and elsewhere; more parkways, more public beaches; and more parks. Especially parks. By the time Moses had finished, New York owned 45 percent of all the nation's acreage devoted to state parks![163]

To build, Moses destroyed. A quarter-million people—the equivalent population of Chattanooga—were dispossessed for his highways. Perhaps another quarter-million saw their homes razed for other kinds of projects. His apartment buildings, parks, and playgrounds, with few exceptions, were built for the white and the wealthy. His expressways slash through a region of 14 million people, carving the metropolis into separate and often mutually hostile enclaves of rich, poor, white, black, and brown.[164]

Moses entered the New York scene in 1924, when Governor Alfred E. Smith asked him to design the State Council on Parks, and he quickly assigned himself as chair with a tenure that extended beyond that of the governor's term. He also exempted the new State Council on Parks from the state civil system, granted it independent bonding and land acquisition powers, and used the Council to further his own ambitions. When Franklin D. Roosevelt succeeded Smith as governor of New York in 1929, Moses' power in state government began to wane. Nevertheless, he was able to keep his position in the State Council on

Parks and began seeking bureaucratic allies in the federal government.

In 1932, FDR was elected president, and in the same year Moses made his alliance with Jesse Jones, who had been appointed by Herbert Hoover as head of the newly created federal Reconstruction Finance Corporation (RFC). Both staunch Republicans, Jones and Moses disliked the Democrat Roosevelt, an antipathy that likely cemented their bond. With Jones and his Reconstruction Finance Corporation as his newly found ally in Washington, Moses worked himself into the position of heading up New York State's efforts to put depression-wracked New Yorkers back to work through the creation of capital projects that were financed with federal funds provided by Jones' RFC; and Moses immediately began building the Triborough Bridge with RFC grants.

In 1936, Moses was appointed by the mayor of New York City as chair of the Triborough Bridge Authority, and he served in that capacity until 1966. Using as his power base his position as the state's liaison with the federal public works funding programs, Moses moved forcefully to enhance his chairmanship of the Triborough Bridge Authority by setting up two additional authorities that were approved for federal funding, the Henry Hudson Parkway Authority and the Marine Parkway Authority. To solidify his position, Moses created a board for each authority, but appointed himself as the only board member. In 1938, both authorities were absorbed in the newly created New York City Parkway Authority, and, once again, Moses wrote himself in as the only member of the board.

During this period, Moses was consolidating his power with considerable speed. In 1934 alone, he became president of the Long Island Parkways Commission, commissioner of the New York City Parks System (which he remained until 1960), and chair of the New York State Council on Parks (a position he held until 1963), and he established the Beth Page and Jones Beach park authorities.

Moses was capitalizing on national trends of the time. As one analyst points out, "Moses used building blocks typical of public authority structures: independent financial power, corporate leadership, business patronage, civic reputation, and freedom from the encumbrances of democ-

racy."[165]. Thus, Moses consolidated his power position and political independence by drafting legislation, graciously enacted by the New York State legislature in 1946, that merged the Triborough Bridge Authority, the New York City Parkway Authority (which only eight years earlier had merged the Henry Hudson Parkway Authority and the Marine Parkway Authority under its auspices), and the New York City Tunnel Authority (which had been created in 1945 with Moses as its chief executive officer) into the Triborough Bridge and Tunnel Authority (TBTA). The effect of this exercise in bureaucratic imperialism was to enhance Moses's already considerable influence in New York; ultimately, Moses headed fourteen state and city agencies at the same time.

Significantly, the legislation that Moses had drafted gave TBTA the right to refinance any of its outstanding debt at any time, thus granting Moses an extraordinarily solid power base; as soon as profits were amassed, but just before debts were about to be paid off, Moses could issue new bonds and start a new project. This, in fact, was precisely what Moses did since new projects could be financed with ease in the tax-exempt and laxly regulated municipal bond market.

Triborough's regulations and bonding powers cannot be changed by federal, state, or local governments; its army of Bridge and Tunnel officers and Parkway police reported only to Moses; and its toll booths provide a cornucopia of self-renewing treasure. At its peak (attained in 1960), Triborough controlled a land mass half the size of New York City itself, and annual revenues neared a quarter-billion dollars.

Those who believe that men and women who dedicate their careers to public service face a life of genteel economic modesty should explore the world of government corporations. Moses maintained a yacht for his personal use that was skippered by three captains. Four dining rooms scattered around the city, each with its own full-time staff and chefs, served only Moses and his guests. Triborough secretaries not only were paid higher salaries than were New York City commissioners, but also were given bigger cars and their own chauffeurs, who were on call twenty-four hours a day. The group of Triborough managers known as "Moses Men"—his closest allies—were made millionaires and multimillionaires by Moses.

Moses' period of greatest power and building occurred from 1946 through 1953. During this period, essentially no construction of consequence was even attempted in Gotham without his approval. As we noted in Chapter 4, for thirty-four years, Moses played an important role in establishing the city's priorities, and for seven years, he established all the city's priorities.[166]

Moses was powerful far beyond the boundaries of the country's most important city. He changed the nation, too. In the field of parks, highways, and urban renewal, Moses was a formative force in the country.

In parks, it was Moses who conceived the notion of state and urban recreational complexes linked by landscaped parkways. Prior to Moses, twenty-nine states did not even have a single park, and six had only one. The parks system he bulldozed in New York was widely copied across the nation.

In highways, Moses had completed half a dozen urban expressways in metropolitan New York before Congress passed the Interstate Highway Act of 1956, which funneled federal money into the construction of urban freeways across the country. Prior to the act—which Moses was instrumental in drafting—metropolitan highways were virtually nonexistent except in New York.

Moses also was critical in drafting the Housing Act of 1949, which inaugurated the nation's controversial Urban Renewal program, and Moses was quick to use the federal program that he himself had helped form. Eight years after the passage of the Housing Act, Moses, who controlled all Urban Renewal projects in New York, had spent more than twice the amount of federal urban renewal dollars than all American cities combined! His contracts were used as the model for Urban Renewal administrators across the country.

There was a fourth field in which Moses shaped America: urban planning. He was against it. Although he served on the New York City Planning Commission for eighteen years (1942-1960), he blocked all attempts to establish a rational, comprehensive plan for the city at every turn. The lack of urban planning that is worthy of name in all major American cities reflects the policy biases of the special authorities that Moses directed. As the urban scholar Lewis Mumford, one of Moses' most tenacious foes, has written, "In the twentieth century, the influence of Robert Moses on the cities of America was greater than that of any other person."[167]

Was his influence good or ill for New York and the nation? Moses' special authorities built needed public works that, in all probability, would never have been built without the bold concepts he originated. But the human costs of his Herculean projects, and the physical devastation that highways and Urban Renewal have wrought in America's cities in the absence of local planning, may not have been worth the price.

How did a man, initially dismissed as "Goo Goo" (for "Good Government" reformer) by New York's Tammany Hall, come to wield such power? Moses built his power on an adoring media, the greed of others, tight secrecy (few have ever seen Triborough's detailed financial records), and political savvy that occasionally degenerated into personal vindictiveness. Much of his empire was built on deceptions, the most notable being that the government corporation was "above politics" (an assertion bought with slathering eagerness by the press) and was economically efficient. Through the nickels and dimes collected at his tollbooths, Moses bankrolled huge economic interests in New York and paid off individuals (perfectly legally) who were important to him. The retainers that Triborough granted to public relations firms alone hit about $250,000 a year; legal fees amounted to another quarter-million dollars, and insurance commissions were half-a-million dollars annually. Moses was giving out a million dollars a year to those who played ball in a game he umpired in a modern-day equivalent of Tammany Hall's Christmas turkey baskets.[168]

But a million dollars a year in Tammany turkeys does not compare to the real plums Moses could distribute. Because Moses did not have to be particularly cost conscious, he could let very fat contracts to banks, labor unions, and the private sector. As a consequence, his union and business support was almost unprecedented in the New York metropolitan area. They, like the media, could always be depended upon for support when summoned—a loyalty that was enhanced considerably by the fact that, for twenty years (1948-1968), Moses maintained a secret agreement with the State Department of Public Works that gave him a personal veto over *all* contracts awarded by the department in metropolitan New York.[169]

Moses gave a new meaning to political pressure, boasting that "nothing I have ever done has been tinged with legality."[170] Moreover, he could use political pressure with a savagery that made old-time pols look like Goldilocks. Moses kept on his payroll men whom he called "bloodhounds." Moses' bloodhounds were charged with, among other unpleasantries, building embarrassing dossiers on persons of influence. If a man's past was inadequately juicy, he would visit the sins of their fathers upon him. A well-known and esteemed financier once rose during a City Planning Commission hearing to oppose a zoning change sponsored by Moses, only to hear Moses reply by reading into the hearing transcript newspaper accounts of a scandal, which had no connection whatever with zoning, in which the financier's father had been implicated forty years earlier, when the financier was a child.[171] Moses ruined the careers of at least a dozen public officials with these tactics.

If all else failed, Moses would innovate. Although municipal-level communism is ludicrous on the face of it, two "red scares" and ensuing witch hunts erupted in New York City in 1938 and 1958; both were largely fueled by gossip and misinformation leaked to the press by Moses. For example, when New York City Council member Stanley Isaacs opposed Moses on the grounds that he was razing, on a vast scale, low-income housing in the city, Moses was vicious in his counterattack. Isaacs wanted to reduce the demolition and add antidiscrimination clauses for public housing that was being built. Moses steamrollered Isaacs, citing, among other points, the fact that "Isaacs runs as a Republican among conservatives and is a pinko among radicals."[172] Similarly the Tuscarora Indians objected to the prospective flooding of their land by the construction of Niagara Dam, a pet Moses project. Moses subsequently described the tribal leaders as "utterly incredible and clownish."[173] Another opponent was described by Moses as being "the infant prodigy who continued to be an infant long after he had finished being a prodigy."[174] As one observer has noted, "Moses was probably ruder, more manipulative, and more powerful than other authority managers . . . but regardless of the merits of the results, Moses spoke and acted as can only an authority manager—who will never face election himself or require direct support from community groups and other politicians, and who is not accountable to stockholders, competitors, or questioning board members."[175]

As noted, efficient management, while hardly a watchword in the Triborough empire, nonetheless was a widely accepted Moses myth that was critical to his political success. But the extent of the mismanagement, quite aside from the personal luxury that the unending flow of silver from the tollbooths provided Triborough's administrators, is nonetheless startling; for example, Moses paid $40 million in interest that he did not need to pay on a single bridge, and the state secretly underwrote Triborough to the tune of hundreds of millions of dollars. The city purchased much of the land on which Moses' projects were built; by turning the property over to Moses, Gotham also exempted this valuable land from its own tax rolls.[176]

Although Moses touted the supremacy of business efficiency, his first real venture into the free enterprise marketplace was a total failure. In 1962, Moses took over the second New York World's Fair project and raised funds by promising investors that he could turn the World's Fair into a profit-making event. In fact, Moses was so keen on turning a profit, that he initially opposed cut-rate tickets for schoolchildren. Nevertheless, when the project was completed, Moses defaulted on almost two-thirds of the Fair's debts. Moses failed his first real test of the marketplace.[177]

The myth of government corporations as just another competitor in the marketplace, and its unwarranted image of managerial efficiency, was beginning to fade in the 1960s, and this change in public attitude may have been encouraged by the behavior of Moses. In 1965, a number of bankers (after discovering that Moses, as president of the New York World's Fair, had guaranteed himself $100,000 in salary and annual expenses) resigned from the World's Fair Finance Committee on the grounds that Moses would not give them adequate financial information on how he was running the Fair's operations.

A Rocky Conquest: Rockefeller and His Follies

Robert Moses continued his remarkable successes throughout the 1950s. But in 1958, Nelson A. Rockefeller was elected governor of New York and began to challenge Moses' heretofore undisputed preeminence over the region's public corporations.

Rockefeller's challenge was made easier by the fact that in 1959 Moses had received his first "bad press" as a result of his chairmanship of New York City's Slum Clearance Committee. Scandals erupted in the program that were widely publicized, and since slum clearance contract records were open to the public (unlike most financial records of the enterprises that Moses headed), the opportunities for media criticism were relatively ample.

The essence of Rockefeller's attack on Moses was his aggressive development of his own public authorities at the state level; by so doing, he was creating competition for Moses. In 1963, Rockefeller asked Moses to retire as head of the State Council on Parks, a position he had held since 1934. Rockefeller wished to appoint his brother Lawrence to the position, and Moses objected. Characteristically, Moses relied on a political device that had served him well in the past; he threatened to resign, not only from the State Council on Parks, but from the chairmanship of the New York Power Authority and several other state posts as well. His decision to escalate the conflict was ill advised. Rockefeller happily accepted Moses' departures from all the state posts for which he had tendered resignations!

While Rockefeller had won a battle, his real objective was to reduce Moses' power in the transportation field. To do this, Rockefeller had to gain control over transit finance in the state, and in 1967 he successfully pushed a huge, $2.5 billion, general obligation transportation bond issue. Rockefeller was accorded this bond issue by a statewide referendum, and it gave him the freedom to build transportation facilities that formerly had been controlled almost exclusively by Moses. Rockefeller then went to the state legislature and broadly reorganized New York's transportation policy machinery by creating the Metropolitan Transportation Authority. Central to this reorganization was the inclusion of Moses' Triborough Bridge and Tunnel Authority into Rockefeller's new Metropolitan Transportation Authority. Moses fought this merger on every front, including the courts, and lost on all of them. In 1968, the merger was achieved, and Moses was edged out of regional transportation policy-making. The merger also marked the downfall of the world's greatest builder.

The experiences of Robert Moses illustrate (if on a somewhat larger than life scale) the problems inherent to the operation of government corporations in a democracy: freedom from accountability, both political and financial. The decline of Moses' prestige and power was at least the partial result of a series of direct challenges to Robert Moses by Governor Nelson Rockefeller. The bitter war waged between Rockefeller and Moses illuminates how public authorities can weaken not only the powers of local governments but of state governments as well. As with government corporations at the local level, public authorities at the state level function in a political atmosphere of scant accountability to the public and its elected and appointed representatives. But Rockefeller's experience with public corporations deviated from this pattern. Although the device of the state government corporation is used more extensively in New York that in any other state, public authorities created by Rockefeller were unique in that he, as governor, controlled them absolutely. While this is not to say that these corporations were publicly accountable, at least an elected governor actually governed them—and with a rare thoroughness.

Nelson A. Rockefeller served as governor of New York from 1958 through 1974, and his ambitions to redevelop the physical plant and appearance of the state were rivaled only by Robert Moses and possibly the pharaohs of Egypt. Included in Rockefeller's plans were the redevelopment of Manhattan, for which he committed more than $6 billion to build, among other edifices, the World Trade Center, renovate docks, and renew the face of the city; the creation, virtually out of whole cloth, of a major state university system, which ultimately became the second largest in the country; the construction of massive public housing and public health facilities; the reconstruction and redesign of the capital city of Albany, rendering it, in the words of one observer, "architecturally respectable."[178] (Those who have seen Albany before and after the Rockefeller regime could reasonably conclude that what Rockefeller accomplished there is analogous to building the Great Pyramid in the middle of Altoona, Pennsylvania.) For fillers, Rockefeller built new mental health facilities, established a thoroughbred horse breeding program for the state, and raised private capital for the construction of new nursing homes, colleges, dormitories, hospitals, prisons, and a variety of other projects. All these enormous undertakings were accomplished through public authorities.

Why did Rockefeller rely so extensively on the government corporation to achieve his ends? The reasons are typical of why public authorities have proliferated in recent years. One is that Rockefeller had little regard for the desultory pace of his own state bureaucracy, particularly the hide-bound Department of Public Works. Nor, as an art connoisseur of considerable note, did he care for the kind of architectural design that all too frequently emanated from that department. So Rockefeller turned to the public corporation as a means of building both faster and better, since his public authorities could pay higher architectural fees and avoid reams of red tape.

The government corporation also enabled Rockefeller to bypass voter disapproval of many of his projects. Just two years prior to Rockefeller's taking office, the voters, for example, had voted for a third time to limit a housing bond issue. When Rockefeller became governor in 1958, he quickly created a Housing Finance Agency as a government corporation that built low-income housing. In 1961, New Yorkers defeated for a fourth time a major bond issue for higher education, so Rockefeller created the State University Construction Fund as a public authority designed to raise money for the same purpose that the voters had denied it. In 1965, voters rejected for a fifth time a low-income housing bond proposal, which Rockefeller answered with his creation of the Urban Development Corporation. Through these and other authorities, Rocky could borrow, veil his borrowing from the public eye, and make the legislature pay later.

Finally, Rockefeller found that, in an accounting sense, he could at least convey the appearance of balancing his state budget by creating public authorities, and this had political benefits. In 1962 Rockefeller pushed through a law that changed state accounting methods by striking the requirement that money granted by the state to public authorities be listed in the state budget. The effect of this change was to grant Rockefeller a major political boon because his budgets looked considerably leaner by not listing the costs of his public corporations in them, and such "fiscal responsibility" was in harmony with his "pay as you go" motto that characterized his four gubernatorial campaigns.

We have noted that Rockefeller was unique in that he was a governor who really controlled his own government corporations. How did he accomplish this?

One method was Rockefeller's connections with the New York financial community. Few governors have the fiscal background of a Rockefeller, and, as governor, Rocky capitalized on his network within the limited world of high finance. Rockefeller was able to raise more than $6 billion from Wall Street simply because the bankers trusted him.

Rockefeller also freed his public authorities from the fetters of the state. Although the state of New York was legally responsible for paying off the vast bulk of the public debt that Rockefeller's government corporations incurred, Rocky was adroit in assuring that the legislature and bureaucracy had virtually no control over their policies and operations. Of the twenty-two state corporations that Rockefeller created during his administration, fourteen (including such major ones as the Urban Development Corporation) were completely beyond the scope of New York's public authorities law. This meant that almost two-thirds of the public authorities Rockefeller founded had boards appointed exclusively by Rockefeller, were exempt from state budgetary controls, did not have to submit their policy decisions to the governor for approval, and, in the case of the Urban Development Corporation, not even its own board of directors could review its budget! Moreover, those remaining government corporations created by Rockefeller that did fall under the state's public authorities law often were able to avoid any close supervision. For example, the Metropolitan Transportation Authority (MTA), a Rockefeller creation, submitted such jurisdictionally complex and fiscally convoluted budget reports to the legislature that the legislative staff was understandably confused and effectively gave up trying to conduct responsible oversight of the agency.

But the most spectacular method that Rockefeller used to control his public authorities were his personal administrative appointments to those authorities. Unlike other governors in other states, Rockefeller, using his almost unlimited wealth and a rare political ruthlessness, appointed directors of his various government corporations who were personally committed and loyal only to him. For example, Rockefeller hired Edward J. Logue to head his Urban Development Corporation (UDC) and went to extraordinary lengths to protect Logue politically, including threatening legislators to "take away their judge-ships" if they failed to support Logue. Logue was appointed directly by the governor; in fact, not only did the board of directors of the Urban Development Corporation have no legal voice in the hiring of its own executive director, but the chair of the UDC had no managerial control whatever over its own executive director, who reported directly to Rockefeller. Similarly, Rockefeller appointed his longtime executive secretary, Alton Marshall, as a member of the Urban Development Corporation Board and as a board member of the New York Sports Authority.

While there are many examples of appointees to the board of public corporations who had a total loyalty to Rockefeller, perhaps the most remarkable is William J. Ronan, who, under Rockefeller, was both chair of the board and chief executive officer of the Metropolitan Transport-ation Authority, and later served on the boards of the New York Port Authority (as chair) and the New York Power Authority. So extensive was Ronan's influence, thanks to Rockefeller's unstinting support, that he became known as the "Holy Ronan Empire." Ronan paralleled Robert Moses in that he had been a student of public administration and had conducted some outstand-ing research on the concept of the public author-ity; in fact, prior to his first appointment in the state government in 1959, Ronan had been dean of the Graduate School of Public Administration at New York University.

One of the major reasons that Rockefeller was able to retain the loyalty of people like Logue, Marshall, and Ronan was his generosity. Rocky made them all rich. Ronan received his first gift of $75,000 from Governor Rockefeller in 1958, and it was estimated that, during his sixteen years as governor, Rockefeller eventually gave Ronan as much as $650,000. Logue, as chair of the UDC, received gifts and loans from Rockefeller that totaled more than $175,000, while Marshall was loaned more than $300,000 in 1970 alone.[179] There are many other examples.

Perhaps because Rockefeller's chief appointees were not working in a world of per-sonal fiscal reality, none of them was terribly skilled in financial management and cost control. When Rockefeller turned the state house over to the Democrats in 1974, many of his public corpo-rations were in deep financial trouble. For exam-ple, very soon after Ronan left as chair of the board of the MTA in 1973, virtually all projects under construction (including partially dug tun-nels) had to be halted by his successor because there were no funds left to complete them. The Urban Development Corporation, headed by Logue, was spending $1 million a day in the same year[180] and was in such serious financial diffi-culty that Logue was forced to resign in 1975, shortly after a new governor assumed office.

Rockefeller's government corporations had, among other things, overestimated student hous-ing needs, set up a situation in which private developers could manipulate mental health facili-ties for their own profit, and imposed a highly questionable financial system for state transporta-tion. In sixteen years, Rockefeller had created so many public authorities of such enormous scope that they currently account for more than a third of all revenue bonds issued across the country! Public authorities still are the single most impor-tant sector of public finance in the state of New York. When a Democratic governor took over in 1975, he was confronted with a debt incurred by the state's public authorities of more than $12 bil-lion (in 1962, the outstanding debt of New York's public authorities was only $129 million), or almost four times the amount of debt incurred by the state government itself! Moreover, the state had been obligated to pay off two-thirds of this $12 billion, and the state's public authorities still were planning to embark on projects that would involve legislative appropriations of an additional $1.9 billion during the next five years.[181]

For better or worse, New York symbolizes the rise of the public corporation and its relationships with state and local governments. Public authorities, which are beginning to dominate the financial structures of subnational governments, now largely control critical public programs, particularly in energy, water, communication, and transportation; as some observers have put it, the American experience with government authorities has been one of extending "the public's credit, rather than the public's control"[182] in these and a wide spectrum of other policy areas.

PRIVATIZATION: PRELUDE TO ENTREPRENEURIAL GOVERNMENT?

Government's efforts to implement public policies by using or working with extra-governmental organizations in the private sector and third sector point to a larger crusade that is occurring in the public sector: the attempt to "reinvent government," which refers to a "transformation" of governments that will render the public sector more responsive, effective, efficient, and user-friendly.[183] Increasingly, this movement is being called "entrepreneurial government."

Entrepreneurial government does not mean the selling of the public sector to capitalists for the sake of achieving these worthy ends. It does mean unfettering public administrators from some outdated restrictions so that they can act more like business entrepreneurs in making government more beneficial to the everyday lives of people. This unfettering involves neither a conservative nor a liberal agenda; rather, it involves a creative human agenda that, if attained, likely would result in a significant blurring in what currently is perceived to be the public and private sectors, and what is seen as appropriate administrative behavior in each.

In practice, this means that government agencies could compete with the private sector (and with each other) in securing the authorization to deliver public services most efficiently and effectively. It means that counterproductive and antiquated regulations would be modified or scrapped to assure greater governmental responsiveness, and that much more effort would be made to recognize and fund results, rather than programs. It means that governments should become more attuned to earning money through the selling of byproducts (such as methane gas

produced naturally by city dumps) and services (trash collection) to buyers, rather than just taking money through taxes. Entrepreneurial government means these and many other innovations.

The advent of entrepreneurial government is not being thwarted merely by threatened, ossified, and entrenched bureaucrats who understand little beyond niche defense. It is being resisted by special interests which have long fought governmental "competition" with business (particularly their own business), and by the champions of traditional "good government."

We have reviewed in this chapter the arguments and activities of special interests in resisting government "competition," and we have reviewed in previous chapters the reformist movements of the late nineteenth and early twentieth centuries which resulted in many of the deepest characteristics that we associate with "good government" today: control, checks, impersonality, and rigidity. For very different motivations, both private interest and public reformers have worked in tandem to produce governments that are increasingly unresponsive to the public interest.

If the experience of American governments with privatization shows nothing else, it demonstrates clearly that many of these traditional features of "good government" no longer are useful, and should be reconsidered—perhaps at the expense of those groups which have resisted defining "the public interest" in terms that have threatened their special interests.

This reconsideration would require a sea change in the civic culture itself. It would entail large adjustments in how we have traditionally managed public agencies, and even of how we think of "good government."[184] The focus of public administrators would shift from the governmental hierarchy to the client; the historic emphasis on procedures would decline in favor of an emphasis on innovation; competition among agencies within a government and with private interests would heighten; adherence to rules and policy would be weakened in favor of providing services efficiently, effectively—and even pleasantly; standard methods of operation would be replaced by new and multiple means of service delivery;[185] individual public administrators would be given greater freedom to innovate.

Vice President Al Gore's National Performance Review, better known as the "Reinventing Government" task force, which issued its report on the improvement of the federal management in 1993, provides a revealing example of the potential clash between the values of traditional public administration and entrepreneurial government. The Review, found, for example, that federal managers were particularly critical of the Inspectors General (described in Chapter 7) as bureaucrats who consistently stymied innovative management in Washington. Yet the Inspectors General are generally credited with saving billions in federal funds especially in the field of procurement. The rest is clear.

Without question, entrepreneurial government is less risk aversive than traditional government, and this, in turn, could bring new opportunities for old fashioned pillaging of the public treasure. The procurement culture of the Pentagon and the excesses of Robert Moses should not be dismissed lightly. But accounting, auditing, and information management have made enormous strides over the century, and now stand as far more effective bulwarks against fiscal corruption than they were when the control-oriented reform movement was at its peak; in almost all governments, the practices decried (and properly so) by the reformers of a hundred years ago have been eliminated or at least drastically reduced.

It may be time for more entrepreneurial government. As one indication of its arrival, perhaps, between 1982 and 1988, the use by municipal governments of six relatively exotic mechanisms for delivering services—vouchers, subsidies, franchises, volunteers, self-help, and tax incentives—increased by 60 percent, and were being used to deliver at least 10 percent of all city services. [186] The states' dramatic increases in their use of effectiveness and productivity measures over two decades, as reviewed in Chapter 7, indicate a desire to "reinvent government," just as the Federal Managers Financial Integrity Act of 1990, the Government Performance and Results Act of 1993 (recall Chapter 7), and the National Performance Review of 1993 show a commitment among federal officials to change how Washington works. Certainly all governments' use of private companies, public corporations, and third sector organizations indicates that public managers at all governmental levels think that

the time for entrepreneurial government has come.

Governments' use of each other in the implementation of public policy—that is, intergovernmental administration—is further evidence of the public sector's movement toward entrepreneurial government; we consider it next.

NOTES

1. Robert H. Carver, "Examining the Premises of Contracting Out," *Public Productivity and Management Review*, 13 (Fall 1989), p. 38.
2. Irene S. Rubin, "Who Invented Budgeting in the United States?" *Public Administration Review*, 53 (September/October 1993), p. 443.
3. Annmarie Hauk Walsh, *The Public's Business: The Politics and Practices of Government Corporations* (Cambridge, Mass.: MIT Press, 1978), p. 40.
4. *Ibid.*, p. 29.
5. U.S. Commission on the Organization of the Executive Branch of the Government, *Business Enterprises: A Report to the Congress* (Washington, D.C.: U.S. Government Printing Office, 1955), p. xi.
6. Harold Seidman, *Politics, Position, and Power: The Dynamics of Federal Organization*, 3rd ed. (New York: Oxford University Press, 1980), p. 238. Other attempts to count the number of federal corporations include: Walsh, *The Public's Business*; U.S. General Accounting Office, *Congress Should consider Revising Basic Corporate Control Laws*, GAO/PAD-83-3 (Washington, D.C.: U.S. Accounting Office, 1983); National Academy of Public Administration, *Report on Government Corporations* (Washington, D.C.: National Academy of Public Administration, 1981); U.S. Congressional Research Service, *Administering Public Functions at the Margin of Government: The Case of Federal Corporations*, CRS Report 83-236 (Washington, D.C.: U.S. Congressional Research Service, 1983); and Michael Denning and David J. Olson, "Public Enterprise and the Emerging Character of State Service Provisions," paper presented at the 1981 Annual Meeting of the American Political Science Association, New York: September 3-6, 1981. Walsh lists nineteen federal corporations; the GAO concluded that there were forty-seven federal government corporations; the National Academy of Public Administration found thirty-five; the Congressional Research Service located thirty-one; and Denning and Olson unearthed fifty-eight. The varying statements by scholars and federal agencies on how many federal corporations exist indicates little is known about them. But we know far more about federal corporations than we know about government corporations at the subnational levels.
7. Jack R. Kemp, "Statement," Committee on Post Office and Civil Service, U.S. House of Representatives, *Contracting Out of Jobs and Services* (Washington, D.C.: U.S. Government Printing Office, 1977), p. 43.

8. Walsh, *The Public's Business*, p. 33.

9. Timothy Chandler and Peter Ferrille, "Municipal Unions and Privatization," *Public Administration Review*, 51 (January/February 1991), p. 15. The authors received 1,541 usable responses which were obtained from public works directors in 1989, for a response rate of 56 percent.

10. Jerry Mitchell, "Education and Skills for Public Authority Management," *Public Administration Review*, 51 (September/October 1991), p. 436. Paralleling the federal situation, but more strikingly, an indication of the dismal state of our knowledge about government corporations at the subnational levels can be inferred from the widely varying estimates about such a basic datum as how many of them there are. Annmarie Hauk Walsh concludes that there are from 5,000 to 7,000 public authorities, a number which excludes authorities that are not organizationally independent of government agencies. Donald Axelrod, using, more or less, Walsh's criteria pegs the number at around 6,000. Later Walsh with David Mammen, says that there are about 10,000 public authorities. But Charles E. Lindblom contends that if those public corporations are counted which are authorized to issue general obligation bonds, the number jumps to 18,000. See: Walsh, *The Public's Business*, p. 5; Charles E. Lindblom, *Politics and Markets: The World's Political Economic Systems* (New York: Basic Books, 1977), p. 114; Annmarie Hauk Walsh and David Mammen, *State Public Corporations: A Guide for Decision Making* (New York: Institute for Public Administration, 1983); and Donald Axelrod, *A Budget Quartet: Critical Policy and Management Issues* (New York: St. Martin's Press, 1989), p. 28.

11. Unless noted otherwise, the following discussion is drawn from: Ira Sharkansky, "Government Contracting," *State Government*, 53 (Winter 1980), pp. 23-24; and Donna Wilson Kirchheimer, "Entrepreneurial Implementation in the U.S. Welfare State," paper presented at the 1986 Annual Meeting of the American Political Science Association, Washington, D.C., August 28-31, 1986.

12. Gerald W. Johnson and John G. Heilman, "Metapolicy Transition and Policy Implementation: New Federalism and Privatization," *Public Administration Review*, 47 (November/December 1987), p. 468.

13. Carver, "Examining the Premises of Contracting Out," p. 38.

14. Johnson and Heilman, "Metapolicy Transition and Policy Implementation," p. 468.

15. Federal Procurement Data System, *Special Analysis 1: Federal Contract Awards over $10,000 by Type Preliminary Data of Contractor*, Fourth Quarter Fiscal Year 1979 (Washington, D.C.: Federal Procurement Data Center, 1979), p. 3. In Fiscal Year 1986, more than $183 billion was spent by the federal government for goods and services. See: Federal Procurement Data Center, U.S. General Services Administration Federal Procurement Data System, *Standard Report, Fiscal Year 1987* First Quarter (October 1, 1986 through December 31, 1986) (Washington, D.C.: Federal Procurement Data Center, 1987), p. 7. See also:

National Academy of Public Administration, *Privatization: The Challenge to Public Management* (Washington, D.C.: National Academy of Public Administration, 1989), p. 12. The Academy estimates that Washington contracts net about $200 billion a year.

16. Federal Procurement Data System, *Special Analysis I*, p. 3, and *Federal Procurement Data System Standard Report, FY 87*, p. 7.

17. National Science Foundation, as cited in "National R&D spending to Exceed $57 Billion in 1980," *Research Management*, 22 (July 1979), p. 3.

18. Barbara Blumenthal, "Uncle Sam's Invisible Army of Employees," *National Journal* (May 5, 1979), p. 732.

19. U.S. House of Representatives, Committee on Post Office and Civil Service, *Contracting Out of Jobs and Services* (Washington, D.C.: U.S. Government Printing Office, 1977), p. 31.

20. Federal Procurement Data System, *Special Analysis*, p. 11; and U.S. Census Bureau study, as cited in Spencer Rich, "California Cashes in on Federal Contracts," *Washington Post* (March 27, 1987).

21. U.S. Office of Management and Budget, as cited in U.S. General Accounting Office, *Civil Servants and Contract Employees: Who Should Do What for the Federal Government?* (Washington, D.C.: General Accounting Office, 1981), p. 18. In 1981, OMB identified 11,637 such activities, and their annual costs may have been as high as $30 billion. OMB suggested that perhaps $18.5 billion could be saved by privatizing them.

22. U.S. General Accounting Office, *Government Contractors: Are Service Contractors Performing Inherently Governmental Functions?* GAO/GGO 92-11 (Washington, D.C.: General Accounting Office, November 1991), p. 19.

23. Katherine C. Naff, "Labor-Management Relations and Privatization: A Federal Perspective," *Public Administration Review*, (January/February 1991), p. 27. Emphasis is original.

24. "Bush Signs Order for Privatization by Governments," *Wall Street Journal* (May 16, 1992).

25. Federal Procurement Data System, as cited in T. R. Reid, "Protection for Nation's Largest Consumer," *Washington Post* (October 30, 1981); and "Federal Procurement Institute Gets Going," *Contract Management*, 17 (November 1977), p. 10.

26. Study conducted by the Center for Strategic and International Studies, as cited in George Melloan, "Even Generals Get the Arms-Procurement Blues," *Wall Street Journal* (June 23, 1987).

27. Phillip J. Cooper, "Government Contracts in Public Administration: The Role and Environment of the Contracting Officer," *Public Administration Review*, 40 (September/October 1980), pp. 460-461.

28. *Ibid.*, p. 462.

29. *Ibid.*, p. 463.

30. John O'Mally, editor of *Commerce Business Daily*, and Vince Villa, Washington consultant, as quoted in "Most Ads for Contractors Meaningless," *Washington Post* (June 25, 1980).

31. Cooper, "Government Contracts in Public

Administration," p. 462. See also: Richard E. Speidell, "The Judicial and Administrative Review of Government Contract Awards," *Law and Contemporary Problems* (Winter 1972), p. 63; and William J. Spriggs, "The Judicial Role of the Contracting Officer in U.S. Government Contracting," *Washburn Law Journal* (Fall 1971), p. 213. It is possible (although, in our view, doubtful) that this pattern may change as a result of the Competition in Contracting Act of 1984, which permits the GAO to hold up work awarded to one contractor if another bidder has filed a legitimate protest. However, the U.S. Assistant Attorney General has stated that he considers the Act to be unconstitutional. See: Myron Struck, "Clash Looms on New Contracting Act," *Washington Post* (October 31, 1984).

32. Gordon Rule, quoted in William Proxmire, *Report from the Wasteland: America's Military Industrial Complex* (New York: Praeger, 1970), p. 83. Rule was a civilian cost containment expert for the Navy.

33. Former federal administrators averaged a 72 percent increase in wages when they entered industry; former members of Congress increased their salaries by 100 percent; former judges were in between. See: Federal Pay Commission Study, as cited in United Press International, "Private Firms Prize Ex-Officials," *The Arizona Republic* (November 17, 1976).

34. Knight News Service, "Pentagon Retirees' Expertise Eagerly Snapped Up by Defense Firms," *Baltimore Sun* (December 5, 1982). The study analyzed retirees' records from 1980 through 1982.

35. As derived from figures reported in a Knight-Ridder survey of 500 military retirees' files, cited in *ibid.*

36. Figures are for 1970 through 1979. See Gordon Adams, Council on Economic Priorities, as cited in *ibid.*

37. Newchy Mignone, as cited in: Jonathan Neumann and Ted Gup, "The Revolving Door: Industry Plums Await Retired U.S. Officials," *The Washington Post* (June 25, 1980).

38. *Ibid.* The case involved the Navy and ManTech, Inc.

39. *Ibid.*

40. General Accounting Office, as cited in Associated Press, "Pentagon Management Pacts Awarded without Competition, Probe Finds," *The Arizona Republic* (April 8, 1981). The GAO reviewed 256 contracts for management support services valued at $175 million.

41. General Accounting Office study, as quoted in Mary Beth Franklin, "Pentagon-Industry Job Door Still Revolving, GAO Finds," *Washington Post* (May 8, 1987).

42. U.S. General Accounting Office, as cited in Gary Lee, "Trade, National Security, and the Revolving Door," *Washington Post* (April 13, 1992).

43. Gary Lee, "Lobbying Loopholes for Foreign Agents," *Washington Post* (June 21, 1991).

44. Frank J. Guarini, as quoted in Lee, "Trade, National Security, and the Revolving Door."

45. Marcy Kaptur, as quoted in *ibid.*

46. W. Henry Lambright, *Governing Science and Technology* (New York: Oxford University Press, 1976), p. 123.

47. Cooper, "Government Contracts in Public Administration," pp. 462-463.

48. The source for much of this discussion is Raymond G. Hunt, "Cross-purposes in the Federal Contract Procurement System: Military R&D and Beyond," *Public Administration Review*, 44 (May/June 1984), pp. 247-256.

49. *Ibid.*, pp. 248-249.

50. *Ibid.*, pp. 250-251

51. R. H. Charles, "The Short Misunderstood Life of Total Package Procurement," *Innovation* (Winter 1971), p. 10.

52. See, for example, Raymond G. Hunt, Irene S. Rubin, and Franklin S. Perry, *The Use of Incentives in R&D Contracting: A Critical Evaluation of Theory and Method* (Buffalo, N.Y.: State University of New York at Buffalo, Final Report of National Aeronautic and Space Association Grant NGR33-015-061, 1971).

53. Hunt, "Cross-purposes in the Federal Contract Procurement System," p. 251.

54. J. Ronald Fox, *Arming America: How the U.S. Buys Weapons* (Boston: Harvard University Press, 1974), p. 237; and Raymond G. Hung, "R&D Management and Award Fee Contracting," *Journal of the Society of Research Administrators*, 6 (Summer 1974), p. 333.

55. Hunt, "Cross-purposes in the Federal Contract Procurement System," p. 252.

56. Henry Lambright and Albert H. Teich, "The Organizational Context of Scientific Research," in Paul C. Nystrom and William H. Starbuck, eds., *Handbook of Organizational Design*, Vol. II (New York: Oxford University Press, 1981), pp. 305-379.

57. Sharkansky, "Government Contracting," pp. 23-24.

58. Blue Ribbon Defense Panel, *Report to the President and the Secretary of Defense* (Washington, D.C.: U.S. Government Printing Office, 1970), pp. 158-159.

59. The federal contract administrators, in order of quotation, are: Roy Higdon, Environmental Protection Agency; David Webb, Health, Education and Welfare; and William Stevenson, Department of Energy. All are cited in: Jonathan Neumann and Ted Gup "An Epidemic of Waste in U.S. Consulting, Research," *Washington Post* (July 22, 1980).

60. William Farris, cited in *ibid.*

61. Daniel Guttman, appearing on the program "60 Minutes." CBS Television Network, November 30, 1980.

62. David Muscone, quoted in Neumann and Gup, "An Epidemic of Waste in U.S. Consulting, Research."

63. Steve Dorrler, as quoted in *ibid.*

64. Daniel Guttman and Barry Willner, *The Shadow Government* (New York: Pantheon, 1976), p. 167.

65. Response of Dr. Lois Ellen Datta, Chief, Headstart Evaluation Branch, Office of Education, 1970 letter to the Stanford Research Institute, as quoted in *ibid.*, p. 167.

66. *Ibid.*, p. 38.

67. *Ibid.*, p. 16.

68. Subcommittee on Investigations, Committee on Post Office and Civil Service, House of Representatives, *Report on the Investigation of the Contract Between Westinghouse Electric Corporation and the U.S.*

Postal Service (Washington, D.C.: U.S. Government Printing Office, October 19, 1971).

69. Ted Gup and Jonathan Neumann, "Federal Contracts: A Litany of Frivolity, Waste," *Washington Post* (June 23, 1980).

70. Jack Blaine, as quoted in *ibid.*

71. Quoted in *ibid.*

72. The estimate applied only to what is now the Departments of Education and Health and Human Services. See: Surveys and Investigation Staff, Committee on Appropriations, House of Representatives, *Report on the Manpower Policies and Practices of the Department of Health, Education and Welfare* (Washington, D.C.: U.S. Government Printing Office, April 1971), as reprinted in: Committee on Appropriations, U.S. House of Representatives, *Department of Labor and Department of Health, Education and Welfare Appropriations for Fiscal Year 1972*, hearing before a Subcommittee of the Committee on Appropriations, Part IV (Washington, D.C.: U.S. Government Printing Office, 1971), pp. 1061-1066.

73. Guttman and Willner, *The Shadow Government*, pp. 45-46.

74. As cited in United Press International, "Suspended Firms Still Get Contracts, Senate Panel Says," *Washington Post* (July 5, 1981). However, on-site inspections by Pentagon officials doubled from 40,000 in 1984 to more than 80,000 in 1985. See: Melloan, "Even Generals Get the Arms-Procurement Blues."

75. Larkin Dudley, "Managing Efficiency: Examples from Contract Administration," *Public Administration Review*, 50 (July/August 1990), p. 487.

76. U.S. House of Representatives Subcommittee on Human Resources of the Committee on Post Office and Civil Service, *Contracting Out and Its Impact on Federal Personnel and Operations* (Washington: U.S. Government Printing Office, 1990), as cited in *ibid.*

77. Senator Jim Sasser, as quoted in John E. Yang, "Reagan-Era Efficiency Program Called Wasteful," *Washington Post* (April 28, 1990).

78. U.S. General Accounting Office, *Civil Servants and Contract Employees*, p. 6.

79. Al Stapleton, as quoted in "Consultants: New Target for Budget Trimmers," p. 40.

80. Guttman and Willner, *The Shadow Government*, p. 113.

81. *Ibid.*, p. 119. This kind of policy domination by the private sector is hardly unique to Energy. For other examples, see: U.S. General Accounting Office, *Civil Servants and Contract Employees*, pp. 6-14.

82. U.S. General Accounting Office, *Government Contractors: Are Service Contractors Performing Inherently Governmental Functions?* GAO/GGO 92-11 (Washington, D.C.: General Accounting Office, November 1991), pp. 14, 48. In 1989, the federal government spent $48 billion on service contracts; in 1979, it spent $23 billion.

83. *Ibid.*, p. 14.

84. *Ibid.*, p. 5. GAO reviewed 108 consulting contracts let by the Departments of Transportation, Energy, and Defense, and the Environmental Protection Agency, and found twenty-eight that may have involved "inherently governmental functions."

85. General Accounting Office, as cited in Stuart Auerbach, "Disclosure Rules on Consultants Held Insufficient," *Washington Post* (November 2, 1990). The GAO's best shot in making a determination of how much the federal government spends on consultants is to analyze service contracts, which consumed $48 billion in 1989. On the other hand, the U.S. General Services Administration says Washington spent $14 billion on consultants in 1989. See: General Accounting Office, *Government Contractors*, p. 14.

86. Professional Services Council and OMB, as cited in Frank Greve, "Hired Guns Running the U.S.," *Philadelphia Inquirer* (May 19, 1992). The federal civilian payroll was $97 billion in 1992.

87. Walsh, *The Public's Business*, p. 49.

88. *Ibid.*, p. 50.

89. In 1979, there were 19,212 management, public relations, and general consulting services employees working for 1,311 firms. These figures represented an increase of almost 30 percent each in the number of consultants and firms from five years earlier. See: "Consultants: New Target for Budget Trimmers," *U.S. News & World Report* (December 21, 1981), p. 39.

90. Steven Pearlstein, "Reigning in the Pentagon's Think Tanks," *Washington Post* (July 28, 1991). But see also: Guttman and Willner, *The Shadow Government*, p. 21.

91. Seidman, *Politics, Position, and Power*, pp. 268-269.

92. National Science Foundation, *Scientific Activities of Independent Nonprofit Institutions* (Washington, D.C.: U.S. Government Printing Office, 1971).

93. As appearing on the program, "60 Minutes."

94. Auerbach, "Disclosure Rules on Consultants Held Insufficient."

95. Daniel Guttman, "60 Minutes."

96. Richard W. Stevenson, "Many Caught but Few Are Hurt for Arms Contract Fraud in U.S.," *Washington Post* (November 12, 1990).

97. Ronald J. Ostrow and John M. Broder, "New Indictments a Possibility in Pentagon Probe," *Philadelphia Inquirer* (November 26, 1990).

98. The following information in this paragraph is drawn from: Stevenson, "Many Caught but Few Are Hurt for Arms Contract Fraud in U.S."

99. Quoted in: Russell Mitchell, "It Was Mr. Fixit Vs. the Pentagon—and the Pentagon Won," *Business Week* (December 24, 1990), p. 52.

100. David T. Irwin, "Privatization in America," *Municipal Year Book, 1988* (Washington, D.C.: International City Management Association, 1988), p. 43.

101. The Reason Foundation, as cited in Martin Dickson, "America's Sale of the Century," *Financial Times* (June 1, 1992).

102. Irwin, "Privatization in America," p. 52.

103. *Ibid.*, p. 50.

104. *Ibid.*, p. 44

105. Robert M. Stein, "Alternative Means of Delivering Municipal Services: 1982-1988," *Intergovernmental*

Perspective, 19 (Winter 1993), p. 29. In 1982, over 30 percent of municipal services were delivered by contract, and in 1988 over 28 percent were. The surveys covered all cities of 10,000 people or more, and sixty four functions; about a third of the cities responded.

106. Lori M. Henderson, "Intergovernmental Service Arrangements and Transfer of Functions," *Municipal Year Book, 1985* (Washington, D.C.: International City Management Association, 1985), p. 201.

107. Elaine Morley, "Patterns in the Use of Alternative Service Delivery Approaches," *Municipal Year Book, 1989* (Washington, D.C.: International City Management Association, 1989), p. 38.

108. The Independent Sector, as cited in, Joanne Desky, "Non-Profits Increase Service Production," *Public Administration Times*, 15 (January 1, 1992), p. 1.

109. Annie Millar, Carol De Vita, and Lester M. Salamon, *The Phoenix Nonprofit Sector in a Time of Government Retrenchment* (Washington, D.C.: The Urban Institute, 1986), p. 41. Figure is for 1982.

110. Michael Lipsky and Steven Rathgeb Smith, "Nonprofit Organizations, Government, and the Welfare State," *Political Science Quarterly*, 104 (Spring 1990), pp. 625-648.

111. Millar, DeVita, and Salamon, *The Phoenix Nonprofit Sector in a Time of Retrenchment*, p. 41. Figures are for 1982.

112. Lester M. Salamon, "Government and the Voluntary Sector in an Era of Retrenchment: The American Experience," *Journal of Public Policy*, 6 (January-March 1986), p. 7. But see also: John Stuart Hall, *et al., Government Spending and the Nonprofit Sector in Two Arizona Communities: Phoenix/Maricopa County and Pinal County* (Washington, D.C.: The Urban Institute, 1985), p. 47. Figure is for 1982.

113. Salamon, "Government and the Voluntary Sector in an Era of Retrenchment," p. 7. Figures in the paragraph are for 1982.

114. Judith R. Saidel, "Resource Interdependence: The Relationship between State Agencies and Nonprofit Organizations," *Public Administration Review*, 51 (November/December 1991), p. 546.

115. U.S. Bureau of the Census, *Statistical Abstract of the United States, 1992* (Washington, D.C.: U.S. Government Printing Office, 1992), p. 374. Table 601. This figure is based on the U.S. Current Population Survey and is for 1989. Over 38 million American adults volunteered.

116. Gallup Poll, as cited in Desky, "Non-Profits Increase Service Production," p. 1. Figure is for 1990. Gallup found that over 98 million American adults volunteered over 20 billion hours, up from 80 million Americans in 1988. The Gallup figures, however, have been questioned as inflated. See: Jeffrey Brudney, "The Availability of Volunteers: Implications for Local Government," *Administration and Society*, 21 (February 1990), pp. 72-76.

117. U.S. Bureau of the Census, *Statistical Abstract of the United States, 1992*, p. 374. Table 601.

118. National Sheriffs' Association, as cited in Owen Thomas, "Citizen Patrols: Self-Help to an Extreme?"

Christian Science Monitor (July 5, 1988). Figure is for 1988.

119. Sydney Duncombe, "Volunteers in City Government: Advantages, Disadvantages, and Uses," *National Civic Review*, 74 (September 1985), pp. 356-364.

120. Stein, "Alternative Means of Delivering Municipal Services," p. 29.

121. Robert S. Montjoy and Jeffrey L. Brudney, "Volunteers in the Delivery of Public Services: Hidden Costs . . . and Benefits," *American Review of Public Administration*, 21 (December 1991), pp. 327-344; and David Osborne and Ted Gaebler, *Reinventing Government: How the Entrepreneurial Spirit Is Transforming the Public Sector* (Reading, Mass.: Addison-Wesley, 1992), pp. 68, 75, 196, and 340.

122. Kenneth Perkins, *Volunteer Fire Fighters in the United States: A Sociological Profile of America's Bravest* (Farmville, Va.: National Volunteer Fire Fighters Council, 1987).

123. Jeffrey L. Brudney and William D. Duncombe, "An Economic Evaluation of Paid, Volunteer, and Mixed Staffing Options for Public Services," *Public Administration Review*, 52 (September/October 1992), p. 474.

124. In 1975, 24 percent, or $36 billion, of state and local expenditures went to purchases of goods and services. See Donald Fisk, Herbert Kiesling, and Thomas Muller, *Private Provision of Public Services: An Overview* (Washington, D.C.: the Urban Institute, 1978), p. 87.

125. David, "Privatization in America," p. 51. An earlier survey found that more than 97 percent of American cities (1,350 cities responded) required sealed bids on purchasing contracts. On the other hand, nearly 87 percent of these same cities permitted bidding to be waived under certain circumstances. See Dan H. Davidson and Solon G. Bennett, "Municipal Purchasing Practices," *Municipal Year Book, 1980* (Washington, D.C.: International City Management Association, 1980), pp. 236-237, Tables 3/10 and 3/12.

126. Fisk, *et al., Private Provision of Public Services*, p. 92.

127. David, "Privatization in America," p. 45.

128. *Ibid.*, p. 43.

129. *Ibid.*, p. 47.

130. Susan A. MacManus, "Why Businesses Are Reluctant to Sell to Governments," *Public Administration Review*, 51 (July/August 1991), p. 334.

131. Based on Sharkansky, "Government Contracting," p. 25. See also: Ruth Hoogland De Hoog, *Contracting Out for Human Services: Economic, Political, and Organizational Perspectives* (Albany: State University of New York Press, 1984), especially pp. 1-33.

132. "Federal Procurement Institute Gets Going," p. 10.

133. U.S. House of Representatives Armed Services Committee, Investigations Subcommittee, *Life Is Too Short: A Review of the Brief Periods Managers of Major Defense Acquisition Programs Stay on the Job* (Washington, D.C.: U.S. Government Printing Office, 1990), as cited in Molly Moore, "Military Revolving Door Quickens," *Washington Post* (July 3, 1990).

134. Representative Nicholas Mavroules, as quoted in Moore, "Military Revolving Door Quickens."

135. Denning and Olson, "Public Enterprise and the Emerging Character of State Service Provisions," pp. 6, 9.

136. Walsh, *The Public's Business*, p. 6.

137. See notes 5 and 10.

138. U.S. Bureau of the Census, *Statistical Abstract of the United States, 1992*, p. 549, Table 880. In 1990, the U.S. Postal Service employed 809,000 people, and had revenues of just over $40 billion.

139. *Ibid.*, p. 323. Table 504. The U.S. Office of Management and Budget defines government-sponsored enterprises as "financial intermediaries directing capital to particular sectors of the economy." See: U.S. Office of Management and Budget, *Special Analyses: Budget of the United States Government, Fiscal Year 1990* (Washington, D.C.: U.S. Government Printing Office, 1988), p. F-21. A more rigorous definition of a *government-sponsored enterprise* is as follows: a privately owned, federally chartered financial institution with nationwide scope and limited lending powers that benefits from an implicit federal guarantee to enhance its ability to borrow money. See: Thomas H. Stanton, *Government-Sponsored Enterprises: Their Benefits and Costs as Instruments of Federal Policy* (Washington, D.C.: Association of Reserve City Bankers, 1988), p. iv. Using this definition, the seven government-sponsored enterprises in the United State are: the Farm Credit System Banks (FCS), founded in 1916; the Federal National Mortgage Corporation (Freddie Mac, 1970), the Federal Home Loan Banks (FHLB, 1932), the Student Loan Marketing Association (Sallie Mae, 1972), the College Construction Loan Insurance Corporation (Connie Lee, 1986), and the Federal Agricultural Mortgage Corporation (Farmer Mac, 1988). Additional government-sponsored enterprises are under consideration. Most observers agree that the GSEs are not well regulated.

140. Walsh, *The Public's Business*, p. 6.

141. Denning and Olson, "Public Enterprise and the Emerging Character of State Service Provisions," pp. 10, 42.

142. U.S. Bureau of the Census, *Statistical Abstract of the United States, 1992*, p. 285, Table 458. Figure is for 1990.

143. James L. Regans and Thomas P. Lauth, "Buy Now, Pay Later: Trends in State Indebtedness, 1950-1989," *Public Administration Review*, 52 (March/April 1992), p. 158.

144. Roy Bahl and William Duncombe, "State and Local Debt Burdens in the 1980s: A Study in Contrast," *Public Administration Review*, 53 (January/February 1993), p. 34. Nonguaranteed state and local debt increased from 60 percent of total debt in 1982 to over 70 percent in 1989.

145. Irene S. Rubin, "Municipal Enterprises: Exploring Budgetary and Political Implications," *Public Administration Review*, 48 (January/February 1988), p. 548.

146. Charlie B. Tyer, "Municipal Enterprises and Taxing and Spending Policies: Public Avoidance and Fiscal Illusions," *Public Administration Review*, 49 (May/June 1989), p. 255.

147. For example, *Williamsburg Savings Bank* v. *State of New York* (1928), and *Robertson* v. *Zimmerman* (1935).

148. Bahl and Duncombe, "State and Local Debt Burdens in the 1980s," p. 34.

149. Ann Crittenden, "The Hoover Way to Help Sick Companies," *New York Times* (January 24, 1982).

150. This discussion is drawn from Walsh, *The Public's Business*, pp. 27-29.

151. John Carver, *Boards That Make a Difference* (San Francisco: Jossey-Bass, 1990), and Joel Sokloff, *Handbook for Commissioners* (Washington, D.C.: National Association of Housing and Redevelopment Officials, 1980).

152. James Leigland and Robert Lamb, *WPP$$: Who Is to Blame for the WPPSS Disaster* (Boston: Ballinger, 1986), and Walsh, *The Public's Business*.

153. Unless noted otherwise, the data in this and the following paragraph are drawn from: Mitchell, "Education and Skills for Public Authority Management," pp. 429-437. Mitchell surveyed 6,352 state and local public authorities in the United States, and obtained a response rate of 60 percent.

154. International Personnel Management Association, *Pay Rates in the Public Service: Survey of 62 Common Job Classes in the Public Sector* (Washington, D.C.: International Personnel Management Association, 1985). According to this thorough survey, special districts pay their employees more for virtually every type of administrative position than do the federal, state, municipal, and county governments, and many special districts, perhaps most, are public authorities. Another indicator of high pay in public authorities can be found in the earnings of the executive directors of the federal government sponsored enterprises, such as, Sallie Mae, which are in the millions.

155. Tari Renner, "Appointed Local Government Managers: Stability and Change," *Municipal Year Book, 1990* (Washington, D.C.: International City Management Association, 1990), pp. 30-35.

156. Richard J. Stillman II, "Local Public Management in Transition: A Report on the Current State of the Profession," *Municipal Year Book, 1982* (Washington, D.C.: International City Management Association, 1982), p. 163. The figure for city managers is about ten years older than that for authority executives, so there may be an even greater disparity in educational levels.

157. Mitchell, "Education and Skills for Public Authority Management," pp. 434-435.

158. Walsh, *The Public Business*, p. 289.

159. Nathanial S. Preston, "The Use and Control of Public Authorities in American State and Local Government," Ph.D. dissertation, Princeton University, 1960.

160. Walsh, *The Public's Business*, p. 237.

161. *Ibid.*, p. 4.

162. Jameson W. Doig, "'If I See A Murderous Fellow Sharpening a Knife Cleverly . . .': The Wilsonian Dichotomy and the Public Authority Tradition,"

Public Administration Review, 44 (July/August 1983), pp. 292-303.

163. Robert A. Caro, *The Power Broker: Robert Moses and the Fall of New York* (New York: Alfred A. Knopf, 1974), pp. 5-10.

164. *Ibid.*, pp. 19-20.

165. Walsh, *The Public's Business*, p. 213.

166. Caro, *The Power Broker*, p. 38.

167. Quoted in *ibid.*, p. 12.

168. *Ibid.*, p. 18

169. *Ibid.*, p. 15

170. United Press International, "'Master Builder' Robert Moses, 92, Dies," *The Arizona Republic* (July 30, 1981).

171. Caro, *The Power Broker*, p. 15.

172. Robert Moses, *Public Works: A Dangerous Trade* (New York: McGraw-Hill, 1970), p. 438.

173. *Ibid.*, p. 394.

174. United Press International, "'Master Builder.'"

175. Walsh, *The Public's Business*, p. 220

176. Caro, *The Power Broker*, p. 17.

177. Walsh, *The Public's Business*, p. 220.

178. *Ibid.*, p. 265.

179. *Ibid.*, pp. 271-272.

180. *Ibid.*, p. 275.

181. *Ibid.*, pp. 263-264 and 276.

182. Denning and Olson, "Public Enterprise," p. 6.

183. Osborne and Gaebler, *Reinventing Government*.

184. Some of the following points, but not all, are found in: John Rehfuss, " A Leaner, Tougher Public Management? Public Agency Competition with Private Contractors," *Public Administration Quarterly*, 15 (Summer 1992), pp. 239-252.

185. Osborne and Gaebler identify thirty-six "alternatives" to the delivery of public services by public employees, including regulation, deregulation, tax policies, grants privatization, vouchers, volunteers, and public investment policy. But despite their claim, not all of their alternatives exclude public employees, such as the provision by governments of technical assistance to business, or the dissemination by governments of information. Most of these alternatives have been addressed, at least implicitly, in this book. See: Osborne and Gaebler, *Reinventing Government*, pp. 332-348.

186. As derived from Stein, "Alternative Means of Delivering Municipal Services," Table 2, p. 29.

CHAPTER 12

INTERGOVERNMENTAL ADMINISTRATION

Domestic public policy is implemented not merely by government, but by governments. The administration of a "single" public policy often involves a pastiche of funding sources and public administrators interacting through all three levels of government, and the field of public administration calls this pastiche *intergovernmental relations*, or the series of financial, legal, political, and administrative relationships established among all units of government which possess varying degrees of authority and jurisdictional autonomy. These relationships are called *federalism* when applied more narrowly to the federal government's relations with state governments, and the states' relationships with each other, although, in this book, we usually use "intergovernmental relations" and "federalism" interchangeably. *Intergovernmental administration*, sometimes called *intergovernmental management*, is the management and coordination of intergovernmental relationships for the purpose of achieving specific policy goals.[1]

THOUSANDS AND THOUSANDS OF GOVERNMENTS

Considering how opinions differ among scholars on the nature of intergovernmental relations, it is not surprising to learn that we are dealing with an extraordinarily complex system. These complexities are administrative, jurisdictional, political, and financial—a list that is hardly surprising when we consider the enormous number of governments thriving in the United States. Table 12-1 identifies the 86,743 governments in the United States by type, and indicates their fluctuations between 1942, 1962, 1982, and 1992.

Much of the proliferation of units of local government occurred in the years following World War II, particularly around the fringes of big cities. It was largely due to white flight from the inner cities and unplanned metropolitan growth. The lack of prior planning for urban regions is particularly noticeable when we consider these examples of growth: Forty-four new suburban governments were created between 1945 and 1950 around St. Louis by builders desirous of escaping strict municipal building codes. New towns were formed around Minneapolis solely as a means of taxing a newly arrived industry, and one village was incorporated for the single purpose of issuing a liquor license. Bryan City, California, was created so that a circus owner could zone for animal populations as he saw fit. The town of New Squier, New York, was established so that a kosher slaughterhouse could be operated. Gardenia, California, was incorporated so that its residents might play poker legally.[2] Yet, eager as Americans appear to be to set up

TABLE 12-1 **Number of Governments in the United States by Type of Government, 1942, 1962, 1982, and 1992**

Level of Government	1942	1962	1982	1992
Total	155,116	91,237	81,831	86,743
U. S. Government	1	1	1	1
State Governments	48	50	50	50
Local Governments	155,067	91,186	81,780	86,692
Counties	3,050	3,043	3,041	3,043
Municipalities	16,220	18,000	19,076	19,296
Townships and Towns	18,919	17,142	16,734	16,666
School Districts	108,579	34,678	14,851	14,556
Special Districts	8,299	18,323	28,078	33,131

Source: U. S. Bureau of the Census, *Statistical Abstract of the United States*, 1985 (Washington, D. C.: U. S. Government Printing Office, 1984), p. 261, Table 433; and U. S. Bureau of the Census, as cited in: Jeff Fletcher, "Census Report 3600 New Special Districts Created Since 1987," *Nation's Cities Weekly* (February 22, 1993).

small towns, they are wary of creating large ones. Community efforts to merge urban and suburban governments have generally failed, despite frequently intensive efforts by urban political elites.

With the exceptions of school districts, which have been diminishing in number since the 1930s, and special districts, which have been steadily multiplying, the numbers of governmental units in all categories have remained more or less the same since 1942. The total number of American governments reached its nadir in the second half of the twentieth century in 1972 (78,269); it is the proliferation of special districts that largely accounts for the overall growth of governments since then.

THE CONSTITUTION AND THE COURTS: SETTING THE RULES

How these thousands of American governments act and react to each other is based on broad rules of the game set by the Constitution and court decisions.

Much of the federal government's relationship with state governments is specified by the Constitution, which organized the federal system around three basic ideas: drawing boundaries between governmental activities of the states and the nation; establishing and maintaining the identity of state and national governments; and politically integrating the nation and the states.[3]

Section 8 of Article I of the Constitution was instrumental in making distinctions between state and national functions. It delegated seventeen specific powers to the national government, including defense, general welfare, and commerce, and left the remaining powers to the states. These remaining powers are now known as "reserved powers," a phrase taken from the Tenth Amendment, which was added rather hastily by the Founders in response to such populist rabble-rousers as Patrick Henry. The Tenth Amendment was designed to grant the states a more visible and defined territory for exercising their powers. Section 9 of Article I also dealt with states' boundaries by preventing the national government from doing certain things, such as suspending the writ of *habeas corpus*, and also forbidding the states from doing certain things, such as entering into treaties with foreign nations and coining money.

The second area of constitutional federalism deals with establishing and maintaining the identities between state and nation. The most important clause here is Section 2, Article IV, which stipulates that "no new States shall be Formed or Erected within the jurisdiction of any other State; nor any State be formed by the junction of two or more States, or Parts of States, without the Consent of the Legislature of the States concerned."

Finally, the Constitution dealt with the integration of national and state governments, primarily by providing for cooperation among them in the performance of certain functions. For example, the states and the nation cooperate in amending the Constitution and electing a president. "Perhaps the most important factor in making possible political integration between the two levels is the scarcity of officials with a clearly defined identification with the states, resulting in the creation of a group of national officeholders who also have links to the states."[4] This arrangement, of course, was designed by the founders. As James Madison noted in the *Federalist* papers, "a local spirit will infallibly prevail much more in the members of Congress than a national spirit will prevail in the Legislatures of the particular states."[5]

These three major features of the relations between the state governments and the national government—boundary settlement, separate identities, and national and state integration—were refined by the courts over time. Without question, the most influential single case in this process of refinement was *McCulloch* v. *Maryland*, which was settled by the Supreme Court under Chief Justice John Marshall in 1819. Marshall and his colleagues supported the expansion of national powers under the commerce clause of the Constitution, which gave the national government a powerful ability to interpret what was necessary and proper in the way of making policy under the Constitution. The case involved the state of Maryland's attempt to tax the second United States Bank, which was located in Maryland. Alexander Hamilton, as secretary of the treasury, had proposed a national bank and argued that it could be established under a strong national government, which could and should adopt such measures because they were "implied powers" under the Constitution, even though the Constitution did not specifically authorize such policies as the establishment of the bank. The Marshall Court agreed with Hamilton's argument, stating that, although a bank was not explicitly authorized as a power granted to Congress under the Constitution, it nonetheless was implied under Congress' abilities to establish and collect taxes, regulate commerce, raise and support armies, and so on. Hence, Congress had the ability to adopt appropriate measures for the realization of the powers granted to it by the Constitution to do whatever is "necessary and proper to implement its specified functions." This notion of implied powers as an interpretation of

the "necessary and proper" clause of the Constitution is with us today, and (with the exception of the Civil War) remains the single strongest statement of national power as opposed to state power. Table 12-2 lists the principal powers of the federal government and the implied powers of the states.

THE EVOLUTION OF INTERGOVERNMENTAL ADMINISTRATION

Operating within the formal rules of the game established by the Constitution and by subsequent judicial interpretation, localities, states, and the federal government have gone through a number

TABLE 12-2   The Constitution's Federal Divisions of Powers

Major powers of the federal government:

Tax for federal purposes.

Borrow on the nation's credit.

Regulate foreign and interstate commerce.

Provide currency and coinage.

Conduct foreign relations and make treaties.

Provide an army and navy.

Establish and maintain a postal service.

Protect patents and copyrights.

Regulate weights and measures.

Admit new states.

"Make all laws which shall be necessary and proper" for the execution of all powers vested in the U.S. government.

Major implied powers of the states:

Tax for local purposes.

Borrow on the state's credit.

Regulate trade within the state.

Make and enforce civil and criminal law.

Maintain a police force.

Furnish public education.

Control local government.

Regulate charities.

Establish voting and election laws.

"Powers not delegated to the United States by the Constitution, nor prohibited by it to the states are reserved to the states respectively, or to the people."

of phases in their administrative relationships. During the twentieth century, we can discern at least seven such phases, often overlapping in time, but each possessing its own set of unique characteristics.[6]

Layer Cake Federalism, 1890–1930

The first of these phases occurred from the late nineteenth century to 1930, and was characterized by the conflict between states, localities, and Washington. The major problems centered around defining the boundaries and proper spheres of influence among various governmental jurisdictions, and intergovernmental actors (*i.e.,* relevant public officials at all governmental levels) saw themselves in an adversary and antagonistic relationship with each other. The mechanisms of intergovernmental relationships prior to 1930 were relatively simple and relied largely on legislative statutes, judicial rulings, and federal regulations. What Deil S. Wright calls the "federalism metaphor"—that is, how intergovernmental relations were perceived and described in metaphorical terms—during this period was "Layer Cake Federalism." In other words, people saw the relationships between governments as a series of layers: localities on the bottom, states in the middle, and the federal government on top. There was little, if any, interaction among the layers other than each governmental level defending its autonomy from encroachment by the other levels.

Marble Cake Federalism, 1930–1960

The next federal phase occurred during the 1930s and the 1950s and represented quite an opposite composite of relationships than the previous period of intergovernmental conflict. The thirties, forties, and fifties were decades of "Cooperative Federalism" in which everyone faced up, essentially as an intergovernmental team, to common problems of the Depression, World War II, and the rise of international Communism. In stark contrast to the pre-1930s, officials involved in intergovernmental relations stressed collaboration and supportive relationships. The mechanisms of working relationships among governments moved from simple statutes and court orders to a national planning mode

involving the introduction of formula grants and more sophisticated versions of intergovernmental tax credits. The federalism metaphor changed from "Layer Cake Federalism" to "Marble Cake Federalism"; increasingly, it was difficult to separate the governmental activities of localities, states, and nation.

Water Tap Federalism, 1940–1970

The next phase, which occurred during the 1940s through the 1960s, has been called "Concentrated Federalism." During this period, the shape of intergovernmental relations was increasingly functional, focused, and specific. The federal government attempted more aggressively to meet the public service obligations and the physical development needs of states and communities. In terms of the working styles of officials who participated in intergovernmental relations during this period, "politics" were largely "out" and "professionalism" was largely "in"; a kind of engineering mentality predominated. The new mechanisms of intergovernmental relations evolved from a national planning format to an emphasis on detailed and targeted categorical grants and the monitoring of certain service standards. The federalism metaphor changed from a "marble cake" to "water taps," stressing the focused and channeled nature of the concentrated federalism phase; that is, federal grants, released by Congress from the federal spigot, flowed from Washington to the states, and from the states to the localities.

Federalism in Flower, 1950–1970

The 1950s and 1960s saw the emergence of "Creative Federalism." Here the emphasis was on meeting the problems of urban America, the poor, the dispossessed, and minorities. The apolitical, engineering mentality held by officials who were involved in intergovernmental relationships during the concentrated period of federalism gave way to a more political view, focusing on the achievement of national goals as they pertained to President Lyndon Johnson's Great Society programs. The mechanisms for achieving all this largely were participation by the citizenry, program planning, and an increasing emphasis on aid given by the federal government to states and localities for the completion of specific projects. The federal metaphor that had relied on plumbing ("water taps") was replaced with one that focused on botany; suddenly there was a "flowering" of federalism, a metaphor that emphasized the verdant proliferation of various intergovernmental programs.

Picket Fence Federalism, 1960–1980

The 1960s and 1970s saw the emergence of a new phase of federalism which stressed competition among governmental jurisdictions. After federalism's flowering phase, new problems emerged involving coordination, program effectiveness, the competency of delivery systems, and the accessibility of citizens to the policymaking process. As in the conflictually oriented phase of intergovernmental relations, a renewed emphasis was seen on disagreement, tension, and rivalry among competitors for federal grants. The mechanisms of intergovernmental relations shifted from project grants and participation to the consolidation of federal grants through such devices as block grants, revenue sharing, and the reorganization of categorical grants. The operative metaphor of federalism's competitive phase became "Picket Fence Federalism," which stressed the fragmented, discrete nature of the hundreds of different kinds of categorical and project grants that developed during this phase.

Federalism as Facade, 1970–1980

The 1970s saw the emergence of "Calculative Federalism." Calculative federalism amounted to the intergovernmental system's way of coping with new regulatory constraints. The main problems were ones of accountability, fiscal dependency, and diminishing public confidence in the institutions of government. The state and local officials who participated in intergovernmental relations perceived the shape of federalism to be one of gamesmanship, and concentrated their energies on such endeavors as using federal grants for the attainment of local goals that were not necessarily envisioned by federal policymakers, and of coping with an overload of demands for governmental services while often functioning under budgetary constraints. Increasingly, the

mechanisms of dealing with the relationships between governments stressed loans, entitlements, Washington's bypassing of state governments and working directly with localities, and a variety of crosscutting regulations.

The metaphor of intergovernmental administration during this period was "facade." In other words, intergovernmental management and relations, as they had been traditionally understood, no longer existed; so powerful and dominant had the federal government become that the powers of states and localities, at least in relative terms, were no longer of consequence.

Fend-for-Yourself Federalism, 1980–Present

Finally, the 1980s and 1990s have witnessed the emergence of "Competitive Federalism," or "Fend-for-Yourself Federalism."[7] The federal government's intergovernmental preeminence of the seventies began to dissipate after 1978, when (as we later detail) the federal government's contribution to the finances of state and local governments peaked as a share of their budgets, and began a decline that has yet to be arrested. Late in the 1980s, the federal government became increasingly mired by "the uncontrollables" (described in Chapter 8), and crushed by its own staggering deficit. In 1981, the annual federal deficit exceeded $100 billion for the first time, in 1986 it topped $200 billion, and by 1992 was nearing $300 billion a year.[8]

The effects of the feds' withdrawal of their fiscal support of subnational governments, combined with the federal deficit, have resulted in a situation in which all governments have had to become more innovative and more competitive to deliver services. But "competition" no longer refers to state and local governments competing among themselves for federal grants, as it did during the phase of Picket Fence Federalism. Today, competition means that all governments are competing with each other for revenues, regardless of the source. "The essence of [Fend-for-Yourself Federalism] is that now Washington policymakers as well as state and local officials must go back, hat-in-hand, to a common source—the nation's taxpayers—when additional revenue is needed. . . . There is growing evidence to suggest that absent a national crisis, Washington does not have the inside track in the emerging intergovernmental race for taxpayer support."[9]

Indeed not. Public opinion polls taken since 1972 show that the federal government has steadily slipped in the public's perception as the most efficient and effective level of government, relative to state and local governments. As Figure 12-1 shows, state governments first surpassed the federal government on this dimension in 1979, and local governments, long the butt of American political humor, now are almost at a par with the

BACK TO BASICS: A FOUNDER ON FEDERALISM

The following excerpt is taken from Federalist Paper 51, written in 1788. In this brief condensation, the writer explores the nature of governmental relationships.

In order to lay a due foundation for that separate and distinct exercise of the different powers of government, which to a certain extent is admitted on all hands to be essential to the preservation of liberty, it is evident that each department should have a will of its own; and consequently should be so constituted that the members of each should have as little agency as possible in the appointment of the members of the others. Were this principle rigorously adhered to, it would require that all the appointments for the supreme executive, legislative, and judiciary magistracies should be drawn from the same fountain of authority, the people, through channels having no communication whatever with one another. Perhaps such a plan of constructing the several departments would be less difficult in practice than it may in contemplation appear. . . .

But what is government itself but the greatest of all reflections on human nature? If men were angels, no government would be necessary. If angels were to govern men, neither external nor internal controls on government would be necessary. In framing a government which is to be administered by men over men, the great difficulty lies in this: you must first enable the government to control the governed, and in the next place oblige it to control itself. A dependence on the people is, no doubt, the primary control on the government, but experience has taught mankind the necessity of auxiliary precautions. . . .

In the compound republic of America, the power surrendered by the people is first divided between two distinct governments, and then the portion allotted to each subdivided among distinct and separate departments. Hence a double security arises to the rights of the people. The different governments will control each other at the same time that each will be controlled by itself. . . .

It is of great importance in a republic not only to guard the society against the oppression of its rulers, but to guard one part of the society against the injustice of the other part. Whilst all authority in it will be derived from and dependent on the society, the society itself will be broken into so many parts, interests, and classes of citizens that the rights of individuals or of the minority, will be in little danger from interested combinations of the majority. . . .

Justice is the end of government. It is the end of civil society. It ever has been and ever will be pursued until it be obtained, or until liberty be lost in the pursuit. . . .

In the extended republic of the United States, and among the great variety of interests, parties, and sects which it embraces, a coalition of a majority of the whole society could seldom take place on any other principles than those of justice and the general good; whilst there being thus less danger to a minor from the will of a major party, there must be less pretext also to provide for the security of the former by introducing into the government a will not dependent on the latter, or, in other words, a will independent of the society itself. It is no less certain than it is important, notwithstanding the contrary opinions which have been entertained, that the larger the society, provided it lie within a practical sphere, the more duly capable it will be of self-government. And happily for the *republican cause*, the practical sphere may be carried to a very great extent by a judicious modification and mixture of the *federal principle*.

James Madison

FIGURE 12-1 Comparison of Opinions Regarding from Which Level of Government Do You Feel You Get the Most for Your Money—Federal, State, or Local? 1972–1991

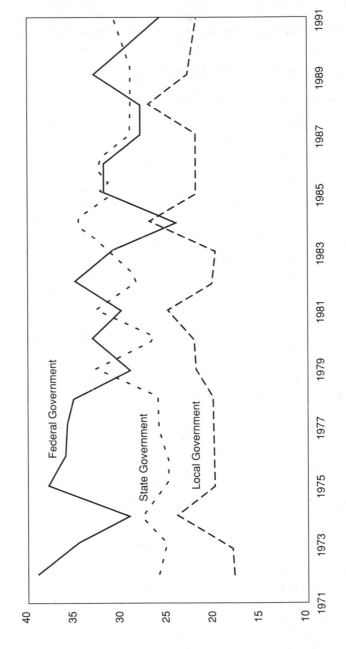

Source: Advisory Commission on Intergovernmental Relations, *Changing Public Attitudes on Governments and Taxes, 1991* (Washington, D.C.: U.S. Government Printing Office, 1991), p. 7.

federal government when Americans are asked which level of government gives them the most for their money.

Over time, Americans have grown to view the federal, state, and local governments as increasingly alike in terms of their abilities to deliver services efficiently and effectively. This developing popular perspective has evolved at the expense of the federal government and to the greatest benefit of the state governments. The principal point, however, is that the competence of each level of government is perceived by the people to be increasingly comparable in an age of reduced governmental revenues. As a consequence, federal, state, and local public administrators must compete with one another as never before to earn the respect and trust of their taxpayers if they are to increase their government's revenues. Fend for yourself.

In describing these phases of federalism, we have relied on hyperbole and caricature as methods of getting the main ideas across. This point should be kept in mind, particularly as it applies to our description of our present federal phase, "Fend-for-Yourself Federalism," because exaggeration can be misleading, and it is not our intention to promote what one wag has called, "the Henny Penny school of federalism"; that is, the notion that the sky of the intergovernmental system is falling, either because of too much or too little federal activity.[10]

Nevertheless, characterizing federalism along these seven phases is useful as a background in gaining a more complete understanding of the relations among America's governments—especially their fiscal relations, which typically have been the dominant, though by no means only, factor in each of these phases of federalism.

FISCAL FEDERALISM

The old question in politics of who gets what, when, where, and how is nowhere more evident than in the intergovernmental money game. During the twentieth century, these fiscal and political patterns have changed radically.

A World Turned Upside Down: A Century of Fiscal Change

The fiscal scene throughout the intergovernmental system has undergone some dramatic alterations during this century.[11] Between 1927 and 1991, government revenues as a percentage of personal income in the United States tripled from less than 15 percent to 44 percent. But the relative tax bite of each level of government changed considerably during these years, and illustrate the comparative power of each governmental level in American society.

Clearly, the federal government waxed at the expense of both the state and local levels. Its revenues quintupled from slightly more than 5 percent of personal income in 1927 to almost a fourth of personal income sixty-four years later.

Much the same story was unfolding among the states. In 1927, state government revenues which were derived from the states' own revenue sources (in other words, not counting federal and local financial aid to the states) stood at over 2 percent of personal income. By 1991, this figure had quadrupled to almost 11 percent—not quite as long a leap as that taken by the feds, but nonetheless impressive.

It was the local governments which were not keeping up. In 1927, local governments were the dominant players in public finance. The revenues of local governments which were derived from their own sources (*i.e.*, not counting aid to localities from the federal and state governments) amounted to almost 7 percent of personal income—a figure almost a fourth larger than that of the federal government, and nearly three times larger than that of the states. By 1991, the local governments' share of personal income had increased to less than 9 percent—a relatively paltry rise of only 25 percent over sixty-four years—and one which was over two-thirds less than the feds' share of personal income and nearly one-third less than that of the states.

The Revenue Rise and Fiscal Fall of the Feds

Both the federal and state governments have displaced the local governments in the public finance of the United States, but the federal government—which collects more than half of all government revenues and expends close to two-thirds of all government expenditures[12] (the difference lies in Washington's propensity to deficit

FIGURE 12-2 Federal Grants-in-Aid in Relation to State-Local Outlays and Payments to Individuals 1965–1992

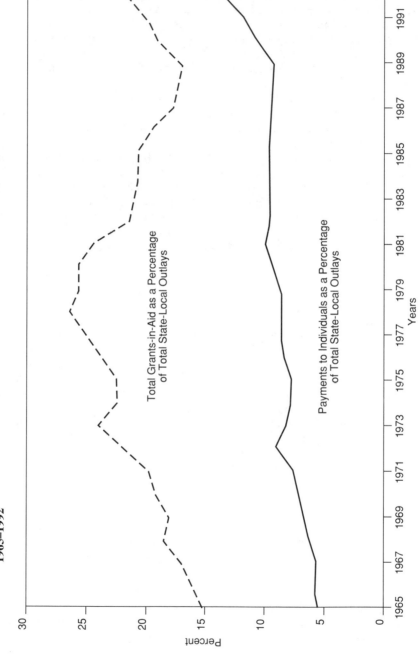

Source: Advisory Commission on Intergovernmental Relations, *Significant Features of Fiscal Federalism, 1993*, Vol. 2, M-185-II (Washington, D.C.: U.S. Government Printing Office, 1993), p.3.

spend)—clearly is the reigning fiscal figure in public finance.

The unquestioned reason for this federal dominance is the ratification in 1913 of the Sixteenth Amendment to the Constitution, which permitted governments to tax personal income. Today, individual income taxes account for over 72 percent of federal revenues, over 31 percent of state revenues, and almost 5 percent of local revenues.[13] The effective "ownership" of the personal income tax by Washington (in contrast to states, which derive nearly half of their revenues from sales taxes, and local governments, which gain almost three-quarters of their revenues from property taxes), together with its incredible productivity as a tax, has led to the federal government's preeminence as a revenue harvester.

The growing wealth of the national government compared to the subnational governments following the ratification of the Sixteenth Amendment led to Washington's becoming deeply involved in giving federal fiscal aid to both state and local governments.[14] In 1927, federal aid accounted for less than 5 percent of state revenues and an iota (well under 1 percent) of local revenues. By 1978, the peak year for federal transfers of funds to state and local governments, federal aid accounted for over 22 percent of all state revenues, and over 9 percent of local revenues. These were historic figures, and would never be repeated.

After 1978, the federal role in state and local budgets fell. By 1991, federal aid to states had decreased to 20 percent of total state revenues, and federal assistance as a percentage of local revenues had been slashed by two-thirds, and amounted to only 3 percent of all local revenues. Were it not for a sharp rise in federal Medicaid grants (Medicaid is a health program for the poor), which increased by a fourth in 1990 and 1991, these figures would be lower. Figure 12-2 illustrates this precipitous federal fall in terms of both state and local outlays and payments to individuals. As it indicates, the federal contribution to state and local budgets has regressed to the levels of the late 1950s.

What, if anything, has filled the fiscal vacuum left by Washington's departure? Clearly, the states are the governments most willing to assume the responsibilities placed by the feds on the doorstep of the subnational jurisdictions, and the states,

confronted with truly trying circumstances, have managed to keep state aid to local governments constant since 1978 at about 30 percent of all local revenues. As two analysts have concluded, "we find that the most important developments [of the 1980s on intergovernmental relations] are twofold—the relative decline in the federal role and the rising role of the state governments."[15]

State spending levels, held constant for inflation, support this assessment; state spending from their own sources of revenues began a sharp upward swing in 1981 that still continues. Figure 12-3 illustrates this quite proactive fiscal posture that the states started to assume as the federal government withdrew from their affairs in the 1980s. All in all, the states warrant praise for attempting to protect their communities in the context of a federal withdrawal, and doing so under conditions that, in the view of many analysts, have been made harder for the states because of federal actions.[16]

The Politics of Federal Grants-in-Aid: Categorical Grants, Block Grants, and the Brief but Edifying Life of General Revenue Sharing

Even though Washington's clout in the intergovernmental fiscal system is in decline, the federal government nonetheless remains dominant. As its dominance began to grow, Washington increasingly relied on *grants-in-aid*—which are transfers of federal funds to state and local governments—to, at first, help them, and, later, to help itself.

Prior to 1960, federal grants were used to help state and local governments to achieve their own policy objectives, but following that year the increasing tendency was evident for the federal government to use the intergovernmental grants system to, in effect, bribe state and local governments to accomplish national objectives.[17] Between 1960 and 1981, the number of federal grants programs quadrupled from 132 to 539, indicating the new reliance that the federal government was placing on the grants system to achieve its ends.[18]

Categorical grants. Washington uses two major types of grants to pass money to the state

FIGURE 12-3   **State Direct General Expenditures in Constant (1986) Dollars**

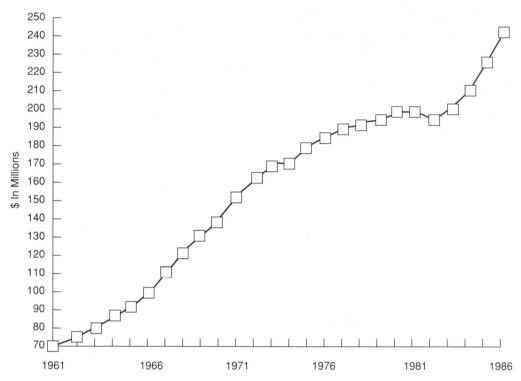

Source: Richard P. Nathan and John R. Lago, "Intergovernmental Relations in the Reagan Era," *Public Budgeting and Finance,* 8 (Autumn 1988), p. 28.

and local governments: categorical grants and block grants. *Categorical grants* are highly specific and rather rigid programs that address narrow policy issues. The typical categorical grant has a number of strings attached, and each qualification must be met by the recipient in order to receive the grant. Categorical grants account for over 88 percent of the money that the state and local governments receive from the federal government.[19] Washington obviously favors these categorical grants since they offer the most opportunity for retaining control over the expenditures of its money on the policy objectives for which federal dollars are spent.

There are three kinds of categorical grants. *Formula grants* are grants distributed by an administratively or legislatively prescribed formula, and the federal government pays without limit (unless one is contained in the formula)

according to the formula. *Project grants,* or *discretionary grants,* are distributed to state or local governments at the discretion of federal administrators. Nearly 73 percent of categorical grants are project grants, and they are growing as a proportion of categorical grants. Finally, there are *formula/project grants,* which are grants that are awarded at the discretion of federal administrators, but within the bounds of a formula, such as the amount of dollars that may be awarded to a state.

Block Grants.   Block grants account for about 11 percent of the money that Washington expends. A *block grant* is a formula grant which allows the recipient to exercise more discretion in the way that federal dollars granted to it are expended in comparison to categorical grants. Most block grants are awarded to states, although some, such as the Community Development Block Grants, go directly to local governments. Until 1965, essentially all federal grants were categorical grants; in that year, some categorical grant programs in health were consolidated, and constituted the first block grant.

Block grants generate substantial political heat. At the center of the argument is the level of trust that one has in state and local officials, as opposed to national officials, and the kinds of programs that each level of government would fund with block grant money. Those who favor focusing federal dollars toward the needs of the poor and the deprived tend to favor the use of categorical grants to achieve these ends, while those who favor letting state and local governments— or those governments that are somehow "closer to the needs of the people"—decide how money should be spent and in what areas favor the use of block grants.

Investigations do indicate that when state and local governments receive block grants, they tend to use the money for programs other than those related to the impoverished. For example, when Congress, at President Richard Nixon's urging, consolidated seven basic national programs under the Housing and Community Development Act of 1974, essentially converting them from categorical to block grants, and thereby giving local leaders more control over how the funds underwriting these programs were to be used, The Brookings Institution found that poverty programs had fared better under the old Model Cities program initiated during the 1960s than under the new Community Development programs. (Model Cities was one of those programs that were subsumed by the Housing and Community Development acts.) There had been a shift, both in funding and decision making, away from the poorest people in the neighborhoods to more mixed patterns, and programs had changed from an emphasis on social services, such as health and education, to short-term capital spending for projects, such as parking lots and downtown renewal. Social services spending was found to be low under the Community Development programs.[20]

General Revenue Sharing. Analyses of a much more liberal block grant program ("liberal" in the sense that it permitted the widest discretion by recipients in the spending of federal grants) found comparable patterns. The program was *General Revenue Sharing*, which between 1972 and 1986, transferred about $84 billion in federal grants to 39,000 state and local governments. At its height[21] (in 1975), General Revenue Sharing amounted to over 14 percent of the federal aid package, and these funds were distributed according to a formula based on the proportion of personal income tax funds paid to the federal government in each state and community; once these dollars were received, essentially no strings were attached on how state and local governments could spend them.

Studies found that, whereas small cities and towns used about three-quarters of their Revenue Sharing funds for new spending programs (mostly for capital projects), bigger urban areas with 100,000 people or more used only half of the money for new spending programs; the remaining half went to keep taxes down or to avoid borrowing. Among the states, only a third of shared revenues were used for new programs, and the tendency of both state and local governments to use Revenue Sharing funds for keeping a muzzle on the tax bite rather than initiating new spending programs was the norm.

In sum, state and larger local governments used shared revenues mainly to keep their fiscal heads above water by maintaining existing services without raising taxes; merged General Revenue Sharing funds with other revenue sources, thus reducing the political visibility of General Revenue Sharing; retained traditional patterns of political power and enhanced the clout of entrenched special interests; and, contrary to widespread speculation (and hope), reinforced the existing inefficiencies of public management systems.[22]

Revenue sharing remains with us ("general purpose" grants account for less than 2 percent of the dollars transferred by the federal government to other governments), but only in a technical sense, and refers largely to such programs as grazing fees and mineral rights leases.[23]

Categorical Grants: A Favored Federal Commitment. Nixon's steps toward decentralization of the intergovernmental grants system, which he took in part by increasing the stature of block grants, were accelerated by the Reagan administration. In 1981, Congress enacted the Omnibus Budget Reconciliation Act, which consolidated seventy-seven categorical grants and one block grant into seven new block grants, raising to twelve the total number of block grants; prior to 1981, the nation had only five block grant programs (including General Revenue Sharing). In addition, sixty-two categorical grant programs were eliminated altogether.

The effects of these consolidations and eliminations were dramatic, at least if we use the number and types of federal assistance programs as a measure. In 1981, Congress had funded 534 categorical grant programs and five block grants; in 1984, 392 categorical grants and twelve block grants (including General Revenue Sharing) were funded.[24] But Washington's propensity to use the categorical grant, despite Ronald Reagan's efforts to alter the federal government's reliance on the form, seems undiminished. By 1993, the number of categorical grants had rebounded to 578, General Revenue Sharing had been struck, and the remaining block grant programs stood at a modest fifteen. Moreover, when we use money as a measure, in contrast to numbers of grant types, the effects of Reagan's reforms are even less visible; block grants (other than General Revenue Sharing) peaked in their percentage of grant dollars expended at 15 percent in 1978 (and categorical grants reached their all-time low in that year of 73 percent), but by 1993 accounted for only 11 percent of the federal funds granted to states and localities.[25]

A Regional Rivalry

One of the major effects of the dramatic growth of fiscal federalism during the 1960s and 1970s, and its subsequent withdrawal in the 1980s and 1990s, was the fostering of an increasingly cutthroat competitiveness among state and local governments for federal dollars. Despite the fact that they are among the wealthiest of the nation's regions, the Northeast and Midwest, beginning in the 1970s, have complained that they are losing industry and jobs to other sections of the country, especially to the Western and Sunbelt states. These regions argue that, since they have supported other regions in the country over the years through a variety of federal grants programs that have favored those regions that his-

torically have been less wealthy, it is now time for the federal government to tilt its grants programs toward the Northeast and Midwest.

The contention that certain regions are favored by the federal grants system more than others is a controversial one. One reason why is the problem of determining what kinds of federal payments to regions that one wants to include in the mix, for there are more transfers of federal funds to regions than merely grants to governments.

Figure 12-4 illustrates the distribution of federal funds to the states, including not only those funds constituting intergovernmental aid, but welfare payments, salaries of federal employees, payments to individuals, procurement contracts, and other payments, after federal taxes paid by each state have been subtracted. Regional inequities, as defined by how much a region transfers to the federal government in taxes compared to how much is transferred back to the region in the forms of federal grants and payments, have been lessening over the past several decades, and are now relatively marginal. At mid-century, the Mideastern states in particular transferred more to Washington than they received back, whereas the situation was the opposite for the Southeastern states.

More recent analyses substantiate that the diversion of federal funds from the Frostbelt to the Sunbelt as a consequence of tax and spending policies continues to equalize, although "any lessening of the inequalities has been almost entirely accidental," and the federal government "has not intentionally adjusted spending and tax policies to help one region or punish another."[26]

MONEY AND MANDATES: FEDERAL INSTRUMENTS OF IMPLEMENTATION

The federal attitude toward state and local governments as prospective executors of federal policies can be reduced to three periods. The first occurred during the years prior to 1960, when federal officials more or less tried to help out their colleagues at the subnational levels by slipping the occasional project grant to them. Federal grants in the 1950s never attained 15 percent of all state and local expenditures, and were usually closer to 10 percent. An even greater indicator of federal indifference to the state and local role in

FIGURE 12-4 Per Capita Net Flow (Federal Expenditures Minus Federal Tax Burden) of Federal Funds, 1988-1990

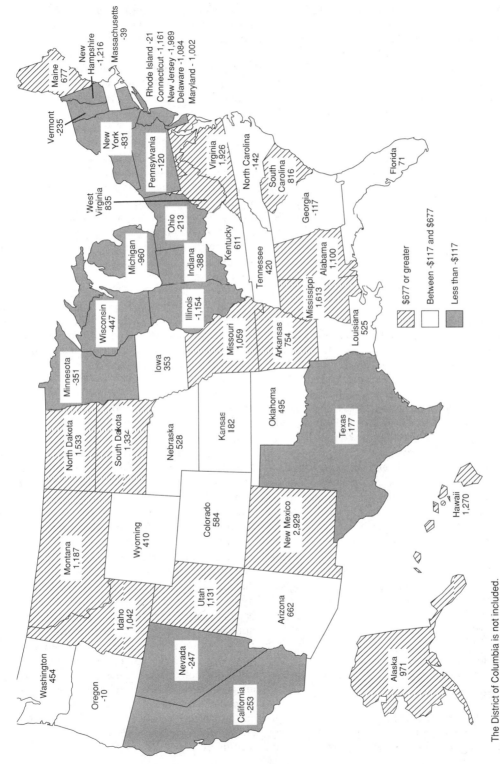

$677 or greater

Between -$117 and $677

Less than -$117

The District of Columbia is not included.

Source: Advisory Commission on Intergovernmental Relations, *Significant Features of Fiscal Federalism, 1991, Vol. 2* (Washington, D.C.: U.S. Government Printing Office, 1991), p. 9.

intergovernmental administration was the fact that no new federal mandates were enacted that applied to state and local governments during the entire two decades of the 1940s and 1950s,[27] and there were hardly any in the first place. The idea of pressuring state and local governments to enforce federal policies had not, prior to 1960 (more or less), really occurred to federal officials.

After 1960, however, a new attitude emerged in Washington. Increasingly, grants were being used as bribes to state and local governments to accomplish federal ends. By 1978, federal grants accounted for an astonishing 27 percent of all state and local outlays combined, and the subnational governments' craving for their federal fiscal fix was clearly distorting policy choices in states and communities. Federal regulations on state and local governments also burgeoned between 1960 and 1980, but at a lesser rate of expansion than the federal dollars flowing to these jurisdictions.

With the advent of unprecedented deficit spending by Washington during the 1980s and the inauguration of two conservative presidents, federal grants-in-aid to state and local governments began their precipitous decline, from more than a quarter for every dollar in state and local budgets to about a dime by the early 1990s. Despite an almost obsessive ideological bent toward deregulation in the administrations of Ronald Reagan and George Bush, however, a decline in federally promulgated intergovernmental regulations did not accompany the decline in federal dollars. In fact, the eighties saw the enactment of more federal mandates applying to state and local governments than in any preceding decade!

In sum, Washington has experimented with both honey (in the form of federal money) and vinegar (federal mandates) as inducements to state and local governments to assist Washington in the implementation and enforcement of national policies. We consider next how these approaches have worked.

Does National Money Make Subnational Policy? Lessons from the Sixties and Seventies

The heavy fiscal role that Washington played in state and local budgets during the 1970s not only consumed the time and energies of state and local officials, but had a perverse effect on the policy choices that were made by them for their citizens.

Grants and Governments: The States. Governors in the 1960s devoted less of their time to state-federal business than did governors in the 1970s, but by the end of the seventies the typical governor spent almost a full working day in a six-day working week on these concerns. The impact of Washington on the states is clearly apparent, and only 3 percent of more than 100 former governors responding to one survey stated that they would advise new governors to spend less time than they did on state-federal relations. Even so, more than 86 percent of the governors expressed genuine concern about the intergovernmental system of grants-in-aid, saying that it needed a "major overhaul."[28]

State administrators also believed that state-federal relations were important, but went a step farther: They contended that federal governmental programs had distorted policymaking itself in their states. Seventy percent of state administrators in 1978 (up from 52 percent in 1964) felt that they would use federal assistance grants for different purposes if the "strings" attached to those grants were relaxed, indicating the distorting effect that federal aid was having on state priorities.[29]

There is a more subtle, but potentially equally harmful, impact of federal assistance on state governments that continues today. Because federal aid flows directly to state agency heads— federal intergovernmental funds for environmental improvements, for example, go directly from Washington to state environmental protection agencies—rather than to the states' chief executive officers, the governors, it has been suggested that those state agencies that are heavily funded by Washington are also more autonomous because they are less dependent upon their governors and legislatures for their budgets. Hence, Washington, through its intergovernmental programs, has made the governors' management task more difficult. And, despite the fact that virtually all governors believe that Washington's dollars helped them implement their programs for their states, there is some reason to believe that the conjecture is valid: Surveys of state administrators taken since 1964 have found that from 44 percent to 48 percent of state administrators admit they are less subject to supervision by the governors and the legislatures because of federal aid.[30]

Grants and Governments: The Communities. If anything, the federal government's grants programs have had a greater impact on local governments than on state governments. The formal linkage between local governments and the national government is called "direct federalism," indicating that state governments are frequently bypassed. Nevertheless, the major impact of the federal government on local governments is more accidental than planned. For example, Rand Corporation studies have shown that federal officials may often have more control than local office holders over the shape of the economy in a particular locality. The Rand studies indicated the following: In St. Louis, federal housing and highway policies attracted many central-city residents to the suburbs; in San Jose, federal military procurement procedures accelerated the local growth rate; in Seattle, Federal Civil Aviation policies were probably detrimental to the area's major employer.[31]

There is, in fact, substantial evidence to warrant the conclusion that "federal stimulation produced independent housing authorities, a type of special district, and federal encouragement of the growth of suburbia through underwriting liberal mortgage arrangements indirectly led to the creation of many new suburban governments," and that the creation of the federal Department of Housing and Urban Development and Department of Transportation are "both institutional examples of recognition by the national government of its deep involvement in metropolitan affairs."[32]

From 1960 to 1980, this "deep involvement" by the federal government in local affairs increased. Although local governments received only 10 percent of the total federal aid package in 1965, by 1980 the figure had hit 30 percent.[33]

Federal intergovernmental funds, in the view of local officials during the seventies, also distorted local policy—a view that, as we noted, was shared by state administrators. A survey of local administrators in all cities and counties that had received federal aid in 1976 found that officials in about two-thirds of the cities, and roughly 80 per-

cent of the counties, stated that they would have made different budgetary allocations had not federal grants been available. Seventy-five percent of both city and county administrators would have made moderate to substantial changes. More than two-thirds of the city administrators, and more than three-quarters of the county administrators believed that their governments would shift their local funds to other efforts if their federal grants were cut off.[34]

This policy shift is highly likely. As we have noted, federal contributions to the general revenues of local governments plummeted by two-thirds in about a decade. The termination of General Revenue Sharing (which was far and away the single federal assistance program most cherished by local officials) by Congress in 1986 had a disproportionately adverse impact on local governments (which had received about two-thirds of these funds), and this was particularly true for smaller and poorer local governments, some of which had relied on General Revenue Sharing for nearly two-thirds of their total revenues; the National Association of Towns and Townships reports that 78 percent of the nation's 36,000 local governments with 25,000 people or fewer are receiving *no* federal assistance after the cancellation of General Revenue Sharing.[35] The thirty-nine federal grants-in-aid that dealt directly and exclusively with local administrators in 1980[36] had been slashed to sixteen by 1987.[37]

The pain accompanying this wrenching of the feds' fiscal hook from the financial flesh of local governments has been acute. A 1990 survey of 576 cities with populations of 10,000 or more found that over three-quarters (76 percent) had increased user fees over the course of the past year, and 41 percent had raised property taxes, the traditional main source of local revenues; yet, two-thirds of these municipalities reported that they were less able to balance their budgets than they had been a year earlier![38] It is among the local governments, apparently, where Fend-for-Yourself Federalism functions at its most basic level.

As federal dollars have departed local governments, however, so, in effect, have federal administrators. A survey taken in 1988 of mayors and city managers in Colorado found that more than 39 percent of them perceived their contacts with federal officials to be less frequent than they had been in 1980 (less than 12 percent thought that these contacts had increased), nearly 53 percent believed that their contacts with state officials had increased (less than 6 percent felt that these contacts had decreased in frequency), and almost 70 percent reported that their contacts with other local officials had increased since 1980 (compared to less than 2 percent who believed that these contacts were less frequent).[39] The presence of federal administrators in intergovernmental relations appears to be declining in proportion to the funds that the federal government commits to those relations.

Do National Mandates Make Subnational Policy? Lessons from the Eighties and Nineties

If, however, federal bureaucrats are less involved in the system of intergovernmental administration than they were before the decline in federal dollars to state and local governments began, the federal bureaucracy is more involved in state and local affairs than ever. This is because of the proliferation of federal regulations on state and local governments that were enacted during the seventies and eighties, and which are continuing to be imposed in the nineties. One study found that nearly 1,300 federal regulations have been placed on state and local governments, and that the average number of regulations affecting these jurisdictions was 570 regulations per government![40]

The Federal Mandates Maw. The great bulk of these regulations deal with what one would expect in the way of assuring fiscal accountability and programmatic propriety in the administration of intergovernmental programs, but not all. Some—sixty-three—are highly intrusive federal "mandates" that are designed to make state and local governments extended enforcers of Washington in implementing federal policies within their jurisdictions.[41]

A *mandate* is a federally imposed intergovernmental regulation that requires the government receiving a federal grant to advance specific social and national goals, or meet certain national standards, which may or may not pertain to the accompanying grant; in some mandates, these compulsory clauses state that financial sanctions will be applied in one federally funded program for violations occurring in another, or that civil or criminal penalties will be invoked in cases of noncompliance. Federal intergovernmental mandates come in four types:[42]

- *Crosscutting requirements* are mandates that stipulate compliance with specific federal policies by all governments receiving federal grants. They are the most numerous, and they apply to virtually all federal assistance programs. For example, nondiscrimination clauses are in all federal intergovernmental programs, and if a state violates the clause, Washington can withdraw the program—or never grant it.
- A *partial preemption* occurs when the subnational governments are, in limited ways, denied their traditional prerogatives because the federal government demands that the states adopt and administer program standards set by Washington, rather than by the states, if the states want federal aid.
- *Crossover sanctions* permit the federal government to punish a state by reducing or withdrawing federal aid in one or more programs if its standards are not being satisfied in another program.
- A *direct order* is an instruction from the federal government to state and local governments that, if not followed, can result in civil or criminal penalties. An eyeball-to-eyeball standoff between a state capitol or local government and the national capitol is the last occurrence federal officials want, so these are the least used; to pit Congress against the states raises serious constitutional questions. Nevertheless, Congress has shown a revitalized interest in mandating direct orders to subnational governments beginning in the 1970s, such as its direct order in 1977 prohibiting cities from dumping sewerage at sea.

Figure 12-5 shows the dramatic proliferation of all four types of mandates in federal intergovernmental programs since the 1930s. Even though the dollars available in federal grants was falling, mandates grew more rapidly in the eighties than in any previous decade—by twenty-seven, compared to twenty-two during the seventies. The largest increases during the eighties were in both

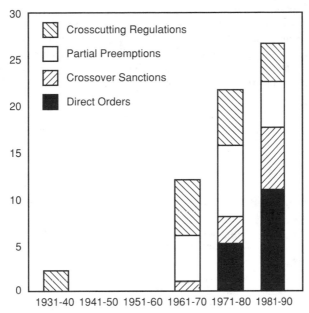

Note—Includes new programs and major amendments.

Source: Advisory Commission on Intergovernmental Relations, *Federal Regulation of State and Local Governments: The Mixed Record of the 1980s*, A-126 (Washington, D.C.: U.S. Government Printing Office, July, 1993), p. 46.

FIGURE 12-5   The Growth of Federal Mandates on State and Local Governments, by Decade, 1931–1990

crossover sanctions and direct orders, "the two most openly coercive" types of mandates, of the four kinds that we have described.[43]

The tilt from the traditional federal reliance on providing financial subsidies to state and local governments to regulating them is unambiguous. One study found that "the total number of intergovernmental regulations grew by almost 160 percent during the 1970s."[44] "Whereas intergovernmental grants outnumbered intergovernmental regulations nearly two to one during the 1950s and 1960s, grants and regulations were employed with almost equal frequency during" the seventies and eighties.[45] "This surprising record of continued intergovernmental regulatory activity for the 1980s was all the more significant given the overall decline of legislative output" compared to the preceding two decades, "so the influx of new mandates [and other regulations] represented a larger proportion of a shrinking legislative agenda."[46]

All of the growth in intergovernmental regula-

tion was accompanied by much talk in Washington about deregulation. The Paperwork Reduction Act of 1980, the Regulatory Flexibility Act of 1980, and the State and Local Government Cost Estimate Act of 1981 all were designed, at least in part, to provide regulatory relief to subnational governments, but have not been noticeably successful. In 1981, President Reagan issued Executive Order 12612, designed to minimize the impact of federal policies on the grassroots governments, but, by informed accounts, it has been followed barely, if at all, by federal agencies.[47] In 1982, Reagan proposed a sorting out of appropriate federal, state, and local functions that, while innovative and in many ways well conceived, went nowhere. In 1991, President Bush announced his intention to turn over $15 billion in federal grant programs to the states in the form of a single large block grant; again, no action by Congress.

A comprehensive estimate of the costs of federal intergovernmental regulation is difficult to obtain, but they appear to be significant. The Congressional Budget Office states that federal regulations cost state and local governments between $2.2 billion and $3.6 billion a year, and that, since 1986, federally mandated costs to these governments have been growing at a pace which exceeds that of overall federal aid.[48] However, this analysis excludes a number of additional federal regulatory costs in the intergovernmental system, so that true costs may be much higher.

State and Local Burdens. The burdens of federal mandates and regulations have not gone unnoticed by state and local officials. Governors who served their states in the 1960s and 1970s believed strongly that intergovernmental regulations had encroached on states' rights and responsibilities. More than 88 percent in one survey said that the federal government had assumed many of the responsibilities that appropriately belonged to the states.[49] Other surveys of state administrators taken during the 1970s found that three quarters of them believed that federal aid led to inappropriate national interference in state affairs, and over four-fifths thought that there should be more decentralization of federal authority to the states.[50]

A survey of incumbent governors, attorneys general, community affairs departments, and state advisory commissions on intergovernmental regulations found that these perceptions among state officials had changed little by the late 1980s. Forty percent of the governors, over half of the attorneys general, more than a third of the community affairs directors, and over a fifth of the state intergovernmental commission respondents reported that federal preemptions had prevented their states from pursuing policies preferred by their states "several times." "There is a consensus among state officials. . . . that there is too much federal preemption and that the Congress delegates too much authority to federal administrators."[51]

It is at the local level, however, where federal regulations seem most onerous. Of the nearly 1,300 federal regulations built into the intergovernmental grant system, a surprising number, 911, apply only to local governments or directly affect local governments through the states.[52]

It is predictable, perhaps, that local officials

had developed a less than trusting attitude concerning the federal government by the early 1980s. A national study of cities found that pluralities or majorities of local office holders believed in most cases that federal regulations on local governments resulted from Washington playing an inappropriate role in urban affairs (40 percent); that their cities did not have the resources to comply with federal regulations (39 percent); that inefficient federal management made compliance difficult (65 percent); that Washington went too far in stipulating how its requirements should be met (51 percent); and that the mandates themselves were unrealistic (50 percent).[53]

Such opinions should not be surprising in light of the federally imposed regulatory costs on local jurisdictions. One examination of the economic impact of federal regulations on seven localities in only five grant programs concluded that the cost borne by these local governments in complying with them was about $25 per citizen! Compliance costs in these five programs alone equaled 19 percent of the total federal aid received by the seven local governments, effectively canceling out what they had received from Washington under General Revenue Sharing![54]

The citizenry seems to sense that state and local governments are under duress as a result of federal regulations. One survey found that a majority of Americans believe that the costs of federal mandates should be shared among all governmental levels,[55] and another survey detected rather sophisticated responses among Americans concerning which level of government should be responsible for various public programs: Most respondents favored federal regulation of interstate banking and food labeling, state regulation of insurance companies, and local regulation of pesticide use and low income housing.[56]

FEDERALISM: A NEW SORTING OUT

For the past fifty years, few people have been happy with federalism. State and local officials feel that Washington, through money and mandates, has muscled its way into their jurisdictions and has inappropriately altered how their governments work. Federal officials believe that subnational governments are indifferent at best and subversive at worst in the attainment of basic national goals; as one Senate staffer put it, "Mandates wouldn't be necessary if [states] were doing what they should have been doing in the first place."[57]

The scholarly community shares these frustrations. At one pole, academic observers have attacked some variations of federalism, as overly decentralized, inducing a "crisis of public authority" antithetical to the national interest, and indicative of "the end of liberalism."[58] At the opposite pole, scholars have applauded what they see as the decentralizing overtones of new ventures in federal relations as beneficial to the assurance of a "compound republic"—that is, one where multiple and jurisdictionally overlapping administrative units are most responsive to the needs of the individual citizen.[59]

Dwight D. Eisenhower was the first president to attempt to clarify what was becoming an intergovernmental hash even in the 1950s;[60] Richard Nixon, Ronald Reagan, and George Bush made similar efforts, all to little or no avail. But these failures simply illustrate the magnitude of the problem, and it is worth concluding our discussion of the federal role in intergovernmental administration with some of the more cogent thoughts expressed by experienced administrators and observant academics on what should be some basic precepts about how federalism should work.[61]

Any sorting out of what public responsibilities are appropriately controlled by which level of government necessarily must deal with the present level of public debt—the highest in American history—and the fact that governments' fiscal crisis is worsening. Similarly, any approach must also consider the reality that Americans generally are disaffected with their governments, although they seem to have a relatively growing trust in those governments which are closest to home (recall Figure 12-1).

By far the greatest generator of deficit spending and public debt is health care, notably Medicaid and Medicare, which are health programs whose costs are shared between Washington and the states. It makes sense for the federal government to relieve the states of this shared responsibility, and fully take over health care; in addition, Washington should begin pressing the brakes on spiraling health costs, which, in the United States, are among the highest in the world. This take-over of health care, regardless of how much health costs might be controlled, likely would necessitate a new federal tax.

Second, responsibility for what one writer calls "a productivity agenda of reforms"—for example, education, skills training, housing, child care, highways, infrastructures, and economic development—could be turned over to the states, and the states placed "clearly in charge" of these and related responsibilities: In brief, "federal programs in these areas are devolved to the states or just wither away."[62]

Finally, the states could adopt some *common taxes*, or taxes which have the same revenue base and the same tax rate in each state, and share the proceeds among them. These common taxes would ameliorate two old and stubborn problems that have long handicapped the states' efforts to improve services: Poorer states must tax at a higher rate than wealthier states to even approach the service levels of wealthier states (thus rendering poorer states less competitive in luring new taxpayers and jobs and keeping old ones), and ever more complex and different tax systems in each state which discourage corporate taxpayers from investing in new locations. The federal government could collect these common taxes, such as a common corporate income tax, and distribute the revenues to the states by formula.

Similar (if far less reaching) "sorting out" scenarios have been proposed in the past (notably President Reagan's 1982 proposal to turn back a massive array of federal programs to the states), but have run into buzz saws of politics. That is not to conclude, however, that attempting intergovernmental reform is pointless. As a former director of the Congressional Budget Office has put it, "We do not need to be stuck in this particular political swamp forever."[63]

INTERGOVERNMENTAL ADMINISTRATION: THE STATE AND LOCAL PERSPECTIVE

So far we have been discussing federalism largely from the viewpoint of the government in Washington. But the states and localities also have active governments. In this section we review the states' relations with each other and their involvement (or lack of it) in the business of their cities, counties, towns, and other local jurisdictions.

Interstate Cooperation—and Conflict

States have been known to cooperate and not cooperate with each other, although the Constitution requires that "full faith and credit shall be given in each state to the public acts, records, and judicial proceedings of every state." Since the clause applies only to civil matters and not necessarily to criminal violations, we occasionally witness states harboring fugitives from other states if public officials feel that the fugitive has been treated unjustly in the state from which he or she fled. States also cooperate to create interstate compacts and interstate agencies.

There are 179 interstate compacts in operation, the great majority of which have been entered into during the past three decades. Only fifty-seven interstate compacts were agreed to between 1789 and 1940, but during the next five decades, an additional 122 of these agreements emerged.

Interstate compacts normally require congressional approval to be set into motion, and many have evolved into ongoing interstate agencies. There are more than sixty such agencies dealing with educational concerns, river basin management, transportation, water fronts, fisheries, and energy. Perhaps the most notable example of an interstate agency is the Port Authority of New York and New Jersey. Established in 1921 and headed by six commissioners appointed by the governor of each member state, the Port Authority is in charge of virtually all transportation in the New York and New Jersey areas. It has 6,000 employees, more employees than any other interstate agency (few interstate agencies exceed fifty employees and a number have none).

In addition to interstate compacts, however, a number of more general interstate associations have cropped up which are designed to advance regional interests. For example, in 1977 the thirteen Western states formed the Western Governors' Policy Office (WESTPO) with a fully staffed office in Denver to conduct regional analyses of sensitive issues, but primarily energy policy. Similarly, in 1976 seven states in the Northeast (Connecticut, Massachusetts, New Jersey, New York, Pennsylvania, Rhode Island, and Vermont) formed a Coalition of Northeastern Governors and stated as one of its principal objectives the presentation of a united front before the Congress to gain more federal funds. The founding of WESTPO and the Coalition of Northeastern Governors was in part a reaction to the founding in 1972 of the Southern Growth Policies Board, a thirteen-state organization that conducts research on economic growth management in the South and has a well-staffed office in Washington.

In Congress, states have banded together in a variety of regional formats including the New England Congressional Caucus, the Northeast-Midwest Economic Advancement Coalition, the Great Lakes Conference, the Sunbelt Conference, and the Western States Coalition (not to mention a Suburban Caucus, a Rural Caucus, and a Metropolitan Area Caucus), all of which symbolize a growing recognition that cooperation can acquire more than competition.

Although most analysts delineate the kinds of cooperative activity between states, few discuss the kinds of conflict in which states engage. The most obvious example occurred in 1861 when the nation went to war with itself, an event that in the North is called the Civil War, but in the South is still referred to as the War Between the States.

A more recent example concerns the gradually developing shortage of water in the nation.[64] Although this shortage is more pronounced in the West than in other parts of the country, some researchers have estimated that by the year 2000 only three of the nation's nineteen water regions will be able to live even close to comfortably within their water supplies. (The three exceptions are New England, the Ohio Basin, and the South Atlantic-Eastern Gulf areas.)

This possible serious shortage in the nation's water is already straining relationships among states. Montana and Idaho threatened to sue the state of Washington if that state seeded clouds over the Pacific Ocean, thereby "stealing" water that might have fallen as rain farther inland. Oregon and Washington have resisted attempts to divert water to areas in the western Sunbelt states. When Boston embarked on a program to divert water from the Connecticut River, Connecticut objected because it did not wish to give up water rights that it might need in the future. The eight states and two Canadian provinces that surround the Great Lakes—the world's largest reservoir of fresh water—agreed in 1982 to block attempts to divert their water unless all ten governments agreed. Iowa, Nebraska, and Missouri filed suit opposing South Dakota's efforts to divert part of the Missouri River to Wyoming, and El Paso, Texas, challenged New Mexico's law that forbids all out-of-staters from using its groundwater.

Although water wars long have erupted among the states, and will continue to do so as long as water supplies deplete, hydraulic technology innovates, and rivers meander, interstate antagonism is surfacing in other fields as well. Thirty-nine states use some sort of *severance tax*—that is, a tariff on natural resources exported to other states—and some states have been using the device, according to some regional analysts, as a weapon against other states to recruit new industry by lowering taxes. One estimate contends that the dozen states that export energy to other states (such as Montana, which has a 10 to 15 percent severance tax on coal) will gain close to $200 billion over ten years through their severance taxes on their energy supplies.[65] Some states have threatened reciprocity; for example, the governor of Iowa floated the notion of introducing a severance tax on corn.

Other statewide "exports" are free of severance taxes, such as pollution spawned in one state but which ends up in another states. Northeastern states long have argued that they are the primary recipients of Midwestern air pollutants that produce acid rain. Other states export other kinds of undesirable items. Over a five-year period, for example, South Dakota gave ninety-three people charged with burglary, forgery, theft, and other felonies the choice of facing prosecution or moving to California; all ninety-three moved to the Golden State, whose officials promptly dubbed South Dakota's actions as outrageous. In 1984, Oregon hiked by up to $400 the income tax that it levies on some 40,000 Washington State residents who work in Oregon; Washington retaliated with a $30-a-month tax on Oregonians who work in Washington. Texan welfare officials take pains to inform their clients that benefits are higher in every other state except Mississippi and that welfare payments in Texas show no prospects of rising, while Florida officials have carefully explained to their Haitian refugees that ten other states might offer better relief aid.

All is not happy in the realm of the American states.

The States Tame Their "Creatures"

The states can cooperate with each other as equals, but their relationships with their own local governments are quite different. The phrase, "creatures of the states," describes the place of local governments relative to their state governments more than adequately. It is drawn from a statement made by Judge John F. Dillon in 1868 that is now known as "Dillon's rule." "Creatures of the state," a concept upheld by the U.S. Supreme Court in 1923, simply means that such units of government as counties, towns, townships, school districts, special districts, multipurpose districts, cities, and villages have no independence beyond what the state grants them. The state government determines the area of political and administrative discretion its subunits of government may or may not have and sometimes this state oversight can be miasmic in detail, including stipulating, that "a city cannot operate a peanut stand at the city zoo without first getting the state legislature to pass an enabling law, unless, perchance, the city's charter or some previously enacted law unmistakably covers the sale of peanuts."[66]

Municipalities: Docile Creatures. State legislatures achieve this kind of control through the type of charter that they grant a municipality (that is, a city or a town). Most city charters are quite long (New York City's, for example, fills several hundred pages) because the states often want to retain minute degrees of control. There are four general types of charters: special act charters, general act charters, optional charter laws, and home rule charters.

The *special act charters* are charters that have been drawn specifically for a particular city. Such cities remain completely under state legislative control; often these charters help state legislatures to pass laws that are written specifically for a particular city, such as the law stating that "Fall River be authorized to appropriate money for the purchase of uniforms for the park police and watershed guards of said city."[67]

General act charters tend to categorize cities by population and then apply state legislation to all cities in each size category. Usual divisions are cities with less than 10,000 people, with 10,000 to 25,000 people, and so on.

Optional charter laws give city governments relatively more free choice. They offer optional forms of government that a city may wish to adopt, such as council-manager, commission, or whatever.

Finally, *home rule charters* provide cities with the greatest degree of self-governance, although home rule charters are furnished by the state legislature or the state constitution and may be taken away as easily as they are granted. Home rule got its start in 1875 in Missouri; today more than half of the states have constitutional clauses that provide for home rule charters. Roughly two-thirds of the cities in the United States with populations of more than 200,000 people have some form of home rule. Political battles over acquiring urban home rule often are bloody, with good government groups, city mayors, and city managers usually pitted against rural legislators and large municipal taxpayer groups.

Regardless of the type of charter that a city may have, the point remains that these charters are granted according to the discretion of the state polity. Nevertheless, municipalities have considerably more autonomy than that other major form of local government: counties.

Counties: Strange Creatures. Nowhere are the creatures of the state a stranger beast than in the case of counties.[68] The United States adopted counties from England, where they had existed for six centuries as "shires" administered by sheriffs before the first European settlers arrived in America. Virginia created the first American counties in 1634, followed by Massachusetts nine years later. The kinds of counties established by Virginia and Massachusetts were quite different. In Virginia, the counties were strong governments, with distinct electoral, managerial, judicial, and even military responsibilities; "county home rule," an idea arguing that counties should be autonomous units of government with their own elected officials, got its start in Virginia. But in Massachusetts, the original counties were run by officials appointed by the governor; as with

England's shires, the Massachusetts counties were perceived as being administrative arms of the king—or, in the case of Massachusetts, the king's designate, the governor.

Virginia's model of county government spread throughout the South, and even today Southern counties seem to be more significant jurisdictions in their states than elsewhere. The Virginia model, by and large, spread westward, with permutations added by Pennsylvania, which originated the concept of a governing body for counties—the county board of commissioners, or supervisors—elected by each county's citizens. The Massachusetts model was heavily influential in the Northeast; because counties were simply extensions of the state governments in the Northeast, self-governing towns and townships became the predominant units of local governments.

Even though the Virginia model, which espoused the notion that counties should be independent local governments, was clearly gaining in popularity as the nation moved West, the early court decisions on the place of counties in the federal framework advocated the traditional Massachusetts model, which conceived of the counties as administrative arms of the state. In 1845, the U. S. Supreme Court ruled in *Maryland v. Baltimore and Ohio Railroad* that the "counties are nothing more than certain portions of the territory into which the state is divided for more convenient exercise of the powers of the government." This and later rulings by the courts sharply constricted the services that counties would be able to provide their citizens as independent governments.

But if counties could not provide their own services, they could—and did—provide their own elected officials, who were duly paid out of their states' treasuries. As new states were admitted to the Union, they adopted—kind of—the Virginia model. By that we mean that the symbols of county independence were touted, but not the reality. The symbols were the counties' elected "row officers," a term covering county sheriffs, prosecuting attorneys, clerks, auditors, recorders, assessors, treasurers, coroners, and commissioners. While some of these row officers have authority, notably, those associated with the criminal justice system, not all do because the state governments have granted them few if any policymaking responsibilities. For example, county commissioners in most counties—supposedly the policymaking bodies of county government—have little if any policy to make because the state legislature calls the tune, and then simply orders the counties to play it. Similarly, most of the other county row officers (*e.g.*, clerks, auditors, recorders, assessors, treasurers, and coroners) have responsibilities that are purely clerical in nature, responsibilities that hardly warrant their election to office by county voters. Thus, most counties appear to combine the worst of both worlds: little authority, but lots of responsibility, at least in the eyes of the counties' residents.

As a result, counties tend to have significantly less freedom from state oversight than do cities; cities enjoy their greatest freedoms from state controls in functional areas, such as sanitation, and have the least liberty in the area of finance; counties have the most freedom in personnel matters (uniquely, in fact, a bit more freedom than cities), but, like municipalities, are most restricted by their states in the finance area. States clearly seem concerned with the fiscal health of their local governments.[69]

State Urban Policy: A New Responsiveness

As the foregoing review implies, states can treat their creatures with severity or laxity, and may play the roles of inhibitor, facilitator, or initiator in their relations with their own local governments.[70] Over time, the states have made strides in contributing constructively to urban government.

All states have established offices specifically endowed with responsibilities pertaining to local affairs, although only five existed prior to 1966.[71] These offices provide advisory services and assist the state in coordinating local administrative functions. Most are concerned primarily with regional planning; relatively few have responsibility for specific programs such as urban renewal, housing, and poverty.

The states have taken a variety of managerial and policy steps in dealing with their local governments. Twenty-six states have created their own Advisory Commissions on Intergovernmental Relations patterned after the federal model (up from four in 1974),[72] and another twenty-one have created similar advisory panels of local officials. Forty-three states have commissions on intergovernmental cooperation, and all states have departments of community affairs.[73]

Research indicates that those state commissions which focus on local governments tend to stress the desirability of fiscal reforms, of reducing functional fragmentation among local governments, and providing greater authority and more home rule for local jurisdictions.[74] In a few states, these and related bodies are beginning to take on a genuine policymaking role for their urban and local governments. Texas, for example, has been active in discouraging the separate incorporation of satellite cities, as have Indiana and Minnesota, although to lesser degrees. In 1968 Connecticut abolished counties as a unit of government and, as a result, "state government may in effect become the metropolitan government unit in Connecticut, since Connecticut transferred county functions to the state."[75]

What of the larger panorama of relationships between the states and their local governments? Is the role of the states declining, or is it actually increasing?

The typical answer to these questions, at least in the past, has been that the states have often proven to be more of a hindrance than a facilitator in resolving the problems of local governments. By the 1970s, however, such views were beginning to change. In part, this change resulted from the simple fact that more empirical and systematic investigations were being conducted on the relationships between states and their local governments. Studies indicate that the states tend to emphasize four policy areas when they deal with local governments: physical development, such as upgrading industrial and residential infrastructures; the enhancement of cooperation between the public and private sectors; fiscal incentives to help local development patterns; and citizen participation in the development of local objectives.[76]

Related research has concluded that states are increasingly sensitive to the needs of their more depressed cities, at least when this sensitivity is measured by the amounts of money that states transfer to their needier urban areas. Localities receive grants from other governments in three forms: direct aid from their states, direct aid from the federal government, and aid from state governments that combine state funds with federal funds received by the states (or what are known as "passthrough" funds, since federal money is being passed through state governments to local governments). One analysis found that depressed cities benefitted most favorably when they received intergovernmental grants through this final method, indicating an awareness by states of their more pressing urban problems.[77] Another study concluded that federal and state aid to needy cities were roughly comparable in terms of targeting assistance effectively, although federal aid may have been slightly more effective in meeting urban needs of particularly distressed inner cities.[78]

Regardless of how sophisticated the approach that states may take in aiding their local governments, it is clear that states are at least trying to shoulder the burdens of their local governments that are being left on their doorsteps by Washington's withdrawal of dollars. Although state assistance appears not to have fully offset the loss of federal aid to cities, "state aid to local governments has been increasing slowly but steadily over time" since the drop-off in federal grants to localities.[79]

As a consequence of these shifts at the national level, plus a growing body of information about state and local governmental relationships, the overall scholarly assessment of the states' role in local affairs is showing indications of positive change. As a leading scholar of intergovernmental relations has observed, "The states have been roundly and soundly chastised for their neglect of urban distress and decline. The criticisms are not without foundation. Yet a balanced view . . . shows the states on record as taking numerous and varied urban-oriented policy initiatives."[80]

Managing Intergovernmental Programs in the States

State governments have their own sets of intergovernmental relationships, but they conduct them quite differently from the feds. In fact, there is a difference in philosophy, and control over intergovernmental programs seems, on the whole, tighter at the state levels than at the national one. States, more frequently than the federal government, simply order their local governments to implement programs on the basis of clear directives given by state agencies; "bargaining" with recipients is rare in the states.[81]

One of the local benefits of the states being a "simpler" source of local funding than the federal government is that local administrative costs can be held down. An analysis of public school districts across the United States found that, because federal education grants were much more complex, fragmented, and formal than were state fiscal transfers to school districts, those districts that had to rely more on federal funds than they did on state funds generated significantly more administrative positions. Interestingly, even locally funded school districts produced more administrative positions than did those which were more dependent on state funds (though still fewer than did districts which relied on federal grants), because local funding politics and procedures were more complex than were those of the states.[82]

Another difference between the state style of implementation and the federal style is that the legislature is directly involved in how state assistance to local governments is to be implemented. This implies, among other things, that the state legislators give their bureaucrats far less leeway than do their federal counterparts. It also implies, however, that state legislators are able to take a more responsible and detailed interest in state assistance to local governments, and that they have developed their assistance programs with the advice and input of officials from the local levels of government.[83]

How much of an impact local governments have in determining implementation procedures and processes that are required by state government tends to be a function of statewide wealth, urbanism, and high levels of population. The Advisory Commission on Intergovernmental Relations found, for example, that some statewide intergovernmental assistance systems are dominated by state government (in these states, the state government provides local assistance directly), while in others they are dominated by local governments (in these states, a federal-style grants system is used). State government dominance of the statewide intergovernmental assistance system seems to associate with the more populous, urbanized, and wealthy states.[84]

Another study, this one focusing more specifically on the states' use of mandates in dealing with their local governments, also found a strong correlation between a state's high affluence and a high tendency to issue mandates to its localities. The competitiveness of a state's political parties and a high quality of state public administration also associated with a state's propensity to mandate local governments.[85]

By and large, states have avoided the use of federal-style mandates in their relations with their local governments, but they are by no means immune to their use. Illinois, for example, imposes an average of seventeen mandates on its communities per legislative session.[86] State mandates, however, unlike their federal counterparts, appear to be more flexible, less harsh, and even fairer. Forty-two state legislatures (like Congress) stipulate that the probable fiscal impact of each state mandate on local governments be determined, and fourteen states (unlike Congress) require that the state reimburse local jurisdictions for the costs of implementing state mandates.[87]

Still, local officials resent state mandates, and ten states, as a result of local political mobilization, have voted in constitutional amendments prohibiting the imposition of unfunded state mandates on local governments.[88] But local motivation to push for antimandate amendments is not merely monetary; there is an element of pride, too. As one observer of state mandates notes, "What cities and counties most want is to be recognized as legitimate governing bodies. They want to work with state governments to form better policy.[89]

Quite another problem of intergovernmental administration is less the question of states loading new responsibilities on their local governments, and more that of states providing adequate authority to their local jurisdictions to effectively implement policy, whether it is state or local policy. Nowhere is this dilemma more evident than in county governments.

We have noted the ambivalence of authority in county governments as a product of their odd evolution over a thousand years. But this ambivalence does not mean that counties have not been saddled with new and onerous responsibilities by state legislatures as arms of state government. One national survey of chief county administrators, elected executives, and commission chairs, found that, whereas the responsibilities of county governments had increased markedly over the past five years in virtually every county (at least in the view of 93 percent of the respondents), fewer than half (46 percent) of county officials thought that their states had increased their policymaking or self-governing authority proportionately. Only 31 percent thought that they had adequate authority to execute their duties as public officers, and adequately meet local needs.[90]

Whether it is too little money, too many mandates, or inadequate authority to implement public policy, local governments are stressed. The states have made progress in developing intelligent means of supporting their local governments, but there is still some distance to travel.

Regionalism in the States: Councils and Coordination

One effort to include local governments in the loop of intergovernmental administration is the on-again, off-again movement to establish and use regional councils in the states, which often are constituted of officials representing all three levels of government. *Regional councils* are coordinating associations of public officials who represent jurisdictions in a substate region; often they specialize in functional areas, such as growth management, and have widely varying degrees of authority, ranging from planning to policy.

Largely as a result of federal requirements or financial incentives that can be traced back to at least the early 1950s, state and local governments have created over the years a vast network of substate intergovernmental and interagency coordinating bodies.[91] There are roughly 2,000 of them. Some 600 of these are regional councils. About 70 percent of the regional councils are various kinds of policy councils. Some of these are controlled by the federal government, such as Economic Development Districts (administered through the Department of Commerce) and Rural Area Development Committees (managed by the Department of Agriculture). But almost half of the original policy councils are planning councils, usually established by state legislation, and another 30 percent are voluntary Councils of Governments, composed dominantly or exclusively of local government representatives, and which coordinate intergovernmental planning.

With the advent of the Reagan administration in 1981, Washington walked away from its traditional role of encouraging the use of regional councils as a means of coordinating policy implementation.

First, Congress began withdrawing funds that it had long allocated in support of various kinds of substate regional coordinating councils, such as Councils of Governments. Among the more important acts of this cutting back by Washington was the elimination of "701" funding in 1982. The "701" program was established under Section 701 of the Urban Planning Assistance Act of 1954, and over the twenty-eight years of its existence it disbursed more than $200 million to state, regional, and local planning agencies for the purpose of improving coordinated planning.

Many of these regional associations could not survive severe cutbacks in federal aid, and an estimated 10 percent of them closed their doors within a year of the reductions.[92]

Second, and perhaps more significantly, the "A-95" process was eliminated in 1982 by Executive Order 12372.[93] The "A-95" process was established in 1969 by the Office of Management and Budget (OMB) Circular A-95. OMB Circular A-95 drew together federal mandates for state and local planning that were found in several federal statutes, particularly the Demonstration Cities and Metropolitan Development Act of 1966 (Model Cities), the Intergovernmental Cooperation Act of 1968, and the National Environmental Policy Act of 1969. It effectively required states and localities to set up OMB-recognized "clearinghouses" empowered to approve state and local grant requests if states and localities were to receive federal grants in a wide variety of fields. Although subnational jurisdictions formed these clearinghouses in various ways, most set up voluntary Councils of Governments.

Reagan's Executive Order 12372 replaced OMB Circular A-95 (which had, in many ways, permanently altered the face of intergovernmental administration) and permitted state and local governments to create their own review and planning procedures and reduce federal regulations. Prior to Reagan's Executive Order of 1982, review and planning procedures under "A-95" had been stipulated by the Office of Management and Budget.

The costs of Washington's walk-out in 1982 can be measured only imprecisely, but it is reasonable to agree with the statement that in the 1980s the federal government "abandoned the few national inducements to metropolitan coherence [and, for that matter, rural coherence] it had in place."[94]

Since the Reagan administration, Washington has taken a renewed interest in encouraging regional coordination in the states. In 1990, Congress established large and broadly representative Rural Development Councils in eight states on a pilot basis to coordinate rural development and establish collaborative relationships[95] among federal agencies, state and local governments, and the private sector. In 1991, Congress passed the Intermodal Surface Transportation Efficiency Act, a major piece of legislation, which, among other things, required an inclusive transportation planning process in metropolitan regions, if governments wanted federal transportation grants of considerable size under the Act's auspices. The Act empowers metropolitan planning organizations (usually Councils of Governments) to make hard choices between highways and mass transit, and authorizes significant funds to them to enforce their choices.[96]

The states, meanwhile, have continued their differential and incremental efforts, begun in 1961 in Hawaii, to rationalize land use planning and growth policies through the use of regional councils. Overall, these efforts have been modestly effective, but more important, the states continue to show a quiet determination to make headway in these areas.[97]

Interlocal Agreements: Regionalism That Works

If there is tension among the levels of government, local governments themselves seem to be getting on famously with each other. Cities and counties have devised a number of ways of working together as a means of providing more, better, and cheaper services to their citizens, and they are cooperating with each other enthusiastically.[98]

One method is the *intergovernmental service contract*, as when one jurisdiction pays another to deliver certain services to its residents. More than half—52 percent—of cities and counties have entered into intergovernmental service contracts. Cities and counties contract most frequently with each other for jails, sewage disposal, animal control, and tax assessing.

Another form of interlocal agreement is the *joint service agreement*, or agreements between two or more governments for the joint planning, financing, and delivering of certain services to the residents of all participating jurisdictions. Sixty percent of cities and 54 percent of counties have entered into joint service agreements. The services most frequently provided under these agreements are libraries, communications among police and fire departments, fire control, and sewage disposal.

Cities have moved away (albeit marginally) from entering into intergovernmental service contracts since 1972 (when the first national survey on the practice was conducted) and have shown an increasing preference for contracting with private firms and negotiating joint service agreements with other local governments. Joint service agreements in particular are experiencing an upsurge in popularity, from 35 percent of cities that were involved in them in 1972 to 55 percent in 1983.[99]

A third type of interlocal agreement is the *intergovernmental service transfer*, or the permanent transfer of a responsibility from a jurisdiction to another entity, another government, a private corporation, or a nonprofit agency. Transferring a responsibility permanently is a serious matter for any government because it is a sacrifice of authority and power, so it is perhaps surprising that 40 percent of cities and counties executed such transfers between 1976 and 1983. Favored areas of transfer were public works and utilities, health and welfare, and general government and finance.[100]

Regardless of the type of interlocal agreement, patterns emerge. Larger jurisdictions are far more willing to enter into them than are smaller ones. Council-manager cities and counties with a county administrator tend to favor them, as do inner cities over suburbs and metropolitan counties more than nonmetropolitan ones. The motivation of local officials to enter into interlocal agreements is usually "economies of scale"—they believe that some services can be delivered more effectively and efficiently over larger tracts of territory, or by larger jurisdictions.[101]

"Micro-Federalism": Neighborhoods and Cities

One of the more intriguing expressions of the many permutations surrounding the uniquely public question of reconciling area with power in ways that maximize efficiency, effectiveness, responsiveness, and democratic control can be found in the local movement toward "neighborhood governance." It began in the mid-1960s, and at least some of its origins can be traced to a reaction against what was (and often still is) perceived as the condescension of "professional managers" in the urban bureaucracy. Neighborhood governance advocates a limited disannexation of neighborhood communities rather than outright secession from city hall.[102] Three practical consequences of the neighborhood governance movement have been the rise of neighborhood corporations, neighborhood associations, and residential community associations.

Neighborhood corporations are nonprofit organizations, chartered by the state, and managed for the public benefit of specialized urban areas by area residents. Many received their initial funding in 1966 under the provisions of the Economic Opportunity Act of 1964, and later under the Model Cities program. An analysis of these groups concluded that, although their record of success had been spotty, neighborhood corporations had established a genuine rapport with residents. Nevertheless, just how representative the corporations are is open to question when it is realized that resident turnout to elect the directors of these organizations has been fewer than 5 percent of the eligible voters,[103] and it appears that more informal neighborhood associations have filled this role in recent years.

Like neighborhood corporations, neighborhood associations, or community action groups, received at least some of their initial impetus from the federal government: There are, in fact, 155 specific provisos in federal grants programs mandating citizen participation.[104] Probably the most significant of these is Congress' 1976 extension of General Revenue Sharing, which required citizen participation in the budgetary processes of the 39,000 local governments that received shared revenues; despite the demise of General Revenue Sharing a decade later, the impact of this mandate lives on.

Neighborhood associations are voluntary groups of citizens who work toward what they perceive to be the betterment of their communities; unlike neighborhood corporations, they have no state charter. There are an estimated 200 major neighborhood associations in the United States, ranging from the Bois d'Arc Patriots in Dallas to the Citizens to Bring Broadway Back in Cleveland.[105] Most neighborhood associations concern themselves with issues of planning and development, housing, freeway construction, race relations, taxes, and education, and they are estimated to comprise from 6 to 19 percent of a community's adult population.[106]

Finally, *residential community associations* are private organizations of home owners, condominium owners, and members of residential cooperatives that are governed under local real estate contract laws; their members typically elect a policymaking council from their ranks, impose mandatory fees on their members, and conduct certain kinds of public business, such as land management. They have been called "private governments," and they are growing; in 1960, there were fewer than 1,000 residential community associations, but today there are around 130,000 and they have some 12 to 15 percent of the American population as members.[107]

Most residential community associations are in the Sunbelt and Mideastern states, and they bring with them new concepts of governance. Their members, in effect, pay dual taxes, with some going to local governments and some going to the association as the price of a level of service superior to the base level provided by the local government. They often exclude local officials from providing local services in their communities. Some have argued that the members of residential community associations exercise rights of dual citizenship.

Certainly residential community associations seem to exercise rights of sovereign governments, and deal directly with local officials as peers on such questions as traffic, water, sewerage, parks, zoning, animal control, pollution, taxes, and a host of other public issues. Fifty-six percent of the officers of residential community associations responding to a national survey of them said that the level of cooperation between their associations and the local government was good, and 71 percent stated that they had been treated fairly by local officials.[108]

Residential community associations appear to be led by a handful of zealots who "represent" a dues-paying membership that is content with or indifferent to a detailed agenda. A study of residential community associations in California found that less than 1 percent of their members had ever served on their association's board of directors or any committees, and only 11 percent had ever served as an association volunteer.[109]

Neighborhood corporations, neighborhood associations, and residential community associations (and, we must note, these distinctions are not neat ones) are working within local jurisdictions as both a lobby and a government, and they are effective in both capacities. A study of 115 city council members in California found that 94 percent of the council members perceived these groups as a welcomed civic association phenomenon; only 28 percent identified organized economic interests as major political actors in their cities. Only 16 percent of the council members did not view any group as being influential in the formation of urban policy, and more than two-thirds identified two or more groups as influential.[110] This appears to be a recognition rate that is twice that of state legislators' perceptions of the power of civic associations and economic interest groups.[111]

More significantly, however, participation by these neighborhood associations in the local policy process brings results. More than four out of every ten local officials believe that the participation by these groups and other members of the public in their counties' and cities' budget processes has a measurable effect on the setting of local priorities; more than 60 percent of local officials have developed new federal grant proposals and sent them to Washington solely because of citizen participation.[112] As an assistant secretary in the Department of Housing and Urban Development has put it, "Twenty neighborhood groups have accomplished more . . . than all of the federal programs."[113]

INTERGOVERNMENTAL ADMINISTRATION AND THE PYRAMIDING OF POWER

A final summing up on the nature of relations between governments in the United States points to one conclusion: Governmental power is centralizing despite Americans' ultralocalist leanings.

Perhaps the clearest indication of this can be seen by examining certain measures, such as financial resources and intergovernmental regulations. The nation's nearly 87,000 local governments raise less money today than do the nation's fifty state governments and considerably fewer dollars than does the national government. Although money is paid to the national government and part of these revenues are sent back to the state and local governments through grants, this practice, as well as proliferating intergovernmental mandates and regulations promulgated by Washington, connotes, at least in the view of some, a centralization of governmental power at the national level.

But such centralization also may be happening at the state level. By ranking the local proportions of financial resources, services, and worker availability by state, G. Ross Stephens found that certain states were quite centralized in relation to their local governments, while others were relatively decentralized. Stephens concluded that larger states tend to be decentralized governmentally, whereas smaller states are more centralized. Nevertheless, there is a remarkably clear trend toward state centralization, and a growing dominance by state governments over their local governments.[114] Other studies by and large confirm Stephens's findings.[115]

There is additional evidence that governments are centralizing. Not only is centralization occurring at the state level, but at the local level, too. In national studies conducted since 1972, it has been found that, generally speaking, larger local governments are taking over the responsibilities of smaller ones.[116] Fifty-six percent of the intergovernmental service contracts let by cities, for example, are given to counties.[117] A plurality (48 percent) of all joint service agreements are entered into with counties, and counties are the principal service providers for more than half of all services provided through these agreements.[118] Most significantly, however, counties and regional organizations receive most of the intergovernmental service transfers; in other words, these relatively large units of local government are *permanently* taking over the traditional duties of cities and towns, *and at the request* of those cities and towns. Fifty-four percent of all intergovernmental service transfers go to counties, and 14 percent (the next highest) to regional organizations, such as councils of governments.[119]

Whatever the cause and whatever the outcome, it appears that subnational governments are moving power not only *up* the intergovernmental pyramid, to higher levels of government, but also *out* of smaller jurisdictions and into larger ones. If, it seems, the American people like ultralocalist government, the people whom Americans elect and appoint to run their governments do not. State and local officials have been engaged in a slow but steady process of centralizing and shifting responsibilities for service deliveries both upward and outward for many years in an effort to meet the needs of their citizens more effectively and efficiently. It is a process that shows no signs of reversing.

If this assessment is accurate, then it is a tribute to the professionalism and inventiveness of America's grassroots bureaucrats, because they have gradually centralized and consolidated major governmental functions over the years, while working within the confines of a national political culture that places an unusually high value on maintaining ultralocalist "responsiveness," and often at the price of impairing governmental efficiency and effectiveness.

In Part Four, we have been reviewing the ways that public administrators implement public policies. But implementation rests on decision making, and decision making in the public sector, in turn, is based on underlying moral and ethical assumptions held by individual decision makers about how the world works and what is right or wrong about how the world works. We consider this final, and perhaps most important, aspect of public administration next.

NOTES

1. Two good discussions of the definitional differences among the terms used in this paragraph are: Deil S. Wright, "Federalism, Intergovernmental Relations, and Intergovernmental Management: Historical Reflections and Conceptual Comparisons," *Public Administration Review*, 50 (March/April 1990), pp. 168-178, and Vincent L. Marando and Patricia S. Florestano, "Intergovernmental Management: The State of the Discipline," in Naomi B. Lynn and Aaron Wildavsky, eds., *Public Administration: The State of the Discipline* (Chatham, N.J.: Chatham House, 1990), pp. 287-317.

2. Henry S. Reuss, *Revenue Sharing: Crutch or Catalyst for State and Local Governments?* (New York: Praeger, 1970), pp. 53-56.

3. This discussion is drawn largely from: Kenneth N. Vines, "The Federal Setting of State Politics," in Herbert Jacob and Kenneth N. Vines, eds., *Politics in the American States*, 3rd ed., (Boston: Little, Brown, 1976), p. 4.

4. *Ibid.*, p. 7.

5. Alexander Hamilton, John Jay, and James Madison, *The Federalist* (New York: Random House, 1937), p. 347.

6. Unless noted otherwise, the following discussion is drawn from: Deil S. Wright, *Understanding Intergovernmental Relations*, 2nd ed. (Monterey, Calif.: Brooks/Cole, 1982), pp. 43-82.

7. The following discussion is drawn from: John Shannon, "The Return to Fend-For-Yourself Federalism: The Reagan Mark," in Advisory Commission on Intergovernmental Relations, *Readings in Federalism: Perspectives on a Decade of Change*, SR-11 (Washington, D.C.: U.S. Government Printing Office, 1989), pp. 119-122; John Shannon, "Competitive Federalism—Three Driving Forces," *Intergovernmental Perspective*, 15 (Fall 1989), pp. 17-18; and John Shannon and James Edwin Kee, "The Rise of Competitive Federalism," *Public Budgeting and Finance*, 9 (Winter 1989), pp. 3-20.

8. U. S. General Accounting Office, *Budget Issues*, Transition Series, GAO/OCG -93-ITR (Washington, D. C.: General Accounting Office, December 1992), p. 20. In 1992, federal deficit spending was $290 billion.

9. Shannon and Kee, "The Rise of Competitive Federalism," p. 11.

10. Donna Wilson Kirchheimer, "Entrepreneurial Implementation of the U. S. Welfare State," paper presented at the 1986 Annual Meeting of the American Political Science Association, (Washington, D. C.) August 28-31, 1986, p. 1.

11. All of the following figures on government revenues as percentages of personal income are drawn from: Advisory Commission on Intergovernmental Relations, *Significant Features of Fiscal Federalism, 1993*, Vol. 2, M-185-II (Washington, D.C.: U.S. Government Printing Office, 1993), p. 80.

12. *Ibid.*, pp. 50, 53.

13. Advisory Commission on Intergovernmental Relations, *Significant Features of Fiscal Federalism, 1991*, Vol. 2, M-176-II (Washington, D.C.: U. S. Government Printing Office, 1991), p. 11.

14. The following figures on federal and state aid are derived from Advisory Commission on Intergovernmental Relations, *Significant Features of Fiscal Federalism, 1993*, p. 50.

15. Richard P. Nathan and John R. Lago, "Intergovernmental Relations in the Reagan Era," *Public Budgeting and Finance*, 8 (Autumn 1988), p. 27.

16. See for example, Steven D. Gold, "The Federal Role in State Fiscal Stress," *Publius*, 22 (Summer 1992), p. 33-47, and J. Edwin Benton, "The Effects of Changes in Federal Aid on State and Local Government Spending," *Publius*, 22 (Winter 1992), pp. 71-82.

17. James L. Sundquist and David W. Davis, *Making Federalism Work* (Washington, D.C.: Brookings Institution, 1969).

18. Advisory Commission on Intergovernmental Relations, *Significant Features of Fiscal Federalism, 1989*, Vol. II, M-163-II (Washington, D. C.: U. S. Government Printing Office), p. 21, for 1960 figure, and Advisory Committee on Intergovernmental Relations, *Characteristics of Federal Grants-in-Aid Programs to State and Local Governments: Grants Funded, FY 1993*, M-183 (Washington, D. C.: U. S. Government Printing Office, January, 1994), p. 1, for 1981 figure.

19. The figures for the dollars expended through each grant type, and the number of grant types, in this discussion are for 1993, and drawn from Advisory Commission on Intergovernmental Relations, *Characteristics of Federal Grant-in-Aid Programs to State and Local Governments*, pp. 1, 7.

20. Paul R. Dommel, *et al.*, *Decentralizing Community Development: Second Report of the Brookings Institution Monitoring Study of the Community Development Block Grant Program* (Washington, D.C.: Brookings Institution, 1978).

21. Advisory Commission on Intergovernmental Relations, *Characteristics of Federal Grant-in-Aid Programs to State and Local Governments*, p. 5.

22. Richard P. Nathan, *et al.*, *Monitoring Revenue Sharing* (Washington, D.C.: Brookings Institution, 1975), and Richard P. Nathan and Charles F. Adams, Jr., *Revenue Sharing: The Second Round* (Washington, D.C.: Brookings Institution, 1977).

23. Bruce D. McDowell, "Grant Reform Reconsidered," *Intergovernmental Perspective*, 17 (Summer 1991), p. 10.

24. Advisory Commission on Intergovernmental Relations, *Characteristics of Federal Grant-in-Aid Programs to State and Local Governments*, p. 1.

25. *Ibid.*, p. 7.
26. Joel Havemann and Rochelle L. Stanfield, "'Neutral' Federal Policies are Reducing Frostbelt-Sunbelt Spending Imbalances," *National Journal* (February 7, 1981), p. 233. This analysis covered the years 1975 and 1979.
27. Timothy J. Conlan and David R. Beam, "Federal Mandates: The Record of Reform and Future Prospects," *Intergovernmental Perspective*, 18 (Fall 1992), p. 9.
28. Dennis O. Grady, "American Governors and State-Federal Relations: Attitudes and Activities, 1960-1980," *State Government*, 57, No. 3 (1984), pp. 110-111.
29. Advisory Commission on Intergovernmental Relations, *State Administrators' Opinions on Administrative Change, Federal Aid, Federal Relationships*, M-120 (Washington, D.C.: U.S. Government Printing Office, 1980), pp. 39-59.
30. *Ibid.*, p. 51.
31. R. B. Rainey, *et al.*, *Seattle: Adaptation to Recession*; Barbara R. Williams, *St. Louis: A City and Its Suburbs*; Daniel Atesch and Robert Arvine, *Growth in San Jose: A Summary Policy Statement* (all published in Santa Monica: Rand Corporation, 1973).
32. John C. Bollens and Henry J. Schmandt, *The Metropolis*, 3rd ed. (New York: Harper & Row, 1975), p. 60.
33. Carl W. Stenberg, "Federalism in Transition, 1959-79," *Intergovernmental Perspective*, 6 (Winter 1980), pp. 6-7.
34. Albert J. Richter, "Federal Grants Management: The City and County View," *Municipal Year Book, 1977* (Washington, D.C.: International City Management Association, 1977), pp. 183-184.
35. Robert Gleason, "Federalism 1986-87: Signals of a New Era," *Intergovernmental Perspective*, 14 (Winter 1988), p. 12.
36. Stenberg, "Federalism in Transition, 1959-79," p. 7.
37. Gleason, "Federalism 1986-87," p. 12. In addition to the sixteen federal grants-in-aid that dealt only with local officials, forty-five federal grant programs went to both state and local governments.
38. John Herbers, "The Cavalry is Not Coming to Save the Besieged Cities," *Governing*, 3 (September 1990), p. 9. See also: Gary J. Reid, "How Cities in California Have Responded to Fiscal Pressures Since Proposition 13," *Public Budgeting and Finance*, 8 (Spring 1988), pp. 20-37.
39. Robert W. Gage, "Intergovernmental Change: A Denver Area Perspective," *Intergovernmental Perspective*, 14 (Summer 1988), p. 15.
40. Catherine H. Lovell, *et al.*, *Federal and State Mandating on Local Governments: An Exploration of Issues and Impacts* (Riverside: Graduate School of Administration, University of California, 1979), p. 82. Lovell and her colleagues found 1,259 federal mandates affecting state and local governments. See also: Catherine Lovell and Charles Tobin, "The Mandate Issue," *Public Administration Review*, 41 (May/June 1981), pp. 318-339.
41. Advisory Commission on Intergovernmental Relations, *Federal Regulation of State and Local Government: The Mixed Record of the 1980s*, A-126 (Washington, D.C.: U. S. Government Printing Office, July 1993), p. 46.
42. The following typology is described more fully in Advisory Commission on Intergovernmental Relations, *Regulatory Federalism: Policy, Process, Impact and Reform*, A-95 (Washington, D.C.: U.S. Government Printing Office, 1984), pp. 7-10. For another good treatment of this problem, see: Academy for State and Local Government, *Preemption: Drawing the Line* (Washington, D.C.: Academy for State and Local Government, 1986).
43. Timothy J. Conlan and David R. Beam, "Federal Mandates: The Record of Reform and Future Prospects," *Intergovernmental Perspective*, 18 (Fall 1992), p. 8.
44. Timothy J. Conlan, as cited in: Advisory Council on Intergovernmental Relations, *Federal Regulation of State and Local Governments*, p. 9.
45. *Ibid.*, p. 55.
46. Conlan and Beam, "Federal Mandates," p. 8.
47. *Ibid.*, p. 11.
48. *Ibid.*, p. 9. Figures are for 1991.
49. Grady, "American Governors and State-Federal Relations," p. 107.
50. Advisory Commission on Intergovernmental Relations, *State Administrators' Opinions on Administrative Change, Federal Aid, Federal Relationships*, p. 50.
51. Advisory Commission on Intergovernmental Relations, *Federal Statutory Preemption of State and Local Authority: History, Inventory, and Issues*, A-121 (Washington, D. C · U. S. Government Printing Office, September 1992), pp. 34, 36. The survey was taken in 1988.
52. Lovell, *Federal and State Mandating on Local Governments*, p. 82.
53. National League of Cities, *Municipal Policy and Program Survey* (Washington, D.C.: National League of Cities, 1981), as cited in Advisory Commission on Intergovernmental Relations, *Regulatory Federalism*, p. 175. But see also Jeffrey L. Pressman, *Federal Programs and City Politics: The Dynamics of the Aid Process in Oakland* (Berkeley: University of California Press, 1975), p. 85. Another survey taken in 1981 found that most local officials believed that some relief from federal rules was "urgent." See: Advisory Commission on Intergovernmental Relations, *Federal Regulation of State and Local Government*, p. 10.
54. Thomas Muller and Michael Fix, "The Impact of Selected Federal Actions on Municipal Outlays," in *Government Regulation: Achieving Social and Economic Balance*, Vol. 5 of *Special Study on Economic Change*, Joint Economic Committee, U.S. Congress (Washington, D.C.: U.S. Government Printing Office, 1980), pp. 327, 330, and 368.
55. Advisory Commission on Intergovernmental Relations, *Changing Public Attitudes on Governments and Taxes, 1991*, S-20 (Washington, D. C.: U. S.

Government Printing Office, 1991), p. 10.

56. Advisory Commission on Intergovernmental Relations, *Changing Public Attitudes on Government and Taxes, 1992*, S-21 (Washington, D. C.: U. S. Government Printing Office, 1992), p. 1.

57. Quoted in Julie Rovner, "Governors Ask Congress for Relief from Burdensome Medicaid Mandates," *Congressional Quarterly Weekly Report* (February 16, 1981), p. 417.

58. Theodore J. Lowi, *The End of Liberalism* (New York: Norton, 1969), p. 250-266.

59. Vincent Ostrom, *The Intellectual Crisis in American Public Administration* (Tuscaloosa, Ala.: University of Alabama Press, 1973), p. 10-11.

60. McDowell, "Grant Reform Reconsidered," p. 9.

61. Much of this discussion is drawn from: Alice M. Rivlin, " A New Vision of American Federalism," *Public Administration Review*, 52 (July/August 1992), pp. 315-320, and Rivlin, *Reviving the American Dream: The Economy, the States, and the Federal Government* (Washington, D. C.: Brookings, 1992). But see also: James Edwin Kee and John Shannon, "The Crisis and Anticrisis Dynamic: Rebalancing the American Federal System," *Public Administration Review*, 52 (July/August 1992), pp. 321-329.

62. Rivlin, "A New Vision of American Federalism," p. 320.

63. *Ibid.*

64. Much of the following discussion on interstate conflict is drawn from Joanne Omang, "In This Economic Slump, It's a State-Eat-State Nation," *Washington Post* (June 14, 1982); and Richard Benedetto, "States Skirmish in 'Border War,'" *USA Today* (February 24, 1984).

65. The twelve energy exporting states were projected to reap $193 billion in severance taxes between 1982 and 1992 by the Northeast-Midwest Economic Advancement Coalition, as cited in Omang, "In This Economic Slump."

66. Edward C. Banfield and James Q. Wilson, *City Politics* (Cambridge, Mass.: Harvard University Press, 1963), p. 65.

67. Quoted in *ibid.*, p. 66.

68. Unless noted otherwise, this discussion is drawn from Robert Sydney Duncombe, *County Government in America* (Washington, D. C.: National Association of Counties, 1966), pp. 20-23.

69. Carl W. Stenberg, "The New Federalism: Early Readings," *Public Management* (March 1982), p. 5, and Joseph E. Zimmerman, *The Discretionary Authority of Local Governments*, Urban Data Service Reports, Vol. 13, No. 11 (Washington, D.C.: International City Management Association, 1981), p. 11.

70. Joseph F. Zimmerman, "The Role of the States in Metropolitan Governance," Paper presented at Conference at Temple University, Philadelphia, August 17, 1973. Cited in Bollens and Schmandt, *The Metropolis*, p. 58.

71. National Research Council, *Toward an Understanding of Metropolitan America* (San Francisco: Canfield, 1975), p. 109.

72. Andree E. Reeves, "State ACIRs: Elements of Success," *Intergovernmental Perspective*, 17 (Summer 1991), p. 12.

73. Advisory Commission on Intergovernmental Relations, *State-Local Relations Bodies: State ACIRs and Other Approaches* (Washington, D.C.: U.S. Government Printing Office, 1981), p. 3; and Jane Roberts, Jerry Fensterman, and Donald Lief, "States, Localities Continue to Adopt Strategic Policies," *Intergovernmental Perspective*, 11 (Winter 1985), p. 29.

74. Patricia S. Florestano and Vincent L. Marando, "Urban Problems as Viewed from State Commissions: A Research Note," *Urban Affairs Quarterly* 15 (March 1980), pp. 337-338.

75. National Research Council, *Toward an Understanding of Metropolitan America*, p. 109.

76. Advisory Commission on Intergovernmental Relations, *State Community Assistance Initiatives: Innovations of the Late 1970s* (Washington, D.C.: U.S. Government Printing Office, 1979), pp. 15-36.

77. Fred Teitelbaum, "The Relative Responsiveness of State and Federal Aid to Distressed Cities," *Policy Studies Review* (November 1981), p. 320. "Distressed cities" in this study referred to those municipalities identified as in severe hardship by the Brookings Institution's "central city hardship" index. See: Richard P. Nathan and Charles Adams, "Understanding Central City Hardship," *Political Science Quarterly*, 91 (Spring 1976), pp. 44-52.

78. David R. Morgan and Mei-Chian Shih, "Targeting State and Federal Aid to City Needs," *State and Local Government Review*, 23 (Spring 1991), pp. 60-68. But see also: Michael J. Rich, "Targeting Federal Grants: The Community Development Experience, 1950-1986," *Publius*, 21 (Winter 1991), pp. 29-49. Rich did not find the federal government responsive to changing urban needs.

79. John Yinger, "States to the Rescue? Aid to Central Cities Under the New Federalism," *Public Budgeting and Finance*, 10 (Summer 1990), p. 31.

80. Wright, *Understanding Intergovernmental Relations*, p. 389.

81. For a good review of state practices in this area, see Patricia S. Florestano and Vincent L. Marando, *The States and the Metropolis* (New York: Marcel Dekker, 1981).

82. John Meyer, W. Richard Scott, and David Strang, "Centralization, Fragmentation, and School District Complexity," *Administrative Science Quarterly*, 32 (June 1987), pp. 188-201.

83. Catherine Lovell, *Federal and State Mandating on Local Governments: An Explanation of Issues and Impacts*, National Science Foundation Grant #DAR 77-20482 (Washington, D.C.: National Science Foundation, 1977).

84. Advisory Commission on Intergovernmental Relations, *State Mandating of Local Expenditures* (Washington, D.C.: U.S. Government Printing Office, 1978).

85. Rodney E. Hero and Jody L. Fitzpatrick, "State Mandating of Local Government Activities: An

Exploration," paper presented at the 1986 Annual Meeting of the American Political Science Association, Washington, D.C., August 28-31, 1986, p. 18.

86. Linda Wagar, "A Declaration of War," *State Government News* (April 1993), p. 20.

87. Advisory Commission on Intergovernmental Relations, *Mandates: Cases in State-Local Relations*, M-173 (Washington, D. C.: U. S. Government Printing Office, September 1990), p. 7.

88. Wagar, "A Declaration of War," p. 18.

89. Janet Kelly, quoted in *ibid.*, p. 21.

90. Gregory Streib and William L. Waugh, Jr., "The Changing Responsibilities of County Governments: Data from a Survey of County Leaders," *American Review of Public Administration*, 21 (June 1991), p. 144. All counties were surveyed in 1989, and the response rate was 40 percent.

91. The facts in this paragraph are drawn from: David B. Walker and Albert J. Richter, "Regionalism and the Counties," *County Year Book, 1975* (Washington, D. C.: National Association of Counties and International City Management Association, 1975), p. 15.

92. John F. Shirey, "National Actions Affecting Local Government: Cutbacks and Lowered Expectations," *Municipal Year Book, 1982* (Washington, D. C.: International City Management Association, 1982), p. 47.

93. "Intergovernmental Focus," *Intergovernmental Perspective*, 8 (Summer 1982), p. 5.

94. Neal R. Pierce, with Curtis W. Johnson and John Stuart Hall, *Citistates: How Urban America Can Prosper in a Competitive World* (Washington, D. C.: Seven Locks Press, 1993), p. 6.

95. Beryl A. Radin, "Rural Development Councils: An Intergovernmental Coordination Experiment," *Publius*, 22 (Summer 1992), pp. 111-127.

96. "Ready or Not, Here Comes Regional Power," *Governing* (April 1992), pp. 67-68, and Pierce, Johnson, and Hall, *Citistates*, p. 6.

97. Forster Ndubisi and Mary Dyer, "The Role of Regional Entities in Formulating and Implementing Statewide Growth Policies," *State and Local Government Review*, 24 (Fall 1992), pp. 117-127.

98. The following typology is drawn from Lori M. Henderson, "Intergovernmental Service Arrangements and the Transfer of Functions," *Municipal Year Book, 1985* (Washington, D.C.: International City Management Association, 1985), p. 194.

99. *Ibid.*, p. 201. The 1972 survey is in Advisory Commission on Intergovernmental Relations, *The Challenge of Local Government Reorganization*, A-44 (Washington, D.C.: U.S. Government Printing Office, 1976).

100. Henderson, "Intergovernmental Service Arrangements," pp. 199-200.

101. *Ibid.*, pp. 196-198, 201.

102. See: Joseph F. Zimmerman, *The Federated City: Community Control in Large Cities* (New York: St. Martin's, 1972); Milton Kotler, *Neighborhood Government* (Indianapolis: Bobbs-Merrill, 1969); and Alan A. Altshuler, *Community Control: The Black*

Demand for Participation in Large American Cities (New York: Pegasus, 1970).

103. Howard W. Hallman, "Guidelines for Neighborhood Management," *Public Management* (January 1971), pp. 3-5.

104. Advisory Commission on Intergovernmental Relations, *Citizen Participation in the American Federal System*, A-73 (Washington, D.C.: U.S. Government Printing Office, 1979), p. 4.

105. John Herbers, "Neighborhood Activists Are Gaining Credence as a Political Force," *New York Times*, as reprinted in *The Arizona Republic* (August 12, 1979).

106. Frank X. Steggert, *Community Action Groups and City Government* (Cambridge, Mass.: Ballinger, 1975), pp. 6-8.

107. Robert J. Dilger, "Residential Community Associations: Issues, Impacts, and Relevance for Local Government," *State and Local Government Review*, 23 (Winter 1991), p. 18.

108. Advisory Commission on Intergovernmental Relations, *Residential Community Associations: Private Governments in the Intergovernmental System?* A-112 (Washington, D.C.: U.S. Government Printing Office, 1989), p. 1.

109. Stephen E. Barton and Carol J. Silverman, "Common Interest Homeowners' Associations: Private Government and Public Interest Revisited," *Public Affairs Report* (May 1988), pp. 5-9.

110. Betty A. Zisk, Heinz Eulau, and Kenneth Prewitt, "City Councilmen and the Group Struggle," *Journal of Politics*, 27 (August 1965), p. 633.

111. Thomas R. Dye, *Politics in States and Communities*, 3rd ed. (Englewood Cliffs, N.J.: Prentice Hall, 1977), p. 300.

112. John Rehfuss, "Citizen Participation in Urban Fiscal Decisions," *Municipal Year Book, 1979* (Washington, D.C.: International City Management Association, 1979), p. 87. Rehfuss surveyed all municipalities with 10,000 people or more, and all counties with 50,000 people or more. He obtained responses from 1,817 governments, a response rate of 57 percent.

113. Monsignor Geno Baroni, quoted in Herbers, "Neighborhood Activists."

114. G. Ross Stephens, "State Centralization and the Erosion of Local Autonomy," *Journal of Politics*, 36 (February 1974), pp 44-76, and Stephens, "State Centralization Revisited," paper presented at the annual meeting of the American Political Science Association, New Orleans, August 29-September 1, 1985. In 1957, four states were categorized as "centralized"; by 1982, sixteen were.

115. See, for example, Advisory Commission on Intergovernmental Relations, *The Condition of Contemporary Federalism: Conflicting Theories and Collapsing Constraints* (Washington, D.C.: U.S. Government Printing Office, 1981), pp. 68-70; Jeffrey M. Stonecash, "Fiscal Centralization in the American States: Increasing Similarity and Persisting Diversity," *Publius*, 13 (Fall 1983), pp. 123-137; and Stonecash, "Fiscal Centralization in the American Status: Findings from Another Perspective," *Public Budgeting and Finance*, 8 (Winter 1988), pp. 81-89.

116. Henderson, "Intergovernmental Service Arrangements," pp. 194-202, for 1983 data; Advisory Commission on Intergovernmental Relations, *Pragmatic Federalism: The Reassignment of Functional Responsibility* (Washington, D.C.: U.S. Government Printing Office, 1976) for 1975 data; and Advisory Commission on Intergovernmental Relations, *The Challenge of Local Government Reorganization*, for 1972 data. For a detailed treatment of all three studies, see: Advisory Commission on Intergovernmental Relations, *Intergovernmental Service Arrangements for Delivering Local Public Services: Update 1983*, A-103 (Washington, D.C.: U.S. Government Printing Office, 1985).

117. Henderson, "Intergovernmental Service Arrangements," p. 196. All information in this paragraph is for 1983.

118. *Ibid.*, p. 198.

119. *Ibid.*, p. 202.

CHAPTER 13

TOWARD A BUREAUCRATIC ETHIC

The notion that the public bureaucracy stands in need of ethical sensitivity in order to serve the public interest is a fairly new one. Although the first code of ethics for public administrators was adopted in 1924 by the International City Management Association, it was a code that reflected the anticorruption and antipolitics values of the municipal reform movement of the period, rather than a statement of professional ethics in the tradition established by the fields of education, engineering, law, and medicine, among other professions.

Congress imposed a code of ethics on federal administrators in 1958, and twenty years later expanded the code and founded the federal government's Office of Government Ethics as part of the Ethics in Government Act of 1978. In 1992, the Office of Government Ethics released the federal government's first comprehensive set of standards of ethical conduct, consolidating, in the process, a jumble of ethics codes that had been promulgated by federal agencies over the years. Consuming some forty pages in the *Federal Register*, the standards cover gifts, conflicts of financial interest, impartiality, misuse of office, seeking outside employment, and outside activities.

The first state code of ethics was established in 1967; it was only in 1984 that the chief association of public administrators at all levels of government, the American Society for Public Administration, saw fit to write and adopt a code of ethics for professionals in the public sector.

There were reasons for this lethargy, and the reasons had less to do with a determination among public administrators to permit and condone unethical practices in their field, and can be ascribed more to a common assumption held by society (including public administrators) about what the proper role of public administration and government was. Prior to the abandonment of the politics/administration dichotomy and the principles of administration, the public administrator needed morality no more than a hotel clerk carrying out his or her daily duties. After all, of what use was morality to a person who did no more than execute the will of the state according to certain scientific principles? Provided that public administrators accomplished their given tasks efficiently and economically, they were by definition, moral in the sense that they were responsible. (In fact, the original city managers' and federal codes of ethics placed notable stress on efficiency as an ethical concept—a notion that many ethicists might find puzzling.) Morality, after all, necessitates ethical choice, and, as the literature was wont to stress, ethical choice simply was not a function of the functionaries.

PUBLIC ADMINISTRATION'S ETHICAL EVOLVEMENT

The Demise of the Politics/Administration Dichotomy

Three developments have been instrumental in the emergence of the concept that ethics are, in fact, pertinent to public administration. One, of course, was the abandonment of the politics/administration dichotomy. When this naive bifurcation was eliminated, when politics and administration were recognized as being part of the same parcel, it was also admitted implicitly that morality had to be relevant to the bureaucracy. Now the public administrator was forced to make decisions not only on the comfortable bases of efficiency, economy, and administrative principles, but on the more agonizing criteria of morality as well. Public administrators had to ask themselves: What is *the* public interest?

The Emergence of Decision-Making Theory

The second development was the new role of decision-making theory in public administration. Herbert A. Simon had called for the rigorous analysis of decision-making behavior as central to the future study of administration; he simultaneously decimated as simplistic the "proverbs of administration" in his *Administrative Behavior*.[1] Simon argued that administrators made decisions on bases other than those of economy and efficiency. He contended that social and psychological factors had a significant effect on the decisions that decision makers made. And, before the appearance of *Administrative Behavior*, Harold Lasswell in *Psychopathology and Politics*[2] and Chester I. Barnard in *The Functions of the Executive*[3] had made essentially the same argument. The contention that decision makers made

decisions on the bases of feeling, emotion, and mental sets, as well as on "rationality," implied that public administrators could make highly questionable, even immoral, public policies that possibly would affect whole populations. This was a serious matter. Public administrationists became increasingly cognizant of the disquieting notion that a sense of ethics—a sense of the public interest—was a genuine need in the practice of public administration.

This concern was exacerbated by the appearance of a new body of literature that addressed the topic of morality in public administration in a different manner. Paul H. Appleby, in *Morality and Administration in Democratic Government*, took on the ethical problems posed by the tensions between pluralistic politics and bureaucratic hierarchy. In Appleby's view, the pressures of politics and hierarchy forced moral dilemmas "up" to the highest appropriate policymaking levels in legislatures and bureaucracies and simultaneously simplified the number of choices available to public bureaucrats, usually leaving them with only two options. This was a realistic appraisal of the moral situation of the public bureaucrat; it emphasized the lack of ethical subtlety that the bureaucrat was permitted in making decisions. Although a situation might have "gray" areas in reality, decisions usually had to be either "black" or "white."[4] Similarly, Norton Long explained the connections between moral choice and administrative decision making in the public bureaucracy by his survival thesis. In Long's opinion, all decisions made by public administrators could be explained by their desire that their agencies survive. Long perceived this situation as beneficial to the public interest more often than not, but his reasoning did not rest easily with many of his colleagues as one that cultivated moral rectitude in government.[5] Likewise, Joseph Harris, in *Congressional Control of Administration*, implied that federal public administrators made their decisions primarily on the basis of satisfying a few men who headed powerful committees in Congress; his logic did not strike many as a sound rationale for promoting the public interest.[6]

Perhaps the most shattering analyses of the public administrator's relationship to the public interest were Gordon Tullock's *The Politics of Bureaucracy*[7] and Dwaine Marvick's *Career Per-*

spectives in a Bureaucratic Setting (1954).[8] Although we reviewed their contributions in Chapter 5, a brief consideration of their works' implications for bureaucratic ethics is warranted. By arguing that all decision making in bureaucracies is predicated on the individual "reference politician" getting ahead in the hierarchy, Tullock implied that, among public administrators, what is good for the public, or even for the organization, is at best an incidental consideration. Marvick's empirical study of public administrators hypothesized that all individual behavior in public organizations was a matter of conscious or sublimated self-interest. Some participants had deep security needs that obstructed organizational innovation. Others needed simply the opportunity to "do their own thing" and had no commitment beyond protecting that opportunity. Still others were consciously willing and able to disrupt, disorient, and undermine the organization if they felt such behavior would advance their own career goals. In brief, research such as Tullock's and Marvick's was disconcerting not only to public administrationists, but to democratic theorists as well. As Ferrell Heady observed, with the experiences of France and Germany chiefly in mind, public bureaucrats "have obediently and even subserviently responded to whatever political leaders have gained power."[9]

The Counterculture Critique

A third development that has led scholars and practitioners in public administration to dwell more acutely on the meaning of the public interest is the emergence in America of the "counterculture." The term *counterculture* is here used to refer to that body of literature that criticizes the American administrative state as being inhumane, technocratic, impersonal, and "faceless." The counterculture's critique of the public bureaucracy is an especially fundamental one: It states that the typical public administrator is not *immoral* but *amoral*—that is, he or she has been so seduced in this thinking by the values, pressures, and propaganda of the technocratic state that he or she no longer is capable of comprehending what morality is or is not. Thus, even if public administrators wanted to do the "right" thing—indeed, even if they thought that they were doing the right thing—they neither would

be able to make the proper moral decision nor recognize it should they happen to stumble on it.

The counterculture's argument is essentially a linguistic one. It holds that the symbols and values of technological society prevent individual men and women from choosing the life styles that they in fact would probably choose if they were not propagandized by the technocracy to be aggressive, amoral, competitive, even war-like "consumer hedonists." Herbert Marcuse, for example, stresses the symbolic aspects of this view. He contends that the media and institutions of society represent a profound kind of authoritarianism, one that coopts protest via the continual repetition of certain phrases over the mass media that restrict, by their drilling meaninglessness, alternative thinking; for example, the quite deliberate and unending repetition of the phrase, "warmongering capitalist imperialism" over the media of the former Soviet Union squelched the objective analysis of Western economic and foreign policies on the part of Soviet citizens while encouraging popular paranoia.[10]

Likewise Jacques Ellul states that citizens in technological societies dwell on "technique" to the exclusion of "reality"; thus, moral choices are "defined out" of administrative problems, and technical means become far more important than ethical ends.[11] Similarly, Theodore J. Roszak argues that "scientism" is inadequate as a way to analyze social problems because it "hexes" our thinking on moral issues. As Roszak states:

We have produced the scientized jargon which currently dominates official parlance and the social sciences. When knowledgeable men talk, they no longer talk of substances and accidents, of being and spirit, of virtue and vice, of sin and salvation, of deities and demons. Instead, we have a vocabulary filled with nebulous quantities of things that have every appearance of precise calibration, and decorated with vaguely mechanistic-mathematical terms like "parameters," "structures," "variables," "inputs and outputs," "correlations," "inventories," "maximizations," and "optimizations." ... the more such language and numerology one packs into a document, the more "objective" the document becomes—which normally means the less morally abrasive. . . .

Thus to bomb more hell out of a tiny Asian country in one year than was bombed out of Europe in the whole Second World War becomes "escalation."... A comparison of the slaughter on both sides in a war is called a "kill ratio." Totaling up the corpses is called a "body count." Running the blacks out of town is called "urban renewal." Discovering ingenious new ways to bilk the public is called "market research." Outflanking the discontent of employees is called "personnel management." . . . On the other hand, one can be certain that where more colorful, emotive terms are used—"the war on poverty," "the war for the hearts and minds of men," "the race for space," "the New Frontier," "the Great Society,"—the matters referred to exist only as propagandistic fiction or pure distraction.[12]

Charles Reich dubs this situation "Consciousness II" and lists its characteristics as a critique of the administrative state: The reduction of personal freedom via the amalgamation and integration of the public and private interests of society; the value-neutral, even value-less, bureaucracy that is consistently biased in favor of existing policy; the autonomy of the administrative bureaucracy, which makes particular decisions untraceable to particular sources; the displacing of traditional private property, such as land owned by people, by "the new property" of people belonging to organizations—thus, status and identification conferred by the organizations replace private property in humanity's traditional structure of values; and, finally, law as an "inhuman medium" that relates to classes and categories in society, but not to individual people. These features combine to produce the major symptoms of the administrative state, the essence of which "is that it is relentlessly single-minded; it has just one value . . . technology as represented by organization, efficiency, growth, progress." The effect on the individual public administrator of this relentless single-mindedness is the development of "a profound schizophrenia." Not only is his or her working self separated from his or her private self by the creation of unwanted needs and status drives via advertising, but there also is a split between the public self and the private self, which is accomplished through the nourishment of his or her "liberal" feelings of elitist paternal-

ism for the dispossessed as well as cultivating his or her own needs for status and identity in a consumer-oriented society.[13]

PUBLIC ADMINISTRATION AND THE RECOGNITION OF THE PUBLIC INTEREST: TWO INTELLECTUAL ATTEMPTS

The counterculture critique of the moral dilemma of public administrators (*i.e.*, that they are amoral because of the obfuscation of their language and symbols and the fractionalization of their sense of identity) is a profound one. Public administrationists, while increasingly concerned with administrative ethics and decision making, have not yet addressed themselves to the necessary chore of defining a workable framework of moral choice for the public administrator.

Bureaucratic "Responsibility"

In fact, public administrationists have avoided this task by implying that a moral framework is really not needed when they examine instead the various ways in which "responsibility" and "accountability" are assured in public bureaucracies.[14] For example, some scholars, such as Carl Friedrich and Norton Long, contend that the normal scruples and professional commitments that public administrators glean from being socialized into the public service, along with the "representative elite" nature of their bureaucracies, act as internal constraints against the perpetuation of antidemocratic policies.

Most public administrationists, however, argue that a plethora of external checks exist as well, assuring compliance with the public interest. Charles Hyneman and Herbert Finer, for instance, believe that legislative surveillance is an adequate check. J. D. Lewis and L. Von Mises contend that citizen participation in bureaucratic decision making accomplishes the task of matching bureaucratic behavior with the public interest. Henry J. Abraham makes a case for the use of Ombudsman (a figure in Scandinavian governments and elsewhere who has no official power but great personal prestige, which he or she uses to rectify unjust bureaucratic decisions on an individual basis) as an effective means for assuring administrative responsibility. Dwight Waldo, John M. Pfiffner, and Robert Presthus have stated that decentralization of the bureaucracy provides an effective means of implementing the public interest. Gordon Tullock and Harold Wilensky urge the use of publicizing bureaucratic information to insure accordance with the public interest. And K. C. Davis believes that judicial review of administrative decisions checks policies not in the public interest.

In a very real sense, however, these efforts miss the crucial point: Public administrators do make political decisions, but no effective moral and philosophic guidelines (as opposed to *mechanisms* for correcting "bad" decisions) exist for their making these decisions in the public interest.

Organizational Humanism

What some writers have called "organizational humanism" represents another kind of skirting of the issue; rather than denying the appropriateness of bureaucratic ethics, however, organizational humanism dances a baroque minuet around the problem of moral choice. In an unusually solid review of this literature, Robert B. Denhardt observes that organizational humanism contains at least three themes that are of particular utility to the development of a theory of bureaucratic ethics: Treating members of an organization humanely leads to greater organizational efficiency; treating organizational members humanely promotes organizational change; and treating the individual in an organization in a humane way is in and of itself a desirable objective.[15]

Organizational humanism was spawned in the literature of human relations and organization development—literary traditions that constitute two of the significant streams of the open model of organizations that we reviewed in Chapter 3. It focuses on the individual in the organization and his or her personal development. As we shall see, organizational humanism verges on addressing the question of bureaucratic ethics, but like the literature of bureaucratic responsibility, ultimately draws short of it.

Some of the early studies in the open model of organizations brought out questions—often morally-tinged questions—concerning the individual's role in the organization. Chester I. Bar-

nard's recognition of the "informal organization"; the Hawthorne studies that focused on the importance of social and psychological rewards for workers; Douglas McGregor's development of the "Theory Y" model of workers' personalities; and Robert Blake and Jane Mouton's notion of the "managerial grid," in which they argued that a high organizational concern for people and the team approach to management most closely corresponded with high organizational productivity, all had the effect of teasing out the idea that the satisfaction and happiness of the individual person in an organization was an important element in organizational effectiveness.[16]

Chris Argyris is among the better-known writers in developing the argument that organizations would improve themselves if they were able to develop the full human potentiality of their members. In *Personality and Organization*, for example, Argyris argued that the normal dynamic of organizations was to "dematurize" people in organizations and, that if organizations changed their internal dynamics, more creative and contributing organizational members would result. Argyris conceived of learning as the primary means through which individual members could develop their human capabilities, and "learning" to Argyris meant learning not only about the organization, but about one's self; learning, in Argyris's mind, equated with the maturation of both the organization and the individual.[17]

In a perceptive critique of Argyris's work, Denhardt observes that by emphasizing learning, Argyris "implies a relationship involving shared meanings and raises the possibilities for creating not only conditions of trust, openness, and self-esteem, but also conditions of community."[18] But for whatever reason, Argyris chose not to extrapolate the implications of learning in organizations, which in Denhardt's view constitutes the "potentially radical implication of Argyris's work," because by inference, Argyris's idea of learning ultimately forces the issue of developing a set of bureaucratic ethics. Fundamentally, Argyris is still "bound to an instrumentalist perspective," or one that places the organization's needs above that of the individual's happiness.[19]

Robert T. Golembiewski, on the other hand, goes a step further. Rather than arguing for the desirability of emotionally mature organizational members, as does Argyris, Golembiewski directly addresses the problem of morality within the organization and the prospects of freedom for the individual worker. Golembiewski asserts that "moral sensitivity can be associated with satisfactory output and employee satisfaction."[20] Golembiewski's major contribution is that he confronts the question of morality in organizations, arguing that organization development, particularly the laboratory approach (recall Chapter 3), represents an unusually useful method of bringing morality to organizations.

The literature that we have been covering so far is drawn largely from organization theory and, with the occasional exception of Golembiewski, this literature was not written by nor directed to the world of public administration. With the advent of the "new public administration" in the early 1970s, however, this situation began to change. We reviewed the new public administration in Chapter 2 in terms of its effects on the intellectual evolution of the field. Although its impact was not particularly lasting and, as has been pointed out, it was "a movement from the beginning more fictional than real,"[21] the literature associated with the new public administration nonetheless has overriding tones of moral and ethical concerns, and thus has pertinence here. Writers in the tradition of the new public administration emphasized the paramountcy of equity over efficiency, and of participation by organizational members over hierarchy.[22]

One of the more interesting contributions to this literature has been written by Eugene P. Dvorin and Robert H. Simmons, who observe that "little of the literature of public administration reflects on the nature of public interest, and virtually none reflects belief in the dignity of man as the ultimate value." Conversely, they add, the other branches of the government do have operational definitions of the public interest. Both the legislative and adjudicative branches "have their myths and techniques by which they serve these myths." In the legislature, the operational concept is majority rule as the fundamental precondition of democracy. In the judiciary, the concept is *stare decisis*, or judicial precedent, by which the evolutionary development of legal principles is perceived as the basic method for obtaining a system of justice that reflects the public interest. In both of these examples there are, of course, flaws. As Dvorin and Simmons say, the "myths" of

majority rule and *stare decisis* in reality "serve several functions—to meet the psychoemotional needs of the society and to protect and defend both legislators and judges." Nevertheless, the point stands that these concepts do not pretend to be value-neutral, and they do go far toward defining the abstract notion of the public interest in workable terms that meet the needs of the legislative and adjudicative institutions of society. Not so, however, with the executive branch, which has no such operational definition.

Dvorin and Simmons urge that "radical humanism" be accepted as the public bureaucracy's functional concept of the public interest. In their words:

'Radical humanism' forwards the proposition that the ends of man are the ends of man. . . . Radical humanism is radical because it is not willing to compromise its human values on any grounds. . . . Radical humanism calls for the ultimate capitulation of operational mechanics and political strategies to a concept of the public interest based on man as the most important concern of bureaucratic power.[23]

This statement is fine as far as it goes. Regrettably, Dvorin and Simmons go no further, and a serious problem arises in terms of what "radical humanism" means when it is applied to particular administrative problems. The same may be said, in fact, for organizational humanism in general.

AN EXAMPLE OF APPLIED ETHICAL CHOICE IN PUBLIC ADMINISTRATION

Consider, for an example, a classic dilemma in that traditionally hidebound field of public human resource management: hiring members of socially disadvantaged groups. There are two positions. One is that government should make special efforts, including the reduction of entrance standards, to hire members of those segments of American society that have endured various forms of racial, religious, disability, ethnic, or sexual discrimination. The reasoning is that, because of cultural bias in testing, lack of educational opportunity, and general social prejudice, government owes those people who have suffered these injustices a special chance to get ahead. If this should entail some bending of the civil service regulations (as is done for veterans), then so be it. Such rule-bending will, after all, only balance the social equities for those applicants who have had to suffer bigotry in the past, and this is only as it should be since government is the single institution most responsible for assuring equality of opportunity in society.

The other position is that no "lowering of standards" should be considered, regardless of the applicant's past tribulations. The logic for this viewpoint is that government owes the best governance possible to all the governed. To hire applicants who do not score as well on tests as other applicants, or who do not have comparable educational attainments, or who are just less qualified, irrespective of the tough breaks in their backgrounds, is to do a disservice to the populace generally, deprived groups included. Governmental economy, efficiency, effectiveness, and responsiveness will deteriorate to the detriment of us all, unless only the top applicants are hired.

(It must be noted here that both arguments, pro and con, have been simplified considerably in order to emphasize the ethical aspects of each. Other pertinent facets, such as the efficacy of tests in measuring administrative ability and the role of strict civil service standards in protecting applicants from disadvantaged groups against discrimination, among others, were reviewed in Chapter 9.)

It is reasonably apparent from this example that organizational humanism does not offer much of a guide to the public administrator in formulating a decision in terms of promoting the public interest. Organizational humanism states that treating people humanely should be the ultimate end in bureaucratic decision making, but which option should the public administrator choose in the case cited? Is humanity best served by hiring or promoting a deprived group member who may not execute his or her duties especially well, or is humanity best served by not hiring (or by holding back) the same disadvantaged group member, thus never permitting him or her to try realizing his or her full human potential nor aiding the cause of his or her people? This dilemma can be rendered even more exquisite by making the hypothetical deprived-group member in ques-

tion an applicant to an agency designed to end discrimination against deprived groups, such as the Equal Employment Opportunity Commission; thus, to hire or not to hire him or her implies a lack of sincerity in advancing the cause of disadvantaged groups, depending on one's point of view. In any event, organizational humanism would seem to lack a viable framework of clearcut referent points for a public administrator in making an ethical choice that is in "the public interest."

JUSTICE-AS-FAIRNESS: A VIEW OF THE PUBLIC INTEREST

What is needed for the public administrator is a simple and operational articulation of the public interest that permits him or her to make a moral choice on the basis of rational thinking. It is suggested in this book that such a useful concept may exist in the form of a theory of justice offered by philosopher John Rawls.

Rawls extends the notion of a social contract formulated by John Locke, Jean-Jacques Rousseau, and Thomas Hobbes, and contends implicitly that the public interest can be discerned in most situations by applying two "principles of justice": (1) that "each person is to have an equal right to the most extensive basic liberty compatible with a similar liberty for others," and (2) that "social and economic inequalities are to be arranged so that they are both (a) reasonably expected to be to everyone's advantage, and (b) attached to positions and offices open to all." Should these principles come into conflict, the second is expected to yield to the first; thus, just as in organizational humanism, the dignity of the individual person is considered to be of paramount importance.[24]

Rawls's theory of justice goes further, however. His principles necessarily lead to the conclusion that inequalities of wealth, authority, and social opportunity "are just only if they result in compensating benefits for everyone, and in particular for the least advantaged members of society. These principles rule out justifying institutions on the grounds that the hardships of some are offset by a greater good in the aggregate. It may be expedient but it is not just that some should have less in order that others may prosper."[25]

In short, as Rawls observes, his principles in essence are a rigorous statement of the traditional Anglo-Saxon concept of fairness. In the context of managing organizations, "fairness" is comprised of trust, consistency, truthfulness, integrity, clearly stated expectations, equitable treatment, a sense of ownership and influence in the organization, impartial decision making, and mutual respect.[26]

INTUITIONISM, PERFECTIONISM, AND UTILITARIANISM

The usefulness of Rawls's justice-as-fairness philosophy can be elucidated by contrasting it with other philosophies of the public interest. One is the *intuitionist* philosophy, expressed by Brian Barry, Nicholas Rescher, and W. D. Ross, among others.[27] Intuitionist theories expound a plurality of first principles, which may conflict when applied to particular situations but which offer no precise method for choosing the principle that should take precedence in cases of conflict. Such dilemmas are resolved by intuition, by what seems most nearly right. Intuitionist philosophies do not help the conscientious public administrator to make a rational decision in light of an explicit theory of the public interest, other than rendering him or her some solace in justifying present practices. In other words, public administrators already make decisions on the basis of intuitionist theories—that is, they do what seem to be to them most nearly right on an individual basis and given particularistic circumstances. The view here, however, is that this practice—an ethical "muddling through"—is increasingly inadequate for a society in which rapid change is the only constant.

A second major philosophical school that addresses the public interest is *perfectionism*. The first and sole principle of perfectionism is to promote, via society's institutions, the attainment of excellence in art, science, and culture. There are, however, two forms of perfectionism. In its relative form, as advocated by Aristotle, the perfectionist principle is one among many first principles, and thus overlaps with intuitionism. In its absolutist form, by contrast, there are no problems of ambiguity: the public administrator should always strive to support the upper intellectual crust of his or her society; any misfortune for

society's least fortunate segments that accrues from the necessary allocation of resources and that results from implementing the perfectionist principle is morally justified by the benefits incurred by the best members that the society has. As Nietzsche put it so pithily, the deepest meaning that can be given to the human experience is "your living for the rarest and most valuable specimens."[28]

Perfectionism is a counterpoise to the egalitarian notions rife in a democratic society, and for that reason we shall not dwell on it as an appropriate ethical decision-making framework for American public administrators. Nevertheless, this is not to imply that perfectionism has not been used as an operating premise by American bureaucrats in making decisions. The National Science Foundation's traditional criterion for financing "pure" scientific research (which has been, with few exceptions, the only kind of research that the Foundation financed)—that science should be funded for the sake of science—would appear to be an implementation of the perfectionist principle, although this emphasis has been changing in recent years.

A third ethical framework for the determination of the public interest is *utilitarianism*, as represented by Jeremy Bentham, Adam Smith, David Hume, and John Stuart Mill.[29] Of the philosophies that have had the most influence on public administrators in terms of intellectual rigor and social appropriateness, utilitarianism holds first place in theory, if not in actual practice.

The reasoning of utilitarianism is both democratic in values and systematic in thought. It holds that a public policy will be in the public interest provided the policy increases the net balance of social satisfaction summed over all the individuals belonging to the society. In other words, if a public policy makes everybody slightly better off, even if some individuals are left slightly worse off in other ways as a result of that policy, then the policy is just and the public interest is served. An example of a utilitarian public policy would be one that increased the income of medical doctors by raising everyone's taxes and turning over these new revenues to doctors, thereby increasing everyone's net balance of health by inducing a greater net balance of individuals to enter the medical profession. Even though society's least well-off individuals would lose money under this arrangement, the policy nevertheless would be just and in the public interest under a utilitarian theory because everyone's net balance of health would be increased, including that of the least well-off. The logic behind this justification of such a public policy is that since individuals try to advance as far as possible their own welfare in terms of net increases, it therefore follows that the group should do the same, and the society likewise.

The ethical theory of justice-as-fairness, however, would hold that such a public policy was not just and not in the public interest because it reduced the welfare of the least well-off people in society, even if it is for the net benefit for the whole society. With some alterations, our hypothetical policy could be made just under Rawls's principles; for instance, by not taxing the poor but still letting them take part in the overall health benefits that derive from the policy. It is on the same logic that the United States has a mildly "progressive" income tax structure which is supposed to tax the rich proportionately more than the poor, rather than a "regressive" income tax structure that taxes the poor proportionately more than the rich, or even a "proportional" tax that taxes the indigent and the wealthy at the same rate.

Although, as we noted earlier, utilitarianism is practiced more by chance than by choice among American bureaucrats, occasionally agencies will select utilitarianism quite consciously as their operational definition of the public interest. An example is provided by the U.S. Army Corps of Engineers, which has adopted benefit/cost analysis as its method of deciding which engineering projects are in the best interests of the nation. But the assumptions underlying the Corps' use of benefit/cost analysis are squarely set in a utilitarian philosophy, and can bring utilitarian consequences.

For instance, in 1983, the Corps of Engineers conducted a benefit/cost analysis of flood control for the La Puerta del Norte, a frequently-flooded community of 150 families living in mobile homes near the Santa Cruz River in Pima County, Arizona. The Corps' study concluded that flood control projects for La Puerta del Norte would not be cost-effective because the potential flood damage that could be wreaked on mobile homes would not be great in terms of dollar losses. If, however, La Puerta del Norte had consisted of expensive homes, then the Corps' analysis likely would have justified a flood control project because the Corps' benefit/cost formula was predicated on estimating the potential dollar loss in property damage that might result from floods.[30] Thus, costlier homes (and wealthier people) are favored over cheaper homes (and poorer people) in the Corps' benefit/cost analyses because the technique itself is based on utilitarian precepts.

APPLYING THE JUSTICE-AS-FAIRNESS THEORY

Intuitionism, perfectionism, and utilitarianism illuminate by contrast the usefulness of justice-as-fairness as an ethical framework for public administrators in making decisions that are in the public interest. But how would justice-as-fairness help the public administrator in deciding our original dilemma, that of hiring "less qualified" applicants from disadvantaged groups in society? It would, by the inevitability of its logic, argue for the hiring of these applicants on these grounds:

1. *Not* hiring them would be further depriving society's most deprived groups for the sake of the whole society.
2. Hiring them would facilitate the full realization of their "basic liberty" (or personal dignity) without encroaching on the basic liberty of others.
3. Hiring them helps assure that all positions and offices are open to all.
4. Hiring them helps assure that privileges innate to such offices continue to work toward the advantage of all in a reasonably equal way, because the privileges and positions are being extended to the least well-off in society.

Moreover, of the ethical frameworks considered, only justice-as-fairness would by its logic permit the public administrator the decisional choice of making a special effort to hire members from disadvantaged groups. Utilitarianism would demand that the good of the whole be the first priority, regardless of consequences for society's least well-off. Perfectionism, in effect, would say to hell with society's least well-off since they are not considered at all in its value structure. Intuitionism, which most public administrators practice, permits the choice of hiring members of minority groups, but only as a coincidental happenstance and not by the force of its theory.

Justice-as-fairness offers the public administrator a workable way for determining the public interest. So, for that matter, do utilitarianism and perfectionism, but we are rejecting those frameworks in this book; the former because it logically permits the least advantaged persons in society to be disadvantaged further and thus is "unfair" and not in the public interest in all instances, and the latter because its antidemocratic values are incompatible with the dominant values of American society. The choice in this book of justice-as-fairness as an operating moral logic for the public administrator is, of course, a value choice by the author and should be recognized as such by the reader. But it is believed to be a reasonable one under the circumstances.

PRACTICING ETHICAL PUBLIC ADMINISTRATION

Whatever ethical standard a public administrator chooses, and however each public administrator elects to employ that standard, it is reasonably apparent that career public administrators take the practice of ethical administration seriously. A national survey of public administrators at all levels of government in the United States found that almost 70 percent believe that the interest in ethical issues among public administrators seemed to be "steadily growing over time"; close to 60 percent disagree that ethics is "meaningless because organizational cultures encourage a Machiavellian philosophy of power, survival, and expediency"; about two-thirds think that "ethical concerns can be empowering in organizations" (only 6 percent disagree), and reject the position that "expressions of ethical concern . . . evoke cynicism, self-righteousness, paranoia, and/or laughter"; and 90 percent take issue with the statement that there "is no real need for codes of ethics in work organizations."[31] These responses seem to substantiate the proposition that public administrators maintain a belief set that codes of ethics and ethical behavior in their profession are needed, good, and growing.

Data from the private sector appear to support the notion that good ethics are good business. In a careful study of twenty retail stores in the United States, researchers found that when nonsupervisory employees "report organizational climates deficient in these so-called 'soft' areas [of ethical behavior, *i.e.*, trust, truthfulness, integrity and justice], the company can expect to bear significantly higher bottom-line costs in the area of employee sickness and accident compensation costs. The data are strikingly clear: Out in the real world, not just in the college-freshmen psychology experiment, fairness does make a difference."[32]

Irrespective of its practical uses, however, practicing ethical administration in the public sector remains a challenging chore. Reflecting a fundamental theme of this book—that the task environment is far more penetrating of the public organization than of the private one—half of public administrators report that "supervisors are under pressure to compromise personal standards." The lower that one descends through the strata of the public organization, and the more youthful and politically liberal the public administrator, the stronger this belief becomes. Much of this perception is enmeshed in the on-going tensions between career and noncareer public executives, described in Chapter 9. Sixty percent of the respondents doubted that the "ethical standards of elected and appointed officials are as high as those held by career civil servants" (only 25 percent accepted the contention that the ethical standards of both groups are comparable), and almost three-fourths took umbrage at the idea that "senior management has a stronger set of ethical standards than I do."[33] Senior managers, however, seem serene in their belief that not only do they have high ethical standards, but, according to one survey of city and county employees, it appears that the higher one advances up the governmental ladder, the less likely one is to perceive ethical lapses in their governments.[34]

In light of these views, it is perhaps not surprising that public administrators, are more critical of the ethics of corporate culture than government (nearly 90 percent spurn the notion that "government morality in America is lower than business morality"[35]), and one review of ethics surveys found that "the findings in which public and private employees differ . . . . most often

ETIQUETTE, IMAGE, AND ETHICS IN PUBLIC ADMINISTRATION

Beginning in the late 1980s, it became clear that the United States' biggest bankruptcy—the failure of much of the savings and loan (S&L) industry—could not be staved off, and the American taxpayers would be the losers. Congress and a conservative White House had, at one and the same time, insured (with federal funds) the deposits of citizens who invested their money in savings and loan associations; radically deregulated the S&Ls, allowing them to invest their depositors' savings in extremely questionable pursuits; and significantly cut back on the federal government's oversight and inspection of the savings-and-loan associations.

The results of these policies were perhaps predictable, but not their colossal dimensions: Hundreds of S&Ls (also known, ironically, as "thrifts"), beginning in the late 1980s, declared bankruptcy, and the estimates of the final federal bill to the taxpayer to cover these losses run as high at $500 billion over thirty years.

To administer the S&L bailout, Congress in 1989 created the Resolution Trust Corporation (RTC), which was charged with selling or liquidating insolvent or mismanaged savings and loan associations. The RTC typically sends a team of 20 to 100 auditors unannounced to the thrift in question on a Friday, which works with the S&L's staff over the weekend to determine the level of its fiscal soundness, and completes its work by Monday. The S&L then is either reopened under new ownership, or liquidated, in which case its depositors receive federal insurance checks covering their lost deposits.

The following memorandum was written by the RTC's administrator of its East Region to his regional audit teams. It unwittingly captures the macabre interrelationships among the maintenance of business etiquette, the unremitting pressure to manage an agency's image in the public sector, and the ethical collapse inherent in the S&L debacle.

"As representatives of the Resolution Trust Corporation we must be cognizant of the fact that we are under the watchful eye of the press, the public, the General Accounting Office, and other oversight agencies. Our actions and activities must be above reproach. In that regard there are a few things that I wish to remind you of or admonish you to consider as we move forward with resolution activity.

"First, over the closing weekend we allow you to dress in 'casual attire.' This is often referred to as `golf attire'—clothing that is comfortable, but not worn or ragged. Shorts are not deemed acceptable attire for thrift-closing activities. Of course, in the event we reopen the thrift on Saturday morning, business attire is required. Think about what you are going to wear and whether it would look appropriate on television.

"Many of you have recently acquired RTC T-shirts with the slogan WANNA BUY AN S&L? on the front and 141 OR BUST on the back. [The RTC recently had established as a goal the resolutions of 141 S&Ls by the end of the month.] Obviously, there is a time and a place to wear these shirts. The closing, with the stress that the thrift's employees are under, is not the time or the place.

"Second, we must treat the employees of the thrift with courtesy and respect. The staff remaining after the association has been placed in conservatorship are not at fault for its problems. They have been under a tremendous amount of pressure and now have the added burden of concern about their future employment.

"Although it is certainly not a widespread problem, I have heard of a few instances when members of our closing team were rude or disrespectful to association employees. This behavior will not be tolerated. Closing managers are instructed to respond to such behavior by sending the employee home immediately and providing a memorandum to this writer stating that the individual should not be considered for future closing activity.

"Third, the confidentiality of this transaction prior to the closing hour must be stressed. The resolution date is not disclosed to the public prior to the press release issued at the closing hour. Keep this in mind at all times. Further, hotel reservation for closing activity should not be made in the name of the Federal Deposit Insurance Corporation or the RTC, and you should not register with the corporate Diners Club card until after the closing has occurred.

"Fourth, those of you who have attended closings prior to the creation of the RTC probably remember the days of pizza on closing night. Those days are gone.

Due to the focus on our activities by the media, it would not be appropriate to read in the paper how we ate pizza on the taxpayers' money.

"Closing activity is not one great big party. Certainly some of the cities where you may be sent are great places to visit. While you are there you will want to have a little fun. However, remember that we are in the spotlight, and do not embarrass the corporation.

"Finally, think about our image when you rent a car for corporation business. It is not how much you actually pay for the rental car that is most important but how it looks. The public may not understand that a Lincoln Continental is the same price as a Pontiac Sunbird. Therefore, stick with a reasonable-size vehicle.

"This memorandum is not all-inclusive as to issues of a sensitive nature that we must consider in the closing routine. However, I trust that it will cause you to consider the ramifications of your actions. We are constantly in the fishbowl and must act accordingly."

Craig A. Francis, Jr., Administrator, East Region, Resolution Trust Corporation, June 18, 1990

Sources: *For the information contained in the explanation introducing the memorandum, the sources are Janet L. Fix, "Mind-Boggling Bill for S&Ls,"* Philadelphia Inquirer *(September 9, 1990) and Michael Gartner, "Biggest Robbery in History—You're the Victim,"* Wall Street Journal *(August 9, 1990).*

---

reflect more positively on the values and perceived behavior of public employees." [36] Still, public administrators nonetheless are relatively remorseless in their hostility to the ethical failures of government. Not only do public administrators appear to register more outrage than the average citizen over government scandals, but their despondency over these scandals is deepening over time.

For example, more than 90 percent of the public administrators believed that the corruption involved in overcharging the Pentagon by private contractors in 1988 was "a scandal just waiting to happen," compared to 82 percent of the general public.[37] Over three-quarters of the public administrators dismiss the notion that the administration of Ronald Reagan "did a good job in enforcing ethical standards," compared to only 43 percent of the citizenry who reject this statement.

And public administrators are becoming increasingly depressed and alienated over public corruption. In 1977, a poll of federal administrators in the United States found that over 60 percent of the respondents disagreed with the view that "governmental practices today suffer from a 'moral numbness' following a decade of strife ...",[38] while only 28 percent of public administrators in 1990 disagreed with the statement that "society suffers a 'moral numbness' following a decade of scandals. . . ."[39] Although the surveys differ slightly, the trend of professional opinion seems clear. Buttressing the conclusion that public administrators are concerned about public ethics, one survey of local employees in Florida found that about three out of ten respondents reported that they had "observed one or more acts of unethical behavior" in their governments over the past twelve months.[40]

In sum, public administrators in the United States seem to believe that ethics in government is extraordinarily important; that they are under pressures to engage in unethical behavior; and that, compared to business, government still is the more ethical institution. Public administrators appear to be more critical of ethical lapses in government than are the taxpayers themselves, and they may be, with time, becoming even more irate over those lapses.

These perspectives among public administrators are encouraging ethical auguries.

CONCLUSION: POLITICS AIN'T BEANBAG AND MANAGEMENT AIN'T FOOD STAMPS

It is fitting to close this book on what the public administrator should and should not do as a moral, amoral, or immoral actor in the public bureaucracy. One can learn the techniques of management science, the notions of organization theory, and the intricacies of policy formulation and implementation, but ultimately public administration is a field of thought and practice in which personal ethical choices are made. Those who enter the field, either as thinkers or practitioners (and, one hopes, some of both), are, not infrequently, required to make decisions about moral questions that have far-reaching social consequences. Public administration is a profession of large responsibilities, and moral choices and ethical obligations will always be an integral part of those responsibilities.

We observed in Chapter 2 that the academic field of public administration combined both political science and management, and thus is not only larger than either but different from both. What holds for the study of public administration holds equally for its practice.

Practicing politicians, in explaining their craft, state simply that "politics ain't beanbag." Like most *clichés*, the phrase when new was insightful, witty, and accurate, and it remains so. "Politics ain't beanbag" summarizes professional politics: individuals competing ruthlessly against other individuals for power in an arena in which few if any rules apply—a refined variant of the Hobbesian state of nature.

To this verity of political life we might add one that describes the practice of management: "Management ain't food stamps." Managers, in other words, are charged with advancing organizations and policies, but they are not charged with advancing (or even maintaining) the welfare of individuals. Of course, it is often true that when certain kinds of organizations and policies progress, so do the fortunes and welfare of those individuals associated with them or affected by them, and one can argue (persuasively) that society created organizations and policies to benefit itself and the people comprising it. But these happy occurrences are incidental to the fundamental duty of managers. The prime directive of management is to look after the system.

Because public administration combines the professions of both politics and management, we have in some ways the worst of both worlds: individual political and managerial actors competing against others to advance their own ends and the ends of their own systems and clienteles. The profession of public administration thus becomes both unusually brutal ("politics ain't beanbag") and unusually insensitive to the welfare of the individual members of the public organization ("management ain't food stamps").

This condition can elide easily into a potentially nasty administrative structure. It is a condition unique to the practice of public administration, and public administrators should always be keenly aware that, as a consequence, their profession offers an unusually rich variety of opportunities to make moral or immoral decisions, to make ethical or unethical choices, to do good or evil things to people.

As one who both practices and thinks about public administration, this writer asks that, if you enter the field, you remember when making your choices to ask yourself how people will be helped or hurt by your decisions. Few questions are more important in any context, but in the context of the public life of the nation, none is more important.

Public administration is neither beanbag nor food stamps.

NOTES

1. Herbert A. Simon, *Administrative Behavior: A Study of Decision-Making Processes in Administration Organization* (New York: Free Press, 1947).
2. Harold Lasswell, *Psychopathology and Politics* (New York: Viking, 1930).
3. Chester I. Barnard, *The Functions of the Executive* (Cambridge, Mass.: Harvard University Press, 1938).
4. Paul H. Appleby, *Morality and Administration in Democratic Government* (Baton Rouge: Louisiana State University Press, 1952).
5. Norton Long, *The Polity* (Chicago: Rand McNally, 1962).
6. Joseph P. Harris, *Congressional Control of Administration* (Washington, D.C.: Brookings Institution, 1964).
7. Gordon Tullock, *The Politics of Bureaucracy* (Washington, D.C.: Public Affairs Press, 1965).
8. Dwaine Marvick, *Career Perspectives in a Bureaucratic Setting* (Ann Arbor: University of Michigan Press, 1954).
9. Ferrel Heady, *Public Administration: A Comparative Perspective* (Englewood Cliffs, N.J.: Prentice Hall, 1966), p. 45.
10. Herbert Marcuse, *One Dimensional Man: Studies in the Ideology of Advanced Industrial Society* (Boston: Beacon Press, 1964).
11. Jacques Ellul, *The Technological Society* (New York: Knopf, 1964).
12. Theodore J. Roszak, *The Making of a Counter Culture* (New York: Doubleday, 1969), pp. 142-144.
13. Charles A. Reich, *The Greening of America: How the Youth Revolution is Trying to Make America Livable* (New York: Random House, 1970).
14. The following works are germane to this paragraph: Carl J. Friedrich and Taylor Cole, *Responsible Bureaucracy* (Cambridge, Mass.: Harvard University Press, 1932); Long, *The Polity*; Charles S. Hyneman, *Bureaucracy* (New York: Harper & Row, 1950); Herbert Finer, "Administrative Responsibility in a Democratic Government," *Public Administration*

Review, 1 (Summer 1941), pp. 335-350; J. D. Lewis, "Democratic Planning in Agriculture," *American Political Science Review*, 35 (April and June 1941), pp. 232-249, 454-469; L. Von Mises, *Bureaucracy* (New Haven, Conn.: Yale University Press, 1944); Henry J. Abraham, "A People's Watchdog Against Abuse of Power," *Public Administration Review*, 20 (Summer 1960), pp. 152-157; Dwight Waldo, "Development of a Theory of Democratic Administration," *American Political Science Review*, 46 (March 1952), pp. 81-103; John M. Pfiffner and Robert Presthus, *Public Administration*, 5th ed. (New York: Ronald Press, 1967); Gordon Tullock, *The Politics of Bureaucracy* (Washington, D.C.: Public Affairs Press, 1965); Harold L. Wilensky, *Organizational Intelligence: Knowledge and Policy in Government and Industry* (New York: Basic Books, 1967); K. C. Davis, *Administrative Law* (St. Paul, Minn.: West Publishing, 1951).

15. Robert B. Denhardt, *Theories of Public Organization* (Monterey, Calif.: Brooks/Cole, 1984), p. 92.

16. Barnard, *The Functions of the Executive*, p. 120; Fritz Roethlisberger and William Dickson, *Management and the Worker* (Cambridge, Mass.: Harvard University Press, 1940), p. 562; Douglas McGregor, *The Human Side of Enterprise* (New York: McGraw-Hill, 1960), pp. 47-48; and Robert Blake and Jane Mouton, *The Academic Administrator Grid* (San Francisco: Jossey-Bass, 1981), p. 128.

17. Chris Argyris, *Personality and Organization* (New York: Harper & Row, 1957); but see also Argyris's *Interpersonal Confidence and Organizational Effectiveness* (Homewood, Ill.: Dorsey Press, 1962).

18. Denhardt, *Theories of Public Organization*, p. 99.

19. *Ibid.*, pp. 99, 101.

20. Robert T. Golembiewski, *Men, Management, and Morality* (New York: McGraw-Hill, 1967), p. 53.

21. Denhardt, *Theories of Public Organization*, p. 108.

22. Among the contributors who are associated with the new public administration and who emphasize bureaucratic ethics are: Larry Kirkhart, "Toward a Theory of Public Administration," in *Toward a New Public Administration: The Minnowbrook Perspective*, Frank Marini, ed. (San Francisco: Chandler, 1971), pp. 127-163; Todd LaPorte, "The Recovery of Relevance in the Study of Public Organization," in *ibid.*, pp. 17-47; Dwight Waldo, ed. *Public Administration in a Time of Turbulence* (San Francisco: Chandler, 1971); Frederick E. Thayer, *An End to Hierarchy! An End to Competition!* (New York: New Viewpoints, 1973); and David K. Hart, "Social Equity, Justice, and the Equitable Administrator," *Public Administration Review*, 34 (January/February 1974), pp. 3-10.

23. Eugene P. Dvorin and Robert H. Simmons, *From Amoral to Humane Bureaucracy* (San Francisco: Canfield Press, 1972), pp. 60-61. For an update, see: Omar Aktouf, "Management and Theories of Organizations in the 1990s: Toward a Critical Radical Humanism?" *Academy of Management Review*, 17 (July 1992), pp. 407-431.

24. John Rawls, *A Theory of Justice* (Cambridge, Mass.:

25. *Ibid.*, pp. 14-15.

26. Marshall Sashkin and Richard L. Williams, "Does Fairness Make a Difference?" *Organizational Dynamics* (Autumn 1990), pp. 56-71.

27. See, for example: Brian Barry, *Political Argument* (London: Routledge and Kegan Paul, 1965); Nicholas Rescher, *Distributive Justice* (New York: Bobbs-Merrill, 1966); and W. D. Ross, *The Right and the Good* (Oxford: Clarendon Press, 1930).

28. Friedrich Nietzsche, as quoted in J. R. Hollingsdale, *Nietzsche: The Man and His Philosophy* (Baton Rouge: Louisiana State University Press, 1965), p. 127.

29. See, for example: Jeremy Bentham, *An Introduction to the Principles of Morals and Legislation*, J. H. Burns and H. L. A. Hart, eds. (London: Athlone, 1970); Adam Smith, *The Wealth of Nations*, Edwin Cannan, ed. (New York: Modern Library, 1937); David Hume, *Theory of Politics*, Frederick Watkins, ed. (Edinburgh: Nelson, 1951); and John Stuart Mill, *Essays on Politics and Culture*, Gertrude Himmelfarb, ed. (New York: Doubleday, 1962).

30. Laura Mumford, "Policy Analysis and the U.S. Army Corps of Engineer," paper submitted to a graduate course in public administration, December 11, 1984, School of Public Affairs, College of Public Programs, Arizona State University, Tempe, Arizona, Nicholas Henry, instructor.

31. James S. Bowman, "Ethics in Government: A National Survey of Public Administrators," *Public Administration Review*, 50 (May/June 1990), p. 346. Bowman contacted 750 randomly selected members of the American Society for Public Administration, and obtained responses from 441, or a response rate of 59 percent.

32. Sashkin and Williams, "Does Fairness Make a Difference?" pp. 66-67.

33. Bowman, "Ethics in Government," p. 347.

34. Donald C. Menzel, "Ethics, Attitudes, and Behaviors in Local Governments: An Empirical Analysis," *State and Local Government Review*, 24 (Spring 1992), p. 101.

35. Bowman, "Ethics in Government," p. 346.

36. J. Norman Baldwin, "Public Versus Private Employees: Debunking Stereotypes," *Review of Public Personnel Administration*, 11 (Fall 1990-Spring 1991), p. 16.

37. The material in this paragraph is drawn from: Associated Press, "Poll: Americans Believe Bribery Rampant," *Tallahassee Democrat* (October 4, 1988).

38. James S. Bowman, "Ethics in the Federal Service: A Post-Watergate View," *Midwest Review of Public Administration*, 11 (March 1977), pp. 7-8.

39. Bowman, "Ethics in Government," p. 346.

40. Menzel, "Ethics Attitudes and Behaviors in Local Governments," p.100. The survey covered 730 employees of a city and county in Florida (the response rate was 62 percent), and was conducted in 1990.

Belknap Press of Harvard University Press, 1971), p. 60.

APPENDIX A

ANNOTATED INFORMATION SOURCES IN PUBLIC ADMINISTRATION AND RELATED FIELDS

This appendix annotates major bibliographies, guides, dictionaries, directories, and encyclopedias in public administration and related fields, including political science, management, American government, law, statistics, and the social sciences. Entries are listed under their organizing category alphabetically by title. Numbers appearing in the right-hand margin are the entries' Library of Congress call numbers, and should facilitate your locating the work. The appendix is organized as follows:

Contents of Appendix A

I. Public Administration
   A. General Works
   B. Public Budgeting and Finance
   C. Public Human Resource Management
   D. Community Planning
   E. Education, Internships, and Jobs
II. Related Topics: Political Science, Management, Law, and Statistics
   A. Political Science and Public Policy
   B. Management and Business Administration
   C. Law and Justice
   D. General Statistical and Data Sources
III. American Government: Federal, State, and Local
   A. Federal Government
   B. State Government
   C. Local Government and Urban Affairs
IV. Miscellaneous Useful Materials

Browsing through library shelves often can produce the richest lodes of knowledge. The following list provides Library of Congress call numbers that are among the most useful to students of public administration:

Call Numbers Most Specific to Public Administration

- HD 216-244 (public land)
- HD 3611-4730 (state and industry, public works)
- HD 8000-8030 (state labor)
- HJ (public finance)
- HT 1-399 (cities and towns, planning)
- JF (constitution and administration)
- JK (U.S., constitution and government)

- JL (British and Latin America, constitution and government)
- JN (Europe, constitution and government)
- JQ (Asia, Africa, Australia, Oceania, constitution and government)
- JS (local government)

I. PUBLIC ADMINISTRATION

This portion of Appendix A deals with information resources that focus directly on public administration and its subfields, public budgeting and finance, public personnel administration and human resource management, and community planning. A final section lists sources dealing with educational programs, internships, and jobs in public administration.

Contents of Section I

A. General Works
B. Public Budgeting and Finance
C. Public Human Resource Management
D. Community Planning
E. Education, Internships, and Jobs

A. General Works

A Centennial History of the American Administrative State. Ralph Clark Chandler, ed. New York: Free Press, 1987. A commemoration of Woodrow Wilson's seminal essay on public administration of 1887, the book's seventeen original chapters use that essay as a "pivot point" from which both the past and future of the practice and theory of public administration are addressed. A very useful work in that it provides a concise thorough understanding of the field's historical development and its evolution of defining ideas. `JK 411 .C46`

Basic Documents of American Public Administration 1776–1950. Frederick C. Mosher. New York: Holmes and Meier, 1976. Just as the title states, the book covers the basic early American documents of public administration. An excellent compendium. `JK 411 .B3`

Basic Documents of American Public Administration Since 1950. Richard J. Stillman II. New York: Holmes and Meier, 1982. Editor's introductions place each topic and document into perspective. The 1976 edition organizes documents under "The Foundations, The Management Movement, Depression and New Deal, and the Post War Period." The book reveals postwar reforms in organization, personnel, budgeting, and accountability. `JK 411 .B32 1982`

Directory of Organizations and Individuals Professionally Engaged in Governmental Research. Austin, Tex.: Governmental Research Association, 1981. Notes national, state and local agencies concerned with the improvement of governmental organizations, administration, and efficiency. Indexed by name of organizations and individuals. `JK 3 .G627`

Documentation in Public Administration. New Delhi: Indian Institute of Public Administration, 1973–. (Previous title *Public Administration Abstracts and Index of articles, 1957–1972*.) Indexes articles from a few selected journals relating to public administration. Issued monthly without cumulations. The coverage is limited, but still useful for long abstracts of major articles and some emphasis on administration in developing areas. `Z 7164 .82D6`

Guide to Library Research in Public Administration. Antony Simpson. New York: Center for Productive Public Management. John Jay College of Criminal Justice, 1976. Excellent, comprehensive guide to the literature. Opens with an overview of the field of public administration, discusses research, and then details resources. `JF 1411 .S5`

Guide to Public Administration. D. A. Cutchin. Itasca, Ill.: Peacock, 1981. An excellent review of the field, Cutchin's *Guide* covers concepts, theories, and facts and lists them alphabetically; provides annotated bibliographies of research sources and journals; and furnishes organization charts of agencies in the federal executive branch. `JA 61 .C87`

Handbook of Information Sources and Research Strategies in Public Administration. Mary G. Rock. San Diego, Calif.: Institute of Public and Urban Affairs, San Diego State University, 1979. A guidebook to the major research sources and retrieval tools for public administration and public affairs information. Includes evaluation of basic texts and readers. Beginning researchers and practitioners will profit from its perusal. `JF 1351 .R63`

Handbook of Public Administration. James L. Perry, ed. San Francisco: Jossey-Bass, 1989. A remarkably solid compendium, published in cooperation with the American Society for Public Administration, that covers the waterfront of the field and more. Forty-nine original chapters written by some of the leaders of the profession are "designed to meet the needs of the range of the professionals who work in government or who interact with public agencies." `JF 1351 .H276`

Public Administration: A Bibliographic Guide to the Literature. Howard E. McCurdy. New York: Marcel Dekker, Inc., 1986. Some 1,200 books and articles are listed and annotated in thirty-three categories, focusing on the 181 most frequently cited books in the field. Essays on the evolution of public administration as both a scholarly field and a profession are included. The book is an update of the 1973 edition. `JF 1351 .M23`

Public Administration Dictionary. Ralph Chandler and Jack C. Plano. New York: John Wiley, `JA 61`

1982. Terms are alphabetized within seven chapter headings, but the index gives a term's location. In addition to a definitional interpretation the authors include a section explaining the "significance" of the term. .C47

Public Administration in American Society: A Guide to Information Sources. John E. Rouse, Jr. Detroit, Mich.: Gale Research, 1980. The 1,700 annotated entries cover the literature of public administration, "a professional discipline with no fixed principles, ideology or methodology." Author, title and subject index. Appendices describe the American Society for Public Administration and National Association of Schools of Public Affairs and Administration. JK 421 .R63

Public Administration Series: Bibliography. Monticello, IL: Vance Bibliographies, 1978–. Bibliographies vary in length and quality. Cover a wide range of topics related to public affairs, local to international. Treatment may be empirical, theoretical, or practical. JT 1351 .A1 B38

Public Administration: The State of the Discipline. Naomi B. Lynn and Aaron Wildavsky, eds. Chatham, N.J.: Chatham House, 1990. Jointly sponsored by the American Society for Public Administration and the American Political Science Association, this collection of twenty original chapters covers the academic side of public administration's house. Among the topics covered are organization theory and behavior, comparative public administration, intergovernmental administration, budgeting, human resource management, public policy, methodology, and implementation. A welcome addition to the literature. JF 1351 .P8185

Public Affairs Service Bulletin. New York: Public Affairs Service, 1915–. This index, with annual cumulations, unifies a wide variety of sources concerned with public affairs. It lists books, pamphlets, periodicals, and government documents. Most articles include brief explanatory items. Z 7163 .P9761B

Public Policy: A Yearbook of the Graduate School of Public Administration, Harvard University. Cambridge, Mass.: Harvard University Press, 1940–. Each volume contains several essays on various subjects, emphasizing public administration. JA 51 .P8

Recent Publications on Government Problems. Chicago: Merriam Center Library, 1932–. Semimonthly. Lists and briefly annotates new acquisitions received by the pioneer Merriam Center Library, a resource center jointly sponsored by such public administration organizations as American Planning Association, American Public Works Association, Public Administration Service and Council of Planning Libraries. Entries are arranged by subject. Good current awareness tool with an emphasis on local and regional issues. Selective indexing of journal articles. Annual cumulation by subject. Z 1223 .Z7C4

Sage Public Administration Abstracts. Beverly Hills, Calif.: Sage, 1974–. A quarterly publication that lists and abstracts more than 1,000 publications in the field annually. Abstracts are indexed by author, title, and subject, and a year-end cumulative index is published. JA 1 .S27

Subject Catalog of the Institute of Governmental Studies Library. University of California, Berkeley. Boston, Mass.: G.K. Hall and Co., 1970; *First Supplement*, 1978. Listing this as just a bibliography is misleading, for it is, in fact, a reproduction in book format of the subject card catalog of an extremely valuable, in-depth public administration collection dating back to 1918. Specialized subject headings, developed at Berkeley and used in the Catalog, are compiled in Volume 1. Consult the list for terms to search. Pamphlets, articles in periodicals and government documents comprise the bulk of the entries. Z 7166 .C3

B. Public Budgeting and Finance

Budget in Brief, U.S. Washington, D.C.: Executive Office of the President, Office of Management and Budget. Abridged explanation of the budget. Describes federal budget plans in all major policy areas. PR Ex 2.8/2

Budget of the U.S. Government. Washington, D.C.: Executive Office of the President, Office of Management and Budget. Presentation of the president's budget proposals and how they were formulated. Includes president's budget message and general assumptions about the economy; analysis of the U.S. budget system; budget breakdowns by function (national defense, education, health, etc.). Lists the amount each agency receives. PR Ex 2.8

Budget of the U.S. Government, Appendix. Washington, D.C.: Executive Office of the President, Office of Management and Budget. Most precise and detailed of all budget documents. Contains the specific language of every proposal for each agency, as well as the functions the agency performs. Also lists permanent positions in each agency by number and federal grade level. PR Ex 2.8: Appendix

Budget of the U.S. Government, Special Analysis. Washington, D.C.: Executive Office of the President, Office of Management and Budget. Analyses of specific programs financed from the budget. Gives financial information on employment, health, income security, civil rights, crime reduction programs, research and development, environmental protection, and other aspects of the economy. PR Ex 2.8/3

Budget Revisions (by fiscal year). Washington, D.C.: Executive Office of the President, Office of Management and Budget. Summary of the administration's revisions to the budget. PR Ex 2.8/7

Catalog and Quick Index to Taxpayer Information Publications. Washington, D.C.: U.S. Department of the Treasury, Internal Revenue Service. Provides a reference to taxpayer information publications. Part I gives a list of taxpayer information publications; Part 2 provides an index to the T 22 .44/3 subjects discussed in each document; and Part 3 is a list of forms and schedules and the documents in which they are illustrated.

Economic Report of the President. Washington, D.C.: U.S. Government Printing Office. Annual. President's report for the past fiscal year. Review of personal consumption, business fixed investment, housing, exports, wages, corporate profitability, monetary policy, energy, and agricultural developments. Also gives information on world economy. — PR 33 .10

Facts and Figures on Government Finance. Washington, D.C.: Tax Foundation. 1941–. Biennial. Information about taxes, expenditures, and debt at federal, state, and local levels. Statistics also cover selected national economic series, social insurance programs, and government enterprise operations. Glossary and Index. — HJ 257 .T25

Terms Used in the Budgetary Process. Washington, D.C.: U.S. General Accounting Office, 1977. Glossary divided into three sections: a compilation of general terms; terms applicable to zero-based budgeting; and economic terms used in connection with the budget. Arranged alphabetically within each section. — GA 1.2 B85/2

C. Public Human Resource Management

Directory of National Unions and Employee Associations, 1979. Washington, D.C.: U.S. Department of Labor, 1980. Comprehensive listing of unions, including information on structure and membership. Indexed. — L 2.3 2079

Human Resources Abstracts. Beverly Hills, Calif.: Sage Publications, 1966–. Quarterly. (Previous title, *Poverty and Human Resources Abstracts.*) Information on human, social, and manpower problems and solutions as they relate to public policy is arranged by broad topic with author and subject indexes. Cumulative index for each year. Includes books, reports, periodicals, and government documents. — Z 7165 .U5P2 —— Z 7164 .C4P115

Human Resources Yearbook. Craig T. Norback, ed., Englewood Cliffs, N.J.: Prentice Hall. Annual. A yearly compendium of all aspects of personnel administration, both public and private. — HF 5549.2 .U5H85

Labor-Management Relations in the Public Sector: An Annotated Bibliography. N. Joseph Cayer and Sherry Dickerson. New York: Garland, 1983. Topical arrangement of scholarly articles, monographs and books published since 1962 and dealing with public sector relations. Appendices list journals publishing articles in this area and organizations. — HD 8005 .6.U5

Michigan Index to Labor Union Periodicals. Ann Arbor, Mich.: Bureau of Industrial Relations, Graduate School of Business Administration, University of Michigan, 1960–. Covers about 50 publications and issued monthly with annual cumulations. — Z 7164 .T7U6

Paul Felix Warburg Union Catalog of Arbitration. A Selective Bibliography and Subject Index of Peaceful Dispute Settlement Procedures. Compiled and edited by Katharine Seide. Totawa, N.J.: Rowan and Littlefield, 1974. A joint listing of the arbitration materials in 19 libraries in the U.S., including the U.N. Dag Hammerskjold Library. Part three of V. II notes "International Public Arbitration," and V. III includes "Community Dispute Settlement Procedures." Volume I is an alphabetical listing of all documents; volumes II and III provide these entries by subject. — Z 7164 .L1S43

Personnel Bibliography Series. U.S. Office of Personnel Management Library. Washington, D.C.: U.S. Government Printing Office, 1970. A comprehensive annotated listing of books and articles on themes of relevance to public personnel administration. Each issue concerns a particular theme, such as "Scientists and Engineers in the Federal Government," or "Managing Human Behavior." Although the series began earlier, only titles beginning in 1970 are presently available. — PM 1 .22/2

Personnel Literature. U.S. Office of Personnel Management Library. Washington, D.C.: U.S. Government Printing Office, 1969–. A monthly annotated listing of a wide range of public personnel materials. — HF 5549 .A3 —— Z7164 .C81U4 5683

D. Community Planning

Geo Abstracts Regional and Community Planning. Norwich, England: Geo Abstracts Ltd., 1972–. Six issues per year. Subject arrangement of articles on planning theory and methodology as well as economic, environmental, and social planning. Annual cumulative index in last issue is arranged by region and by author. — HT 390 .G4

Housing and Planning References. Washington, D.C.: U.S. Department of Housing and Urban Development, 1962–. Six times a year. Good coverage of the subject, including both U.S. Government and nongovernment sources, periodicals, and monographs. Major disadvantage is that it does not cumulate, although each issue is arranged by subject. — HH 1 .23/3

International Handbook on Land Use Planning. Nicholas N. Patricios, ed., Westport, Conn.: Greenwood Press, 1986. The first comprehensive treatment of land use planning techniques used around the globe. — HD 108 .6I58

Land Use Planning Abstracts: A Select Guide to Land and Water Resources. New York: EIC Intelligence, 1974–. Annual. Abstracts key land use articles, conferences proceedings, governmental reports, and special studies. Covers power plant siting, strip mining, transportation controls, and Western water problems. Also includes annual review of events in these fields and a statistical section with maps and graphs. Subject, geography, and author index. — HD 171 .A1L35

E. Education, Internships, and Jobs

Complete Guide to Public Employment. Ronald S. Krannich and Caryl Rae Krannich. Manassas, VA: Impact Publications, 1986. Projects employment prospects in the public sector, explains effective job search skills, details how to approach government in exploring job opportunities, and has special sections on "third sector" and international job opportunities.
JU 716 .U68

Directory of Graduate Programs in Public Affairs and Administration. Washington, D.C.: National Association of Schools of Public Affairs and Administration, 1972–. Published biennially, the *Directory* is a rich information resource on graduate programs in public administration in the United States and Canada.
JF 1338 .A2N2 8a

Directory of Public Service Internships: Opportunities for the Graduate, Post-Graduate Graduate and Mid-Career Professional. Debra L. Mann, ed. Washington, D.C.: National Society for Internships and Experimental Education, 1981. Entries for programs throughout the United States include the name, address, phone numbers, contact person, administering agency, number of interns accepted, program objectives and design, eligibility, selection, and remuneration. Lists programs in federal, state and local government, public policy, and urban affairs.
JK 2480 .16N37 1981

Internships: 16,000 On-the-Job Training Opportunities for all Types of Careers. Cincinnati, Ohio: Writer's Digest Books, 1983. Views internship as experiential education and offers advice on applications. Subject breakdown includes Public Interest/Public Service Groups and Government/Public Administration.
L 901 .166 1983

The Student Guide to Fellowships and Internships. New York: E.P. Dutton, 1980. Written by students of Amherst College, this guide presents advice on applying for internships, including sample resumes. Each subject area opens with a general introduction followed by listing of specific programs, with "The Inside Word" giving inside advice.
LB 2338 .S843

II. RELATED TOPICS: POLITICAL SCIENCE, MANAGEMENT, LAW, AND STATISTICS

Political science and public policy, management and business administration, law and justice, and general statistical and data bases all are highly pertinent to an understanding of public administration. This section covers information sources in these areas. Some statistical and data sources are listed under other headings that are directly applicable to them.

Contents of Section II

A. Political Science and Public Policy
B. Management and Business Administration
C. Law and Justice
D. General Statistical and Data Sources

A. Political Science and Public Policy

ABC - POL SCI: A Bibliography of Contents: Political Science and Government. Santa Barbara, Calif.: American Bibliographical Center, Clio Press, 1969–. Five issues per year. Students may use this title to keep up with the latest articles in political science, government, and public policy. It reproduces the tables of contents from about 300 journals, with indexes for authors and subjects. Index cumulates.
Z 674.5 .A45B 45

Almanac of American Politics. Michael Baron. New York E.P. Dutton, 1979–. Annual. Provides political information by state on governors, senators, representatives; district information (population, voter profile, economic base, tax burden); and political group ratings of representatives and senators.
JK 271 .A45 Year

American Political Dictionary. 6th ed. Jack C. Plano and Milton Greenberg. New York: Holt, Rinehart and Winston, 1982. Unlike an A to Z dictionary, words are alphabetical under 14 chapter headings. Useful will be "Public Administration: Organization and Personnel" and "State and Local Government." In addition to definition, authors explain terms' significance.
JK 9 .P55 1982

American Politics Yearbook. Jarol B. Manheim. New York: Longmans, 1982–. Chapter 4 notes policy planning organizations and Part Three lists alphabetically "Policies and Issues" with citations to articles in the *New York Times*, departments, agencies, and interest groups involved, search terms for finding the subject in basic indexes and bibliographic references.
JK 1 .A49

Combined Retrospective Index to Journals in Political Science, 1866–1974. Arlington, Va.: Carrollton Press, 1978. Provides retrospective bibliographic access to many journals never previously covered. Supplies in one search citations which formerly would have required searching many different indexes, volume by volume. Entries in hierarchical subject arrangement under keywords. Chronological arrangement within categories. Author index in V. VII and VIII. Take time to locate pertinent categories using the listing at the front of the volume (*i.e.*, V. 3 "Public Administration"). Journal titles are entered by code numbers. Code list is at front and back of the volume.
Z 7161 .C18

Energy Abstracts for Policy Analysis. Oak Ridge, Tenn.: U.S. Department of Energy, Technical Information Center, 1975–. Monthly. *EAPA* abstracts and indexes nontechnical literature contributing to energy-related analysis and evaluation. Publications covered are government reports,
E 1 .11

regional and state government documents, books, conference proceedings, periodicals, and papers. Abstracts are arranged by broad subject area. Corporate author, personal author, subject, and report number indexes are cumulated annually.

Guide to Resources and Services. Ann Arbor, Mich.: Inter-University Consortium for Political and Social Research. Annual. Cooperative repository for survey, election, census, and roll call data. Information supplied to member units on magnetic tape or punch cards. Guide notes holdings in "Community and Urban Studies," "Governmental Structures, Policies and Capabilities," and "Legislative and Deliberative Bodies." [H 62 .A1158]

International Bibliography of the Social Sciences: Political Science. London: Tavistock Publications, 1952–. Annual. An extensive bibliography covering 5,000 books, journals, and national and international documents. One section is devoted to "Government and Public Administration." Published by the International Committee for Social Science Information and Documentation. Subject and author indexes. [Z 7164 .E2I58]

International Political Science Abstracts. Paris: International Science Association. 1951–. Bimonthly. Abstracts the leading U.S. and foreign scholarly journals, although not all articles in each journal are abstracted. Probably the best starting point for literature searches in the field of foreign and comparative government and political theory. Abstracts are in English for English language articles; foreign language publications abstracted in French. Index, cumulated annually, is in English by subject and by author. [JA 36 .15]

Lexicon of Historical and Political Terms. Robert R. Davis, Jr. Palo Alto, CA: R and E Research Associates, 1982. A brief guide intended to introduce the undergraduate to the terminology used by historians and political scientists. [JA 61 .D36 1982]

Perspective: Monthly Reviews of New Books on Government/Politics/International Affairs. Washington, D.C.: Perspective, 1972–. Eight times per year. Reviews in this publication are substantive and signed. The scope is international. Annual index for previous year appears in January/February of following year. [JA 1 .P47]

Policy Research Centers Directory. Urbana, Ill.: Policy Studies Organization, 1978. Essays about policy research centers precede survey information from both university and nonuniversity centers. Questionnaire responses note policies, clients, disciplines, funding and suggestions for researchers. Indexed by research subject. Companion volume is *Policy Studies Personnel Directory* (H 62.5 .U5P65x). [H 62.5 .U5P59]

Political and Social Science Journals: A Handbook for Writers and Reviewers. Santa Barbara, CA: ABC-Clio Press, 1983. Index of journal titles by subject creates useful list for researcher wanting to survey journals. While geared to the writ- [JA 74 .P62 1983]

ers' needs, the focus and institutional affiliation under journal entry proves especially useful.

Political Science Abstracts. (formerly *Universal Reference System*). New York: IFI Penum, 1966–. Annual supplements since 1967 update the base set of ten volumes. Volumes are organized around broad subjects, that is, V. IV covers "Administrative Management: Public and Private Bureaucracy;" V. IX, "Public Policy and the Management of Science." Valuable because entries include not only books, pamphlets, and periodical articles, but chapters of books as well. A challenge to use because of its complicated arrangement and indexing system, but extremely worthwhile. [Z 7161 .U643]

Statesman's Yearbook: Statistical and Historical Annual of the States of the World. New York: St. Martin's Press, 1864–. Annual. Published continuously for more than 120 years, the *Yearbook* covers international organizations and countries, A to Z. History; area and population; government and constitution; defense, international relations; economy; energy and natural resources; industry and trade; communications; justice, religion, education, and welfare; diplomatic representatives, and books of reference are narrated for each country. Great for comparative studies. [JA 51 .S7]

United States Political Science Documents. Pittsburgh, Pa.: NASA Industrial Applications Center, University of Pittsburgh, 1975–. Annual. Detailed abstracts and indexing from selected major American journals publishing scholarly articles in the broad area of political science. Coverage includes public administration, political and policy sciences. Published annually in two volumes, indexes are available for author/contributor, subject, geographical area, proper name, and journal. Journal index valuable for comparisons of annual output among journals in like fields. *Political Science Thesaurus II* (Z 695.1.P63B4 1979) serves as terminology control volume for *USPSD*. [Z 7163 .U58H 9]

World Encyclopedia of Political Systems and Parties. George E. Delury, ed. New York: Facts on File, 1983. An A to Z study of 169 sovereign nations and eight dependent territories. Each entry discusses the system of government, including executive, legislative, judicial, and local; the political parties and political forces and each nation's prospects for continuing or attaining political stability through the mid-1980s. For addresses, phone numbers and forms of addresses for country officials consult *Lambert's Worldwide Government Directory with Inter-Governmental Organizations.* (JF 37.L34 1983). [JF 2011 .D44 1983]

B. Management and Business Administration

Business Periodicals Index. New York: H.W. Wilson Co., 1958–. Monthly except August. Subject index to business periodicals. Includes a book [Z 7193 .A66] review index under author name. Quarterly and annual cumulations. Good for management, personnel, budget and finance. Easy to use with its A to Z entries.

Encyclopedia of Management. 3rd ed. Carl Heyel, ed., New York: Van Nostrand Reinhold, 1982. Theories noted in this volume transpose effectively into public sector administration. Definitions are followed by listings of associations, journals, cross references, and information sources. 203 authorities contributed to this 1371 page volume. Indexed. HD 30.15 .E49 1982

International Review of Administrative Science (Revue Internationale des Sciences Administratives). Brussels: Institut Internationale des Sciences Administratives, 1928–. Each quarterly issue has a "Bibliographical Section" which contains abstracts of recent books on administration, plus a list of periodical articles. JA 26 .I58

Management Contents. Northbrook, Ill.: Management Contents, 1975-. Biweekly. Tables of contents of over 350 business-management journals stressing decision making and forecasting. Z 7164 .07M2 834

Management Research. Amherst, Mass.: University of Massachusetts School of Business Administration, 1968-. Monthly. An annotated bibliography of considerable use, covering periodical articles dealing with administration, organization, social responsibilities, personnel policy, personnel testing and selection, motivation and performance, human behavior, human resources development, etc. Also contains a list of new books and editorial notes about periodical publications. HD 28 .M397

C. Law and Justice

Basic Documents in International Law. 3rd ed. Ian Brownlee, ed. New York: Oxford University Press, 1983. Emphasizes documents of significance in international relations. Includes charters of organizations, laws of the sea, outer space, diplomatic relations, natural resources, human rights and self determination, treaties, and judicial settlement of disputes. JX 68 .B78 1983

Black's Law Dictionary. 5th ed. Minneapolis, Minn.: West Publishing Company, 1979. The latest edition of this classic in the field reflects new legal concepts and doctrines while retaining old English, European, and federal terms. Pronunciation guides have been added, as have a U.S. government organizational chart, the U.S. Constitution, and a listing of U.S. Supreme Court Justices and terms. KF 156 .B53 1979

CIS/Annual: Abstracts of Congressional Publications and Legislative History Citations. Washington, D.C.: Congressional Information Service, 1970–. Monthly. In the Abstract volume, the section "Legislative History Citations" is arranged by Public Law number. Besides noting the KF 49 .C62

hearings and committee prints, the entry reveals references appearing in the *Weekly Compilation of Presidential Documents* (GS 4.114).

Code of Federal Regulations. Agency regulations which have the force of law are arranged by subject in separate volumes (titles), each with its own index. A multi-volume extensive index is available (KF 70.A3415x). GS 4 .108

Congressional Bills and Resolutions. The Government Printing Office now issues current bills on microfiche with a *Cumulative Finding Aid* (GP 3.28:Congress #) which indicates, by bill number, the microfiche and grid location where the bill may be found. Y 1.4 #

Congressional Hearings. Since 1970, Congressional hearings are available as part of the CIS Microfich Collection, accessed through the *CIS Index*. Paper copies of pre-1970 hearings are accessed through the *Monthly Catalog of U.S. Government Publications. CIS U.S. Congressional Committee Hearings Index* (KF 49.C6225x) is in publication and now available for the 79th through 91st Congresses. KF 40 .C56

Congressional Index. Chicago, Ill: Commerce Clearing House, 1953/54–. Looseleaf, updated service indexes legislation by subject, author, and bill number. Includes summaries, statutes, and voting records. J 69 .C6

Directory of Criminal Justice Information Sources. Thomas Ketterman. Washington, D.C.: U.S. Department of Justice, National Institute of Law Enforcement and Criminal Justice. Lists agencies that provide information on criminal justice, including telephone numbers, directors or head, and information on area of activity. J 26 .2In3

Federal Register. Agency regulations, proposed and adopted, first appear in the *Federal Register*, published daily Monday through Friday, with monthly, quarterly, and annual indexes. GS 4 .170 v/#

Finding the Law: A Workbook on Legal Research for Laypersons. Al Coco. Bureau of Land Management. Washington, D.C.: U.S. Government Printing Office, 1982. Prepared by the Law Librarian, who also teaches law librarianship at the University of Denver. Excellent workbook on federal law with illustrations, definitions, and resource citations. L 41 .153:2

Index to Legal Periodicals. New York: H.W. Wilson Co., 1908–. Monthly. Subject and author and book review indexes are accompanied by table of cases. Urban headings: public finance, documents and records, public officials and employees, etc. Annual cumulations. K .1213

Law and Legal Information Directory. Paul Wasserman and Marech Kaszubski, eds. Detroit, Mich.: Gale Research, 1980. Guides user to sources of information including organizations, associations, schools, libraries, research centers, periodicals, and publishers. KF 190 .L35

Legal Thesaurus. Burton, William C. New York: KF Macmillan, 1980. Establishes nuances among terms 156 and allows the writer a chance to vary word usage. .B856 The index refers users to entry under which index terms appear.

Major Legislation of the Congress. Washington, LC D.C. U.S. Government Printing Office, 1979–. 14 Monthly during sessions. Classified subject arrange- .18 ment. Discusses issues surrounding major legislation Con- under consideration. Summary issue published at gress # end of each Congress.

Shepard's Acts and Cases by Popular Name, KF *Federal and State*. Colorado Springs, Colo.: 80 Shepard's Inc., 1979–. Cases are listed alphabetical- .S5 ly by popular name. Covers cases to October 1979. 1979 Cites sources in which act can be found. Updates by pamphlets.

Shepard's Code of Federal Regulations KF *Citations*. Colorado Springs, Colo.: Shepard's 78 McGraw Hill, 1981. The first edition follows the for- .S54 mat of other Shepard's citations, noting citations to the other CFR (by title number); Presidential Proclamations and Executive Orders (by numbers); and Reorganization Plans (by years), then listing source of citation. Pamphlet updates.

Shepard's United States Citations, Statutes. 6th KF ed. Colorado Springs, Colo.: Shepard's Citations, 78 Inc., 1968. The statute edition of Supreme Court .S56 coverage involves tracing subsequent action on a specific law and judicial action construing that legis- lation. Helps determine the applicability of statutes and cases for use in specific situations. Supplement covers 1968–1974. Pamphlet updates.

Sourcebook of Criminal Justice Statistics. U.S. J Department of Justice, Bureau of Justice Statistics. 29.9 Washington, D.C.: U.S. Government Printing SD-SB Office, 1972–. Issued annually since 1972, the *Sourcebook* describes the criminal justice systems, traces public attitudes on crime, record crime rates, and analyzes arrestees, defendants, prisoners, and parolees.

Sources of Compiled Legislative Histories. KF Nancy P. Johnson. Littleton, Colo.: Rothman, 1979. 42 Guides student to sources for study of legislative his- .2 tory of specific public laws. Sources may be govern- 1979 ment documents, periodical articles or books. Covers first through 94th Congress; does not include all public laws enacted. Looseleaf format.

Statutes-at-Large of the United States of GS *America*. Published at the end of each session of 4 Congress since 1789, the volumes include public .111 laws, reorganization plans, private laws, congres- sional resolutions and proclamations. Often the sole source of text of private and temporary legislation not included in statutory compilations. Organized by date of enactment of law. Indexed.

Subject Compilation of State Laws: Research KF *Guide and Annotated Bibliography*. Lynn Foster and 1 Carol Boast. Westport, Conn.: Greenwood Press, .F67

1981. Facilitates comparative studies of state laws by subject areas. Includes indexes.

United States Code. These 16 basic volumes plus Y annual supplements arranged by subject laws that 1 are currently in effect. Table translates *Statutes-at-* .2/5 *Large* numbers to *U.S. Code* entries. 1976

United States Reports. Bound volumes are JU issued for each court term and include full text of all 6 decisions. Prior to issue of bound volume, opinions .8 appear in pamphlet form as they are released.

D. General Statistical and Data Sources

American Statistics Index. Washington, D.C.: Z Congressional Information Service, 1974–. 7554 Monthly. Guide and index to the statistical publica- .U5A46 tions of the U.S. Government. The index is by sub- —— ject, geographic area, and category (*i.e.*, statistics by Z race, sex, and geographic area). Publications in the 7554 abstract sections are analyzed in detail with refer- .U5A51 ences to page and table numbers. This is a major and 2 unique index in the field of statistics and one that should be consulted. Will prove useful in subject searches, since narrative publications which contain statistics are included. Annual and five year cumula- tions.

Bureau of the Census Catalog. Washington, C D.C.: U.S. Bureau of the Census. Annual. Guides 3 user to the wealth of publications resulting from cen- .163/3 sus activities. Data covers population, housing, gov- Year ernments, transportation, etc. Includes data products produced by the reformatting of census statistics.

Regional Statistics: A Guide to Information HA *Sources*. M. Balanchandrian. Detroit, MI: Gale 217 Research, 1980. Identifies by subject the sources of .B34 socio-economic data for small areas. Includes publi- —— cations of federal, state, chamber of commerce, and Z7554 utility company offices. .U5D34

Social Indicators III: Selected Data on Social C *Conditions and Trends in the United States*. 3 Washington, D.C.: U.S. Office of Management and .2: Budget, 1980. Sections on public safety, health, So 1/2 housing, leisure, etc., depict data on graphs and 1979 tables. An attempt to address quality of life on a national level.

Statistical Abstract of the United States. U.S. HA Bureau of the Census. Washington, D.C.: U.S. 202 Government Printing Office. Annual. Statistical .A388 compilations from federal agencies are presented. —— Notation of information source leads researchers to C 3 additional information. The best single source for .134 national data on every topic.

Statistical Reference Index. Washington, D.C.: HA Congressional Information Service, 1980–. 214 Monthly. Companion to *ASI*, this resource indexes .S8 statistics published by sources other than the federal —— government, such as publications from trade, profes- Z sional, and nonprofit associations and institutions; 7554 business organizations; commercial publishers; independent research centers; state government agencies, and university research centers. *SRI* covers business, industry, finance, economic and social conditions, government, and politics, the environment, and population. Includes data on foreign countries. Issued in index and abstracts sections. Indexes are cumulated annually. Indexing is by subject and names, categories, (geographic, economic, and demographic), issuing sources and titles. .U557

Statistics Sources, A Subject Guide to Data on Industrial, Business, Social, Educational, Financial, and Other Topics for the United States and Internationally. 9th ed. Detroit, Mich.: Gale Research, 1984. Alphabetical subject approach for U.S.; information for other countries is under country name and subtopics. Entries appear under headings such as cities, SMSAs, and government. HA 36 .S84 1984 —— Z 7551 .S84 1984

World Handbook of Political and Social Indicators. 3rd ed., Charles Lewis Taylor and Davis A. Jodice. New Haven, Conn.: Yale University Press, 1983. 2 v. The authors quantitatively assess nation-states for "Cross National Attributes and Rates of Change" (V. 1), and "Political Protest and Government Change" (V. 2). Useful data for the comparative researcher. HN 25 .T39 1983

III. AMERICAN GOVERNMENT: FEDERAL, STATE, AND LOCAL

Section III covers information sources for the federal government, state governments, and local governments, including urban affairs. Federal budget resources are covered under Section I, A of this Appendix.

Contents of Section III

A. Federal Government
B. State Government
C. Local Governments and Urban Affairs

A. Federal Government

Catalog of Federal Domestic Assistance. Washington, D.C.: Executive Office of the President, Office of Management and Budget, 1980. Compendium of federal programs that provide financial assistance to state and local governments, for-profit and nonprofit organizations, and individuals. Lists eligibility requirements, amount of money available, application procedures, and related programs. PR Ex2 .20

CIS/Annual: Index to Congressional Publications and Public Laws. Washington, D.C.: K 49

Congressional Information Service, 1970–. Monthly. Indexes by subject, personal name, and agency, all Congressional publications, that is, House and Senate reports, documents, hearings, and committee prints. Abstract section actually analyzes the *contents* of the documents, giving page numbers for pertinent sections. May be used to some extent as an index to the documents themselves. Annual cumulative index and abstract volumes. .C62

Congressional Directory. Washington, D.C.: U.S. Government Printing Office. Gives brief biographies of each member of Congress, terms of service, committee assignments. Includes statistical tables on sessions of Congress and election results of recent Congressional elections. Y 4 .P93/1

Congressional Quarterly Weekly Report. Washington, D.C.: Congressional Quarterly, Inc., 1971–. Current awareness tool provides narrative background for intent of legislation. Summaries of bills and voting records. *Congressional Quarterly Almanac* (JK 8.C66) cumulates same information on an annual basis. Includes special reports and presidential messages. JK 1 .C15

Congressional Record. Washington, D.C.: U.S. Government Printing Office. Daily during sessions. The fortnightly index that accompanies the daily record of congressional debates; includes an Index to Proceedings and a History of Bills and Resolutions. Access is by subject, sponsor and bill number. The final bound issue published at the end of a session includes a comprehensive status table for bills enacted into law. X/ Congress/ Session

Congressional Staff Directory. Charles B. Brownson. Washington, D.C.: Congressional Staff Directory, Ltd., 1990. Contains information concerning Congress, with emphasis on the staffs of legislators and members of the committees and subcommittees. JK 1012 .C74

Directory of Federal Regional Structure. Washington, D.C.: National Archives of the United States, 1980. Provides a map showing the Standard Federal Regions and lists the key officials, addresses, and telephone numbers of the agencies. GS 4 .119 Year

Encyclopedia of Governmental Advisory Organizations. 5th ed., Linda E. Sullivan and Anthony T. Kruzas, eds. Detroit, Mich.: Gale Research Company, 1985. Guide to public advisory committees, boards, panels, task forces, commissions, conferences, etc. Grouped by subject, with subject and key word index. Each entry has information on history of the committee, membership, program, publications, and reports. JK 901 .E5

Federal Information Sources and Systems. A Directory Issued by the Comptroller General. Washington, D.C.: General Accounting Office, 1981. Directory of executive agencies with sources of fiscal, budgetary and program-related data and information. GA 1 .22 IN 3/980

Federal-State-Local Government Directory. JK

Bonnie A. Stern, ed. Washington, D.C.: Braddock Publications, Inc., 1977. Federal government offices with names and telephone numbers, and their state and local offices. Arranged by state. 6 .B73

Federal Yellow Book. Teri Calabrese, ed. Washington, D.C.: Washington Monitor, Inc. Annual. Loose-leaf directory of federal departments and agencies; names, titles, room and telephone numbers of 25,000 principal federal employees. Updated throughout the year. JK 6 .F440

Government Periodicals and Subscription Service. Washington, D.C.: U.S. Government Printing Office. Alphabetical listing of government periodicals with prices. GP 3.9 36

Government Reports, Announcements and Index. Washington, D.C.: U.S. Department of Commerce, National Technical Information Service, 1964–. Biweekly. Indexes and abstracts government-sponsored research and development reports and other government analyses prepared by federal agencies, their contractors or grantees. Indexes are by key word, personal author, corporate author, contract/grant number, NTIS Order/report number. C 51 .9/3

Guide to U.S. Government Directories, 1970–1980. Donna Rae Larson. Phoenix, Ariz.: Oryx Press, 1981. A subject-indexed list of directories published by or for a government agency. J 83 .L37 —— Z 1223 .A12L 37 1981

Guide to U.S. Government Directories, 1980–1984. Donna Rae Larson. Phoenix, Ariz.: Oryx Press, 1984. A subject-indexed list of directories published by or for a government agency. J 83 .L37 —— Z 1223 .A12L 37 1984

Historic Documents of (YEAR). Washington, D.C.: Congressional Quarterly, 1972–. Full text or pertinent excerpts of documents are preceded by background information and, on occasion, relevant subsequent developments. Chronological by month, entries highlight development of policy from issues. E 839.5 .H57

Index to U.S. Government Periodicals. Chicago, Ill.: Infordata International, Inc., 1970–. Quarterly. Indexes substantive articles of lasting research and reference value that have appeared in the major periodicals published by the U.S. Government. Annual cumulations. Z 1223 .Z9I5

Monthly Catalog of United States Government Publications. Washington, D.C.: U.S. Government Printing Office, 1895–. Monthly. Principal index for government documents. Lists all U.S. Government Printing Office publications by issuing agency, with monthly, cumulative semiannual and annual indexes. Multiple access points are available for recent years; authors; title; subject (Library of Congress subject headings); series/reports; stock number and title keyword. *Cumulative Subject Index to the Monthly Catalog, 1895–1971 and Cumulative Title* GP 3 .8

Index to United States Public Documents, 1789–1976 make it possible to check quickly such entries for those years.

Official Congressional Directory. Washington, D.C.: U.S. Government Printing Office, 1898–. Annual. Contains biographical sketches of members of Congress, their addresses, party affiliation, terms of service, committee assignments and names of administrative assistants; committee staff members; memberships of committees and boards; lists of principal administrative officers of executive departments and independent agencies; biographies of the President, Vice President and Justices of the Supreme Court; lists of officials of international organizations, foreign diplomatic and consular officers in the U.S. and U.S. officers abroad; and election statistics. JK 1011 .U5 —— Y 4 :93/1 1 Congress/ Session Year

United States Government Manual. Washington, D.C.: U.S. Government Printing Office. Annual. This annual "official handbook of the federal government" has descriptions of all government agencies, including a statement of purpose or authority for each, addresses, tables of organization, and lists of key officials. Similar information is provided for international organizations in which the U.S. participates. JK 421 .A3 —— C 3 .134

U.S. Organization Chart Service. Washington, D.C.: U.S. Organization Chart Service, Inc., 1980. Personnel charts for U.S. government agencies as well as major contractors with the government. HD 9711 .5.U6 .U5 vol. 1

Washington Information Directory. Mary M. Neumann, ed. Washington, D.C.: Congressional Quarterly, Inc. Lists top-level appointments in the government, all congressional assignments, plus revised and updated sources of information available in Washington. Agency and organization index as well as subject index. F 192 .3 .W33

B. State Government

Book of the States. Lexington, Ky.: Council of State Governments, 1935–. Biennial. Contains a mass of descriptive and statistical data concerning state governments, their organization, finances, programs and services, and intergovernmental relations. Elective and administrative officials of each state are listed in supplements. JK 2403 .B6

Guide to State Legislative Materials. Mary L. Fisher. Littleton, Colo.: Fred B. Rothman Co., 1979. One-stop resource noting for each state the availability of bills, hearings, debates, committee reports, legislative digests, journals and proceedings, slip laws, session laws, legislative reference services, bar association legislative recommendations, attorney general opinions, executive orders, administrative regulations, legislative manuals, state law guides, and contact personnel. KF 1 .G8

Handbook of State Policy Indicators. 4th ed. HC

David R. Morgan. Norma, Okla.: Bureau of Government Research, University of Oklahoma, 1982. Comparative ranking of state in such areas as demography, state revenue and expenditures, and political and governmental features. `106.7 .M67 1982`

Monthly Checklist of State Publications. Library of Congress. Washington, D.C.: U.S. Government Printing Office, 1910–. Monthly. Published by the Library of Congress since 1910, this *Checklist* includes state publications arranged under state name, then by issuing agency. It includes only those items received from each state by the Library of Congress. Periodicals of state agencies are listed each year in the June issue and then cumulated in the December issue. The *Checklist* also includes publications of associations of state officials, regional organizations, library surveys, studies, manuals, and statistical reports. There is an annual index arranged by subject. `LC 30 .9`

National Directory of State Agencies. Arlington, Va.: Information Resource Press. Biennial. Includes listing of state agencies by both state and by function, giving names of individuals, full addresses, and phone numbers for state services in all areas. *State Information Book* (JK 2443.L84 1980) includes federal offices in each state. `JK 2443 .N37`

State Government Research Checklist. Lexington, Ky.: The Council of State Governments, 1957–. Bimonthly. Accessions list of materials received by the States Information Center of the Council of State Governments. Concentration here is on research reports issued by legislative service agencies, state study commissions, the Council, university bureaus of governmental research, and the Advisory Commission on Intergovernmental Relations. `Z 1223.5 .A1L51`

C. Local Government and Urban Affairs

City Data: A Catalog of Data Sources for Small Cities. Stephen J. Carroll, *et al.* Santa Monica, Calif.: Rand Corp., 1980. More than 270 sources of data on the quality of life in small cities with at least 2,500 population. Entries note source, contact, description, geographic coverage, frequency, years covered, caveats, form (machine readable, hard copy), availability and comments. `Q 180 .A1R41 6 R-2612-HUD`

County and City Data Book. U.S. Bureau of the Census. Washington, D.C.: U.S. Government Printing Office. Quinquennial. The most convenient format for extracting statistics from the many different Census Bureau series, such as the Census of Government. Access by county, by SMSA, and by city for all places over 25,000 population. Data comes from census of population, manufacturing, retail trade, etc. Equally useful is the *State and Metropolitan Area Data Book* (C 3.134/5:982). `HA 202 .A36 —— C 3.134./2 C83 1982`

Directory of National Bodies Concerned with Urban and Regional Research. New York: United `ECE/ HBP/23` Nations, 1978. Arranged alphabetically by country, this directory lists the ways urban and regional research is organized in the country, followed by a list of bodies involved in research. Includes U.S. entries.

Index to Current Urban Documents. Westpoint, Conn.: Greenwood Press, 1972–. Quarterly. Bibliographic guide to publications of over 280 of the larger U.S. cities, counties, and regions. Indexed by subject and geographic identity. `Z 7165 .U5I65 4 —— Z 1223 .Z7I36`

Language of Cities: A Glossary of Terms. Charles Abrams. New York: Viking Press, 1971. Terms relevant to urban study are defined and interpreted. `HT 108.5 .A24`

Metropolitan Area Annual. Albany: Graduate School of Public Affairs, State University of New York at Albany, 1966–. An annual reference volume with section entitled "Metropolitan Area Bibliography," which lists recent books, articles, and pamphlets, plus a "Metropolitan Surveys" section listing studies in progress or recently completed on metropolitan problems. `HT 334 .U5M5 6`

Metropolitan Area Problems: News and Digest. New York: Conference on Metropolitan Area Problems, 1957–. Each bimonthly issue has a section entitled "Recent Publications on Metropolitan Area Problems," which contains a selective listing of books and articles. `HT 101 .M47`

Municipal Year Book. Washington, D.C.: International City Management Association, 1935–. Annual survey of detailed data for local governments in U.S. (including counties) and Canada. Narrative sections discuss trends and issues. Directory section notes organizations, administrators, and officials. "Sources of Information" section identifies books, reports, monographs, reference sources, and periodicals for major municipal departments. `JS 342 .A2152`

Periodical Literature on United States Cities. Compiled by Barbara Smith Shearer and Benjamin F. Shearer. Westport, Conn.: Greenwood Press, 1983. Lists 4,919 articles in widely available journals for cities with populations exceeding 100,000. Arrangement is by name of city. Among subjects covered are "Housing and Urban Development" and "Government and Politics." Subject and author indexes. `HT 123 .S464 —— Z 5942 .S464 1983`

Quality of Life Indicators in U.S. Metropolitan Areas, 1970. Ben-Chieh Lin. U.S. Washington Environmental Research Center. Washington, D.C.: Environmental Protection Agency, 1975. First attempt to quantitatively analyze and compare quality of life in U.S. metropolitan areas. Includes economic, political, environmental, health and education, and social components—with ratings for 243 SMSA's, divided by size: over 500,000 population, 200,000 to 500,000 and under 200,000. Reprinted in full by Praeger with call number HN 60.L58 and in summary form by Midwest Research Institute under HT 334.U5L57x. `EP 1.2: Q2/4 1975`

Reform of Local Government Structures in the `JS`

United States 1945–1971. Greenwich, Conn.: JAI Press, 1976. Following World War II, dramatic urban growth led to demands for reform in local government. This bibliography documents reports of such reform from cities, states, and regions. It indexes them by geographic locations, authors, and institutions. Subject indexing is poor, but the material valuable. `345 .R430`

Sage Urban Studies Abstracts. Beverly Hill, Calif.: Sage Publications, 1973–. Quarterly. Indexes same type of publications as *Sage Public Administration Abstract* and is particularly good for planning and land use. The cumulative index is arranged by author and by subject. `HT 51 .S24`

Urban Affairs Abstracts. Washington, D.C.: National League of Cities, 1972–. Weekly. Covers up-to-date, relevant urban literature. Quarterly and annual cumulations have an author and a geographic index. `HT 123 .U7`

Urban Affairs Annual Reviews. Beverly Hills, Calif.: Sage Publications, 1967–. A series of "annual reference volumes designed to present critical analyses" in various fields of urban studies. `HT 108 .U7`

Urban America: A Historical Bibliography. Neil L. Shumsky and Timothy Crimmins, eds. Santa Barbara, Calif.: ABC-Clio Press, 1983. More than 4,000 entries dealing with urban life were selected from *America: History and Life*, V. 11 through V. 17. Sections cover both historical and contemporary American urban life; Canadian urban life; American Indian urban settlements; and historiography, methodology, bibliography, and teaching. Author index and extensive subject index. `HT 123 .U725 1983`

Urban Policy: A Guide to Information Sources. Dennis J. Palumbo and George A. Taylor. Detroit, Mich.: Gale Research, 1979. Items on government policy which impacts on urban areas are included. Covers policy demands, formation, implementation, and evaluation. `HT 123 .P34 —— Z 7164 .S68P34`

Urban Studies: A Guide to Information Sources. Thomas P. Murphy. Detroit, Mich.: Gale Research, 1980. Charting social progress by means of indicators has become an integral part of urban policymaking and evaluation. The author lists entries tracing the history, types, problems, use, and future of urban indicators. `HT 167 .M87`

IV. MISCELLANEOUS USEFUL MATERIAL

Section IV lists miscellaneous information resources, concentrating on the social sciences, that are of particular utility to students of public administration.

American Behavioral Scientist. Beverly Hills, Calif.: Sage Publications, 1957–. Each monthly `HM 1`

issue contains an insertion section entitled "New Studies: A Guide to Recent Publications in the Social and Behavorial Sciences." This consists of brief abstracts of articles selected from over 300 journals, plus significant new books. `.A45`

Bibliographic Index: A Cumulative Bibliography of Bibliographies. New York: H.W. Wilson Co., 1938–. Three times per year. Bound cumulation in December issue. Subject and author index to bibliographies with 50 or more citations. Bibliographies may be published separately or as sections within books, pamphlets, or periodicals. Easy to use. `Z 1002 .B595`

Changing Attitudes on Governments and Taxes. Advisory Commission on Intergovernmental Relations. Washington, D.C.: U.S. Government Printing Office. Annual. A very useful survey sponsored each year by the ACIR on public perceptions of governmental services, policies, and taxes. Each new issue replicates past surveys going back to 1972. `Y3 .Ad 9 8:17 Year`

Civil Rights Directory. Washington, D.C.: U.S. Commission on Civil Rights. List of agencies with civil rights responsibilities. Includes federal, state, and private organizations; research and women's organizations; and state and local commissions on the status of women. `CR 1 .10:15- 3`

Combined Retrospective Index to Journals in Sociology, 1895–1974. Arlington, Va.: Carrollton Press, 1978. Follows format of companion volume for political science. Use sections in V. II, "Institutions, Bureaucratic Structures;" V. III, "Political Institutions;" V. V, "Urban Systems and Structures." `H 1 .C17 —— Z 7161 .C17`

Current Contents: Social and Behavioral Sciences. Philadelphia, Pa.: Institute for Scientific Information, 1969–. Weekly. Reproduces the tables of contents of over 1,300 journals, world-wide. Includes sections on Demography, International Relations, Management Sciences, Planning and Development, Public Administration, Transportation, and Urban Affairs. Index in each issue is by key words in the title of the article. `H 1 .C92`

Directory of Directories. 2nd ed. James M. Ethridge, ed., Detroit, Mich.: Gale Research, 1983. Directories are listed under broad subject areas and indexed by title and subject. Biennial with supplements. Section on "Law and Government (Including Military)" is useful. "Public Affairs and Social Concerns" concentrates on social work; is good for locating foundation directories. `AY 2001 .D52 1983`

Dissertation Abstracts International: A. The Humanities and Social Sciences; B. The Sciences and Engineering; C. European Abstracts. Ann Arbor, Mich.: University Microforms International, 1861-. Monthly. Cumulative indexes make it possible to check for all dissertations completed from 1861 to 1972; 5-year cumulations and annuals supplement these. Dissertations owned by your library will be located in the card catalog, treated as monographs. Dissertations not owned by your library can be purchased on microfilm from University Microfilms or requested through Interlibrary Loan. `AC 801 .D542/ .D544 —— Z 5055 .U49D 57`

Effective Research and Report Writing in Government. Judson Monroe. New York: McGraw-Hill, 1980. Extolls skills necessary for effective written communication in public sector field. Also useful is *Research and Report Handbook: For Managers and Executives in Business, Industry and Government* by Ruth Moyer (HF 5719.M69).   JF 1525 .R46M 65

Guide to Grants: Governmental and Nongovernmental. Donald Levitan. Washington, D.C.: Government Research, 1985. Designed for the grants seeker in virtually every area.   AS 911 .A2L4 x

International Encyclopedia of Sociology. 15 volumes. Michael Mann, ed. New York: Macmillan and Free Press, 1984. This work supplements the old *Encyclopedia of the Social Sciences*, published in the early 1930s. A synthesis and summary of the "state of the art" in all the social sciences. Consisting of original articles contributed by leading social scientists, it covers the disciplines of Anthropology, Economics, Geography, History, Law, Political Science, Psychiatry, Psychology, Sociology, and Statistics. There are a number of articles on organization theory, administrative science, and one on public administration by Dwight Waldo.   HM 17 .I153 1984

Journal of Economic Abstracts. Chicago: American Economic Association, 1963–. A quarterly journal containing lengthy abstracts of articles in the major economic periodicals, both English and foreign. Supplemented by a five-volume *Index of Economic Journals* (Homewood, Ill.: Irwin, 1961–62) which indexes, but does not abstract, economic articles published from 1886 to 1963.   HB 1 .J6

London Bibliography of the Social Sciences. London: London School of Economics, 1931–. Annual Supplements. A major bibliography in the broad field of social science. Listing is by subject. Strong in legislative and administrative reports and official publications. International in coverage with periodic cumulations.   Z 7161 .L84

Masters Abstracts. Ann Arbor, Mich.: University Microfilms International, 1962–. Quarterly. Selectively lists Masters theses from cooperating universities. "Political Science, Public Administration," and "Urban and Regional Planning" listings. Annual cumulative subject and author indexes.   Z 5055 .U5A5 4

PAC Directory: A Complete Guide to Political Action Committees. Compiled by Marvin Weinberger and David U. Greevy. Cambridge, Mass.: Ballinger Publishing Co., 1982. In addition to listing Political Action Committees (PACs), the directory notes contributions, names, and Standard Industrial Classification of company sponsors and indexes of PAC support.   JK 1991 .W44

Psychological Abstracts. Arlington, Va.: American Psychological Association, 1927–. Monthly. Classified arrangement. Monthly, with semiannual and annual cumulative author and subject indexes. Use *Thesaurus of Psychological Index Terms* to find subject headings and related terms.   BF 1 .P65

Index refers you to abstract number in a specific volume and year. Full citation includes titles in italics. Includes books, pre-1980 dissertations, reports, and periodical articles. Good for personnel and training issues, applied psychology.

Research Centers Directory. Detroit, Mich.: Gale Research Co., 1982. University-related and nonprofit research organizations are described in terms of their governance, research activities and fields, and publications and services. Updated supplement, *New Research Centers* (AS 8.N4).   AS 8 .R4

Selected Rand Abstracts. Santa Monica, Calif.: Rand Corporation. 1963–. Irregular. The Rand Corporation publishes in such areas as decision making, policymaking, urban planning and services, and transportation.   AS 36 .R284 —— A 180 .A1R1 8/ Rand #

Social Science Citation Index. Philadelphia, Pa.: Institute for Scientific Information, 1969–. Quarterly. Appears three times per year with annual cumulations. Covers approximately 1,400 of the most frequently cited international journals in the social sciences in toto and another 3,000 selectively.   Z 7161 .S65

Social Sciences Index. New York: H.W. Wilson Co., 1974–. Quarterly. (Previously titled, *Social Science and Humanities Index*, 1965–73, and *International Index to Periodicals*, 1907–1965.) Author and subject index with annual cumulations. Indexes journals of a scholarly nature, and is easier to use than such indexes as *Psychological Abstracts* or *Sociological Abstracts*.   AI 3 .S62

Sociological Abstracts. San Diego, Calif.: Sociological Abstract, Inc., 1952–. Five issues per year. Includes abstracts of books and articles from all the major sociological journals. Particularly useful for its coverage of the literature of political sociology, public opinion, bureaucracy, political interactions, economic development, and research methodology. Author and subject indexes cumulate annually. Additional cumulated indexes cover 1953–62, 1963–67, 1967–70.   HM 1 .S67

State of Black America. Washington, D.C.: National Urban League. Annual. A particularly authoritative compendium on the yearly status of black Americans.   E 185.5 .N317

Using Government Publications. 2 vols. Jean L. Sears and Marilyn Moody. Phoenix, Ariz.: Oryx Press, 1985, 1986. Volume I provides guidelines by subject and agency; Volume II is more specialized, and concentrates on statistical and other techniques.   J 83 .S4x

Work Related Abstracts. Detroit, Mich.: Information Coordinators, Inc., 1979–. Monthly. Succinct abstracts from over 250 management, labor, government, professional, and university periodicals. Articles concerning public affairs are found throughout the twenty broad subject divisions, such as "Personnel Management," "Socioeconomic and Political Issues," and "Government Policies and Actions." Looseleaf.   HD 4901 .W68 —— Z 7164 .L1W6 8

APPENDIX B

SELECTED ANNOTATED JOURNALS RELEVANT TO PUBLIC ADMINISTRATION

The following list identifies and describes journals that are particularly germane to public administration on a general level. That is, it encompasses such areas as public policy analysis; public personnel administration, budgeting, and so forth, but does not delve deeply into those journals identified with fields of tangential relevance to public administration, such as political science, economics, and sociology.

There are a number of new journals bearing on public administration that, while worthwhile, are not well known. These have been included, as have foreign journals published in the English language.

Journals are listed alphabetically by title. Brief descriptions accompany each title. Library of Congress call numbers appear in the right-hand margins for your convenience.

Academy of Management Executive. The Executive focuses new research to the practical needs of practicing executives. HD 28 .A251

Academy of Management Journal. A high-quality publication on general management with a mathematical and behavioral orientation. HD 28 .A24

Academy of Management Review. A more youthful version of *Academy of Management Journal*, and also of high quality. *The Review* has a thematically oriented book review section, while the *Journal* does not. HD 28 .A242x

Administration. Devoted to Irish administration with an occasional article on Western European administration. JA 26 .A35

Administration and Society. Formerly the *Journal of Comparative Administration, its contents* no longer bear any resemblance to those of its ancestor. An excellent journal covering the broad spectrum of public administration. JA 3 .J65

Administrative Management. A quantitatively directed journal with a technical emphasis. Issued monthly. HF 5500 .A203

Administrative Science Quarterly. Perhaps the foremost journal in administrative theory and in organization theory of special relevance to public administration. HD 28 .A25

American City and County. Formerly *American City Magazine*, this is among the best periodicals in the field of planning and urban management. Articles are straightforward and practical. HT 101 .A5

American Journal of Public Health. Concerns policy and administration aspects of public health in the U.S. RA 421 .A41

American Journal of Sociology. Publishes occasional articles relevant to public administration theory and public policy. Excellent book review section. HM 1 .A7

American Political Science Review. Occasional articles on public policymaking and the political aspects of public organizations. Book reviews on boundary topics. JA 1 .A6

American Review of Public Administration. Formerly *The Midwest Review of Public Administration*, this quarterly ranks among the best public administration journals in the field after Public Administration Review. JK 1 .M5

American Sociological Review. Has articles relevant to administrative behavior, bureaucracy, organization theory, and social issues. Quality book reviews. HM 1 .A75

Annals of Public Administration. Published annually since 1981, the *Annals* provide overview articles on a wide variety of topics related to public administration. JF 1351 .P817

Annals of the American Academy of Political and Social Science. Each issue concentrates on a specific area in the social sciences, and produces an extensive book review and notes section covering the social sciences. H 1 .A4

Baseline Data Report. Published bi-monthly by the International City Management Association, the periodical covers a wide array of municipal issues. Formerly was *Urban Service Data Report*. JS 39 .U72x

Behavioral Science. Five to ten well-documented articles appear in this academic, largely theoretical journal on human behavior. Each issue contains a section on computer applications in the field. H 1 .B44

Brookings Review. An informative, slim quarterly that outlines in article form recent books and studies published by The Brookings Institution on matters of public policy. Formerly called *The Brookings Bulletin*. H 1 .B76

Business and Society Review/Innovation. A journal that absorbed *Innovation* and began publication in 1972. Published quarterly, it addresses the "role of business in a free society." HD 60.5 .U5 B855

California Management Review. A high-quality journal in the style of *Harvard Business Review*, but more data conscious. HD 28 .C18

Canadian Public Administration. Devoted to Canadian public administration and comparative analysis. JL 1 .C35

Citizen Participation. A bimonthly newspaper on activities involving citizen participation in policy formation at all levels of government. JK 1 .C58x

Current Municipal Problems. A quarterly journal dealing with policy and administrative issues at the local level. JS 39 .C85

Data Access News. Issued six to eight times a year, this bulletin covers various statistical bureaus HA 37 .U5C56

of the federal government. 5

Decision Sciences. The journal for the American Institute for Decision Sciences, this quarterly focuses on quantitative management techniques. HD 30.23 .D4

Dialogue. A quarterly journal published by the Public Administration Theory Network that attempts to express the cutting edge of theory in public administration. JA 1 D52

Economic Development and Cultural Change. Concerns research findings in development. HC 10 .C453

Evaluation Review. A journal on evaluation research in the public sector. Formerly was *Evaluation Quarterly*. HM 1 E8

Evaluation Practice. Practical articles on public program evaluation. Formerly was *Evaluation News*. AZ 191 .E93x

Federal Labor Relations Reporter. Published since 1979, the *Reporter* follows developments in the public sector labor force. KF 5365 .F43

Financial Accountability and Management. A quarterly journal published in Britain since 1985 specializing in the financial management of governments, public services, charities, and "third-sector" organizations. HJ 9701 .F55x

Futures. An international journal of forecasting and planning. HB 3730 .F8

GAO Review. Published quarterly by the U.S. General Accounting Office, this is a journal of high quality focusing on the whole spectrum of accountability in government. GA 1 .I5

Governing. A new monthly magazine focusing on the management of state and local governments In 1994, it absorbed *City and State*. JK 2403 G686

Government Accountants Journal. Published quarterly by the Association of Government Accountants, the *Journal* focuses on problems of accountancy at all levels of government. HJ 9801 .F4

Government Data Systems. A magazine published bimonthly on all facets of electronic data processing as applied to its use by public administrators at all levels of government. JK 468 .A8G65

Government Executive. Published monthly, and billing itself as "government's business magazine," *Government Executive* focuses on management issues and agencies exclusively at the federal level. JK 1 .G58

Government Finance Review. A bimonthly journal on municipal finance published by the Government Finance Officers Association. It supersedes *Governmental Finance* (1972–1984), which in turn had superseded *Municipal Finance*. HJ 9103 .G68x

Government Publications Review. An international guide to government information and bibliographic resources. Z 7164 .G7 G71

Government Union Review. Published since HD

1979 by the Public Service Research Foundation, the review traces labor management relations at the federal, state, and local levels. 8008 .A1 663

Grants Magazine. A journal for grants seekers and grant makers aimed toward those interested in sponsored research. H 62 .A1G72

Harvard Business Review. Concerns a variety of administrative processes. An outstanding journal of quality. HF 5001 .H3

Human Organization. A journal of applied anthropology that focuses on problems of urban and modernizing societies. GN 1 .H83

Human Relations. A behavioral journal of excellent quality, often dealing with organization theory. H 1 .H8

Human Resource Management. A quarterly journal on personnel administration which makes no distinction between the public and private sectors; each issue concentrates on a theme. HF 5549 .A2

Indian Administrative and Management Review. Devoted to administrative aspect of policy and development in India. HD 28 .I42

Indian Journal of Public Administration. Relates to administration in India, comparative analysis, and development administration. JQ 201 .I55

Industrial and Labor Relations Review. Devoted to industrial relations in both public and private sectors. Substantial book review section. HD 4802 .I53

Intergovernmental Perspective. A quarterly magazine published by the Advisory Commission on Intergovernmental Relations on problems of federalism. One of the most informative journals on this topic available. Y 3 .AD 9/8, 11

International Development Review. Published quarterly by the Society for International Development. Short articles devoted to development. Comprehensive book review section. HC 60 .I546

International Journal of Government Auditing. A journal that covers all aspects of government accounting and auditing. JA 1 .A1

International Journal of Public Administration. A quarterly journal with a comparative bent. JA 1 .A1I593

International Organization. Occasional articles on international administration. JX 1901 .I55

International Review of Administrative Sciences. Devoted exclusively to comparative public administration and international administration. JA 26 .I58

Journal of Accounting and Public Policy. A quarterly journal that specializes on "the effects of accounting on public policy and vice versa." Both the private and public sectors are covered. H 97 .J56

Journal of Administration Overseas. Concerned with development administration. JS 40 .J6

Journal of African Administration. Deals with problems of public administration in Africa. JQ 1881 .A1J6

Journal of Applied Behavioral Science. Devoted to applied behaviorism and organization development. H 1 .J53

Journal of Collective Negotiations in the Public LB

Sector. A quarterly publication designed to help public managers and employees understand each other's perspectives. 2842.2 .J68

Journal of Criminal Justice. Published bimonthly, the *Journal* focuses on systemic issues of justice. HV 7231 .J62

Journal of Criminal Law and Criminology. Devoted to policy and administration of law enforcement. HV 6001 .J68

Journal of Management Studies. A Scottish journal that concerns applied behavioral theory. HD 28 .J6

Journal of Organizational Behavior. A British journal published quarterly which deals with human behavior in organizations at a fairly abstract level. HD 6951 .J681

Journal of Organizational Behavior and Management. A quarterly journal devoted to behavior management in business, government, and service organizations; quantitatively oriented. HD 58.7 .J68

Journal of Police Science and Administration. Published quarterly by the International Association of Chiefs of Police. HV 7935 .J6x

Journal of Policy Analysis and Management. Published quarterly by the Association for Public Policy Analysis and Management, the journal replaced the *Journal of Policy Analysis* and *Public Policy* in 1981. The journal tends to publish articles of substantive rather than methodological nature. H 1 .J552x

Journal of Public Administration Research and Theory. A journal begun in 1991, *J-PART* is dedicated to tying research in the field to theory, and is published in affiliation with the Section on Public Administration Research of the American Society for Public Administration. JA1 .J65

Journal of Public Policy. A quarterly journal published in England which first appeared in 1981. The journal covers a wide range of policy issues from cutback management to government regulation. H 1 .J65

Journal of State Government. Called simply *State Government* until 1986, *The Journal of State Government* is published quarterly by the National Conference of State Legislatures and the Council of State Governments; articles are generally good, and cover a wide range of state issues. JK 2403 .S7

Journal of Taxation. A monthly magazine with a news orientation aimed at financial professionals. HJ 2360 .J6

Journal of the American Institute of Planners. Devoted to public planning. NA 9000 .A45

Journal of the American Planning Association. A quarterly publication devoted to land-use planning in the public sector. HD 87.5 .A46a

Journal of Urban Planning and Development. Published quarterly by the American Society of Civil Engineers, the focus is somewhat technical. NA 9000 .A5786

Management Information Service Report. A monthly publication of the International City Management Association dealing with local government that is practitioner oriented. JS 308 .M35x

Management: The Magazine for Government Managers. Formerly *The Civil Service Journal, Management* is published quarterly by the U.S. Office of Personnel Management. The publication focuses on public personnel administration. — PM 1 .11/2

Management Review. Monthly publication, first put out by the American Management Association in 1914. Includes survey of books for executives, critical reviews of between ten and twenty recent works, and a listing of recent publications received from publishers. — T 58.A2 .M37

Management Science. Oriented to mathematics, systems, and scientific method in administration. — HD 28 .I453

Minerva. A philosophic journal devoted to the relationships among government, higher education, and science policy. — AS 121 .M5

Monthly Digest of Tax Articles. A publication that does precisely what its title claims; the meaning of the complete article is well preserved in each synopsis. — HJ 236D .N65

National Civic Review. Published every month except August by the National Municipal League, the *Review* provides short but informative articles on a wide variety of urban problems. — JS 39 .N3

National Journal. Founded by a group of editors and reporters in 1970 who left *Congressional Quarterly* because they felt it did not pay enough attention to bureaucratic decision making. The *Journal* is published weekly and designed as a monitor of all government actions. It analyzes details surrounding such actions, focusing mainly on the relationships among the various agencies. It also contains in-depth reports on federal programs, biographical information on government officials, and analyses of congressional districts. — JK 1 .N28

National Public Accountant. The journal of the National Society of Public Accountants. Published monthly. — HF 5601 .N335

National Tax Journal. Published quarterly by the National Tax Association and the Tax Institute of America, the *Journal* is the nation's foremost periodical on issues of government finance and taxation. — HJ 2240 .N32x

New England Journal of Human Services. A quarterly journal that focuses on problems of social work and welfare. — HV 1 .N45

New Zealand Journal of Public Administration. Devoted to New Zealand administration. — JA .N12

Nonprofit Management and Leadership. A quarterly journal devoted to the managing and leading of non-government not-for-profit organizations. Quite good. — HD 62.6 .N663

Organizational Behavior and Human Decision Processes. A high-quality journal focusing on interaction in small groups, conflict resolution, and the social psychology of organizations. Until 1985, it was called *Organizational Behavior and Human Performance.* — BF 638 .A107

Organizational Dynamics. A quarterly review on organizational behavior written mostly by academics — HD 28

but aimed at professional managers, primarily in the private sector. Published by the American Management Association. — .O76

Organizational Science. Published quarterly by the Institute of of Management Sciences, each issue focuses on a theoretical theme, such as organizational decline. — HD 28 .O74

Personnel. Short articles on personnel; published monthly by the American Management Association. — HF 5549 .A2P38

Personnel Administrator. Useful for public personnel administration. Published by the Society for Human Resource Management. — HF 5549 .A2P39

Personnel Journal. A monthly magazine billing itself as "the business magazine for leaders in human resources," its articles concentrate on the private sector. — HF 5549 .A2

Personnel Management. A journal that concerns public personnel administration, often with a comparative orientation. — HD 28 .I463

Personnel Manager's Legal Reporter. A monthly newsletter about legislation and court rulings affecting personnel managers in the public and private sectors. — KF 3302 .P475

Philippine Journal of Public Administration. Devoted to Southeast Asia administration, comparative analysis, and development administration. — JA 26 .P5

Policy Sciences. Concerns public policy theory and methodology. — H 1 .P7

Policy Studies Journal. One of two journals published by the Policy Studies Organization on a quarterly basis. The *Journal* has a political science orientation. — H 1 .P72

Policy Studies Review. Published jointly by the Morrison Institute for Public Policy at Arizona State University and the Policy Studies Organization, *Policy Studies Review* is an excellent journal in the field of public policy analysis and has a distinctly public administration flavor. — H 97 .P66

Political Quarterly. Devoted to public policy issues and public administration in England. — JA 8 .P72

Public Administration. Devoted to British administration and comparative analysis. Lists recent British government publications. — JA 8 .P8

Public Administration. Devoted to Australian administration. — JA 8 .N12

Public Administration in Israel and Abroad. Articles on Israeli administration and comparative administration. — JQ 1825 .P3P8

Public Administration Newsletter. Published by the Public Administration Division of the United Nations, the newsletter contains occasional articles in development administration, but is devoted principally to reports of field projects conducted by U.N. officials in developing countries. — JF 251 .P8

Public Administration Quarterly. Formerly *Southern Review of Public Administration,* a good new journal on public administration with a broad orientation. An employment listing is available. — JA1 .S68

Public Administration Review. The most significant American journal concerned with public administration. *Review* articles are of high quality; research notes are provided. JK 1 .P85

Public Administration Survey. A bimonthly publication of the Bureau of Governmental Research at the University of Mississippi. JK 4601 .M57

Public Administration Times. A biweekly newsletter with employment opportunities. Published by the American Society for Public Administration. JA 1 .P975

Public Affairs. A public affairs, public policy journal. JK 6501 .P83

Public Budgeting and Finance. A good quarterly journal on questions of public finance and budgeting that is sponsored by the American Association for Budgeting and Program Analysis and the Section on Budgeting and Financial Management of the American Society for Public Administration. HJ 2052 .A2P8

Public Budgeting and Financial Management. A quarterly journal with an international orientation. HJ 101 .P78

Public Choice. A policy journal with a political economy orientation. H 35 .P33

Public Finance. Devoted to comparative public finance. HJ 109 .N4P8

Public Finance Quarterly. A journal emphasizing economic approaches to budgeting in the United States. HJ 101 .P83

Public Interest, The. High quality articles with a neo-conservative orientation on public policy issues. H 1 .P86

Public Management. Short articles devoted to urban administration. Published monthly by the International City Management Association. JS 39 .P97

Public Manager. A quarterly journal with a federal emphasis featuring a thematic "Forum" section, an ethics column, and an "irreverent" slant. Until 1992, it was titled *The Bureaucrat.* JK1 .B861

Public Personnel Management. Directed at personnel administrators at all governmental levels, each issue has ten to twelve brief articles with a practical orientation. It is published by the International Personnel Management Association. JK 671 .P48x

Public Productivity and Management Review. Initiated in 1975, the *Review* combines case studies and articles by academics and practitioners that focus on questions of program evaluation and productivity. Formerly was *Public Productivity Review.* JF 1411 .P8

Public Welfare. Devoted to policy and administration of public welfare in the United States. HV 1 .P75

Publius. A journal devoted to intergovernmental relations and federalism. JK 1 .P88

Research Management. Concerns problems of managing research-and-development units in large organizations. T 175.5 .R4

Review of Public Data Use. A quarterly journal designed to encourage the use of publicly available data for research or analysis applied to local, regional, or national problems. H 62 .A1R47

Review of Public Personnel Administration. Published three times a year, the *Review* began publication in 1980 and covers all aspects of the field, particularly at the state and local levels of government. JF 1601 .R4

Sage Professional Papers in Administrative and Policy Studies. Twelve academic papers are published annually in three issues, devoted to the administrative sciences. H 31 .S24

Science. The major science journal of the nation; extremely useful for articles and reports on public science policy. Q 1 .S35

Society. Applies social science research to contemporary social and public policy problems. Formerly called *Transaction.* H 1 .T7

State and Local Government Review. A good journal covering a variety of aspects of state and local government with an emphasis in public administration. JK 2403 .S684

Urban Affairs Quarterly. Devoted primarily to sociological and political treatments of urban areas. HT 101 .U7

Urban and Social Change Review. A journal with a social services orientation that attempts to appeal to both practitioners and academics. HT 101 .U672

Urban Interest, The. A highly readable journal that aids professionals in analyzing and solving urban problems. Published twice a year. JS 39 .U75

Washington Monthly. A liberal journalistic publication of high quality. It focuses on the injustices of the public bureaucracy, as well as on policy issues. E 838 .W37

Western City. Articles on urban administration in the West; published monthly. TD 1 .W4

APPENDIX C

SELECTED ACADEMIC, PROFESSIONAL, AND PUBLIC INTEREST ORGANIZATIONS, WITH DESCRIPTIONS AND ADDRESSES

The following national groups all have a direct relevance to public administration. Virtually all of them publish journals and newsletters on topics of interest; you may wish to contact some of them for their materials. The organizations, together with a brief description and their addresses, are listed in alphabetical order.

Academy for State and Local Government. 444 North Capitol Street, N.W., Suite 349, Washington, DC 20001. Supported by seven major organizations representing state and local interests, the Academy publishes original research on state and local issues. Its former title was the Academy for Contemporary Problems.

Advisory Commission on Intergovernmental Relations. 1111 Twentieth Street, N.W., Washington, DC 20036. Founded in 1959, the ACIR publishes significant studies of the federal system.

American Association of School Administrators. 1801 North Moore Street, Arlington, VA 22209. The largest association of school managers.

American Association of State Highway and Transportation Officials. 444 North Capitol Street, Washington, DC 20001. The major association of state transit officials.

American Correctional Association. 4321 Hartwick Road, Suite L-208, College Park, MD 20740. The major association of correctional officials.

American Institute for Decision Sciences. 33 Gilmer Street S.E., Atlanta, GA 30303. Perhaps the premiere organization of quantitatively oriented academics interested in decision making.

American Management Association. 135 West 50th Street, New York, NY 10020. The major association of private sector managers.

American Planning Association. 1776 Massachusetts Avenue, N.W., Washington, DC 20036. An important organization of public planning officials. Formerly the American Society of Planning Officials.

American Political Science Association. 1527 New Hampshire Avenue, N.W., Washington, DC 20036. The chief academic association of political scientists.

American Productivity Center. 123 N. Post Oak Lane, Houston, TX 77024. Conducts and publishes case studies on productivity and the quality of work life.

American Public Transit Association. 1201 New York Avenue, N.W., Washington, DC 20005. The major association of public officials interested in mass transit.

American Public Welfare Association. 1125 Fifteenth Street, N.W., Washington, DC 20005. The major organization of public welfare officials.

American Public Works Association. 1313 East Sixtieth Street, Chicago, IL 60637. The principal association of public works administrators.

American Society for Public Administration. 1120 G Street, N.W., Washington, DC 20005. The major organization of academics and professionals in public administration at all levels of government.

Brookings Institution. 1775 Massachusetts Avenue, N.W., Washington, DC 20036. A major academic think tank with important concerns in domestic public affairs.

Center for Community Change. 1000 Wisconsin Avenue, N.W., Washington, DC 20007. Provides technical assistance to communities.

Center for Science in the Public Interest. 1779 Church Street, N.W., Washington, DC 20036. A coalition of scientists interested in the impact of public policy on science and society.

Committee for Economic Development. 477 Madison Avenue, New York, NY 10022. A private group that studies issues relating to business and public policy.

Common Cause. 2030 M Street, N.W., Washington, DC 20036. An organization of more than 300,000 members dedicated to political reform.

Conference Board, Inc. 845 Third Avenue, New York, NY 10022. A business group that often addresses public issues.

Conference of Minority Public Administrators. 1220 G Street, N.W., Washington, DC 20005. The major national association of minority public administrators.

Congressional Quarterly Service. 1735 K Street, N.W., Washington, DC 20006. Publishers of *Congressional Quarterly* and other publications relating to congressional action.

Council of State Community Affairs Agencies. Hall of the States, 444 North Capitol Street, Room 251, Washington, DC 20001. The major association of state community affairs officers.

Council of State Governments. Ironworks Pike, P. O. Box 11910, Lexington, KY 40511. Publishers of *The Book of the States* and other publications relating directly to state governments.

Council on Municipal Performance. 30 Irving Place, New York, NY 10003. Conducts research on urban service efficiency.

Environmental Action, Inc. 1525 New Hampshire Avenue, N.W., Washington, DC 20036. Environmentalists who are interested primarily in solid waste disposal.

Freedom of Information Center. School of Journalism, University of Missouri, P. O. Box 858, Columbia, MO 65201. Conducts studies on the public's uses of federal, state and local Freedom of Information Acts.

Government Finance Officers Association. 180 North Michigan Avenue, Suite 800, Chicago, IL 60601. Major organization of state and local finance officials, with an emphasis on local government. Formerly the Municipal Finance Officers Association.

Governmental Research Association. 24 Providence Street, Boston, MA 02108. One of the granddaddys of the municipal research bureaus, the Governmental Research Association was established in 1914 and is a national organization of individuals professionally engaged in governmental research.

Institute of Public Administration. 55 West 44th Street, New York, NY 10036. A public affairs research group that was one of the first public interest organizations.

International Association of Chiefs of Police. P. O. Box 6010, 13 First Field Road, Gaithersburg, MD 20878. The major organization of police chiefs.

International Association of Fire Chiefs. 1329 Eighteenth Street, N.W., Washington, DC 20036. The major organization of fire chiefs.

International City Management Association. 1120 G Street, N.W., Washington, D.C. 20005. The major organization of city managers and other individuals interested in city management.

International Institute of Municipal Clerks. 160 North Altadena Drive, Pasadena, CA 91107. The major association of municipal clerks, who, in small towns, often function as the town manager.

International Personnel Management Association. 1617 Duke Street, Alexandria, VA 22314. The major organization of public personnel administrators at all levels of government.

Labor-Management Relations Service. 1620 Eye Street, N.W., 4th Floor, Washington, DC 20006. Sponsored by the U.S. Conference of Mayors, this organization specializes in research on local labor problems.

National Association for the Advancement of Colored People. 733 Fifteenth Street, N.W., Washington, DC 20005. One of the most prestigious political organizations of African-Americans.

National Association of Counties. 440 First Street, N.W., Washington, DC 20001. The major organization of county officials, and publishers of research on county government.

National Association of Housing and Redevelopment Officials. 1320 Eighteenth Street, N.W., Suite 500, Washington, DC 20036. The major association of state and local officials concerned with community development.

National Association of Regional Councils, 1700 K Street, N.W., Washington, DC 20036. The major organization of Councils of Governments and related organizations.

National Association of Schools of Public Affairs and Administration. 1120 G Street, N.W., Suite 520, Washington, DC 20005. The accrediting body for masters degree programs in public administration and public affairs.

National Association of Towns and Townships. 1522 K Street, N.W., Suite 780, Washington, DC 20005. Major organization representing towns and townships.

National Center for Public Productivity. 445 West 59th Street, New York, NY 10019. The Center gathers and disseminates information about productivity in public service and publishes a catalog of research on productivity improvement in the public sector.

National Conference of State Legislatures. Hall of the States, 444 North Capitol Street, N.W., Washington, DC 20001. The national association of state legislatures.

National Governors' Association. Hall of the States, 444 North Capitol Street, Suite 250, Washington, DC 20001. The organization of American governors.

National Institute of Governmental Purchasing. 115 Hillwood Avenue, Suite 201, Falls Church, VA 22046. Promotes improved procurement practices in government.

National Institute of Public Management. 1612 K Street, N.W., Washington, DC 20006. A research organization in public administration.

National League of Cities. 1301 Pennsylvania Avenue, N.W., Washington, DC 20004. One of the major associations of urban governments.

National Municipal League. 55 West 44th Street, New York, NY 10036. One of the major and oldest associations dedicated to improving urban governments.

National Public Employer Labor Relations Association. 1620 I Street, N.W., 4th Floor, Washington, DC 20006. Promotes better labor relations management at all levels of government.

National Recreation and Park Association. 3101 Park Center Drive, 12th Floor, Alexandria, VA 22302. The major organization of public parks and recreation professionals.

National Society for Internships and Experiential Education. 122 St. Mary's Street, Raleigh, NC 27605. Promotes public service internships, especially in the area of the environment. Formerly the National Center for Public Service Internship Programs.

Policy Studies Organization. 361 Lincoln Hall, University of Illinois, Urbana, IL 61801. The Policy Studies Organization consists largely of academics with an interest in public policy analysis.

Public Administration Service. 1497 Chain Bridge Road, McLean, VA 22101. An organization conducting significant research on public administration questions.

Public Service Research Foundation. 8330 Old Courthouse Road, Suite 600, Vienna, VA 22180. The Public Service Research Foundation was founded in 1977 and is an independent nonprofit public education group whose purpose is to increase research and public awareness regarding public sector employee and employer relations.

Rand Corporation. 1700 Main Street, Santa Monica, CA 90406. A major think tank concerned in part with public problems.

Tax Foundation, Inc. One Thomas Circle, N.W., Suite 500, Washington, DC 20005. A private association concerned with tax issues.

United States Conference of Mayors. 1620 I Street, N.W., Fourth Floor, Washington, DC 20006. The major association of American mayors.

Urban Institute. 2100 M Street, N.W., Washington, DC 20037. A research organization devoted to urban issues.

APPENDIX D

CORRECT FORMS OF ADDRESS FOR PUBLIC OFFICIALS

Information, like money, is one of those things of which there is never enough. When you need information on a public issue that is not publicly available, it often is a good idea to write and ask someone who knows. A correct form of address can add to the effectiveness of your request to a public official, so this Appendix lists the proper ways of addressing public officials.

Public Official	*Form of Address*	*Salutation*
alderman	The Honorable John (or Joan) Green	Dear Mr. Green: (or Dear Ms. Green:)
assemblyman	—see representative, state	
associate justice, Supreme Court	Justice Green The Supreme Court of the United States	Dear Justice Green:
Cabinet officers (as Secretary of State and the Attorney General)	The Honorable John (or Joan) Green, Secretary of State The Honorable John Green Attorney General of the United States	Dear Sir: (or Dear Madam:)
chief justice, Supreme Court	The Chief Justice of the United States	Dear Chief Justice Green:
commissioner	The Honorable John Green	Dear Mr. Green:
council member	The Honorable Joan Green	Dear Ms. Green:
former U.S. president	The Honorable John Green	Dear Mr. Green:
governor	The Honorable Joan Green Governor of _____	Dear Governor Green:
judge, federal	The Honorable John Green United States District Judge	Dear Judge Green:
judge, state or local	The Honorable Joan Green Chief Judge of the Court of Appeals	Dear Judge Green:
lieutenant governor	The Honorable John Green Lieutenant Governor of _____	Dear Mr. Green:
mayor	The Honorable Joan Green Mayor of _____	Dear Mayor Green:
president, U.S.	The President	Dear Mr. President:
representative, state (same format for assemblyman)	The Honorable Joan Green House of Representatives State Capitol	Dear Ms. Green:
representative, U.S.	The Honorable John Green The United States House of Representatives	Dear Mr. Green:
senator, state	The Honorable Joan Green The State Senate State Capitol	Dear Senator Green:
senator, U.S.	The Honorable John Green United States Senate	Dear Senator Green:
speaker, U.S. House of Representatives	The Honorable John Green Speaker of the House of Representatives	Dear Mr. Speaker:
vice-president	The Vice-President United States Senate	Dear Mr. Vice-President

APPENDIX E

BECOMING A PUBLIC ADMINISTRATOR

Now that you have read about public administration, why not consider working in it, too? Public administrators are in one of the world's most rewarding professions: The people's interests are served, the job security is high, the pay is good, and the field of public administration is fascinating.

And the popular appeal of public administration seems to be on the upswing. As one writer in the *Los Angeles Times* noted, "That scruffy orphan of the Me Generation, that woebegone villain of the Ronald Reagan epoch, that doleful survivor of a kinder and gentler past — that pursuit we know as public service—stands ready for a comeback."

JOBS! JOBS! JOBS!

There is a relatively high probability that you can get a good job in government. Employment in the public sector has been going up almost every year for the past three decades, and today there are some 18 million full-time and part-time public employees, or about one for every six workers. The U.S. Bureau of Labor Statistics projects an increase of 8.4 percent in general government jobs between 1988 and 2000. Most are in local government (58 percent); state government accounts for almost a quarter of public employment, and the federal government for less than a sixth. The fastest growth rates in public employment are among the state and local governments, and opportunities are quite good at these levels.

The MPA: A Door Opener

The single best educational qualification for a management position in the public sector is the Master of Public Administration (MPA) degree—a point on which both employees and employers agree. MPA degree holders believe that the MPA has made them significantly more knowledgeable and confident in entering government service, and four-fifths of them, according to a survey by George Grode and Marc Holzer, think that the MPA has been more beneficial to them as professionals than any other kind of master's degree.

The same research found that employers seemed to agree. Nearly three-quarters of the supervisors of these graduates stated that the performance of their employees who held MPAs was slightly to "clearly superior" to the performance of holders of other kinds of advanced degrees who also were under their supervision.

The success rate of MPAs in the public bureaucracy validates these views. Gregory B. Lewis studied a large sample of federal employees with graduate degrees and found not only that graduate degree holders as a class advanced significantly higher and faster in the federal service than those without such credentials, but also that MPAs held a higher federal rank, on the average, than did the holders of any other kind of advanced degree (with the exception of law degrees); earned larger salaries than most; and were more likely to hold administrative positions of authority. (The other advanced degrees were in business administration, law, social science, and the ubiquitous "other.") Federal employees seem to recognize that the MPA is the coming degree; the number of MPAs working in the federal government has more than doubled in eight years (1974–1982), a far greater rate of growth than any other kind of degree.

For successful employment in the public sector, the Master of Public Administration degree is the credential of choice.

Minorities and Women: Better Possibilities

More minorities and women are hired and earn more money in the public sector than in the private sector.

As we noted in Chapter 9, 27 percent of all federal full-time employees are minorities; 17 percent are African-Americans, and 5 percent are Hispanic. Forty-eight percent of federal white-collar workers are women. Twenty-seven percent of all state and local employees (excluding those in education) are minorities and 43 percent are women. It appears that state and local governments may do a better job in promoting minorities and women and paying them more than does the federal government and the private sector. See Chapter 9 for details.

MONEY! MONEY! MONEY!

Public sector pay rates have gone up by about 5 percent a year since 1970, and, despite tax revolts in the states, pay rates for state and local employees have increased more rapidly than have pay rates for federal employees. With the enactment of the Federal Employees Pay Comparability Act of 1990, however, federal salaries may begin to rise at a faster pace than their subnational counterparts.

Federal Public Administration

There are nearly 3 million people working full-time or part-time in the federal civilian work force. Nearly two-thirds of these employees (outside of the U.S. Postal Service) have administrative or policy responsibilities. In addition, there are 2.1 million service men and women in the armed forces, and perhaps 3 million civilian employees in the private sector who are working under federal contracts.

Federal salaries at the executive levels are good, and, since 1970, have increased about 4 to 5 percent a year. With the passage of the Federal Employees Pay Comparability Act in 1990, federal salaries likely will get even better. The Act ties federal salaries to comparable positions in the non-federal sector and to local costs of living. The top salary in the General Schedule is not quite $80,000, and the average federal salary is over $31,000. Entry level administrative salaries begin at the level of Grade 7 of the General Schedule (about $22,000), although it is possible to enter at a higher grade.

State Public Administration

There are more than 4.1 million state employees, a figure that includes 1.8 million state employees in education. The Council of State Governments reports that there are over 120 categories of top state officials, ranging from directors of state lotteries to secretaries of education to directors of emergency management. Few data have been compiled about compensation rates for state public administrators. However, $80,000 to more than $100,000 seems to be the salary level for the top state administrative jobs in the more populous states, and in these states, salaries at all administrative ranks appear to be roughly comparable to federal pay rates. But even in the least populated states, it is rare to find the top major job salaries at less than $50,000. Southern states tend to pay their public administrators the least, followed by Eastern states; Western states generally have the highest rates of pay. It is increasingly common to find top administrators in state government (particularly in higher education) to be paid more than the governor.

Local Public Administration

Local governments employ more than 10 million people, a figure that includes nearly 5.6 million local employees in education. Considerably more is known about administrative salaries at the local level than at the state level.

The top positions in urban governments are nearing an average salary of $64,000, and salaries are increasing by about 5 percent a year. However, in the largest cities and counties, top administrators typically earn more than $100,000 (Los Angeles, with the highest salaries in the nation, pays its top city and county administrators almost $170,000); typically, school superintendents and, to a lesser degree, police chiefs, in cities with more than 500,000 people are paid more than the city administrator. West Coast governments pay their public administrators the most; Northeastern cities pay the least — often a third less than Western cities. Entry level administrative positions in small cities (5,000–10,000 people) typically pay around $25,000, and it is not uncommon to enter municipal service in small towns as head of an entire department.

County salaries usually are larger than city salaries. County managers earn, on the average, over $71,000, and county salaries generally are higher than are municipal pay rates for comparable positions. North Central counties seem to pay the least, and, as with cities, Western counties pay the most. County pay patterns generally reflect those of cities, and county salaries also are increasing by about 5 percent a year.

It appears that the best salaries, including entry-level salaries, in the public sector are offered by the special districts, such as water districts, transportation districts, and other single function jurisdictions. These governments, many of which are also public corporations, pay better, on the average, than any other type of government.

GETTING A JOB IN GOVERNMENT

When perusing the job announcements and want ads, it is important to know which jobs are appropriate for public administration students. Being new to the field, some students may not even be sure what job titles are related to public administration. For the most part, trainee and intern positions are for the less experienced and may not lead to permanent positions. A "I" after a title, such as Analyst I, usually indicates an entry-level position. An Analyst II or Analyst III would indicate that more extensive education or experience is required.

At the federal level, Executive Order 12364 in 1982 reconstituted the Presidential Management Intern Program (PMI) which was established by Executive Order in 1977. The goal of the PMI program is to attract outstanding men and women who are completing a master's degree from a variety of academic backgrounds to the federal service. The PMI seeks out those who have a clear interest in, and commitment to, a career in the analysis and management of public policies and programs, so the MPA is the preferred degree.

Each year up to 200 interns receive two-year appointments to developmental positions throughout the executive branch of the federal government. These positions differ from most entry-level positions in terms of pay and the emphasis on career development. While most entry level positions begin at GS-7, PMIs enter at GS-9, are promoted to GS-11 at the end of the first year, and routinely convert to regular civil service appointments upon the successful completion of the internship at the end of the second year. Professional positions at the GS-11 level normally require a doctorate, three years of full-time graduate study, or specialized work experience equivalent to one or more years at the GS-9 level. See Tables 9-1 and 9-2 in Chapter 9 for the range of federal salaries in the General Schedule.

Entry into the PMI program is competitive. Each educational institution is limited in the number of candidates it may nominate. In recent years, almost 500 masters level students complete applications each year.

Of course, the new federal examination, Administrative Careers with America, for entry-level administrative positions is now in operation, and should not be overlooked. Begun in 1990, after a nine-year hiatus, it tests applicants for suitability in 118 position classifications. Your campus placement office can provide you with the schedule for the examination. The test admits around 5,000 of its takers to the federal service each year.

Regardless of the level of government that you are interested in, summarize your abilities in a resumé format that presents your most important assets first. What things were you able to accomplish in your job and education? State your case in terms of projects that you have directed, designed, developed, implemented, researched, reported, managed, controlled, planned, organized, edited, or built.

Human resource managers have suggested in the past that those who are new or are returning to the job market can be disadvantaged by using the traditional *chronological resumé*, and have stated that they should use a *functional resumé* format that highlights their training, analytic skills, ability to get along with others, knowledge of organization dynamics, budgeting strategies, and management tools, for example. The latest thinking, however, is that one's resumé should combine both chronological and fuctional resumé, which, by themselves, leave too many questions that need answering in the minds of their readers: the chronological resumé if there are unexplained gaps in one's career history (which can and should be addressed), and the functional resumé if it is left unclear what one's job history precisely is (and job histories are very difficult to make clear in functional resumé). A sample of a consolidated resumé follows this appendix.

It is also considered old fashioned to get too personal. The resumé reader may be safely assumed to conclude that your health is "excellent" without being told as much, and your age, gender, and marital status are your own business. Listing hobbies and pasttimes can be a plus if they can be construed as giving you an edge for a job, but noting that you like "reading" as a hobby probably is a waste of space. For entrants new to the marketplace, most professionals advise that their resumé be limited to a single page, although references (including title, full address, and telephone number, with area code) may constitute a second page or the reverse side of the resumé. If you include references (it is appropriate to say instead that they are available on request), list at least three.

Do not be shy in asking for help in polishing up your resumé; your campus's career services or placement office can be a genuine asset in not only developing a presentable resumé but often in helping you practice interviewing skills as well.

An excellent way to develop job contacts is to join the American Society for Public Administration, or ASPA. ASPA has local chapters in cities across the country comprised of public administrators from all levels of government. Typically, ASPA chapters sponsor monthly luncheons and regional conferences where new contacts are easily made. To learn how to join, ask your course instructor, or write

American Society for Public Administration
1120 G Street, N.W., Suite 500
Washington, DC 20005
ASPA's telephone number is (202) 393-7878.

An internship, paid or voluntary, can be an important step toward gaining needed relevant work experience for students lacking public sector experience. Often, schools of public administration or departments of political science work with governmental agencies in developing local internship opportunities in personnel, budgeting, planning, policy analysis, and so forth. A satisfactory internship can provide strong recommendations and strengthen one's resumé.

CONCLUSION

If you are interested in becoming a public administrator, two recommendations are paramount. First, join the American Society for Public Administration. Not only does it provide unique networking opportunities, but also it publishes a biweekly newsletter *Public Administration Times*, listing professional job openings around the country.

Second, consider entering an MPA degree program. Increasingly, these programs cater to the scheduling needs of students who already have jobs, and the MPA itself is regarded as an important qualification for entry and advancement in the public sector. To learn more about the Master of Public Administration degree, contact your local university or the National Association of Schools of Public Administration (NASPAA) and ask for its highly informative pamphlet, *MPA: The Master of Public Administration Degree*, which is available at no charge. NASPAA also publishes *In the Public Interest*, a useful quarterly newsletter on employment trends in the public service with a special emphasis on internships. A detailed *Directory* of about 200 MPA programs is also available from NASPAA for $12.50. NASPAA's address is the same as ASPA's:

National Association of Schools of Public Affairs and
    Administration
1120 G Street, N.W.
Washington, DC 20005

NASPAA's telephone number is (202) 628-8965.

SOURCES

John Balzar, "Public Service Making a Comeback," *Los Angeles Times* (April 1, 1990).

Bureau of the Census, *Statistical Abstract of the United States, 1990* (Washington, D.C.: U.S. Government Printing Office, 1990).

"Governing's 1990 Salary Survey," *Governing*, 4 (December 1990), pp. 65–67.

George Grode and Marc Holzer, "The Perceived Utility of MPA Degrees," *Public Administration Review*, 35 (July/August 1975), pp. 403–412.

International Personnel Management Association, *Pay Rates in the Public Service: Survey of 62 Common Job Classes in the Public Sector* (Washington, D.C.: International Personnel Management Association, 1985).

Gregory B. Lewis, "How Much Is an MPA Worth? Public Administration Education and Federal Career Success," *International Journal of Public Administration*, 9 (April 1987), pp. 397–415.

State Administrative Officials Classified by Function, 1985–86 (Lexington, Ky.: Council of State Governments, 1985).

The Municipal Year Book, 1993 (Washington, D.C.: International City Management Association, 1993).

SAMPLE CONSOLIDATED résumé

résumé

VIVIAN LOOK

1234 East University Drive   (602) 000-0000 (work)
Tempe, Arizona 85281   (602) 000-0000 (home)

OBJECTIVE:

  To work in an area of public administration related to legislation or public
policy. The ideal position would allow me to utilize my skills in research
analysis, interpersonal relations, and communication, both oral and written.

CAREER CHRONOLOGY

*Administrative Intern, Maricopa County Office of Management Analysis, Phoenix,
Arizona. 1-93 to present.*

*Research Assistant, School of Public Affairs, Arizona State University, Tempe,
Arizona. 8-92 to present.*

*Project Nutrition Consultant, Bureau of Nutritional Services, Arizona
Department of Health Services, Tempe, Arizona. 10-89 to 8-92.*

*Nutritionist, Health Division, Lane County Department of Health and Social
Services, Eugene, Oregon. 7-84 to 7-88.*

*Special Vocational Educational Teacher, Springfield School District No. 19,
Springfield, Oregon. 9-83 to 6-84.*

*Trainer/Nutritionist, Community Nutrition Institute, Washington, D.C. 10-82 to
6-83.*

EDUCATION:
Arizona State University   1-92 to present   —   Public Administration
Tempe, Arizona
University of Michigan   9-88 to 8-89   MPH   Public Health
                                                         Ann Arbor, Michigan
University of California   3-78 to 7-81   BS   Nutritional Sciences,
                                                         Economics, Psychology
  Other training: Food Services Division, Milwaukee Public Schools, Milwaukee,
Wisconsin. 9-76 to 6-77. Administrative dietetic internship focusing on the man-
agement of school food service programs.

SKILLS AND EXPERIENCE

  Conducted management audits of county departments to investigate efficiency
and effectiveness of services provided. Assessed present and future staffing
requirements and make recommendations for improving the service delivery system.

Contract Negotiation

Served as the primary contact person from the Bureau of Nutrition for county and tribal health departments, as assigned. In this capacity, monitored local agency programs for compliance to program and contract requirements, provided assistance in program management, and served as an advocate for local projects, participating in negotiations when appropriate.

At the Bureau level, participated in planning, development, and review of policies and procedures and budget allocation process for state-subvened funds. Researched alternative methods of carrying out the program and completed comparative cost studies. Developed and presented final recommendations for improving the program and reducing costs, which were ultimately adopted by the agency.

Assisted in developing a master copier plan for use by the county in the next five years.

Management Analysis and Performance Assessment

Work on research projects has included assisting in computer-based management and analysis of educational enrollment data for the Phoenix Town Hall, citizen surveys for the city of Glendale, and library research on public choice theory.

RECENT PROFESSIONAL ACTIVITIES AND HONORS:

1992 to present	Regents Graduate Academic Scholarship, Arizona State University, Tempe, Arizona
	Member, American Society for Public Administration, Arizona Chapter
1991–92	Co-editor, Legislative Newsletter, Arizona Dietitians for Legislative Action
1990–91	Community Nutrition Section Chairperson and Executive Board Member, Central Arizona District Dietetic Association
1988–89	U.S. Public Health Traineeship, University of Michigan, Ann Arbor, Michigan
1987–88	Member, Task Force on Dental Health, Nutrition, and Health Education, Western Oregon Health Systems Agency Member, Nutrition Task Force, Oregon Public Health Association

REFERENCES

Dr. John Adams
Professor of Public Administration
Georgia Southern University
Statesboro, Georgia 30460
(912) 681-0000

The Honorable Mary Currin
State Representative
House of Representatives
Phoenix, Arizona 85287
(602) 961-0000

Ms. Jane Morton
Vice President for Human Resource Management
Cave Creek Corporation
Scottsdale, Arizona 85283
(602) 841-0000

NAME INDEX

SUBJECT INDEX